he Soviet Union

T. M. Oberlander

cuse University / Department of Geography

Scale

200   400   600   800   1000

Miles

Geography of the U.S.S.R.

The Moscow Kremlin   Courtesy of the Foreign Languages Publishing House, Moscow

RANDALL SALE, *Cartographer*

Geography of the U.S.S.R.

Second Edition

PAUL E. LYDOLPH

Professor of Geography

University of Wisconsin—Milwaukee

JOHN WILEY & SONS, INC.   NEW YORK • LONDON • SYDNEY • TORONTO

Library of Congress Catalogue Card Number: 78-112594

SBN 471 55725 0

Printed in the United States of America

10 9 8 7 6 5 4 3 2 1

To Mary

Preface

The second edition of *Geography of the U.S.S.R.* is written in response to a wide demand by colleagues and students, and attempts have been made to incorporate their helpful suggestions for updating and revision. After weighing the various pros and cons, the format of the first edition has been retained, with the regional analysis first and then the topical analysis. It is better to introduce students to actual locations and their interworkings before presenting them with more abstract discussions of cultural and economic phenomena. The original regional breakdown has been retained. To a large extent it reflects Russian traditional thought, and it is relatively simple. It attempts to encompass all tangible and intangible factors that go into the making of regional concepts within a country, and therefore it is not based on precise criteria measured in terms of a set of economic factors, an ecosystem, or any such narrow consideration. Such restricted regional distributions are shown under individual discussions in the topical chapters.

The revision of the book, then, lies in the updating and strengthening of the chapters in the first edition. The topical chapters particularly have been greatly lengthened to include background analyses that will help the student to understand the present-day geography. Throughout the book a great deal more attention has been given to historical and ethnological per-spectives than was done previously. The evolution of the nationality groups and their struggles with the Russians are more fully treated in the chapter concerned with population, as well as in appropriate regional chapters.

In all cases, the latest possible information has been incorporated. In this respect, Theodore Shabad's news notes in *Soviet Geography: Review and Translation,* as well as personal communications from Mr. Shabad himself, have been invaluable. The many statistical handbooks and fine atlas materials constantly being published by the Soviets have provided data which, in most cases, are no more than two years old. Except where otherwise specified, population estimates are all as of July 1, 1967. So are territorial and name changes, although here adjustments have sometimes had to be made for typically Soviet weird omissions, or "unplaces." For instance, places whose names were derived from Stalin that have undergone name changes since 1957 largely are omitted from Soviet lists of place name changes. In the case of an older city, such as Volgograd, which had the original name of Tsaritsyn before it became Stalingrad, it is shown in such lists as "Volgograd" with its previous name as "Tsaritsyn" only, with no mention of Stalingrad. Apparently the present Soviet regime prefers the Tsars to Stalin! Such omissions have been corrected in the city discussions at the ends of the regional chapters as well as in Table 13–13 which lists all the Soviet cities with populations of more than 100,000.

The thumbnail sketches of the largest cities have been retained at the ends of the regional chapters, although this sort of information appears to be rather encyclopedic. In many cases it appears that the larger cities are not characterized by any particular industry or other distinguishing feature in the regional discussion itself, and therefore the student is liable to end up with limited knowledge of the region discussed. A large city is a primary phenomenon on the landscape which pervades the activities of all the surrounding areas. If a student travels to a given area in the future he might be astonished to find that here is a large urban complex of which he is not even aware. Therefore I think it is important, after all has been said about individual industries and other phenomena in a region, to list in order of size the larger cities so that a student can gain a proper prospective of the urban build-up of the area.

An added feature at the end of most chapters is a short section which attempts to forecast developments in the immediate future. This is a little safer to do now as the world has moved farther away from the extremely disrupting effects of World War II and the Soviet Union has displayed more or less persistent trends through the fairly normal development period of the last two decades. Also, much more information is available now than it was at the time of the first writing.

A year or two hence might be an even more auspicious time to be writing, since at the present one is caught in the last phases of an economic plan, is reliant upon 10-year-old census data, and is faced with the prospects of a new constitution which might effect significant changes in internal political regions. If a census is taken in 1970, as is now planned, the population data then should be much more uniform and reliable than they are now, and the initiation of a new plan period in 1970 should provide economic guideposts for several years into the future.* Nevertheless, it has been deemed necessary to revise the book now since the Soviet Union has moved ahead so fast during the past 6 years. Also, there has been a full flowering of western analytical writing about the Soviet scene.

Accordingly, the reading lists at the end of chapters have been greatly expanded to include much of the recent information appearing in English as well as some of the more significant works in the Russian language. In addition to these specific citations, the following general sources are recommended.

Bibliographies

1. For a list of the basic books, serials, atlases, and bibliographic references published in Russian in the Soviet Union about the geography of the U.S.S.R. see Harris, Chauncy D., "The Land," Chapter II, in *Basic Russian Publications, a Selected and Annotated Bibliography on Russia and the Soviet Union,* edited by Paul L. Horecky, University of Chicago Press, Chicago, 1962, pp. 25–48. Other chapters cover the people and economic and social structure, among other topics.
2. Horecky, Paul L., ed., *Russia and the Soviet Union: A Bibliographic Guide to Western Language Publications,* University of Chicago Press, Chicago, 1965, 473 pp. Lists the most important works that have been published in English, French, and German.
3. The *Referativnyy Zhurnal* (published in the U.S.S.R. in Russian) section on geography is one of the most complete abstract journals in the world. It lists titles and summaries of periodical

---

* The 1970 census was taken, and preliminary result have been released. These are presented as an ap-pendix at the end of the book.

articles and monographs published all over the world.

4. The U.S. Library of Congress *Monthly Index of Russian Accessions* has been a major bibliographic source for American researchers.

5. *The American Bibliography of Russian and East European Studies,* published yearly by Indiana University.

6. For an extensive list of American doctoral research on all aspects of the Soviet Union see Dossick, Jesse J., *Doctoral Research on Russia and the Soviet Union,* New York University Press, New York, 1960. More recent dissertation titles have been listed by Dossick in certain issues of *The Slavic Review.*

7. Maichel, Karol, *Guide to Russian Reference Books,* Stanford University Press, Stanford, 1962 and 1964. Volume 1 lists general bibliographies and reference books. Volume 2 covers history, auxiliary historical sciences, ethnography, and geography. Chapter F in Volume 2, pp. 189–227, entitled "Geography," contains a list of 300 annotated bibliographies on the geography of the U.S.S.R. classified by region and topic.

8. Hammond, Thomas Taylor, *Soviet Foreign Relations and World Communism: A Selected, Annotated Bibliography of 700 Books in 30 Languages,* Princeton University Press, 1965, 1240 pp.

9. Pokshishevskiy, V. V., ed., *Ekonomicheskiye administrativnye rayony SSSR: ukazatel novoy literatury po prirode, resursam, i khozyaystvu* (Economic administrative regions of the U.S.S.R.: index of new literature on nature, resources, and economy) Akademiya Nauk SSSR, Moskva, 1957–1958, 14 volumes (in Russian).

Atlases

The Soviets have published many excellent atlases and single maps of the world, the U.S.S.R., and regions within the U.S.R.R. In most cases the information is detailed and up-to-date and the cartography is superb. A listing of a few of the most significant and most recent U.S.S.R. and world atlases follows. In addition, the Soviets are in the process of publishing separate atlases for each oblast and kray in the U.S.S.R. which give detailed, complete information on all aspects of the regions covered. A considerable number of these regional atlases already are available.

1. *Atlas SSSR* (Atlas of the U.S.S.R.), Moscow, 1969, 2nd ed., 199 pp. (in Russian). The best and most recent general atlas on the U.S.S.R. Pages 6–64 are general regional maps showing great detail of landform and location. Pages 66–123 are maps of the entire country showing many aspects of the physical and economic geography of the area. Pages 124–147 are regional economic maps. The remainder of the atlas is primarily an exhaustive gazetteer of place names.

2. *Atlas razvitiya khozyaystva i kultury SSSR: 1917–1967* (Atlas of the growth of the economy and culture of the U.S.S.R.: 1917–1967), Moscow, 1967, 172 pp. (in Russian). Excellent maps of all aspects of economy and culture. Map symbols are generally divided into time periods to illustrate the growth of the economy.

3. *Atlas selskogo khozyaystva SSSR* (Atlas of agriculture of the U.S.S.R.), Moscow, 1960, 309 pp. (in Russian). The last word on agricultural distributions in the country as of about 1957. In addition, there are many maps on the physical geography of the country, many aspects of climate, as it pertains to agriculture, as well as political and population maps. Although the agricultural data are becoming obsolete, nothing more recent matches this monumental mapping job.

4. *Fiziko-Geograficheskiy Atlas Mira* (Physical Geographical Atlas of the World), Moscow, 1964, 298 pp. (in Russian). All printed material has been translated by Theodore Shabad and published in

Soviet Geography: Review and Translation, May–June 1965. One of the best world atlases available.

5. *Morskoy Atlas* (Marine Atlas), Moscow, 1950, 3 volumes. (in Russian). English key published by Telberg Book Co., 1958.

6. *Atlas avtomobilnykh dorog SSSR* (Atlas of highways of the U.S.S.R.), Moscow, 1966, 166 pp. (in Russian). This atlas is revised frequently and contains many regional maps at fairly large scales. Thus it is useful for detailed location purposes.

In addition, two-non-Soviet atlases are worthy of note:

7. *The U.S.S.R. and Eastern Europe,* Regional Economic Atlas, Oxford University Press, London, 1956, 134 pp.

8. Taaffe, Robert N. and Kingsbury, R. C., *An Atlas of Soviet Affairs,* Methuen, London, 1965, 143 pp.

Encyclopedias

1. Florinsky, Michael T., ed., *Encyclopedia of Russia and the Soviet Union,* McGraw-Hill, New York, 1961, 624 pp.

2. Karger, Adolf, *Europaische Sowjetunion,* Westermanns Lexikon der Geographie, Wolf Tietze, ed., George Westermann Verlag, Braunschweig, 1968, 206 pp. (in German).

3. *Kratkaya geograficheskaya entsiklopediya* (Short geographical encyclopedia), Moscow, 1960, 5 volumes (in Russian).

4. Kubijovyc, Volodymyr, ed., *Ukraine: A Concise Encylopaedia,* University of Toronto Press, 1963, 1185 pp.

5. Maxwell, Robert, ed., *Information U.S.S.R.* (translation of most of volume 50 of the *Great Soviet Encyclopedia*), Pergamon Press, New York, 1962, 982 pp.

6. Plaschka, O., *Sowjetunion (Asiatischer Teil),* Westermanns Lexikon der Geographie, Wolf Tietze, ed., George Westermann Verlag, Braunschweig, 1968, 121 pp. (in German).

7. *Ukrainska Radianska Entsiklopediya,* Ukrainian Academy of Sciences, Kiev, 1967, volume 17, 807 pp. (in Ukrainian).

8. Utechin, S. V., *Everyman's Concise Encyclopedia of Russia,* Dutton, New York, 1961, 623 pp.

Serials

Among English-language periodicals the following are the most useful for geographic information on the U.S.S.R.

1. *Soviet Geography: Review and Translation,* published by the American Geographical Society, edited by Theodore Shabad. An indispensable publication of translated articles from professional geographical journals in the Soviet Union. Materials from this journal have been used extensively throughout the book.

2. *Soviet Studies,* published by the University of Glasgow, Scotland. A scholarly journal with occasional articles pertinent to geography.

3. *The Annals of the Association of American Geographers.* A few articles pertaining to the Soviet Union.

4. *The Geographical Review.* A few articles pertaining to the Soviet Union.

5. *Economic Geography.* A few articles pertaining to the Soviet Union.

6. *The Geographical Journal.* A few articles pertaining to the Soviet Union.

7. *Bulletin of the Institute for the Study of the U.S.S.R.,* published in Munich primarily by Russian emigres. Many brief analyses of current events in all aspects of the U.S.S.R., especially political and economic.

8. *The Current Digest of the Soviet Press* (weekly since 1949) and *Current Abstracts of the Soviet Press* (monthly, except July and August, since April 1968). Translations of key news items from Soviet newspapers and magazines, published by the Joint Com-

mittee on Slavic Studies of the American Council of Learned Societies and the Social Science Research Council. Many news items of interest, especially full texts of plan goals, plan fulfillments, international agreements, and so forth. Human interest items give pungent insight into the domestic situation.

9. *Slavic Review.* The professional journal of the American Association for the Advancement of Slavic Studies. Articles predominately dealing with literature, political science, history, and economics.

10. *Central Asian Review.* Many articles on agriculture and life in Soviet Middle Asia.

Russian language serials of a geographical nature are:

11. *Akademiya nauk SSSR, izvestiya, seriya geograficheskaya* (Bulletin of the academy of sciences of the U.S.S.R., series in geography).

12. *Vsesoyuznoye geograficheskoye obshchestvo, izvestiya* (Bulletin of the all-union geographical society).

13. *Voprosy geografii* (Problems of geography). A monograph series published by the University of Moscow.

14. *Leningrad Universitet, Vestnik, Seriya geologii i geografii* (Leningrad University, Bulletin, Series in Geology and Geography).

15. *Moskva Universitet, Vestnik, Seriya geografiya* (Moscow University, Bulletin, Series in Geography).

Books of Direct Geographical Interest

1. Baransky, N. N., *Economic Geography of the U.S.S.R.,* Foreign Languages Publishing House, Moscow, 1956, 413 pp. (in English).

2. Berg, L. S., *Natural Regions of the U.S.S.R.,* translated into English and published by the Macmillan Company, New York, 1950, 436 pp.

3. Breyterman, A. D., *Ekonomicheskaya geografiya SSSR, chast 1, geografiya tyazheloy promyshlennosti* (Economic geography of the U.S.S.R., part 1, geography of heavy industry), Moscow, 1965, 370 pp. (in Russian).

4. Cherdantsev, G. N., Nikitin, N. N., and Tutykhin, B. A., *Ekonomicheskaya Geografiya SSSR;* 3 volumes: *obshchiy obzor,* 1958, 280 pp.; *R.S.F.S.R.,* 1956, 490 pp.; and *SSSR,* 1957, 371 pp. (in Russian).

5. Cole, J. P. and German, F. C., *A Geography of the U.S.S.R.,* 1961, 290 pp.

6. Davydova, M. I., Kamenskii, A. I., Nekliukova, N. P., and Tushinskii, G. K., *Fizicheskaya geografiya SSSR,* Moscow, 1966, 2nd ed., 847 pp. (in Russian).

7. Dewdney, John C., *A Geography of the Soviet Union,* Pergamon, Oxford, 1965, 154 pp.

8. Fitzsimmons, Thomas, Malof, Peter, and Fiske, John C., *U.S.S.R., Its People, Its Society, Its Culture,* HRAF Press, New Haven, 1960, 590 pp.

9. Gregory, James S., *Russian Land-Soviet People,* Pegasus, New York, 1968, 928 pp.

10. Gvozdetskiy, N. A. and Mikhaylov, N. I., *Fizicheskaya geografiya SSSR,* Asiatic part, Moscow, 1963, 571 pp. (in Russian).

11. Hooson, David, *The Soviet Union: People and Regions,* Wadsworth, Belmont, Calif., 1966, 376 pp.

12. Lavrishchev, A. N., *Ekonomicheskaya geografiya SSSR,* Moscow, 1967, 478 pp. (in Russian).

13. Lyalikov, N. I., *Ekonomicheskaya Geografiya SSSR,* 1960, 343 pp. (in Russian).

14. Maslov, Yevgeny, *The Russian Federation,* Foreign Languages Publishing House, Moscow, 1960, 215 pp.

15. Mellor, Roy E. H., *Geography of the U.S.S.R.,* Macmillan, London, 1964, 403 pp.

16. Mikhailov, Nicholas, *Soviet Russia: The*

Land and its People, Sheridan House, 1948, 370 pp.

17. Mikhailov, Nicholas, *Glimpses of the U.S.S.R., its Economy and Geography,* Foreign Languages Publishing House, Moscow, 1960, 199 pp.

18. Milkov, F. N. and Gvozdetskiy, N. A., *Fizicheskaya geografiya SSSR,* European part, Moscow, 1962, 475 pp. (in Russian).

19. Nikitin, N. P., Prozorov, E. D., and Tutykhin, B. A., eds., *Ekonomicheskaya Geografiya SSSR,* Izd. Prosveshcheniye, Moscow, 1966 (in Russian).

20. Parker, W. H., *An Historical Geography of Russia,* Aldine, Chicago, 1969, 416 pp.

21. Saushkin, Yu. G., Nikolskiy, I. V., and Korovitsyn, V. P., *Ekonomicheskaya Geografiya Sovetskogo Soyuza,* Chast I, Izd. Moskovskogo Universiteta, Moscow, 1967 (in Russian).

22. *Soviet Geography: Accomplishments and Tasks,* a symposium of 50 chapters contributed by 56 leading Soviet geographers, English translation edited by Chauncy D. Harris, and published by the American Geographical Society, New York, 1962, 409 pp.

23. Suslov, S. P., *Physical Geography of Asiatic Russia,* translated into English, published by Freeman and Co., San Francisco, 1961, 594 pp.

Regional Monographs and Statistical Handbooks Published in the U.S.S.R.

1. The Institute of Geography of the U.S.S.R. Academy of Sciences has published the so-called blue series of regional physical and economic geographies of the U.S.S.R. (in Russian).

2. The Academy of Sciences has published about 20 other occasional regional monographs (in Russian).

3. *Sovetskiy Soyuz* (Soviet Union), new series consisting of 22 volumes of regional monographs covering physical landscape history, ethnography, culture, economy, and regional subdivisions. First volume published in 1966. Izdatelstvo Mysl, Moscow (in Russian).

4. *SSSR: Administrativno-territorialnoye deleniye soyuznykh respublik,* Moscow, yearly. A statistical compilation of all political administrative units of the country with their areas, populations, and subdivisions (in Russian).

5. *Narodnoye khozyaystvo* (national economy), annual statistical abstracts of U.S.S.R. and regions. Listed in the January issues of *Soviet Studies* beginning in 1959 (in Russian).

6. *Strana Sovetov za 50 let* (Country of the Soviets for 50 years), Moscow, 1967, 351 pp. Published in lieu of *Narodnoye khozyaystvo* for 1966 (in Russian).

7. *Promyshlennost SSSR* (Industry of the U.S.S.R.), Moscow. Statistical abstract published in 1957 and 1964 (in Russian).

8. *Transport i svyaz SSSR* (Transport and Communications of the U.S.S.R.), Moscow. Statistical abstract published in 1957 and 1967 (in Russian).

9. *Vneshnyaya torgovlya SSSR* (Foreign trade of the U.S.S.R.), Moscow. Statistical abstract published yearly (in Russian).

General Reference Materials for International Comparisons

1. *United Nations Yearbook* and *Monthly Bulletin of Statistics.*

2. *Commodity Yearbook.*

3. *The Economic Survey of Europe,* United Nations, Geneva, published yearly. Contains summary chapters on the economy of the Soviet Union.

Materials for Background on the Economy and Society of the U.S.S.R.

1. Ames, Edward, *Soviet Economic Processes,* Richard D. Irwin, Inc., Homewood, Ill., 1965, 257 pp.

2. Bauer, Raymond A., Inkeles, Alex, and Kluckhohn, Clyde. *How the Soviet System Works,* Harvard University Press, Cambridge, 1956, 274 pp.
3. Bergson, Abram, *The Economics of Soviet Planning,* Yale University Press, New Haven, 1964, 394 pp.
4. ———, *Planning and Productivity under Soviet Socialism,* Columbia University Press, New York, 1968, 95 pp.
5. Campbell, Robert Wellington, *Soviet Economic Power: Its Organization, Growth, and Challenge,* Houghton Mifflin, Boston, 1966, 2nd ed., 184 pp.
6. Clark, Colin, *The Real Productivity of Soviet Russia,* United States Government Printing Office, Washington, 1961, 61 pp.
7. Degras, Jane and Nove, Alec, eds., *Soviet Planning,* Blackwell, Oxford, 1964, 225 pp.
8. Dobb, Maurice H., *Soviet Economic Development Since 1917,* International Publishers, New York, 1948, 475 pp.
9. Dunn, Stephen P. and Dunn, Ethel, *The Peasants of Central Russia,* Holt, Rinehart, and Winston, New York, 1967, 139 pp.
10. Goldman, Marshall I., *Soviet Marketing: Distribution in a Controlled Economy,* Free Press of Glencoe, New York, 1963, 229 pp.
11. Granick, David, *Management of the Industrial Firm in the U.S.S.R., a Study in Soviet Economic Planning,* Columbia University Press, New York, 1959, 346 pp.
12. Grossman, Gregory, ed., *Value and Plan,* University of California Press, Berkeley, 1960, 370 pp.
13. Holzman, Franklyn D., *Readings on the Soviet Economy,* Rand McNally, New York, 1962, 763 pp.
14. Hopkins, Mark, many editorials on first-hand observations and analyses of various social and economic phenomena in the U.S.S.R., in various issues of the *Milwaukee Journal* since 1960.
15. Inkeles, Alex, and Geiger, Kent, *Soviet Society, A Book of Readings,* Houghton Mifflin, Boston, 1961, 703 pp.
16. Kassof, Allen, *Prospects for Soviet Society,* Praeger, New York, 1968, 586 pp.
17. Katkoff, Vladimir, *Soviet Economy, 1940–1965,* Dangary Publishing Co., Baltimore, 1961, 559 pp.
18. Lyashchenko, Peter I., *History of the National Economy of Russia to 1917,* translated by L. M. Herman, Macmillan, New York, 1949, 880 pp.
19. Nove, Alec, *The Soviet Economy,* Praeger, New York, 1968, 2nd ed., 376 pp.
20. Reports of the Joint Economic Committee, Congress of the United States: 1959, *Comparisons of the United States and Soviet Economies;* 1962, *Dimensions of Soviet Economic Power;* 1964, *Annual Economic Indicators for the U.S.S.R.;* 1965, *Current Economic Indicators for the U.S.S.R.;* 1966, *New Directions in the Soviet Economy;* and 1968, *Soviet Economic Performance: 1966–67.* All together, these reports comprise thousands of pages of factual information and mature analyses of all phases of Soviet economic life written by United States governmental and academic experts on the Soviet Union.
21. Salisbury, Harrison E., ed., *The Soviet Union: The Fifty Years,* Harcourt, Brace, and World, New York, 1967, 484 pp.
22. Sorlin, Pierre, *The Soviet People and Their Society,* Praeger, 1968, 288 pp.
23. Spulber, Nicolas, *The Soviet Economy: Structure, Principles, Problems,* Norton and Co., New York, 1962, 311 pp.
24. ———, *Soviet Strategy for Economic Growth,* Indiana University Press, Bloomington, 1964, 175 pp.
25. Treml, Vladimir G. and Farrell, Robert, eds., *The Development of the Soviet Economy: Plan and Performance,* Praeger, New York, 1968, 298 pp.
26. Whiting, Kenneth R., *The Soviet Union Today,* revised edition, Praeger, 1966, 433 pp.

Quantities in the tables and illustrations have been expressed in some cases in English units, in some cases in metric or other units commonly used in the U.S.S.R., usually depending on the source of information. There has been no particular attempt to standardize, and indeed I believe that students should be exposed to the various units of measure used. To facilitate conversion from one system to another, a table of equivalent measures is given at the end of the book. Unless otherwise stated, all quantities in tables expressed in tons are in metric tons.

Accent marks are shown on place names in the index so that the index may double as a pronouncing gazeteer. In general, place names have been transliterated according to the system proposed by the United States Board on Geographic Names, except that the hard and soft signs have been ignored. Names have been transliterated literally except for those familiar to non-Russians in Anglicized form, such as Moscow, Archangel, the Caspian Sea, the Dnieper River, and so forth. Names from Central Asia and the Far East have been transliterated from Russian, rather than from Chinese or some other language in the area. Thus Tyan Shans, rather than Tien Shans. So far as possible, standard Russian map symbols have been used on illustrations to acquaint students with the Russian symbols and thereby to facilitate use of Russian wall maps and atlases.

I express thanks to my many colleagues and students who took the trouble to comment on the first edition. Particularly I am grateful to Theodore Shabad for providing up-to-date factual information, reading the manuscript, and checking graphic illustrations; to Hlib Hayuk, who was helpful in the bibliographic stages of the work; and to Don Temple, who drafted the map revisions under the direction of Randall Sale. My greatest appreciation goes to my wife, Mary, who willingly typed the entire mess, several times, and cheerfully aided in all phases of the editorial work.

PAUL E. LYDOLPH

Elkhart Lake, Wisconsin
March 1969

Contents

Chapter

   1. Introduction to the U.S.S.R.   3

Part One   The Regions of the U.S.S.R.   **29**

   2. The Central Industrial Region   35
   3. The Central Black Earth Region   57
   4. The Povolzhye and the Lower Don   67
   5. Ukraine and Moldavia   91
   6. The European West   125
   7. The European North   147
   8. The Urals   165
   9. The Caucasus and the North Caucasian Foreland   185
  10. Soviet Middle Asia and Southern Kazakhstan   217
  11. Western Siberia and Northern Kazakhstan   271
  12. Eastern Siberia and the Far East   299

Part Two   Topical Analysis of Cultural and Economic Phenomena   **333**

  13. Population, Nationalities, Manpower, and Employment   335
  14. Agriculture   398
  15. Industry   460
  16. Transportation and Domestic Trade   551
  17. Foreign Trade, Aid, and International Relations   590
Equivalent Measures   653
Appendix. Preliminary Results of the 1970 Soviet Census   657
Index   669

Geography of the U.S.S.R.

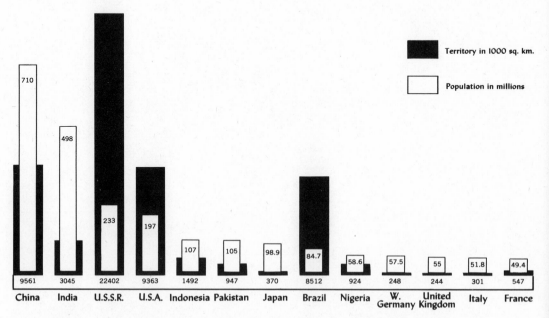

Figure 1–1   Areas and populations of leading countries, mid 1966. Data from United Nations Demographic Yearbook.

Introduction to the U.S.S.R.

The geography of the U.S.S.R. is the geography of one sixth of the earth's land surface. Part East, part West, the country sprawls across two continents. Progeny of the old Russian Empire, the U.S.S.R. is the result of more than a thousand years of acquisition and consolidation of lands on all sides. Its expansion at times has been explosive across vast empty areas, at times painfully slow and faltering against major adversaries in Europe and eastern Asia. Occasionally submerged by strong neighbors or internal strife, it sometimes appeared on the verge of breaking up and dissolving altogether as one of the world's great powers. But like the phoenix, each time it rose from seeming extinction to size and strength never attained before.

Gradually it has taken on somewhat stable form. International boundaries have been established where its power has been matched by some other strong country; generally the international boundaries between the major contenders have been set in intermediate zones, in which weak buffer countries have been maintained. Boundaries in the fracture zones have been subject to wide oscillations as major power blocks have shifted in the backgrounds.

The U.S.S.R. presently bounds on Finland, Norway, and the satellite countries in eastern Europe; on Turkey, Iran, and Af-ghanistan in the Middle East; and on China, the Mongolian People's Republic, Korea, and Japan in the Far East. There is no territorial contact with other major military powers of the world. But it is the major power blocks that have established these boundaries and that now maintain the identities and status quo of the states that border directly on the U.S.S.R.

World War I and subsequent revolutions and civil wars appeared for a while to have torn the Russian Empire asunder. But once again the area was resurrected into a stronger state than before. The most important net result of World War I was the establishment of the Soviet Union. And World War II was the catalyst that coagulated its diverse units into a consolidated country. The Soviet Union now is larger, more integrated, and more powerful than the Russian Empire ever was.

The U.S.S.R. is not a homogeneous state. In its growth by accretion of peripheral territories, the Russian Empire acquired many diversified pieces of land peopled by widely varying nationalities. The old Russian Empire has been referred to as "a prison of nations." The Soviet Union today is, therefore, a multinational state with many non-Russian peoples living in non-Russian ways. And in spite of the fact that the Soviet system has been imposed on

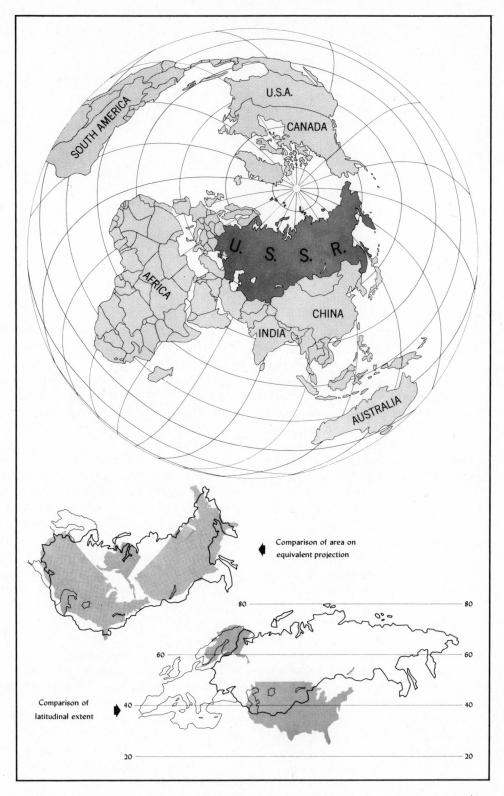

Figure 1–2   The U.S.S.R. in its world setting. The U.S.S.R. occupies an area nearly 2½ times that of the United States, most of which lies at a latitude north of the Canadian border.

everyone, individual responses to this system reflect the indigenous cultures.

Thus the U.S.S.R. is a very large country that contains widely varying landscapes, both cultural and physical. For discussion purposes it will be divided into its various regions and each region will be dealt with in its entirety. Then the regions will be welded together by considerations of separate items of culture and economy that transcend regional boundaries. But first, a brief look at the history of territorial growth of the country and at its broad zones of natural environment and cultural development is necessary to set the perspectives for regional discussions.

Emergence of the Russian State and Subsequent Territorial Acquisition

The Russian State emerged on the east European plain after centuries of invasion, conquest, and sporadic settlement. Wave after wave of nomadic peoples, presumably from somewhere in Central Asia, swept across the Black Sea steppes and into Central Europe long before the Christian era. Scythians, Goths, Huns, Avars, and many other tribal groups crisscrossed the area during the period from 1000 B.C. to A.D. 800. Some settled for brief periods in what was to become the Russian plain, only to be assimilated by indigenous peoples or driven on by succeeding movements.

The origin of the Slavs is not clear, but they emerged in the area that is now Ukraine in the eighth and ninth centuries as a sedentary peasant people engaged in agriculture. The first Slavic state was organized in 862 under a Scandinavian prince named Rurik. This governmental control under the Scandinavians, or the Varangians, as they were called, was established to secure the trade route from the Baltic Sea to Constantinople. Two cities that became focal points on this trade route were Kiev along the Dnieper River in the south and Novgorod along the Volkhov River in the north. Kiev quickly became established as the primary center of the Slavic area, and Kievan Rus flourished until the Tatar invasion in A.D. 1240 under Batu, the grandson of Genghis Khan. At the same time, Novgorod became a great trading city, one of the Hanseatic League cities in the north with connections westward along the Baltic. But Novgorod was peopled by a cosmopolitan group of central and west Europeans, as well as by eastern Slavs and was always looked upon as an alien city, not a center of Slavic culture. During the period of Kievan Rus, A.D. 862–1240, the middle portion of the Russian plain, which was to become so important later, was primeval forest.

With the fall of Kiev to the Tatars, the Slavic peoples in the southern part of the plain either fled into the forest or perished. There is no agreement on the fate of these peoples. Although Novgorod was never captured by the Tatars, and flourished commercially for 200 years more, it did not serve as a center of the Slavic peoples as Kiev had. It appeared for a time after the Tatar invasion that the Slavic state might be doomed forever. The record becomes quite obscure here; apparently the area in the central European plain was broken up into a great number of small feudal-type states with the Tatars exacting tribute from everyone. The Tatars established themselves first in the town of Sarai, near the present site of Volgograd (Stalingrad) on the lower Volga, and controlled much of what is now European Russia from this strongpoint. Later, with the breakup of the Tatar tribes into separate groups, centers were established at Kazan at the great bend of the Volga, at Astrakhan on the north coast of the Caspian, and in the Crimea.

While the Tatars were in control and were exacting tribute from the eastern Slavs, several major Slavic princely states were beginning to emerge from the many smaller states that had existed immediately after the Tatar invasion. By a series of

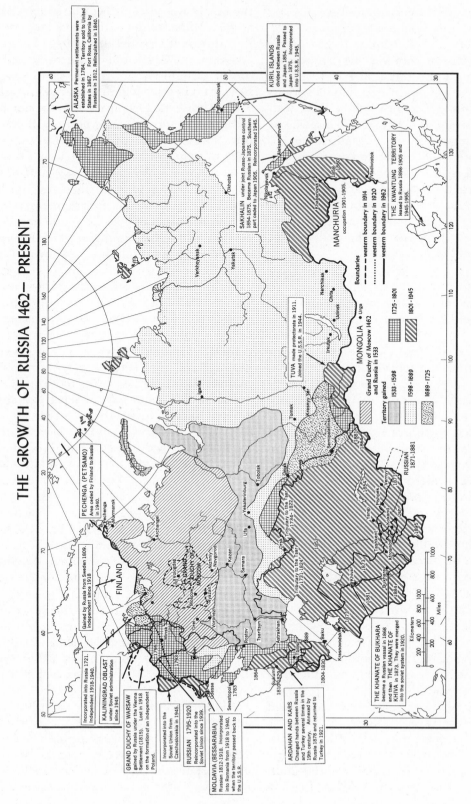

THE GROWTH OF RUSSIA 1462– PRESENT

Figure 1–3 Expansion of the Russian Empire. Part of the information on this map was derived from the Oxford Regional Economic Atlas of the U.S.S.R. and Eastern Europe, pp. 98–99, by permission of the Clarendon Press, Oxford, England.

Figure 1-4   The walled city of Novgorod on the bank of the Volkhov River north of Lake Ilmen. Novosti.

clever maneuvers by unscrupulous rulers over a period of 100 years or more, Moscow emerged as the predominant princely state, and the Moscow prince was named the Grand Prince of all the Russias by the Tatars more often than were any of the other Slavic princes.

It was during the reign of Ivan III, or Ivan the Great, from 1462–1505, that the Muscovy state finally emerged supreme over all the other princely states. During his reign, Novgorod, with all its lands to the north, fell to Muscovy. It was also during his reign that the Muscovy state became strong enough to tackle the Tatars themselves, and a major stalemate was reached with the Tatars on a battleground near the Ugra River south of Moscow in 1480. This date often is given as the end of the so-called Tatar Yoke, because no more tribute was paid from then on, but the Tatars continued to harass the Slavic area for another century. Kazan was not captured until 1552 during the reign of Ivan IV, or Ivan the Terrible, and as late as 1571 much of Moscow was burned to the ground by an expedition of Tatars from Crimea.

All during this period when the Slavic princely states were fighting among themselves for supremacy and were resisting the Tatar horde, various Slavic princes also were gathering armies to repulse the Swedes, the Germans, the Poles, and the Lithuanians in the north and west, and later the Ottoman Turks in the south, who had taken over the Byzantine Empire with the fall of Constantinople in 1453. The struggle along the Baltic dates back to Alexander Nevsky's battle with the Swedes on the Neva River in 1240, the very same year that Kiev in the south was falling to the Tatars, and to the defeat of the Germans on Lake Peipus (Chudskoe) in 1242. In 1410, at the Battle of Tannenberg, a great Pan-Slav army under a Polish-Lithuanian prince defeated the so-called Livonian Knights and thereby set the eastern limits of German penetration for centuries to follow. During the sixteenth century, Poland, which had joined with the Duchy of Lithuania, was the largest state in Europe and stretched from the Baltic to the Black Sea. It controlled much of what is now western Russia, Belorussia, and

Ukraine, and even succeeded in placing a king on the throne in Moscow from 1610–1613.

While all this was going on in the west, during the reign of Ivan IV an expedition under the leadership of a Cossack named Yermak to open up Siberia was sponsored by the fur trading family of Stroganov. His little band of Cossacks crossed the Urals and conquered the town of Sibir, a Tatar stronghold in western Siberia. Within half a century the quest for furs took the Russian explorers across Siberia to the shores of the Pacific, where in 1649 Okhotsk became the first Russian settlement on the eastern coast. The movement through Siberia met with little resistance, for the area was practically devoid of population. Only a few tribes of Paleo-Asiatic nomads occupied the area at the time. Since the climate of the area was so harsh, there was little inducement for settlement; the Russians did not stop to take up land, but continued across the continent in their race to the sea. In 1652 a fort was established on the Amur River on the site of the modern city of Khabarovsk. Here the Russian pioneers came into conflict with the northernmost Chinese, and in 1689 the Far Eastern territories were partitioned between the two countries by the Treaty of Nerchinsk.

Russian fur traders continued on across the Bering Straits into Alaska, where in 1784 permanent settlements were established, and they continued on down the coast of North America until in 1812 they founded their southernmost fort, Fort Ross, only a few miles north of present-day San Francisco. Later, pressures on the central government in Moscow from the Crimean War and from the opposition of British fur trading companies in Canada induced the Muscovy government in 1867 to sell Alaska to the United States and to relinquish all claims to the south along the west coast of North America.

Also during the reign of Ivan the Terrible the movement southward to reoccupy the steppes of southern Russia and Ukraine was begun under the impetus of the oppression of Ivan's government in Moscow. People escaped from the central area and moved southward into the "no man's" land of the steppes to either settle and become farmers or to join in semi-nomadic bands to become so-called Cossacks. It is this Russian movement southward into the steppes, and not the movement eastward through Siberia, that corresponds so closely in character to the movement westward into the Great Plains of North America. The movement southward occupied a semiarid region of open grasslands and good soils with great farming possibilities. The economy of the time was a mixture of sedentary agriculture and a seminomadic cowboy-like existence.

The roving Cossacks consisted of diverse nationalities, mainly Ukrainian and Russian, who had escaped the jurisdiction of the central government to establish a law of their own in the "wild field." Usually they joined in bands and either preyed on the settlers, robbing and looting, or hired themselves out to the central government to carry on some military campaign in the outlying provinces. It was such a group of

Figure 1–5 River station at Aksay, the old Don Cossack stronghold on the high west bluff near the mouth of the Don River just upstream from the present large city of Rostov. Most river stations in the Soviet Union are old river boats that have been permanently lashed to the shore. Photograph by the author.

men, banded together under Yermak, who were commissioned to open up Siberia.

Although the Cossacks were scattered widely over the southern plains, they were concentrated in two or three localities. The so-called Don Cossacks occupied the lower Don River area and established a center at Aksay only a few miles northeast of the present large city of Rostov. The other concentrations of Cossacks were in Ukraine around Kiev and farther south on some islands in the rapids of the Dnieper River near the present site of Zaporozhye. It was the Cossacks in Ukraine who during the seventeenth century rebelled against the Polish-Lithuanian state and finally established their independence of the power, bringing on the weakening of Poland. But the independence of Ukraine was short-lived; in 1654 it recognized the supremacy of the Duchy of Moscow. During the same year, the old city of Smolensk, in the western part of European Russia, was ceded to Moscow by Poland.

Consolidation of these gains in the south under an organized governmental control was begun by Peter I, or Peter the Great, during his reign from 1698–1725. After a few skirmishes along the Sea of Azov with the Ottoman Turks, however, his attention was diverted to the north by the Swedes in the Baltic, where he first suffered a major defeat from Charles XII near the city of Narva. But in 1709 he recuperated his armies to defeat Charles decisively in Ukraine at the town of Poltava, a battle which the Russians consider one of the decisive battles of history, since it insured continued control of Ukraine. Even though this was a major victory for the Russians, the Swedes harassed them in the Baltic area throughout Peter's reign. The opening up of the south remained undone for another half century until the accession to the throne of Catherine the Great. Nevertheless, Peter's war with Sweden established a Russian hold on the Baltic and weakened Swedish power from then on. In 1703 Peter the Great began building St. Petersburg on the Baltic Sea, and in 1713 he moved the national government from Moscow to his new city, where it remained until 1918. This move shifted the center of influence of the Russian government and assured a stronghold on the Baltic and a western position on the European plain.

During the reign of Catherine the Great (1762–1796) the offensive to the south was reopened, and many battles were fought with and against the Austrians, the Prussians, and the Turks until by the end of the reign the entire north shore of the Black Sea was secured to Russia. The Crimea was occupied in 1783. The ancient city of Odisseos, near the site of the present city of Odessa, which had been captured from the Greeks by the Turks was captured by the Russians in 1774, was lost again, and was recaptured in 1789. Bukovina, west of the Dniester, which had been occupied by the Austrians in 1773, and Bessarabia, which was still in Turkish hands, both were ceded to Russia in 1812. It was also during the reign of Catherine that the three partitions of Poland took place, which led to the decision incorporated in the Paris Treaty in 1814 to put almost all of the territory of Poland, including Warsaw, under the Russian throne, where it remained with varying degrees of autonomy until 1915. Thus by the end of Catherine's reign the boundaries of the Russian Empire extended from their most western limit in Poland eastward to the Pacific. Expansion to the northwest was completed in 1809 when Finland was acquired from Sweden.

Two more great advances remained to be carried out in the nineteenth century to round out the Russian Empire as it existed in its greatest extent in 1904. The first of these was the advance into the Caucasus, a movement that began by the founding of towns along the northern foothills of the Great Caucasus during the latter part of Catherine's reign. The movement continued across the Caucasus during the reign of Alexander I in the early part of the nineteenth century. Tbilisi, the capital of Georgia, fell to Russia in 1801. Baku, later to become the capital of the Azerbaydzhan Republic, came under Russian control in 1806, and the Black Sea coast south to Sukhumi was secured by 1810. The advance was completed in 1828 when, after the capture of Yerevan, Russia met stiff resistance from Turkey and growing British influence in Persia.

The second advance proceeded into the deserts of Middle Asia from such established bases as Orenburg along the southern fringe of the Ural Mountains. Tashkent was captured in 1865 and Bukhara and Samarkand (Afrosiab) in 1868. The last remaining khanates of Khiva and Kokand were subjugated in 1873 and 1876 respectively. Although many Moslem towns remained nominally independent of the Russian "protectorate" until after the Revolution in 1920, the Russians controlled the area to the high mountains in the south. The Russians occupied this area primarily to subjugate the nomadic tribes that periodically foraged northward into southwestern Siberia and the southeastern part of the European plain to harass the Russian settlers. In Central Asia British influence was met again, and in 1883 the frontier between Russia and India was agreed on, with Afghanistan established as a buffer state.

In 1860 Russian expansion was revived in the Far East after the weakening of the Chinese influence and in response to the expansionist tendencies of Japan. Vladivostok was founded in 1860 after the annexation of the Amur Provinces from China. Three decades later, in 1892, construction was begun on the Trans-Siberian Railway, and great pressure was brought to bear on China to allow the extension of the railway through northern Manchuria to Vladivostok. Finally, in 1904, after the Boxer Rebellion in China, Russia occupied the whole of northern Manchuria. This action brought

on the Russo-Japanese War in 1905 in which Russia was defeated decisively, and thus ended Russian expansion in the Far East. The loss of southern Sakhalin to Japan in 1905 was the first diminution in Russia's frontiers since the fifteenth century, and the year 1904 marks the greatest expanse of the territory controlled by the tsars. The total area of the country at that time was approximately 8,550,000 square miles, about 50,000 square miles less than the present area of the Soviet Union.

The ultimate result of defeat in World War I, followed by revolution, civil war, and intervention by the Allies, was the loss of Finland, Estonia, Latvia, Lithuania, and Poland, which became independent countries, and Bessarabia and Northern Bukovina in the southwest to Rumania. Various national areas such as Ukraine, the Transcaucasian areas of Georgia, Armenia, and Azerbaydzhan, and some of the areas in Middle Asia east of the Caspian declared their independence and set up their own governments. So-called White Republics were established within Russia by such military monarchists as Denikin in the Northern Caucasus and Kolchak in Siberia. But such resistance forces failed to integrate their efforts and one by one they were crushed by the Red Army as Lenin appealed to the non-Russian nationalities by proclaiming national self-determination. The result was that essentially all of these areas were brought within the boundaries of the newly constituted Soviet Union in 1923.

All the territories lost as a result of World War I, except for Finland and part of the Polish area, were regained at the end of World War II, and some territory which never had been under the Russian Empire also was acquired at this time. Poland was partitioned again in 1939 between Germany and the Soviet Union, but this partition did not stand after Germany's attack on the U.S.S.R. After the war, all of eastern Poland became part of Belorussia or Ukraine within the Soviet Union, whereas the country of Poland was shifted westward to occupy much of what had been eastern Germany. The Baltic States of Estonia, Latvia, and Lithuania were regained by the Soviet Union during the early part of the war. Bessarabia was later regained and Bukovina newly gained from Rumania to be incorporated partly into the new republic of Moldavia and partly into western Ukraine. Small pieces of territory were taken over from Finland, particularly the Pechenga area in the far north, which contains important nickel and copper deposits, and the Karelian Isthmus in the south next to Leningrad. Two areas in the west that were taken after World War II which had never been under Russian control were the Ruthenian area of Czechoslovakia, which became Transcarpathian Ukraine, and the northern half of East Prussia, which became Kaliningrad Oblast. In the Far East, southern Sakhalin and the Kuril Islands were regained from Japan. Also, in 1944, Tuva joined the Soviet Union, after the establishment of a protectorate which dated back to 1911. In 1946 the area of the Soviet Union was given as 8,606,300 square miles, which compares to 3,615,210 square miles in the United States.

The Physical Setting

Topography As has been seen, the Soviet Union is a huge country, nearly three times the area of the United States. We would expect to find within such an expanse of territory much variety of landforms, climate, soils, and natural vegetation, and we do. But there are some generalizations that can be made. Very simply, the landforms of the Soviet Union can be described as an extensive plain, only a few hundred feet above sea level in the central and western portions, surrounded by high mountains and rugged plateaus on the south and east. This arrangement of landforms, as will be seen later, has a great

effect on the climate and the zonations of soil and natural vegetation.

Geologically, the European plain, from the western borders of the country to the Urals, is an old stable block of the earth's crust underlain by ancient crystalline rocks of igneous and metamorphic origin that over millions of centuries have been planed down by stream erosion to a rough, rolling surface. This crystalline basement rock outcrops at the surface in the northwestern part of the country in the so-called Karelian and Kola Peninsula areas. It also outcrops at the surface in a few places in the southern part of the plain where the major streams have eroded channels deep enough to expose it. But over most of the plain the crystalline rock is covered to a depth of several hundred feet by younger sedimentary rocks lying in nearly horizontal positions. Dating from Paleozoic times, these sediments compare in age, type, and present attitudes to the rock layers in the Middle West of the United States.

Here and there the European plain has been warped gently into broad swells and shallow swales, which inject some variety into the landscape; the higher portions of the plain have undergone more severe stream dissection, and differential erosion on the dipping sedimentary layers has produced a system of low-lying cuestas that have exercised considerable control on the development of the major stream pattern. The broadest upwarps have resulted in the Central Russian Uplands, which run northwest to southeast through the center of the plain, and the Volga Heights, which lie to the west of the Volga River in its central portion. There also has been a broad upwarp in the south through Ukraine and Moldavia, which runs essentially west-east across the major south-flowing rivers and forces an abrupt eastward bend of the rivers as they cross the axis of uplift. This upwarp is known in the west as the Podolian Plateau and in the east as the Donets Ridge.

At what is usually considered to be the

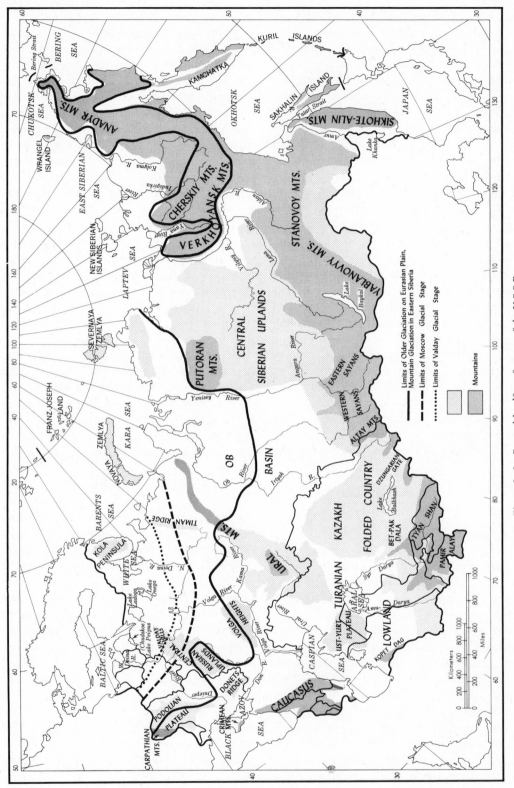

Figure 1–6 General landform features of the U.S.S.R.

boundary between Europe and Asia, the plain is interrupted by the low range of the Ural Mountains. These old, worn-down mountains of Paleozoic age correspond in elevations to the Appalachian Range in the United States. No doubt they have been much higher in the past, but erosion has worn them down to the bare stumps and has exposed old Paleozoic sedimentary rocks on the western slopes and even older crystalline rocks on the eastern slopes. The greatest heights in the Urals are now little above 6000 feet and general elevations are no more than 2000 feet. In the middle, most heavily populated section, the range splits into numerous individual ridges which here and there become discontinuous and are very low in altitude so that sections of the area are not mountainous at all. The range therefore is no barrier to transportation or other cultural endeavors or to physical phenomena such as climate and soils.

East of the Urals, the plain continues until it reaches the River Yenisey where it stops abruptly against the Central Siberian Upland. This plain between the Urals and the Yenisey River, drained by the mighty Ob, is as flat as a floor. It represents a recently uplifted part of the Continental Shelf which had been inundated by Arctic waters during postglacial time. The surface materials are young marine sediments, in many cases very poorly consolidated, with no outcrops of older rock, and everywhere the drainage is exceedingly poor.

Surrounding the east European and west Siberian plains on the south and east are rugged, young, folded mountains and associated plateaus. In the very southwestern part of the country, in the area that was acquired from Czechoslovakia after World War II, the Carpathian Mountains reach heights above 6000 feet. Farther east, on the Crimean Peninsula, the Crimean Mountains reach elevations above 5000 feet and plunge abruptly to the sea on the southeast along a fault system that continues into the Caucasus between the Black and Caspian Seas. The Great Caucasus, with elevations over 18,000 feet, have no low passes and are a definite barrier for climate and other phenomena.

The high mountains continue eastward around the southern end of the Caspian Sea where the Elburz Mountains in northern Iran reach an elevation of more than 19,000 feet. Without a break, these ranges continue eastward along the border of Iran and the Soviet Union as the Kopet Dag, or "Dry Mountains," which reach elevations of about 10,000 feet in the Soviet Union and are extremely arid. Farther east, in Afghanistan, the Hindu Kush Range leads up to the "Roof of the World," the Pamirs.

The Pamir-Alay Mountains and the Tyan Shan to the north are the highest mountains in the Soviet Union. In the southeastern corner of Soviet Middle Asia they reach elevations well above 20,000 feet. These high mountains form a complete barrier to climate and to communication between the Soviet Union and adjacent countries. Their snow-capped peaks provide abundant irrigation water to the cotton-growing areas of Soviet Middle Asia. Their west-to-east-oriented ranges are broken here and there by rather broad synclinal valleys, the broadest of which, the so-called Dzungarian Gate, lies east of Lake Balkhash.

The extensive lowland lying to the north of the broad arc of Central Asian mountains is a desert of low plateaus, eroded hills, expansive sand dunes, and basins of interior drainage, the chief ones of which contain the three large bodies of water: the Caspian Sea, the Aral Sea, and Lake Balkhash. This lowland opens northward onto the Ob Basin in western Siberia, from which it is distinguished more by climate than by topography.

The high mountains continue northeast of the Dzungarian Gate in ranges oriented roughly northwest-southeast. The western-most ranges, on the border between Kazakhstan and Siberia, are the Altay

Mountains. These mountains are considerably older geologically than those to the southwest and have been eroded down somewhat more and are not quite as high or rugged as are the Tyan Shans and Pamirs. They do reach elevations of more than 16,000 feet, however, and their importance will become obvious in the discussion of mineral resources. These high mountains and intervening basins continue eastward along the border of the Soviet Union and Mongolia and further east between the Soviet Union and China.

To the north, stretching all the way to the Arctic Sea between the Yenisey and Lena Rivers, is a broad roughly dissected upland known as the Central Siberian Uplands or the East Siberian Plateaus. Different sections are known by different names that correspond to the major river systems. The general elevation of the upland is only about 2000 feet above sea level, but locally it rises to 6000 feet. It has been deeply dissected everywhere by streams, which in some cases lie in true canyons. Much of the upland is underlain by an old crystalline rock platform, a stable block that has resisted tectonic movement as younger mountains have been folded up along its flanks. In places the crystalline rocks outcrop at the surface, but more often they are covered by younger sedimentary rocks, many of which are coal bearing, or by recent outflows of lava. The southern fringe has been splintered by recent faults that have divided the area into a series of horsts and grabens. Lake Baykal lies in one of the deep grabens.

Beyond the Lena River, high mountains and intervening river basins continue eastward to the Bering Sea. These ranges are part of the arcuate mountain ranges that run the full length of the east coast of Asia and continue offshore in a series of islands and peninsulas. The island of Sakhalin, and particularly the peninsula of Kamchatka, are part of this arcuate mountain system which is a zone of contemporary intensive disastrophism and vulcanism.

Kamchatka has approximately one hundred active volcanoes, the highest of which, Mt. Klyuchevskaya, reaches an elevation of more than 16,000 feet. It is one of the world's great volcanoes, rising from nearly sea level to its lofty peak, which is perpetually snow capped.

Climate   The climate of the Soviet Union reflects the high latitude of the country, the enormous land area, and the rim of high mountains along the south and east. Everywhere it shows strong influences of continentality; precipitation in most cases is only moderate or deficient, and temperatures are extreme. Most of the moisture that comes to the Soviet Union comes from the Atlantic Ocean. By the time the air reaches European Russia it has lost much of its capacity for precipitation.

Cyclonic storms follow northeasterly tracks across the European plain, and usually dissipate along the Arctic Coast of Western Siberia. This is particularly true during winter when storms are squeezed off the continent by the strong and persistent Siberian high-pressure cell. The precipitation is most adequate in the northwestern part of Russia and diminishes southeastward into Middle Asia. Yearly totals in northwestern Russia amount to approximately 25 inches, but along the northern shore of the Black Sea this total has dropped to less than 16 inches, and it continues to diminish eastward until around the northern end of the Caspian Sea it is only 8 inches. Farther east, in the area around the Aral Sea, an extensive area of desert receives less than 4 inches of precipitation per year. Much of Siberia, except for parts of the southern fringe, can be classified as humid, but this classification stems not so much from abundant precipitation as it does from cool temperatures and low evaporation rates. In the Far East, particularly in the south, precipitation increases again as a result of monsoonal influences from the Pacific. Precipitation in the Far East is heavily concentrated in mid-

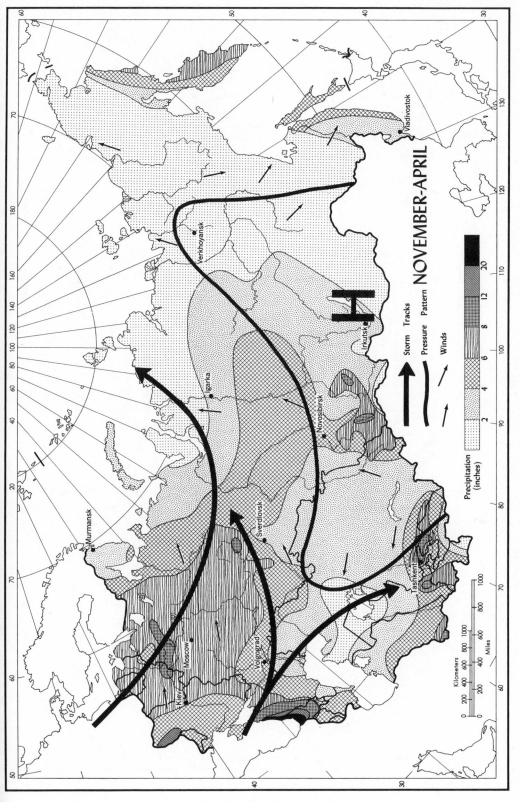

Figure 1–7 Storm tracks and precipitation in the U.S.S.R., November–April. Adapted from Davydova and Alisov.

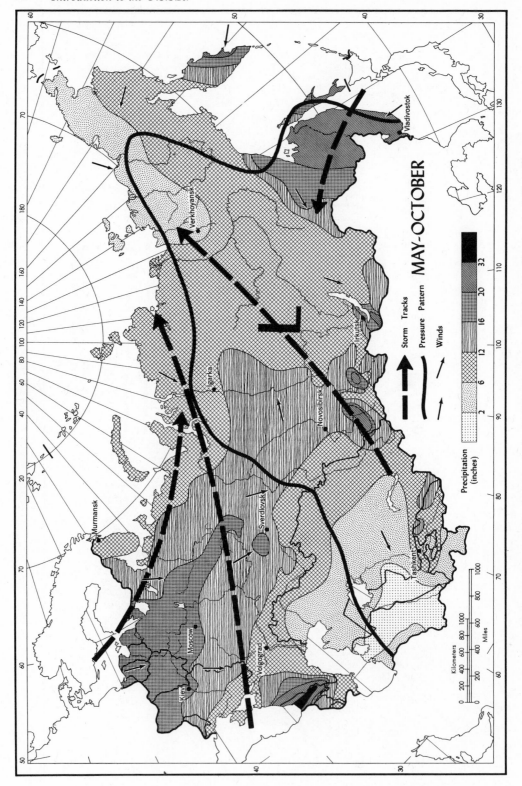

Figure 1–8   Storm tracks and precipitation in the U.S.S.R., May–October. Adapted from Davydova and Alisov. The summer storm tracks are shown by dashed arrows to indicate that they are less frequented by cyclones than the winter tracks are.

dle and late summer when monsoon winds blow into the land from the Pacific Ocean. This rainfall regime is not very favorable for crop growth, since the heaviest rain often falls during the harvest time.

The high mountains along the southern fringes of the country may catch as much as 40 inches of precipitation on their windward slopes, much of it coming in the form of snow during the wintertime. Parts of Transcaucasia and Middle Asia are in latitudes that are affected by cyclonic storms during the winter that follow a southern track through the Mediterranean Sea and eastward across southwestern Asia along the southern fringes of the Siberian High. The heavy fall of snow in the wintertime in the southern mountains is of great significance to irrigation agriculture in the adjoining plains since the precipitation is held over in the form of snow until midsummer when it reaches its maximum melting at the time of greatest need.

Only two small spots in the Soviet Union receive what might be called excessive precipitation. These are at either end of Transcaucasia, bordering on the eastern end of the Black Sea and on the southwestern side of the Caspian. The Colchis Lowland at the eastern end of the Black Sea receives 60 inches or more of rain per year and totals as high as 90 inches are received in the mountain foothills around Batumi. Summers here are hot and humid and the precipitation comes mainly in the form of thundershowers, whereas winter precipitation is due primarily to cyclonic storms that move in from the Mediterranean across the Black Sea. On the Caspian side of Transcaucasia, a much smaller area known as the Lenkoran Lowland receives around 60 inches of rainfall. Both the Colchis Lowland and the Lenkoran Lowland have mild winters and hot, humid summers and thereby classify as having humid subtropical climates.

The climate of nearly all the Soviet Union is either humid continental and subarctic or dry. The winters are always severe.

Even in Middle Asia the plain is wide open to cold blasts of air during the winter. Much of European Russia classifies as a humid continental, cool summer type of climate, similar to the Great Lakes and adjacent parts of the United States and Canada. Moscow sits approximately in the center of this belt of climate in a latitude corresponding roughly to the southern part of Hudson Bay. In southeastern European Russia the summers become longer and warmer, but they also become drier. Before the summers become long and warm enough for a wide variety of crops, the precipitation has diminished to the point where the climate no longer classifies as humid. The Soviet Union does not have the combination of long, hot, moist summers that prevail in the North American Corn Belt. Traveling from Moscow to southern Ukraine climatically corresponds to traveling from Minnesota to eastern Montana. Hence corn has not been a major crop in the Soviet Union, although now it has been introduced under governmental decree.

The northern part of European Russia has a subarctic climate and lies beyond the limits of most agriculture. This type of climate extends eastward across the Urals and expands latitudinally until it engulfs much of Siberia. Most of this subarctic region still is covered by virgin coniferous forests. The northern fringe along the Arctic seas and some of the mountainous areas east of the Lena River in eastern Siberia have a tundra climate in which no month averages above 50°F. These areas are largely devoid of trees and contain only sparse tundra vegetation of mosses and lichens.

Only the southern fringes of Siberia are warm enough to be classified as other than subarctic. This particularly pertains to southwestern Siberia, but it also applies to mountain basins along the southern fringes of Siberia all the way to the Pacific. In Maritime Kray and along the lower Amur River the climate once again is of a humid

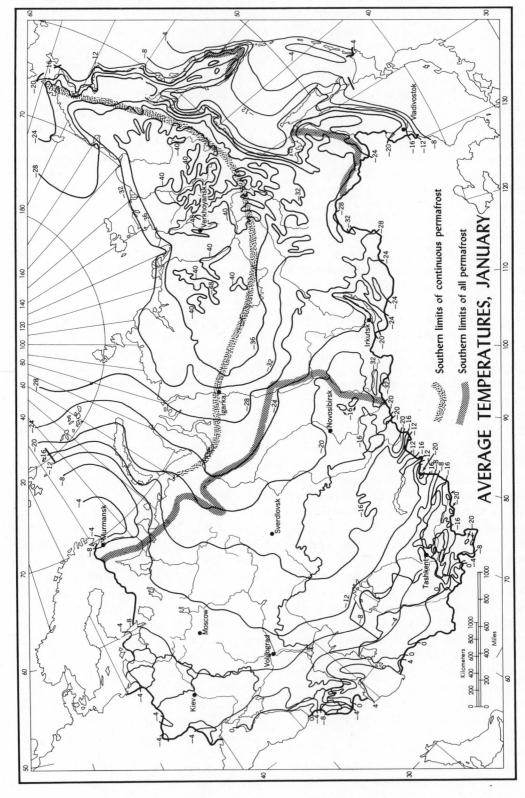

Figure 1-9   Average temperatures in degrees centigrade, January. From Atlas selskogo khozyaystva SSSR, p. 10.

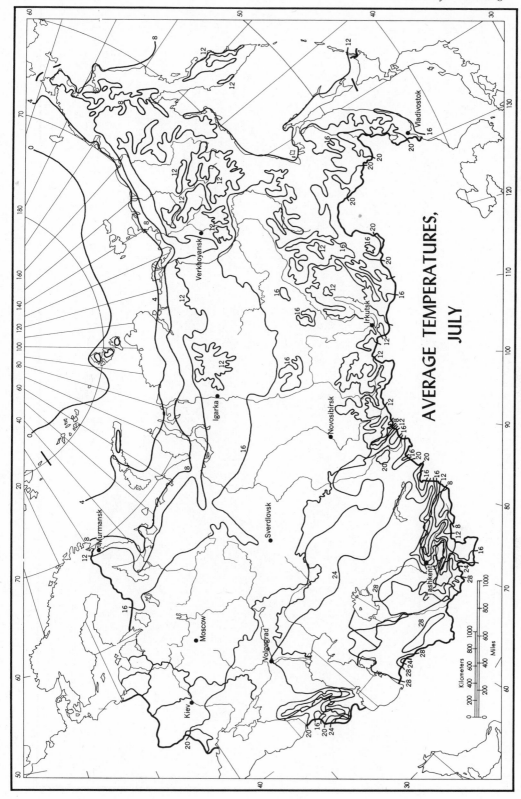

Figure 1–10 Average temperatures in degrees centigrade, July. From Atlas selskogo khozyaystva SSSR, p. 11.

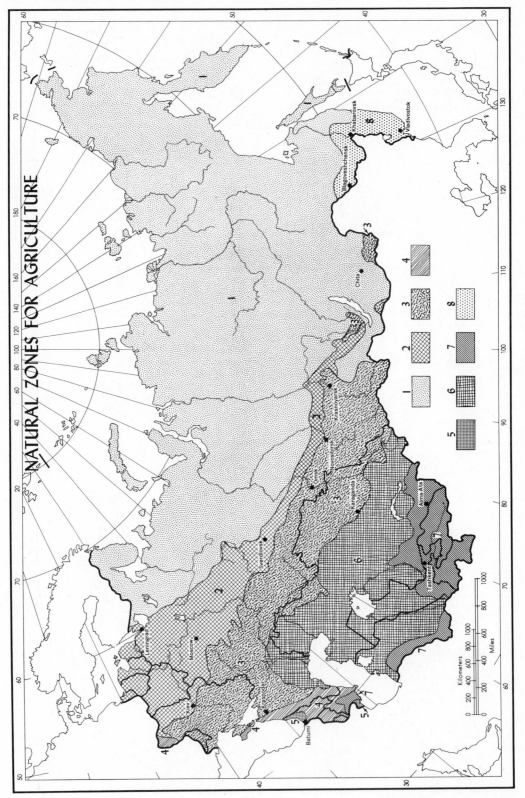

NATURAL ZONES FOR AGRICULTURE

Figure 1–11   For descriptive legend see following page.

continental, cool summer type, but here the precipitation is more concentrated in summer owing to the monsoonal flow of air from the Pacific at that season. During the winter, much of eastern Asia is covered by a very intensive high-pressure cell usually centered somewhere south of Lake Baykal, and the winds, circulating clockwise about the high, blow from the northwest across Maritime Kray to the Pacific and strictly limit precipitation. In addition they bring severe temperatures even to the coastal areas of the Pacific.

South of a line running from the western Ukraine to southwestern Siberia, the Eurasian plain is an area of dry climates. The fringes generally are steppe or semiarid, but an extensive region from the eastern shore of the Caspian Sea to the eastern end of Lake Balkhash classifies as true desert. The more humid fringes of the steppe regions contain the best soils in the country, and hence an intensive grain-growing agricultural economy is practiced in spite of the droughty climate.

Only three small spots in the south classify as humid mesothermal climates. These are the two limited areas of humid subtropical climate at either end of Transcaucasia and the southern side of the Crimean Peninsula. In each spot mountains to the north protect these areas from cold winter winds, so that winter temperatures average above freezing. The climate along the south-east shore of Crimea classifies as a Mediterranean type which receives almost all its rain in the wintertime from cyclonic storms.

Natural Vegetation, Soils, and Land Use The natural vegetation and soils are distributed in zones oriented roughly west-east, which closely correspond to the zones of climate. The northern fringe of the country is covered by tundra vegetation and infertile tundra soils. Further south, a broad expanse of coniferous forest, the taiga, occupies much of European Russia north of 56° latitude and widens east of the Ural Mountains until it engulfs much of Siberia. Associated with the coniferous forests are heavily leached, gray, infertile podzol soils. The drainage throughout much of the tundra and the northern coniferous forest is very poor. Much of the area in Siberia is underlain by permafrost, which makes drainage even poorer, since downward percolation of water during the warm season largely is prevented by the frozen subsoil. Possibilities of agriculture throughout the entire region are very limited.

South of the coniferous forest lies a belt of mixed forest dominated by broad-leaf deciduous trees. Along the western border of the Soviet Union this forest occupies a wide band from the shores of the Baltic nearly to the Black Sea. The belt narrows rapidly eastward in a triangular shape until at the Urals it has been largely pinched out between the taiga to the north and the steppes to the south. The soils throughout this region are gray-brown podzolic, which are somewhat leached of plant minerals but which can be made quite productive through proper management and gener-

Figure 1–11   Natural zones for agriculture. Adapted from Atlas selskogo khozyaystva SSSR, *p. 8.*

1. Northern forests and tundra, podzol and tundra soils, little agriculture. 2. Mixed forests, podzolic soils, general farming (flax, potatoes, oats, rye, barley, hay, livestock). 3. Wooded steppe and steppe zones, Chernozem and chestnut soils, cash farming (wheat, sugar beets, sunflowers, corn, livestock). 4. Mountain forests and soils of the Carpathians, Crimea, and Caucasia; little agriculture. 5. Humid subtropical climate and soils of the Colchis and Lenkoran Lowlands; citrus, tea, tobacco, grapes, other fruits and vege- *tables, corn, rice, livestock. 6. Desert vegetation and soils; extensive grazing, scattered irrigation agriculture. 7. Mountains and mountain forelands with semidesert climates and serozem soils; dry farming of wheat and intensive irrigation of cotton, alfalfa, and other crops; transhumance of livestock. 8. Low mountains and basins of the Far East; cool monsoon climate, mixed forests, forest and steppe soils; wheat, sugar beets, soy beans, rice, grain sorghums, livestock.*

ous additions of fertilizers. General farming has developed here based on crops that are adapted to cool, moist, acidic soil conditions such as potatoes, flax, rye, barley, oats, hay, and a variety of hardy vegetables, particularly cabbage and beets. Dairying and livestock raising are very important.

South and east of the mixed forest lies a rather narrow zone of so-called wooded steppe in which the natural vegetation is tall grasses interspersed by clumps of trees, particularly along streams. Further south lies the true steppe, a rolling, open grassland devoid of trees. It is within the zone of wooded steppe and the northern parts of the steppe that the famous black earth or chernozem soils of Russia exist. The black earth belt of Russia begins in the west-central Ukraine and extends east-northeast across the middle Volga and southern Urals into southwestern Siberia and northern Kazakhstan, where it narrows to a belt approximately 150 miles wide, straddling the 55th parallel of latitude. The black soils are encountered here and there farther east along similar latitudes in the steppe basins that lie between the mountains of southern Siberia. These are the best soils of Russia, and indeed, some of the best soils in the world. The area is hampered by its droughty climate and desiccating flows of hot, dry air, the famous Russian "sukhovey," so that it is not as productive as some areas of the world that have less fertile soils. Nevertheless, this is the heart of the farming country in the Soviet Union. The main crops here are wheat, corn, sugar beets, and sunflowers, but a great variety of other crops are grown, and livestock raising is very important. Farming here is done on a more commercial level than it is further north.

The steppes extend south to the northern coast of the Black Sea, southeast into the North Caucasian Foreland, and east across northern Kazakhstan. The soils continue to be good, but the climate becomes drier further south, and agriculture becomes more commercial and more spe-

cialized. Wheat and sunflowers are grown on extensive scales. Only in the Kuban District in Krasnodar Kray along the north-western slopes of the Caucasus does the climate once again become humid enough for such crops as sugar beets and corn. The Kuban District rivals the better parts of Ukraine in agricultural potentialities and production.

South of the Caucasus, the humid subtropical Colchis and Lenkoran Lowlands are utilized for specialty crops such as citrus fruits, tea, and tobacco, which are exotic to the rest of the Soviet Union and enjoy monopolies on nationwide markets. The drier Kura Lowland is important for its irrigated cotton and alfalfa.

The large area of Middle Asia between the Caspian Sea and Lake Balkhash has a desert climate, and, hence, desert vegetation and desert soils. The vegetation here is a sparse cover of saxaul trees, brush, and certain types of cactus. Much of the surface is not covered by vegetation; hence, the soils are largely lacking in humus. The mineral content is high, however, and wherever irrigation water can be applied, the soils prove to be quite productive. In border areas on the southeast sides of the deserts the great cotton-growing areas of the Soviet Union have developed on a discontinuous belt of thick loess deposits, utilizing irrigation waters from northwest-ward-flowing streams which come down from the Tyan Shans and the Pamir-Alay Ranges.

In the Far East, Amur Oblast and Maritime Kray are areas of mixed forests and gray-brown podzolic soils similar to those in central European Russia and northern Ukraine. Here the general farming of Ukraine and western Russia has mingled with the rice paddies, soy beans, and grain sorghums of Manchuria and North Korea.

The effectively occupied territory of the Soviet Union is limited primarily to the wedge of agriculturally productive land, in the contiguous zones of the mixed forest, the wooded steppe, and the steppe, which stretch from the Baltic to the Black Sea in the west and taper to a narrow belt in western Siberia. Three major outliers of settlement are the basins of Transcaucasia, the oases of Middle Asia, and the southern valleys of the Far East. The total area of these cultivated lands is approximately equal to the area under cultivation in the United States, and in general the cultivated land in the United States lies in warmer and moister climates. Thus, although the U.S.S.R. contains nearly three times the area of the United States, the agricultural potential of the two countries is approximately equal. The United States might even be slightly better endowed. So far, the United States certainly has produced much more than the U.S.S.R. has, largely because agriculture in the United States has been much better organized and more efficient; 40 million farmers in the U.S.S.R. produce somewhat less agricultural produce than do approximately 5 million farmers in the United States. With a total population of approximately 35 million more people than are in the United States, the U.S.S.R. obviously has a considerably lower per capita consumption of farm products than does the United States.

Political and Economic Subdivisions

The Soviet Union is divided into subregions on the bases of nationality and administrative convenience. Soviet ideology on the one hand calls for national self determination, and on the other it says that the political structure should reflect the economic structure. In practice this duality of ideology has led to conflict on several occasions; adherence to the principle of political recognition of nationality groups tends to stabilize internal boundaries, whereas economic determination of political boundaries in such a rapidly developing country calls for almost constant change. Although boundary and name changes have occurred frequently enough in the Soviet Union to excite comment, in general traditionalism has induced an element of ultraconservatism in the laying out of subregions, even where nationality is not a question. The administrative subdivisions of European Russia look very much the same as they did when they were first formed by the government of Catherine the Great in the latter part of the eighteenth century.

At present, the U.S.S.R. is divided into fifteen Soviet Socialist Republics (S.S.R.), sometimes called Union Republics, on the basis of nationalities. These fifteen republics represent fifteen of the most populous and most culturally advanced groups of peoples in the U.S.S.R. Administratively, they would correspond somewhat to the fifty states of the United States. Actually,

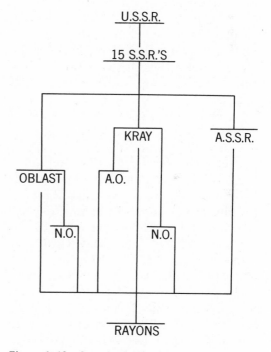

Figure 1–12 Organizational structure of political administrative units in the U.S.S.R. Exceptions to the general scheme depicted above are (1) Maritime Kray in the Far East has no subdivision, (2) small SSR's are divided directly into rayons, and (3) some of the larger cities have been placed under the direct jurisdictions of their respective SSR's.

according to the constitution of the U.S.S.R., the Union Republics have a wider latitude of jurisdiction than do the states of the United States. The constitution of the U.S.S.R. is really a confederate one, reserving the rights to the individual member republics to coin money, enter into foreign agreements, and secede from the Union at any time. In actuality, little attention is paid to the constitution in the Soviet Union, and the individual republics have very little latitude of operation outside the surveillance of Moscow. The Russian Republic is much bigger and much more populous than any of the other republics and it definitely is the "first among equals." The provisions of the constitution are adhered to only when it is expedient to do so. A good illustration of this is the fact that three seats are occupied in the United Nations by the Soviet Union; one for the U.S.S.R., one for the Ukrainian Republic, and one for the Belorussian Republic, with the contention that these republics really are independent countries.

The Union Republics, except for some of the smaller ones, are divided into oblasts, krays, and Autonomous Soviet Socialist Republics (A.S.S.R.), all of which are on a commensurate level of jurisdiction, and all of which are directly responsible to their respective Union Republics. The oblast is purely an administrative subdivision that contains no significant nationality group other than the titular nationality of the Union Republic within which it is located. The A.S.S.R. administratively serves the same function as the oblast, but its boundaries have been drawn to give political recognition to an important minority nationality group. The kray is a kind of combination of the other two. Its boundaries have been laid out rather arbitrarily, primarily for administrative facility, but it contains within it lesser political subdivisions that are based on nationality groups—autonomous oblasts (A.O.) or national okrugs (N.O.) or both. Theoretically, any administrative unit can contain within it nationality-based political units on any of the lower echelons. For instance, several oblasts encompass national okrugs. But an oblast cannot contain an autonomous oblast. An administrative unit containing an autonomous oblast would become a kray. In a sense, then, the kray is a higher unit than is the oblast, but they are both directly responsible to the Union Republic.

A nationality group is given political recognition in one of the following four administrative units ranked in decreasing order of importance: (1) S.S.R., (2) A.S.S.R., (3) A.O., and (4) N.O. The national okrug is usually assigned to large remote areas of sparse population such as areas in northern Siberia occupied by semi-nomadic reindeer herders. In cultural development these areas might be likened to Indian reservations in the United States. However, the national okrugs in the Soviet Union do have some representation in the national government. There are many small nationality groups in the U.S.S.R. that have no political identities because of their limited numbers. There are also some larger and more significant groups, particularly the Germans and Poles, who have no regional identities because their people are scattered.

At the lowest level of administration, all areas are divided into "rayons." There are rural rayons and city rayons. Most Soviet production statistics and other information are not broken down for individual rayons; rarely are they reported for units smaller than oblasts, if that. In this book, discussion will be based on oblasts, krays, and A.S.S.R.'s. These units administratively might be likened to counties in the United States, but generally their areas are much larger. The rural and city rayons might be likened to townships and city wards. Outside this hierarchy of administrative regions, a number of cities have been given a special status which excludes them from the governmental jurisdiction of the regions within which they are located and

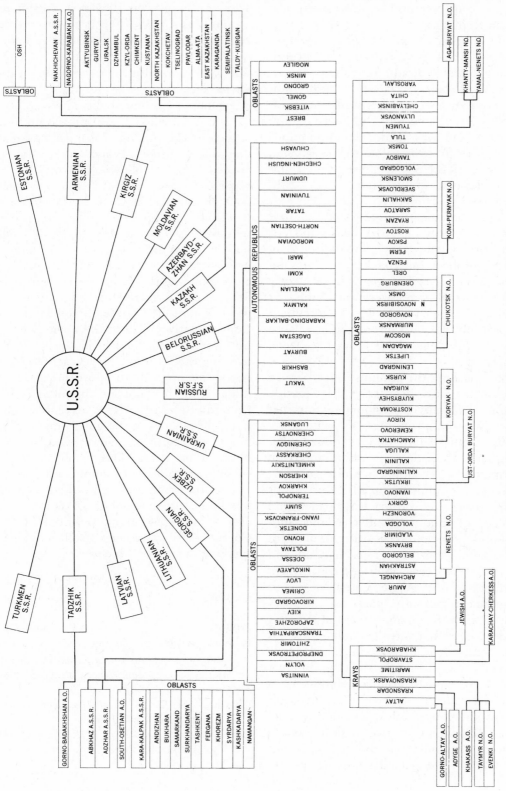

Figure 1-13 Political subdivisions of the U.S.S.R. as of October, 1968.

makes them responsible directly to their Union Republics.

The political administrative organization of the U.S.S.R. is rather complex. It embodies elements of administrative convenience, nationality recognition, and traditionalism. It also contains some inconsistencies. Tuva came into the Soviet Union in 1944 and was made an autonomous oblast directly responsible to the Russian Republic (R.S.F.S.R.). Since then it has been elevated to the status of A.S.S.R. Primorskiy (Maritime) Kray in the Far East has no nationality-based political unit within it. It once included oblasts and was therefore called a kray. The oblasts were later abolished, but the kray designation remained. For a few years in the early 1960s, several krays were established in Kazakhstan, each of which contained several oblasts but no nationality-based subdivisions. Now these krays have been abolished.

Complicating the administrative picture still further have been several frequently changing systems of economic regions that have involved groupings of political regions. From 1940 to 1960 economic planning and production was based largely on thirteen gross economic regions. In 1957, when the administration of industry was reorganized, the country was divided into 105 economic administrative regions. Subsequently, the boundaries and numbers of these administrative regions changed, and in 1965 they were abolished altogether. Remaining is a single system of major economic regions for planning purposes only. The branch management of industry under centrally controlled ministries has once again been firmly established. However, there is much talk and experimentation these days to establish some sort of objectively determined system of territorial-production complexes. Under the doctrine that administrative regions should reflect economic conditions, constant changes can be expected in regional boundaries. Although the 1965 reestablishment of ministries was a step backward in the regionalization process, perhaps someday political administrative regions will coincide with rational economic regions if the Soviet social system eventually can erase the influences of nationality and tradition.

Each nationality-based political unit has representation in the House of Nationalities in the legislative branch of the national government as follows: each S.S.R., 32 representatives; each A.S.S.R., 11; each A.O., 5; and each N.O., 1. In the House of the Union, on the other hand, one representative is chosen for every 300,000 people. Thus the U.S.S.R. has a bicameral legislature with a House of Nationalities corresponding roughly to the United States Senate and a House of the Union corresponding to the United States House of Representatives. There the analogy ends, however, for the houses in the U.S.S.R., forming the Supreme Soviet, act only as a rubber stamp body to approve legislation initiated by the Central Committee of the Communist Party. The executive and judicial branches of the government grow out of the Supreme Soviet and are dependent on it. A Council of Ministers, stemming from the economic administrative setup, is the real political administrative body, and since many of its members also hold high-ranking positions in the Communist Party, it does an efficient job of carrying out party directives.

Reading List

HISTORY

Adams, Arthur E., Matley, Ian M., and McCagg, William O., *An Atlas of Russian and East European History,* Praeger, New York, 1967, 216 pp.

Charques, R. D., *A Short History of Russia,* Dutton, New York, 1956.

Chew, Allen F., *An Atlas of Russian History,* Yale University Press, New Haven, 1967, 113 pp.

Florinsky, Michael T., *Russia: A History and Interpretation,* Macmillan, New York, 1953, 2 vols., 1511 pp.

——, *Russia: A Short History,* Macmillan, New York, 1964, 653 pp.

Robinson, Geroid T., *Rural Russia under the Old Regime,* University of California Press, 1967.

Sumner, Benedict H., *A Short History of Russia,* Reynal and Hitchcock, New York, 1943, 469 pp.

GEOLOGY AND HYDROLOGY

Davydov, L. K., *Gidrografiya SSSR* (Hydrography of the U.S.S.R.), Leningrad, 1955 (in Russian), Part II, pp. 321–389, translated by Office of Technical Services, Joint Publications Research Service.

Markov, K. K. and Popov, A. J., eds., *Lednikovyy period na territorii yevropeyskoy chasti SSSR i Sibiri* (The Ice Age in the European Section of the U.S.S.R. and in Siberia), Moscow, 1959, 560 pp. (in Russian).

Nalivkin, D. V., *The Geology of the U.S.S.R.,* English translation edited by J. E. Richey, Pergamon Press, New York, 1960, 170 pp.

CLIMATE

Agroclimatic handbooks, published for most oblasts, krays, and autonomous republics (in Russian).

Alisov, B. P., *Klimat SSSR* (Climate of the U.S.S.R.), Moscow, 1956, 126 pp. (in Russian).

Borisov, A. A., *Climates of the U.S.S.R.,* English translation edited by Cyril A. Halstead, Aldine, Chicago, 1965, 255 pp.

Davitaya, F. F., Drozdov, O. A., and Rubinshteyn, Ye. S., "Study of the Climatic Resources of the U.S.S.R. and their Economic Utilization," *Soviet Geography: Review and Translation,* June 1960, pp. 11–35.

Grigorev, A. A. and Budyko, M. I., "Classification of Climates of the U.S.S.R.," *Soviet Geography: Review and Translation,* May 1960, pp. 3–23.

Klimat SSSR (Climate of the U.S.S.R.), Leningrad, 1958–1963, 6 vols., the most complete compendium on the climate of the U.S.S.R. (in Russian).

Lydolph, Paul E., "The Russian Sukhovey," *Annals of the Association of American Geographers,* September 1964, pp. 291–309.

——, "Schemes for the Amelioration of Soil and Climate in the U.S.S.R.," in Laird, Roy D., *Soviet Agricultural and Peasant Affairs,* University of Kansas Press, Lawrence, 1963, pp. 204–212.

Stroitelnye normy i pravila, chast II, razdel A, glava 6, *stroitelnaya klimatologiya i geofizika, osnovnye polozheniya proyektirovaniya,* Moscow, 1963, 215 pp., the most extensive tables available on the climatic statistics of the U.S.S.R. (in Russian).

SOIL

Gvozdetskiy, N. A. and Mikhaylov, N. I., *Fiziko-geograficheskoye rayonirovaniye SSSR* (Physical geographical regionalization of the U.S.S.R.), Moscow, 1960, 286 pp. (in Russian).

Soil Geographical Zoning of the U.S.S.R., published by the Dokuchayev Soil Institute of the Academy of Sciences of the U.S.S.R., translated into English by the Israel Program for Scientific Translations, Jerusalem, 1963, 480 pp.

GOVERNMENT

Armstrong, John A., *Ideology, Politics, and Government in the Soviet Union; an Introduction,* Praeger, New York, 1967, 173 pp.

Hazard, John N., *The Soviet System of Government,* The University of Chicago Press, 1968, 4th ed. 288 pp.

Pipes, Richard, *The Formation of the Soviet Union,* Harvard University Press, Cambridge, 1964, 365 pp.

PART ONE

The Regions of the U.S.S.R.

SPLITTING THEIR COUNTRY INTO "NATURAL" REGIONS has become almost a national pastime for Soviet geographers and economists. Since they are all apparently committed to the principle that natural divisions do exist to be discovered, they search for them and they argue vehemently in print about them. Many maps have been drawn, and each has been offered as the final word on regionalization of the country. On each, purportedly, boundaries have been set according to objective criteria. But as much as the Soviets would like to believe that the Revolution released them from the fetters of the past, their thinking is still beclouded much more than they realize by traditional premises that have become ingrained in their minds. And, often as not, a scheme of regionalization, which was conceived on the bases of objective criteria, in the final presentation degenerates into a reiteration of traditional boundaries.

A good case in point is the resultant regionalization of the 1957 reorganization of industry. The movement started with a sweeping abolishment of most of the ministries in Moscow and a revolutionary reform to regional control based on a relatively small number of rather larger regions. But in the demarcation of regions the movement bogged down and finally stagnated within boundaries of oblasts and autonomous areas that have existed almost in their original forms since Catherine the Great, and even before. The so-called economic regions set up in 1957 corresponded generally to political regions and bore little relation to economic phenomena.

To some degree political regions affect the regional schemes that have been discussed by economic geographers in articles and textbooks. Although general economic regions have been devised in various fashions, combining several political administrative units into one geographical region, the boundaries of the larger regions follow along administrative boundaries and do not cut across oblasts. Hence the traditional oblast is held inviolate and the entire oblast is either included or excluded from a geographical region as a unit. Thus it is that sections of oblasts of a very primitive nature with absolutely no industrial development are included in such a highly developed area as the Central Industrial Region.

In devising the regionalization scheme

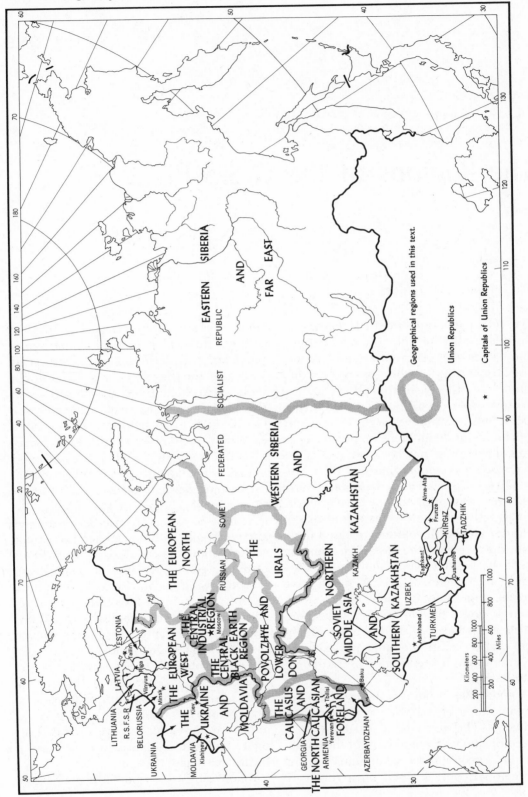

Figure 1–14 Geographical regions used in this book.

used in this book, three things have been taken into account. First, there are reasonably well-defined zones of agricultural production which are closely related to the natural environment; second, there are recognizable industrial nodal areas which lie within and transgress the boundaries of the agricultural regions; and third, there are traditional areas whose names have a real but unclearly defined significance in the minds of the Soviet people. Just as the regional terms "New England," "the South," "the Middle West" have meaning to an American, so the terms "Central Chernozem Region," "Ukraine," "the North Caucasian Foreland," and "the Povolzhye" have meaning to a Russian. These regional concepts are part of the life and the thinking of the Soviet people. Although no layman has stopped to draw boundaries around these regional concepts, the whereabouts of the core areas are tacitly understood and need no definition. The geographer who is attempting to catch the content and spirit of the Soviet Union cannot deny the existence of such conceptual regions. Therefore these concepts must be weighed against economic phenomena and other criteria for regionalization.

The author of this book, like many Soviet authors, has often found these traditional regions to have more real significance than regions based purely on economic criteria. Thus the regionalization used here is primarily the traditional one. But tradition has been tempered, or more precisely, focused, by a consideration of present economic conditions in drawing boundaries of the traditional regions. The individual oblast has not been held inviolate, nor has the Union Republic, in some instances. Only where the Union Republic has some significance in the regional thinking of the people, as in Ukraine, has the Union Republic been treated as a unit. (The very word "Ukraine" stems from regional concepts; it means "extremity" or "borderland.") The sprawling Kazakh Re-

public, however, a political unit newly conceived under the Soviet regime, has been divided and its parts included with adjacent areas.

The regions within the R.S.F.S.R. have also not been dealt with in their entirety before areas in other Union Republics were taken up, as seems to be the rule in Soviet texts. Contiguous and adjacent areas are discussed in succession, regardless of political boundaries, beginning in the heart of the country and spiralling outward in clockwise fashion to include the most highly developed and interconnected regions of the U.S.S.R. before moving out into remote border areas. Figure 1–14 shows the eleven regions that will be used as the basis for discussion in this text.

Reading List

Alampiev, P. M., *Ekonomicheskoye rayonrovaniye SSSR* (Economical regionalization of the U.S.S.R.), Moscow, Vol. 1, 1959; Vol. 2, 1963 (in Russian).

Bone, Robert M., "Regional Planning and Economic Regionalization in the Soviet Union," *Land Economics*, August 1967, pp. 347–354.

Dewdney, John C., *Patterns and Problems of Regionalization in the U.S.S.R.*, Research Papers Series No. 8, Department of Geography, University of Durham, 1967, 42 pp.

Geografiya SSSR, No. 2: *Economic Regionalization of the U.S.S.R.*, Institute of Scientific Information, Academy of Sciences U.S.S.R., Moscow, 1965, 147 pp. (in Russian); key articles and long bibliography published in English in *Soviet Geography: Review and Translation*, May 1966, entire issue.

Hoeffding, Oleg, "The Soviet Industrial Reorganization of 1957," *American Economic Review*, May 1959, pp. 65–77.

Kolotievskiy, A. M., *Voprosy teorii i metodiki ekonomicheskogo rayonirovaniya* (Theoretical and methodological problems of economic regionalization), Riga, 1967, 251 pp. (in Russian).

Lonsdale, R. E., "The Soviet Concept of the

Territorial-Production Complex," *Slavic Review,* September 1965, pp. 466–478.

Lydolph, Paul E., "The Soviet Reorganization of Industry," *American Slavic and East European Review,* October 1958, pp. 293–301.

Melezin, Abraham, "Soviet Regionalization: An Attempt at the Delineation of Socioeconomic Integrated Regions," *Geographical Review,* October 1968, pp. 593–621.

Mieczkowski, Z., "The 1962–63 Reforms in Soviet Economic Regionalization," *Slavic Review,* September 1965, pp. 479–496.

———, "The Major Economic Regions of the U.S.S.R. in the Khrushchev Era," *Canadian Geographer,* September 1965, pp. 19–30.

———, "The Economic Regionalization of the Soviet Union in the Lenin and Stalin Periods," *The Canadian Slavonic Papers,* 1966, pp. 89–124.

———, "The Economic Administrative Regions in the U.S.S.R.," *Tijdschrift voor Econ. en Soc. Geografie,* July–August 1967, pp. 209–219.

Morrison, John, "The Evolution of the Territorial-Administrative System of the U.S.S.R.," *American Quarterly on the Soviet Union,* Vol. I, No. 3, 1938, pp. 25–46.

Pavlenko, V., "Ekonomicheskoye rayonirovaniye v novykh uslovyakh," *Ekonomicheskaya Gazeta,* October 19, 1963, pp. 12–13; English translation, "Economic Regions in New Conditions," published in *The Current Digest of the Soviet Press,* November 13, 1963, pp. 3–5, 18.

Poulsen, Thomas Martin, *The Provinces of Russia: Changing Patterns in the Regional Allocation of Authority, 1708–1962,* Ph.D. Dissertation, University of Wisconsin, 1963, 318 pp.

Shabad, Theodore, "Political Administrative Divisions of the U.S.S.R. in 1945," *Geographical Review,* April 1946, pp. 303–312.

———, "The Soviet Concept of Economic Regionalization," *Geographical Review,* April 1953, pp. 214–222.

Soviet Geography: Review and Translation has printed a large number of translated Soviet papers pertaining to regionalization and has also included news notes by Theodore Shabad relating to current changes in economic and political administrative regions. The following issues and pages are of particular interest: November 1962, pp. 49–55; March 1963, pp. 49–52; December 1963, pp. 60–67; December 1964, pp. 19–33; November 1965, pp. 43–66; May 1966, entire issue.

The Central Industrial Region

Circumscribed by a circle centered at Sobinka 15 miles southwest of Vladimir with a radius of approximately 150 miles. Contains all or most urbanized parts of the following regions:

Region	Area (sq mi)	Population	People (sq mile)	% Urban [a]
Moscow City	340	6,422,000	18,900	100
Moscow Oblast	18,060 [b]	5,372,000 [b]	298	67
Yaroslavl Oblast	14,200 [b]	1,398,000 [b]	98	68
Vladimir Oblast	11,300	1,496,000	132	65
Ivanovo Oblast	9,400	1,352,000	144	73
Kostroma Oblast	6,000 [c]	420,000 [c]	70	51
Gorky Oblast	11,400 [c]	2,332,000 [c]	204	62
Ryazan Oblast	15,500 [b]	1,439,000 [b]	93	41
Tula Oblast	4,000 [c]	1,026,000 [c]	256	69
Kaluga Oblast	2,400 [c]	322,000 [c]	134	47
Kalinin Oblast	6,500 [c]	647,000 [c]	99	53
Total	99,100 [d]	22,226,000 [d]		

[a] All figures are for entire oblasts.
[b] Populations and areas of entire oblasts, although small portions lie outside Central Industrial Region.
[c] Estimated populations and areas of portions of oblasts lying within Central Industrial Region.
[d] Does not include northwestern corner of Mordovian A.S.S.R., which falls within circle.

2

The Central Industrial Region

Let us start the regional discussion of the Soviet Union with the very heart of the country at the central position on the European Plain around Moscow. This region emerged as an area of relatively dense population some time after the fall of Kiev in the thirteenth century, and two centuries later the Russian State began to expand and to take form from this center. The cultural and economic focus of the country today, it is known universally as the Central Industrial Region.

Definition of the Region

Although the Central Industrial Region has become a traditional area in the minds of the Russian people, and although everyone is agreed that the core of the area consists of a region of closely spaced cities, its boundaries have been defined in various ways.

Russian geographers, in their reluctance to violate political boundaries, always include entire oblasts, in spite of the fact that large sections of some of the outlying oblasts are not urbanized at all. For instance, the city of Kalinin is definitely part of the Central Industrial Region, but the city lies near the eastern border of Kalinin Oblast. The rest of the oblast is a poor agricultural

area at best, and the northern part is sparsely inhabited forest land. The same is true of Kostroma Oblast to the northeast. In the southeast, the cities along the Oka should be included within the Central Industrial Region, but the southern and eastern portions of the oblasts within which these cities lie, and of which they often are the political centers, are largely rich agricultural lands. They contain good-sized towns, but the towns are simply regional centers for the rural population, and most are not industrialized. Similarly, in the south, the city of Tula and its satellite cities are heavily industrialized and belong very definitely to the Central Industrial Region, but the southern part of Tula Oblast is a rural agricultural area.

We might fairly well define the boundaries of the Central Industrial Region by drawing straight lines between four corner cities, Kalinin in the northwest, Vologda in the north, Gorky in the east, and Tula in the south. Such a quadrilateral would well demonstrate the eccentric position of Moscow within this industrial complex, for Moscow is not in the center of the area but is on the western edge of the concentration of cities, and the urban growth has taken place primarily to the northeast, to the east, and to the south of Moscow. However, this four-sided figure

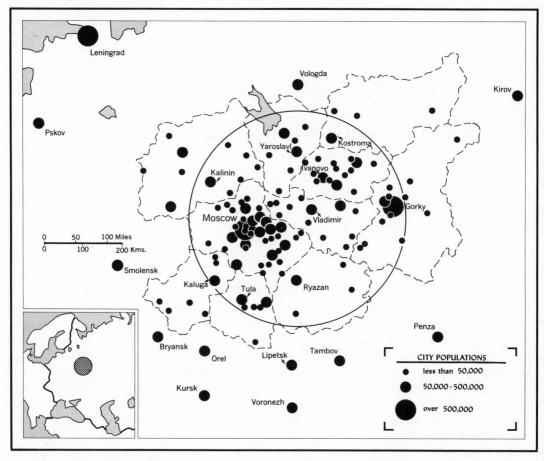

Figure 2–1   The Central Industrial Region. A circle centered southwest of Vladimir with a radius of approximately 150 miles separates an enclosed area with dense urban concentration from a surrounding area containing only scattered cities.

leaves out some of the important cities in the southeast along the Oka River. It also eliminates Kaluga and some other important towns in the southwest, and it includes some territory in the north which is very sparsely populated.

The region of urban concentration can best be circumscribed by a circle with a radius of approximately 150 miles centered near the town of Sobinka, just southwest of the old city of Vladimir. Thus will the Central Industrial Region be defined here. Such a circle passes through Gorky in the east, Tula in the south, Kalinin in the west, and a few miles north of the concentration of cities along the Volga in the northeast. It includes all or most of Moscow, Yaroslavl, Vladimir, Ivanovo and Ryazan

Oblasts, and parts of the surrounding oblasts of Kalinin, Kostroma, Gorky, Tula, and Kaluga. In addition, the city of Moscow is a separate political entity outside the jurisdiction of the oblast in which it is located. The area thus encompassed contains around 22 million people, almost 75 per cent of which are now classified as urban. More than half of these people live in the city of Moscow and heavily urbanized Moscow Oblast.

The Physical Setting

The natural resources of this region are limited. The area is comprised of a rather flat plain underlain by sedimentary mate-

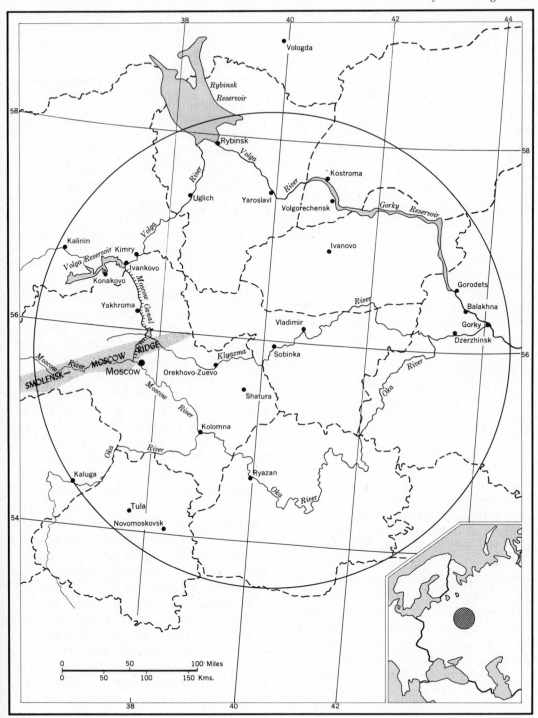

Figure 2–2   The Central Industrial Region.

rials that is gently upwarped to the west of Moscow along the eastern flanks of the Central Russian Uplands. The entire area has been glaciated, but only the northern half has been affected by the most recent glacial advance and today displays the features of continental glaciation. The so-called Smolensk-Moscow Ridge, running from west-southwest to east-northeast just north of the city of Moscow, is the terminal moraine that marks the southern limits of the most recent glaciation. North of this line the drainage is universally poor, and lakes and swamps abound. The drainage is poor in the southeast also along the very flat floodplains of the Oka River and its tributaries. The area is best drained in its southwestern portion where the bulge of the Central Russian Uplands has elevated the surface slightly and induced enough stream erosion to produce a rolling topography.

The Central Industrial Region lies in a cool, humid climate similar to that of southern Canada, with relatively short summers and long, cold winters. The length of the winter is more depressing than its temperatures. Although Moscow has experienced −44°F, its January average temperature of +14°F is no colder than Minneapolis. But winter seems to drag all the way through spring. Atlantic air from the Baltic tends to ameliorate winter temperatures, but it adds to the gloominess by causing gray overcast days that follow monotonously one after another. December averages only 19 hours of sunshine.

The precipitation is modest, somewhere between 20 and 25 inches per year, but the cool temperatures limit evaporation and make for effective dampening of the soil. Such conditions have been conducive to the growth of a forest vegetation. This is largely an area of mixed forest, with coniferous trees predominating in the north and deciduous trees predominating in the south. The forest vegetation and abundant soil moisture have led to a podzolization of the soil, which has leached away much of the mineral content and has added only a minimum of organic matter. The resultant gray-brown forest soils are rather low in fertility, although they can be made to be quite productive under the correct adaptations of crops and farming methods and generous applications of fertilizers.

Agriculture   A general farming has developed that in the past has been more subsistence than commercial, although this is gradually changing. Flax, being well adapted to cool, moist conditions and acidic soils, is the chief cash crop, and this region, together with the European West, is the main area of flax growing in the country. Potatoes occupy more acreage, however, and serve both as a staple food and as a base for ethyl alcohol for the chemical industry. The Russians have used the potato for everything from drinking to riding. Vodka is made from potatoes, and synthetic tires were long made from potato alcohol.

The small hardy grains, rye, barley, and oats, and a variety of hay crops, take up most of the rest of the cultivated land. Dairying and grazing of livestock for meat are important, utilizing fairly good pastures during most of the summer and hay in the winter. Dairying is particularly developed in the cooler, moister areas in the north and around the larger cities. The meat supply of the area has recently been increased by a great expansion in hog and poultry raising, utilizing garbage and waste produce from canneries, potato alcohol distilleries, and the like.

A variety of fruits and vegetables are raised, particularly around the larger cities to serve the urban markets. A number of state farms have been formed in the area specifically oriented toward urban supply. In general, farming improves from north to south in the region as the climate becomes a little milder and the soil improves.

Minerals   Mineral resources as a basis for industrialization in the Central Industrial Region largely are lacking. The most important mineral resource in the area is the brown coal of the so-called Moscow

Coal Basin, which provides fuel for heating and electrical generation, but which is not of coking quality and cannot be used in metallurgical industries. In spite of the low grade of the coal, local demand for it is so great that the Moscow Basin ranks fourth among producing basins in the U.S.S.R., annually producing about 6 per cent of the country's coal.

Next in importance are the iron ore deposits in the south around the city of Tula, that, however small, were the basis for the development of the first iron industry in the Russian Empire in the eighteenth century and which still support some iron and steel industries in the cities of Tula and Lipetsk. The vast iron ore deposits outside of this region to the south in the oblasts of Kursk and Belgorod are beginning to revive this steel industry and in the near future they might raise it to heights never known before, but this iron ore lies in another region and has to be shipped into the Central Industrial Region.

Other than low-grade coal and minor deposits of iron ore, about the only mineral resources are various types of building stones and clays and scattered deposits of phosphate rock, which are becoming important in the agricultural fertilizer industry and in certain chemical industries. Such resources cannot explain the growth of this area into the most urbanized and industrialized region of the Soviet Union; it contains approximately 10 per cent of the population of the country and produces approximately 20 per cent of the country's industrial output. We must turn to economic considerations of market, labor, early start, central position, and the like for an explanation of this industrialization.

Urban Growth and Industrialization

Located in the forest zone among the headwaters of the great Volga River system, the Central Industrial Region enjoyed a somewhat strategic position with regard to water routes and to defense from the Tatar hordes to the south. It thereby got an early start as a center of relatively dense population, which in the seventeenth and eighteenth centuries provided the basis for the beginning of industrialization in the form of home industry. Thus the emergence of this region as the most important industrial area in the country was prompted by an early concentration of people that provided both labor and market and that accumulated capital for the basis of a growing economy.

Larger towns grew up early on the main river routes along the headwaters of the Volga. Northwest of Moscow, at a strategic point of navigation on the Volga, the old city of Tver, now named Kalinin, during the thirteenth and fourteenth centuries challenged the position of Moscow for supremacy over the central part of the Russian Plain. About 150 miles northeast of Moscow a string of cities along the Volga River early grew into a major manufacturing district. Here lie the old cities of Yaroslavl, Kostroma, Ivanovo, and many lesser towns. Farther down the river to the southeast the large industrial city of Gorky, the old city of Nizhny Novgorod, grew up at the junction of the Volga and its main right-bank tributary, the Oka.

A string of lesser cities has grown up along the Oka. Cities such as Ryazan and Kolomna date back to medieval times. Today they perform important functions in industry, commerce, and government, but none of them has reached the size or preeminence of the cities along the Volga.

It is between the Volga River and its tributary, the Oka, however, that the greatest urban development has taken place. Cities grouped around Moscow extend in two lines eastward along two minor streams, the Moscow River, which flows through the city of Moscow and joins the Oka at Kolomna, and the Klyazma River, which flows eastward north of the city of Moscow.

A smaller concentration of urban settlements has developed in the iron and phosphate ore district about 100 miles south of Moscow around the city of Tula.

Thus the urbanization of the area proceeded from several positions: from the city of Kalinin in the northwest, from the concentration of cities along the Volga to the northeast, from the port and industrial center of Gorky at the most important river junction, from a central position along the minor streams around Moscow, and from Tula in the south. Gradually the area between these centers has filled in with urban settlements until today there is a close concentration of cities throughout the region that distinguishes it from its surroundings.

Industrialization began with the textile industries, primarily in Moscow and in the cities to the northeast along the Volga. Very early the city of Ivanovo became known as the "Manchester of Russia" because of its concentration on cheap cotton textiles. At first the cotton textile industry in Russia was largely dependent on imports of raw cotton. As late as 1928, over half the raw cotton used in the Soviet Union was supplied by imports from Egypt, India, and the United States. Since then cotton growing in Soviet Middle Asia and Transcaucasia has been expanded to almost entirely meet the needs of the country. Although textile plants have been built in the cotton-growing areas, the Central Industrial Region still produces almost 80 per cent of the cotton textiles in the U.S.S.R.

The manufacture of linen, based on locally grown flax, also became important in this region, particularly in the city of Kostroma. Russia has always led the world in flax production, and Kalinin Oblast northwest of Moscow raises more flax than any other political unit in the Soviet Union.

Later, with the development of the iron and steel industry around Tula, then in the Urals, and finally in eastern Ukraine, the machine-building industries got started in the Central Industrial Region. Moscow became the primary center for this industry, but many other cities shared in it and some of them came to concentrate heavily on one particular item. Kolomna became known for its manufacture of railroad locomotives, and Kalinin for the manufacture of railroad rolling stock. Gorky, the most important port on the Volga, became the center of the ship-building industry and then later of the automobile industry. Yaroslavl, upstream from Gorky, in the 1930s became the center of the new synthetic rubber industry.

At the same time that the textile and machine-building industries were developing, the whole range of food-processing industries were growing to serve the large urban markets. These are dispersed throughout most of the cities, but are concentrated somewhat in intermediate-sized cities in the better farming regions of the south.

At present the fastest growing group of industries in the Central Industrial Region are the chemical industries, which until recently have been based primarily on potato and grain alcohol and on local phosphate deposits. In the last few years a rapid shift to the utilization of natural gas and by-product gases of oil refining, which are being piped into this area from the south and east in ever-increasing quantities, has greatly speeded their development.

With the construction of pipelines into the area from major oil- and gas-producing areas in the Volga-Urals, the Caucasus, and Ukraine, oil refining is becoming important in new refineries in Moscow, Yaroslavl, and Ryazan, and fuel oil and gas are becoming major power fuels for the generation of electricity. In this power-hungry area of many industries, thermal plants must produce much of the electricity. Recently, some monster thermal stations have been built to utilize the new fluid fuels. The Konakovo plant, with a 2.4 million kilowatt capacity, transmits power from its site in Kalinin Oblast over an experimental 750-kilowatt AC power transmission line to Moscow. Construction began in 1965 on what is advertised as the world's largest thermal complex at the new town of Volgorechensk 25 miles southeast of Kostroma. This has a designed capacity of 5.2 million kilowatts, about equal to all the hydroelectric plants on the Volga River. In addition to electricity, the thermal plants in the Central Industrial Region supply about 25 per cent of all the domestic heating in the region.

So far, among industries of the Central Industrial Region the textile industries still occupy first place, in terms of workers employed. The textile industries employ 28 per cent of all factory workers, and machine construction and metalworking employ 21 per cent. In Moscow Oblast in 1956 workers were employed as is shown in Table 2–1.

Chemical and metallurgical industries usually require far fewer workers for a given value added by manufacture than do such industries as textiles and food processing. Thus, when the industries are ranked according to numbers of workers, the role of heavy industries is minimized in comparison to light industries. Textiles are most dominant in some of the intermediate and smaller sized cities. This is especially true of cotton and linen goods, as can be seen in Table 2–2.

Table 2–2   Textile Production in Millions of Running Meters, 1965 [a]

Region	Cotton	Linen	Wool	Silk (Including Artificial)
U.S.S.R.	7080	587	365	935
Central Industrial Region	5156	374	198	624
Ivanovo Oblast	1908	60	—	179
Moscow Oblast	1295	—	83	60
Moscow City	507	—	72	305
Kostroma Oblast	—	68	—	—
Vladimir Oblast	816	164	—	—
Kalinin Oblast	420	—	—	55
Yaroslavl Oblast	—	51	—	—

[a] *Source: Narodnoye khozyaystvo SSSR v 1965 g.,* pp. 225–228 and *Narodnoye khozyaystvo RSFSR v 1965 g.,* pp. 135–137. Dash indicates that the region did not rank among the five leading political units in the country.

Table 2–1   Workers Employed by Industry in Moscow Oblast in 1956, in Per Cents of Total

Industry	Per Cent of All Workers
Textiles	30.2
Machine construction and metalworking	29.8
Construction materials	6.6
Chemicals	5.7
Woodworking	2.2
Food	2.2
Peat	2.1
Electric generation and heat	0.9
Heavy metallurgy	0.8
Leather working, furs, and shoes	0.7
Other	18.8

Source: Voprosy geografii, Vol. 49, 1960, p. 21.

The Central Industrial Region is credited with almost one-fourth of all the industrial output of the U.S.S.R. and the city of Moscow alone with approximately 8 per cent.

Transportation

Since both the industry and the concentrated population of the Central Industrial Region depend on large imports of raw materials and foodstuffs from other parts of the country, the transportation system is all important to the area. It focuses on Moscow in a radial pattern from all other parts of the Union. Many of the finished products of manufacturing also are

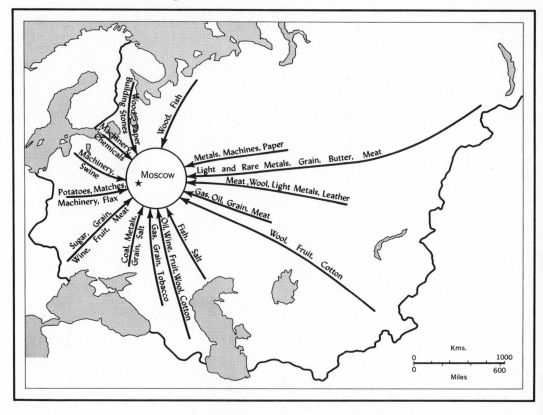

Figure 2–3   Goods shipped into the Central Industrial Region.

shipped out of this area to all parts of the country, and these, too, have fostered a close network of transportation lines. Although the rivers were primary means of transport when this area was emerging in the Middle Ages, today the eleven trunk railroads have greatly superseded the streams in total traffic. As in most parts of the Soviet Union, the railroads in the Central Industrial Region handle over 80 per cent of incoming and outgoing freight. Rapid conversion to electrical traction is further enhancing their position. True, the Volga River is the most heavily traversed river in the Soviet Union, but remember that in the Moscow area it is closed by ice at least 5 months of the year. Also, river traffic is slow and is economical only with regard to the handling of bulky, low-cost goods. Lumber, coal, petroleum, and grain make up the bulk of water ship-

ments, and much of these commodities is brought in by rail.

The railways must bring in cotton and wool from the southeast; grain, meat, butter, and milk from the east; timber and fish from the north; machine tools and finished products from the Baltic Republics to the northwest; and sugar, grain, meat, coal, and steel from the south in Ukraine. They must carry out a great variety of finished products in all directions. Since much of the incoming freight is bulky raw materials and the outgoing freight is more compact finished goods, import tonnages are about five times greater than export tonnages.

Highways serve simply to supplement the role of the railroads; intercity truck traffic is not well developed in the Soviet Union. The average length of truck hauls is about 14 miles, indicating that trucks serve only in distributing produce once it is brought into the city by rail.

To supplement the railroads, pipelines to carry oil and gas from the Caucasus, from Ukraine, from the Volga Region, and from Western Siberia are being constructed into the Central Industrial Region. As the fuel balance shifts from predominantly coal to predominantly oil and gas, pipelines are becoming increasingly important.

Water Construction Projects Although river traffic's share of total traffic has been decreasing, river traffic has been increasing through the years, and during the Soviet period improvements to navigation, which also serve other functions, have been made on the Volga and its tributary streams. The main obstacle to navigation on the Volga, other than ice, was its large seasonal fluctuation in flow, with floods in spring and shoals in late summer and fall. The small Moscow River was not navigable for boats of appreciable size.

To provide Moscow with a navigable waterway, the 80-mile-long Moscow Canal was completed in 1937. It joins the Moscow River in Moscow, through a system of eight locks, with the Volga 128 kilometers to the north. A dam with a hydroelectric power plant of 30,000 kilowatts capacity was constructed on the Volga River near Ivankovo, which raised the water level on the Volga as far as 100 kilometers above the city of Kalinin to form the Volga Reservoir. One third of the water collected in the reservoir is used to feed the Moscow Canal, and the rest goes down the Volga into the Uglich Reservoir. The Uglich dam and power plant, with a capacity of 110,000 kilowatts, was put in operation in 1940. In 1941 the Rybinsk Reservoir was formed by two dams on the Volga and its tributary, the Sheksna. With a surface area of 4550 square kilometers, it was the largest man-made body of water in the world at the time. The power plant at Rybinsk (Shcherbakov), with a capacity of 330,000 kilowatts, provides electricity to Moscow, Yaroslavl, and Kalinin Oblasts.

These reservoirs have regulated the flow of the upper Volga and have supplied additional water to the Moscow River via the Moscow Canal to provide an 18-foot-deep water route for navigation from the city of Moscow to the Volga River. The reservoirs and the canal also have assured recreational facilities and a domestic water supply for the city of Moscow, which previously drank about half of the Moscow River. Moscow's

Figure 2–4   Moscow canal.

expanding industries and population today use more than half of all the additional water being dumped into the canalized river. The function of supplying water to Moscow has transcended the Moscow Canal's importance as a transportation artery.

The deepened channel of the Moscow River meanders through Moscow between granite-lined embankments and landscaped parks. Pleasure craft make regular runs between river stations, which in most cases consist of old double-decked river boats that have been lashed securely to the river bank and converted into combination restaurants and dance halls. If one desires, he can spend a weekend making a round trip up the Moscow Canal to Kimry. The locks along the way have been constructed to blend esthetically with the landscape.

In 1955 the Gorky Sea, 420 kilometers long, was formed by the dam at Gorodets 55 kilometers upstream from Gorky. Its power plant, with a capacity of 400,000 kilowatts, supplies electricity to the cities of Gorky and Moscow as well as to Gorky and Ivanovo Oblasts. The construction of larger dams downstream from Gorky has enhanced navigation all along the Volga. With the opening of the Volga-Don Canal near Volgograd in 1952, the waters of the Volga were united with the traffic of the open sea, so the Volga River system no longer ends in a dead end in the Caspian. Moscow is now connected to the Azov, Black, and Caspian Seas in the south and, through other canal systems, lakes, and rivers, to the Baltic and the White Seas in the north. Hence, the Russians' references to Moscow as the "Port of Five Seas."

Cities

Moscow Moscow is the metropolis of the Soviet Union. Besides serving as the governmental and cultural center of the U.S.S.R. and the R.S.F.S.R., it is the coun-

try's largest industrial producer. On July 1, 1967 its population was estimated at 6,422,000. Thus, it is one of the great cities of the world. Since Moscow is the nerve center of the entire country, it will be described in considerable detail. The city will be discussed as an example of both the prototype and the ultimate in city planning and development in the Soviet Union.

The city of Moscow is roughly circular, with streets and railways radiating outward in all directions from the center and crossing circular boulevards and railways in an ever-widening pattern. Its form reflects the historical process of city building throughout much of old Russia. The kremlin, or citadel, erected in 1147, was a construction of high walls along the bank of the Moscow River surrounding an area of perhaps three or four blocks which contained all the important governmental and religious buildings as well as most of the individual dwellings at the time (see frontispiece). As the city grew, new walls were constructed around successive peripheries of the expanding city to defend it from marauding nomads from the south and east.

The present Moscow Kremlin walls of weathered red brick date back to the fifteenth century. Early in the sixteenth century the so-called White Wall was constructed, delineating the boundaries of the city, and later in the sixteenth century, after Tatar attacks, another rampart of wood and earth was built around the periphery of the city. Since then the city has far outgrown the area enclosed within these walls and has outgrown the function that the walls served, but the imprint of the walls remains in the present street pattern. In 1943, a Ten-Year Plan was launched to revamp the city of Moscow, and all the old walls, except for the Kremlin walls, were pulled down, and the areas they occupied were used for the construction of wide, circular boulevards. The outermost of these boulevards, which lies a little more than a mile from the Kremlin, is called "Sadovaya Ulitsa" (Garden Street) or "Garden Ring" after the old earthen wall that preceded it. The squares that are formed where the radiating streets cross the circular streets still are known by the names of gates, reminders that previously these streets passed through gates in the walls of the city.

Between this simple lattice of intersecting radial and circular main streets lies a

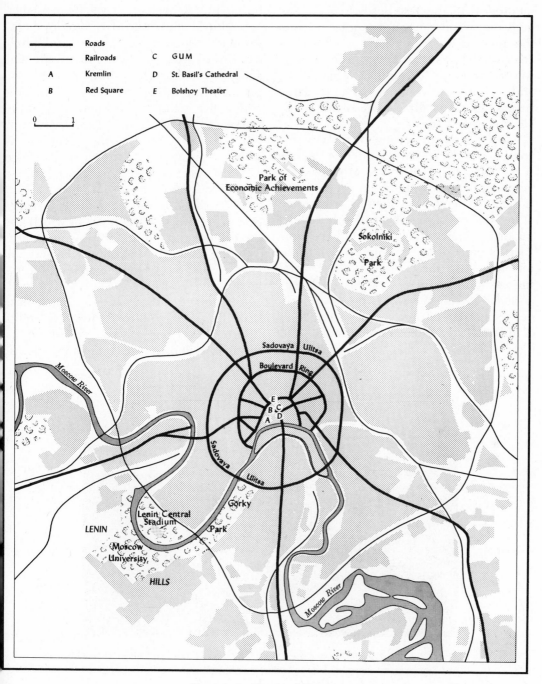

Figure 2–5 The city of Moscow.

maze of narrow, crooked, discontinuous secondary streets reminiscent of the old cities of western Europe. They stand in great contrast to boulevards such as Sadovaya Ulitsa, whose broad expanse of unmarked lanes is bewildering in its immenseness to the few buses, trucks, and taxis that wander upon it, not to mention the poor pedestrian who must plan his crossing well to seek islands of refuge from wildly careening occasional vehicles. To add to the confusion, small and large streets alike typically change names every block or so!

Farther from the center of the city, beyond Sadovaya Ulitsa, is a circular railway that completely encircles Moscow and eliminates train traffic from the heart of the city. Several train stations are located along the circular railway at the ends of major rail lines coming into the area from various parts of the country. Train traffic terminates at these stations, and communication with the central part of the city is made by subway, which now is a well-developed system of three branching lines diametrically crossing under the city and intersecting with a line that encircles the city. New lines constantly are being extended into the suburbs.

A double belt highway 109 kilometers long has been completed recently around the newly expanded city limits. Beyond this a so-called green belt approximately 6 miles wide has been preserved from further agricultural and industrial development. Primarily wooded with pines and birch trees, this green belt contains residential suburbs and dachas, or summer homes, of people living in Moscow. Almost 1 million people live within its confines. This belt is under the jurisdiction of Moscow Oblast, but two main airports lying beyond it, as well as various water supply and sewage disposal systems, have been placed under the jurisdiction of the city of Moscow. The city of Moscow is under the direct jurisdiction of the Russian Republic, of which it is the capital, and not under Moscow Oblast.

In the center of Moscow, the 64 acres of land within the triangular-shaped Kremlin are covered with governmental palaces, onion-domed cathedrals, and museums. Recently a magnificent new "Kremlin Palace" has been constructed within its confines to house large congresses, operas,

Figure 2–6   Red Square, looking north from Saint Basil's Cathedral. Statue to Minin and Pozharsky in foreground, historical museum in background, Kremlin on left, GUM on right. Photograph by the author.

Figure 2–7   Inside GUM (State Department Store). Courtesy of Virgil Petty.

and the like. Many of the streets around Red Square outside the Kremlin also are lined with government buildings, historical museums, and hotels. Across Red Square to the east of the Kremlin the block-long state department store, GUM, with its high-arched glass ceilings, houses two floors of individual bazaar-like stalls.

Down the hill toward the river from Red Square conspicuously stands the brightly painted baroque onion-domed spires of St. Basil's Cathedral. A short distance to the north of the Kremlin is the Bolshoy Theater, or large theater, the Malyy Theater, or small theater, and the Hall of Columns. Not far away is the Lenin Library, perhaps the largest library in the world, which contains some 20 million volumes. Several art museums round out the major buildings in the civic center.

Figure 2–8   The main building of the University of Moscow. Photograph by the author.

Figure 2–9   The main auditorium in the University of Moscow. Photograph by Lois Barland.

In the southwestern portion of the city, where the Moscow River cuts through the so-called Lenin Hills, stands the University of Moscow with its magnificent central building rising to a height of thirty-two stories, the tallest building in the Soviet Union. Together with six other widely spaced, similarly constructed "skyscrapers" of varying functions, it pierces the other-wise squat skyline of the flat city. Across the river from the University is the new Central Lenin Stadium and other facilities forming a complete sports area within one of the loops of the Moscow River. This southwestern portion of the city is the newer, more sought-after residential area, known as the Lenin Hills, although it is indeed about as flat as the rest of the city.

Figure 2–10   View from the top of Moscow University. Formal gardens in foreground and Central Lenin Stadium across Moscow River in background. Photograph by the author.

About the only topographic feature of any note is the high bank along the western side of the Moscow River which rises perhaps 200 feet above the level of the water. Eventually many of the embassies of foreign countries will be relocated in new buildings in this area from the ancient structures that they now occupy, which are scattered about the central portion of the city.

Beginning about a mile and a half south of the Kremlin and stretching for another mile and a half along the river is Gorky Park, which at present is the most highly developed park within the city. Here there are all sorts of sports facilities, theaters, outdoor bandshells, areas for chess and other games, a huge ferris wheel, and many other features. And, as in all the parks of the Soviet Union, there are many billboards and banners proclaiming the goals and ideals of the Soviet system and loudspeakers adding to the din, exhorting people to produce to their utmost. In the north-northeast part of the city lies Sokolniki Park, site of the American Exhibition in 1959, and, to the northwest of that, the Park of Economic Achievements.

The Park of Economic Achievements is a 490-acre permanent exhibition of agricultural and industrial products. Each type of industry has a large pavilion in which to show its wares. Other pavilions house displays of new scientific achievements such as space travel.

All the parks are minutely landscaped and neatly kept. Formal gardens seem to be a fetish with the Russians. They are found not only in parks but about many public buildings. The formal gardens surrounding the University of Moscow are outstanding. Perhaps part of the painstaking care of these gardens is explained by the fact that many old or unskilled people are kept busy by digging at the flowers in these parks. Thus the Soviets are able to boast that there is no unemployment.

Much of the industry is in the east and southeast portions of the city. Large new factories have pushed southeastward onto formerly vacant marshy land.

The Moscow subways are something at which to marvel. They are truly outstanding among the subways of the world, in both splendor and cleanliness and service. The Soviets seem to have put their hearts and souls into the construction of a monumental showpiece in the form of a 55-mile

Figure 2–11   Entrance to the Park of Economic Achievements. Photograph by the author.

Figure 2–12   Map in the Park of Economic Achievements. Different colored lights show construction of industrial plants by periods. Photograph by the author.

labyrinth of passages and more than seventy stations deep beneath the city. Extensive use has been made of statuary, chandeliers, mosaics, marble, porcelain, bronze, and stainless steel to express the

Figure 2–13   Arbatskaya Station, Moscow Subway. Photograph by the author.

motif of each station. The escalators leading down to the subways themselves are awe inspiring. Plunging at inclines of 45 degrees, they are so long that one cannot see one end from the other. In 1964 more than 3 million people were moved daily by subway. At nearly any time of day, all public transportation facilities are jammed to capacity by commuters. The subways, busses, and street cars are augmented by a surprising number of taxis. Private vehicles, however, are at a minimum.

Gorky   Next in size of population is the city of Gorky at the important river confluence of the Oka and the Volga. Gorky, on July 1, 1967, was listed as having 1,120,000 people. This, together with the population of several important industrial suburbs, brings the Gorky metropolitan area to third place in total population in the Soviet Union, after Moscow and Leningrad. However, the population for the city of Gorky alone falls behind that of Kiev, Tashkent, Baku, and Kharkov.

Gorky is the most important automotive center in the country, and has been dubbed "the Detroit of the Soviet Union." Approximately 50 per cent of the industrial production in Gorky is in the machine-building industries, which, besides auto-

Figure 2–14   The Kremlin at Gorky on the confluence of the Oka and the Volga. Novosti.

mobiles, include ship building, aircraft industries, and many others. The other 50 per cent of Gorky's industry is made up of food and diversified industries. Southwest of Gorky, the suburban city of Dzerzhinsk, with a 1967 population of 201,000, is a new city concentrating on chemical industries. Northwest of Gorky is the suburban city of Balakhna, a paper-processing city, which, among other things, produces all the newsprint for *Pravda,* the leading newspaper in the Soviet Union.

Gorky was founded in 1219 as the fortress of Nizhniy Novgorod in defense against the Volga Bulgars and Mordva.

During later days of the Russian Empire, Nizhniy Novgorod was known for its annual trade fairs that attracted business people from all over Russia. Since the death of the writer Maxim Gorky, the city has been renamed after him. His life was linked to the city along the Volga much as Mark Twain's life was linked to Hannibal, Missouri, along the Mississippi.

Yaroslavl   The third most populous city in the Central Industrial Region is Yaroslavl, with a 1967 population of 498,000. It was founded in A.D. 950 as the major city within a group of cities that were established very early along the Volga, northeast of Moscow, and until the seventeenth century it was second in size only to Moscow. It has maintained its supremacy among this group of cities concentrated on the textile industries, and in recent years has grown steadily under the impetus of the synthetic rubber industry.

Yaroslavl has been called "the Akron of the Soviet Union" because it is the leading tire-producing city in the country. Originally the rubber was produced from potato alcohol, but now it is being made from by-product gases derived from the oil refinery that was constructed during the last few years to refine crude oil from the Volga-Urals fields. Yaroslavl is one of the most intensively industrialized cities in the Soviet Union. Approximately 60 per cent of its gainfully employed actually work in factories. Such percentages are much higher than anything experienced in the United States because the tertiary activities, the service industries, so important in the United States, are very little developed in the Soviet Union.

Ivanovo   Fourth in size of population is the city of Ivanovo northeast of Moscow in the same general region as Yaroslavl, which in 1967 had a population of 407,000. As has been mentioned, Ivanovo early became the leading center of the cotton-textile industry, and it has been dubbed "the Manchester of the Soviet Union."

Tula   Fifth in population within the Central Industrial Region is the city of Tula, which in 1967 had a population of 372,000. It was founded in 1146 south of Moscow, on the northern border of the rich agricultural area of the Central Black Earth Region. Located among some minor iron ore deposits, it was first to develop an iron and steel industry. Today it still is an important center for heavy metallurgy, but it is not of first-rank importance in that respect. About 65 per cent of its production is in machine-building industries of

various sorts, and much of the rest is in heavy metallurgy. A large iron and steel plant, now beginning operation utilizing iron ore from the Kursk Magnetic Anomaly, should considerably revitalize the city. Just to the southeast of Tula is the relatively new important chemical city of Novomoskovsk, which until 1961 was named Stalinogorsk. It uses natural gas as the raw material for a nitrogen industry providing agricultural fertilizers and various other products.

Kalinin   Sixth in size is Kalinin, on the upper Volga northwest of Moscow, which in 1967 had a population of 318,000. The town was founded in 1180 as the city of Tver, which during the thirteenth to fifteenth centuries vied with Moscow for supremacy over the central Russian plain. It early became an important center for textile industries, and more recently an important center for the manufacture of railroad rolling stock. In 1931 it was renamed Kalinin after Mikhail Kalinin, a party revolutionary and onetime President of the U.S.S.R.

Ryazan   To the southeast of Moscow lies the city of Ryazan, one of the old centers on the Oka River, which was the frontier of settlement during the time of the Tatar hordes. Many times it withstood the first onslaught of the Tatars in their punitive expeditions from Sarai to Moscow. It was founded in 1095 as Pereyaslav. Today, with a population of 311,000, Ryazan is a city of diversified industries, with some emphasis on forging equipment, heavy machine tools, and calculating machines. At present it seems to be experiencing a spurt in industrialization after the construction of an electric steel furnace, a rayon plant using the viscose process, and an oil refinery to process crude oil from the Tatar A.S.S.R. to the east.

Rybinsk, Vladimir, and Kostroma
Northeast of Moscow are three more im-

portant old cities. Rybinsk, with a population of 212,000, sits at the site of the dam that forms the Rybinsk Reservoir. It is especially known as a ship building and woodworking center. Known alternately as Shcherbakov, the city reverted to its previous name, Rybinsk, in 1957. Vladimir, founded in 1108, was the center of one of the princely states that rivaled Moscow. For a short time in the twelfth century it was the center of the Orthodox Slavic area and the central seat of government as well. After its fall to Muscovy it faded from prominence, but now it is beginning to industrialize and grow with the rest of the region. In 1967 it had a population of 211,000. Kostroma, the most concentrated center in the Soviet Union of the linen textile industry, in 1967 had a population of 209,000.

Other Cities In the vicinity of Moscow, particularly to the east, are many industrial cities with populations in the 100,000–200,000 class which concentrate on textile industries, machine-building industries, and chemicals. Three newer cities that are heavily concentrated on chemicals are Orekhovo-Zuevo, Shatura, and Yakhroma. Other cities also are concentrated in the important textile region along the Volga northeast of Moscow and along the Oka River between Moscow and Gorky.

Kolomna, at the confluence of the Moscow and Oka Rivers, already has been mentioned for its railroad locomotive industry. This industry was established by French capital in the latter half of the nineteenth century, and for a long time Kolomna was the only city in Russia producing locomotives.

Prospects

The Central Industrial Region undoubtedly will continue to be the leading industrial area in the country and also the most populous. Socialist policies to limit the growth of big cities and to spread industries evenly across the country for the most part have been unsuccessful, and economic principles have worked in favor of already established industrial centers, just as they do in any country. Moscow grew from a population of 5,046,000 in 1959 to 6,422,000 in 1967. True, it incorporated some surrounding territories during that period, but even discounting this, it grew by about 500,000 during the 8½ years. During the same time, Gorky grew from 942,000 to 1,120,000; Yaroslavl, from 407,000 to 498,000; and so forth. All the leading cities registered considerable growth, and new cities filled in spaces between major urban centers. Although outmigration from the area is generally heavy, this, in the final analysis, is fed by the rural population, which will continue to decrease as the urban population increases.

The region might even grow in importance in relation to the rest of the country now that the Soviet leaders have largely abandoned ideological policies that were in conflict with economic realities. The allocation of large shares of capital investment during the immediate future to the location of industries in small and medium size cities in the European part of the country, in order to utilize surplus pools of labor and the advantages of concentration, should tend to fill in the Central Industrial Region even more. The growth of large cities might slow down, but the filling in of spaces between large cities should accelerate. Also, the newly found mobility of energy fuels, oil and gas, largely has erased one of the traditional industrial ailments of the region. Most of the new oil refineries of the country are being built in consuming areas rather than in producing regions. Thus large consuming areas suddenly find themselves on the threshold of another leap forward for a whole range of industries, particularly the chemical industries based on by-products of oil refining.

Reading List

Fuchs, Roland J., "Moscow," *Focus,* American Geographical Society, New York, January 1966, 6 pp.

Mints, A. A., *Podmoskovye* (The Moscow Region), Moscow, 1961 (in Russian).

Mishchenko, G. Ye., "Satellite Cities and Towns of Moscow," *Soviet Geography: Review and Translation,* March 1962, pp. 35–42.

Moskva i podmoskovnye rayony (Moscow and the Moscow region), *Voprosy geografii,* No. 51, Moscow, 1961, 220 pp. (in Russian).

Saushkin, Yu. G., *Moskva* (Moscow), Mysl, geograficheskaya seriya, Moscow, 1964, 240 pp. (in Russian).

Tsentralno-promyshlennyy rayon (Central Industrial Region), *Voprosy geografii,* No. 49, Moscow, 1960, 157 pp. (in Russian).

Tsentralnyy Rayon: Ekonomiko-geograficheskaya kharakteristika (Central Region: Economic geographic characteristics), Akademiya Nauk SSSR, Institut geografii, Moscow, 1962, 800 pp. (in Russian).

The Central Black Earth Region

Region	Area (sq mile)	Population	People (sq mile)	% Urban [a]
Orel Oblast	9,700	937,000	97	34
Kursk Oblast	11,600	1,492,000	129	28
Belgorod Oblast	10,600	1,248,000	118	29
Lipetsk Oblast	9,400	1,221,000	130	39
Voronezh Oblast	20,400	2,495,000	122	43
Tambov Oblast	13,400	1,523,000	114	34
Penza Oblast	16,800	1,534,000	91	40
Mordovian A.S.S.R.	10,200	1,014,000 [b]	99	30
Tula Oblast	6,000 [c]	940,000 [c]	157	68
Total	108,100 [d]	12,404,000 [d]		

[a] All figures are for entire regions.

[b] Population of entire region, although northwest corner lies within circle defining Central Industrial Region.

[c] Estimated population and area of portion of oblast lying within the Central Black Earth Region.

[d] Does not include southern fringe of Ryazan Oblast, which lies within the Central Black Earth Region.

3

The Central Black Earth Region

Southward, beyond the circle delimiting the Central Industrial Region, a rapid change takes place from a northern area that is predominantly urban to a southern one that is predominantly rural. The rural region to the south, known as the Central Black Earth Region, is in many ways analogous to the Middle West in the United States. It is one of the better farming regions in the country; on one side it borders on the main industrial belt of the country, and on all other sides it merges imperceptibly with adjoining regions. Although it is a traditional region in the minds of the Russian people, they would be hard put to define its boundaries precisely. As defined by Russian geographers it lies wholly within the Russian Republic, its southwestern boundary being the political boundary of Ukraine. But as far as climate, soil, natural vegetation, and land use are concerned, the area continues westward into Ukraine. On the east the region merges imperceptibly with the middle Volga Valley.

In deference to tradition, the boundary on the south will be taken as the republic boundary, and the whole Ukraine will be considered later. On the east, again traditional Russian boundaries will be accepted between the Central Black Earth and Volga Regions. This puts Penza Oblast in the Central Black Earth Region, which is quite in keeping with its agricultural character but ignores the fact that the industries of Penza Oblast are more directly tied to the economy of the Volga Region. In the north, traditional Russian boundaries have been ignored in the definiton of the Central Industrial Region, and a line has been drawn to separate a predominantly urban area from a predominantly rural one. The Central Black Earth Region thus contains the southern half of Tula Oblast and the southern fringe of Ryazan Oblast. As is shown on the summary sheet at the beginning of this chapter, the region here defined contains an area of approximately 108,000 square miles with a population of around 12 million people who are predominantly Russian. Its outstanding characteristic is its relatively dense population, more than 100 people per square mile, 65 per cent or more of whom are rural. A prime agricultural area that has not undergone extensive industrialization, the rural-urban ratio only now is beginning to undergo significant change.

Agricultural Resources and Development

Topographically the Central Black Earth Region lies in much the same position as

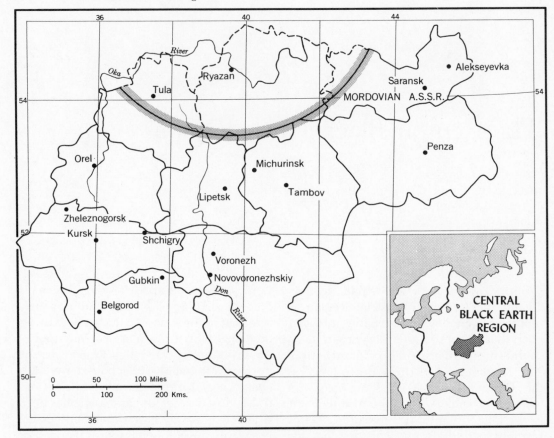

Figure 3–1   The Central Black Earth Region.

does the Central Industrial Region. The western half of the area, on the Central Russian Uplands, is a stream-dissected rolling plain, whereas the eastern half is the flatter Oka-Don Lowland, sometimes known as the Tambov Plain. The Oka River drains this plain to the northeast and the Don River drains it to the south.

Climatically the Central Black Earth Region is a little warmer and a little drier than the Central Industrial Region. The seemingly small gradient in moisture toward the southeast induces an all-significant change in natural vegetation and soil development. Much of the region lies in the belt of wooded steppe with its chernozem soils, hence its name. The northwestern fringe, in Orel and Tula Oblasts, originally was covered by deciduous trees,

which were conducive to the development of a gray-brown forest soil. The southeastern fringe, in Voronezh and Tambov Oblasts, was vegetated by steppe grasses and contains the best chernozem soil. In general, the drainage throughout the area is adequate.

During the Tatar dominance on the Russian plain much of the Central Black Earth Region was a no man's land between the Russian-dominated area around Moscow and the Tatar stronghold at Sarai on the lower Volga. As the Tatar hold began to weaken, particularly in the fifteenth to seventeenth centuries, some of the bolder Russians escaped from the oppression of the Russian princes and migrated southward into what was then known as the "wild field" to either settle and cultivate the land or to band into seminomadic groups of horsemen to carry on forays against the Tatars, against Moscow, against the Turks to the south, and against the settlers in the area. Hence in the fifteenth to seventeenth centuries the Central Black Earth Region served as a frontier land that was being reopened by settlers from the north, much as the Great Plains of the United States were opened by settlers from the east two centuries later. The physical environment and the mode of settlement in both was much the same.

The Don Cossacks, as the horsemen of the plains were known, worked hard, fought hard, and were ready for any adventure. In attitudes and actions they much resembled the cowboys of the early days of the American West. Often they derived their livelihood by serving as a military arm to the Tsar in Moscow, from whose rule they had previously escaped, to bring some order to outlying regions where men lived by their own laws. During the eighteenth century the wild field disappeared; the Central Black Earth Region became a completely settled integral part of the Russian Empire, and the frontier moved southward, and the Cossacks with

it, to the steppes of the Black Sea and the lower Don.

During the eighteenth and nineteenth centuries the Central Black Earth Region, being nearer to the populous center around Moscow than was Ukraine to the southwest, became one of the most productive agricultural areas in the country with one of the densest rural populations. The peasants, as was the case throughout the Russian Empire, were serfs in a feudal system of land holding, a system which led to the neglect of the fertile soils, excessive erosion, and the ultimate near collapse of the rural economy. Thus, owing to overpopulation and a feudal land tenure system, one of the richest naturally endowed agricultural regions of the country remained an area of underdevelopment and rural poverty. Collectivization of the land under the Soviets thus far has shown little gain either in agricultural production or mode of life. Although the land is now held in large collective farms, most of the people have not been consolidated into larger villages or cities; they still live in their haphazardly scattered villages along muddy stream valleys. The typical rural dwelling in the forests of the north is the log cabin

Figure 3–2   The village "waterworks." A well with a windlass serves a row of seven cabins in a village near Tula. Courtesy of Clara Dundas Taylor.

izba, and in the steppes of the south the adobe *khata.* About the only change in dwelling type that has taken place thus far has been a gradual substitution of corrugated sheet metal roofs for the thatched roofs of yesteryear. Only since the accession of Khrushchev, with his interest in agriculture, has much official attention been paid to conservation methods in farming and the heavy use of fertilizers to increase yields per acre.

The Central Black Earth Region is an area of general farming, transitional between the potato, small grain, flax-growing area of the Central Industrial Region and the commercial wheat fields and sunflower fields of the steppes to the southeast. Wheat always has been produced in some quantity, but only in Voronezh Oblast does it occupy the largest portion of the cultivated land. The other small grains — oats, barley, and rye — are important throughout the region, particularly in the north. Potatoes are important in the northeast. The sunflower belt begins in the drier southeast and culminates in the steppes of the lower Don and North Caucasus. Sugar beets are the main cash crop in Kursk and Belgorod Oblasts in the southwest. Belgorod Oblast provides about

a fifth of the sugar beets of the Russian Republic, and cash from sugar beets provides about a third of the monetary income of collective farmers in the area. The sugar beet belt continues southwestward into west-central Ukraine. Much of the hemp raised in the Soviet Union is raised in the Central Black Earth Region. Tambov Oblast is the principal producer of millet in the Soviet Union. Recently corn has been introduced, both for grain and for silage. The raising of dairy cattle, beef cattle, and hogs is very important. Until shortly after World War II, the experimental raising of kok-sagyz and tau-sagyz, two dandelion-like rubber-bearing plants, was being pushed very strongly in this region, but during the last two decades little mention has been made of them.

The expansion of sugar beet and corn growing is the most important trend in the agriculture of the region at the present time. Sugar beets are being extended to oblasts other than Kursk and Belgorod and are rapidly becoming the chief industrial crop. Initially, much of the expansion of sugar beet growing was at the expense of the growing of sunflowers or other technical crops such as the makhorka, a low-grade tobacco, even in the traditional

Figure 3–3   Hemp field. Courtesy of D. A. Davidson.

makhorka growing region of Lipetsk Oblast, whereas the acreage in grain had remained much the same. But during the last decade some reversal of this trend took place, with a considerable increase in the growing and yield of oil crops for vegetable oils and the expansion of sugar beet growing at the expense of grain, which, since the initiation of the virgin lands program, is being grown over vast areas in western Siberia, northern Kazakhstan, and the Transvolga Region. The Central Black Earth Region now plays only a secondary role in grain production. It is hoped that by means of heavy fertilization and better farming methods grain production in this area can be maintained at its present level and the acreage reduced. Corn, which yields more heavily than do the small grains, is being substituted more and more for the small grains.

Industrial Resources and Development

Until recently, the Central Black Earth Region had little basis or little reason for industrial development. No rich coal basins underlay the area and no great rivers existed for harnessing. The development of local mineral resources had been limited primarily to the small deposits of iron ore in the Tula and Lipetsk areas. But these minor resources had long since been largely exhausted, and even the small steel plants at Tula and Lipetsk for a number of years had been securing the bulk of their iron ore from Krivoy Rog in Ukraine. Other than the small iron industry, about the only significant development was the utilization of the Belgorod chalk, a thick limestone which forms a prominent escarpment in Belgorod Oblast and provides the basis for an important cement industry. Belgorod Oblast, along with the city of Novorossiisk on the Caucasian coast of the Black Sea, has provided much of the high-grade cement for distribution throughout the Soviet Union.

The region was not industrialized to any great extent and much of the industrialization that had taken place had developed rather irrationally in light of the local resources and market. The manufacture of farm machinery, which would appear to be needed in the Central Black Earth Region more than any other kind of industry, was poorly developed. Lipetsk had a tractor plant, but it was still turning out clumsy caterpillar-type tractors although the need was primarily for wheel-type lighter tractors. The building-materials industry, in spite of its entirely adequate and well-distributed supply of raw materials, was inadequately developed and did not provide for all the region's requirements. The cement industry, for example, was too concentrated in Belgorod and Voronezh Oblasts, and should have been more dispersed throughout the area. A rather large proportion of the industries that had been established in the largest oblast capitals depended entirely on materials from the outside and to a large extent exported their products to regions outside the Central Black Earth Region. There was no industrial economic unity in the Central Black Earth Region. Now a number of factors are slowly beginning to change all this. Chief among these is the long-awaited opening of the Kursk Magnetic Anomaly.

The Kursk Magnetic Anomaly is a large body of iron-rich quartzites lying mainly in Belgorod and Kursk Oblasts. Its existence had been known for years because of the extreme compass variations in its vicinity. Hence, its name. Reserves are now estimated at approximately 50 billion tons, which make it one of the largest deposits in the country. About two thirds of the ore consists of magnetite quartzite, which has an iron content of between 25 and 45 per cent; the other third has an iron content somewhere between 50 and 65 per cent. Much of the richer ore lies at depths of more than 500 meters and is covered by thick water-bearing strata. These conditions largely explain why the deposit had not been exploited earlier, in spite of its strategic location between the Central Industrial Region and the heavy industry area in eastern Ukraine. Toward the edges of the basin the ore is nearer the surface, and a few open-pit mines have been developed. They have raised production to about 15 million tons a year. In 1956 this region, together with small-scale mining around Tula and Lipetsk, produced only 1.8 million tons of iron ore.

The present production is all high-grade ore, about two thirds of which is produced by open-pit mines in the vicinity of Gubkin in Belgorod Oblast and one third of which comes from Zheleznogorsk in Kursk Oblast. Concentrators are being built in both the Gubkin and Zheleznogorsk areas to facilitate the large-scale utilization of low-grade iron quartzites. In conjunction with the expansion of iron mining, the iron and steel plants at Tula and Lipetsk are being greatly expanded. The Novolipetsk plant eventually is to rival Magnitogorsk, now the largest single plant in the country, in size. New blast furnaces and oxygen converters have already greatly increased the capacity of these two plants. In addition a third large iron and steel plant has been planned for some undetermined location within the general area of the Kursk Magnetic Anomaly. This mill is planned to exceed the capacity of Magnitogorsk in the Urals.

Both the Kursk and Belgorod regional councils have put forward plans for the development of iron and steel plants in their respective regions at strategic points where the movements of iron ore and coal cross. Water supply seems to be the critical item in these locations. Some planners have pointed out that construction of large iron and steel plants in these areas would leave important cities without an adequate water supply.

The "KMA" ore eventually will serve not only the needs of the local plants, but also the Donbass plants, to some extent. This will make rational use of railroad equipment by utilizing returning cars which have brought coal from the Donbass to the Tula and Lipetsk steel plants. Coal will be shipped northward and iron ore southward. Also, as sources of iron ore in the European north dwindle, the Kursk ore will be used to supplement the operation at Cherepovets on the north shore of the Rybinsk Reservoir. It is also intended to substitute KMA ore for the Krivoy Rog ore that is being exported to various east European satellites. This will help to forestall the rapid dwindling of the Krivoy Rog reserves, which are all important to the iron and steel industry in eastern Ukraine.

The KMA development has sparked the construction of a 105-kilometer rail line directly from the iron mines at Zheleznogorsk to Orel and hence to the consuming areas of Tula and Lipetsk. This line will shorten ore hauls to Tula by 236 kilometers and to Lipetsk by 155 kilometers. Previously, rail connections were very roundabout.

Another new construction is taking place in the northeast in the Mordovian A.S.S.R. A new city with a planned population of 50,000 is being built at the site of the Alekseyevka cement and roofing-slate plants, which is planned to become one of the most important cement-producing centers in the Soviet Union. When completed, this will be the second largest city in the Mordovian A.S.S.R., after the capital city, Saransk.

Undoubtedly, the greatest future resources for industrial development in the Central Black Earth Region are, first, its intermediate location on the dense network of railroads that run between the Central Industrial Region to the north and the heavy industries area of Ukraine to the south, and second, its large rural population, which represents a rich potential source of industrial labor supply. The greatest single drawback has been the power shortage. No integrated electrical grid system existed until recently; adequate electrification was limited to oblast capitals where thermal plants fueled by Donets coal generated the power. This condition is beginning to be corrected by the completion of gas pipelines running through the area from the gas fields of the North Caucasus and eastern Ukraine to the Central Industrial Region and the northwest, and by the trunk oil line which carries crude oil from the Volga oil fields westward to Hungary, Czechoslovakia, Poland, and East Germany via Kuybyshev, Penza, Michurinsk, Lipetsk, and Bryansk. The Central Black Earth Region again benefits by its intermediate location between main suppliers and main consumers, and can tap these gas and oil lines to fuel new thermal electric stations and to provide for the conversion of synthetic rubber and products of other chemical industries from their original vegetable bases. In 1964 the first reactor of the Novovoronezhskiy atomic power plant was put into operation 25 miles south of Voronezh on the left bank of the Don River. This is one of the two major civilian atomic power plants in operation in the Soviet Union. Eventually it is to have a capacity of 1.5 million kilowatts.

Cities

The largest cities of the Central Black Earth Region are the capitals of the respective oblasts, and they serve primarily as regional centers providing governmental and commercial services. Although industrialization in general has not been great, at least one of the cities has become an industrial city, and other cities have developed particular types of industry. A consideration of the largest cities and their industries follows.

Voronezh   Voronezh is the metropolis of the region, with a population of 611,000. It has transcended its original role of governmental center and has become an industrial city in its own right. Half of its industry is concerned with the production of many types of machines such as ore-concentration equipment, excavators, forge and press equipment, machine tools, grain-cleaning machines, small electric motors, radio and television sets, and machines and equipment for the food industry and the production of building materials. The city is probably better known, however, for its chemical industries, particularly the synthetic rubber industry and automobile tire industry. Voronezh early became established, along with Yaroslavl in the Central Industrial Region, as one of the main centers for the synthetic rubber industry. In Yaroslavl the industry was based on potato alcohol; in Voronezh it was based on grain alcohol. The rubber industry in Voronezh is now being converted to the use of natural gas as pipelines are being built through the area. The highly developed food industries are based on local raw materials: grain, sunflower seeds, and sugar beets. The processing of sugar is becoming more important as the growing of sugar beets is extended. Industries producing building materials also are important.

Penza   Penza, with a population of 333,000, is second in importance to Voronezh, both in population and in industrialization. Although Penza Oblast is included within the Central Black Earth Region, the industries of Penza are more oriented toward the needs of the Volga Valley. Approximately half of the industries of the city of Penza are concerned with the production of machines such as equipment for ship building and the extraction and refining of petroleum, chemical equipment, textile equipment, compressors, diesels, and various instruments. Paper manufacturing and food industries also are important.

Kursk   Third in size is Kursk with a population of 255,000. It is primarily the governmental and commercial center of Kursk Oblast. The industries of Kursk are concentrated on machine building, chemicals, and food. Just to the east of Kursk is the smaller city of Shchigry whose industries are concentrated totally on ground phosphate derived from phosphorite deposits in the vicinity.

Lipetsk   Lipetsk has already been mentioned for its rejuvenated steel industry and the present construction of a super iron and steel plant, which will be one of the largest in the country. With a population of 253,000, Lipetsk is the most rapidly growing city in the Central Black Earth Region. It appears to be in the process of transformation from merely a regional center to a truly industrial city. Its industries are classified as about half heavy metallurgy and half machine building. Chemical and building material industries also are important. Among its machine industries, the caterpillar tractor plant is outstanding.

Tambov   Fifth in size is Tambov with a population of 211,000. Like Kursk, its industries are divided among machine building, chemicals, and food. The machine industries turn out equipment for sugar and alcohol plants and auto and tractor spare parts. The chemical industries furnish some rubber and asbestos materials for the lining of tractor and automobile engines and aniline dyes for textile factories. The food industries process local products such as sugar, alcohol, fruit, and tobacco.

Orel   In the northwestern part of the region, Orel, with a population of 209,000, is the governmental and commercial center for Orel Oblast. Its industries are rather diversified with about one third concentrating on machine building and one third on food.

Saransk   In the northeast, Saransk, with a population of 154,000, is the capital of the Mordovian A.S.S.R. Its role as capital

of the Autonomous Republic is its chief function. Its industries are concentrated on machine building, woodworking, and food. The Mordovians are a Finno-Ugrian group of people who now are somewhat outnumbered by Russians in their own Republic.

Belgorod   In the south, Belgorod, with a population of 129,000, is the remaining oblast center. Two thirds of its industries are concerned with the building construction materials derived from the chalk escarpment in the vicinity. As has been pointed out, it is one of the main cement-producing centers of the Soviet Union. Its other industries are primarily food processing. It appears to be benefiting from the KMA exploitation in Belgorod Oblast, as it grew from 72,000 in 1959 to 129,000 in 1967.

Michurinsk   Lying just north of the midway point between Lipetsk and Tambov is the smaller city of Michurinsk, with a population of 91,000. It is primarily known as the home of Michurin, "the Soviet Luther Burbank." His experimental nurseries have developed special strains of plums, peaches, apples, and other fruits and vegetables. The diversified industries of Michurinsk include machine building, textiles, and food.

Prospects

With the development of the Kursk Magnetic Anomaly and its attendant establishment of large iron and steel plants at Tula and Lipetsk, the coming of natural gas and oil to the region, and the utilization of the region's advantageous location and potential labor supply, the Central Black Earth Region may develop industrially very rapidly during the next couple of decades, and a continuous industrial belt may finally be established from the

Central Industrial Region to eastern Ukraine. So far there has been no announcement of a grand scheme to accomplish this, but the economic and cultural conditions appear to be ripe for such a development.

Reading List

Kapitonov, Ye.I., "The Kursk Magnetic Anomaly and its Development," *Soviet Geography: Review and Translation,* May 1963, pp. 10–15.

The Povolzhye and Lower Don

Region	Area (sq mile)	Population	People (sq mile)	% Urban [a]
Gorky Oblast (Eastern three-fifths)	17,200 [b]	1,341,000 [b]	78	62
Kirov Oblast (Southern half, including Kirov City)	23,900 [b]	1,076,000 [b]	45	52
Mari A.S.S.R.	9,100	653,000	72	38
Chuvash A.S.S.R.	7,100	1,192,000	168	32
Tatar A.S.S.R.	26,600	3,127,000	118	49
Ulyanovsk Oblast	14,600	1,187,000	81	45
Kuybyshev Oblast	21,000	2,602,000	124	72
Saratov Oblast	39,200	2,412,000	62	61
Volgograd Oblast	44,600	2,201,000	49	63
Astrakhan Oblast	17,200	811,000	47	58
Kalmyk A.S.S.R.	29,600	248,000	8	36
Rostov Oblast [c]	39,300	3,771,000	96	65
Total	289,400	20,621,000		

[a] All figures are for entire regions.
[b] Estimated population and area of portion of region lying within the Povolzhye.
[c] Rostov City and the coal-bearing area to the north of the city are included here for convenience, although economically they are closely tied to the Donets Basin in eastern Ukraine.

4

The Povolzhye and the Lower Don

East of the Central Industrial Region and the Central Black Earth Region is an elongated area that stretches from the city of Gorky east and then south to the mouth of the Volga on the Caspian Sea, generally known as the Povolzhye, or "Along the Volga." Extending from the cool, humid forestland of the north to the hot, dry deserts of the Caspian, this region shows much variety in natural and cultural landscapes. But the region is held together by the great Volga River itself, the major navigational waterway in the Soviet Union, which exchanges the products of the different areas up and down the river. To the Povolzhye now must be added the lower Don, because the Volga-Don Canal, opened in 1952, links the lower Volga southwestward with the Sea of Azov. Thus the lower Don is now a vital part of the Volga waterway system.

Nationalities and Political Units

Politically this region includes the following oblasts and autonomous republics: Gorky Oblast east of the city of Gorky, Kirov Oblast south of and including the city of Kirov, the Mari A.S.S.R., the Chuvash A.S.S.R., the Tatar A.S.S.R., Ulyanovsk Oblast, Kuybyshev Oblast, Saratov Oblast, Volgograd Oblast, Astrakhan Oblast, the Kalmyk A.S.S.R., and Rostov Oblast.

The "ethnological museum" of the Middle Volga presents a political checkerboard of Russian oblasts and non-Russian autonomous republics. During the ninth to twelfth centuries, the Volga Bend area was settled by Bulgar farmers and traders, Turkish in language and Moslem in religion. They had subdued earlier Finnish-speaking settlers, and all in turn were overwhelmed in the early thirteenth century by the Tatars. Finally, during the second half of the sixteenth century, the Russians gained control of the entire Volga, established scattered farming colonies and towns such as Samara and Saratov, and attempted to Russify their subject peoples. In the seventeenth century, the Mongol Kalmyks established themselves in the semidesert west of the Volga delta, and later German colonists centered on the Middle Volga around Saratov.

After the Revolution most of these non-Russian peoples were given political recognition as autonomous oblasts or autonomous republics within the Middle Volga Kray or Gorky Kray and eventually were elevated to the status of A.S.S.R. The Tatar A.S.S.R., formed in 1920, was one of the first autonomous republics in the country.

1

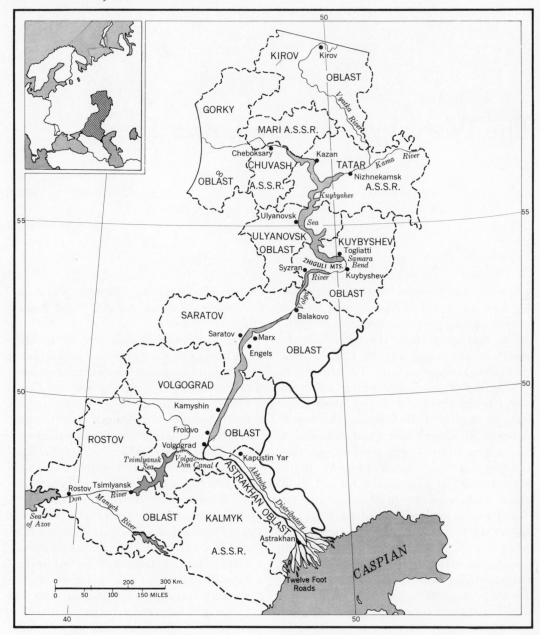

Figure 4–1   The Povolzhye.

During World War II the Volga German and Kalmyk A.S.S.R.'s were abrogated, allegedly for collaborating with the Germans, and their peoples were scattered throughout the Russian and Middle Asian Republics. In 1956 the Kalmyks were reinstated as an autonomous oblast within Stavropol Kray and very soon thereafter as an A.S.S.R.

Russians constantly have been moving into the non-Russian autonomous republics of the Volga Region as well as into the Russian-dominated oblasts. This is particularly true in the larger cities where most of the industrialization is taking place. In the Tatar and Chuvash A.S.S.R.'s, the titular Turkic groups constitute about 50 and 80 per cent of the populations respectively. In the Mari A.S.S.R., the Mari, a Finno-Ugrian group, make up about 50 per cent of the total population. Much of the remaining population in these three republics is Russian.

Two other non-Russian autonomous republics lie just to the east of the region under consideration. The Bashkir A.S.S.R., peopled by a Turkic group, and the Udmurt A.S.S.R., peopled by a Finno-Ugrian group, traditionally are included in the region of the Urals. They might just as well be included with the other non-Russian republics in the Povolzhye, particularly now that the Volga-Urals oil fields, which overlap these regions, have somewhat united their economies. The Bashkir and Udmurt Republics still have strong economic ties with the Urals, however, and they do not touch on the Volga River, so until more justification is forthcoming for their inclusion in the Povolzhye, they shall continue to be grouped with the Urals.

Physical Landscape

Topographically the Povolzhye is divided into two parts, east and west, along the Volga River itself. Along the right bank, the west side, lie the so-called Volga Heights, which geologically are a counterpart of the Central Russian Uplands farther west, an old upwarp with some faulting. The Volga in its process of erosion has exposed different strata of sedimentary rocks, all dipping southwestward, and has adjusted its valley to follow along the strike of one of the hardrock layers. A cuesta of hard sandstone underlain by weaker limestone has been etched along the western bank of the river. In places the top of the escarpment stands as high as 500 feet above the river. The highest part of the cuesta lies within the Samara Bend near Kuybyshev where it is known as the Zhiguli Mountains. This spot has long been a haunt of people seeking recreation in the hilly wooded area surrounded on three sides by water. Although this is not a mountainous area, the topography is truly rugged; the edge of the cuesta is deeply dissected by steep, short tributaries which run down into the Volga. The sandstone uplands are forested primarily by coniferous trees, whereas the ravines are clothed in a lighter green of deciduous trees. Before the construction of the Kuybyshev Dam, the short Usa River flowed northward through this narrow band of hills into the Volga. A favorite trip of young people was to leave Kuybyshev by rowboat, float downstream on the Volga to the point opposite the headwater of the Usa, carry their small boat up over the hills for a distance of approximately one mile, and then embark down the Usa back to the Volga and down the Volga again to Kuybyshev. This jaunt they called "the Round the World Cruise." The entire trip took about a fortnight. Now the Usa Valley is flooded by the great Kuybyshev Sea.

The left bank, or east side of the Volga, is almost the antithesis of the right bank. The left bank is a very flat marshy lowland, which represents the "slip-off slope" that the Volga River has leveled out in its process of shifting westward with the dip of the rocks. The contrast between the two sides of the river is greatest from Kazan to Volgograd and disappears both to the north and to the south. Between Volgograd and the Caspian the river flows through a flat desert plain, a part of the previous bed of the Caspian. To a lesser degree, the relation of topography to river and rock strata along the lower Don is a replica of the middle Volga.

Not only is the topography markedly different on the two sides of the Volga, but also the river seems to be something of a climatic divide. Apparently the extra elevation along the west side of the stream alters the air flow enough to produce additional

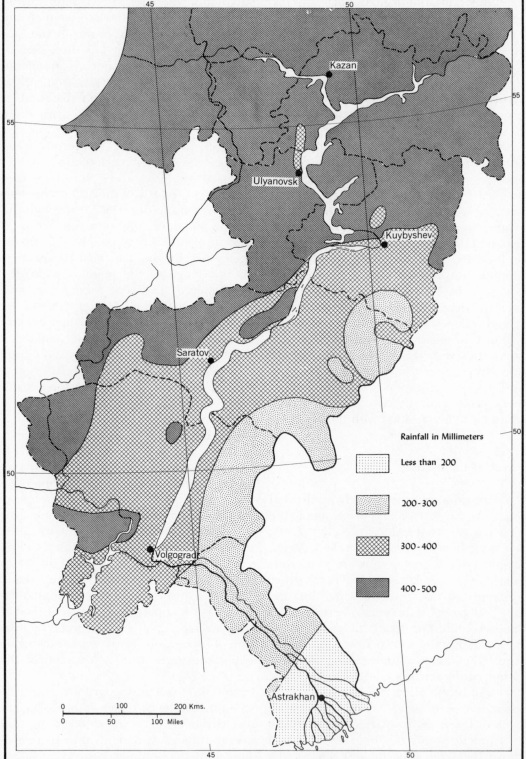

Figure 4–2   Annual precipitation in the Povolzhye. After Lyalikov.

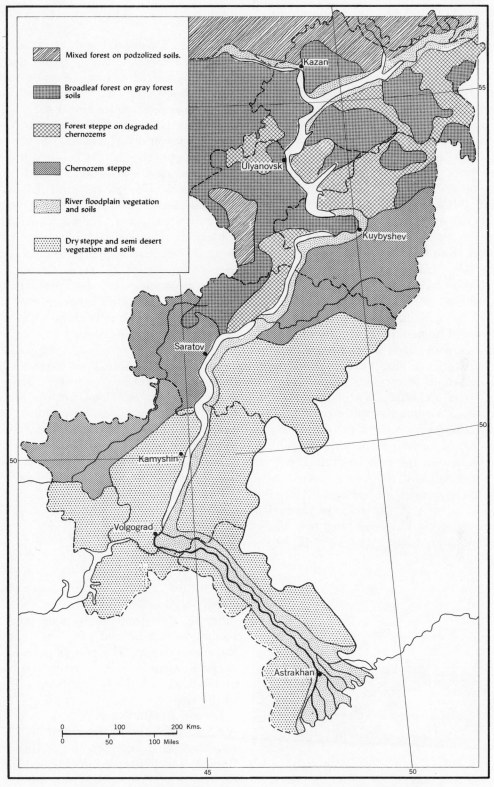

Figure 4–3 Natural vegetation and soil zones of the Povolzhye. After Cherdantsev.

precipitation and to reduce temperatures slightly, so that the upland on the west appears to be considerably more humid than the lowland to the east. The forests, which in the north cover the entire width of the area under consideration, extend southward much farther along the west side of the river on the Volga Heights than they do on the east in the so-called Transvolga Meadows. East of the river from Kuybyshev south, the forests have almost entirely disappeared and open steppeland is at hand. Thus the climate changes significantly in two directions in this region, from north to south and from west to east.

Cool, humid conditions in the north have been conducive to the growth of coniferous trees and the development of podzol soils in Kirov Oblast and in the Mari A.S.S.R. Southward the forest changes to one of mixed deciduous trees which continue southward on the western bank to the vicinity of Saratov. East of the river the deciduous forest ends in the center of the Tatar Republic. Within the area of deciduous forests, the soils are of a gray-brown forest variety similar to those around Moscow. Southward, in the vicinity of Kuybyshev on the east bank and Saratov on the west bank, the forest rapidly gives way to the wooded steppe and then to the true steppe, and the soils become rich chernozems and chestnut-browns. These conditions gradually give way to the semi-

desert and desert downstream from Volgograd.

Between Volgograd and Astrakhan the Volga becomes an exotic stream and divides into a series of intertwining distributary channels that make their way through the sands, eventually to empty their waters into the Caspian Sea. Between the Volga on the west and its main distributary, the Akhtuba, on the east, a floodplain 10 to 20 miles wide is available for irrigation agriculture. The delta itself is poorly drained and is overgrown by a tangled mass of water-loving reeds. A myriad of wild animals and water fowl occupy this delta region. The Soviets have been trying to put the wealth of reeds to some use; such things as walls for prefabricated houses and mats of all varieties have been tried, but so far none of these ideas seem to have been very practical.

Southwest of Volgograd, along the route of the Volga-Don Canal and the lower Don River, lies an extensive area of open steppe. Here the climate is semiarid, the natural vegetation is grass, and the soils are a deep, rich chestnut-brown with occasional patches of sand. In places between the lower Don and the lower Volga the soils become too saline for use.

Agriculture

The Volga Region is not as good an agricultural area as is the Central Black Earth Region. In the north the soils are infertile, the drainage is poor, and the summers are cool and short; in the south the area is desert. The middle portion, between Kazan and Saratov, particularly west of the Volga, is the best agricultural part of the region.

In the north, Kirov Oblast and Mari A.S.S.R. correspond agriculturally to the northern fringe of the Central Industrial Region. The fields are interspersed among the forests, and the chief crops are flax for

Figure 4–4   Steppe lands and river breaks at a small river station along the lower Don. Photograph by the author.

cash, potatoes, hay, and small grains. Dairying is very important.

Southward more general farming is practiced on the dissected western upland where wheat, hay, and other small grains now are being interspersed with significant acreages of corn and sugar beets. Since 1954 much of the drier Transvolga Meadows east of Kuybyshev has been plowed up under the "Virgin Lands Project" and seeded to spring wheat. Winters here are too severe for the survival of winter wheat. Scattered fields of sunflowers are found on both sides of the river all the way from Kazan to Volgograd, but this is not part of the major sunflower belt. Millet is grown in some of the drier parts of the region. Beef cattle, sheep, and pigs are being raised in ever-increasing numbers.

On the floodplain between the Volga and the Akhtuba from Volgograd to Astrakhan a strip of intensively irrigated agriculture cuts through the dry desert. Melons, fruit, vegetables, rice, and a little cotton are grown in the irrigated strip. Otherwise the lower Volga is a dry grazing land.

The steppes of the lower Don are used for the extensive growing of such drought-resistant crops as wheat, sunflowers, and millet and for the grazing of cattle and sheep. This is the midsection of the main crescent-shaped belt of sunflower growing which has two nodes of more intense cultivation, one on either side of the lower Don, in eastern Ukraine and in the North Caucasus. On the delta of the Don near the head of the Sea of Azov overhead irrigation is now being used to grow some alfalfa, vegetables, and fruit.

Industrial Development

The industrial revolution, which came belatedly to the Moscow region and eastern Ukraine during the latter part of the nineteenth century, passed by the Volga Region. At the turn of the century only 5 per cent of the population in the area were employed in industry, and cottage or craft industries were much more important than factories. What factories existed were engaged primarily in processing local agricultural produce; flour milling, distilling, soap making, tanning, and leather working were outstanding. Other industries were ship building, cement, and timber. Lime kilns still dot the west side of the Volga where limestone outcrops at the base of the escarpment. The processed lime and cement are loaded directly into river boats for distribution.

In 1917 a cursory report on the prospects for the development of the Volga basin concluded that since it was mainly an agricultural district the question of the provision of power was not important. It was stated that the use of the river for water power was precluded not only by the weakness of the current because of the slight gradient, but also by ice in winter and drought in summer. Apart from some asphalt and oil shale near Syzran, no minerals, metals, or industrial fuel of any kind were obtainable from the Middle Volga.

During the first twenty years following the Revolution the Volga Region remained a Cinderella among the rapidly developing industrial regions of the Moscow area, eastern Ukraine, the Urals, and western Siberia. In 1937 the Volga Region still had virtually no power supply of its own. Although the Volga-Ural oil-bearing region had been discovered, its great extent was not yet known, and it was being exploited only at scattered points. Only in the mid 1930s were the foundations laid for the metal-using industries, and even then the emphasis was primarily on the production of agricultural machinery.*

World War II, with its attendant move-

* Much of the preceding discussion of the historical development of the Volga Region derives from David J. M. Hooson, "The Middle Volga—An Emerging Focal Region in the Soviet Union," *The Geographical Journal*, Vol. CXXVI, Part 2, June 1960, pp. 180–190.

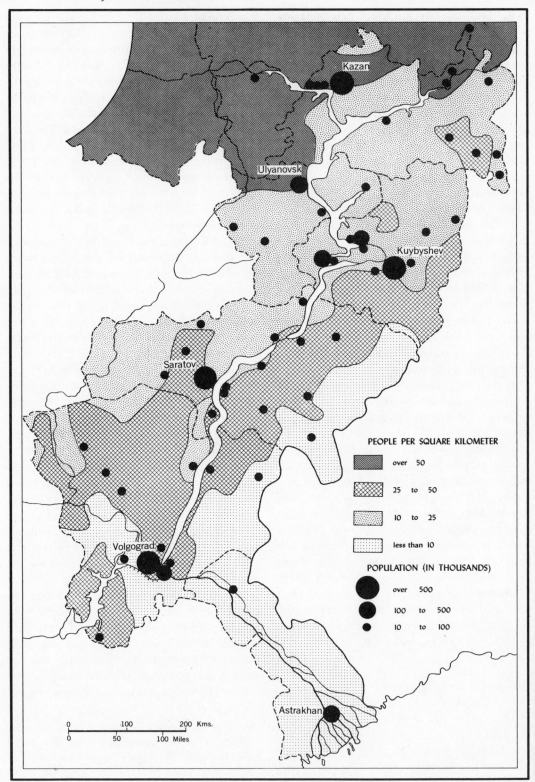

Figure 4–5   Population in the Povolzhye. After Lyalikov.

ment of industries eastward, was the catalyst that triggered the development of the Middle Volga Region that has continued since the war at an undiminished pace. For a time during the war when Moscow was under heavy siege, even the central government was relocated largely in Kuybyshev. Since 1940 the Middle Volga and adjacent "pre-Ural" Regions have been the most rapidly developing regions in the country in terms of growth of industrial production, trade, and major cities. Only Novosibirsk Oblast in western Siberia even approaches the growth rates of the Middle Volga and pre-Ural Regions. The much-vaunted growth of production in the rest of Siberia, the Far East, and Middle Asia is in no way comparable to that in the Middle Volga. This fact often is obscured by Soviet statements stressing the importance of the eastern regions and by methods of reporting production statistics which split the Middle Volga–pre-Ural Regions down the middle and include the eastern half with the Urals, whose production statistics in turn are included in "the eastern regions," a catchall that includes Middle Asia and extends to the Pacific.

In 1965, the industrial production of the U.S.S.R. was 791 per cent of what it had been in 1940. By comparison, the industrial output in Kuybyshev Oblast in 1965 was 2507 per cent of what it had been in 1940; in the Bashkir A.S.S.R., 2644 per cent; and in the Tatar A.S.S.R., 1715 per cent. Other indices of growth similarly reveal the preeminence of the Middle Volga. Employed manpower and railroad freight traffic also have increased the most rapidly in the Middle Volga–pre-Ural area. Such indications of sustained growth have given rise to predictions that the Middle Volga is an emerging focal region of the Soviet Union. There is little doubt now that the Volga Region is the greatest powerhouse in the Soviet Union. This is due to oil and gas deposits on the one hand and hydroelectric developments on the other.

The Volga Waterway

Trade The unity of the Povolzhye depends on the Volga River, for it is the river and the traffic on it that historically has bound together the ends of the region and induced the establishment of towns along its banks. Now the towns have transcended their original functions and grown into great industrial cities, and the river traffic has been eclipsed by rail traffic. Although the trade function of the cities and the water transport of the total freight have been relegated to minor roles, both have increased greatly during the Soviet period. In 1960 the Volga carried 40 billion ton-miles of freight, which was twice what it had carried in 1950 and three times the amount carried in 1913. However, in 1913 the Volga had accounted for about three quarters of the total river traffic in the country, whereas in 1960 it accounted for only two thirds of the total. Within the Volga Region, the river carried 12.2 per cent of all the freight traffic in 1963, whereas railroads carried 67.1 per cent. Pipelines had surpassed river traffic, accounting for 16.5 per cent of the freight of the region. The Volga Region accounted for 81 per cent of all the pipeline loadings in the country in 1963.

Historically, wheat, coal, and pig iron from Ukraine, fish from the Caspian, salt from the lower Volga, and oil from Baku have gone up the river in great quantities to supply the population concentrations in the Central Industrial Region, the Northwest, and the Urals, while timber and finished products have moved down the river to the lower Volga and Ukraine.

The wheat trade has diminished considerably as the wheat base has shifted from Ukraine to Western Siberia and Northern Kazakhstan; the oil traffic has diminished somewhat and shifted its direction as the Baku fields have faded in importance and the Volga-Urals fields

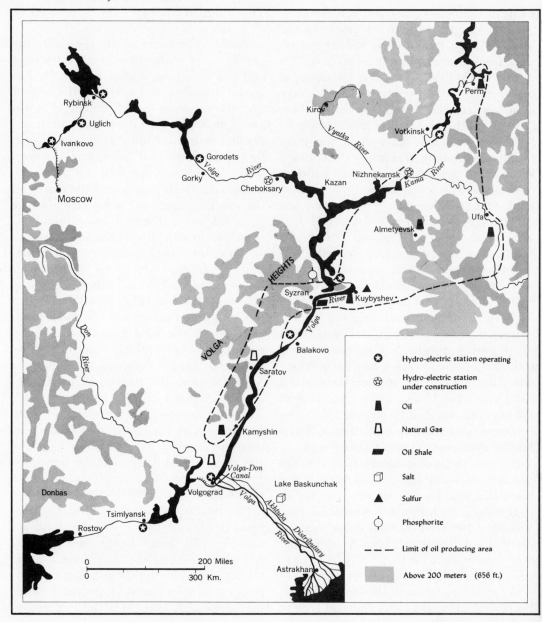

Figure 4–6   Mineral resources and water power of the Volga and adjacent regions.

have become the dominant suppliers. Timber has remained the primary freight on the river. The most significant change in the freight makeup has been the rapid growth of short-distance hauling of mineral construction materials. As the large cities along the Volga have grown at very rapid rates, great quantities of cement and other construction materials, generally derived locally within the region, have been hauled to myriad construction sites. The construction of the system of large dams and associated facilities on the river itself necessitated the movement of almost incredible quantities of bulky construction materials. Such materials recently have

Figure 4–7   Traffic on the Volga near Gorky. Novosti.

been averaging about one quarter of all Volga freight handled, although they account for only about 7 per cent of the total traffic, because of the short distances involved. Timber has retained its number one position with something over 40 per cent of the total freight and one third of total Volga traffic, whereas oil has declined a little to approximately 20 per cent of total freight and total traffic. Thus, timber, petroleum, and mineral construction materials now comprise about 90 per cent of the Volga tonnage and two thirds of its total traffic.

The Great Volga Scheme   The continued growth of traffic on the Volga has prompted the grand scheme to completely control the flow of the river, by constructing a stairway of huge reservoirs, each of which would reach upstream to the dam forming the next reservoir. This would assure complete navigability during the 6 or 7 months when the river is free of ice and incidentally would provide large amounts of hydroelectric power and some water for irrigation of the steppes from Kuybyshev southward. The construction projects on the upper Volga already

have been discussed within the context of the Central Industrial Region.

The first project to be completed on the lower Volga was the Volga-Don Canal, which in 1952 connected the Volga with the Don at the point where they bend most closely toward each other; it provided an outlet for the Volga traffic to the sea. The

Figure 4–8   Log rafts floating down the Volga near Volgograd. A log cabin is built on each raft to house the workmen who accompany the rafts to their destinations where both rafts and cabins are sold. This practice explains the presence of log cabin dwellings in the treeless Caspian Lowland. The raftmen return to their places of employment by rail. Photograph by the author.

78   *The Povolzhye and the Lower Don*

canal starts along the west bank of the Volga a few miles below Volgograd and follows a looping course for 62 miles across the lowest part of the divide to the Don River. (Fig. 4–6) Thirteen locks, each with a lift of about 30 feet, lift the water 145 feet above the Don and drop it 290 feet to the Volga. The Volga at Volgograd is just about at sea level. To provide water for the canal and to improve the channel on the lower Don, an earthen dam was strung for more than 7 miles across the broad, shallow valley of the Don River at the town of Tsimlyansk. The Tsimlyansk Dam raised the water 85 feet and backed it up the Don Valley 216 miles to form the Tsimlyansk Sea. With a surface area of approximately 1000 square miles, the Tsimlyansk Sea surpassed the Rybinsk Reservoir in size and was the largest man-

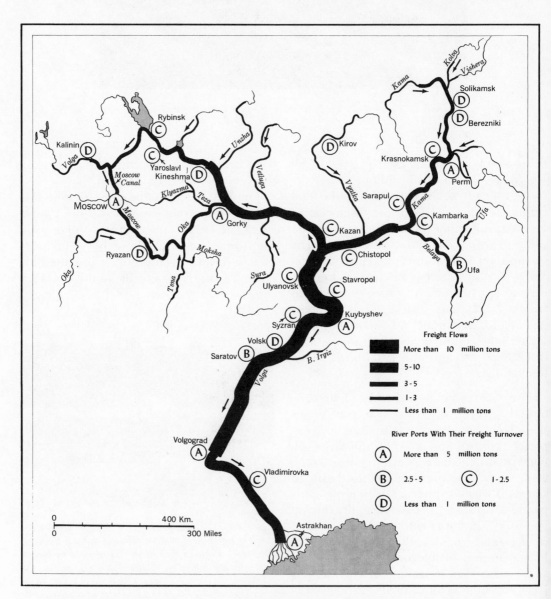

Figure 4–9   Freight traffic densities and major ports on the rivers of the Volga Basin. From Soviet Geography: Review and Translation, *June 1961, p. 86.*

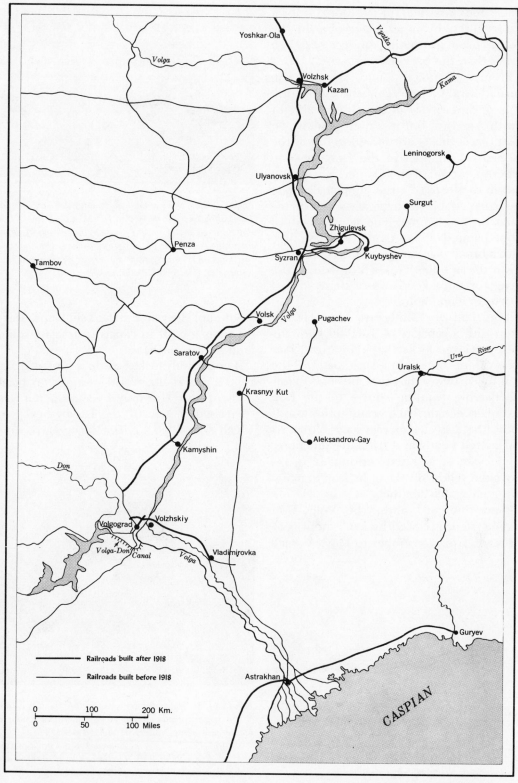

Figure 4–10 Railroads of the Povolzhye. From Soviet Geography: Review and Translation, *June 1961, p. 80.*

made body of water in the world until it was eclipsed by other reservoirs on the Volga. Each succeeding project has been larger than the previous one.

From the vantage point of a steamer in the middle of the reservoir, the Tsimlyansk Sea appears as vast as the Great Lakes of North America, but it is quite shallow. In most places, boats are forced to follow the submerged channel of the Don River in order to stay out of shoal water. Navigation aids in the form of large signboards along the banks enable the navigators to keep the boats in the channel. The signs consist of white-painted billboards about 10 feet high with a broad black stripe painted vertically down the middle. To keep on course the navigator must keep two of these striped boards in alignment.

The dam at Tsimlyansk has a power plant with a capacity of 160,000 kilowatts and two large locks that raise and lower boats from the Tsimlyansk Sea to the Don River. Below the dam, the boats follow the narrow, winding course of the Don River between the willows and cottonwoods lining the dissected dryish loess bluffs. At constricted bends and tributary junctions, dredges must be used continually to remove the yellow silt from the Don to maintain a navigable channel.

Even this far south, the Volga-Don Canal system is closed by ice 5 months of the year, from December to May. A small

Figure 4–12   *Navigational aids along the banks of the Tsimlyansk Sea in the Volga-Don Canal System. The ship's navigator stays on the course of the submerged channel of the Don River by lining up the black stripes on two successive sign boards. Note the dry steppe nature of the countryside. Photograph by the author.*

amount of the water in the Tsimlyansk Reservoir is led off in canals to irrigate some land to the southeast.

The Tsimlyansk Sea had enjoyed its reputation as the world's largest artificial body of water for only 4 years when it was surpassed in size by the Kuybyshev Sea, which was filled in 1956. The earth and

Figure 4–13   *Passenger boats navigating the Volga-Don System stop frequently at small river stations to unload and take on passengers. Natives are on hand to sell fresh produce to the travelers. Note the thick chernozem soil profile developed on a mantle of loess. The Don here is thickly silted with yellow mud. Photograph by the author.*

Figure 4–11   *The Volga entrance to the Volga-Don Canal. The statue of Stalin sits a few hundred yards to the south of the entrance. Photograph by the author.*

concrete spillway dam upstream from Kuybyshev raises the Volga water 80 feet and backs up a reservoir some 380 miles up the Volga and its tributaries, the Kama River, and others. The city of Kazan, which formerly was 2 miles east of the Volga up the small Kazanka River, now sits on the shore of the Kuybyshev Sea. The dock facilities of Kazan had to be relocated, and a 20-mile earthen dike was built to protect the city. Some 280 villages containing more than 40,000 houses had to be moved to prepare for the flooding of the reservoir. With a capacity of 2,100,000 kilowatts, the hydroelectric plant is somewhat larger than that of Grand Coulee Dam in the United States. Hence, at the time of its dedication in 1957, it was the largest hydroelectric plant in the world. High-voltage transmission lines (500,000-volts) carry power west to Moscow and east through the Tatar and Bashkir oil fields to Zlatoust in the Urals. A double canal and lock system by-pass the dam and allow for simultaneous passage of boats in both directions. Also, a 3-kilometer stretch in the by-pass canal provides a winter harbor with repair docks. It is planned that eventually 1 million hectares of land southeast of Kuybyshev will be irrigated.

Since 1957 the Kuybyshev Dam and Reservoir have been surpassed in size by those at Volgograd. The capacity of the hydroelectric plant at Volgograd is more than 2,500,000 kilowatts. The reservoir extends about 400 miles upstream. About 40 per cent of the power is transmitted all the way to Moscow over 500,000-volt transmission lines. Power is also transmitted 300 miles west to the Donets Basin over an experimental 800,000-volt direct current line. It is planned to irrigate some land on both sides of the Volga downstream from Volgograd. Originally a 400-mile canal was projected to carry Volga water eastward to the Ural River and provide irrigation along the way for 60,000 square kilometers of land in the North Caspian Lowland. There

is not enough surplus water in the Volga to accomplish this, however, and there is no indication that construction ever was started.

At the end of 1967 the first units of the Saratov hydroelectric plant went into operation. The plant is situated at Balakovo upstream from Saratov where the Volgograd Reservoir ends. The Saratov Dam raises the water level 13 meters and extends a reservoir upstream all around the east side of the Zhiguli Bend past Kuybyshev to the Kuybyshev dam site. Ultimate capacity of the hydroelectric plant is scheduled to be 1.3 million kilowatts. The Saratov Dam, seventh on the Volga, leaves only the proposed Cheboksary Dam to complete the great stairstep of reservoirs. Construction is scheduled to begin in 1969 15 miles east of Cheboksary at the new workers' settlement of Novocheboksarsk, which already had a population of 24,000 in 1967. This settlement is to be retained as a permanent town after the dam is built and will be developed into a chemical industrial complex. The first of eighteen generating units are scheduled to be installed in 1974 in the power plant that is to have an ultimate capacity of 1.4 million kilowatts. A ninth dam, originally envisaged for the lower Volga below Volgograd, apparently has been abandoned because of its unfeasibility in the flat, dry Caspian lowland. The system of dams regulates the highly seasonal flow of the Volga and maintains a minimum navigational depth of 9½ feet.

The construction projects on the Volga have not been entirely beneficial to navigation. The transformation of a flowing stream into a staircase of extremely large, quiet bodies of water has rendered timber rafting virtually impossible. Log rafts must be towed through the reservoirs, and even that is not very satisfactory. Storm waves on these "inland seas" break up the rafts and cause hazards to life and property, and the intricate system of locks between reservoirs necessitates delays which have lengthened the movement of logs from the upper Volga to Astrakhan from 30–40 days to 60–80 days. These difficulties are inducing a shift in the lumber-milling industry from traditional market areas in the larger cities of the south to smaller towns in the logging areas of the north, where the logs can be sawed into lumber and the lumber loaded onto river barges or railroad cars for shipment southward.

Irrigation of land along the Volga is severely curtailed by the limited flow of the Volga, which if diminished will cause a damaging drop in the water level of the Caspian. In fact, the Caspian, which receives about three fourths of its water from the Volga, already has suffered an alarming drop in level, owing to a slightly warmer, drier climate since 1929 and increased evaporation of Volga River water from the extensive surfaces of the man-made reservoirs. The delta shoreline has extended out into the shallow northern end of the sea until at present Astrakhan lies about 40 miles inland, and a transfer point known as "Twelve-Foot Roads" has to be maintained near the edge of the delta to transship oil and other freight from large Caspian steamers to smaller river boats. (Fig. 4–1) Although new shallow-draft vessels have been devised that can negotiate both sea and river, a continued drop in the Caspian level would make navigation all the more difficult and seriously impair the rich fishing grounds of the northern banks.

The maintenance of the level of the Caspian Sea has been deemed such an important problem in the Soviet Union that an all-Union conference was called on April 11, 1960 to discuss the question. The results of this conference and a more complete description of the Caspian are included in the chapter on Middle Asia and Southern Kazakhstan (Chapter 10), after all the surrounding territories have been discussed.

Petroleum and Natural Gas

The Volga-Urals oil fields, stretching from Volgograd northeastward to Perm, contain some of the greatest reserves of oil in the Soviet Union and since 1956 have been producing more than 65 per cent of the country's petroleum. The Tatar A.S.S.R. is now first in the production of petroleum, Kuybyshev Oblast is third, after the Bashkir A.S.S.R., to the east, and Volgograd Oblast is fifth. The Tatar A.S.S.R. and Kuybyshev Oblast each considerably outproduce the famous old area of production in Transcaucasia around Baku.

Production costs in the Volga-Urals oil fields are several times lower than they are in most other oil fields in the Soviet Union. The oil in the Volga-Urals fields is found in a number of essentially flat-lying strata which are particularly adaptable to contour flooding. As oil wells are drilled into the tops of oil-bearing structures, holes are driven downslope on the rock structure in all directions, and water is pumped in at approximately the same rate as oil is extracted. Natural pressure thereby is maintained, ultimate recovery is greatly increased, and production costs are reduced.

Kuybyshev and Syzran have become important centers for oil refining, and other cities in the region will have new refineries. The city of Almetyevsk in the center of the Tatar A.S.S.R. has grown to a population of 74,000 acting as a center for the oil fields and as one of the main collection points for crude oil that enters the so-called Friendship pipeline that carries crude oil to the refineries of some of the East European satellites. This trunkline, completed in September 1964, runs westward from Kuybyshev through the Central Black Earth Region to Belorussia where it splits into two sections, one running northwest to Germany and Poland and the other southwest to Czechoslovakia and Hungary. Other pipelines have been built to the west and to the east to distribute Volga-Urals oil to a region stretching from Leningrad in the west to Irkutsk in the east.

A new oil center, Nizhnekamsk, is being built in the midst of the Kama River oil field, opened up in the Tatar A.S.S.R in 1958. It is planned for an ultimate population of 250,000, which will make it the second largest city in the republic, after Kazan. (Fig. 4–6) The Lower Kama hydroelectric plant is to be built in the vicinity; its reservoir will flood part of the oil field. Therefore oil rigs in the area of the future reservoir are being installed on marine platforms.

A major gas deposit near Saratov was developed during World War II, and in 1946 a gas pipeline was laid from Saratov to Moscow. Since then another pipeline has been laid to carry this gas northwestward to Gorky, Ivanovo, and Cherepovets. Lesser gas fields are now in production northwest of Volgograd and in the Tatar Republic. Tatar oil field gas is being piped to the steel plant in Magnitogorsk and a synthetic rubber plant in Kazan.

The high development of the oil and gas industries in the Volga Region have resulted in a reduction of long, expensive coal hauls into the region from the Donets, Kuznetsk, and Karaganda basins. Also, natural gas and gaseous by-products of oil refining have provided a new broad base for the development of a variety of chemical industries in the Volga Region, particularly those producing synthetic rubber, artificial fibers, fertilizers, and alcohol.

Synthetic rubber plants have also been established at the chemical center of Stavropol (recently renamed Togliatti) on the Volga River upstream from Kuybyshev and at Volzhskiy, the new city across the river from Volgograd, which was originally established as a workers' settlement to house the construction workers for the Volgograd Dam project. A chemical fiber plant and a pipe mill for 56-inch oil pipe are also being established in Volzhskiy.

A nitrate fertilizer plant has been built in Togliatti. Oil and gas products are also speeding the construction of thermal electric stations, such as the Zainsk station in the Tatar A.S.S.R., which has a designed capacity of 1,200,000 kilowatts. Such stations are necessary to supplement the electrical output from the huge hydroelectric stations along the Volga which frequently operate at far below capacity because of ice or lack of sufficient water.

Other Resources and Industries Extensive deposits of oil shale exist in Ulyanovsk and Kuybyshev Oblasts, and a significant production of oil from shale has been carried on for a number of years, particularly in the vicinity of Syzran. Some oil is still being produced from shale in this area in spite of the growth of the petroleum industry.

In the same general areas as the oil shales are important deposits of phosphorites and limestone for the agricultural fertilizer industries. In addition, in the Samara Bend area there are some deposits of sulfur important to fertilizer and other chemical industries.

Along the lower Volga, southeast of Volgograd in the Caspian Lowland, lie several salt lakes which are developed over underlying salt plugs. These lakes supply a large portion of the Soviet Union's salt. The chief producing lake beds are Baskunchak and Elton. The salt produced here is important to the fishing industry in the northern Caspian, which for many years was the richest fishing ground of the Soviet Union and still is of major importance. Much of the world's black caviar is produced from sturgeon caught in the shallow northern end of the Caspian.

Other than the mineral resources and the fish of the Caspian, the chief natural resource is the forests of the north in Kirov Oblast and in the Mari A.S.S.R. This is a significant lumbering area, and logs are floated down tributary streams such as the Vyatka into the Volga to go to the treeless

Caspian Plain in the south or through the Volga-Don Canal and down the Don River to Ukraine.

The local natural resources are reflected in only part of the industries along the Volga. For a number of years before the oil boom breathed new life into the region, the major cities had been growing steadily, primarily due to the development of the machine-building industries. And in spite of the recent emphasis on chemicals, machine industries still account for the greatest portion of manufactured value and factory labor in this area. Chemical industries are still relatively undeveloped, and constitute somewhat less than 10 per cent of the industrial production of the Volga Region. Everything from business machines to major aircraft components are manufactured in the larger cities. The caterpillar tractor plant at Volgograd has been famous for years, as has the Red October metallurgical works which supplies the steel. Recently, the most exciting development in this respect has been the establishment of the Fiat plant at Togliatti, which is scheduled to turn out about 660,-000 passenger cars each year.

Cities

The Volga Region is rapidly becoming a string of great cities, each of which marks an important rail crossing of the river. As noted before, these cities, which started as defense outposts and evolved through a stage when trade was their primary function, under the Soviets have developed into full-fledged industrial centers.

Kuybyshev Gorky excluded, the largest city on the Volga is Kuybyshev, a preeminence only recently attained. At the time of the Revolution it was smaller than both Kazan and Saratov. With its present population of 992,000 and several good-sized suburbial towns around it, Kuybyshev is becoming the focal center of the entire Volga Region. The largest of these satellite towns is Syzran about 50 miles around the Samara Bend to the west on the other side of the river. Together, Kuybyshev and Syzran are the chief refining centers of the Volga-Urals oil fields. A long railroad bridge crosses the river between Syzran and Kuybyshev and continues eastward to join with the Trans-Siberian Railroad.

Kuybyshev is the old city of Samara, which was established in 1596 as a fortress at the mouth of the small Samara River where it flows into the Volga from the southeast. Samara early distinguished itself as the financial capital of the Volga wheat trade during the days of the Russian Empire. The wheat barons constructed bank buildings along the main street facing the river, and further out in the countryside they established large estates. Many of the bank buildings and mansions still stand, but they now serve as government buildings, rest homes, children's homes, and so forth. In 1935 the city was renamed after the Bolshevik leader, V. V. Kuybyshev.

Today Kuybyshev is a great industrial city concentrating on machine building, oil refining, and food processing. Now that this region is the major oil-producing area in the country, we can expect a growing importance of oil refining and the development of a whole range of chemical industries associated with the by-products of oil refining. During the last decade, the chemical industries have grown about six times as fast as the machine-building industries. It may be that in the future oil refining and oil-based chemicals will become even more important than the machine industries in this region.

Kazan The second largest city in the Volga Region is Kazan, the old center of the Tatars which now serves as the capital of the Tatar A.S.S.R. Founded in 1437 by the Tatars, it was captured by Muskovy in 1552 when its kremlin was undermined and blown up. In 1967 Kazan had a population of 821,000. It is growing at a rate similar to that of Kuybyshev and is being industrialized in much the same way. It also lies within the Volga-Urals oil fields, the Tatar Republic being the main producer of oil in the Soviet Union at present. So far, however, Kazan has not become the center of oil refining that Kuybyshev has. It early became a center for buying cattle hides and furs, and this trade determined its first development of industries. Tanning, shoe making, and the tallow industry for soap and candles became of first importance. These industries still occupy about a fourth of the manufactures of Kazan, but the machine-building industries and chemical industries each make up a fourth of Kazan's industry, and the other fourth is made up by food industries. Kazan is particularly known for its manufacture of a variety of business machines — typewriters, calculators, etc. It has a major university which has become famous in the Soviet Union, because for a time Lenin studied law there. We might expect that machine-building and chemical industries will become even more important in the future.

Volgograd   Third in size is Volgograd with a population of 743,000. Volgograd is the old city of Tsaritsyn, which gained Union-wide fame during the Civil War following the Bolshevik Revolution, and then gained worldwide fame in World War II when it withstood the onslaught of the Germans and eventually proved to be the battle that signified the turning point in the war. Stalin distinguished himself here as a leader in the Red Army after the Revolution and the name "Tsaritsyn," which was derived from "Tsarina" or "Tsar's wife," was changed to Stalingrad. With the posthumous purge of Stalin in 1961, the name was changed once more to Volgograd.

Tsaritsyn was founded in 1589 as a Russian fort overlooking the steppes to the southeast. In the late nineteenth century it became an important transshipping point between rail and water for oil, lumber, coal, and fish. Lying just east of the heavy industrial area in eastern Ukraine, Volgograd has been the recipient of some heavy metallurgy and much machine building based on the iron and steel supply of Ukraine. At present the industrial makeup of Volgograd is one fifth heavy metallurgy, one fifth machine building, one fifth chemicals, one fifth food industry, and one fifth diversified. Volgograd has been known all through the Soviet period as one of the two great centers of tractor building. The caterpillar tractor plant and the Red October metallurgical works on the narrow floodplain on the north side of the city are still the largest industries in Volgograd. Chemical and lumber industries dominate the floodplain to the south of the city.

The city holds a strategic position on the high right bank of the Volga where the Volga makes its major bend toward the southeast. The city stretches in a crescent-shaped arc for about 35 miles along the west side of the river. A low narrow floodplain exists between the high right bank and the river, and on this floodplain much of the industry of the city is located.

The city suffered much damage during World War II and has been designated as one of the "hero cities" of the Soviet Union. Much of the rubble has been cleared away since World War II, and most of the city has been reconstructed. But near the center of town overlooking the Volga, a large bombed-out shell of a building has been left standing as a war memorial. A tall graceful obelisk dominates the central square of the city, on the base of which are commemorated the fallen heroes of World War II. The Soviet people keep this monument smothered in flowers. The entire tone of the city of Volgograd is one of war-stricken grief from which the people have never recovered. Their remembrances are much too vivid for them to view the war with any sort of objectivity.

With the completion of the Volga-Don Canal in 1952, Volgograd occupies a much more strategic position on the river than it did previously. It now has become the point from which trade goes either on down the Volga southeast to the Caspian or through the Volga-Don Canal and down the Don River southwest into the Sea of Azov and the important industrial areas of Ukraine. It is also on a major rail line that parallels the west bank of the river from the north, and then crosses the river in the vicinity of Volgograd and continues on southeastward to Astrakhan, passing through the important testing grounds for intercontinental ballistic missiles at Kap-. ustin Yar. Railroads also connect Volgograd to the northwest with Moscow and to the west and southwest with Ukraine and the Northern Caucasus.

The building of the dam about 10 miles north of the city has assured the area of an abundance of electrical power. The dam has an ultimate capacity of 2,563,000 kilowatts, which makes it the largest power plant on the river. The workers' settlement of Volzhskiy near the east end of the dam has been turned into a chemical industrial complex using electrical power and natural and by-product gases to produce synthetic fibers, rubber, and plastics. By 1967 its population had already grown to 114,000.

Important gas fields lie near Frolovo about 50 miles northwest of Volgograd, and a gas pipeline connecting the two centers has existed for some years. An aluminum industry has been located in Volgograd to make use of the hydroelectric power for converting alumina from the Urals to aluminum.

Saratov   Nearly as large as Volgograd is Saratov, located halfway between Volgograd and Kuybyshev on the high bluff of the river, with a 1967 population of 720,-000. Saratov occupies the site of one of the major rail crossings of the Volga. The rail line continues on eastward to the southern Urals and eventually connects with the Trans-Siberian Railroad. Saratov is the center of one of the major gas fields on the Volga. At present Saratov has about one third of its industry engaged in machine building, one third in chemicals, and one third in food industries. We can probably expect the chemical industries to grow at a more rapid rate than the others in the future.

Across the river from Saratov are the towns of Marx and Engels, which lay in the Volga German A.S.S.R. before World War II. During the war, the Volga Germans were accused of collaboration with Germany and were dispersed throughout the Soviet Union, many of them being sent as far east as Soviet Middle Asia or eastern Siberia. The Volga German Republic is one of the two remaining political units that were abolished during World War II which have not been restored to their previous status since the death of Stalin.

Astrakhan   Astrakhan, founded as a fortress in 1558 at the mouth of the Volga, has been growing at a much slower rate than the four previously mentioned cities. In 1967 it had a population of 368,000. It lies on a dead-end branch of the waterway off the mainstream of products going between Ukraine, the Central Industrial Region, and the Urals, and it cannot be expected to grow in the future at a rate commensurate with the rest of the cities. Its function remains primarily that of a port city handling products of the local water area: fish, oil, and salt. It has the largest fish-processing plant in the country. Its industries are about one third food processing, one third machine building, and one third diversified. With the diminishing of the flow of oil from Baku up the Volga, the role of Astrakhan might actually diminish.

Kirov   The sixth city in size in the Povolzhye is Kirov, lying on the northern boundary of the region. It was founded as Khlynov in 1174 and became known as

Vyatka in 1781, after the Vyatka River, which is a tributary of the Kama. In 1934 it was renamed Kirov after Sergey Kirov, Bolshevik revolutionary and Leningrad party boss, who had been born in Vyatka region and who was assassinated in 1934. The present population of the city is 309,-000. Lying in the forest zone, it has become an important center for wood processing and fur processing. Thirty per cent of the teaching aids in the U.S.S.R. are made in Kirov. Besides these, such things as matches, prefabricated houses, and furniture are made from local wood supplies. At present the industry of Kirov is characterized as being one fourth machine building, one fourth chemical, one fourth woodworking, and one fourth food processing. The city is situated at just about the northern limit of concentrated agriculture, with only scattered dairying, potato growing, some flax growing, and very little grain growing to the north. It is the site of annual winter games for the U.S.S.R.

Ulyanovsk Next in size is the city of Ulyanovsk located on the Volga about halfway between Kuybyshev and Kazan. It was founded in 1648 as the fortress of Simbirsk and was renamed Ulyanovsk in 1924 after Lenin, because it was his birthplace. In 1967 Ulyanovsk had a population of 294,-000. It has been sharing in the growth of all the cities along the river. Its industry is characterized as being about 65 per cent machine construction and 35 per cent food processing.

Other Cities Other than these major cities, there are numerous ones of the 50,-000–200,000 class. Syzran, west of Kuybyshev, has already been mentioned as a center of the oil and gas industry. About half of its industry is machine construction. Another city of similar size is Kamyshin, located about halfway between Volgograd and Saratov, which is concentrated on the textile industries, particularly cotton textiles. Volzhskiy, at the eastern end of the

Volgograd Dam, has rapidly grown into an important industrial complex. And Togliatti, just upstream from Kuybyshev, is a city of 130,000 which produces synthetic rubber, cement, and mercury rectifiers for electric transmission lines. Until 1964 it was known as Stavropol, but was renamed after the Italian Communist leader, Palmiro Togliatti, when it was decided that the large Fiat automobile plant would be located there.

The large city of Rostov and the coal-mining area to the north of it will be discussed along with the rest of the Donets Basin in eastern Ukraine.

Prospects

The Volga Region is in an intermediate position on major transport routes between the three great industrial nodes of the Soviet Union — the Central Industrial Region to the west, the Urals to the east, and the Donets Basin to the southwest. With the building of the Volga-Don Canal, the Moscow Canal, and the large reservoirs on the Volga and Kama Rivers, a navigable all-water route in the shape of a large Y has been formed between the three industrial nodes; the Middle Volga occupies the strategic point at the fork of the Y. Major rail lines connecting west and east have been constructed across the Volga at Kazan, Ulyanovsk, Kuybyshev, and Saratov, and during World War II a line was laid along the western bluffs parallel to the river. This line crosses the river at Volgograd and continues along the eastern side to Astrakhan. With the growth in exchange of products between the three industrial nodes across the Middle Volga via the rail and water transport systems, the Middle Volga could hardly have escaped eventual economic development, even if it had been completely devoid of local resources. The opening up of the huge petroleum deposits has, of course, greatly speeded this development. Undoubtedly the rapid expansion will continue in the foreseeable future.

The greater rate of industrial development in the Middle Volga Valley compared to that at either end, plus the fact that the rapid industrialization and the oil fields continue eastward into the Bashkir A.S.S.R. and Perm and Orenburg Oblasts, eventually may warrant the consideration of this area as a separate region, cutting across and breaking down the traditional regional divisions of the Volga and the Urals. As yet, industrialization in this area has not progressed so far as to induce a change in the views of Russian geographers about these regions.

Reading List

Dolgolopov, K. V. and Fedorova, E. F., *Povolzhye: ekonomiko-geograficheskiy ocherk* (Volga Region: Economic-Geographic Study), Moscow, 1967, 206 pp. (in Russian).

Dzhimbinov, B., *Sovetskaya Kalmikiya* (Soviet Kalmyk), Moscow, 1960, 144 pp. (in Russian).

Hooson, David J. M., "The Middle Volga — An Emerging Focal Region in the Soviet Union," *The Geographical Journal*, June 1960, pp. 182–190.

———, *A New Soviet Heartland?* Van Nostrand, New York, 1964, 132 pp.

Muckleston, Keith W., "The Volga in the Pre-revolutionary Industrialization of Russia," *Yearbook of the Association of Pacific Coast Geographers*, 1965, pp. 67–76.

Muckleston, Keith W. and Dohrs, Fred E., "The Relative Importance of Transport on the Volga Before and After the Communist Revolution," *Professional Geographer*, March 1965, pp. 22–25.

Padick, Clement, "Reorientation in Power Generation in the Volga Basin, U.S.S.R.," *Yearbook of the Association of Pacific Coast Geographers*, 1965, pp. 27–37.

Povolzhye: Ekonomiko-geograficheskaya kharakteristika (Volga Region: Economic-geographic characteristics), Akademiya Nauk SSSR, Institut geografii, Moscow, 1957, 464 pp. (in Russian).

Prociuk, Stephan G., "The Territorial Pattern of Industrialization in the U.S.S.R.: A Case Study in Location of Industry," *Soviet Studies*, July 1961, pp. 69–95.

Soviet Geography: Review and Translation, February 1967; entire issue is devoted to the Volga Region.

Taaffe, Robert N., "Volga River Transportation: Problems and Prospects," in Thoman, Richard S. and Patton, Donald J., *Focus on Geographic Activity*, McGraw-Hill, New York, 1964, pp. 185–193.

Vendrov, S. L., Gangardt, G. G., Geller, S. Yu., Korenistov, L. V., and Sarukhanov, G. L., "The Problem of Transformation and Utilization of the Water Resources of the Volga River and the Caspian Sea," *Soviet Geography: Review and Translation*, September 1964, pp. 23–34.

Ukraine and Moldavia [a]

Region	Area (sq mile)	Population	People (sq mile)	% Urban
Ukrainian S.S.R.	234,000	45,966,000	196	53
Vinnitsa Oblast	10,600	2,136,000	202	22
Volyn Oblast	7,700	968,000	126	32
Dnepropetrovsk Oblast	12,600	3,212,000	255	76
Donetsk Oblast	10,200	4,856,000	476	88
Zhitomir Oblast	11,600	1,591,000	137	32
Transcarpathia Oblast	5,000	1,040,000	208	29
Zaporozhye Oblast	10,400	1,707,000	164	64
Ivano-Frankovsk Oblast	5,400	1,220,000	226	29
Kiev Oblast	10,900	1,817,000	166	32
Kiev City	—	1,413,000	—	100
Kirovograd Oblast	9,600	1,270,000	132	40
Crimea Oblast [b]	10,000	1,623,000	162	88
Lugansk Oblast	10,300	2,796,000	271	84
Lvov Oblast	8,300	2,381,000	287	46
Nikolayev Oblast	7,500	1,100,000	147	47
Odessa Oblast	15,600	2,255,000	145	53
Poltava Oblast	13,200	1,682,000	127	37
Rovno Oblast	8,000	1,021,000	128	25
Sumy Oblast	9,400	1,511,000	161	40
Ternopol Oblast	5,300	1,157,000	218	23
Kharkov Oblast	12,000	2,694,000	225	70
Kherson Oblast	10,600	976,000	92	52
Khmelnitsky Oblast	8,000	1,617,000	202	25
Cherkassy Oblast	7,000	1,513,000	216	34
Chernigov Oblast	12,200	1,576,000	129	33
Chernovtsy Oblast	3,200	834,000	261	32
Moldavian S.S.R.	13,200	3,425,000	259	29

[a] Since the industries of the city of Rostov and the coal-mining area to the north are tied intimately to those of the rest of the Donets Basin, the economy of the western part of Rostov Oblast will be discussed with that of eastern Ukraine, although the entire area and population of Rostov Oblast were included in the Povolzhye.

[b] Since 1948 the city of Sevastopol has been under the direct jurisdiction of the Ukrainian S.S.R. But its territory and population are not customarily listed separately from those of Crimea Oblast.

Ukraine and Moldavia

The Ukrainian S.S.R., in the southwest corner of the Soviet Union, is in many respects a continuation of the parts of the Russian Republic that lie along its northeastern border. The Central Black Earth Region of Kursk and Belgorod Oblasts penetrates southwestward into Ukraine and perhaps even into northern Moldavia, and the steppes of the lower Volga roll unbroken over Ukraine's southeast. In the northwest the forests of the Pripyat Marshes spread into adjacent areas of the Russian Republic and Belorussia. Thus the character of this constituent republic of the U.S.S.R. changes from region to region as its terrain merges imperceptibly with that of neighboring republics. A discussion of Ukraine as a separate unit can probably be justified, however, for it is known throughout the world as a political and economic entity, second in importance in the U.S.S.R. only to the Russian Republic.

Ukraine represents 2.7 per cent of the area of the U.S.S.R. and 19.7 per cent of its population. In 1966 it accounted for 34 per cent of the coal, 56 per cent of the coking coal, about half the iron ore, half of the manganese, half of the pig iron, 42 per cent of the steel, 59 per cent of the corn, 59 per cent of the sugar beets, 48 per cent of the sunflowers, 27 per cent of the wheat, 22 per cent of the meat, 26 per cent of the

butter, and 28 per cent of the vegetable oil produced in the Soviet Union. At the time of the Revolution it had been even more significant to the total economy of the country. In 1913 Ukraine produced 78 per cent of the coal, 69 per cent of the iron, 58 per cent of the steel, and 35 per cent of the wheat and had long been the primary source of grain for export, an item vital to the establishment of foreign exchange which paid for the initial industrialization in the 1920s and 1930s.

Outside the U.S.S.R., Ukraine compares favorably in area, population, and primary production with the leading countries of Europe. (Tables 5–1 to 5–5) Its 234,000 square miles make it larger than any country on that continent, with the exception of the remainder of the Soviet Union, and its 45,966,000 citizens constitute one of Europe's most populous political units.

The 1959 census listed 37,000,000 Ukrainians, of whom 32,000,000 spoke their native language. Next to Russian, Ukrainian is the most widely spoken Slavic tongue. The Poles in 1960 numbered only 29,000,000.

The postwar republic of Moldavia is discussed with Ukraine because it is not large enough nor is its role in the economy of the Soviet Union important enough to

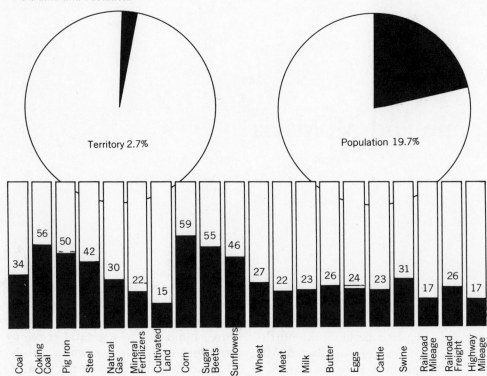

5

Figure 5–1   Ukraine's share of the U.S.S.R. territory, population, and production, 1965–1967, in per cent.

warrant separate study. In many ways it is similar to Ukraine, on which it borders. In addition, the western third of Rostov Oblast, including the city of Rostov, in the Russian Republic, is treated with eastern Ukraine because economically and geographically it is tied to the all-important Donets Coal Basin, which overlaps the boundary between Ukraine and the R.S.F.S.R.

Table 5–1   Comparison of Ukraine and Some European Countries by Area (in Square Miles)

Country	Area
Ukraine	234,000
France	216,000
Spain	197,000
Poland	122,000
Itlay	118,000
Yugoslavia	100,000
West Germany	97,000
United Kingdom	95,000

Source: United Nations Demographic Yearbook, 1966.

Table 5–2   Comparison of Ukraine and Some European Countries by Population, mid 1966

Country	Population
West Germany	57,485,000
United Kingdom	54,965,000
Italy	51,859,000
France	49,440,000
Ukraine	45,728,000
Spain	31,871,000
Poland	31,698,000
Yugoslavia	19,756,000

Source: United Nations Demographic Yearbook, 1966.

Table 5–3   Comparison of Ukraine with Leading European Countries in Coal Production, 1966 (in Millions of Metric Tons)

Country	Coal Production
Ukraine	185
United Kingdom	177
West Germany	126
Poland	122
France	50

Source: United Nations Statistical Yearbook, 1967, pp. 180–181.

Table 5–4   Comparison of Ukraine with Leading European Countries in Pig Iron and Steel Production, 1966 (in Millions of Metric Tons)

Country	Pig Iron and Ferro-Alloys	Crude Steel
Ukraine *a*	35	40
West Germany	26	35
United Kingdom	16	25
France	16	20

Source: United Nations Statistical Yearbook, 1967, pp. 299–300.
a Ukraine also produces about one fourth of the world's manganese.

Table 5–5   Comparison of Ukraine with Leading Producing Countries of Sugar, 1966 (in Thousands of Metric Tons)

Country	Sugar Production
Ukraine	5950 (beet)
Cuba	4867 (cane)
India	3633 (cane)
United States	2570 (cane and beet)

Source: United Nations Statistical Yearbook, 1967, pp. 238–239.

Political History

The word "ukraine" means extremity or borderland. During the rise of Moscow after the Tatar invasion, this area was the frontier, a no man's land between the Russians, the Poles, the Lithuanians, the Tatars, the Turks, and various nomadic tribes to the south. Gradually it was resettled, primarily by people from the north and west, and was incorporated into the Polish-Lithuanian state, which in the sixteenth and seventeenth centuries stretched from the Baltic to the Black Sea. Toward the middle of the seventeenth century a successful Cossack revolt under the leadership of Bogdan Khmelnitsky liberated Ukraine from Poland, but a few years later it fell to the power of Moscow, under which it remained until World War I.

The war and subsequent revolution resulted in the loss of the Polish provinces to a newly organized Poland, and Moldavia and Bessarabia fell to Rumania. For a short time after the Revolution the Ukrainians, independent of Russia, governed the land that remained theirs, and several years of bitter war ensued before Ukraine was finally absorbed by the Soviet Union. Civil war broke out again in 1929 and in 1930 when the farmers were forced to collectivize.

During World War II Moldavia, Bessarabia, Bukovina, and the two southeastern provinces of Poland, Volhynia and Galicia, were regained by the Soviet Union and were constituted into what is now known as Western Ukraine and the newly established Moldavian S.S.R. At the end of the war the Soviet Union demanded and was given the eastern end of Czechoslovakia on the basis that it was inhabited by Ukrainians. This territory is distinguished from those previously mentioned in that it had never been part of the Russian Empire. The Soviet Union now extends over the Carpathians onto the floor of the Hungarian Plain in so-called Transcarpathian Ukraine. In 1954 the Crimean

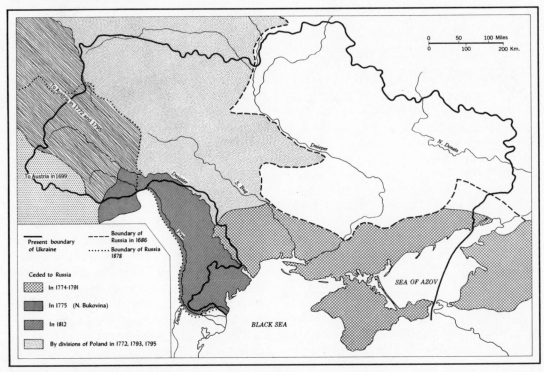

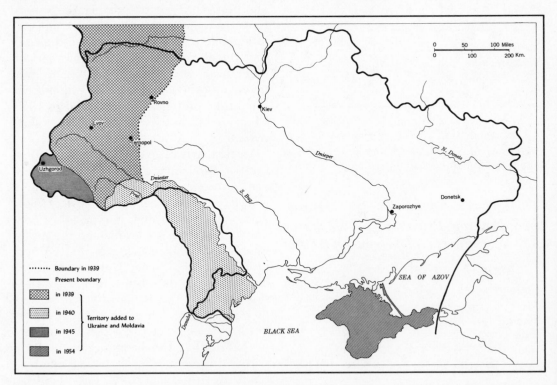

Figure 5–2   Historical exchanges of territory in the Ukraine. Upper map: The Ukraine from 1686 to 1917 and at present. Lower map: Acquisitions of territory during and since World War II. After Cherdantsev.

Peninsula was transferred from the Russian Republic to its southern neighbor.

Thus Ukraine is now larger and more populous than it has ever been before. About 77 per cent of its people are Ukrainians, 17 per cent are Russians, and the rest are Jews, Poles, Belorussians, Moldavians, Bulgarians, Hungarians, Greeks, and various other nationalities from adjacent areas. Fifty-three per cent of the people are classified as urban dwellers, which places Ukraine 2 per cent below the national average for urbanization. Moldavia and Ukraine have the highest average population densities of all the union republics.

General Survey

Geology and Topography Topographically and geologically Ukraine throughout most of its territory is a flat-lying sedimentary plain that is now undergoing some stream dissection. In the center a broad upwarp has induced more erosion, which has resulted in a rolling, broken landscape and the exposure of older rocks. The higher western part of the upwarp, known as the Podolian Plateau, covers much of southwestern Ukraine and Moldavia along the northeastern base of the Carpathian Mountains. The eastern part of the upwarp north of the Sea of Azov is known as the Donets Ridge. (Fig. 5–10) Between the two, the Dnieper River has cut through the sedimentary strata to the hard crystalline basement rock below, which produces a series of rapids in the vicinity of Zaporozhye. At this point the river makes a pronounced bend as it alters its course along the strike of the surface formations to flow directly down the dip slope of the rock into the Black Sea.

The Carpathians in western Ukraine

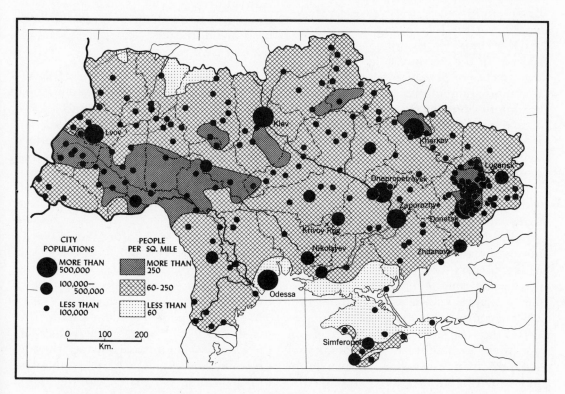

Figure 5–3 Population densities and cities of Ukraine and Moldavia. Updated from Cherdantsev.

reach altitudes of 6000 to 7000 feet. Their steep slopes on both sides are heavily forested, and recent glaciation has given the landscape an alpine character. In Crimea the mountains rise abruptly from the Black Sea coast to an altitude of more than 5000 feet. Composed primarily of limestone rocks that have undergone considerable underground solution, these mountains exhibit a rugged appearance. The south slopes dropping off to the sea are especially steep because of recent movement along a major fault zone that borders the north edge of the Black Sea.

Climate, Vegetation, and Soils   Climatically, the Russians look upon Ukraine as a mild region, but actually it has severe winters and relatively cool summers, except along portions of the Black Sea coast. And everywhere but in the northwest it is plagued by drought. January temperatures in Kiev average 21°F, and annual precipitation averages 21 inches. These conditions closely approximate those of central Nebraska, but the July average temperature of 67°F is more like that of northern North Dakota. In the northwest there are 24 or more inches of precipitation each year, an amount that diminishes steadily southeastward until along the coast of the Black Sea annual precipitation varies between 8 and 16 inches. In the warmer summers of the southern fringe this amount of rainfall is insufficient for many crops.

Periodically in summer clear Arctic air with low absolute humidity penetrates the region and allows strong insulation to heat rapidly the surface of the earth, which warms the air and drops the relative humidity to very low values and suddenly produces a condition extremely desiccating to plants, known as the "sukhovey."

The natural vegetation of Ukraine reflects the transition in moisture from northwest to southeast. Vegetation and soil zones are oriented generally in a southwest to northeast direction, perpendicular to the moisture gradient. In the northwest,

extending southeastward beyond the city of Kiev, is an area of pine and mixed deciduous forest, similar to that in adjacent parts of the Russian Republic and Belorussia. In this region the soils are gray-brown podzolic, and in the poorly drained area of the "Polesye" the soils are groundwater podzol and bog. Just south of Kiev is the "wooded steppe," characterized by extensive areas of open grassland interspersed with clumps of trees, particularly along the stream valleys. This region, which is the beginning of fertile chernozem soils, continues to Zaporozhye, beyond which lie the chernozem and chestnut soils of the open steppes.

The soils of Ukraine are in general quite good, as is to be expected in an area of subhumid and semiarid climates. In addition, over much of the land a mantle of loess has greatly increased their mineral constituents. The chief drawback to agriculture is the cool and droughty climate. Agriculture as a rule is commercial; specialty crops raised on an extensive cash basis are distributed according to the climate of each region.

The Dnieper River   The Dnieper River, like the Volga, has been harnessed by dams that have remade the stream into a large stairway of reservoirs. The chief function of most of these structures is to produce hydroelectric power, but navigation has also been improved. Irrigation is the primary purpose of the southernmost dam and is an auxiliary function of some of the other dams.

The first dam built before World War II was the Dnieper, just north of the city of Zaporozhye where the river cuts into the old crystalline basement rock and flows through a constricted channel over a series of nine large rapids. The name Zaporozhye means "across the rapids." This dam raised the water level more than 100 feet, thereby drowning the rapids and connecting the upper portion of the river with the lower, both of which are navigable. With a gen-

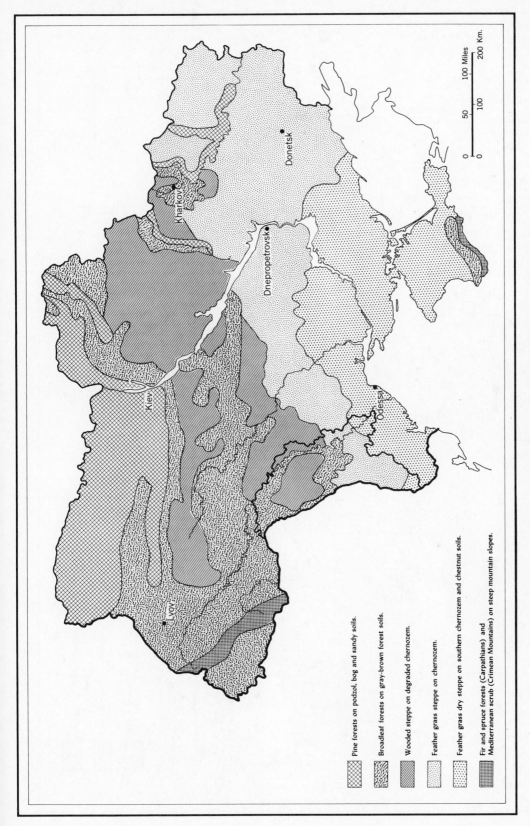

Pine forests on podzol, bog and sandy soils.

Broadleaf forests on gray-brown forest soils.

Wooded steppe on degraded chernozem.

Feather grass steppe on chernozem.

Feather grass dry steppe on southern chernozem and chestnut soils.

Fir and spruce forests (Carpathians) and Mediterranean scrub (Crimean Mountains) on steep mountain slopes.

Figure 5–4 Soil and natural vegetation zones of the Ukraine and Moldavia. After Cherdantsev.

97

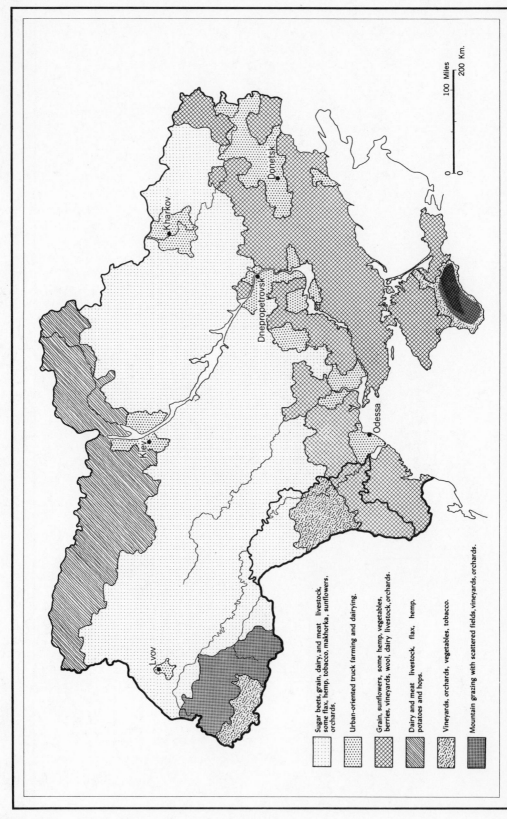

Sugar beets, grain, dairy, and meat livestock,
some flax, hemp, tobacco, makhorka, sunflowers,
orchards.

Urban-oriented truck farming and dairying.

Grain, sunflowers, some hemp, vegetables,
berries, vineyards, wool, dairy livestock, orchards.

Dairy and meat livestock, flax, hemp,
potatoes and hops.

Vineyards, orchards, vegetables, tobacco.

Mountain grazing with scattered fields, vineyards, orchards.

Figure 5–5   Agricultural regions of the Ukraine and Moldavia. From Atlas selskogo khozyaystva SSSR, pp. 238, 239, 243.

erating capacity of 650,000 kilowatts, the power station was the largest in Europe at that time. Early in World War II, in the face of the advancing Germans the Russians dismantled the power plant and carried away all movable equipment. Later, as they retreated, the Germans blew up the dam; at the end of the war there was nothing left but a pile of concrete rubble and twisted steel in the river bed. This was more than just a mortal blow to a power station; it was a blow to the young ego of the Soviet Union, for the Dnieper Dam, as the first major construction project in the new country, had become a symbol of Soviet strength, even though the work had been

directed by American engineers. After the the war the dam was quickly reconstructed, and since then five more dams have been built.

The second dam was built in the 1950s at the town of Kakhovka near the mouth of the Dnieper River. It has a 300,000-kilowatt power station, but its primary functions are irrigation and navigation. (Fig. 5–6) The Crimean irrigation canal has been built from the reservoir southeastward 125 kilometers to the Perekop Isthmus where it is projected to extend onto the Crimean Peninsula. Another canal 10 to 20 feet deep has been built westward 165 kilometers to Krasnoznamenka. Feeder

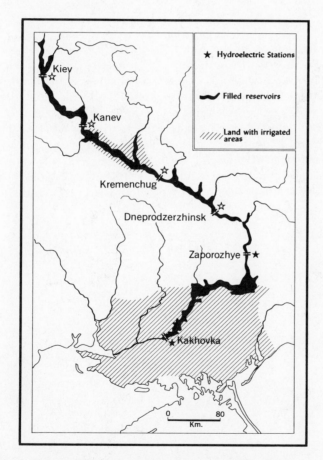

Figure 5–6 Construction projects on the Dnieper River.
From Soviet Geography: Review and Translation, *January 1961, p. 78. Updated from Newsnotes in subsequent issues.*

Figure 5–7   The Dnieper Dam. Novosti.

canals are now being added to the Kakhovka irrigation project which, when completed around 1980, is to water 570,000 hectares of land of which 150,000 hectares are to be sown to rice. The completed system is to have 12,000 kilometers of canals and ditches, which will make it one of the most extensive systems in the world. By 1970 about 40,000 hectares of land are to be under irrigation, 13,000 hectares of which are to be sown to rice. It is interesting to note that the Soviets are not returning to cotton as a main crop on this land, in spite of the fact that they wasted quite a number of years in the 1930s and 1940s trying to grow it in this area as a dry-farmed crop before irrigation water was available. Obviously, lack of water was not the primary limiting factor. The growing season is simply too cool and short.

Figure 5–8   The submerged rapids of the Dnieper at Zaporozhye. Photograph by the author.

The Kremenchug hydroelectric station, with a capacity of 625,000 kilowatts, was completed in 1960, and the Dneprodzerzhinsk plant became fully operative in 1964. The Kiev plant began operation with its first generating unit in 1964, and the Kanev plant, with a generating capacity of 420,000 kilowatts, was scheduled to be completed in the late 1960s.

These six dams and reservoirs will greatly enhance navigation along the river, which is surprisingly heavy for a stream no larger than it is. River craft ply the stream in both directions; timber is floated downstream from the Polesye to the treeless south. Eventually, a canal is to connect the headwaters of the Pripyat River, the main right bank tributary of the Dnieper, in southern Belorussia, to the Neman River which flows northwestward to the Baltic. But this waterway will require approximately seventeen locks and its construction probably will not take place for some time.

In addition to the navigational benefits, the Dnieper dams generate a considerable amount of electricity for this heavy consuming area. Thermal electric plants being built in the area tend to dwarf the hydroelectric plants, however. The Pridneprovsk thermal station on Chapli Island in the river near Dnepropetrovsk has a generating capacity of 2.4 million kilowatts. It is fueled by natural gas from the Shebelinka field just to the northeast. Thermal stations of similar size are also being built farther east to serve the electric needs of the heavy industries in the Donets Basin.

Mineral Resources   In addition to the enormous agricultural potential of Ukraine, there are rich mineral resources as the basis for industry. Most valuable are the coal fields of the Donets Basin, the nearby iron deposits at Krivoy Rog and Kerch, and the manganese at Nikopol. There are also substantial supplies of oil, natural gas, salt, mercury, uranium, antimony, potash, phosphate, and several other minerals.

Railroads   Another important resource, which must not be overlooked, is Ukraine's excellent transport network. Railway construction began around 1860 and proceeded rapidly as industrialization took place in the Donets Basin. Rail lines were also needed to ship grain and other food products to the central regions of Russia for domestic consumption and to Black Sea ports for export. The heaviest rail traffic in the Soviet Union moves between eastern Ukraine and the Central Industrial Region, and, in spite of the fact that a good all-water route, via the Volga-Don Canal, now exists between the two areas, rail shipment is much more direct, much faster, and much the preferred method of transport among Soviet shippers.

Regional Division   Industries based on the mineral, waterpower, and transport strength of the country have given it an aspect other than agricultural; hence the subregions of Ukraine are complicated by two unrelated economies, urban industrial and rural agricultural. Crop complexes correspond closely to the climate and soils; they cut across the area in broad zones oriented southwest-northeast perpendicular to the moisture gradient. The belt of heavy industry in eastern Ukraine ignores the agricultural zones. For convenience of discussion, the Donets-Dnieper Bend-Azov industrial area has been lifted from its agricultural context and discussed separately, and the rest of Ukraine is divided into four somewhat traditional regions: (1) Central and Western Ukraine, (2) Carpathian Ukraine, (3) the Polesye, and (4) the Black Sea Steppes and Crimea. (Fig. 5–10) Moldavia is treated as a separate region.

The Donets-Dnieper Bend-Azov Heavy Industry Area

Rich deposits of coal, iron, and manganese, the main raw materials for heavy

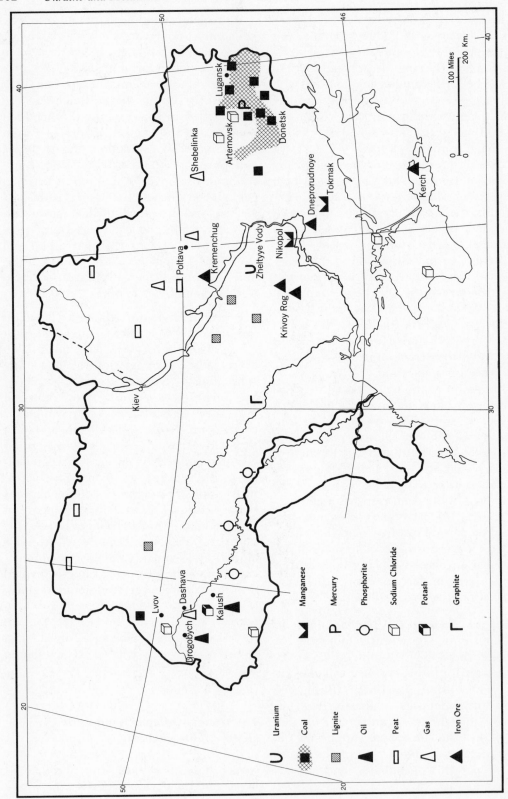

Figure 5–9 Mineral resources of the Ukraine.

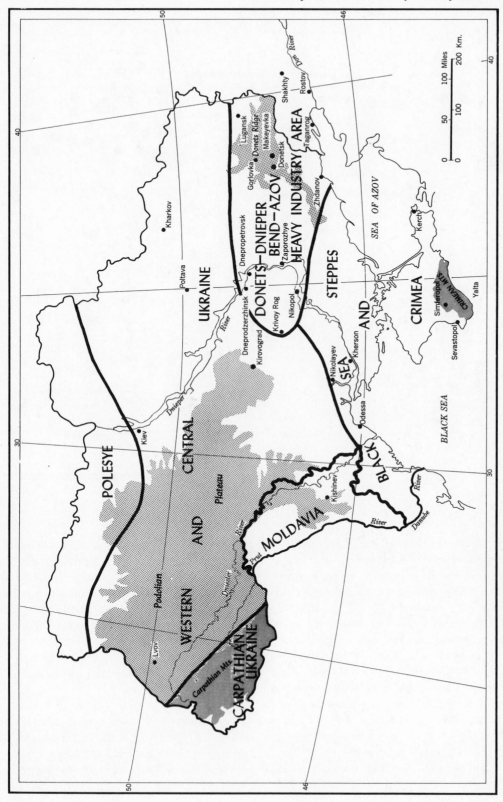

Figure 5–10 Subdivisions and landform regions of the Ukraine and Moldavia.

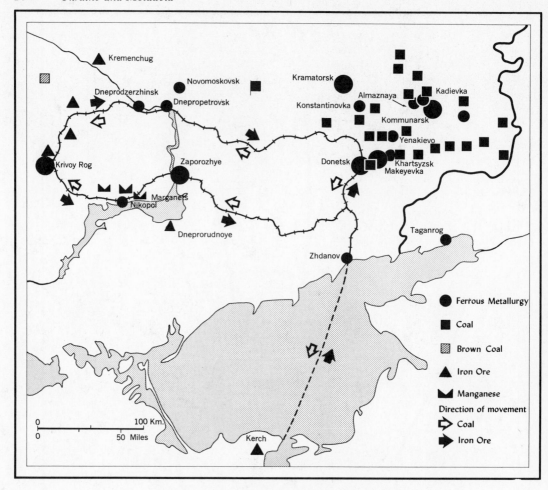

Figure 5–11   Donets-Dnieper Bend-Azov metallurgical area.

industry, as well as rock salt, limestone for fluxing, and lesser amounts of a variety of minerals lying in proximity in the eastern third of Ukraine have induced the development of a broad industrial area within which lie three nodes of more intensive concentration.

The Donets Coal Basin in Donetsk and Lugansk Oblasts in eastern Ukraine and the western fringe of Rostov Oblast in the Russian Republic, by no means contains the richest coal fields in the Soviet Union, but it is the most highly developed mining area. Mining began here in the 1840s, and the basin quickly became Russia's major coal producer. In 1913 it was responsible for 87 per cent of the country's supply. Although under the present regime its share of the total production has diminished, owing to the development of other coal basins, its absolute production has continued to increase until today the basin is mining more coal than ever before. In 1966 the Donbas still led the country with one third of the coal and more than half of the coking coal.

Coal in the Donets lies in a series of rather thin seams interbedded among the essentially flat-lying sedimentary rocks of Carboniferous age along the lower portion of the "little Don," or Donets River, in eastern Ukraine. Actually, the seams extend northwestward into Kharkov Oblast, but until recently only the southeastern part of the basin had been extensively developed. Here and there the rocks are more steeply tilted along the flanks of the Donets Ridge, where tectonic movement has been more severe and metamorphosis has been more extreme. The beds in Donetsk Oblast and adjacent areas supply most of the coking coal and yield a high-grade bituminous product; those of more highly metamorphosed tipping beds in the vicinity of Lugansk contain higher grade anthracite, which is required for purposes other than those of the metallurgical industries. Hence the iron and steel industry has concentrated in Donetsk Oblast. Almost everywhere the seams lie deep below the surface, so that until recently shaft mining was the only practical method. The average depth of the mines is about 1000 feet, but some reach about three quarters of a mile into the ground. During World War II the mines were largely disabled by the Soviet Army in the wake of the German invasion, and, when in retreat, the Germans flooded the shafts with millions of gallons of water. Nevertheless, by 1948 the mines had been rehabilitated and the prewar production level regained. In the last few years some open-pit mining has been used to exploit the shallower edges of the basin, and a significant shift of new mining activity toward the western part of the basin has taken place.

Eastern Ukraine is credited with containing more than 40 per cent of the country's iron ore. Within the bend of the Dnieper River, the Krivoy Rog deposits consist of more than 2 billion tons of rich ore containing 53 to 64 per cent iron and more than 18 billion tons of iron quartzites containing 30 to 36 per cent iron. This is about double the reserves of the Kursk Magnetic Anomaly. On the eastern tip of the Crimean Peninsula, the low-grade Kerch deposit is estimated at about 2 billion tons. Just east of Krivoy Rog, at the towns of Nikopol and Marganets on the west

bank of the Dnieper River, lies the world's greatest reserve of manganese.

Krivoy Rog iron and Nikopol manganese were exploited in the last two decades of the nineteenth century with the rapid development of the iron and steel industry in the Donets Basin. Major plants were established in the coal area of what is now Donetsk and Lugansk Oblasts, and in the 1930s others were built in the Dnieper Bend area. Iron and manganese are now moved eastward into the Donets Basin, and coal is transported westward into the Dnieper Bend to serve steel industries at both ends. Krivoy Rog iron ore is also shipped westward to Poland and East Germany. The Soviets hope to supplant this consumption in the satellites with ore from the Kursk Magnetic Anomaly as mining is developed in that area.

Although the primary centers of the steel industry continue to operate in the Donets Basin, both this nodal region and the one around the Dnieper Bend have been expanding at a rapid rate until at present they have become almost one continuous belt of heavy industry. The building of the Dnieper Dam at Zaporozhye increased the industrial growth of that area by adding to its resources an abundant supply of hydroelectricity and also by improving navigation on the river.

In the last decade or two a third nodal area of heavy industry, in the form of a short string of cities along the northwest coast of the Sea of Azov, has reached the point of merging on the north with the industrial belt just described. The cities along the Azov coast, such as Zhdanov and Taganrog, lie between the iron ore of the Kerch Peninsula to the south and the Donets Coal Field to the north. Iron ore is transported from Kerch by water directly to these cities and coal is carried the short distance from the Donets Basin by rail. Some of the Donets coal that is brought to Zhdanov by rail is transferred to boats and sent on to Kerch. Some of the iron ore shipped from Kerch to Zhdanov is transferred to the empty coal cars returning to the Donets Basin. Hence some Kerch ore is mixed with the Krivoy Rog ore in the Donbas.

High amounts of sulfur and phosphorus delayed use of the Kerch iron ore until smelting processes were perfected to extract these elements in usable forms. They have now become important by-products of the iron industry as the bases for mineral fertilizer and other chemicals.

Within the last decade a number of new deposits and mining activities have been made known. The Krivoy Rog iron mines have been expanded northward toward Kremenchug as lower grade quartzites (35 per cent ore) have been put to use through the process of concentration. Such concentrates made up about half of the 80 million tons of usable ore produced by the Krivoy Rog Basin in 1966, which produced roughly half of all the ore in the U.S.S.R. In this part of the Krivoy Rog Basin, near the town of Zheltyye Vody (Yellow Water), important uranium mines have been producing much of the Soviet uranium for a number of years. (Fig. 5–9) This has only recently been made known. In October 1967 new iron-mining operations began in the high-grade Belozerka deposit discovered in the mid 1950s on the left bank of the Dnieper about 45 miles southwest of Zaporozhye. Part of the deposit consists of open-hearth grade ore with an iron content of 66 per cent and low silica, phosphorus, and sulfur. The mining town of Dneprorudnoye was founded in 1963 on the south shore of the Kakhovka Reservoir.

Since the mid 1950s Krivoy Rog has been reconstructed into the second largest iron and steel center in the country, after Magnitogorsk in the southern Urals. The eighth blast furnace was inaugurated in November 1967 and was heralded as the largest in the world. It is the first of a series with working capacities of 2700 cubic meters (95,000 cubic feet) that are to be installed in the Soviet Union. New iron and steel capacities have also been installed

in many other towns of the Donets-Dnieper-Azov area, and new rolling mills and pipe plants have been added in such towns as Zhdanov, Novomoskovsk, Kommunarsk, and Khartsyzsk. Four Soviet pipe plants, three of them in Ukraine, are now capable of producing 40-inch and larger pipe that is used in such transcontinental gas and oil pipelines as the Bukhara-Urals gas line, the international "Friendship" oil pipeline, and the Volga-West Siberia oil lines. In addition, new ferroalloy plants have come into being in this area and a wide range of coke-chemical plants have been established in conjunction with coking operations in order to use by-product gases and tars.

Cities and Industries in the Donets Basin   The major cities in the Donets Basin are Donetsk, with a population of 840,000, Makeyevka, with a population of 414,000, and Gorlovka, with a population of 343,000. These three cities lie close together in Donetsk Oblast and are the major producers of coal; Donetsk and Makeyevka are the major producers of pig iron and steel. They also support other industrial activity, chief among which is the production of chemicals based on coal tars and gases derived from coke. To the northeast, Lugansk, a less highly industrialized city of 352,000, is situated in the heart of the anthracite coal-mining area. It is noted for the manufacture of railroad locomotives and other heavy machinery. Until 1957 Lugansk was named Voroshilovgrad in honor of Voroshilov, who from 1953 to 1960 held the figurehead position of president of the Soviet Union; until 1961 Donetsk was named Stalino. Both Stalin and Voroshilov distinguished themselves in the Red Army on the lower Volga after the Revolution. Now both have been somewhat downgraded, and cities named after them have been renamed.

Smaller iron and steel centers in the Donets Basin are Kommunarsk (formerly known as Alchevsk and then Voroshilovsk),

Kramatorsk, Konstantinovka, Kadievka, Yenakievo, Almaznaya, and Khartsyzsk. Many of them have chemical industries associated with coking operations. In addition, a number of smaller towns are important coal-mining centers. Among the coal-mining towns of the Donets Basin is Shakhty, which is across the Ukrainian border in the western part of Rostov Oblast in the Russian Republic. Rostov Oblast normally produces about one fifth of the Donbas coal. Artemovsk is known for its salt production. (Fig. 5–9)

Cities and Industries of the Dnieper Bend Several cities have been built in the Dnieper Bend area, the largest of which is Dnepropetrovsk, with a population of 816,000. Next in size is Zaporozhye, downstream from Dnepropetrovsk, with a population of 595,000, and the third is Dneprodzerzhinsk, with a population 224,000. These cities utilize the hydroelectric power generated by the river and carry on considerable trade by water. All are becoming highly industrialized in heavy and light metallurgy, machine building, and chemicals. The abundance of hydroelectric power has attracted the location of aluminum plants to convert alumina shipped in from the Urals.

To the west of these cities, within the bend of the river and in the heart of rich iron-ore deposits, is the city of Krivoy Rog, which now has a population of 510,000 and is rapidly undergoing heavy industrialization. A large new steel plant, which has been dubbed the "Magnitogorsk of Ukraine," is under construction, and it has been speculated that steel from this plant may be utilized to satisfy the needs of satellite countries in eastern Europe. Nikopol, on the Dnieper downstream from Zaporozhye, with a population of 110,000, has been mentioned before as the site of the world's largest manganese deposit.

Cities and Industries of the Azov Coast Along the north shore of the Sea of Azov two important iron and steel cities get their iron ore from Kerch in Crimea and their coal from the Donets Basin. The first of these is Zhdanov, in Ukraine, which until 1948 was named Mariupol. Zhdanov is the principal port for the Donbas and now has the Azovstal metallurgical works, which is one of the largest in the vicinity of the Donets Basin. In 1967 Zhdanov had a population of 385,000. The other steel city is Taganrog, across the border in Rostov Oblast. Taganrog has a population of 245,000. Like Zhdanov, it is an important seaport and has recently added important heavy industries.

Characterizations and Analogues of Cities The cities within this belt of heavy industry might be characterized as follows. Donetsk and Makeyevka have heavy concentrations of fuel-oriented metallurgical and chemical industries and might be compared to Pittsburgh in the United States, to the Ruhr in Germany, or to metallurgical centers of northeastern England. Krivoy Rog in the Dnieper Bend is a secondary metallurgical center dependent on iron ore, and it corresponds closely to Duluth in the United States, although it is now outgrowing this role. Zaporozhye, Dnepropetrovsk, and Dneprodzerzhinsk in the Dnieper Bend and Taganrog and Zhdanov on the north shore of the Sea of Azov are metal-working and machine-building cities located between iron and coal much as are the Great Lakes centers of Chicago, Gary, and Cleveland in the United States. The three cities on the Dnieper, like Buffalo, New York, have hydroelectric power to supplement their industrial complexes. These cities make up the largest urban areas of the three core regions within the belt of heavy industry, and all are concentrated on primary metal working.

Ringing these cities are others that utilize the products of heavy industry to turn out machinery of all types. Nikolayev, to the west, at the mouth of the Southern Bug River, specializes in ship building; Kirovograd, to the northwest, builds agricultural machinery; Kharkov, in the north, is the greatest general manufacturer of machinery in the Soviet Union; Lugansk, to the northeast, has already been mentioned as an important producer of railroad locomotives; and far to the east, Volgograd is known for its auto-tractors.

Beyond this ring, cities more diversified in function, some of them even larger in population than those in the heavy-industry belt, take from it many of their raw materials. Among them are Kiev in the northwest, Odessa in the southwest, Simferopol in Crimea, and Rostov at the mouth of the Don River. These peripheral and outlying cities are discussed in their respective regions.

Rostov-on-Don   Rostov is fairly close to the Donets Basin and might well be discussed as part of it, but it stands somewhat alone as a major city in its own right, and its industries are not concentrated on any one item. Heavy metallurgy occupies only a small portion of its economic activity. Its principal factory is "Rostselmash," which is probably the largest agricultural machine plant in the U.S.S.R. Besides its function in industry, Rostov is a busy seaport controlling the mouth of the Don River whose traffic now has been greatly increased by the Volga-Don Canal. In 1967 Rostov had a population of 757,000 which can be expected to increase at a rapid rate. It is a surprisingly pleasant city, situated on the delta of the Don. In the evenings soft breezes from the Sea of Azov cool the streets, and an air of lightness, so often lacking in Soviet cities, is evident among the pedestrians. The main boulevards, divided by grassy strips, are wide and are bordered by broad, tree-lined sidewalks.

Agriculture   The fact that the Donets-Dnieper area is heavily industrialized should not obscure the fact that it is agriculturally important. The relatively long warm summers and fertile steppe soils are conducive to the production of crops that can withstand the drought conditions. Wheat and sunflowers, which are grown extensively, are most adaptable to this environment. This is the western half of the sunflower belt, which wraps around the head of the Sea of Azov and continues southeastward into the northern Caucasus. Other small grains and grain-sorghums are harvested in significant amounts, and dairying and livestock raising around centers of dense urban population are developing rapidly. In the last few years corn

Figure 5–12   Theater in Rostov constructed to look like a caterpillar tractor, which signifies the importance of the city as an agricultural machine builder. Photograph by the author.

Figure 5–13   Orchards and mine heaps, Donetsk Oblast. Photograph by the author.

has been introduced into the region; in 1960 it occupied more than 30 per cent of the cultivated area.

Central and Western Ukraine

The second region to be considered is the general farming area in central and western Ukraine, which covers much of the rest of the republic outside the industrial belt. This broad section has rich soils and a good agricultural climate, long summers, and in most cases sufficient moisture for a great variety of crops. It might be subdivided on the basis of crop complexes or on historical development, for there are variations in these elements from one part of Ukraine to another. But suffice it to say that physically it becomes moister toward the northwest; natural vegetation changes gradually from steppe grasses in the southeast to mixed forests in the north, and soils and crops differ accordingly. Also, there is a general transition in land form from east to west, from an exceedingly flat plain with little stream dissection to a rather rough, rolling stream-dissected plain in the foothills of the Carpathian Mountains.

This region is not traditional in the Soviet Union; rather it incorporates three areas, all of which have been given some local designation by the Ukrainians. The area lying to the east of the Dnieper is usually referred to as "Left Bank Ukraine" and that lying to the west as "Right Bank Ukraine." The newly acquired area farther west is known as "Western Ukraine." There is some topographic break along the Dnieper, since the river occupies a position along the base of a cuesta escarpment similar to those of the Volga and Don Rivers. The area to the east is lower and generally flat, but to the west it is a rolling, stream-dissected upland. Also there is some change in soil moisture conditions and natural vegetation along the river; the east has a drier aspect than the west. But zones of soil types and crop complexes are continuous across the river and extend into western Ukraine. Thus the area is somewhat of a unit agriculturally; the differences in crop complexes that do exist form zones cutting across the traditional regions from west-southwest to east-northeast to form indistinct subdivisions along a north-south line.

Agriculture   In the middle, in the very heart of Ukraine where soils are best and moisture still sufficient, the traditional crops are sugar beets and wheat. Sugar

Figure 5–14   Brick yard in loess bluffs along the west bank of the Dnieper River between Kiev and Kanev. Photograph by the author.

beets usually account for at least one quarter of the cash income of farms. This is the sugar-beet belt of the Soviet Union which extends from Kursk and Belgorod Oblasts in the Central Black Earth Region southwestward and then westward south of Kiev and on to western Ukraine. The concentration of sugar beets increases westward as the zone widens from Rovno south to the Carpathians and into northern Moldavia. Since 1953 corn has replaced much wheat. Many other crops are grown including grains, sunflowers, potatoes, vegetables, and fruit.

To the northwest lies a somewhat narrower belt in which a transition takes place from the strong concentration on cash crops to a more general type of farming in which sugar beets and wheat are no more important than other grains, potatoes, and flax. This belt is the beginning of the mixed forest where there is greater moisture and somewhat podzolized soils. To the southeast is a region of drier climate more adapted to growing sunflowers than sugar beets. This zone, which begins just north of Kirovograd, extends southward to the region along the Black Sea and continues eastward into the belt of heavy industry. Wheat and sunflowers are the

dominant crops here, and farming is done on a more extensive scale than it is to the northwest. Some other crops are raised, and corn has recently been introduced.

Interspersed within this great agricultural region around the major cities are numerous urban-oriented truck farms.

Rural population, which is heavy throughout central and western Ukraine, increases westward where greater moisture permits more intensive and varied cultivation. In western Ukraine the population density is between three hundred fifty and four hundred persons per square mile. The farmers live in large villages, sometimes reaching populations of several thousands, strung helter-skelter in the stream valleys near sources of water. The typical rural dwelling is a one-room hut of whitewashed adobe walls and thatched or corrugated sheet metal roof. The adobe "khata" of the south reflects the chief local building material (clay) as the log cabin "izba" of the north reflects the forests.

Minerals   In addition to the favorable conditions for agriculture in this large region, there are several sources of minerals, particularly of the mineral fuels. (Fig. 5–9) In western Ukraine along the

Figure 5–15   Ukrainian villages and private plots in the dissected topography of the Podolian Upland east of Kirovograd, central Ukraine. Photograph by the author.

foothills of the Carpathians are significant deposits of coal, oil, and natural gas. The coal fields are exploited to satisfy local needs, but reserves are in no way comparable to those of the Donets Basin; supplies are limited and the quality is insufficient for coking. The oil fields in Drogobych Oblast, also of secondary importance, supply local needs. Refineries are located in Drogobych and Lvov. The natural gas deposits are of more significance to the country as a whole than are either coal or oil. The Dashava gas fields have been producing since before World War II, and pipelines have been constructed to Kiev, Moscow, Leningrad, and the principal cities of Belorussia and the Baltic Republics. Until 1955 the Dashava gas fields were the only ones in Ukraine and were one of the major producing areas in the Soviet Union. Since then new gas deposits have been discovered at Shebelinka, south of

Figure 5–16   Typical Ukrainian khata *with whitewashed adobe walls and thatched roof, in Kanev. Photograph by the author.*

Figure 5–17   Ukrainian farmers in a sugar beet field near Kharkov. Courtesy of J. H. Glen Burke.

Kharkov, in northeastern Ukraine, which appear to be larger than those at Dashava. The production at Shebelinka now approximates that at Dashava. Lying on the main lines of gas transport between the northern Caucasus and the Central Industrial Region, the Shebelinka fields are more fortunately located than are the fields in western Ukraine.

Pipelines now carry Shebelinka gas southwestward to the Dnieper Bend cities and on to Nikolayev and Kishinev and northwestward as far as Kiev. Many other cities are serviced along these routes. Oil

Figure 5–18   Straw stack south of Kiev. After the wheat is combined the straw is raked and then stacked by hand. A line of 15 or 20 farmers armed with pitch forks pass the straw up the sloping end of the stack. Note chernozem soil in field already prepared for new planting. Courtesy of Virgil Petty.

pipelines have also been built to the Dnieper Bend area, branching southward from the "Friendship" pipeline that carries Volga-Urals oil to the East European satellites along a route that passes through northwestern Ukraine. Two refineries have been built at Kremenchug to refine some of this oil.

Also in western Ukraine, near the towns of Kalush and Stebnik, are significant deposits of potash salts, second in value in the Soviet Union only to those of the Urals. A potash plant has been built at Stebnik and other chemical industries are being established in western Ukraine and Belorussia to utilize these potash salts. In the same general area, native sulfur deposits were discovered in the 1950s around the towns of Rozdol, Yavorov, and Nemirov. Open-pit mining began in 1959 in a drained portion of the marshy floodplain of the Dniester River near Rozdol. Mining began near Yavorov in 1968, where both open-pit and hot-water-injection methods are being used. These mining activities have induced a significant shift in sulfur production from the older established areas in the Kara Kum desert of Middle Asia, the Urals, and the Middle Volga Region east of Kuybyshev.

Cities   Kiev, with a population of 1,413,000, Kharkov, with a population of 1,125,000, and Lvov, with a population of 512,000 are the major cities in this region and all are focal points for the railroads of Ukraine. Kiev and Kharkov are the largest cities in Ukraine and rank third and sixth in the Soviet Union respectively.

Kiev, of course, is the historical center of Ukraine. It flourished during the ninth to thirteenth centuries as the capital of Kievan Rus and again from the fifteenth century onwards as the cultural and religious focus of the Ukrainian Cossacks. In 1934 it was made the capital of the Ukrainian S.S.R. Damaged severely during World War II, Kiev has been rebuilt into perhaps the most beautiful city of the Soviet Union.

Figure 5–19   Traffic on the blue Dnieper viewed from the high west bluff at Kiev. Unlike the muddy Volga and Don rivers, the Dnieper contains beautiful clear water interspersed by bars of white glacial sands washed down from the Polesye to the north. Photograph by the author.

The opportunity has been taken during the reconstruction to lay out modern sewage, gas, and water lines and to build the first subway in the city.

The natural setting is magnificent. Situated on the high loess-covered western bluff of the Dnieper, at the confluence of its main left-bank tributary, the Desna, the city overlooks the blue water and white sandbars of the many-channeled river to the east. Beautiful beaches abound along the banks of the river, for great quantities of white glacial sand have been carried down from the Polesye in the north. The wind has whipped some of this sand out of the immediate floodplain of the river and has created extensive areas of sand dunes on the flat, low-lying meadowland to the east. A surprising number of boats ply the river, and considerable quantities of timber are floated down from the northern forests. With the completion of all the reservoirs, navigation has been greatly improved, but many of the sandy beaches have been submerged.

Tree-lined double boulevards with broad sidewalks are modern innovations; but the gilded domes of St. Sophia's Cathedral and the catacombs of the monastery in the loess bluffs are reminders of the old

Kiev. A tall, graceful obelisk commemorating the heroes of World War II stands in a park along the rim of the high western bluff, overlooking the huge gray statue of Saint Vladimir facing down the Dnieper.

Kharkov was founded in 1650 by Ukrainian Cossacks. From 1922 to 1934 it served as the capital of the Ukrainian S.S.R. It is a very important regional center, a major rail hub, and one of the most important machine-building centers in the Soviet Union.

Lvov was founded in 1241. It has retained a medieval aspect with cobbled streets and high, narrow, steep-roofed houses. It was in the Austro-Hungarian Empire until 1920. With the breakup of the Empire after World War I, it became part of Poland. In 1939 the Soviet Union annexed the territory and made it part of Ukraine. As the cultural and religious center of western Ukraine, it is growing rapidly. New electronics industries have been established in the city, as well as an automobile plant to assemble passenger buses.

Other cities in central Ukraine are Poltava, with a population of 184,000, Kirovograd, with a population of 168,000, and a number of smaller oblast centers which serve primarily as governmental and trading centers for rich agricultural regions. Poltava, west of Kharkov, is the site of the decisive victory of Peter the Great over Charles XII of Sweden in 1709.

Carpathian Ukraine

The third region to be considered is that in the western part of the republic, which includes the Carpathian Mountains and Transcarpathian Ukraine. This region was taken over from Czechoslovakia in 1944 and includes a small portion of the Hungarian Plain southwest of the Carpathians. It is inhabited by Ukrainians.

The Carpathians in this section rise to elevations of more than 6000 feet; they are heavily forested by coniferous growth on the higher slopes and have been strongly dissected by the headwaters of the Dniester and the Danube. The higher portions of the mountains underwent strong mountain glaciation during the Pleistocene, which left their slopes exceedingly steep.

Lumbering and cattle and sheep grazing are carried on in the highlands ("Polonyny"). The small area of the Hungarian Plain southwest of the mountains is occupied by vineyards, truck gardens, and orchards and a mixture of wheat fields, sunflowers, sugar beets, and tobacco. One third of Transcarpathia is still covered by forests. Uzhgorod, the oblast center, is the only town of any size, and it has only 61,000 people.

Polesye

In the northwest, bordering on the Belorussian Republic, lies the fourth region of Ukraine, the so-called Polesye, or woodland. This is the southern limit of an area that lies primarily in Belorussia in the basin of the Pripyat River, which flows from west to east into the Dnieper. It is a proglacial lake bed that is almost as flat as a floor and is everywhere poorly drained. More than 30 per cent of the area is still forested. In many places vegetation has failed to gain a permanent foothold because of active wind deflation in loose glacial outwash sands. Agriculture at best is meager; the cultivated land is on poor podzolic soils. The chief crops are flax, potatoes, and small grains, including buckwheat, which is a staple food crop throughout much of the western part of the Soviet Union. Considerable timber cut in the Polesye is floated down the Dnieper to southern markets.

Black Sea Steppes and Crimea

The fifth and last region of Ukraine is comprised of the Black Sea Steppes and the Crimean Peninsula. This area extends from the mouth of the Danube on the border of Rumania eastward along the Black Sea in a strip of land 50 to 100 miles wide across the mouths of the Dniester River, the Southern Bug, and the Dnieper to the northwestern shores of the Sea of Azov. It includes the entire peninsula of Crimea. The western extremity of this region, the so-called Izmail District, was taken from Rumania during World War II and was incorporated into Ukraine rather than into the Moldavian Republic; the reason was that the region contained a majority of Ukrainians.

The Black Sea Steppes The strip of land along the northern shore of the Black Sea is a flat coastal plain with a dry steppe climate. The mineral-rich steppe soils are conducive to extensive crop growing, but drought conditions make agriculture hazardous. Here the desiccating "sukhovey" occurs frequently and with considerable intensity. These climatic and soil conditions extend across the narrow Perekop Isthmus onto the northern plains of the Crimea, which occupy about two thirds of the peninsula. The crops in this region are primarily wheat and sunflowers, grown on an extensive scale. However, corn, melons, grapes, and apples are also important. Seemingly endless apple orchards have been set out in strips of ten or fifteen rows on either side of many of the roads. Typically, a major road is flanked on either side by a 100-meter width or so of scraggly trees and bushes planted to form a most effective windbreak, back of which the rows of apple trees are planted. The open fields lie beyond these, generally obscured from view from the road. Contrary to what many of my tourists have contended, these shelter belts and orchards have been planted to reduce effects of the wind rather than to hide the fields. The orchards serve the dual purpose of producing fruit and affording wind protection. The shelter belts have been planted in nonuniform fashion purposely, because in this way the greatest

Figure 5–20 Sunflowers and bee hives, Black Sea Steppes. Novosti.

Figure 5–21   Cultivation of a young shelter belt in the Black Sea Steppes. Novosti.

air turbulence will be created, which will have maximum effect on slowing the wind. Most of these apple trees have been planted since 1955 as part of a nationwide effort to solve the fruit shortage forever. As has so often been the case in the Soviet Union, it appears that once again a crash agricultural program on a grand scale is going to provide a great overproduction of a single commodity. As all these apple trees come into prime production during the next few years, the Ukrainians should have apple sauce running out of their ears! The fact that the trees have survived and thrived for 10 or 15 consecutive years in this dry steppe area would seem to indicate that drought conditions are not as severe as originally thought. Some experimentation with dry-farmed cotton has been carried out but has proved unsuccessful, primarily because of the shortness of the growing season. With the construction of the dam at Kakhovka on the lower Dnieper, irrigation has been made possible over several hundred thousand acres of the plain and across the Perekop Isthmus into Crimea. Much irrigated rice is planned for this area.

In many places along the Black Sea the land descends to the water in a series of low, sandy terraces fronting on shallow, salty, stagnant lagoons, or limans, which are hemmed in from the sea by elongated offshore sand bars. Many of the sandy terraces in this mild climatic region are planted in vineyards. Some of the most stagnant water lies in the area between the Crimean Peninsula and the mainland coast of Ukraine on both sides of the Perekop Isthmus. The most completely surrounded body of water, known as the Sivash Sea, or putrid sea, is east of the Perekop Isthmus and adjacent to the Sea of Azov. Some salt is taken from it. The shallow water of the Sea of Azov and adjacent parts of the Black Sea abounds in fish.

The major cities in the Black Sea Steppes are Odessa in the west, Nikolayev on the estuary of the Southern Bug, and Kherson near the mouth of the Dnieper. All three serve as ports, although Odessa is much more active than the other two in this respect. Odessa has traditionally been the primary wheat-exporting port of the Soviet Union and has also handled considerable quantities of lumber. Since 1963 it has served as the primary wheat-importing port for the Soviet Union. It is the chief entrepot for Caucasian oil products which are shipped across the Black Sea for distribution in Ukraine. In 1967 Odessa had a population of 776,000, fifth in size in Ukraine. Nikolayev is noted for ship building. Kherson, although the smallest of the three, has the longest history. It was a thriving city in the fifteenth century when it was transferred to Muscovy by the Byzantine emperor at Constantinople on the occasion of the marriage of his niece to Ivan the Great.

All the Black Sea ports of southwestern Ukraine have experienced considerable growth of shipping tonnage during the last few years. This growth has been hampered, however, by a lag in the construction of adequate port facilities and adequate rail lines connecting the ports to their interiors. One result has been specialization of ports according to destinations. Odessa, which once traded with forty countries, now trades with only ten. Another result has been the development of alternate ports to handle traffic during peak periods. This is especially true of Izmail and Reni up the mouth of the Danube. A new port, Ilyichevsk, was founded in 1952 just southwest of Odessa, and has grown to a population of about 20,000.

The Crimean Mountains The southeastern third of the Crimean Peninsula is made up of the Crimean Mountains, which rise abruptly from a fault system along the northern shore of the Black Sea to elevations of more than 5000 feet. This western extremity of the young folded belt of mountains that extends eastward into the Caucasus displays the features of recent

Figure 5–22 The southern slopes of the Crimean Mountains. Note the sheer limestone cliffs in the background. Vineyards are interspersed on the steep foothills that plunge abruptly to the sea. Photograph by the author.

faulting and mild volcanism. The mass of the Crimean Mountains is made up of limestone, which comprises three belts and forms three separate ridges. The highest of these ridges is the southernmost, where the limestone is not as crumbly as in the others. The middle slopes of the Crimean Mountains are covered with a rather sparse forest, but the summits are alpine meadows. These upland grassy areas are known as "Yaila," a Tatar term designating communal pastures. It is sometimes erroneously applied to the entire mountain range. Along the eastern end of the mountains and extending eastward into the Kerch Peninsula are mud volcanoes and fumaroles which indicate recent volcanic activity.

The Crimean Mountains are not high, but their altitude is sufficient to protect the southeast coast of Crimea from the cold blasts of northern winds, so that the strip of coast from Yalta to Alushta has a Mediterranean-type climate. Its winters average above-freezing temperatures and its summers are long, warm, and dry. This section of the Black Sea Coast has become one of the most popular resort areas in the Soviet Union. Its principal city, Yalta, received world attention during World War II as the site of a conference between Premier Stalin, President Roosevelt, and Prime Minister Churchill. Many impressive white buildings stand out in bold relief against the backdrop of shrubs and trees among the steep hills overlooking the sea far below. Some of these buildings date back to Tsarist times when they served as summer palaces for the imperial court, but many have been built under the Soviet regime. Apparently the new rulers know no other grandeur to aspire to than that effected by the nobles of fifty or more years ago, for the new buildings have been constructed in the prerevolutionary style, and it is impossible to distinguish the new from the old. Both now serve as resort hotels and sanatoria for Soviet citizens who are lucky enough to be sent there for recreational or health purposes.

Two other cities, considerably larger in size, lie on the Crimean Peninsula. The first is Simferopol, with a population of 223,000, on the northern slopes of the Crimean Mountains, which is the seat of government for Crimea Oblast. It serves as the governmental, transport, and cultural center for Crimea, but its industries are only of local importance. To the southwest

Figure 5–23   Tobacco and orchards on the northern slope of the Crimean Mountains South of Simferopol. Courtesy of Roy Meyer.

Figure 5–24   The beach at Yalta. Photograph by the author.

of Simferopol, on the southwest tip of the peninsula, is the important port and naval base of Sevastopol, population 209,000. Twice during the last century Sevastopol gained world renown as a stronghold that stood up under long siege: first in the Crimean War, when it became the subject of Tennyson's famous poem, "The Charge of the Light Brigade," and again during World War II when it was attacked by the Germans.

One other Crimean city, Kerch, at the extreme eastern end of the peninsula has already been mentioned in conjunction with the industrial belt. In addition to being the center of the iron-mining district, Kerch is a seaport and a fish-processing center.

The Moldavian S.S.R.

The Moldavian Republic lies in the extreme southwestern corner of the Soviet Union in the Podolian Upland between the Dniester and Prut Rivers. It was formed in 1940 largely from parts of the regions known as Bessarabia and Bukovina, which had just been annexed from Rumania, and from a small portion of southwestern Ukraine, which had been part of the Moldavian A.S.S.R. It is interesting to note that although the Moldavian A.S.S.R. had existed for a number of years within the Ukrainian Republic, much of the territory that had been in the A.S.S.R. was left in Ukraine when the Moldavian S.S.R. was established. This seems to indicate that the Moldavian A.S.S.R. had never had a majority of Moldavians in its population, which is supposedly the basis for the formation of such a political unit. Apparently the Moldavian A.S.S.R. had been created along the boundary of Rumania to induce the Moldavians in eastern Rumania to agitate for incorporation in the Soviet Union. (This technique has been used again and again along the borders of the Soviet Union and may be demonstrated in the north in the now defunct Karelo-Finnish Republic and in Soviet Middle Asia in the Tadzhik Republic bordering on Iran.) Sixty-five per cent of the people in this area are Moldavians who speak a Rumanian dialect and use the Cyrillic alphabet. Approximately 14 per cent are Ukrainians, 10 per cent are Russians, mainly in the cities, and the remainder are Jews, Bulgars, Gypsies, Greeks, and Armenians.

Moldavia is the most densely populated

(two hundred sixty persons per square mile) republic in the Soviet Union. Large rural villages, with populations of more than five thousand people, line the river valleys and crowd the landscape in a dense pattern; only 29 per cent of the population is classified as urban. Kishinev, the capital, is its only city of any size; in 1967 it had a population of 302,000. Although this is more than double the 1939 population, the growth of Kishinev has been more the result of its function as a capital than of its industrialization.

Moldavia has few natural resources other than the fertile soils and favorable climate for agriculture, so we might expect the region to remain predominantly rural. Climatically, it is one of the mildest parts of the Soviet Union.

Agriculturally, the Moldavian Republic may be divided into three parts: the central zone is considerably higher and more rolling than either the north or the south. Elevations of slightly more than 1400 feet are reached where the loess-covered limestone upland has been deeply dissected from both sides by the tributaries of the Dniester and the Prut. The rougher portions of this upland are still covered by forest, whence comes the name "Kodry" (forest). The trees are oak, ash, maple, and other deciduous varieties, and the soils are gray-brown podzols. To the north of the Kodry lies the level Beltsy Steppe, which has good black soils and a fairly abundant supply of moisture. To the south lies the drier Budzhak Steppe, which also has black soils but is severly hampered by drought.

Grain and livestock raising predominate, but viticulture and the raising of fruits, nuts, and vegetables are most characteristic of the region. More than one fourth of all the vineyards of the U.S.S.R. are located in Moldavia. One might say that Moldavia is the Champagne of the Soviet Union. The principal wine-producing districts are in the Kodry, in the picturesque hills around Kishinev.

Grain occupies 75 per cent of the sown area in Moldavia, principally in the northern and southern steppes, and corn is the chief grain crop, occupying at least one third of the grain fields. The entire corn plant is put to use; corn porridge is a staple food, and the stalks are used for fuel, in the building of fences, and in the thatching of roofs. Winter wheat is a valuable crop in the northern and southern portions of the republic, as are barley and winter rye. Since this is a very mild area climatically, experimentation with a wide variety of crops has been carried on. Tobacco, sugar beets, soybeans, sunflowers, flax, hemp, opium poppies, mustard seed, kok-sagyz, castor beans, caraway seed, mint, rice in the Danube delta in the Izmail District, and cotton have been tried. Dairy cattle and hogs are raised in the north and sheep and goats in the south. In its middle and lower portions the Dniester flows entirely within the Moldavian Republic on a broad, well-watered floodplain, on which are found irrigated vegetable gardens flanked by strips of orchards. The banks of the valley are covered by vineyards, and grain, particularly corn, occupies the dry uplands away from the river.

Prospects

With the opening of new iron, coal, and manganese mines and the enlargement and additions of blast furnaces, steel mills, and rolling and pipe mills, eastern Ukraine seems destined to retain its foremost position in heavy industry in the U.S.S.R. or even to increase it, after three decades of tapering off while new plants were being established in the Urals, western Siberia, northern Kazakhstan, and elsewhere. As official policy shifts to more economic considerations, the Soviets are finding it more expedient to revitalize old plants and build new large industrial complexes in the western part of the country where concentrations of population and existing urban and

Figure 5–25   Grape harvesting in Moldavia. Novosti.

commercial agglomerations have already laid the basis for further industrialization. Eastern Ukraine, with its high population density, urban buildup, and good intraregional and interregional transportation connections, under a freer choice of industrial locations based on the profit motive, is bound to attract much additional industry. The new gas and oil pipelines crisscrossing Ukraine present opportunities for the development of new industries, particularly a wide variety of chemical industries, and further enhance the general urban-industrial process.

In agriculture, Ukraine has witnessed something of a transformation during the past 15 years due primarily to the intense injection of corn into the crop complex made possible by a concomitant development of the Virgin Lands in western Siberia and northern Kazakhstan which allowed a major shift of wheat out of Ukraine. Regions that for a century or more had experienced stable crop complexes and farming methods suddenly found themselves in a period of great transition in which they were called upon annually to institute abrupt changes as they were ordered to experiment with new crash programs. Now that the broader shifts have been effected and corn has been established as a major crop, agriculture in the area is once more assuming a more consistent posture from one year to the next as attention now focuses on ways to increase production on the land already under cultivation by crops now being grown. A great shelter belt network, associated with the widespread planting of orchards, has been established in the drier areas, and more and more land is being brought under irrigation as water construction projects are being completed. As irrigation in the Black Sea Steppes increases, rice is becoming a major crop.

The growth in Moldavia is a continuation of events of the past. Some urbanization is taking place, but this is due more to government and trade functions than to industrialization. So far, no important mineral deposits have been found in the republic and no basic industries have been established. With its mild climate and good soils, Moldavia undoubtedly will continue to be primarily agricultural.

Reading List

Allen, William E. D., *The Ukraine; a History,* Cambridge University Press, 1941, 404 pp.

Anuchin, V., *Geografiya Sovetskogo Zakarpatya* (Geography of Soviet Transcarpathia), Moscow, 1956, 294 pp. (in Russian).

Armstrong, John A., *Ukrainian Nationalism,* Columbia University Press, New York, 1963.

Atlas silskoho hospodarstva ukraynskoi RSR (Atlas of Agriculture of the Ukrainian SSR), Kiev, 1958, (in Ukrainian).

Blazhko, N. I., "The System of Urban Places of the Donets Territorial-Production Complex," *Soviet Geography: Review and Translation,* February 1964, pp. 11–16.

Bondarchuk, B. G., et al., "The Natural Resources of the Ukrainian SSR and Ways of Using Them Rationally," *Soviet Geography: Review and Translation,* January 1961, pp. 35–43.

Bondarchuk, Volodymyr, *Ukraina Radianska* (Soviet Ukraine), Kiev, 1958, 266 pp. (in Ukrainian).

Chamberlin, William Henry, *The Ukraine: A Submerged Nation,* Macmillan, New York, 1944.

Dmytrishyn, Basil, *Moscow and the Ukraine: 1918–1953,* Bookman Associates, New York, 1956.

Fox, David J., "Odessa," *Scottish Geographical Magazine,* January 1963, pp. 5–22.

Gnatyuk, L. V., "Some Aspects of the Economic-Geographic Situation of Odessa," *Soviet Geography: Review and Translation,* November 1963, pp. 43–51.

Hayuk, Hlib S., *Changes in the Ethnic Structure and in Regional Distribution of Population in Ukraine, 1897–1959,* M.A. Thesis, University of Wisconsin—Milwaukee, August 1967, 106 pp.

Jolsten, Joachim, "Hitler's Fiasco in the Ukraine," *Foreign Affairs,* January 1943, pp. 331–339.

Khizhak, A. A., *Nizhneye Pridneprovye; ekonomiko-geograficheskiy ocherk* (The Lower Dneiper Region: An Economic-Geographic Study), Moscow, 1956, 80 pp. (in Russian).

Kiev; Putevoditel-spravochnik (Kiev; traveler's handbook), 1962, 350 pp. (in Russian).

Kryven, P., *Ukrainska RSR; ekonomiko-geografichna kharakterystyka* (Ukrainian SSR; economic-geographic characteristics), Kiev, 1961, 208 pp. (in Ukrainian).

Kugukalo, I. A., et al., "Economic Regionalization of the Ukrainian SSR," *Soviet Geography: Review and Translation,* October 1960, pp. 23–32.

Lanko, A. I., et al., "The Physical-Geographic

Regionalization of the Ukrainian SSR for Agricultural Purposes," *Soviet Geography: Review and Translation*, December 1960, pp. 33–50.

Laponogov, Aleksandr N., *Dnepr; posobie dlya uchitelya* (The Dnieper; a guide for teachers), Moscow, 1965, 102 pp. (in Russian).

Lyalikov, N. I., *Sovetskaya Ukraina; ocherk ekonomicheskoy geografii* (Soviet Ukraine: a study of economic geography), Moscow, 1954, 216 pp. (in Russian).

Manning, Clarence A., *The Story of the Ukraine*, Philosophical Library, New York, 1947, 325 pp.

———, *Twentieth-Century Ukraine*, Bookman Associates, New York, 1951, 243 pp.

Odud, A. L., *Moldavskaya SSR* (Moldavian SSR), Moscow, 1955, (in Russian).

Pityurenko, E. I., "Tipy gorodskikh poseleniy Donetskoy oblasti i perspektivy ikh razvitiya" (Types of urban places in Donets Oblast and prospects of their development), in Pavlovskiy, E. N. and Konstantinov, O. A., *Geografiya naseleniya v SSSR* (*Geography of Population in the U.S.S.R.*), Akademiya Nauk SSSR, Moscow, 1964, pp. 168–182 (in Russian).

Popov, V. P., et al., "The Study of the Heat and Moisture Balance of the Ukraine as a Basis for Measures to Raise the Productivity of Agriculture," *Soviet Geography: Review and Translation*, September 1960, pp. 16–27.

Ukrainskaya SSR (Ukrainian SSR), Akademiya Nauk Ukrainskoy SSR, Institut Ekonomiki, Part 1, Moscow, 1957, 556 pp., and Part 2, Moscow, 1958, 313 pp. (in Russian).

Vernander, N. B., et al., "The Land Resources of the Ukraine; Their Evaluation and Inventory Methods," *Soviet Geography: Review and Translation*, January 1961, pp. 35–43.

The European West

Region	Area (sq mile)	Population	People (sq mile)	% Urban [a]
Within the R.S.F.S.R.				
Bryansk Oblast	13,600	1,573,000	116	43
Kaluga Oblast (Southwest four fifths)	9,200 [b]	642,000 [b]	70	47
Smolensk Oblast	19,500	1,100,000	56	44
Kalinin Oblast (excluding Kalinin City and adjacent area)	26,400 [b]	1,079,000 [b]	41	42
Novgorod Oblast	21,600	726,000	34	50
Pskov Oblast	21,500	870,000	40	48
Leningrad Oblast	33,500	1,366,000	41	60
Leningrad City	—	3,296,000	—	100
Kaliningrad Oblast	5,900	693,000	117	70
Belorussian S.S.R.	81,200	8,744,000	108	41
Brest Oblast	12,600	1,251,000	99	32
Vitebsk Oblast	15,600	1,354,000	87	43
Gomel Oblast	15,800	1,505,000	95	37
Grodno Oblast	9,800	1,111,000	113	32
Minsk Oblast	15,900	1,526,000	96	26
Minsk City	—	772,000	—	100
Mogilev Oblast	11,300	1,225,000	108	39
Lithuanian S.S.R.	25,500	3,026,000	119	45
Latvian S.S.R.	24,900	2,285,000	92	62
Estonian S.S.R.	17,600	1,294,000	74	63
Total	300,400 [c]	26,694,000 [c]		

[a] All figures are for entire regions.
[b] Estimated population and area of portion of region lying within the European West.
[c] Does not include western fringe of Moscow Oblast, which lies within the European West.

6

The European West

The region that here is called the European West stretches from the northern boundary of Ukraine to the Baltic Sea and extends eastward to the boundary of the Central Industrial Region and westward to the international boundary with Poland. In the minds of the Russian people this is not a traditional region; rather, it includes within its boundaries several areas that they traditionally identify individually. Nevertheless, it is a fairly homogeneous area in terms of physical landscape and economic development, and it justifies treatment as a unit in spite of the fact that it combines several oblasts of the Russian Republic and the entire area of Belorussia and the three Baltic Republics — Lithuania, Latvia, and Estonia.

The area within the Russian Republic includes the following oblasts: in the southwest, Bryansk and about two thirds of Kaluga; in the west, Smolensk and the northwestern half of Kalinin Oblast, excluding the city of Kalinin which was included in the Central Industrial Region; and in the northwest, Novgorod, Pskov, and Leningrad Oblasts. In the extreme western part of the Soviet Union, bordering on Poland and the Baltic Sea west of Lithuania, is an isolated segment of the Russian Republic that was formed out of the northern part of what was East Prussia

before World War II. This has been named Kaliningrad Oblast, and the old city of Koenigsberg has been renamed Kaliningrad. This oblast is part of the Russian Republic in spite of the fact that the Baltic Republics lie between it and the rest of the R.S.F.S.R. We might speculate that this region was considered too strategic to be placed under the jurisdiction of one of the adjacent Baltic Republics, and therefore it was placed under the direct jurisdiction of the Russian Republic. With the removal of most of the Germans after the war, Kaliningrad Oblast was resettled primarily by Russians, so as far as nationality is concerned, the Russians can justify its inclusion in the Russian Republic.

Population and Politics

The European West as defined here is part of the no man's land on the plain of Eastern Europe which has been in contention among neighboring powers from time immemorial. Together with western Ukraine to the south, it was part of the Polish-Lithuanian Empire during the sixteenth, seventeenth, and eighteenth centuries, and parts of it changed hands among Russia, Poland, and other powers several times. In the north, the Baltic states

Figure 6–1   The European West.

were frequently under contention which involved the Livonian Knights in early times, then later Sweden, and finally Prussia and Poland. Hence the population is a mixture of diverse elements which retain various loyalties and various ways of life. Much of the area has never enjoyed independence, but Lithuania, Latvia, and Estonia were established as independent countries after World War I and remained as such until their annexation by the Soviet Union in July 1940. The 20-year period of independence between the two world wars fanned the fires of nationalism in the Baltic states and engendered much hostility to-

ward the Soviet takeover, which has been expressed in more or less passive resistance much of the time, but which quickly bubbles to the surface in more active form whenever the political climate of the Soviet Union would seem to allow it without dire consequences. Open clashes occurred frequently after World War II, and it might be said that guerrilla warfare was actually being carried on in Lithuania from 1944 to 1952.

During the past 15 years or so, resistance has tapered off, and the population in all three Baltic Republics and Belorussia has increased considerably, due primarily to an influx of Russian laborers who have been sent in to man the many new industries that have been established somewhat artificially in the region. Thus in the entire European West of the Soviet Union the population increased from 25,416,000 in 1959 to 26,694,000 in 1967. The four non-Russian republics accounted for all of this increase and more, since the oblasts on the western fringes of the R.S.F.S.R. generally declined in population. Kaliningrad Oblast has shown a modest increase since 1959, but its population is nowhere near what it was before World War II. Leningrad Oblast increased almost 100,000 during the same period, and Bryansk Oblast increased a little, but Smolensk, Kalinin, Novgorod, and Pskov Oblasts are all declining in population. These declines no doubt attest to the fact that in spite of the relatively low population density in much of this area, as compared to areas to the south, there is still a population pressure on this relatively poor land which induces outmigration. The rural population, which until 1959 predominated in most of the area, is on the decline practically everywhere, and the population gains shown by Belorussia and the Baltic Republics reflect rapid urbanization in these regions.

Soviet policy during the past 15 years or so has induced the establishment of many new industries, in the Baltic states particularly, which to a large extent have not evolved from the local economy. This has necessitated the import of much raw materials and labor to sustain these industries. The result is that the three Baltic Republics can boast that their industrial production between 1940 and 1965 increased sixteen to eighteen times, but at the same time the percentage of Russians in the population increased in Latvia from 10.6 per cent to 26.6 per cent, in Estonia from 8 per cent to 20.1 per cent, and Lithuania from 2 per cent to 8.5 per cent. There were also unknown numbers of immigrants from Ukraine and

Belorussia. Russification has gone on more slowly in Lithuania than in the other two Baltic Republics because industrialization has lagged somewhat there.

The influx of Russians, coupled with the general tendency to establish Russian schools side by side with the native schools, and the natural tendency for ambitious native youths to learn the Russian language and take on Russian ways in order to enhance their careers, all tend toward a growing process of assimilation which the older Baltic citizens greatly resent. Such tendencies are particularly imminent in the larger cities, such as Riga and Tallin, where it appears that Russians make up at least half of the population. Such situations make the use of the Russian language a daily necessity, encourage mixed marriages, and generally create a Russian elite toward which local youths aspire. Thus the economic and demographic policies of the Soviet Union have combined to create economically dependent industrial melting pots of the Baltic states.

The Physical Landscape

The European West is divided northwest and southeast along the southern limit of most recent glaciation by a rather prominent moraine oriented southwest-northeast through the cities of Minsk, Smolensk, and Moscow. To the northwest of the moraine lies an undulating glacial plain with many lakes and swamps and deranged streams. To the southeast the area generally is slightly hillier and somewhat better drained. Some of the southern portion also suffers from poor drainage, however. A broad swampy region, the Polesye, occupies a large section of land along the Pripyat River in southern Belorussia, and it presents a problem to the development of the republic. Some drainage has already been carried out in the Polesye, and there are plans for considerably more drainage

Figure 6–2   Digging drainage ditches in the swamps of the Polesye, Belorussia. Novosti.

to be done in the future. However, there still are large areas of the Polesye that are unusable, and some Soviet scientists fear that extensive drainage might upset the ground-water balance so important to the drier areas to the south.

Because of the swamps in the northwest due to recent glaciation and in the southwest due to older glaciation and extreme flatness, the Belorussian Republic is best suited for agriculture in the east, and it is here that the population densities are highest and the major cities of the republic are located. The terminal moraine running from Minsk to Moscow, the so-called Smolensk-Moscow Ridge, is a little higher and better drained than the country on either side. On it are laid the major highway and railway from Warsaw to Moscow. It is along this route that armies from the west, including those of Napoleon and Hitler, have invaded Russia to attack Moscow.

To the north of this terminal moraine the country is mainly one of glacial aspect, but in certain areas promontories induced by the structure of the underlying rock transcend the glacial features and rise above the general level of the terrain. One such area lies in eastern Latvia, in what is called Latgale. This is a region of hilly upland underlain by the eroded edge of a resistant sedimentary rock layer surmounted by irregular heaps of glacial detritus. This upland extends into southern Estonia where elevations of over 1500 feet are reached.

Along the southern shore of the Gulf of Finland, in northern Estonia and Leningrad Oblast, the eroded edge of a hard layer of limestone forms an abrupt escarpment a short distance back from the seacoast, which rises as high as 450 feet above the narrow terrace that skirts the Gulf. This long cliff of flinty rock is known as the "Glint"; its eroded remnants form hundreds of islands in the Baltic Sea along the northern coast of Estonia. The eastern arm

Figure 6–3   Flax harvesting near Minsk, Belorussia. Novosti.

of the Baltic and its extension, the Gulf of Finland, lie in an inner lowland along the northern edge of this outcropping cuesta escarpment. Farther west, along the Gulf of Riga and southwestward, the coastal hills become much lower, and long off-shore bars paralleling the coast for many miles provide excellent sandy beaches. One bar, over 50 miles long, has completely enclosed the outlet of the Neman River in Kaliningrad Oblast and western Lithuania to produce a stagnant lagoon and swampy delta plain.

In the Russian Republic northwest of Moscow, the Valday Hills, a dissected cuesta escarpment partially covered by moraines and other glacial debris, reach elevations slightly over 1000 feet and form the drainage divide between the headwaters of the four main river systems of the area — the Volga, the Dnieper, the Western Dvina (Daugava), and the Msta. In effect, these rivers are connected at their sources in a vast, mossy bog overgrown by forest.

Agriculture Climatically the area is cool and moist. These conditions have been conducive to the growth of a mixed forest vegetation and the development of pod-zolic soils. The infertile soils coupled with poor drainage definitely limit agricultural possibilities. The main crops are flax, small grains other than wheat, hay, and potatoes. Sugar beets are being introduced slowly, and corn for silage is now being grown. Other than these crops, a variety of hardy vegetables and fruits are grown for local consumption. Dairying and hog and poultry raising are becoming increasingly important. Much of the agriculture is carried on in almost a subsistence manner, and the rural population is rather sparse and widely scattered. The rural villages diminish in size steadily from Ukraine northward through Belorussia and the Baltic Republics, until we find in Estonia villages of only two or three homesteads, and indeed, even separate homesteads on individual farms. Fields in the north are quite small, averaging only 1.3 hectares in Leningrad Oblast. This retards mechanization. The people of this area have carried on some agriculture for centuries in spite of the shortcomings of the natural environment, but the area has never been a prime agricultural region. In general, agriculture improves southeastward as the climate becomes warmer and drier, the soils become more fertile,

Figure 6–4   Hay drying rack near Novgorod. The cool, moist climate in this region makes hay curing difficult. Courtesy of Ronald Helin.

Figure 6–5 Buckwheat field near Minsk. Courtesy of J. H. Glen Burke.

and the drainage improves. Bryansk Oblast contains the best agricultural land in the region.

In spite of the limited nature of the agricultural resource of this area, it is the main resource, and until recently agricultural products formed the main bases for the light industries in the area. Such industries as food processing, particularly of dairy products, tanning and leather working, flax retting, and brush making from hog bristles utilize the local products and excess rural labor and serve local and, in some cases, national markets.

Forestry Other industries are based on the forest resource, which is the second most important resource in the area. Forests still cover approximately 25 per cent of the total area, and in some places in the Baltic Republics they cover as much as 50 per cent of the land. Woodworking of all sorts is important; the manufacture of furniture, plywood, prefabricated houses, and matches is of nationwide significance.

Fishing, Shipping, and Water Power Fishing is important in the Baltic as well as in the many inland lakes and streams, and the cities along the Baltic are significant to

the Soviet Union as seaports. Leningrad is the largest ship-building center in the Soviet Union. Ice covers the eastern arm of the Baltic part of the year and hampers the Gulf of Riga to a certain extent, but southwest of the Gulf of Riga lie the minor seaports of Ventspils and Liepaya, which are used the year round. Kaliningrad, the old Prussian city of Koenigsberg, at the most westerly position in the Soviet Union, might eventually become one of the major seaports of the country. So far there is no indication that this is to take place; perhaps the Russians are still wary of holding this western position permanently.

Figure 6–6 Seimenphal dairy cattle in Latvia. Novosti.

Figure 6–7   Typical log cabin village in the forest zone south of Leningrad. Photograph by the author.

Inland waterways are limited in size. The chief one connects Leningrad eastward through the Great Lakes to the Baltic-White Sea Canal in the north and the Volga-Baltic Canal system to the south. Canals skirting the southern shores of Lakes Ladoga and Onega link the Neva and Svir Rivers to form a navigable waterway from Lake Onega to the Gulf of Finland. The Great Lakes themselves cannot be used because storm waves on them capsize the small canal boats. A little traffic moves on the two main rivers of the West, the Western Dvina and the Neman, but navigation is limited to very small boats. It now is planned to improve navigation on the Western Dvina and to construct a cascade of reservoirs for the production of hydroelectricity.

A small hydroelectric plant has been in operation for a number of years near the town of Kegums on the lower Western Dvina, about 75 miles upstream from Riga, and in 1967 a plant with a capacity of 825,000 kilowatts was completed at Plavinas about 50 miles farther upstream. Five more plants are scheduled to be built on the Western Dvina at unspecified dates in the future. In 1960 a 100,000-kilowatt

plant was completed at Kaunas on the Neman River. It has been proposed to build a rather elaborate system of dams, locks, and hydroplants that would link the Neman with the Pripyat, and thus the Dnieper, to provide a second transcontinental waterway between the Baltic and the Black Seas, but this scheme will probably not take place until far in the future, if at all. Even if all these proposed hydroelectric projects were completed, their aggregate production would be minimal, and they would be dwarfed by the much more numerous and larger thermal stations that are being built in the area.

Minerals   Mineral resources are limited to the oil shale of eastern Estonia, the bauxite deposits at Boksitogorsk east of Tikhvin in Leningrad Oblast, a newly opened potash deposit in south-central Belorussia near Soligorsk, and widespread deposits of peat. The oil shale covers a fairly extensive area along the shores of Lake Chudskoe and north along the Narva River to the Baltic. A pipeline has been carrying gas products from this area eastward to Leningrad and westward to Tallin for a number of years. The alumina and aluminum plant at Volkhov, opened in 1932 to utilize the bauxite ore at Boksitogorsk and electricity of the newly constructed Volkhov hydroelectric plant, was the first plant to produce aluminum in the country, but the aluminum content in the red clay hills east of Tikhvin is not high, and the plant at Volkhov has been switched partially to the use of nephelite from the Kola Peninsula far to the north. Newer plants in the Urals, Ukraine, and Transcaucasia have eclipsed the operation at Volkhov. The potash deposit in Belorussia is auspiciously located to provide for the development of a large mineral fertilizer industry to serve the needs of this agricultural area with its mineral-poor soils. Other than these minerals, building stone, gypsum and limestone for cement, clay, sand, and so forth are of local significance.

Industries

Obviously, the mineral deposits of the European West cannot support a great amount of industry. Except for Leningrad, what has developed in the past has been primarily in response to rural population pressure on the land and some minor market possibilities outside the region. Such industries as handicrafts, primarily processing the products of agriculture and forests from the local area; small household items, utilizing much labor, some skill, and little raw materials; and other items, which were somewhat distinctive and therefore could find their niche in a wider market, were produced on relatively small scales to help the peasants eke out a meager livelihood from the poor land. In the past few years all of this has been changing rather rapidly. The Soviets have begun to locate relatively heavy machine industries and chemical industries in the area and to establish major power bases to supply electricity and fuels to these industries. Much of this has been made possible by the

construction of gas and oil pipelines into the area from various producing regions of the country.

The large city of Leningrad has attracted the extension of pipelines from the Volga-Urals oil fields, and the so-called Friendship pipeline, which has been constructed to carry oil from the Volga-Urals westward to the East European satellites, has provided the opportunity for branch lines to bring Volga-Urals oil to various parts of the European West of the Soviet Union. Consequently, one of the largest oil refineries in the Soviet Union began operation in 1963 at Polotsk in northern Belorussia. In 1966 another oil refinery was opened at Kirishi just southeast of Leningrad. It was built initially to operate on crude oil brought in from the Ukhta field in northeastern European Russia by tank cars, but it is to switch to the refining of crude oil from the Volga-Urals oil fields as soon as the pipeline is completed from Yaroslavl

Figure 6–8   Plywood factory in Estonia. Novosti.

to Kirishi. A third refinery is being constructed at Mozyr, in southern Belorussia, at the junction of the Friendship pipeline where it branches and goes southwestward to Czechoslovakia and Hungary and northwestward to Poland and East Germany. (Fig.15–6) The port of Ventspils on the Latvian coast has been made into a foreign outlet for oil from the Volga-Urals fields. A marine terminal has been in operation there since 1961 to transship crude oil from tank cars to ships for export. In 1968 a pipeline was completed from Polotsk to Ventspils to serve this marine terminal, and now Volga-Urals crude oil can be brought to Ventspils exclusively by pipe.

A gas pipeline was built from the Dashava fields in western Ukraine to Minsk in 1960, and since then has been extended to Riga. On the way it services such cities as Brest, Grodno, and Vilnyus. In 1967 natural gas accounted for 20 per cent of the total fuel consumption in Belorussia and from 70 to 80 per cent in such cities as Minsk and Gomel, which are serviced by a branch pipeline from the Dashava-Kiev-Moscow pipeline. Smolensk is also serviced from a branch line leading from this main trunk. Natural gas has relieved these larger cities of the necessity of using peat and long-haul steam coals and fuel oils. Recently, Leningrad has been connected by gas pipelines to Moscow, which thus connects it to gas supplies from the large north Caucasian fields and eventually will allow gas flowage all the way from the Central Asian fields in the Uzbek and Turkmen Republics. It also derives some gas from the Saratov field on the Middle Volga, which has been supplying Moscow for a number of years, and minimal amounts of gas that are associated with the Volga-Urals oil fields. In addition, two large pipelines, one using pipe as large as 100 inches in diameter, are being constructed all the way from the West Siberian fields along the Lower Ob southwestward across the Northern Urals through the gas fields of Ukhta to Cherepovets at the northern end of the Rybinsk

Reservoir and thence westward to Leningrad. They will be connected with the Moscow-Leningrad gas mains, and thereby gas can be transmitted into various parts of the European West and Ukraine. (Fig. 15–8.)

With the inflow of natural gas from various producing regions, Leningrad has ceased to use the gas produced from oil shale in Estonia, and the flow of gas has actually been reversed on the old Kokhtla-Yarve–Leningrad pipeline to supply natural gas to a new nitrogenous fertilizer plant at Kokhtla-Yarve and to mix natural gas with oil shale gas that moves westward from Kokhtla-Yarve to Tallin. In spite of this influx of natural gas into the region, oil shale production is being expanded for use in the production of gas, fertilizer, resins, synthetic tanning materials, and fuel for power stations. Estonia annually produces about 65 per cent of all the oil shale in the Soviet Union and much of the rest is produced just across the border in Leningrad Oblast. The mines around Syzran on the Volga account for less than 10 per cent of the total.

Large thermal power stations, which recently have been constructed in the region, are making up for the general lack of hydro power in the area. The Baltic thermal power station near Narva, which operates on oil shale fuel, was doubled in capacity in the early 1960s to 1,600,000 kilowatts. A gas-fueled power station using Dashava gas has been built halfway between Vilnyus and Kaunas. It has a capacity of 1,200,000 kilowatts. Other large stations have been connected to these by high-voltage power lines to form the northwestern power grid, which is sufficient to supply not only the European West of the Soviet Union but also to export electricity to Poland.

With the influx of natural gas into this region the chemical industry has expanded rapidly. A new chemical complex began operations at Novgorod in 1967, where natural gas is taken from the Moscow-

Leningrad transmission main to produce ammonia and other nitrogen compounds. Much of the chemical industry is involved in mineral fertilizer production. Nitrogenous fertilizer plants utilizing natural gas and oil refinery gases as raw materials have been established in a number of cities. Also, superphosphate plants and potash plants have been established to utilize local raw materials. By far the largest development is at Soligorsk in southern Belorussia where three potash mills have been built since 1963. By 1970 this plant is to produce roughly 40 per cent of the total Soviet output of potash, thereby rivaling the older Berezniki-Solikamsk plant on the upper Kama River in the Western Urals and eclipsing the production of the Kalush plant in the Carpathian foothills of western Ukraine. The Soligorsk potash plant is supplied with large amounts of electricity from the Bereza station 100 miles to the west. With a designed capacity of 900,000 kilowatts, this is the largest station in Belorussia. It burns Donets steam coal, fuel oil, and natural gas. In 1966 a superphosphate plant was completed in Gomel. One year later, however, the old superphosphate plant in Riga, established in 1892, was closed down because of growing air pollution. This is the first known case of a major plant being shut down in the Soviet Union because of the growing concern about air pollution.

Recently, there has been some indication that the Soviets are experiencing some success in discovering oil in parts of Belorussia. This might be a northwestward extension of what appears to be a general oil field in northcentral Ukraine. If this is the case, the region may experience another spurt in economic activity.

In spite of all the oil and gas developments in the area, and the associated development of new industries, the machine industries still remain by far the largest group of industries in the area. Leningrad, of course, has always been a major machine-construction center in the Soviet Union. Even before the Revolution, and, in fact, for a number of years thereafter, it served as the research and development center for much of the machine tool industry, as well as for many other heavier machine industries. But under the Soviets, since World War II heavy machine industries have been spreading to other cities of the European West. For instance,

Figure 6–9 Dump trucks at the Zhodino plant east of Minsk. Photograph by the author.

Minsk now has large tractor and automobile assembly plants, and Zhodino, about 20 miles east of Minsk, has been established as a workers' settlement around a plant that turns out huge dump trucks that are utilized in large dam construction projects and so forth. Such industries have been established largely in disregard of local resources and, to some extent, of local labor supplies. In many instances the necessary skills to run such plants were not found in local labor pools, and large groups of people had to be brought in from the outside. This, of course, fostered the process of Russification mentioned earlier. Thus, while the area in general has been industrializing during the past 2 decades, local officials have become more and more concerned with the type of development that has taken place. This is particularly true in the non-Russian areas, especially in the Baltic states, where nationalism still runs strong among the older generations.

Cities

The cities of this western region are not large, except for Leningrad and some of the capitals of the non-Russian republics. In general, the populations of the capital cities have increased rapidly whereas those of other cities have increased slowly or not at all.

Leningrad   By far the largest city in this area, and second largest in the Soviet Union, is Leningrad, which in 1967 had a population of 3,296,000. This is slightly smaller than it was in 1939. Leningrad suffered terribly during World War II, when, for more than 900 consecutive days it was under continuous siege by the German army. Since the war, a principle has been established that population migration into the larger cities, particularly into Leningrad, will be prohibited. Therefore we might expect that the Leningrad population never again will reach its pre-war level.

Nevertheless, Leningrad is a great city, having served as capital of the Russian Empire from its founding by Peter the Great in 1713 until after the Revolution in 1919. It was Peter's "window on the west" which was built in the swamps of the delta of the Neva River at the cost of the lives of many Russian peasants. In spite of the fact that it was situated in a forested wilderness of poorly drained podzol soils with meager possibilities for agriculture, its designation as the capital of the Russian Empire and as the main contact with the rest of Europe caused it to prosper and grow into the largest city of the Russian Empire at the time of the Revolution. From 1713 to 1914 it was known as St. Petersburg, but in 1914, after the beginning of World War I, it was renamed Petrograd, to eliminate the German terminology. In 1924, after Lenin's death, it was named Leningrad to commemorate the foremost leader of the Revolution.

Leningrad has the most vivid history of any of the cities in the Soviet Union, having acted as the capital during the momentous years of the growth of the Russian Empire which culminated in the Revolution and the formation of the Soviet Union. Tsarist society reached its zenith here and left its mark in the many monumental buildings and spacious grounds, and the revolutionary resistance groups formed and grew up in St. Petersburg under the very eyes of the so-called Third Section, the secret police arm of the tsars. Although Leningrad is not looked on so much as an indigenous Russian city as Moscow is, and although it is losing out to Moscow in most aspects of economic and cultural life, it still is a showplace of the Soviet Union for tourists. It is curious to witness the Russian guides expound about the monuments left by the tsars while at the same time consciously trying to eliminate mention of the tsars from their explanations. There are some tsars, such as Peter the Great, who have been adopted by the Soviets as being revolutionaries and ahead of their times, and these are eulogized to a considerable degree. However, it is hard to reconcile present Soviet ideology with the fact that one is being guided through one of the most elaborate displays of material wealth on earth in the Hermitage Museum. And the Russian Museum in Leningrad is perhaps an even greater contradiction; it contains all of what is considered to be great of Russian painting, and practically all of the hugh murals and paintings on the walls have religious themes. It is truly a startling experience to listen to the atheistic Soviet guide explain the religious theme of each

painting when it is quite obvious that she has never read the Bible.

Leningrad is built on the many low, muddy islands that separate the distributaries of the delta of the Neva River. With its more than five hundred bridges, it has been likened to Venice in Italy. Although it is only 50 miles long, the Neva is about a mile wide and it has a consistent flow, because it drains the large glacial Lake Ladoga into the Gulf of Finland. The river does not flood, but the delta on which Leningrad sits is so flat and so low above the sea that a strong west wind can raise the water level in the Gulf of Finland enough to inundate the lower sections of the city. Such floods have occurred from time to

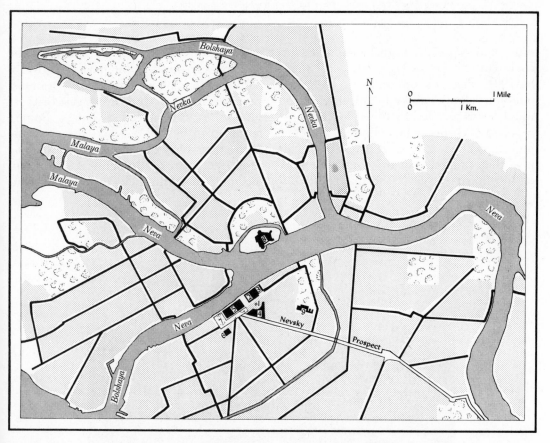

Figure 6–10   Downtown Leningrad. 1. Palace Square. 2. Winter Palace. 3. Hermitage Museum. 4. General Staff Building. 5. Admiralty Building. 6. St. Isaac's Cathedral. 7. Decembrists' Square. 8. Sts. Peter and Paul Fortress. 9. Russian Museum.

Figure 6–11   The Winter Palace across Palace Square, Leningrad. The granite spire commemorates the 1812 victory over Napoleon. It is surmounted by the figure of an angel with the face of Alexander I. Photograph by the author.

time, and especially high floods have occurred exactly 100 years apart, in 1824 and in 1924. Placards on some of the main buildings along Nevsky Prospect mark the water levels reached by these floods.

Nevsky Prospect, the main street of Leningrad, is lined by rows of five-story buildings that culminate at the southeast bank of the Bolshaya Neva, the main distribu-

tary of the Neva River, in a series of large squares surrounded by palaces, government buildings, and monuments reminiscent of Empire days. The largest of these squares is the so-called Palace Square hemmed in by the Winter Palace and the Hermitage Museum along the river, the semicircular arc of the General Staff Building, and the Admiralty Building with its

Figure 6–12   "The Bronze Horseman," Peter the Great, Decembrists' Square, Leningrad. Photograph by the author.

gilded spire. In the center of the square a slender red granite monolith 150 feet high, with the figure of an angel at the top, commemorates the victory over Napoleon. Another square is dominated by the massive St. Isaac's Cathedral, whose dome reaches an elevation of 330 feet, the highest point in the city. In front of it, Decembrists' Square, a broad formal garden, is fronted on the river by a 4000-ton, rough-hewn granite monolith surmounted by the figure of Peter the Great on a rearing horse.

Most of these monumental buildings are painted pale yellow and trimmed in pale green in classic style, although many of them look as if they have had very little paint added to them since the Revolution. The Winter Palace is perhaps the most imposing structure; a five-story green building facing on the Neva River, it served as the home of the royal family during the

Figure 6–14 "Meteor Ship," hydrofoil boat on the Neva River in front of Saints Peter and Paul Fortress. Photograph by the author.

long winters in Petersburg. During the reign of Catherine the Great a large addition was added to the building to provide for a private art gallery for Catherine. This addition became the Hermitage Museum, which now occupies much of the Winter Palace also and houses one of the most elaborate art collections in the world. Outside, the Palace appears as a dull, dirty green building, but inside all is polished mahogany and gold leaf with crystal chandeliers dominating the rooms.

On an island across the broad channel of the River Neva sits the red brick-walled fortress of Sts. Peter and Paul, which in the beginning served as the kremlin for the initial town in the area. At that time the fort was composed of crude buildings enclosed by a log and earthen wall. Later, the wall was replaced by granite and brick, and more imposing cathedrals and governmental buildings were built inside. The cathedrals eventually became the burying places for the tsars, and the casement walls became one of the most infamous prisons in the Russian Empire. During the second half of the nineteenth century, practically every person in Russia who did any thinking at all was imprisoned sooner or later in Sts. Peter and Paul Fortress.

Fringing Leningrad on the south and west are a number of old tsarist estates which in most cases served as the summer homes for the royal family. The best preserved of these is Petrodvorets, about 20

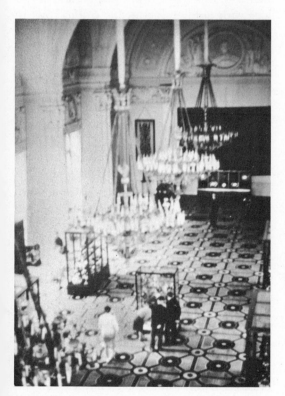

Figure 6–13 In the Hermitage Museum. Courtesy of Clara Dundas Taylor.

miles southwest of Leningrad, along the southern shores of the Gulf of Finland. Here again we find the pale yellow buildings with gold leaf trim, but they are in much better repair and are much shinier in appearance than are the buildings in Leningrad. The huge grounds surrounding the palace are landscaped with hundreds of fountains in various arrays, which are fed by a natural head of water from the limestone escarpment to the south. Farther east are other tsarist grounds, the most elaborate of which is Tsarskoye Selo, the "tsar's village," which since the Revolution has been renamed Pushkin, because Alexander Pushkin attended a lycee near there. Pushkin was occupied by the Germans for a considerable time during World War II. A good deal of damage was wrought, and many art treasures were carried off. The Russians are restoring the area and making it into a combination museum and weekend recreation park.

As has been pointed out before, Leningrad was besieged during World War II for a period of almost 3 years. During this time the German armies had the city nearly encircled, except for a narrow strip along its eastern edge, and they constantly lobbed artillery shells into the city and staged air raids to bomb the city. Throughout this long period the people of Leningrad, in the face of death from starvation, freezing, and disease, as well as from artillery shells and other instruments of war, maintained a spirit of resistance that enabled them to emerge victorious. There was a saying during this period that "one could go to the front by tram." A so-called Road of Life was kept open to the east, through the narrow neck of land that was not held by the Germans, to Lake Ladoga and then across the Lake to what the Russians termed the Mainland, which was unoccupied during the war. Travel across Lake Ladoga was limited primarily to winter when the lake was frozen over and a road could be established across the ice, with trucks moving in long caravans carrying supplies of food and ammunition into Leningrad and women, children, and wounded out of Leningrad. The Germans continually bombed the caravans and blew big holes in the ice, but the Russian Army was able to keep a route posted across the ice, with soldiers acting as traffic cops to guide the trucks around the holes. Such caravans of trucks, however, could not compensate fully for the seven railroads that normally fed the city, and many people died of famine and freezing. Those in the lower age groups were particularly vulnerable; it has been reported that infant mortality rose to 75 per cent. As a result of its great resistance during World War II, Leningrad has been designated as a hero city, and an impressive war memorial cemetery has been established there.

It was in St. Petersburg that the Industrail Revolution made its greatest inroads in the 1890s. Here a semiskilled labor pool, or proletariat, was developed and here the prototypes of all types of industrial products were manufactured. Leningrad produced the first Soviet tractors in 1924 and the first synthetic rubber in the 1930s. Moscow, under the Soviets, largely has preempted these functions of industry and culture from Leningrad, but Leningrad still has a monopoly on certain industries that require special skills, such as the

Figure 6–15   Peterhof (Petrodvorets). Peter the Great's summer palace is noted for its beautiful displays of fountains. Photograph by the author.

manufacture of very fine machine tools and giant hydroelectric turbines. The chief industries in Leningrad at present are the machine-building industries, the chemical industries, textiles, food, and printing. All raw materials for the industry of Leningrad must be brought in from other parts of the Soviet Union, and many of the finished products of the region must find markets in the rest of the country. Leningrad utilizes about 10 per cent of the steel output of the U.S.S.R. The main steel center to serve the machine industries of Leningrad has been established in Cherepovets, at the north end of the Rybinsk Reservoir, utilizing coal from Vorkuta and iron ore from the Kola Peninsula. Ship building is an important industry, as might be expected in the biggest port in the country. Kronshtadt, an important naval base, was constructed during Russian Empire days on Kotlin Island offshore in the Gulf of Finland. In 1955 Leningrad got its first subway.

Minsk   Second in size in the European West is Minsk, the capital of the Belorussian Republic, with a population of 772,000. Minsk long has served as the center of the Belorussian nationality group, although this group has not always enjoyed political identity. In fact, Minsk has never been the capital of an independent country; the area of Belorussia has always existed either within the Russian Empire or within some empire to the west, such as the Polish-Lithuanian Empire in the seventeenth and eighteenth centuries. Since World War II the boundaries of Belorussia have been pushed westward into territory that had been eastern Poland between the world wars, so that now Minsk occupies almost an exact central position in the Belorussian Republic. Serving simply as the capital city of this republic and as the commercial center for the region, Minsk has a variety of light industries and is an important transport center. Recently, machine-building industries, such as a tractor assembly plant, have been introduced into Minsk to bolster the economy of the Republic. In the eight years from 1959 to 1967 the population of Minsk grew 34 per cent.

Riga   The third city in size in the European West is Riga, the capital of Latvia, with a population of 680,000. Riga was founded in 1201 as a fortress and has long served as the focal city of the Latvian nationality group, and between the two world wars it served as the capital of the free republic of Latvia. Sitting on the shore of the Gulf of Riga at the mouth of the Western Dvina River, it has been one of the major ports along the Baltic from early times, and during the Middle Ages it became one of the Hanseatic League cities. Its main function, therefore, is one of commerce, with such industries as ship building and fishing being of prime importance. Other than these functions, its industries are primarily those which serve the local market and make use of some of the local products, such as the food and textile industries. Recently light electronics and precision tools industries have been established.

Tallin   Fourth in size is Tallin, the old city of Reval, which was founded as a Danish fortress in 1154 and now serves as the capital for the Estonian Republic. Besides serving as a capital, Tallin is a fairly important port on the Baltic Sea, and it contains a variety of light industries to utilize the products of local agriculture and fishing and to serve the local market. In 1967 Tallin had a population of 340,000.

Vilnyus   Fifth in size is Vilnyus, the capital of the Lithuanian Republic, which in 1967 had a population of 316,000. Vilnyus apparently was founded in the twelfth century; after the downfall of the Livonian Knights it became the cultural and religious center for Lithuanians and east European Jews. In 1323 Prince Gedimin made it the capital of the Duchy of Lithuania. By the sixteenth century it had lost some of its preeminence due to the merging of Lithuania with Poland. In 1795 it was annexed by Russia. The World War I peace treaty established Lithuania as an independent country, but in 1920 the Poles took over Vilnyus and the surrounding territory. In 1939 the Soviet Union restored Vilnyus to Lithuania as a political gesture to soften up Lithuania for annexation to the Soviet Union.

Vilnyus is located inland, and therefore does not enjoy a port function as do Riga and Tallin, and it has not grown as fast as they have. It is simply the seat of government and a center of light industries and transport within the Lithuanian Republic.

Bryansk   Sixth in size is Bryansk with a population of 288,000. It is a regional center within a rich agricultural area in southwestern R.S.F.S.R.

Kaliningrad   Seventh in size is Kaliningrad with a population of 270,000. Kaliningrad is the old city of Koenigsberg, which was the main seaport in the section of East Prussia that was taken over by the Russians after World War II. The city was first established in 1255 as a fortress of the Livonian Knights. Kaliningrad has only about half the population of the former city of Koenigsberg, and so far it has not assumed the importance as a seaport that Koenigsberg had. However, in the future Kaliningrad might become a more important port to the Soviet Union, since it is the most western of the major ports on the Baltic and is therefore the least hampered by ice during the winter. Perhaps the slowness of the development of Kaliningrad so far has been due to a fear on the part of the Russians that this westernmost point is too exposed to risk a great buildup at present. The Soviets have established some heavy transport equipment and other industries in the city.

Other Cities   Next in size are two cities in the eastern part of the Belorussian Republic: Gomel, with a population of

237,000, and Vitebsk, with a population of 203,000. These cities have largely stagnated during the Soviet period; lack of growth is common throughout this western area with the exception of the capital cities.

One other city that might be mentioned in Russia is Smolensk, with a population of 196,000, which, like Vitebsk, suffered heavily during the war. Smolensk lies on the direct route of invasion from the west toward Moscow, about halfway between Minsk and Moscow along the so-called Smolensk-Moscow Ridge, the terminal moraine or high ground along which the major highway is laid. Founded in 882, Smolensk is one of the oldest cities in the country. It has suffered the first blows of many wars between Muscovy and western powers, and it has changed hands many times among Russia, Poland, and other states. It is the seat of government for Smolensk Oblast and the commercial center for a relatively poor agricultural area.

Besides these major cities, mention should be made of some smaller seaports on the Baltic: Klaypeda, population 131,000, in Lithuania, which is the old town of Memel, and the towns of Liepaya, population 86,000, and Ventspils, population 37,000, in Latvia. Another important old town lies in southeastern Estonia and is now named Tartu, population 85,000. This is the old university city of Dorpat.

Novgorod and Pskov   Two historic towns in northwestern Russia, seemingly stagnant for centuries, have gained some new life since World War II. These are Novgorod and Pskov, which in 1967 had populations of 107,000 and 112,000 respectively. Novgorod was mentioned in the introductory chapter for the historic role it played in Kievan Rus and for several centuries thereafter. Its kremlin was originally built in A.D. 859 by Rurik, the first ruler of an organized Slavic state in this area. With the removal of the seat of government to Kiev after Rurik's death, Novgorod remained the second most important city in Kievan Rus and became an important commercial center peopled by international merchants who had connections with the Hanseatic League cities westward along the Baltic. After its fall to Muscovy in the fifteen century, it declined in importance and practically dropped out of view in the early Soviet period. During World War II heavy German fighting leveled it to the ground. But since the war the Soviets have restored the kremlin and monumental churches and have rebuilt the town into a pleasant city that is now one of the main tourist attractions. A round trip by bus can be made in a day from Leningrad, which provides time for a leisurely tour of the Novgorod kremlin and various religious museums as well as a boat excursion up the Volkhov and around Lake Ilmen.

Since this northwestern area has poor settlement possibilities, particularly for agriculture, such cities as Novgorod and Pskov cannot be expected to grow very much, but Novgorod particularly seems to have experienced a rebirth, with its introduction to the *Intourist* circuit. And now it is experiencing some industrialization as it builds chemical industries to tap the gas mains running between Moscow and Leningrad. Novgorod grew from 61,000 in 1959 to 107,000 in 1967.

Prospects

The European Northwest is something of an economic problem area. It has little resources for either agriculture or industry. But it is an old settled area which has figured prominently historically, and the Russians cannot afford to ignore the political significance of historical facts. Therefore a good deal of attention is being paid to this area and industries are being established, somewhat artificially, to hasten the assimilation of the strongly nationalistic Balts and Belorussians. As a result of political motives behind economic measures,

the non-Russian part of the area has been the most prosperous economically. However, this has been at the sacrifice of nationality identities. It appears inevitable that this process will continue, and perhaps accelerate, as the older generations die off and new generations come to power who have been reared in the Soviet system. If the present low birth rates of the Baltic groups continue, which they probably will, and if Russian laborers keep moving into the new industries of the area at the present rate, which they probably will, the Latvians will be in a minority in their own republic by 1975, and the Estonians by 1985. Lithuania is experiencing less Russification, but the danger lurks that Kaliningrad Oblast adjacent to it on the west might be added to Lithuania. This might well occur when the long-awaited new constitution emerges, perhaps sometime in the early 1970s. Such action would suddenly add about 700,000 Russians to the population of Lithuania, which would reduce Lithuanians to about 60 per cent of the total population in the republic.

Reading List

GENERAL

Altman, L. P. and Dolkart, M. L., "Problems of Economic Development in the Northwest Economic Region during the New Five-year Plan (1966–70), *Soviet Geography: Review and Translation,* January 1968, pp. 11–23.

French, R. A., "Drainage and Economic Development of Polesye, U.S.S.R.," *Economic Geography,* April 1959, pp. 172–180.

Taskin, George A., "The Soviet Northwest: Economic Regionalization," *The Geographical Review,* April 1961, pp. 213–235.

BELORUSSIA

Atlas Belorusskoy SSR (Atlas of the Belorussian SSR), Minsk, 1958, 140 pp. (in Russian).

Belorusskaya SSR (Belorussian SSR), Akademiya Nauk BSSR, Institut Ekonomiki, Moscow, 1957, 487 pp. (in Russian).

Sovetskiy Soyuz: Belorussiya (Soviet Union: Belorussia), Mysl, Moscow, 1967, 309 pp. (in Russian).

Vakar, Nicholas P., *Belorussia: The Making of a Nation,* Harvard University Press, Cambridge, Mass., 1956, 297 pp.

Yurkevich, I., *Geograficheskaya tipologiya i rayonirovaniye lesnoy rastitelnosti Belorussii* (Geographic typology and regionalization of the forest vegetation of Belorussia), Minsk, 1965, 286 pp. (in Russian).

Baltic States

Vardys, V. Stanley, "How the Baltic Republics Fare in the Soviet Union," *Foreign Affairs,* April 1966, pp. 512–517.

Lithuania

Gargasas, Peter, *Litovskaya SSR* (Lithuanian SSR), Moscow, 1960, 126 pp. (in Russian).

Itsikzon, M. R., *Litovskaya SSR* (Lithuanian SSR), Moscow, 1960, 63 pp. (in Russian).

Litovskaya SSR (Lithuanian SSR), Akademiya Nauk Litovskoy SSR, Institut Geografii, Moscow, 1955, 390 pp. (in Russian).

Sovetskiy Soyuz: Litva (Soviet Union: Lithuania), Mysl, Moscow, 1967, 286 pp. (in Russian).

Tavydas, Stasys, *Litva* (Lithuania), Moscow, 1967, 285 pp. (in Russian).

Vardys, V. Stanley, *Lithuania Under the Soviets,* Praeger, New York, 1965, 299 pp.

Latvia

Kolotiyevskiy, Anton M., *Latviyskaya SSR* (Latvian SSR), Moscow, 1955, 117 pp. (in Russian).

Lazdyn, V. K. and Purin, V. R., *Riga; ekonomiko-geograficheskiy ocherk* (Riga; economic-geographic study), Moscow, 1957, 95 pp. (in Russian).

Rostovtsev, M. I., "Zapadno-Dvinskiy Kaskad" (Western Dvina Cascade), *Geografiya v shkole,* 1961, No. 6, pp. 28–31 (in Russian).

Spekke, Arnolds, *History of Latvia,* Goppers, Stockholm, 1957, 436 pp.

Weis, E. E. and Purin, V. R., *Latviyskaya SSR* (Latvian SSR), Moscow, 1967, 439 pp. (in Russian).

Estonia

Estonskaya SSR (Estonian SSR), Akademiya Nauk Estonskoy SSR, Institut Ekonomiki, Moscow, 1957, 366 pp. (in Russian).

Rostovtsev, M. I. and Tarmisto, V. Yu., *Estonskaya SSR* (Estonian SSR), Moscow, 1957, 365 pp. (in Russian).

Sharkov, V. A., *Estonskaya SSR* (Estonian SSR), Moscow, 1956, 118 pp. (in Russian).

Sovetskiy Soyuz: Estoniya (Soviet Union: Estonia), Mysl, Moscow, 1967, 254 pp. (in Russian).

Varep, Endel, *Estoniya* (Estonia), Moscow, 1967, 253 pp. (in Russian).

R.S.F.S.R.

Golovanov, S. S., ed., *Leningradskaya Oblast: priroda i khozyaystvo* (Leningrad Oblast; nature and economy), Leningrad, 1958, 344 pp. (in Russian).

Pavlov, Dmitri V., *Leningrad 1941: The Blockade,* translated by John Clinton Adams, University of Chicago Press, 1965, 186 pp.

Pokshishevskiy, V. V., et al., ed., *Severo-Zapad RSFSR* (The Northwest of the RSFSR), Moscow, 1964 (in Russian).

The European North

Region	Area (sq mile)	Population	People (sq mile)	% Urban [a]
Karelian A.S.S.R.	67,400	707,000	10.5	71
Murmansk Oblast	56,600	727,000	12.8	96
Archangel Oblast	229,000	1,401,000	6.1	67
Nenets National Okrug	69,000	37,000	0.5	49
Vologda Oblast	56,900	1,307,000	23.0	45
Kirov Oblast (Northern half excluding Kirov City)	23,900 [b]	686,000 [b]	28.7	41
Kostroma Oblast (Excluding southwest quarter and Kostroma City)	17,600 [b]	444,000 [b]	25.2	35
Komi A.S.S.R.	163,000	974,000	6.0	65
Total	614,400	6,246,000		

[a] All figures are for entire regions.
[b] Estimated population and area of portion of region lying within the European North.

7

The European North

The vast expanse of territory in eastern Europe lying mostly north of the 60th parallel and extending from the Finnish border on the west to the Ural Mountains in the east is variously known to the Russians as the European North, or, dividing it in two parts, as the European Northwest and the European Northeast. In the south it begins with the transition zones of the various regions previously discussed, the Volga Region in the east, the Central Industrial Region in the center, and the European West in the west, and it stretches northward through a primarily nonagricultural, forested and tundra area to the shores of the Arctic. The northern fringes of the three regions to the south already showed some of the characteristics of this area: the thinning of agriculture, the beginnings of dense stands of coniferous forest, cool moist climatic conditions, and podzol soils. These conditions are dominant in the area now under consideration.

Politically this area includes the Karelian A.S.S.R. and Murmansk Oblast in the west and the large areas of Archangel Oblast and the Komi A.S.S.R. in the east, as well as Vologda Oblast and large northern sections of Kostroma and Kirov Oblasts in the south. Altogether the area is comprised of more than 600,000 square miles and contains a little more than six million people.

With an overall population density of approximately ten people per square mile, this is the emptiest area considered thus far. The entire area lies within the Russian Republic, but it includes three areas of predominantly non-Russian peoples or of populations with large minority non-Russian groups. Two of these non-Russian areas make up two autonomous republics, the Karelian A.S.S.R. in the west and the Komi A.S.S.R. in the east. The third non-Russian area is the Nenets National Okrug, a sparsely populated region of primitive nomads, which lies within Archangel Oblast.

The entire area is quite homogeneous in climate, which is primarily subarctic with a tundra fringe along the north; in soils, which are everywhere podzols and tundra; and in drainage, which everywhere is exceedingly poor. Geologically, however, the west is very different from the east, and on this basis the area is often divided into two regions. The Karelian A.S.S.R. and Murmansk Oblast in the west are part of the Scandinavian Shield, an area of ancient crystalline rocks which has recently acted as the center for continental glaciation. Thus it is a region of ice-scoured bedrock, rough, rolling topography, and thousands of lakes. On the other hand, much of Archangel Oblast and the Komi A.S.S.R.

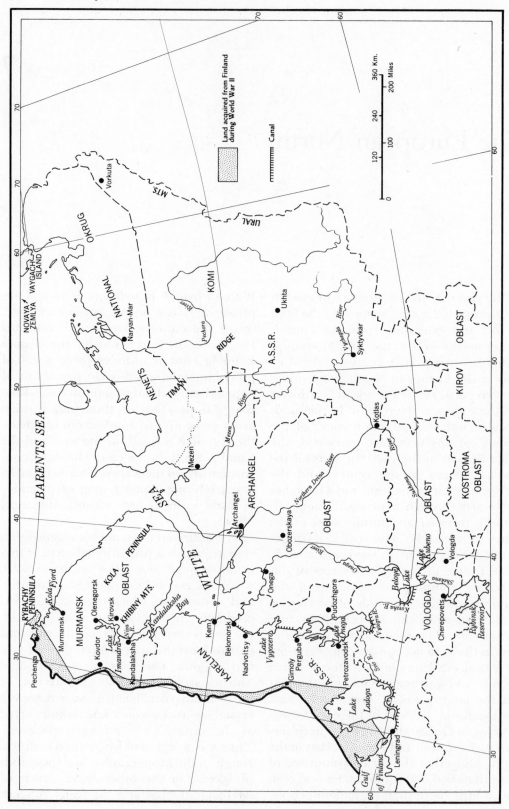

Figure 7-1   The European North.

to the east is an exceedingly flat, low-lying plain underlain by nearly horizontal sedimentary rocks. The eastern part of this section, in the Komi A.S.S.R. and the Nenets National Okrug, is particularly flat because a postglacial inundation from the Arctic seas rewashed what thin glacial deposits there were and produced a surface almost as flat as a floor.

Vologda, Kostroma, and Kirov Oblasts also are underlain by horizontal sedimentary rocks that have recently been covered with glacial till, but they lie in a transition area climatically, so that agricultural possibilities are considerably greater here than they are in the Archangel and Komi areas. Hence this southern region might be considered separately as a third subregion of the European North. Therefore the area will be discussed in three sections: the northwest, the northeast, and the south.

The Karelian A.S.S.R. and Murmansk Oblast

Territorial Development   Parts of the Karelia-Kola Peninsula region have changed hands internationally through the centuries among Russia, Finland, and Sweden. From 1809 to 1918 all of Finland was in the Russian Empire. The peace treaty after World War I established Finland as an independent country, but the Soviets have never fully accepted this arrangement and they took the opportunity early in World War II to invade Finland. Two brief but bitter wars ensued between the two countries. Although the Soviet Union was unsuccessful in taking over Finland, several important boundary adjustments were forced upon the Finns. (Fig. 7–1) The largest areas that were transferred to the Russians lay in the extreme north and the extreme south. The Pechenga area in the north, or Petsamo as it was known by the Finns, is an area with important nickel and copper deposits. This area, along with the Rybachy Peninsula, or

Fishermen's Peninsula, were taken over by the Russians in two different maneuvers in 1940 and in 1944. In the south the entire Karelian Isthmus between Leningrad and Vyborg was ceded to the Soviet Union by the Finns, and this area was placed under the jurisdiction of Leningrad Oblast, probably for strategic and economic reasons. Besides the acquisition of these territories, the Russians acquired the lease of land west of Helsinki for military purposes, but this lease has since been relinquished.

When the Soviet Union was constituted in 1923, the Karelian Area was made into the Karelian A.S.S.R. within the Russian Republic to give recognition to the Karelian nationality group. Then in 1940, with the onset of World War II, the area was reconstituted into the Karelo-Finnish S.S.R., apparently to entice the Finns to be more kindly disposed toward the Russians. It is quite obvious now that tnis was purely a political maneuver, since in 1956, without any forewarning or explanation, the union republic was downgraded once more to an autonomous republic and again was placed under the jurisdiction of the Russian Republic. The area never did warrant union republic status according to the constitution, which states that in order for an area to become a union republic it must have at least one million people with a majority of those people being of the titular nationality. The Karelian A.S.S.R. in 1959 had only 649,000 people; slightly less than one fourth of them were of Karelian and Finnish stock, and over 65 per cent were Russian.

Geology and Topography   As has been stated before, the Karelia-Kola Peninsula area is an ancient crystalline shield that has been worn down essentially to a rough peneplain by millions of years of stream erosion and recently has been heavily ice scoured, since it acted as a center of glaciation during the Pleistocene. Thus the topography is one of a rolling plain that here and there rises into hills or even low,

Figure 7–2   The rocky crystalline shield near Vyborg. Courtesy of Neil Field.

eroded mountains. Rough, bare bedrock outcrops at the surface in many places among the myriad of lakes, swamps, and marshes. Within the Karelian A.S.S.R. elevations do not reach much above 1500 feet, but in Murmansk Oblast the Khibiny Mountains rise to heights of slightly more than 3800 feet. This is well above the tree line at these latitudes so that the mountains have a truly alpine character with tundra vegetation and glacial features.

The contact zone between the ice-scoured crystalline rocks of the north and the ice-drifted sedimentary rocks to the south lies in an east-west inner lowland along the southern boundary of the Karelian A.S.S.R., at the base of a cuesta escarpment that marks the present position of the eroded edge of the rock strata in their erosional retreat southward down the slope of the underlying crystalline complex. The large Lakes Ladoga and Onega, as well as the Gulf of Finland, lie in this cuesta lowland, much as the Great Lakes of North America occupy the contact zone between the Canadian Shield and the Interior Lowland of the United States. And similarly, this is known as the Great Lakes area in the Soviet Union.

Climate, Vegetation, and Soils
Throughout the Karelian area the sub-arctic climate has been conducive to a fairly good stand of coniferous trees, chiefly pine and fir; the Karelian A.S.S.R. is one of the main regions of lumber and paper production in the Soviet Union. Much of Murmansk Oblast, on the other hand, is tundra-like because of its high latitude and somewhat higher elevation; thus lumbering is relatively unimportant in this region. The soils and drainage conditions throughout both areas are extremely poor, and agriculture is significant only in southern Karelia.

Minerals   The complex rocks that outcrop at the surface make for a wide variety of possibilities in mineral resources, and it is largely because of the opening of some mining areas that Murmansk Oblast has developed rather rapidly under the Soviets. The fact that the population of Murmansk Oblast in 1967 was classified as being 96 per cent urban attests to the insignificance of agriculture as compared to the importance of mining, fishing, and trading.

The most significant mining area at present is in the vicinity of the new city of Kirovsk in the Khibiny Mountains in central Murmansk Oblast. Here are found the greatest known deposits of apatite in the world, which serve as the basis for much of the phosphate fertilizer industry in the U.S.S.R., and nephelite, which is now being utilized in the production of aluminum at Kandalaksha, Nadvoitsy, and Volkhov. A transshipment port has been constructed at Perguba on Lake Onega to facilitate the use of the new Volga-Baltic waterway for cheap rail-water combined shipments of apatite and nephelite ores southward. Across Lake Imandra, in the region known as Monche Tundra, lie important ores of nickel and copper. In the far northwestern corner of Murmansk Oblast, in the area known as Pechenga, is another important deposit of nickel and some copper. Low-grade iron deposits are scattered throughout the area, often as residue of leaching in glacial lake beds, with significant deposits at Olenegorsk and Kovdor in Murmansk Oblast and at Gimoly and Pudozhgora in the Karelian A.S.S.R. Iron concentrate is shipped from Olenegorsk and Kovdor to Cherepovets at the northern end of the Rybinsk Reservoir for conversion into steel utilizing coal from Vorkuta. The Olenegorsk concentrator has been in operation since 1955; the Kovdor concentrator began operating in 1962. Besides these major ores, about sixty other useful elements appear in lesser quantities, and some of them are now being utilized. Such things as titanium, radium, zirconium, and molybdenum are being used in small quantities, and the largest mica plant in the Soviet Union is located in Petrozavodsk on the western shore of Lake Onega.

Fish   Other than mining and lumbering, fishing is very important throughout much of the area. Since World War II the Barents Sea has become the second most important fishing area in the Soviet Union, exceeded only by the Sea of Okhotsk in the Far East. In the mixture of waters between the warm Gulf Stream coming around the northern end of Scandinavia and the cold water of the Arctic Ocean a rich growth of plankton feeds large numbers of cod, herring, sea perch, etc. Murmansk is the main base of the fishing fleet in the Barents Sea, and serves as the most important fish canning and processing center as well. Along the western shore of the White Sea lie three other important fishing centers — Kandalaksha in the north and Kem and Belomorsk farther south. Besides these major centers, many small centers of fishing exist, either along the seacoast or along the many interior lakes and streams.

Water Power   Many of the short streams in the area follow swift, rocky courses over steep slopes between lakes, and in spite of the severe winters do not freeze to the point where hydroelectric production would be impossible. Therefore many of the streams are being put to use to provide domestic supplies of electricity to homes, mines, and transportation facilities and to provide large quantities of electricity to power-hungry industries such as the aluminum plants at Kandalaksha and Nadvoitsy. The Niva River flowing southward from the Khibiny Mountains to Kandalaksha Bay has had a hydroelectric station for a number of years, and four small plants were built along the northern section of the White Sea–Baltic Canal when it was constructed in the 1930s. The Kovda hydro system on the border of Karelian A.S.S.R.-Murmansk Oblast, consisting of three power stations with an aggregate capacity of 300,000 kilowatts, was completed in 1963. In 1965 the Tuloma hydro plant on Kola Fjord began to supply electricity to the city of Murmansk and the Kirov railroad leading south to Leningrad. Its ultimate capacity is to be about 230,000 kilowatts. On the Kem River in Karelia, construction began in 1963 on the 84,000-kilowatt Putkinsk plant, which is to be the first of a system of five installations on the Kem. Other stations exist on some of the other rivers, including the short but important Svir River flowing between Lakes Onega and Ladoga. In addition, an atomic power station is being built south of Murmansk.

Figure 7–3   Part of the fishing fleet in Murmansk harbor. Note the barren, rocky cliffs of the ice-scoured, tundra shore. Novosti.

Transportation A major waterway that has been developed by the Soviets is the White Sea–Baltic Canal, which was opened in 1933. This leads southwestward from the White Sea at Belomorsk utilizing many lakes, such as Lake Vygozero, or Crescent Lake, in its course to Lake Onega 140 miles away. From Lake Onega westward this system links up with the canal system that leads down the Svir River to Lake Ladoga, around the southern end of Lake Ladoga, and then down the Neva to Leningrad and the Baltic Sea. The stretch of canal from Belomorsk to Lake Onega utilizes nineteen locks. During World War II the Finns destroyed some of the system, but it was quickly reconstructed after the war.

Of course the canal is closed by ice at least half of the year so that the region still is dependent primarily on the railroad. The main line, the Kirov Railroad, was constructed in 1916 from Leningrad northward to Murmansk. During the early part of World War II, when great quantities of lend-lease materials were being shipped into Murmansk and when Leningrad was almost surrounded by the Germans, the so-called Obozerskaya Bypass was built leading from the Kirov Railroad at Belomorsk and going eastward around the southern end of the White Sea to Obozerskaya, on the rail line running from Archangel to Moscow. This provided an all-rail route from Murmansk to the Moscow area which did not go through occu-

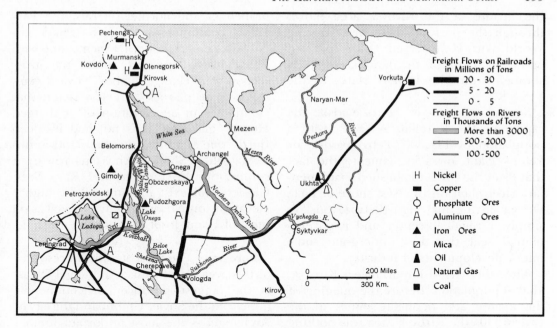

Figure 7–4   *Rail and river freight traffic and mineral resources of the European North. Adapted from* Soviet Geography: Review and Translation, *June 1961, pp. 66–67.*

pied territory. In December 1960 another branch line was opened from Murmansk to Pechenga. A second longitudinal railroad, partly old, partly new, connects towns in west central Karelia with Leningrad via the north shore of Lake Ladoga and Vyborg. But in winter even the railroads are difficult to maintain, and transportation remains a grave problem throughout the area. At the present time sections of the "great north-south highway" from Leningrad to Petrozavodsk to Murmansk are under construction.

Cities   There are few cities in this western region. Murmansk is by far the largest city, with a 1967 population of 287,000. This makes it the largest polar city in the world. Founded in 1915 at the northern terminus of the Kirov Railroad, Murmansk has grown during the Soviet period from a town of 8777 persons in 1926 to its present size because of its importance as a northern seaport in the center of a large fishing industry. The city sits in a somewhat sheltered position near the head of

Kola Fjord about 40 miles from the sea. Although the climate here is cold and raw much of the year, the sea remains ice-free in the winter because of the Gulf Stream. Murmansk replaces Leningrad as the northern port of the Soviet Union from December to May. As the home base for the fishing fleets in the Barents Sea and the western terminus of the Northern Sea Route, it has developed important shipbuilding and ship-repair yards. Much of

Figure 7–5   *Lenin Prospekt in Murmansk. Novosti.*

the apatite of the Kirovsk area moves through the port of Murmansk. During World War II it served as the port of entry for most of the lend-lease goods shipped from the United States to the U.S.S.R.

Second in size is Petrozavodsk, the capital of the Karelian A.S.S.R., with a population of 171,000. Petrozavodsk, or Peter's Plant, owes its name to the fact that Peter the Great established a rudimentary steel plant on the west shore of Lake Onega during his reign. Petrozavodsk is simply a regional center and a governmental seat that has undergone some minor developments of industry.

The other city of importance is Kirovsk, 46,000 population. Before the opening of the apatite and nephelite mines in the early 1930s the Kirovsk area was nothing but open tundra land peopled only by nomadic reindeer herders. Within the course of 2 or 3 years it was developed into a mining boomtown. Founded as Khibinogorsk in 1929, its name was changed to Kirovsk in 1931.

The major lumber port within the area is Belomorsk, 16,000 population, but Leningrad handles more Karelian lumber than any city within Karelia itself.

Archangel Oblast and the Komi A.S.S.R.

Topography The second subregion, consisting of Archangel Oblast and the Komi A.S.S.R., as noted before, is a very flat glacial plain which in recent geological times was inundated by the Arctic seas. A low anticlinal upwarp, the Timan Ridge, forms a slightly higher, more eroded area in the central part and separates the drainage basins of the Northern Dvina and the Pechora rivers. Along the eastern border of the Komi Republic lie the Ural Mountains, but their description will be deferred until the entire chain of mountains is considered. It must be noted here, however, that the northwestward extension of a

branch of the northern Urals, the Pay-Khoy, continues as Vaygach Island and Novaya Zemlya, both of which, along with Franz Josef Land, are under the jurisdiction of Archangel Oblast. Novaya Zemlya is a steep, rocky, treeless island that culminates in an elevation of 3640 feet. Heavily glaciated, it is notched by deep fjords, one of which cuts the island in two at Matochkin Shar, which is a narrow strait connecting the Barents and Kara Seas. Glaciers still exist in some of the higher elevations on Novaya Zemlya as well as on most of Franz Josef Land to the north.

Forestry The most significant resource of this area is its forests; Archangel Oblast is the biggest producer of commercial lumber in the Soviet Union, and the city of Archangel is the most important lumber port. Thirteen per cent of the nation's timber and two thirds of all the sawn lumber exported from the Soviet Union comes from the European Northeast. The most common trees are spruce and Scotch Pine. From May to October logs are floated down the Vychegda and other tributaries of the Northern Dvina. Floating fences of connecting logs across the streams at constrictions and tributary junctions temporarily catch the logs in ponds for sorting and raft formation. The logs are usually rafted together and pulled by tugs over smooth stretches of the rivers and across lakes, but the rafts are broken up and the logs are floated separately down swift stretches containing rapids. Log rafts may be lashed together and broken apart at several different points along the streams before the logs finally reach Archangel. Because of the log rafting, the Northern Dvina ranks second only to the Volga among rivers in the U.S.S.R. in total freight moved.

At Archangel the logs are piled in long rows along the many distributaries in the delta of the Northern Dvina. By fall, Archangel appears to be nothing more than a series of watery corridors between piles of

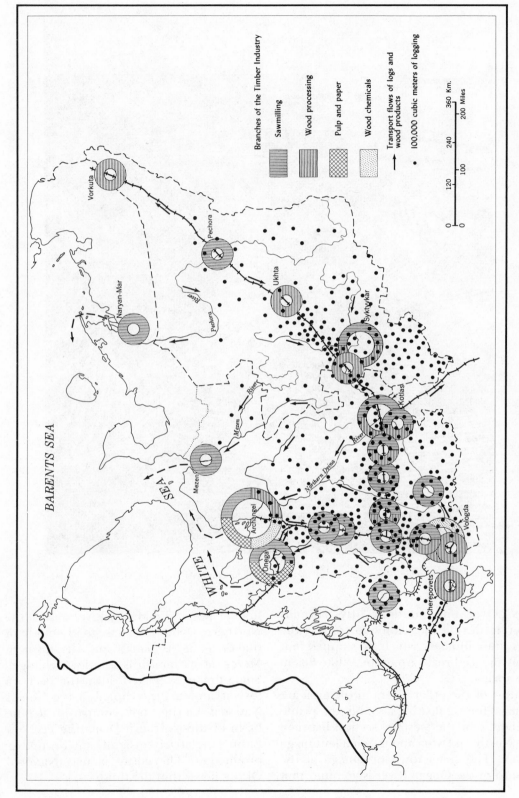

Figure 7–6 The timber industry of northeast European Russia. From Soviet Geography: Review and Translation, April 1961, p. 55.

Figure 7–7   Timber floating in one of the mouths of the Northern Dvina at Archangel. Novosti.

logs. Over one hundred fifty sawmills operate during the winter to convert the logs into lumber, which is shipped out after the ice breaks up in the White Sea in the spring.

Most of the other rivers in the area are utilized for log floating also, but the prime timber is in the western section between the Northern Dvina and the smaller Onega River. The small town of Onega at the mouth of the Onega River is an important lumber port. The Mezen River east of the Northern Dvina also has good stands of timber along its banks, and the town of Mezen at its mouth is a little Archangel. Some timber is floated down the Pechora to Naryan-Mar, the capital of the Nenets National Okrug, but compared to the basin of the Northern Dvina the Pechora Basin is relatively insignificant in lumber production. The entire Nenets National Okrug lies within the tundra.

Several towns in the interior also are important lumber-milling centers such as Syktyvkar, the capital of the Komi Republic, on the Vychegda River, and Kotlas at the important junction of the Vychegda and the Northern Dvina rivers and the Pechora Railroad. Strings of sawmills are located in smaller towns along both the Northern and Pechora railroads. Much of the lumber sawed in these towns moves southward by rail to the heavily urbanized areas of the Central Industrial Region and the Povolzhye. A new lumber railroad has been extended eastward from Archangel to Karpogory to open up new lumber areas along the lower reaches of the Pinega and Mezen rivers.

Minerals Other than the forests, about the only resource in the area is some of the mineral fuels. Since this is a flat sedimentary basin, we would not expect to find metallic ores, but we might find coal, oil, and natural gas. And such is the case. Coal was discovered in the far northeast corner of this area near the city of Vorkuta early in the Soviet period, and during World War II mining was developed to a considerable extent to compensate partially for the loss of Ukraine to the Germans. In 1942 an important railroad was opened from Kotlas to Vorkuta to enable the movement of this coal into the central part of the country. During the war and for several years after, Vorkuta was run as a slave labor camp, but since 1957 it has been stated that all labor in Vorkuta is free, as it is in all other coal-mining areas of the country.

It is claimed that the Vorkuta reserves are even more abundant than those of the Donets Basin in Ukraine and are just as high in quality. But development here cannot be expected to proceed at a consistently rapid rate because of economic reasons: Vorkuta is a long way from markets, and it has a rugged climate. All coal mined in Vorkuta today is utilized at Cherepovets to produce the steel for the Leningrad area and as fuel in the various cities of the European North. Some mention has been made of building a rail line parallel to the Ural Mountains along their western side to bring Vorkuta coal into the heavily industrialized area of the central and southern Urals, but this distance is just as long as the distance from the Donets Basin to the southern Urals, or from Karaganda in Kazakhstan to the southern Urals, so it appears unlikely that Vorkuta will be highly developed or that a railroad paralleling the Urals ever will be built.

Halfway between Vorkuta and Kotlas lies the oil and gas areas of Ukhta and Vuktyl. This is one of the minor oil fields of the U.S.S.R., but it is important locally. Some oil is now being produced and refined at Ukhta, and some gas-based chemical industries have been established in the area. The Vuktyl gas is now being shipped to Vologda, Cherepovets, and Torzhok, where it enters the main Moscow-Leningrad pipelines, and is augmented by Saratov gas that has been brought to the area by pipeline since 1961. The 48-inch pipeline from Vuktyl to Torzhok is the first section of a dual set of pipelines that is being built to bring much larger quantities of gas to Central Russia from the huge gas fields of the lower Ob Basin.

Another mining development that apparently is getting underway is at the recently discovered North Onega bauxite deposit in Archangel Oblast. Not much has been said yet about this deposit. Whether or not it is of significant enough proportions to revitalize the aluminum industry at Volkhov remains to be seen.

Agriculture Agricultural possibilities throughout Archangel Oblast and the Komi Republic are universally poor. The railroad from the city of Vologda cuts straight northward through virgin forest, and very little land clearing is encountered all the way to Archangel. Some agriculture has developed in the southern part of the Komi Republic, particularly around its

Figure 7–8   Greenhouse agriculture near Ukhta, Komi A.S.S.R. Novosti.

capital city, Syktyvkar, but it consists of only hardy grains, flax, hay, pasture, and livestock. Living conditions are almost unbelievably primitive. Syktyvkar, in spite of its status as the capital city of an autonomous republic, is still a sleepy, muddy, backwoods town, with unpainted clapboard houses and grassy streets. A road is maintained from Syktyvkar southward to Kirov during the winter when the ground is frozen, but in the summer the only connection between Syktyvkar and the outside world until 1960 was down the Vychegda River to Kotlas. In December 1960 a railroad was completed from Syktyvkar northwestward to link up with the Pechora mainline northeast of Kotlas.

Cities   The only city of any size in this area is Archangel with a population of 310,000. Archangel was established during the reign of Ivan the Terrible shortly after 1553 when an English ship under the command of Richard Chancellor was driven into the mouth of the Northern Dvina by a storm on the White Sea. The survivors of the shipwreck eventually made their way to Moscow and negotiated a trade agreement with Ivan the Terrible. Archangel then was established in 1584 as the entrepot for goods from England

and the export of goods from Muscovy. At the same time, Vologda to the south was established as the outpost of populated Muscovy on the border of the unbroken forests to the north. Vologda controlled an important portage on the river system between Archangel and Moscow and hence became a center for the transshipment of goods. Actually Vologda was founded in 1147, whereas Archangel was founded in 1583, but both cities got their major impetus from the Russo-English trade in the latter part of the sixteenth century. Other than Archangel, only Syktyvkar, with 102,000 people, and Vorkuta, with 65,000, are cities of notable size. The oil city of Ukhta has grown to a population of 53,000.

Vychegda-Pechora Diversion Project
One of the big construction works that may be undertaken in the future in this area is the Vychegda-Pechora River diversion project, which would not particularly enhance the economy of the local area but which would be of major importance to the Lower Volga Region. Early in the 1930s, when the first five-year plans were being developed, a great deal of talk ensued about the possibilities of constructing a huge reservoir between the headwaters of the Northern Dvina, the Pechora,

and the Kama Rivers that would allow for some reversal of flow in the tributaries of the Northern Dvina and the Pechora to the tributaries of the Kama River. This would transfer water from flowing uselessly to the Arctic Ocean into the Volga River system, which has a deficit of water, particularly in late summer, for all the functions of navigation, electric power, and irrigation that are possible in that region. The Pechora River reaches its greatest flow in summer when the Volga is at its lowest.

It already has been pointed out in the discussion of the Povolzhye that any diversion of irrigation water from the Volga will greatly endanger the maintenance of the level of the Caspian Sea as well as reduce the possibilities of navigation of the Volga itself. Hence it would be very helpful if somehow more water could be dumped into the Volga system. The only feasible solution appears to be this one to divert water from the Pechora and the Northern Dvina, or from its major right-bank tributary, the Vychegda. The project would entail the building of extensive dams on the Pechora, Vychegda, and Kama Rivers, as well as on a few tributary streams, so that the water could be confined in rather well-defined reservoirs and not be allowed to spread up tributary streams to the detriment of general reservoir levels. The three reservoirs would be connected by two canals. The combined areas of the reservoirs would be larger than Lake Ladoga. Such a body of water would inevitably have profound effects on ground-water tables, ice regimes, and microclimate in the surrounding area, and some local officials have shown concern about the lack of knowledge of what these consequences might be. Such deliberations seem to have delayed the beginning of construction work indefinitely, and indeed might have shelved it completely. If such a reservoir and canal system were to be built, it would provide an all-water route

for the transfer of Vorkuta coal to the central Urals. This might completely change the prospects for the development of coal mining in Vorkuta.

Vologda, Kostroma, and Kirov Oblasts

Economy The southern tier of three oblasts that are included in northern European Russia — Vologda, Kostroma, and Kirov — are transitional in character between the severe conditions of the north and the more moderate conditions of the Central Industrial Region and the Povolzhye. Hence considerable agriculture is carried on in these areas as well as considerable lumbering. The agriculture is highly concentrated on dairying and the raising of flax, hardy grains, and potatoes. Vologda Oblast is the most noted dairy region in the country; it might be called the Wisconsin of the Soviet Union. Actually Ukraine produces more dairy products, but dairying makes up a much larger portion of the economy in Vologda Oblast than it does in Ukraine.

No great amount of industry has been established in the area, although Cherepovets now serves as the steel center for the Leningrad area and to a small extent for the Central Industrial Region. Founded in 1777, it remained an insignificant town on the Sheksna, a minor tributary of the Volga, for more than a century and a half. It began to prosper a bit after the filling of the Rybinsk Reservoir located it on the north shore of that major water body. But its spectacular growth has occurred in recent years due to the establishment of the iron and steel plant which is continually undergoing expansion. Pig-iron production began in 1955 and crude-steel production in 1958. In 1960 a hot-rolled mill was completed, and in 1963 one of the largest cold-rolled steel mills in the U.S.S.R. went into operation. The mill supplies sheet metal for the automobile, tractor, combine, refrigerator, and washing-machine industries, as well as many others. In 1967 construction began on one of the huge 2700-cubic-meter blast furnaces that are being installed in a number of the larger steel centers of the country. This will put Cherepovets on something of a par with other first-ranking steel centers. Although the bringing together of iron ore and coal from such far-flung locations as the Kola Peninsula and Vorkuta into a small town which is separated from its major market (Leningrad) by several hundred miles seems to be a very uneconomical way to set up a steel industry, under the Soviet system of decree, at a disregard of cost, Cherepovets has prospered. Perhaps it will find itself more economically located now that the Volga-Baltic waterway has been reconstructed which uses Cherepovets as its southernmost port and connects it by a good deep water route to Leningrad and the White Sea ports. By 1967 Cherepovets had grown to a population of 165,000 and contained an industrial complex that included, in addition to the iron and steel plant, ammonia synthesis processors for the production of ammonium sulfate fertilizer from coke-oven gases and a nitrogenous fertilizer industry that is being expanded to utilize natural gas from the Vuktyl field east of Ukhta. The cities of Kostroma and Kirov have been excluded from this region, so that the only other city of any size that exists here is Vologda. In 1967 Vologda had a population of 170,000.

Volga-Baltic Waterway Through the western part of Vologda Oblast runs the 150-year-old Mariinsk Canal system, which leads up the Sheksna River from the northern end of the Rybinsk Reservoir to Beloe Lake, or White Lake, then up the Kovzha River, across the Kovzha-Vytegra divide, and down the Vytegra River to Lake Onega, where connections are made to the west down the Svir River, Lake Ladoga, and the Neva River to the Gulf of Finland and to the north through the Baltic-White Sea Canal to the White Sea. (Fig. 7–4) The Mariinsk was the deepest of three old canal systems that connected the Center with the Northwest. But even this canal was shallow and slow and involved a system of forty locks, thirty-four of which were wooden, that required hours of waiting for boats making passage. It took between 20 and 30 days for barge caravans to travel from Cherepovets to Leningrad, and the caravans had to be broken up and reformed as many as fourteen times en route in order for barges to be tugged through smaller locks individually. Freight from the Volga traffic had to be transshipped at Cherepovets from the large Volga barges to the smaller Mariinsk barges, and canals had to be maintained around the edges of Beloe, Onega, and Ladoga Lakes because storm waves on the lakes could capsize the small boats. All this made barge freight rates about three times as high as railroad freight rates, so very little freight was moved by barge.

This old waterway has now been revamped into a modern Volga-Baltic waterway to provide a channel 12 feet deep to connect the Center, the Northwest, the Urals, and the South. A dam was built across the Sheksna where the Northern Railroad crosses the river near Cherepovets that backed up water 225 kilometers to form the Cherepovets Sea which completely inundated the valley of the Sheksna as well as Beloe Lake and raised the water level up the Kovzha all the way to the divide. Six large modern locks now lower the boats down the north slope of the divide into the Vytegra River. The large Volga barges are able to navigate all the way to Leningrad. Transport costs have been cut to one third that of railroad freight costs, and travel time from Cherepovets to Leningrad has been reduced to about 10 days for tug-drawn barges and 5 days for self-propelled barges. The waterway was opened in May 1964.

It is hoped that these improvements will

induce increased movements via water of grain, wood, petroleum, salt, cotton fiber, potash, and building materials into the Leningrad area. Also, iron ore from the Kola Peninsula and coal from Vorkuta can be brought to Cherepovets mainly by water to reduce production costs of steel there and make it an economical enterprise. Steel can be shipped from Cherepovets to Leningrad, Gorky, Yaroslavl, and Moscow entirely by water. Wood can be shipped in barges all the way from sawmills in Northern European Russia to the Center, the Volga, and the South. Grain from western Siberia, the Volga, and the Kama areas is expected to move westward along the water route, and apatite from the Kola Peninsula can be shipped through the Baltic-White Sea and Volga-Baltic waterways to nearly all the superphosphate plants of European Russia.

A bonus benefit realized from this system is additional water brought into the upper Volga from Lake Kubeno and the Sukhona River, the major left-bank tributary of the Northern Dvina. Water from Lake Kubeno and the Sukhona River is dumped into the Cherepovets Sea at the rate of about 3.5 cubic kilometers per year, thereby increasing the flow of the Volga. This increase enhances navigation and electric production in the power stations on the upper Volga that cannot benefit from the Pechora-Vychegda diversion project that might bring water into the Volga via the Kama River downstream from Kazan. The Cherepovets Sea on the Sheksna has filled the old Northern Dvina Canal and provides for a better connection between the old Mariinsk and Northern Dvina Canal systems. Additional improvements are to be made later along the Northern Dvina waterway.

Prospects

The European North has definite physical limitations. Except for the southern fringe, little can be done with agriculture, and what can be done, largely has been accomplished already. Thus any further development will probably depend on mineral resources, which have been the impetus for much of the flurry of activity that has taken place so far during the Soviet period. Lumbering and fishing remain mainstays of the economy, and these will undoubtedly continue to expand somewhat, but growth in these sectors will not produce any spectacular developments. So far, except for apatite, mining activity has been only of local significance. Unless unforeseen discoveries of large mineral deposits occur, the region seems destined to remain of secondary importance. The construction of gas lines across the area from the large gas fields of western Siberia will provide an adequate base for power and chemicals, but there is only so much of this type of activity that such a sparsely settled area can absorb. The Volga-Baltic waterway might induce some transcontinental movement of bulky materials between Leningrad and major producing areas of the south, and in time of emergency might prove to be of some strategic significance for transferring small ships from the Baltic or White Sea theaters of operation to the Black and Mediterranean Seas. However, in all cases, most of the traffic will simply move through the region, thus leaving only a minor imprint on it. The continued urban growth in the area, stimulated by mining, lumbering, fishing, and commercial activities, will make the region increasingly more dependent on the rest of European U.S.S.R. for foodstuffs and other amenities of life.

Reading List

Altman, L. P. and Dolkart, M. L., "Problems of Economic Development in the Northwest Economic Region during the New Five-Year Plan (1966–70)," *Soviet Geography:*

Review and Translation, January 1968, pp. 11–23.

Dmitrevskiy, Yu. D., *Geografiya Vologodskoy oblasti* (Geography of Vologda Oblast), Vologda, 1961 (in Russian).

Gorovoy, V. L., "The Timber Industry of Northern European Russia," *Soviet Geography: Review and Translation,* April 1961, pp. 53–59.

Granik, G. I., "Location of Productive Factors in the European Part of the Soviet North," *Problems of the North,* 1965, No. 9, pp. 11–20.

Helin, R. A., "Soviet Fishing in the Barents Sea and the North Atlantic," *Geographical Review,* July 1964, pp. 386–408.

Karelskaya ASSR (Karelian ASSR), Karelskiy filial akademii nauk SSSR, institut geografii, Moscow, 1956, 335 pp. (in Russian).

Pokshishevskiy, V. V., et al., ed., *Severo-Zapad RSFSR* (Northwest RSFSR), Mysl, Moscow, 1964 (in Russian).

Rom, V. Ya., "The Volga-Baltic Waterway," *Soviet Geography: Review and Translation,* November 1961, pp. 32–43.

Shishkin, N. I., "On the Diversion of the Vychegda and Pechora Rivers to the Basin of the Volga," *Soviet Geography: Review and Translation,* May 1962, pp. 46–56.

Vendrov, S. L., "Geographical Aspects of the Problems of Diverting Part of the Flow of the Pechora and Vychegda Rivers to the Volga Basin," *Soviet Geography: Review and Translation,* June 1963, pp. 29–41.

The Urals

Region	Area (sq mile)	Popu- lation	People (sq mile)	% Urban
Perm Oblast	63,500	3,088,000	49	67
Komi-Permyak N.O.	12,800	216,000	17	18
Udmurt A.S.S.R.	16,400	1,379,000	84	55
Bashkir A.S.S.R.	56,200	3,757,000	67	46
Sverdlovsk Oblast	75,400	4,354,000	58	82
Chelyabinsk Oblast	34,400	3,286,000	96	78
Orenburg Oblast	48,500	2,057,000	42	50
Total	294,400	17,921,000		

8

The Urals

Topography

The flat plain of the Pechora Basin ends abruptly on the east with the high ridge of the Ural Mountains, or Stone Belt, as the Russians often call it. In the north about 25 miles inland from the Kara Sea the Urals rise from the flat tundra to a height of over 4000 feet in Konstantinov Kamen. From here southward to a latitude of about 65 degrees, the Urals extend as one continuously high and narrow ridge which is a truly wild and rocky region. This section is well above the tree line and has been heavily glaciated. Local mountain glaciers still exist in some of the protected upper valleys. On either side the ridge drops off abruptly to an extremely flat plain that has recently been washed by the waters of the Arctic Ocean. This northern section, at approximately 65 degrees latitude, contains the highest elevation in the Urals, Narodnaya Gora, or People's Mountain, which reaches an elevation of 6183 feet.

South of here the Urals split into two or more ranges and become softer in outline as pine, fir, and larch forests begin to cover the slopes. From 61 degrees latitude southward to approximately 55 degrees, in the region known usually as the Middle Urals, the mountains are comprised of from two to ten ranges, all rather ill-defined, broken, and low in elevation with only occasional peaks rising to four or five thousand feet. The original vegetation in this region was a mixed forest grading from coniferous forest in the north to wooded steppe in the south. At present much of the area is wooded by second-growth birch and aspen. This middle section has become by far the most important area in the Urals for settlement and industry, and agriculture is carried on to a considerable extent.

In many places this middle section is not mountainous at all; branches of the Trans-Siberian Railroad cross the range without difficulty. Neither do the mountains in this section drop off abruptly on either side. This is particularly true in the west where the land rises gradually eastward from the Volga River in a broad mountain foreland. Much of the foreland has been rather deeply dissected by streams, which in some places have eroded the upland into a series of rounded hills and in others have cut canyon-like stream valleys several hundred feet below plateau- and mesa-like divides. The northern part of this foreland in the Kama River area is known as the Uvaly, or Lumps, the central section is the Ufa Plateau, a tableland deeply dissected by the Ufa River and its tributaries, and farther

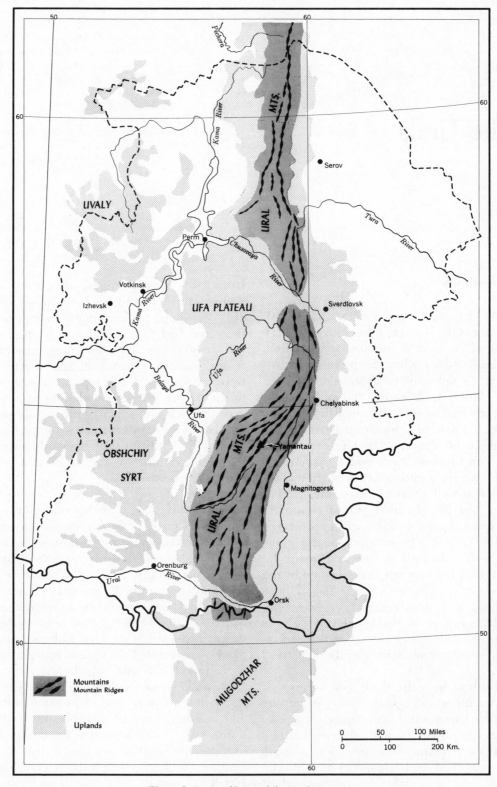

Figure 8–1   Landforms of the Urals Region.

south the upland is known as the Obshchiy Syrt, which means "upland erosion surface."

The Southern Urals, south of 55 degrees latitude, continue to fan out in a series of indistinct ranges that here and there rise to mountainous proportions, among which the highest peak, Yamantau, reaches an elevation of 5375 feet. South of the Russian-Kazakh border the mountains trail out in a broad, eroded, semiarid upland known as the Mugodzhar Mountains, whose highest elevations are little more than 2000 feet.

In all sections the mountains drop off more abruptly on the east than they do on the west. The drainage divide lies along the eastern part of the region and the major rivers drain westward into the Pechora and Volga systems. The Pechora River drains the northern section of the Urals, and the main streams in the center are the Kama, Chusovaya, Belaya, and Ufa rivers. The Ural River drains to the south into the Caspian Sea, and the left-bank tributaries of the Tobol River drain eastward through the Tobol into the Irtysh and finally through the Ob to the Arctic Ocean.

Definition of Region

The Urals extend more than 1200 miles from the Arctic Ocean to the Mugodzhar Mountains, but the discussion here will be limited to the central and southern portions south to the boundary of the Kazakh Republic, the area that presently contains much of the industrial growth and the population. Politically, the following regions are included: in the northwest, Perm Oblast, which includes the Komi-Permyak National Okrug; in the northeast, Sverdlovsk Oblast; in the extreme west, bordering on the Volga Region, the Udmurt A.S.S.R.; and to the south the Bashkir A.S.S.R. Joining the Bashkir Republic on the east is Chelyabinsk Oblast

and in the south is Orenburg Oblast. North of the boundaries of Perm and Sverdlovsk Oblasts the Urals are merely a thin ridge of high rocky, treeless crags which form the boundary between the Komi A.S.S.R. on the west and Tyumen Oblast on the east. This area is practically uninhabited and will not be considered other than as the bounding edge between these two political units.

Settlement and Population

From the time of Ivan the Terrible, when Yermak crossed the Urals with his little band of Cossacks to explore and conquer Siberia, down to the time of the Revolution the Urals were looked on as just about the edge of civilized Russia. But since the Revolution, and particularly since World War II, the Urals have become an integral part of the core of the country, intimately tied industrially to the Central Industrial Region and eastern Ukraine. The Central and Southern Urals in 1967 contained 17,921,000 people, which gives a population density to the area of approximately sixty-one people per square mile. The people in Sverdlovsk and Chelyabinsk Oblasts are more than three fourths urbanized, and in other oblasts urbanization is going on rapidly. The Udmurts and Komi-Permyaks are Finno-Ugrian peoples and the Bashkirs are Turkic. The Udmurts still comprise about one half of the total population of the Udmurt A.S.S.R., but the Bashkirs now account for less than one third of the population of their republic. Russians have been moving into the larger cities and mining areas in great numbers, particularly in the oil fields of the Bashkir A.S.S.R.

Mineral Resources and Industries

The rich mineral deposits of great variety explain the buildup of population and

Figure 8–2   Political units and cities in the Urals.

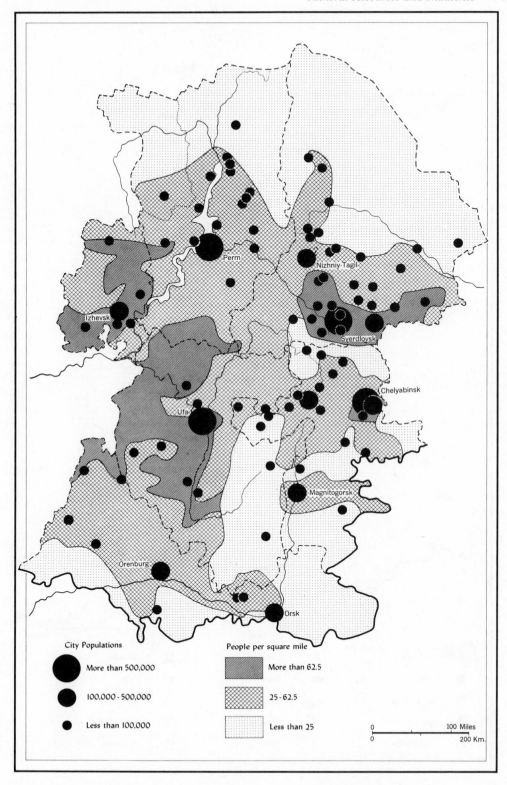

Figure 8–3   Population densities and city sizes. After Cherdantsev.

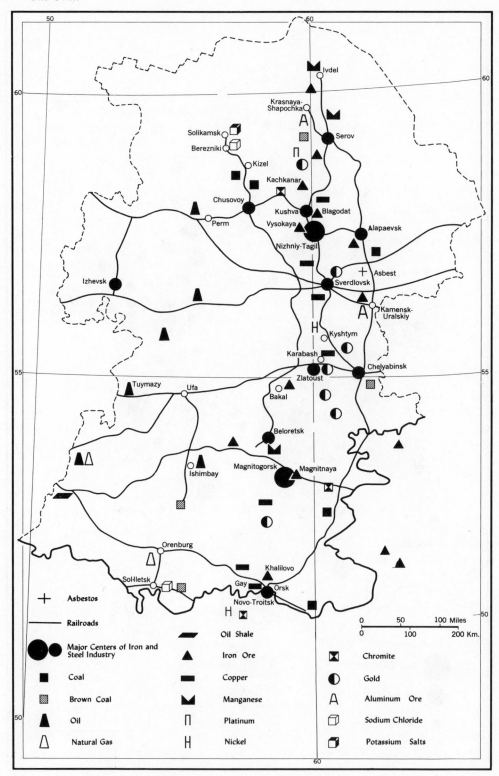

Figure 8–4   Mineral resources, iron and steel industries, and railroads.

industry in the Urals. They range through the entire gamut of resources from ores for various forms of metallurgy to the mineral fuels. There is a saying in Russia that if a schoolboy is asked where a certain mineral is found, if he says "the Urals" he is correct.

The Urals are an old Paleozoic mountain range, corresponding in geological age to the Appalachians in the United States, that have undergone extensive folding, thrust faulting, and some volcanic intrusion on the eastern slopes. The mountains may have been 12,000 feet or more in elevation at one time, but long periods of erosion have worn them down to the bare stumps that remain today. The average elevation at present is little over 1600 feet. In general the Paleozoic sedimentary rocks are still in place on the western slopes, whereas considerable amounts of the underlying intrusive volcanic material is exposed at the surface in the eastern and central portions. Hence a great variety of both sedimentary and igneous rocks are exposed at the surface, and a great potential for mineral deposits exists.

Nonferrous Metals   The Urals have traditionally stood out among mining regions of the Soviet Union because of their nonferrous metals. Copper, zinc, lead, silver, gold, platinum, and asbestos, as well as semiprecious stones, such as emeralds and malachite, have been mined for years in the Urals, and until recently were mined almost exclusively there. Copper and some other metals are now found in greater abundance in other regions. During the last two decades the production of bauxite has become very important in the Urals, surpassing the earlier Tikhvin development in Leningrad Oblast. At present the Urals produce most of the aluminum ore in the country, but other areas are being opened up in Transcaucasia, Middle Asia, Kazakhstan, and Siberia.

Copper ores are scattered up and down the length of the Urals, but the most important copper-smelting centers are two small towns northwest of Chelyabinsk — Karabash and Kyshtym. A newly discovered deposit at Gay, 20 miles north-northwest of Orsk began producing in 1960 and was scheduled to produce more copper than the entire Urals did in 1960. Its reserves are said to be second only to those of Dzhezkazgan in Kazakhstan. The copper content of the ore at Gay is as much as 8 per cent, which is higher than that at Dzhezkazgan. Bauxite is also scattered through the Middle Urals, but the largest deposits and most developed areas are north of Serov in the so-called Krasnaya-Shapochka, or red-cap, mines. Much of this ore is shipped southward to Kamensk-Uralskiy, where the largest alumina smelters in the country are located. Some of the alumina is transformed to aluminum at Kamensk-Uralskiy, but much is now shipped to huge new aluminum plants in Siberia; some is still shipped to Transcaucasia, particularly Yerevan, where large quantities of electricity are available.

Ferrous Metals   Iron mining and smelting has also been a traditional industry in the Urals. It began during the reign of Peter the Great in the first quarter of the eighteenth century when iron was smelted by charcoal furnaces which utilized the local forest resources. Fifty years later, during the reign of Catherine the Great, the Urals experienced a rudimentary industrial revolution and became the primary base for metallurgical industries in the Russian Empire. In fact, during the latter part of the eighteenth century, the Urals were the leading metallurgical area in the world. But within a century, the iron industry of the Urals was eclipsed by rapidly growing new industries in eastern Ukraine, as the larger, richer Krivoy Rog iron mines were opened up and as the fuel emphasis shifted from charcoal to coal. Industrial growth lapsed in the Urals until the 1930s when the Soviets began the construction of the Urals-Kuznetsk Combine based on the newly opened rich iron deposit at Magnitnaya and the large coking coal reserves of the Kuznetsk Basin in Western Siberia.

But the real revitalization of industry in the Urals came with World War II when whole plants were relocated in the area from the western regions. During the war years the Urals once again became the primary metallurgical base as Ukraine was occupied and destroyed by the Germans. By the end of the war it was evident that the higher grade ores were running out at Magnitnaya, which fed the giant blast furnaces of Magnitogorsk, and at Blagodat and Vysokaya on either side of the other large iron-smelting center of Nizhniy Tagil. The old mines at Bakal, which had for years supplied highest grade ore to the fine steel center of Zlatoust, had always been a relatively small operation and could not be expected to take up the slack. For a few years Soviet planners contemplated the gradual diminishing of the iron industry in the Urals and the building of new plants in remote regions of the country.

Then, in the mid 1950s, reports came in from geological survey teams that seemingly inexhaustible supplies of low-grade iron ore lay in widespread deposits in northern Kazakhstan and Western Siberia immediately adjacent to the Urals and within the Urals themselves. Overnight this transformed the picture for the future and plans were changed to develop rapidly large open-pit mines equipped with huge concentrators to process the ore, much of which had no more than 16 per cent iron content, into a pelletized aggregate of iron, manganese, limestone flux, and even coke, to be fed efficiently into the furnaces of the Urals which were to undergo major expansion. It appears that most of these plans are successfully being carried out on schedule and the iron industry of the Urals is assured of a major role for the foreseeable future.

Within the Urals, the outstanding new iron deposits are at Kachkanar northwest of Nizhniy Tagil and in the Orsk-Khalilovo district in the south along the Kazakh border. Outside the region, several large deposits are strung along a north-south line through Tyumen and Kurgan Oblasts in Western Siberia and Kustanay Oblast in Northern Kazakhstan.

Ferrous alloys such as manganese, nickel, tungsten, and chrome are found in some quantities in the Urals, with nickel and chrome being especially abundant in the Orsk-Khalilovo area. The Russians claim that they have found the largest deposit of chrome in the world across the Kazakh border at Chrome-Tau. A new steel industry is being established in this southern extension of the Urals to utilize the iron ore, nickel, and chrome deposits for the production of high-grade nickel-chrome steels.

The last 15 years have witnessed major expansions of iron and steel facilities throughout the Urals. The Kachkanar concentrator began in 1963 to process 16 per cent iron ore containing vanadium and very low percentages of sulfur and phosphorus into naturally alloyed iron-vanadium concentrate for use in two new oxygen converters at Nizhniy Tagil, as well as in the Chelyabinsk and Chusovoy mills. The Kachkanar deposit is now credited with half the iron-ore reserves of the Urals. In 1966 the Number 10 blast furnace went into operation at Magnitogorsk, which completed the expansion program initiated in that plant in 1959 and brought its total capacity to around 12 million tons per year. Much of the iron concentrate for Magnitogorsk now comes from the newly opened Sokolovsk deposit in Kustanay Oblast, Kazakhstan, just to the east. In 1955 some small blast furnaces were put into operation in the new steel center of Novotroitsk to process the naturally alloyed nickel-chrome-iron ore from the nearby Khalilovo mines. These were augmented in 1963 by a large blast furnace which brought the annual pig iron capacity of the plant up to 1 million tons. In 1964 nickel smelting began in the Svetlyy nickel-cobalt smelter, also in Orenburg Oblast. In the northern part of the Urals, the north Peschanka mine began in 1968 to supply the Serov iron and steel industry with 45 per cent magnetite extracted from the deepest iron mines in the Urals, which have shafts extending down to 800 meters. This new deposit, with estimated reserves of 100 million metric tons, is to completely replace ores from the old Pokrovsk-Uralskiy, Rudnichnyy, and Vorontsovka mines in the general vicinity, which are to close down in the early 1970s. These are only some of the largest developments. Many other iron and steel facilities of various kinds have been built in such important centers as Chelyabinsk, Sverdlovsk, Chusovoy, and Zlatoust, as well as in some smaller centers.

Fuels and Power Unfortunately, the Urals are poor in coal. The region contains 0.5 per cent of the country's energy resources and regularly consumes 15 per cent of the country's energy production. The best deposits of coal are in the northwest at Kizel, but even these cannot be used in blast furnaces. Other than the Kizel coals, the Urals are limited to scattered deposits of lignite, generally along the eastern flanks of the mountains and particularly in Chelyabinsk Oblast. Coal must be shipped in for the steel and other metallurgical mills from the Kuznetsk Basin, more than a thousand miles to the east, and from Karaganda, more than 600 miles to the southeast in Kazakhstan. Since the Karaganda coal is high in ash, it cannot be used alone in blast furnaces. Generally, the mix contains one third Karaganda coal and two thirds Kuznetsk coal.

Except for the heavy metallurgical industries, the fuel problems in the Urals may largely be solved by oil and gas, which lie in some abundance on either slope of the Urals, and which can be piped in from the gas fields of Uzbekistan in Middle Asia over 2000 miles to the south and from Berezovo and Tazovskiy in the low Ob Basin of Western Siberia. The most important oil fields in the country lie between the Volga River and the Ural Mountains on the western flanks of the fold. In the Urals Region these fields are concentrated perticularly in the Ufa Plateau in the Bashkir Republic, to the west and south of the capital city of Ufa. The Ishimbay fields lie south of Ufa, and the Tuymazy fields lie to the west of Ufa. Oil pipelines have been constructed from both these areas to the city of Ufa, which is a major refining center. A refining complex has also been built at the twin towns of Ishimbay and Salavat. The Bashkir Republic is the second most important producer of oil in the Soviet Union after the Tatar Republic to the west. Its oil is being piped all the way to Angarsk in Eastern Siberia. Actually oil was first discovered in this western foreland farther north in an operation drilling for potash salts in Perm Oblast. These northern deposits have proved to be minor, however, and production here has not kept up with that in the south. Recently, larger fields have been opened up in the southern part of Perm Oblast.

Only minor gas deposits occur with the oil in the Western Urals, but it appears that major deposits of gas exist on the eastern side of the mountains in the Ob Basin. The gas deposits of the Komi A.S.S.R. near the city of Ukhta have already been mentioned in the discussion of the European North. With the completion of pipelines from the Komi, West Siberian, and Middle Asian fields to the major cities of the Urals, it is planned that more than half of the fuel needs of the Urals will be supplied by oil and gas. This compares to only 12 per cent in 1958 when coal supplied 80 per cent of the fuel needs and wood and peat supplied the rest.

Figure 8–5   The oil fields of Bashkiria. Note the tableland character of the terrain in the Ufa Plateau. Novosti.

The abundant oil and gas supplies are greatly enhancing the generation of electrical power in the Urals. The Urals Region is the biggest power consumer in the R.S.F.S.R., and hydroelectric power in the area is insignificant. About the only hydro plants of any importance are two that have been built on the Kama River during the past 15 years. The first one, the Kama plant, above Perm, was completed in 1956. It has a generating capacity of 504,000 kilowatts. The other, the Votkinsk plant, situated at the town of Chaykovskiy, was completed in 1964; it has a capacity of 1,000,000 kilowatts. A 500,000-volt power line carries electricity from this plant 250 miles east to Sverdlovsk. A third plant, the Lower Kama, is under construction at Naberezhnyye Chelny. It has a planned capacity of 1,080,000 kilowatts. But these amounts are only drops in the bucket, and thermal power stations must supply almost all the electricity used in the Urals. Large thermal plants have operated for many years near most of the big cities, utilizing low-grade coal for fuel. In recent years much larger plants have been constructed to use a combination of Chelyabinsk lignite, fuel oil, and natural gas. Two thermal power plants, each with generating capacities of 3 million kilowatts, were built in the 1960s near Chelyabinsk and Sverdlovsk. They burn lignite from Chelyabinsk and natural gas from Berezovo in Western Siberia. A thermal power station at Troitsk began operations in 1960 using lignite from Chelyabinsk. By 1968 its capacity had grown to 1.5 million kilowatts and its fuel had been switched to coal from Ekibastuz in northeastern Kazakhstan. Another 500,000-kilowatt generator is to be added, which will give it an ultimate capacity of 2 million kilowatts. In 1969 another plant began operations 68 kilometers north of Orsk which eventually is to have a capacity of 2.5 million kilowatts. It is fueled by fuel oil from Orsk in winter and gas from Central Asia in summer. Orsk has a refinery that processes oil brought by pipe from the Emba fields in the North Caspian Lowland.

Twenty-five miles east of Sverdlovsk is the Beloyarskiy atomic power plant which went into operation in 1964 and since has been expanded to a capacity of 300,-000 kilowatts.

Other Minerals   Major deposits of potassium and magnesium salts are located near Solikamsk on the upper Kama River, and potash and other chemical industries based on these salts were established early in Solikamsk and Berezniki. Far to the south, sodium chloride deposits are found near the town of Iletsk in Orenburg Oblast. Sulfur and pyrite deposits, the bases for the all-important constituent of the chemical industries, sulfuric acid, are scattered throughout the central Urals.

The Soviet Union regularly produces about half the world's asbestos, primarily at the mining center of Asbest in the Urals where annual production has recently been expanded to about 1.5 million tons.

With advances in technology some of the rare metals found in this old rock complex of the Urals now are becoming very important. A good illustration are the columbium deposits, which supply the light metal for jet engines.

Agriculture and Lumbering

As might be deduced from the description of the physical landscape, agricultural possibilities in the Urals definitely are limited, and agriculture plays a role in the economy secondary to mining and indus-

Figure 8–6   Threshing wheat in Orenburg Oblast. Novosti.

try. Nevertheless, agriculture has been developed wherever topography, soils, and climate make it feasible. In the Middle Urals the cool humid climate and forest soils have allowed the development of general farming concentrating on flax, dairying, small grains, hay, and livestock raising. To the south this complex gives way to the extensive growing of spring wheat and the grazing of sheep and cattle in the dry steppes of Orenburg and Chelyabinsk Oblasts. In the south the soils are better, but drought becomes a limiting factor. The Bashkir A.S.S.R. has perhaps the best combination of black soils and moderately humid climate. Here sugar beets recently have been introduced into the crop complex.

Lumbering is an important economic activity in the Urals, particularly in the northwest in the upper Kama River Basin. Much lumber is floated down the Kama into the Volga for distribution in the southern steppes, and sawmilling and paper milling are important industries in many of the cities in Perm Oblast and the Udmurt A.S.S.R. Three paper mills on the upper Kama regularly produce about one fourth of the country's paper.

Perm Oblast regularly leads the nation in production of paper, and Sverdlovsk Oblast produces even more lumber than Archangel Oblast, although not as much is of commercial quality. Perm Oblast is generally third in lumber production.

Cities and Industries

With the predominance of mining and the relative unimportance of agriculture, urbanization took place in the Urals almost as soon as settlement began. The cities and industries established by Peter the Great and Catherine the Great in the eighteenth century grew steadily, though slowly, until the Revolution; since the Revolution they have grown much more rapidly, particularly during and since World War II. During the war the Urals had to supply much of the materials that previously had been supplied by Ukraine. Entire factories in the west were evacuated on railway cars and shipped to the Urals to be set up again in new locations. Since the war these industries have not been dismantled; they have continued to grow, and new industries have been added to them. Old metallurgical plants have been reconstructed and modernized at Chusovoy northeast of Perm, at Serov, at Zlatoust, at Beloretsk southeast of Ufa, at Sverdlovsk, and at Izhevsk. The Urals now produce one third of the pig iron of the country and almost one third of the steel.

Machine-building industries have lagged somewhat behind the iron and steel industries; 65 per cent of the rolled steel produced in the Urals is shipped out for use elsewhere. Nevertheless the machine-building industries are second in importance to primary metallurgy.

Third in importance are the chemical industries based on the salts of Solikamsk, the by-products of the large coking industry, and most recently on the by-product gases of oil refining. Such is the petrochemical center at Salavat, which is now producing polyethylene for a variety of plastics industries.

Sverdlovsk   Sverdlovsk, founded in 1722, still is the largest city in the Urals although some others are growing at faster rates. In 1967 Sverdlovsk had a population of 961,000. It is the old city of Yekaterinburg, named after Catherine the Great, because it developed during her reign. In 1924 it was renamed Sverdlovsk after the famous revolutionary. It has often been referred to as the Capital of the Urals, although, of course, the Urals never have been a political unit. Sverdlovsk has some steel industry, but there is more concentration on a variety of machine industries, particularly the electrical machine industries and equipment for mining and metallurgy. It also has

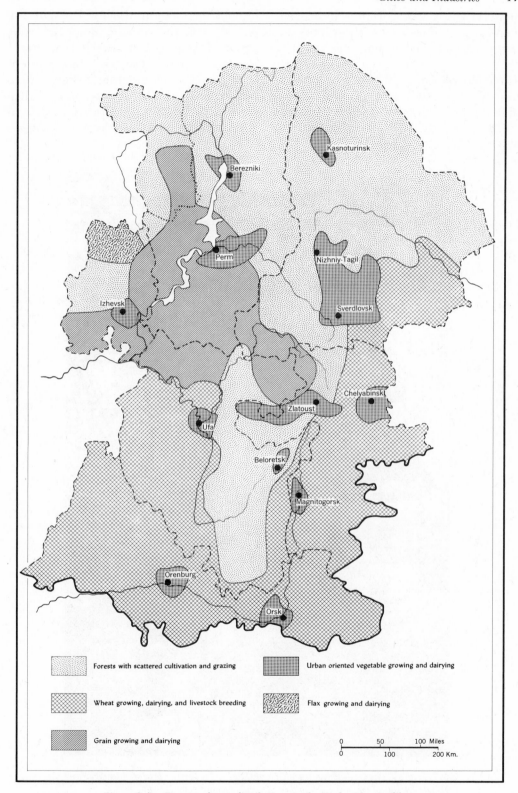

Figure 8–7 Forest and crop distributions in the Urals. After Lyalikov.

chemical and woodworking industries. Seven railroad lines make it the most important rail junction in the Urals.

Chelyabinsk   Second in size is Chelyabinsk, which in 1967 had a population of 836,000. The city was founded as a fortress in 1736. It early labored under an in-

famous reputation during Russian Empire days as the transfer point for exiled peasants awaiting shipment into Siberia. It was largely a barracks town for transients laying over and awaiting assignment to new regions; and, of course, most of them were in a confused, depressed state of mind and they left with very bad impres-

Figure 8–8   The Chelyabinsk tractor plant. Most of the tractors produced in the Soviet Union are still of the heavy caterpillar type with enclosed cabs. Novosti.

sions of the town. With the coming of the Trans-Siberian Railroad in 1890, Chelyabinsk got a great boost in importance and soon replaced Tyumen as the gateway to Siberia.

The city is situated on rather level terrain on the eastern slopes of the Urals, and has more room for expansion than many of the older cities within the Urals. Early in the 1900s Chelyabinsk went through a growth period in which flour milling, based on local wheat growing, was the most significant industry. But today Chelyabinsk has evolved into another important machine-building town like Sverdlovsk. It also has an iron and steel industry and nonferrous metallurgy, as well as chemical industries based on local low-grade coal. It has one of the largest zinc smelters in the country. When the gas pipelines are completed from Uzbekistan and Western Siberia, the chemical industries will expand greatly. Its machine industries range from fine machine tools to aircraft industries, but Chelyabinsk probably still is best known for its tractor works, which, like Volgograd's, are outstanding in the Soviet Union. Much of the agricultural machinery that services Southwestern Siberia and Northern Kazakhstan is built in Chelyabinsk. Recently a large-diameter pipe mill was built to produce pipe for the long gas mains being laid in many regions of the country.

Perm Third in size is the city of Perm, which in 1967 had a population of 796,-000. It was founded in 1780. For a period of about 20 years, up until 1957, the city was renamed Molotov. When it was finally renamed Perm again, geologists around the world breathed a sigh of relief, since it was from this region that the Permian geological period derived its name. Perm has shared in the general growth of population and industry in the Urals and serves as the major center for the northwestern portion of the industrial region in the Kama River area. It has some metallurgy,

Figure 8–9   Oil refinery at Ufa. Novosti.

some oil refining, chemicals, machine industries, and so forth.

Ufa Fourth in size is Ufa, the capital of the Bashkir Republic, with a population of 704,000. As has been mentioned, Ufa serves as the refining center for the important oil fields in the region, and it is also an important city for machine building.

Nizhniy Tagil Fifth in size is the old city of Nizhniy Tagil, which under the Soviets has been revitalized into one of the two major iron and steel centers in the Urals. In 1967 Nizhniy Tagil had a population of 377,000.

Izhevsk Sixth in size is Izhevsk, the capital of the Udmurt Republic, with a population of 376,000. Its foremost industry is the iron and steel industry, but such things as machine building and food industries are important.

Magnitogorsk Seventh in size is Magnitogorsk, which is the second of the two most important iron and steel centers in the Urals. Magnitogorsk now has a population of 357,000, which makes it somewhat smaller than Nizhniy Tagil. Magnitogorsk did not exist at all before 1931, however. It was established next to Magnitnaya Gora, the important iron deposit in the hill just outside of town, as part of the widely publicized Urals-Kuznetsk Combine to utilize the iron ore in the Magnitogorsk area and the coal in the Kuznetsk Basin 1200 miles to the east. Iron and steel mills were built at both ends so that railroad cars could carry coal westward and iron ore eastward. As usual, the most important steel mills were built at the end closest to the markets, in this case Magnitogorsk. By 1939 Magnitogorsk had developed into one of the major metallurgical centers in the U.S.S.R.

During this short 8-year period the town grew like Topsy with no planning whatsoever. Iron and steel mills were erected and laborers were shipped into the area with no living accommodations provided for them. People were living in caves and lean-tos strung without pattern. The citizens of Magnitogorsk are still trying to eliminate the chaos of the past and rebuild the city in a rectangular pattern. The old city is situated on the east side of the Ural River. A new workers' settlement has been established on the west side of the river and most of the people have moved across the river into apartment houses there.

Southeast of the old city a hill of iron ore rises 500 feet above the river to an elevation of about 2000 feet. The steel plant stretches about 3.5 miles between the "magnet mountain" and the river. Ten coke ovens all in a row belch black smoke across the barren landscape as they convert coal to coke for the blast and open-hearth furnaces. A complete chemical complex makes use of the by-product coking gases and tars. The pig iron from the furnaces goes directly as hot metal to the open-hearth shops, where it is joined by scrap metal to make steel ingots. Rolling mills turn out sheet steel for such large

metal-fabricating centers as Chelyabinsk 150 miles to the northeast. Magnitogorsk steel is shipped all over the country and even abroad, since little metal fabrication is done in the city itself.

Until recently, practically all of the iron ore for the plant came from the neighboring magnet mountain. This mining activity has left two enormous pits, one on either side of the hill. The west pit is 7600 feet long, 7000 feet wide, and 1060 feet deep. The east pit is 6400 feet long and 2500 feet wide. The east pit is cut into the side of the hill so that it is level with the terrain on the east and rises to a 300-foot cliff against the hill on the west.

The metallurgical plants use more water than the cities of Moscow and Leningrad combined. This is a problem of the first magnitude in this dryish region. A dam across the small Ural River forms a reservoir just outside of town which provides barely enough water for industrial and domestic use. Little is left over for the maintenance of lawns and gardens. Magnitogorsk is not as pleasant a place to live as are most of the cities farther north in the more humid part of the Urals.

Magnitogorsk and Nizhniy Tagil today are nearly equal in size and are approximately equal in importance in ferrous metallurgy. They are by far the two most outstanding iron and steel centers in the Urals. Although such larger cities as Sverdlovsk and Chelyabinsk also have steel industries, steel does not dominate the scene as it does in Magnitogorsk and Nizhniy Tagil.

Orenburg Eighth in size is Orenburg, in the steppes to the southwest, with a population of 326,000. Orenburg grew as one of a series of Russian fortifications against the steppe peoples to the southeast, and eventually became the center of a rather important agricultural region. After the successful polar flight from Moscow to Los Angeles by Chkalov and his

Figure 8–10   Steel smelting at Magnitogorsk. Novosti.

companions in 1938, Orenburg was re-named Chkalov. However, in 1957, when several towns reverted to their pre-Revolutionary names, Chkalov again became Orenburg. Orenburg serves simply as the center of an important agricultural area in the dry steppes along the Southern Urals, where the main economy is spring-wheat growing and sheep and horse raising.

Orsk Ninth in size is Orsk with a population of 215,000. It also lies in the steppe, to the east of Orenburg, and originally was primarily a center of a farming area. With the development of the Orsk-Khalilovo metallurgical district, Orsk promises to grow rapidly into an industrial city. For a number of years it has been the northern terminus of an oil pipeline from the Emba oil fields in the North Caspian Lowland. It refines oil for distribution to the agricultural areas of Southwestern Siberia and Northern Kazakhstan. A new city, Novotroitsk, has been built in the vicinity of Orsk to serve as the iron and steel center for this important metallurgical region. Its integrated iron and steel plant specializes in high-grade chrome and nickel steels. A huge thermal power plant with a capacity of 2,500,000 kilowatts is being built in the vicinity to be fueled in winter by fuel oil from the refinery in Orsk and in summer by natural gas from Bukhara in Middle Asia.

Other Cities Tenth in size is the old city of Zlatoust, with a population of 178,000. Zlatoust is the site of one of the early steel mills in the Urals, utilizing the high-grade iron ore from the Bakal mines. It still specializes in high-grade steel, and this is the major industry in the town. Its steel compares to high-grade Swedish steels. About the same size as Zlatoust is Kopeysk, 166,000, a suburb of Chelyabinsk. Kamensk-Uralskiy comes next with a population of 161,000. It already has been mentioned as the largest center of alumina production in the Soviet Union.

One other industrial area that should be mentioned is the Berezniki-Solikamsk area on the upper Kama River north of Perm. Berezniki in 1967 had a population of 134,000. The two towns are heavily concentrated on chemical industries, based on the potash and magnesium salts in the Solikamsk area. This is the oldest developed area of potash salts in the country and still is the major producer, although it is being rivaled by Soligorsk in Belorussia.

River Navigation

With the building of dams and reservoirs on the Kama River in conjunction with the great Volga scheme, towns such as Perm and Berezniki are serving important port functions as well as industrial functions. These navigation functions may be greatly enhanced in the future if the proposed Vychegda-Pechora reservoir and canal system is constructed to bring Vychegda and Pechora River water into the Kama.

Prospects

The Urals are the third most important industrial area in the country and the second most important region of primary industry. No longer are they located on the eastern fringe of Russian civilization. They are an integral part of the heart of the country. Recent discoveries of large deposits of low-grade iron ore and associated metals seem to assure a continued rapid industrialization and urbanization of the area. Although adequate coal supplies will remain a problem, oil and gas in great abundance will alleviate the fuel situation except for some of the metallurgical industries. If the Vychegda-Pechora Diversion Project is ever constructed, Vorkuta coal can be brought to the area very cheaply by an all-water route. This will considerably improve the economic picture of the region, which is already quite bright. Undoubtedly, the Urals will continue to be a major supplier of metals to the country, and as population grows in the eastern regions the Urals will take on a more rounded economy.

Reading List

Clark, M. Gardner, "Magnitogorsk: A Soviet Iron and Steel Plant in the Southern Urals," in Thoman, Richard S. and Patton, Donald J., *Focus on Geographic Activity*, McGraw-Hill, New York, 1964, pp. 128–134.

Komar, I. V., *Ural; ekonomiko-geograficheskaya kharakteristika*, Moscow, 1959, 366 pp. (in Russian).

Olenev, A. M., *Ural i Novaya Zemlya: Ocherk prirody* (The Urals and Novaya Zemlya: Natural Conditions), Izdatelstvo mysl, Moscow, 1965, 216 pp. (in Russian).

Stepanov, P. N., *Ural,* Moscow, 1957, 163 pp. (in Russian).

Varlamov, V. S., "On the Economic Links of the Industry of Orenburg," *Soviet Geography: Review and Translation,* March 1961, pp. 54–60.

———, "The Economic-Geographic Situation of Orenburg," *Soviet Geography: Review and Translation,* June 1961, pp. 14–20.

The Caucasus and the North Caucasian Foreland

Region	Area (sq mile)	Population	People (sq mile)	% Urban
Within the R.S.F.S.R.				
Krasnodar Kray	32,700	4,273,000	131	48
Adyge A.O.	1,700	366,000	215	40
Stavropol Kray	31,400	2,177,000	69	39
Karachay-Cherkess A.O.	5,500	330,000	60	33
Kabardino-Balkar A.S.S.R.	4,900	530,000	108	44
North Osetian A.S.S.R.	3,100	518,000	167	63
Chechen-Ingush A.S.S.R.	7,600	1,033,000	136	40
Dagestan A.S.S.R.	19,700	1,361,000	69	35
Georgian S.S.R.	27,200	4,611,000	170	48
Abkhaz A.S.S.R.	3,400	471,000	139	42
Adzhar A.S.S.R.	1,200	301,000	251	48
South Osetian A.O.	1,500	102,000	68	34
Armenian S.S.R.	11,600	2,253,000	194	56
Azerbaydzhanian S.S.R.	33,800	4,802,000	142	51
Nakhichevan A.S.S.R.	2,100	189,000	90	25
Nagorno-Karabakh A.O.	1,700	149,000	88	38
Total	172,000	21,558,000		

9

The Caucasus and the North Caucasian Foreland

In the latter part of the eighteenth century, under the reign of Catherine the Great, when advances were being made all along the Black Sea Coast and toward the west against the Turks, the Austrians, and the Poles, a simultaneous drive was going to the southeast between the Black and Caspian Seas toward the Caucasus. Rostov-on-the-Don was founded in 1761 as an outpost against the Turks, and in 1794 a major settlement was established at Yekaterinodar, the modern Krasnodar. Far to the southeast, in 1784, a fort was set up at Vladikavkaz, the modern Ordzhonikidze. After the turn of the century the Russians moved into Transcaucasia primarily by invitation and default. In 1801 Alexander the First, who was becoming looked on as the "Savior of Europe" because of his resistance against Napoleon, was invited by the Christian Georgian prince to protect the area from the Moslem Persian Shah. Thus the Russian armies crossed the Caucasus and gained a foothold in Tbilisi, the capital city of Georgia, from whence they moved to Baku in 1806 and to Yerevan in 1828. Here Russia met the growing influence of the British in Persia, and a stalemate resulted, which with minor boundary changes, remains to this day.

Thus by 1828 the Russian Empire had acquired an extensive chunk of land peopled largely by non-Russian groups who had national traditions in the local area of over 2000 years duration. The Georgians and Armenians seldom have enjoyed the status of independent countries, but they are both proud old nationality groups who consider themselves culturally ahead of the Russians, the Turks, and the Persians, the three great powers that have surrounded them from time immemorial. Since the Revolution the Transcaucasians have voiced their desires strongly and have played significant roles in national political maneuvering. During the chaotic period of the Civil War following the Revolution, each of the major nationality groups set up independent governments. These governments ultimately were crushed by the Bolsheviks, and the entire Transcaucasian area was included in the newly constituted Soviet Union on December 30, 1922 as the Transcaucasian Soviet Federated Socialist Republic. Agitation for national recognition continued, however, and when the Soviet Union was reconstituted in 1936 each of the three major nationality groups was accorded union republic political status. Thus an area containing approximately 2 per cent of the territory and 8 per cent of

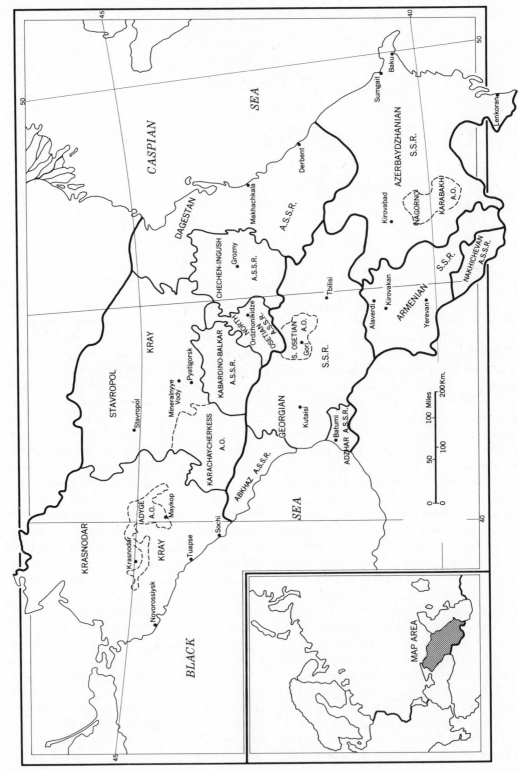

Figure 9–1 The Caucasus.

the total population of the U.S.S.R. accounts for three of the fifteen union republics.

Population

Ethnographically the Caucasus are extremely complex; many small nationality groups have occupied separate valleys and basins for centuries without significant contact with one another or with the outside world. Each of these ethnological groups has maintained a more or less distinct identity, and, under the Soviet policy to recognize nationality groups, has been accorded some sort of political status. Although several of the nationality groups on the north slopes of the Caucasus lost their political identities during World War II as punishment allegedly for collaborating with the Germans, in 1957 the political units were reconstituted almost exactly as they had been before the war. Hence, once again the Caucasus are a crazy quilt of union republics, autonomous republics, and autonomous oblasts.

To simplify a bit, the area north of the crest of the Great Caucasus is essentially a Russian area, and it lies within the Russian Republic. But within it exist several non-Russian nationality groups who have been given political recognition either as autonomous oblasts within krays or as autonomous republics. Many of these are nestled in the valleys on the northern slopes of the Great Caucasus. Besides there are many small groups in the mountains whose numbers have not warranted separate political categories. In Dagestan, for instance, there are many small groups of peoples who differ from one another, but whose numbers individually do not warrant separate political status. They have been lumped together simply as "Dagestani peoples" and have been placed within the Dagestan A.S.S.R.

South of the Great Caucasus, three large nationality groups have been given union republic status: the Georgians, the Armenians, and the Azerbaydzhanians. Again, within these republics live minority groups who differ from the majority groups enough to warrant separate political identity. Within the Georgian Republic lie the Abkhaz A.S.S.R., the Adzhar A.S.S.R., and the South Osetian Autonomous Oblast. And under the jurisdiction of the Azerbaydzhan S.S.R. are the Nagorno-Karabakh Autonomous Oblast and the Nakhichevan A.S.S.R. The Nakhichevan A.S.S.R. is an isolated segment of land surrounded by the Armenian S.S.R. and Iran, but it is attached politically to the Azerbaydzhan Republic because it is peopled primarily by Azerbaydzhanians and because there are adequate communication and transportation lines between it and the parent republic. The Nagorno-Karabakh Autonomous Oblast, however, which lies within Azerbaydzhan territory and is peopled by Armenians, is attached politically to the Azerbaydzhan Republic because it has no good connections with the Armenian Republic. It is the highest part of the Armenian Plateau, which has been deeply dissected by stream canyons, and transportation routes out of the area are tortuous.

In toto, the North Caucasian Foreland has a population of approximately 9,892,000 and Transcaucasia a population of about 11,666,000. Densities of population vary widely from place to place, because of topographic and climatic conditions, from around seventy per square mile in Dagestan to almost two hundred per square mile in Armenia. In the high mountains, of course, population is sparse or absent, whereas the humid lowlands of western Georgia in places contain three hundred to four hundred people per square mile. North of the Great Caucasus the population is predominantly Russian, whereas south of the Caucasus the population is primarily non-Russian. Russians account for only 10 per cent of the total population of Georgia, 14 per cent of Azerbaydzhan, and 3 per cent of Armenia. (Table 9–1)

Table 9–1   Numbers of People by Nationality by Union Republic, 1959

	Number of People	Per Cent of Total
Georgia SSR	4,044,000	100.0
Georgian	2,601,000	64.3
Osetian	141,000	3.5
Abkhazian	63,000	1.6
Armenian	443,000	11.0
Russian	408,000	10.1
Azerbaydzhanian	154,000	3.8
Greek	73,000	1.8
Ukrainian	52,000	1.3
Jew	52,000	1.3
Kurd	16,000	0.4
Armenia SSR	1,763,000	100.0
Armenian	1,552,000	88.0
Azerbaydzhanian	108,000	6.1
Russian	56,000	3.2
Kurd	26,000	1.5
Azerbaydzhan SSR	3,698,000	100.0
Azerbaydzhanian	2,494,000	67.5
Russian	501,000	13.6
Armenian	442,000	12.0
Lezghian	98,000	2.7

Source: Narodnoe khozyaystvo SSSR v 1959 godu, pp. 16–20.

Population is increasing rapidly throughout the region because of high birth rates and in-migration. Between 1959 and 1967 the population of the entire region increased by 21 per cent and that of Azerbaydzhan by 30 per cent.

Physical Characteristics and Agriculture

The Caucasus Mountains are a high, continuous range of young, rugged mountains of Tertiary age, which have been folded along a west, northwest-east, southeast axis by pressures from the north and the south. Basically they are two folds separated by a synclinal valley. But the simple line of folding has been compli-

cated by faulting and outbreaks of vulcanism and also by a transverse axis of folding, which runs roughly south to north through the west-central portion of the area. The higher northern fold, the Great Caucasus, stands out clearly in its overall form; rising in a broad bulge from the North Caucasian Foreland, it plunges steeply to the synclinal valley on the south. But the Lesser Caucasus south of the synclinal valley are harder to distinguish because they merge with portions of a general upland, the Armenian Plateau, in the southern part of Armenia and adjacent Turkey and Iran. The Surami Range follows the north-south axis of folding through eastern Georgia across the Lesser Caucasus and the synclinal valley and divides the valley into two separate basins facing west and east on the Black and Caspian Seas. North of the Great Caucasus the north-south axis of folding can be picked up again in a broad, gentle upwarp in the center of the North Caucasian Foreland.

On either flank of the Great Caucasus, and to some extent in the Lesser Caucasus too, a broad belt of Cretaceous and Jurassic limestones has been conducive to the formation of extensive karst topography honeycombed by innumerable caves and sinks. Within the last few years more than two hundred fifty caverns have been explored in Georgia, some of which rank among the leading caverns of the world. Some of the caves contain ice and were used as early as the twelfth century by the Georgian khans for refrigerating wines. Large underground streams have been tapped for domestic water supplies in such areas as Pyatigorsk and Ordzhonikidze on the northern slopes of the Great Caucasus. Abkhazia, in northwestern Georgia, is most noted for its caves and karst. The Black Sea coast between Novorossiysk and Sochi is full of sea caves and coves, from which pirates have preyed on Black Sea shipping for centuries. Caves also exist to some extent in the volcanic basalt and tuff

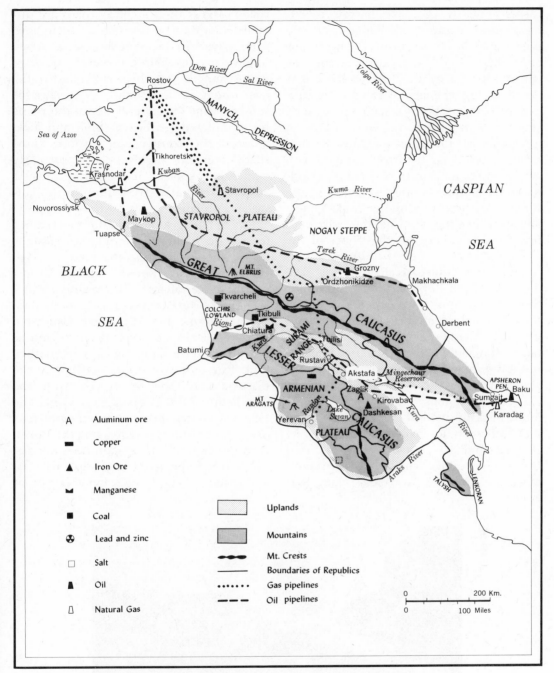

Figure 9–2   Landforms and minerals in the Caucasus.

of the Armenian Plateau in southern Georgia and Armenia. Here, in addition to natural caves, many enclosures have been hollowed out by man for purposes of shelter, military protection, and worship.

The high range of the Great Caucasus extends unbroken for a distance of more than 500 miles from the northeastern shore of the Black Sea to the Apsheron Peninsula jutting into the Caspian and forms a nearly complete barrier to climatic and cultural exchange between north and south. It protects the basins and valleys of the Transcaucasus from the wintry blasts of cold air that sweep across the flat, sloping plain of the North Caucasian Foreland. It induces an atmospheric stagnation in all but the western part of Transcaucasia that causes a generally subsiding mass of air, which, combined with strong insolation, produces a dryish landscape on all but the highest slopes of the mountains. Since the higher peaks generally are above the tree line, there are very few trees anywhere on the slopes of the Great Caucasus east of Mt. Elbrus.

The only railroads connecting the Transcaucasian Republics with the rest of the Soviet Union skirt either end of the Caucasus along the shores of the Black and Caspian Seas. Three roads cross the mountains, all in close proximity to one another in the Georgian Republic; they are known respectively as the Georgian, Sukhumi, and Osetian military highways. Built early after the acquisition of the Transcaucasian areas, these roads had to be guarded by Russian military personnel from wild bands of tribesmen who lived in the mountains and pillaged travelers along the roads. Today these military roads are unguarded and the greater part of them have been paved in two-lane highways. They follow tortuous routes, however, in many places hanging on sheer cliffs, and traffic over them is very light. Avalanches of snow in winter frequently block the roads for prolonged periods of time and have induced the construction of long snow sheds over the highways at particularly vulnerable spots. Hence Transcaucasia is quite separated from the North Caucasian Foreland.

Russian geographers, in their reluctance to violate political boundaries, usually divide this area along the boundary between the Russian Republic and the Transcaucasian Republics, which mainly follows the crest of the Great Caucasus. Many Russian textbooks treat the North Caucasian Foreland with the Lower Don Region as one unit and the Transcaucasus as another unit. But as has been pointed out in the discussion of the Povolzhye, with the completion of the Volga-Don Canal the Lower Don has become an integral part of the navigational system along the Volga. Also the Lower Don Region does not significantly differ from the adjacent area along the Volga; physically it is just as

Figure 9–3   The Georgian Military Highway. Photograph by the author.

closely related to the Volga area as it is to the North Caucasian area. Western Rostov Oblast has been treated with Ukraine because of its common economic ties with the Donets Basin.

Historically the North Caucasian Foreland has been considered an integral part of the Caucasus Region because the entry into the two areas was a continuous one through the northern plain and eventually across the mountains into the southern valleys. The area thus came into the Russian Empire somewhat as a unit. Physically and agriculturally, however, the northern plain is so different from the mountains and valleys to the south that the region will be discussed in two parts.

The North Caucasian Foreland The flat, dryish plain of the Lower Don approaches sea level east of the Sea of Azov in an east-west trough known as the Manych Depression that served as a spillway during Pleistocene times from an enlarged Caspian Sea to the head of the Sea of Azov. From the Manych Depression southward the plain rises gently toward the foothills of the Great Caucasus in what is known as the North Caucasian Foreland. A broad warping of small vertical magnitude along the north-south axis of folding has bulged the southcentral portion of the sedimentary strata a few hundred feet higher than the plain to the east or the west to form what is known as the Stavropol Plateau. This upwarp has undergone a little more stream erosion and is a little hillier than are other parts of the plain. The slight increase in the roughness of the topography does not effect a change in agriculture, however, as much as does the decrease in moisture from west to east.

The entire plain is strongly influenced by continental air masses which produce droughty conditions and seasonal extremes in temperature. During much of the winter air circulates across the region from east to west around the southwestern extremity of the Siberian high-pressure cell. January temperatures average between 20 and 30°F, and a strong push of the Siberian air westward can plunge temperatures on individual nights to −15°F and send cold air spilling over the lower western portion of the Great Caucasus to bring freezing conditions to the otherwise mild seacoast around Novorossiysk. Such "bora wind" conditions frequently whip up the waves of the Black Sea to produce an ice spray over the piers, moorings, and buildings along the beach.

Cyclonic storms, active over the Black Sea during the winter, bring considerable precipitation to the western part of the plain. The northern slopes of the mountains in Krasnodar Kray may receive as much as 25 feet of snow. These storms generally follow a northeasterly course across Krasnodar Kray and Rostov Oblast and have little effect on the plain east of the Stavropol Plateau.

During the summer there is generally a sluggish flow of air across the region from north to south around the eastern end of the Atlantic High. Temperatures average between 65 and 70°F during July, but maximum temperatures over 100°F are experienced. Surface heating, combined with influxes of moisture from the Black Sea, set off frequent thundershowers, which bring a summer maximum of rainfall to the plain. June typically is the rainiest month of the year. The thundershowers are most active in the western part of the plain, but their occurrence does not decrease so sharply eastward as does the occurrence of cyclones during the winter. Hence the summer maximum is most pronounced in the east, although the western part of the plain receives more rainfall than the east during both halves of the year. The precipitation in the west is more evenly distributed throughout the year, and along the immediate Black Sea coast the influence of the winter cyclones becomes predominant and a winter maximum of precipitation is experienced.

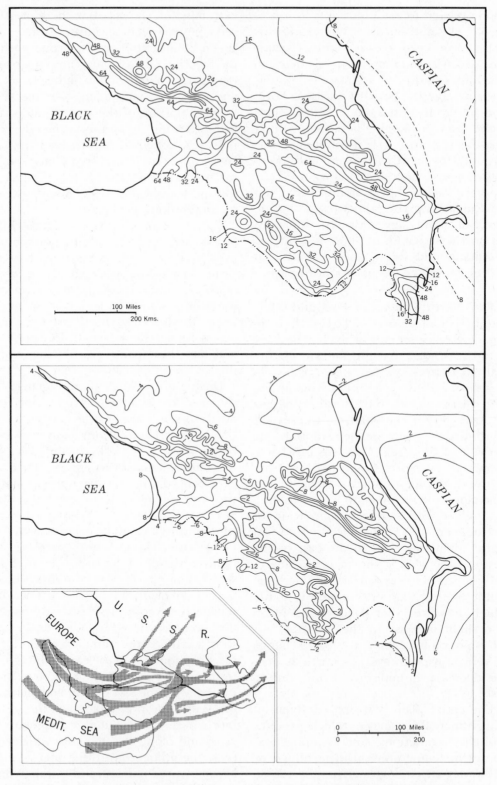

Figure 9–4   Upper map: Annual precipitation in inches. Lower map: Average January temperatures in degrees centigrade. Inset: Cyclone trajectories affecting the Caucasus. From Klimat SSSR, Kavkaz.

Annual precipitation in the west averages between 20 and 25 inches; it decreases steadily northeastward to between 10 and 15 inches in northern Dagestan. Thus the west is subhumid and the east is semiarid. Such climatic conditions have been conducive to the development of a grass and desert shrub type of natural vegetation which has made for the development of chernozem soils in the west and steppe and desert soils in the east. These soils are all quite fertile and except where they are saline, are adaptable to agriculture as long as the moisture is sufficient. Throughout Krasnodar Kray the rainfall normally is sufficient for crop growth of a wide variety without irrigation, but in the eastern portion of the plain cultivation without irrigation is impossible. Streams heading in the snow fields of the Caucasus afford some opportunity for irrigation. Much of the development so far has been on the Middle Terek and its tributaries between Ordzhonikidze and Pyatigorsk and on the Lower Terek where it has formed an extensive delta on the northwestern shore of the Caspian. Many other canals are proposed for the intervening areas, including a long canal taking water from the upper part of the Kuban River northwestward all the way to the eastern part of the Sea of Azov.

The two major streams on the plain head in the central portion of the northern slopes of the Great Caucasus and flow out in either direction to the Black and Caspian Seas. Flowing northwestward into the Sea of Azov is the Kuban River, whose drainage basin is practically coextensive with Krasnodar Kray. This region is often referred to simply as the Kuban. With its rich, black soils and its relatively warm, humid summers, the Kuban rivals central Ukraine in agricultural possibilities. In fact, with the enthusiasm generated by Khrushchev's corn-planting program since 1955, the chairman of the Economic Council of Krasnodar Kray has posed a contest with Iowa in corn production. At present Krasnodar Kray does not compare to Iowa in corn production, and it probably never will closely rival it; the summers average about 5°F cooler and the annual precipitation 5 to 10 inches less than in Iowa. The Kuban suffers from frequent incursions of the dry "sukhovey" winds which are very desiccating to a crop such as corn that reaches its most rapid stage of succulent growth in midsummer. The region is much more suited to its traditional crops, wheat and sunflowers.

The Kuban is the eastern node of the sunflower belt which wraps around the head of the Sea of Azov and extends into eastern Ukraine. In addition both winter and spring wheat are grown, and sugar beets are being introduced into the area in ever-increasing quantities. The Kuban is now the second most important sugar beet-growing area in the Soviet Union, after the main belt in Ukraine and the Central Black Earth Region. The cultivated area of sugar beets in the Kuban multiplied six times from 1957 to 1965. Rice is grown in the swampy delta of the Kuban River where it empties into Sea of Azov.

The Terek River flows eastward into the Caspian through a semiarid region with somewhat poorer soils than those in the Kuban area. Considerable irrigation agriculture is carried on along the Terek, but much of the region is a dry grazing land. North of the Terek the entire area, known as the Nogay Steppe is given over to extensive grazing of sheep and camels. A canal has been proposed to link the Terek and Kuma Rivers and thereby provide irrigation water to portions of this area.

Transcaucasia   The plain extends southward in a long, sweeping upslope and then ends abruptly against the base of the Great Caucasus, whose glaciated volcanic peaks tower to heights above 17,-000 feet. Mount Elbrus, the highest of the peaks, reaches an elevation of 18,481 feet.

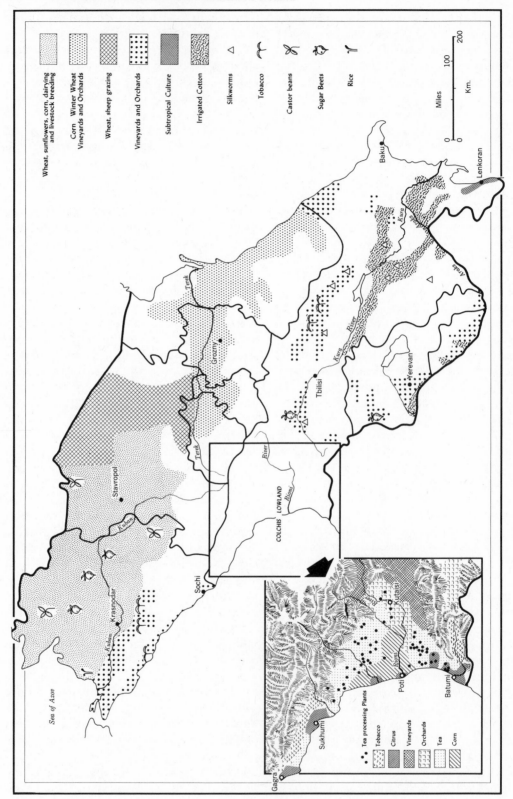

Figure 9–5   Crop distributions in the Caucasus. After Cherdantsev and Lyalikov.

Its horn-like crest is surrounded by mountain glaciers nestled in cirques that lead down to deep U-shaped valleys spotted here and there by glacial tarns. The steep southern slopes of the Great Caucasus frown down on the Kura-Rioni Syncline beyond which lie the Lesser Caucasus and the Armenian Plateau.

The Lesser Caucasus, which do not reach elevations over 8000 feet, in many places merge imperceptibly with the Armenian Plateau to the south, a stream-dissected upland that lies between 3000 and 7000 feet in elevation. Much of the material making up the plateau is of volcanic origin, and the plateau is surmounted here and there by much higher, more recent volcanic cones. The highest of these cones in the Soviet Union is Mt. Aragats, west of Yerevan, which has an elevation of 13,500 feet. These cones get higher across the border in Turkey where Mt. Ararat reaches an elevation of 16,945 feet. Mount Ararat is about 40 miles south of Yerevan, but in the dry crystal-clear air it is plainly visible from Yerevan on days when fresh air sweeps into the basin and cleans out the usual dusty haze. These volcanic peaks reach well above the perpetual frost line, so that they are snow capped year round and lend a grandeur to the scenery of the area.

The low, transverse Surami Range along the north-south axis of folding divides the Kura-Rioni Syncline into two separate basins drained to the east by the Kura River and to the west by the Rioni. These two low-lying alluvial plains at either end of the syncline are the only extensive areas of flat land in Transcaucasia. The Colchis Lowland, as the western basin is known, is a low, swampy, partially filled in extension of the eastern end of the Black Sea. Waves have built a sand bar across the mouth of the Rioni River that has forced the stream to dump its sediment in the embayment. Thus the valley floor is very flat, and drainage is exceedingly poor. Summers here are hot, averaging

between 75 and 80°F, and the winters are mild, with only occasional frosts. Cyclonic storms from the Black Sea in the winter bring heavy rains to the area, and thunderstorms develop in the warm, moist air of the basin in summer. These storms combined make this the most excessively humid area in the entire country. Much of the basin receives more than 60 inches of rain annually, and Batumi, in the foothills to the southwest, receives 93 inches. Throughout most of the basin there is a little more rain in summer than winter, but Batumi records a fairly pronounced winter maximum.

The humid subtropical climate allows the area to specialize in crops that are exotic to the rest of the Soviet Union. Tea and citrus are the most important crops, and they are raised almost exclusively here. They are found primarily on the slopes of the foothills surrounding the basin where they can benefit from both air and soil drainage. (Tables 9–2 and 9–3 and Fig. 9–5) The floor of the lowland is generally too frosty in winter and too poorly drained to be planted to such sensitive crops. Thus, although western Georgia is known primarily for its subtropical produce, such crops occupy no more than 8 per cent of the arable land, whereas corn alone occupies about 40 per cent, generally in lowlands and river

Table 9–2 Major Subtropical Crops in Western Georgia, by Regions, in Percentages of Total Planted Area

Area	Tea	Citrus	Tung
Zugdidi foothills	31.7	5.9	28.9
Southern foothills	21.1	17.8	20.9
Abkhazia	21.2	33.7	27.7
Interior	11.6	0.1	0.9
Adzharia	9.4	39.7	19.4
Colchis Lowland	5.0	2.8	2.2

Source: Adapted from Jensen, *Soviet Subtropical Agriculture,* p. 191.

Table 9–3   Tea Acreages in Georgia, by Regions, 1960, in Percentages of Total

Area	Per Cent of Total
Zugdidi foothills	32.6
Southern foothills	21.8
Abkhazia	17.0
Interior	12.3
Adzharia	11.2
Colchis Lowland	5.1

Source: Bone, *Soviet Tea Cultivation*, p. 166.

valleys where fairly good alluvial soils exist but where poor drainage conditions and frost hazards rule out subtropical trees and shrubs. Another limiting factor are the desiccating foehn winds that blow from east to west across the Surami Range and down the western slope into the Colchis Lowland, which occur as fre-

quently as 114 days per year at Kutaisi. These are primarily a winter and spring phenomenon, but occasionally they blow in summer, and may reach hurricane velocity of 60 meters per second. Under such conditions thick clouds of dust descend upon the area. The dry, hot air burns the leaves on the trees, and the high velocity of the wind strips leaves from the tea bushes and leaves and fruit from the citrus trees. Many shelter belts 40 to 50 feet high have been planted in the region in an attempt to ameliorate the effects of these winds, but much damage is still sustained from them in localized areas where the terrain is such that the air flow is concentrated.

Tea is the national drink in the Soviet Union. In old Russia, afternoon tea pouring was as much of a ceremony as it is in England. Also, the non-Russian nationality groups of the Soviet Middle East are traditional tea drinkers. Therefore the Soviets

Figure 9–6   Tangerine picking in Georgia. Novosti.

Figure 9–7   Mechanized tea picking in Georgia. Novosti.

have been very desirous to expand tea production as much as possible in spite of a rather limited area that is suitable for tea growing. For commercially worthwhile production, tea requires a minimum of about 50 inches of rain per year, well distributed through the year, with no month getting less than about 2 inches. During the bearing season, temperatures less than 55°F may damage the leaves and halt the growth of new leaves; during the dormant season temperatures below 7°F may kill the bush. The well-drained lateritic soils on the foothills immediately to the north and south of the swampy floor of the Colchis Lowland best satisfy these growing requirements, and contain more than 50 per cent of all the tea planting in the Soviet Union. The Zugdidi foothills on the northern side of the lowland contain more than 30 per cent of the tea plantings, and the southern foothills more than 20

per cent. (Table 9–3) The next most important region is the Abkhaz A.S.S.R. which is a northern continuation of the Zugdidi foothills, and plantings here are continued northward along the steep coast of Krasnodar Kray in the Russian Republic. The further north one proceeds, however, the greater the frost hazard and the more severe the erosion problem, since the Caucasus crowd the shoreline in this area and the slopes plunge very steeply down to the sea. In the vicinity of Sochi the slopes are so steep that the tea plantations must be terraced. In this area, frosts limit plantings to below 1000 feet elevation. South of the Colchis Lowland, as winter temperatures become progressively milder, tea is often crowded out by citrus, which generally has less tolerance to frost than tea does. Thus in Adzharia, which has the highest yields of tea in the Soviet Union (Table 9–4), tea occupies only 9.4

Table 9–4   Average Yields of Tea Leaves, 1958, in Pounds per Acre

Area	Pounds per Acre
Georgia S.S.R.	2,251
Adzharia (1957)	3,930
Abkhazia	2,487
Azerbaydzhan S.S.R.	506
Krasnodar Kray	400

Source: Bone, *Soviet Tea Cultivation,* p. 171.

per cent of the cultivated area, whereas citrus occupies 39.7 per cent. (Table 9–2)

In the Colchis Lowland during the years 1910–1960, seven killing frosts occurred, and in the 1949–1950 winter, temperatures as low as −4°F were experienced in the lowest lying areas. Since it takes at least 5 years for the tea plant to reach the bearing stage, seven well-spaced frosts in a 50-year period could wipe out two thirds of the potentially bearing years. Also, minor frosts and other damaging climatic conditions might eliminate or reduce yields even during years when the bush itself is healthy. Thus tea is planted sparingly in the lowland. Outside of western Georgia, tea yields are very low. Although the Azerbaydzhan Republic contains over 6000 hectares of tea land which normally produce about 3 per cent of the country's tea, the yields are less than one quarter the average for the entire Georgian Republic. (Tables 9–4 and 9–5) Azerbaydzhanian tea is raised along the subtropical

foothills of the Talysh Mountains in the very southeastern corner of the Azerbaydzhanian Republic where the eastern slopes facing the Caspian Sea receive 50 to 60 inches of precipitation per year. However, this precipitation is less reliable than it is in the west and the region is subject to frequent hot desiccating winds which reduce yields. The region is definitely a submarginal one for tea planting, and it is questionable whether the Soviets will continue to press their efforts in this area as intensively as they have in the past.

As can be deduced from Table 9–6, the Soviets have done an admirable job in attempting to become self-sufficient in tea. Before the Revolution, tea growing was limited largely to the foothills around Batumi in the warmest, wettest part of the Georgian Republic, which produced less than 1 per cent of the country's consumption. During the years 1928 to 1940 the Soviets planted about 11,000 acres of tea per year and increased the total tea area from only 3500 hectares in 1928 to 55,300 in 1940. (Table 9–5) World War II interrupted the tea-planting program, but after the war there was another rapid expansion, which by 1955 allowed the Soviet Union to become 87 per cent self-supporting. In 1955, however, the per capita consumption of tea was only one third what it had been in 1913. Obviously, the amount of tea being made available to the average citizen did not reflect his desires. After the death of Stalin, relaxations on

Table 9–5   Tea Area and Production, in Thousands of Hectares and Thousands of Metric Tons

	1913		1928		1940		1950		1960		1966	
	Area	Prod.	Area	Prod.	Area	Prod.	Area	Prod.	Area	Prod.	Area	Prod.
U.S.S.R.	0.9	0.55	3.5	1.06	55.3	51.6	54.3	84.9	64.4	163.7	71.3	238.2
Georgian S.S.R.	0.9	0.55	3.5	1.06	49.6	51.3	48.6	83.7	55.6	156.8	62.7	226.2
Azerbaydzhan S.S.R.					5.1	0.24	4.1	0.8	6.4	4.7	6.6	8.3
Krasnodar Kray					0.6	0.01	1.6	0.4	2.4	2.2	2.0	3.7

Source: Strana Sovetov za 50 let, pp. 146–147.

Table 9–6   Production and Consumption of Processed Tea in the U.S.S.R., in Metric Tons

	1913	1940	1955	1960	1966
Production	138	12,900	30,250	40,500	59,550
Imports	75,813	13,135	10,200	22,600	21,300
Exports	488	2,254	5,700	5,300	11,900
Consumption	75,463	23,781	34,750	58,250	68,950
Per Cent Domestic	<1	54	87	70	86
Per Capita Consumption (pounds)	0.99	0.23	0.34	0.61	0.65

Source: Strana Sovetov za 50 let, pp. 146–147; Vneshnyaya Torgovlya SSSR za 1966 god, pp. 35 and 50; Jensen, Soviet Subtropical Agriculture, p. 196; and Bone, Soviet Tea Cultivation, p. 173. Processed tea has been computed at one quarter the weight of freshly harvested tea leaves.

imports of consumer goods allowed the consumption of tea to spurt ahead while the domestic production was growing at a normal pace, and therefore the percentage of consumption supplied domestically declined. Although it rose again dramatically in 1966, that year seems to have been a very good one for tea production and perhaps does not indicate a trend for the future. If anything, it appears that the Soviets are more prone to import more tea in the future than to continue to try to expand tea production into submarginal regions. Contrary to many Soviet statements to the effect that there are abundant opportunities for further expansion of tea production, it appears that all the prime land for tea growing has already been occupied. In fact, some reduction of tea acreage might be expected in the near future as submarginal lands are taken out of production and put to better use.

Citrus growing in Georgia is limited to tangerines, oranges, and lemons. Winter temperatures are too severe for other types such as grapefruit. Of the three fruits grown, lemons are the least frost resistant. A temperature of 22°F damages the leaves and new sprouts, and 16°F kills the trees. Therefore lemons are limited primarily to Adzharia in the far south-

western part of the Georgian Republic, whereas other citrus are grown in Abkhazia in northwestern Georgia and in the foothills surrounding the Colchis Lowland. (Table 9–2) Conditions deteriorate very rapidly from the Black Sea coast inland, so that the interior part of Georgia raises very little citrus.

Citrus fruit is another food product that is very much desired in the Soviet Union. So far the quantity has been limited and the quality has been very poor. Although the Soviets have been very desirous of becoming self-sufficient in citrus, it appears that they have no possibility of coming anywhere near that goal. As can be seen in Table 9–7, the Soviets have never produced more than about 20 per cent of their annual consumption of citrus, and the amount of citrus made available to the public, primarily through imports, probably has never scratched the surface of the potential public demand. If the demand for citrus fruit in the Soviet Union were to be developed and fully satisfied, the domestic production would undoubtedly prove to be only a drop in the bucket.

At the outset of the enthusiasm for the growing of citrus in the late 1930s, the acreage in Georgia was rapidly increased from 8250 acres to 61,552 acres in 1940. Production was always poor, however, and complaints were constantly made regard-

Table 9–7   U.S.S.R. Citrus Production and Imports, in Metric Tons

Year	Production	Imports
1940	23,400	unknown
1950	2,400	unknown
1960	27,700	120,000
1965	28,600	192,100
1966	40,400	208,000
1967	24,700	—

Source: SSSR v tsifrakh v 1967 godu, p. 83; Vneshnyaya Torgovlya SSSR za 1966 god, p. 52; and Jensen, Soviet Subtropical Agriculture, p. 199.

ing the sloppy way in which the citrus crop was being cared for. Then in the winter of 1949–1950 a disastrous freeze killed 47,000 acres of citrus trees, which reduced the remaining acreage in Georgia to less than one third what it had been one decade earlier. Although the acreage has been expanded since then, it has fluctuated up and down drastically, and the latest report seems to indicate that the present acreage is not significantly more than that surviving the 1949–1950 freeze. (Table 9–8) Therefore it would appear that there is not much chance of further expansion of citrus acreage, although production might be increased somewhat be better attention

to the groves that already exist. Also, better marketing methods would reduce much of the spoilage that now occurs before the fruit reaches the market. Therefore the Soviet Union seems destined to remain a large citrus importer, particularly if it tries to satisfy ultimate consumer demands.

The third most important subtropical crop in terms of acreage is tung trees for the production of oil in the use of paints, lacquers, and so forth. In fact, in recent years tung has occupied a little more acreage than citrus fruit has. Generally it is in competition for the same land as tea and citrus. (Table 9–2)

Other important crops traditionally grown in humid Transcaucasia are grapes, tobacco, and a great variety of fruits and vegetables. Tobacco is heavily concentrated on the steep seaward slopes of Abkhazia where it has been a traditional crop for centuries. More than 20,000 acres of tobacco in this region make up over 98 per cent of all the tobacco grown in western Georgia. Grapes are more widely scattered, but are somewhat concentrated on the eastern margins of the subtropics between the Colchis Lowland and the

Table 9–8   Citrus Acreage in Georgia

Year	Acreage
1935	8,250
1940	61,552
1950	20,250
1956	41,000
1960	24,375

Source: Jensen, *Soviet Subtropical Agriculture*, p. 199.

Figure 9–8   The Kura River cuts through the Surami Range at Tbilisi. Photograph by the author.

Figure 9–9   Spring in a rural village near Tbilisi. Novosti.

Surami Range. Grains have always been an important crop for local consumption. Corn has already been mentioned as occupying 40 per cent of the cultivated land in the Georgian subtropics. Here corn is a traditional crop which has been used for human consumption for many centuries. Rice also is a traditional basic food and is being grown more and more extensively on some of the wetter lowlands. Mulberry trees line the banks of many streams and provide the basis for a long-established silk industry.

Drainage is the biggest problem to agriculture in the Colchis Lowland. In 1964 the Soviets claimed that they had drained 200,000 acres of the potentially usable 550,000 acres of the lowland and had eliminated the malarial hazard from the swamps.

The Kura Lowland to the east, fronting on the Caspian Sea, is a considerably more extensive lowland than is the Colchis Low-

land, but climatically it is entirely different. It is primarily a steppe region with dry steppe soils that necessitate irrigation for the intensive raising of crops. The Kura River heads on the western slopes of the Surami Range and cuts across the range to the east where it enters the broad synclinal valley to flow for more than 200 miles

Figure 9–10   Cotton picking in the Kura Lowland, Azerbaydzhan. Novosti.

through the flat alluvial steppe to the Caspian Sea. Wherever water is available for irrigation, land has been planted in cotton, alfalfa, corn, and orchards and vineyards. Rice is grown in the delta and in other marshy areas along the river. Cotton and alfalfa each occupy about one fourth of the irrigated area and corn occupies about 15 per cent. This is the second most important cotton-growing area in the country, after Middle Asia. Mulberry trees typically line the irrigation canals to provide the basis for an important silk industry. Some wheat is grown without irrigation in the moister foothills surrounding the basin, but the largest portions of the lowland still are dry winter grazing lands. The area under irrigation was increased to about 500,000 acres with the opening of the Mingechaur Reservoir on the Kura River in 1953.

Figure 9–11   Transhumance of sheep in the Caucasus. Novosti.

Transhumance of livestock still is practiced in the Kura River area; the sheep and cattle being pastured on the "kishlag," or winter pastures, on the steppes of the lowland in the winter and in the "eilag," or mountain pastures, of the Armenian Plateau in the summer. The livestock are driven seasonally over a distance of a hundred miles or more. The sheep are brought into the Kura Lowland early in the fall where they are shorn and sorted for slaughtering, and the breeding herd is retained to feed on the local pastures and alfalfa hay during the winter.

The wettest part of the Kura Lowland is the extreme southeast around Lenkoran where some citrus and tea as well as some rice are grown. This area is a wet, swampy, and subtropical area, the culture is more oriental than western, and the main beast of burden still is the water buffalo.

The other region of significant cultivation in Transcaucasia is the Araks River Valley cut in the Armenian Plateau along the southern boundary of the country. Beginning at an elevation of around 3300 feet in the basin around the Armenian capital of Yerevan, this agricultural area continues down the short Razdan River and southeastward along the floodplain of the Araks. The entire area is steppe-like, and very little agriculture can be carried on without irrigation. Irrigation water is available from Lake Sevan and from small streams heading in the snow fields on the volcanic peaks dotting the area. The chief crop is cotton, as it is in the Kura Lowland, with a good deal of acreage given over to alfalfa as a rotation crop. A great variety of vegetables and fruit are grown, particularly in the Yerevan Basin, for local consumption.

Other than in these three low-lying valleys (Colchis Lowland, Kura Lowland, and Araks Valley), agriculture is limited largely to grazing, particularly of sheep. The Armenian Plateau is a dry, rolling upland of volcanic soils that sustains fairly good

Figure 9–12 The irrigated basin of Arpa-chaya, Nakhichevan A.S.S.R., Azerbaydzhan. Novosti.

summer pastures. But in general the soils there are too thin and stony and the climate is too dry for cultivation. Armenia is known as the land of stone, because of the prevalence of bare volcanic rock.

At the altitudes at which much of the plateau lies, the climate is no longer sub-tropical; temperatures approximate those of the North Caucasian Foreland, going well below 0°F in winter and above 100°F in summer. The air here is dry and stable, however, and the skies are generally sunny, so that the weather differs considerably from that on the northern plain.

Figure 9–13 Irrigation canal near Lake Sevan, Armenian Plateau. Volcanic cone in background. Courtesy of J. H. Glen Burke.

Water and Power

Mention has already been made of several fairly extensive irrigation districts in the Caucasus area, both in the Kura Lowland of Transcaucasia and along the Terek River Valley on the northern slopes of the Great Caucasus in the central and eastern portions of the North Caucasian Foreland. In addition, there are important irrigation projects in Armenia, particularly those associated with the Yerevan Basin and the connecting Razdan and Araks River Valleys. In conjunction with many of these irrigation districts are large dams and reservoirs which provide the opportunity for the generation of considerable amounts of hydroelectric power. Although the streams throughout the Caucasus are of no great size, their steepness gives this region greater hydroelectric potential than the whole of the European Plain of Russia. Power potentials are enhanced by the fact that most of the streams do not freeze during the winters and they are fed by snow fields and high-level lakes that maintain consistent flows. Many small and medium-sized hydroelectric plants have been operating for a number of years on a great number of these short, swift streams. The largest single station is located at Ingursk on the Inguri River in northwestern Georgia. It has a generating capacity of more than 1 million kilowatts. On the neighboring Rioni River are located three stations which have an aggregate capacity of about 500,000 kilowatts. In eastern Georgia two medium-sized stations are located on a headwater tributary of the Kura River, and three smaller stations are located on the Kura itself. Other small stations are located in several of the streams flowing down the north slope of the Great Caucasus, as well as in the highlands of the Armenian Plateau in southeastern Armenia and southern Azerbaydzhan. Recently, emphasis has been placed on water-construction projects involving multipurpose development of entire river systems. The two outstanding examples are the Mingechaur development on the Kura River and the Sevan-Razdan Cascade.

The Mingechaur Multipurpose Water Management Project was the largest water-construction project to be completed in the Soviet Union during the fifth five-year plan, 1950–1955. Its building required particular engineering skills since the dam was strung across the middle portion of the Kura River Valley which consisted of a gorge flanked by steep dry cliffs made up of weak gypsum clays which were bound to dissolve and slump upon prolonged contact with water. The project was to control floods, provide irrigation water, generate electricity, eradicate malarial swamps, and provide a navigable channel about 2 meters deep. Before the dam was built, the Kura River in its lower portion flowed between natural levees above the general level of the floodplain, and broad flooding occurred annually. Sweeping through the dry sedimentary plain, the river carried 14 million cubic meters of sediment per year, which generally was strewn across the floodplain. Now all the sediment is collected in the reservoir behind the dam. The hydroelectric plant has a capacity of 371,000 kilowatts and sends electricity as far as Tbilisi in eastern Georgia over a 300-kilovolt power transmission line. On completion of the project, 135,000 hectares of new land were immediately put under irrigation, and this is to increase to 335,000 hectares by 1970. Twenty-five per cent of this irrigated land is planted in cotton, 25 per cent in perennial grasses, 15 per cent in corn, 5 per cent in vineyards, 4 per cent in orchards, and the rest in small grains. Rice is grown extensively in areas with controlled flooding. This was the first major project in the U.S.S.R. to be equipped with fish hatcheries and stocking basins to enable an integrated effort to raise fish on a commercial basis.

The Sevan-Razdan Cascade is a project

involving a series of dams and reservoirs on the small Razdan River which drains Lake Sevan southward through Yerevan to the Araks River. The Razdan River is only 65 miles long, but in that distance it drops 3300 feet from Lake Sevan, at an elevation of 6350 feet, to its junction with the Araks. Also, its flow is very consistent since it drains the large lake, so the natural conditions are ideal for the development of water power. Originally, it was planned over the next 50 years to drain Lake Sevan down to a level 160 feet below the present surface and thereby reduce its area to about one seventh of the original size. At this point it was calculated that a balance would be reached between run in, evaporation, and water necessary for power development on the cascade. As it was, about 40 per cent of the annual run in was evaporated. This amounted to a loss of approximately 1 billion cubic meters annually, which is equivalent to a layer 35.5 inches thick from the entire surface of the lake. By 1960 six stations with an aggregate generating capacity of 620,000 kilowatts had been constructed on the Razdan. Two more stations had been projected, but now it appears that they have been shelved because of the development of large thermal

power stations in the area fueled by natural gas piped in from Karadag southwest of Baku. The Yerevan thermal plant was completed in 1965; it has a capacity of 550,000 kilowatts. Another gas-fueled thermal plant with a 150,000-kilowatt capacity has been constructed at Razdan, the northernmost of a string of new cities along the Razdan River.

Now it is planned to reduce the surface area of Lake Sevan by only 13 per cent. To halt the drop in the level of the lake brought about by the diversion tunnel that was constructed to serve the water needs of the Razdan River stations already in operation, a plan has been drawn up to construct a 60-meter-high diversion dam on the Arpa River about 60 kilometers south of the lake. Water from this reservoir will be piped through a 48-kilometer-long tunnel through the Vardenis Range and dumped into a short canal that will carry the water into the southern end of Lake Sevan.

The Sevan-Razdan Cascade has supplied water for irrigation to more than 100,000 hectares of new land along the Razdan Valley and in Yerevan Basin. Combined with other irrigation districts in southern Armenia which utilize water

Figure 9–14 Lake Sevan. Photograph by the author.

from other tributaries of the Araks River, as well as significant areas of irrigation along the southern end of Lake Sevan, the total irrigated area in Armenia amounts to approximately 262,000 hectares, which makes up more than 50 per cent of the cultivated area in the Republic. In addition, the Sevan-Razdan Cascade has generated an urban development along the Razdan River between Yerevan and Lake Sevan of new towns that are planned to be in the 50,000 to 80,000 population bracket and are to house the workers for newly established industrial plants calculated to vitalize the economy of the area.

Three of these new small industrial cities have been constructed as model towns. The first was founded in June 1959 at the former village of Akhta in the northern portion of the Razdan Valley. The new city now has the name of Razdan and has grown to a population of around 20,000. It has a planned size of 80,000. An alumina plant is being established to utilize nearby nephelite-syenite deposits to produce alumina for the aluminum plant in Yerevan, which has been shipping in its alumina all the way from the Urals. The abundant electrical power in the valley makes this an ideal location for the alumi-

num industry, which is a heavy consumer of electricity. A tire cord factory has also been established in Razdan to utilize nylon salt from the Rustavi chemical plant in Georgia to supply cord to the tire factory in Yerevan. The second city was founded in December 1961 and was originally named Lusavan (town of light), but in 1967 it was renamed Charentsavan after an Armenian writer. This town produces iron castings, boring machines, tools and dyes, and prefabricated reinforced concrete building sections. In 1965 its population was 12,000. The third town is Abovyan, 10 miles northeast of Yerevan. It specializes in electronic equipment such as computers and semiconductor devices.

It is interesting to note that although all of these new towns were founded on the sites of new hydroelectric stations, the industries being established in them require more electricity than can be provided by the hydroelectric plants that have actually evolved from the reduced version of the Sevan-Razdan project. Therefore much larger thermal stations are going into operation in the area. For instance, at Razdan a 1.2 million-kilowatt thermal station is to go into operation in the early 1970s to provide adequate electricity for

Figure 9–15   The town of Razdan on the Armenian Plateau. Photograph by the author.

the alumina plant. Armenia, which used to be supplied almost entirely with electricity from hydro plants, now receives more than half of its electricity from thermal plants. The same trend is occurring in the other Transcaucasian Republics. In Azerbaydzhan, a gas-fueled power station at Ali-Bayramli, on the lower Kura River, was expanded to a generating capacity of 900,000 kilowatts in 1967. Ultimately, it is to be expanded to 1.2 million kilowatts. Such thermal stations dwarf even the largest of the hydro power stations in the Caucasian area.

Mineral Resources

The mineral fuels, particularly oil and gas, are outstanding among the mineral resources of the Caucasus. For nearly a hundred years Baku was the leading oil producer in the Soviet Union, and around the turn of the century it was the leading oil producer in the world. Also, important oil fields lie along the northern slopes of the Caucasus in the Grozny area and around Maykop in Krasnodar Kray. Minor deposits exist in eastern Georgia on the southern slopes of the Great Caucasus. Many of these Caucasian fields now are on the decline, and an absolute decline in production has occurred at Baku since World War II. Relative to the country as a whole the Caucasus have become much less significant. They now produce less than 15 per cent of the country's oil, whereas before the Revolution they produced almost all of it. Through deeper drilling and drilling offshore in the Caspian, production at Baku is being increased approximately to its pre-World War II level, but no significant increase beyond that point is expected. Discovery of new oil deposits in deeper strata has also revived the oil industry at Grozny on the northern slope of the Caucasus where oil production had declined to a low of 2 million tons in 1957. By 1968 it had risen

to 16 million tons, which made it almost as important as Baku. A smaller oil boom has recently taken place in Dagestan.

But the big development since 1955 has been the opening up of large gas fields both along the northern Caucasus around Stavropol and Krasnodar and in Transcaucasia southwest of Baku. The Stavropol-Krasnodar fields are some of the largest in the country, and pipelines have rapidly been constructed from these fields northwestward through Rostov and the Donets Basin to Moscow and Leningrad. A gas pipeline has also been built from the Karadag field southwest of Baku, up the Kura River through Kirovabad and Akstafa to Tbilisi, and from Akstafa southwestward to Yerevan. All the new thermal power plants in the Caucasus are being fueled by Karadag gas. Since the Karadag reserves will be exhausted in the next few years, plans have been laid to import gas into the Karadag pipeline system from the Iranian field of Qum south of Teheran. A 48-inch transmission main from Qum would feed gas into the exhausted natural reservoirs at Karadag for distribution westward. A pipeline that was laid across the Great Caucasus along the Georgian Military Highway in 1964 can also provide gas to the Transcaucasian system from the gas fields of Stavropol.

It is hoped that through the greater use of natural gas in Transcaucasia the import of coal from the Donets Basin can be eliminated. The only coal of any significance in Transcaucasia lies in two neighboring areas in the Colchis Lowland at the towns of Tkibuli and Tkvarcheli. These fields are not extensive enough nor of a high enough grade to serve as a basis for large-scale industry, but they do supply much of the local needs for coal.

The second largest deposit of manganese in the Soviet Union is located at Chiatura in the Colchis Lowland. The Ordzhonikidze area on the northern slopes of the Great Caucasus has long been important for its lead and zinc mines.

Copper has been mined in Armenia for a number of years. Alunite mines have been opened up at Zaglik near Kirovabad, in the Azerbaydzhan Republic, and important salt deposits occur in Nakhichevan A.S.S.R. Besides these important minerals, deposits of molybdenum, cobalt, and other minerals exist.

Industries

The Caucasus are still primarily agricultural, but the mineral resources provide a potential basis for considerable industry, and many of the cities are becoming industrialized. Oil for a long time has provided the basis for industry in Baku, Grozny, and Krasnodar, and in the refining towns of Batumi and Tuapse on the eastern Black Sea coast. An oil pipeline running the length of the Kura-Rioni syncline from Baku to Batumi has been serving the area for many years. Also, very early a pipeline was constructed from the oil fields around Maykop across the low northern end of the Caucasus to Tuapse. The oil-refining towns of Tuapse and Batumi ship refined products to the industries of Ukraine via tanker across the Black Sea. Now Novorossiysk is being made into an oil port to receive oil via pipeline from the pumping station at Tikhoretsk.

Also of long standing in Transcaucasia are the textile industries—cotton, wool, and silk. The raw materials for all these textiles are derived locally, and the industries are widely scattered through the major cities of the area. Tbilisi stands out in the silk industry, and Gori, the birthplace of Stalin northwest of Tbilisi, is foremost in cotton textiles.

Since World War II, as part of a drive to make the Transcaucasus semi-independent of the rest of the country, a small-scale primary iron and steel industry has been developed, and chemical industries are growing rapidly. The new town of Rustavi was established southeast of Tbilisi as an iron and steel center to serve the needs of Transcaucasia, particularly steel pipe for oil wells and for pipelines. Rustavi has now reached a population of 95,000 people, which is larger than the 50,000 for which it supposedly was built. It derives its iron ore from Dashkesan nearby and its coal from the Colchis Lowland. Deriving all its raw materials from Transcaucasia and selling all its products in Transcaucasia makes it a self-contained industry.

The chemical industry has been important to some extent in Baku for a number of years, but it is becoming very important now in two other cities, Yerevan and Sumgait. Yerevan early became one of the major centers of the synthetic rubber industry because of its hydroelectric power, which, with local limestone, was used to produce calcium carbide and acetylene, the raw materials for special purpose chloroprene rubber. The industry is being expanded and diversified into all sorts of plastics and synthetics, and the basis for these industries is rapidly being shifted to natural gas, which since 1960 has been piped in from Karadag.

A new city, Sumgait, has been established on the northern side of the Apsheron Peninsula, northwest of Baku, primarily as a chemical industrial center. By 1967 it had already grown to a population of 104,000. Sumgait uses the by-product gases from the oil-refining Baku area and some of the natural gas from Karadag. It is scheduled to produce a wide range of plastics, synthetics, and fertilizers as well as some steel, aluminum, and pipe. Besides Baku, Sumgait, and Yerevan, chemical industries are important in Makhachkala, the capital city of Dagestan; Derbent, a Caspian seaport in Dagestan; Grozny; Kutaisi; Kirovabad; and Kirovakan and Alaverdi in Armenia. In 1968 acetylene production began in a new plastics-chemical fibers plant at Nevinnomyssk in the North Caucasus.

One of the most rapid developments in Transcaucasia at the present time is the aluminum industry. Alumina is shipped from the Urals to Yerevan and Sumgait for refining into aluminum because of the abundant water power supplies at Yerevan and oil and gas power supplies at Sumgait. The aluminum industry in Transcaucasia is being expanded greatly because of recently discovered deposits of alunite in Azerbaydzhan at Zaglik near Kirovabad. Much of the alunite is refined to alumina at Kirovabad and is then shipped to Yerevan and Sumgait for final refining into aluminum.

Machine industries of all types are rapidly being established in the Caucasus to supply local markets and to make use of local metallurgical products. The machine-building industries are located primarily in the larger cities such as Baku, Tbilisi, Yerevan, Kutaisi, Stavropol, Krasnodar, and Novorossiysk. An automobile assembly plant has been established at Kutaisi, the main city of the Colchis Lowland. The cement industry long has been important in Novorossiysk, along the Black Sea coast; Novorossiysk is the largest producer of cement in the Soviet Union. The lead and zinc industries of the Ordzhonikidze area have already been mentioned.

Cities

Baku The largest cities in the region are the three capitals of the Transcaucasian Republics. Baku is first with a population of 1,196,000, if its suburbs are included. Baku was probably founded in the ninth century as a stopover point along a constricted segment of the trade route between the Orient and Europe around the southern end of the Caspian Sea. It grew rapidly in the latter part of the nineteenth century under the impetus of oil production, and because of oil has been maintaining this growth ever since. Although oil production declined during World War II by roughly 50 per cent, it

has been increased slowly since then by deeper drilling and by drilling offshore. Three causeways have been constructed to link offshore islands with the mainland, and entire oil-drilling villages have been constructed on floating platforms. The oil workers come into Baku only on weekends. Besides oil refining, Baku has developed booming industries in chemicals and machine building. The city also serves as the capital of Azerbaydzhan.

Had it not been for oil, Baku undoubtedly would not have gained the eminence that it has today, for it sits on the barren windswept southern shore of the Apsheron Peninsula where the rainfall is less than 8 inches per year. Water supply is a serious problem in the large city. Before 1917 drinking water had to be brought in from the Kura River by tankers. Then a pipeline 120 miles long was constructed to bring in good mountain water for drinking, but it did not supply anything for irrigation. There are no lawns in the city. Plans are underway for diverting more water for domestic purposes in Baku so that greenery can be grown, but at the present time the city is an unpleasant place in which to live. It is very hot and dry in summer and subject to strong winds throughout many months of the year. During summer hot, dry winds funnel around the eastern end of the Great Caucasus and blow dust across the city from the steppes to the north. It is said that in Baku even horses in the streets must wear goggles.

Tbilisi Tbilisi is second in size with a population of 842,000. It was founded in A.D. 458 and it has long been the center of Georgian culture. It now is the capital of the Georgian Republic. Unlike Baku it is a lovely city sitting in the rolling hills and low mountains where the Kura River crosses the Surami Range. Tbilisi is not a heavy industrial town as Baku is, for it has no major local resources, but it has much diversified light industry. Most important

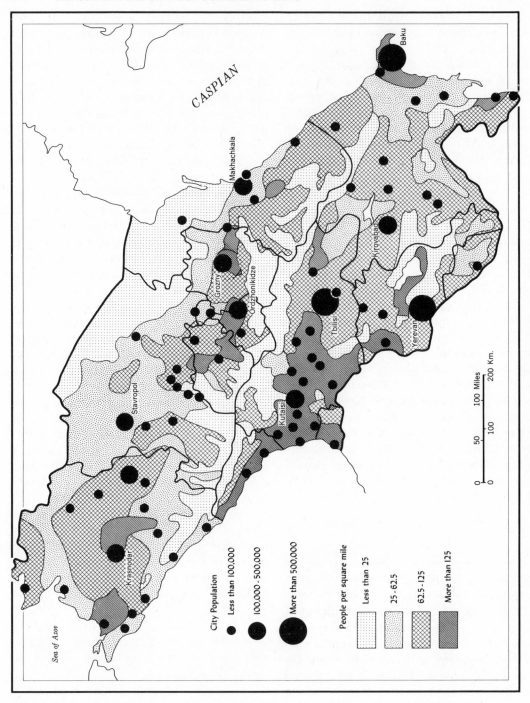

CASPIAN

Baku

Makhachkala

Grozny

Ordzhonikidze

Kirovabad

Tbilisi

Stavropol

Yerevan

Kutaisi

Krasnodar

Sea of Azov

City Population

Less than 100,000

100,000 - 500,000

More than 500,000

People per square mile

Less than 25

25 - 62.5

62.5 - 125

More than 125

0   50   100 Miles

0   100   200 Km.

Figure 9–16   Population densities and city sizes. After Cherdantsev.

Figure 9–17   Cable car in Tbilisi. Photograph by the author.

are the textile industries, concentrating on silk, and machine and food industries. It is famous for its wines, cognac, and champagne.

Yerevan   Third in size is Yerevan, the capital of the Armenian Republic, with a population of 665,000. It was founded in 783 B.C. Like Tbilisi, it has been the cultural center of an important nationality group which has occupied the area for over 2000 years. Under the Soviets it has flourished because of its function as the capital of the Armenian Republic and because of rapid industrialization. It is a lovely old city, sitting at an elevation of 3300 feet in a basin surrounded by higher land on three sides that opens on the south onto the Araks River Valley. Dotted across the Armenian Plateau within sight of the city are several snow-capped volcanic peaks, the highest of which is Mt. Ararat across the border in Turkey. Unfortunately, the stable air in the basin produces a dust haze that generally obscures these magnificent cones from view. Irrigated crops of fruits and vegetables surround Yerevan and serve the urban market. As has been pointed out, Yerevan is rapidly undergoing industrialization in such industries as chemicals, aluminum, and machine

building. These industries originally were based primarily on the hydroelectric power of the Sevan-Razdan Cascade, but recently natural gas from Karadag has augmented this. It appears that Yerevan is destined to become one of the main industrial cities of the Transcaucasus.

Krasnodar   The next four cities in order of size are on the northern plain: Krasnodar, Grozny, Ordzhonikidze, and Stavropol. Krasnodar now has a population of 407,000. It was founded in 1792 by Zaporozhian Cossacks. It is now the economic center of the rich Kuban farming region of Krasnodar Kray. For a long

Figure 9–18   Yerevan. Snow-capped volcanic cones in background. Photograph by the author.

time it has had a minor oil-refining industry, and gas fields have been discovered nearby. The bulk of the industry, however, still reflects the agricultural base. The surrounding region is still heavily peopled by Cossacks.

Grozny   Grozny, a city of 331,000 population, on the other hand, is an industrial city based almost entirely on oil refining. It does serve as a main regional center of a relatively poorer agricultural region and as the capital city of the Chechen-Ingush A.S.S.R. But it owes its eminence to the fact that there is local petroleum available, and it got its start in the oil-refining industry.

Ordzhonikidze   Ordzhonikidze, with a population of 219,000, is outstanding for its lead and zinc industries. It also serves as the seat of government for the North Osetian A.S.S.R. and as a regional center for that area. Much of its industry has located here because of considerable amounts of hydroelectric power derived from the headwater streams of the Terek River which cascade down the mountains at steep gradients from Mt. Kazbek, one of the high, snow-capped peaks of the Caucasus. It was founded in 1784 as the fort of Vladikavkaz (ruler of the Caucasus), so named because it occupied the northern approach to Krestovyy Pass, the lowest route over the Great Caucasus, which is now traversed by the Georgian Military Highway. Its name was changed to Ordzhonikidze in 1931. It was changed again to Dzaudzhikau in 1944, and then back to Ordzhonikidze in 1954.

Stavropol   Stavropol, with a population of 177,000, is almost a replica Krasnodar on a smaller scale. The city sits at the crest of the arch of the Stavropol Plateau in the midst of a relatively good farming region, and what industries it has largely reflect the farming resource. Like Krasnodar, since 1955 large gas fields have been discovered in the area that have added to the industries of Stavropol.

Kirovabad   The ninth city in size is Kirovabad, in the middle Kura River Valley in Azerbaydzhan, with a population of 174,000 people. The economic center of the Kura valley, its importance has been enhanced by the establishment of alumina industries based on the alunite ore to the south.

Makhachkala   Tenth in size is Makhachkala, the capital city of the Dagestan A.S.S.R., with a population of 165,000. Besides being the seat of government for the Dagestan Republic, Makhachkala is an important seaport on the western coast of the Caspian. As the eastern terminus of an oil pipeline, it serves as the transshipping point for oil coming by steamers from Baku and continuing by pipe westward through Grozny to Rostov and Ukraine.

Kutaisi   The eleventh city in size is Kutaisi, the economic center and rail center of the Colchis Lowland, with a population of 159,000. It has diversified light industries, none of which are outstanding. During the last few years an automobile assembly plant has been established in Kutaisi that is to serve the entire needs of Transcaucasia.

Other Cities   Besides these cities there are a number of significant smaller cities with populations between 50,000 and 150,000, such as the oil-refining towns of Maykop (106,000) and Tuapse (49,000) in Krasnodar Kray and Batumi (100,000) in the Georgian Republic, the iron and steel city of Rustavi (95,000), the chemical city of Sumgait (104,000), and the cement-manufacturing town of Novorossiysk (123,000).

The resort towns of Sochi (188,000) and Sukhumi (88,000) along the eastern shore of the Black Sea and Mineralnye Vody on the northern slopes of the Great Caucasus serve recreational and health needs of the entire nation, and are visited by hundreds of thousands of people each year. Like Yalta and other towns of the southeast Crimean coast, the steep slopes of these cities are dotted with whitewashed health resorts and sanatoria.

Sochi is the largest of these resort cities. It sits on a hilly section of land where the mountains plunge abruptly to the Black Sea, and although it is very picturesque, the beaches are narrow and filled with cobbles. Level land in Sochi is so lacking that the city cannot be served directly by air; planes must land at Adler about 20 miles to the south on·a small river delta, and passengers must be conveyed to Sochi by open-air bus over a bumpy, winding mountain road. In 1961 the city limits of Sochi were extended southward to include Adler, which brought the population of the Sochi metropolitan area to seventh in size in the Caucasian Region. In Sochi are all that the Russians consider to be significant to the self indulgence of the idle vacationer: glistening white resort hotels perched on the hills high above the Black Sea, funicular railways, and large expanses of parks with their circus, opera house, and cinema. Besides these strictly resort amenities there is a subtropical botanical garden whose paths are constantly jammed by pedestrains, many of whom are visiting the city in large groups and insist on posing for group pictures.

Sukhumi is better known for its botanical garden for scientific studies than it is for its resort facilities. Mineralnye Vody is noted for its warm mineral baths fed by hot springs issuing from subvolcanic areas. Twenty miles away is the city of Pyatigorsk (Five mountains) which gets its name from five eroded laccolithic low mountains that sit on the northern plain detached from the main body of the Great Caucasus. In 1967 Pyatigorsk had a population of 81,000.

Prospects

Transcaucasia, because of its subtropical climate, holds a unique position in the agriculture of the Soviet Union. Undoubt-

Figure 9–19   Metallurg Sanatorium in Sochi. Photograph by the author.

edly, it will continue to serve as the sole domestic producer of such products as tea and citrus. But the population pressure will force a continued urbanization, and as the Soviets establish basic industries in the area, the urbanization process will be speeded still more.

The Caucasian peoples have some of the highest birth rates in the Soviet Union, which are increasing the population very rapidly. In addition, heavy in-migration of formerly exiled peoples has recently created a large surplus labor pool in the North Caucasus that can be absorbed immediately only by allowing newcomers to work solely on private plots of land. As a consequence, the North Caucasian Foreland now has a higher proportion of its people employed in private agriculture than any other region of the European R.S.F.S.R. Such socially useless labor on a long-term basis is untenable to the Soviets, and thus Gosplan, the State Planning Commission, is studying the situation with the idea of creating labor-intensive medium-scale industries in cities with populations of 50,000 or less.

The Caucasus have lost their prewar monopoly of the Soviet oil industry, but absolutely they are about holding their own, and this production has been augmented since 1955 by the discovery of huge reserves of natural gas. Thus once again in the mineral fuels the Caucasus

Figure 9–20   The approach to Pyatigorsk. Photograph by the author.

(this time the North) have become important to the entire Union. The fluidity of this new fuel and the potentials that it offers for the development of chemical industries tends to spread industrial development more evenly throughout the Caucasus and provide for a better rounded urban economy.

In contrast to the Baltic peoples, the Transcaucasian peoples, because of their extremely high birth rates, are maintaining large majorities in their own republics.

Reading List

CAUCASUS — GENERAL

Geiger, Bernhard, *Peoples and Languages of the Caucasus,* Mouton, the Hague, 1959, 77 pp.

Jensen, Robert G., "Soviet Subtropical Agriculture: A Microcosm," *Geographical Review,* April 1964, pp. 185–202.

Nove, Alec and Newth, J. A., *The Soviet Middle East,* Praeger, New York, 1967, 160 pp.

Shelley, Maryann, *Karst and Caves in the Caucasus,* Field Research Projects, South House, Tyringham, Mass., December 21, 1956, 74 pp.

ARMENIA

Akademiya Nauk SSSR, Institut Geografiya, 1955, *Armyanskoy SSR* (Armenian SSR), 282 pp. (in Russian).

Greenwood, N. H., "Developments in the Irrigation Resources of the Sevan-Razdan Cascade of Soviet Armenia," *Annals of the Association of American Geographers,* June 1965, pp. 291–307.

Shaginyan, Marietta, *Journey through Soviet Armenia,* Foreign Languages Publishing House, Moscow, 1954, 215 pp.

Sovetskiy soyuz: Armeniya (Soviet Union: Armenia), Mysl, Moscow, 1966, 342 pp. (in Russian).

AZERBAYDZHAN

Atlas Azerbaydzhanskoy SSR (Atlas Azerbaydzhan SSR), Akademiya Nauk Azerbaydzhanskoy SSR, Baku, 1963, 213 pp. (in Russian).

Azerbaydzhanskaya SSR (Azerbaydzhan SSR), Akademiya Nauk Azerbaydzhanskoy SSR, Moscow, 1957, 445 pp. (in Russian).

Magakyan, G. L., "The Mingechaur Multi-Purpose Water-Management Project," *Soviet Geography: Review and Translation,* December 1961, pp. 43–50.

GEORGIA

Atlas Gruzinskoy SSR (Atlas of the Georgian Republic), Tbilisi, 1964, 269 pp. (in Russian).

Bone, Robert M., "Soviet Tea Cultivation," *Annals of the Association of American Geographers,* June 1963, pp. 161–173.

Gruzinskaya SSR (Georgian SSR), Akademiya Nauk Gruzinskoy SSR, Moscow, 1958, 400 pp. (in Russian).

Gruzinskaya SSR; ekonomiko-geograficheskaya kharakteristika (Georgian SSR; economic-geographic characteristic), Akademiya Nauk SSSR, Moscow, 1956, 348 pp. (in Russian).

Lang, David Marshall, *The Georgians,* Praeger, New York, 1966, 244 pp.

———, *A Modern History of Soviet Georgia,* Grove Press, New York, 1962, 298 pp.

Sovetskiy Soyuz: Gruziya (Soviet Union: Georgia), Mysl, Moscow, 1967, 318 pp. (in Russian).

Soviet Georgia: Its Geography, History, and Economy, Academy of Sciences of the Georgian SSR, Vakhushti Institute of Geography, Progress Publishers, Moscow, 1967, 182 pp.

NORTH CAUCASUS

Gumilev, L. N., "Khazaria and the Caspian (Landscape and Ethnos, Part I)," *Soviet Geography: Review and Translation,* June 1964, pp. 54–68.

Severnyy Kavkaz (Northern Caucasus), Akademiya Nauk SSSR, Institut Geografiya, Moscow, 1957, 508 pp. (in Russian).

Soviet Middle Asia and Southern Kazakhstan

	Area (sq mile)	Popu- lation	People (sq mile)	% Urban
Within the Kazakh S.S.R.				
Guryev Oblast	109,000	450,000	4	65
Aktyubinsk Oblast (southern) [a]	55,000	—	—	—
Kzyl-Orda Oblast	86,300	426,000	5	51
Chimkent Oblast	47,100	1,037,000	22	40
Dzhambul Oblast	56,500	736,000	13	38
Alma-Ata Oblast	87,200	1,279,000	15	27
Alma-Ata City	—	652,000	—	100
Karaganda Oblast (southern) [a]	56,000	—	—	—
Turkmen S.S.R.	191,000	1,966,000	10	49
Ashkhabad City	—	238,000	—	100
Uzbek S.S.R.	176,000	10,896,000	62	35
Andizhan Oblast	3,500	1,680,000	480	43
Bukhara Oblast	55,800	813,000	15	27
Kashkadarya Oblast	11,100	701,000	63	15
Samarkand Oblast	11,400	1,357,000	119	27
Surkhandarya Oblast	8,100	581,000	72	16
Syrdarya Oblast	9,000	691,000	77	23
Tashkent Oblast	6,100	1,392,000	228	39
Tashkent City	—	1,239,000	—	100
Fergana Oblast	4,000	1,307,000	327	32
Khorezm Oblast	1,800	497,000	276	18
Kara-Kalpak A.S.S.R.	64,000	638,000	10	32
Tadzhik S.S.R.	55,900	2,654,000	47	37
Gorno-Badakhshan A.O.	24,800	93,000	4	13
Dushanbe City	—	333,000	—	100
Kirgiz S.S.R.	77,700	2,749,000	35	39
Frunze City	—	396,000	—	100
Osh Oblast	28,800	1,152,000	40	34
Total	997,700	22,845,000	—	—

[a] Estimated areas of parts of Aktyubinsk and Karaganda Oblasts included in southern Kazakhstan. No attempt has been made to divide the population figures for these oblasts, since the population is very sparse in the southern parts.

Note: In late 1967 two oblasts were reconstituted in this area, but their areas and populations have not been recorded. Taldy-Kurgan Oblast northeast of Alma-Ata in the Kazakh S.S.R. was originally established in March 1944 and was abolished in June 1959. Namangan Oblast in the northern part of the Fergana Valley in the Uzbek S.S.R. was originally established in March 1941 and was abolished in January 1960. Now they both exist once more.

10

Soviet Middle Asia and Southern Kazakhstan

Stretching all the way from the Volga River to China, Kazakhstan and Soviet Middle Asia comprise approximately one and one half million square miles, an area equal to about half that of the United States. Politically this region is composed of five union republics, which are further subdivided into oblasts, autonomous republics, and autonomous oblasts. The Kazakh Republic alone contains a million square miles, and except for the Russian Republic, is larger in area than all the other republics combined. East and west it stretches for a distance of more than 1800 miles, and north and south for a distance of over 1000 miles.

The Soviets usually treat the Kazakh Republic as a separate region, whereas they combine the other four republics under the term "Soviet Middle Asia." The Kazakh Republic alone does not make a good regional unit, however, since it is neither a homogeneous nor a contiguously populated area. The more populous northern and southern portions are divided in the middle by a wide expanse of drier, less populated land. The northern part of Kazakhstan is more closely related physically and culturally to adjacent western Siberia than it is to the rest of the Kazakh Republic, and the southern part of the Kazakh Republic is more closely

related to the adjacent Middle Asian Republics. Therefore the Kazkh Republic will be treated in two separate parts: the southern oblasts with the Middle Asian Republics, as shown on the table at the beginning of this chapter, and the northern and central oblasts with adjacent western Siberia in Chapter 11. It will be expedient, however, occasionally to consider the Kazakh Republic in its entirety.

If there is a theme that unites the Middle Asian Republics and southern Kazakhstan it is a climatic one, that is, drought, because this entire area is afflicted to some degree by lack of water. Only the mountain slopes in the far south have sufficient moisture. Much of the area receives less than 8 inches of precipitation per year, and a large section in the central portion southeast of the Aral Sea, as well as smaller areas along the eastern shore of the Caspian and the western shore of Lake Balkhash, receive less than 4 inches per year. Thus, except for the higher mountains, the area is entirely desert and steppe. This leads to a certain degree of homogeneity in landscape, land utilization, and culture in spite of variations induced by the complex makeup of such factors as geological structure and ethnology. Also, the entire region, which originally was a non-Russian area, during

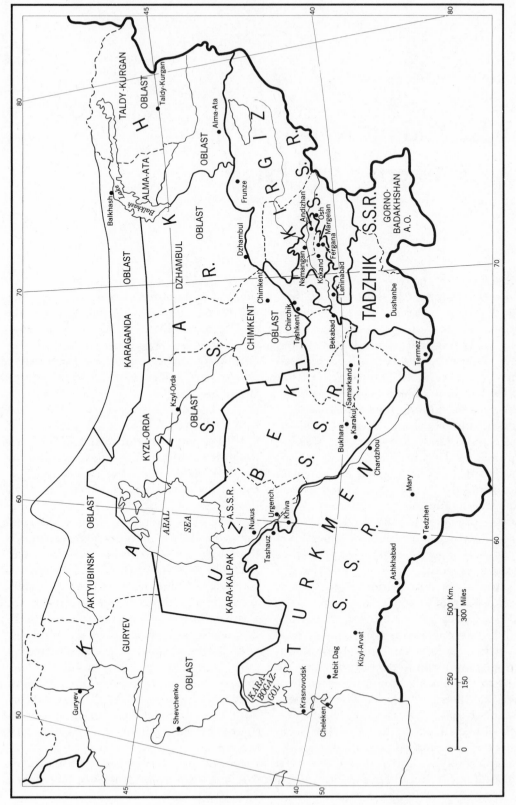

Figure 10–1   Soviet Middle Asia and Southern Kazakhstan.

the last century has undergone a common history of Russian acquisition and organization.

History, Ethnography, and Political Organization

This vast inland region is peopled by a variety of nationalities whose colorful pasts long antedate the Russian incursion into the area and reflect several millennia of nomadic conquests and assimilations in this crossroad between Europe, the Orient, and the Middle East. Archeological evidence in the thick layers of silt deposited on the densely populated flood plains of the annually flooding rivers attest to the existence of various riverain civilizations that date back to at least 3000 B.C. The juxtaposition of loess-covered steppe and desert plains, with long warm summers, and high fringing mountains along the southern border, whose peaks catch considerable amounts of winter precipitation in the form of snow, provide an ideal combination for primitive civilizations based on irrigation agriculture. The mountain snows and glaciers assure reliable flows of summer melt water in the streams that cascade down the northern slopes and partially traverse the desert floors before ending in the sands or depositing their waters in some interior drainage basin, such as the Aral Sea.

Greek and Persian reports of early expeditions into the region of the Oxus (Amu Darya) and Jaxartes (Syr Darya) speak of thriving civilizations that were contemporary with Byzantium, Babylon, and the Nile. Farther north, the nomadic herdsmen roamed the steppes all the way from the Volga to China, and although they left little evidence in the form of permanent settlements, their influences on the present stock of peoples were probably no less than that of their more sedentary neighbors, since they often marauded the towns to the south and became assimilated into these populations.

Thus the area for thousands of years has had identifiable settlements in the river valleys of the south and has been overrun throughout by nomadic herdsmen belonging to many clans. In addition, from time to time it has been overwhelmed by outside invaders from the east and the south, primarily the Mongols and the Arabs. Under Tamerlane the region was organized into an effective power base. But none of the indigenous peoples in the area had much sense of definite territorial occupance or patriotism beyond that of clan or tribal organization. Therefore the area was a sort of no man's land or political vacuum between more powerfully organized neighbors until the nineteenth century when the Russians intervened. Throughout much of this long history, China was more or less an organized state in the east, although its western territories were not very directly attached to China proper, and in the south the Persian and Ottoman Empires exerted some influence, as did India, and later the British in India. Thus, the region was often a stage for a three-way struggle between the encroaching Russians from the north, the anarchic and rebellious indigenous peoples, and other powers on the east and south.

There was little recorded history in the region before the Arab invasions of the seventh and eighth centuries. Therefore it is very difficult to unravel the origins of the many peoples who now are designated as distinct nationalities. Such distinctions were not generally made before the Soviet period. Most of the people in the area identified themselves only with small clans or tribes through blood relations and did not think of themselves as members of larger national groups. The identification of broad national groups as they exist today is largely a product of Sovietization, which, although it made use of traditional group names, nevertheless codified the national classification scheme as it had never been codified before. In fact, the Soviet codification brought to light a great

deal of confusion. The Russians themselves were not very well acquainted with
local ethnic histories. This was particularly
true in the delineation between the
Kazakhs and the Kirgiz. The expansive
steppes of what is now northern Kazakhstan originally were known by the Russians
as the Kirgiz Steppes, and after the Revolution when the Central Asian area was
first constituted into political subdivisions,
the region became known as the Kirgiz
A.S.S.R. It was only in 1925 that this bit of
confusion was eliminated.

Before the seventh century, the only
part of the entire region about which any
coherent information is available was
Sogd, which lay between the Oxus and
Jaxartes Rivers in the region that was later
to become known as Transoxania. The
people of Sogd were of Iranian origin, and
they formed a small part of a vast nomadic
Turkic Empire which stretched from the
Urals to Mongolia and southward into the
mountains bordering on China and India.
During the seventh century the Persian
Empire was overrun by Arab forces
centered on Damascus, and these Arabs
moved northeastward into Transoxania
and occupied what they regarded as
Chinese Turkestan. In spite of the fact that
the Arab power was soon replaced by the
Persians once more, the Arab imprint was
lasting, in the form of religion and rudimentary administration such as law, taxa-
tion, and land tenure. Originally, the
Islamic culture was confined pretty much
to the Iranian settlements of the south, but
by the fifteenth century it had spread to
the Turkic nomads in the northern steppes.

From about A.D. 1000 to A.D. 1200, the
region was under the influence of various
Turkic rulers and dynasties who quickly
embraced Islam. The Mongol invasion
under Genghis Khan early in the thirteenth century quickly overran all of Turkestan and part of the steppe region, but
the Mongol forces consisted largely of
locally recruited Turks, so that the number

of Mongols who settled in the region was
negligible, and the lasting cultural effects
of the conquest were very small. By the
middle of the fourteenth century all the
Mongol rulers had become Turkicized and
had embraced Islam. The Mongol period
reached its zenith under Timur (Tamerlane) and his successors during the fifteenth and early sixteenth centuries when
the Timurid Dynasty was finally over-
thrown by a part of the nomad Kazakhs,
who had embraced Islam and become
known as Uzbeks. They moved southward from the region northwest of the
Aral Sea and overwhelmed the southern
settlements.

Since the Arab invasion had not penetrated northward as far as the Kazakh
Steppes, the early history of the Kazakhs
has never been recorded. In the first half
of the seventeenth century the people in
that area were referred to as Uzbeks. But
by the second half of the seventeenth century a so-called Kazakh Union had been
formed to establish contact with the Russians, who by this time had conquered the
Mongol Khanate of Astrakhan at the
mouth of the Volga. During the seventeenth and early part of the eighteenth
centuries the various Kazakh hordes found
it necessary to become more or less united
against the Kalmyk or Oyrot invasions
directed against their region from what
is now Sinkiang in Western China. It was
partly in order to gain help against these
invasions that some of the Kazakhs submitted to Russian rule around 1730. Thus
the stage was set for Russian occupance.
The Russians were already in possession
of western Siberia and had established a
line of Cossack settlements along the Ural
River in the west. Five years later they
established the city of Orenburg as an outpost to act as a fortress against the steppe
peoples who periodically moved northward toward the Urals. The Cossack settlements and Orenburg were the beginning of what was to become a line of forti-

fied settlements, such as Omsk, Akmolinsk, Semipalatinsk, Pavlodar, and Barnaul, in an effort to form a cordon around the north and eastern borders of the Kazakh area.

Toward the end of the eighteenth century three khanates came into being, in Bukhara, Khorezm (Khiva), and Kokand. At that time, these three khanates occupied most of the territory that now constitutes the four Middle Asian Republics, but there were no clearly defined frontiers and there was constant war among them. For a time the Russians believed that they could negotiate with these khanates which appeared to them to be properly constituted nation states, but by the first part of the nineteenth century the Russians realized that this was far from actuality and that they would have to neutralize these khanates by force if they were to advance until they reached the frontiers of organized states. By this time, Central Asia had become a very isolated region of the world, since the caravan routes, which from the second century B.C. had intimately connected Central Asia with the Middle and Far East, had long since given way to sea routes between southern Chinese ports and the Persian Gulf. Also, events in other parts of the Middle East had cut off the Central Asian area from the rest of the Muslim world. Therefore on the eve of the Russian march southward, the Central Asian khanates, and still more the steppe region to the north, were the most backward parts of the whole Muslim world, and nation-forming processes could hardly be said to have been underway there. In surrounding areas, the Mogul Empire in Persia was beginning to disintegrate, British power in India had not yet been firmly established, and the Chinese government had liquidated the Oyrots in Dzungaria but had failed to formally establish Sinkiang as a province of the Chinese Empire. Thus the Russian expansion southward began at an aus-picious time when other powers adjoining the region had either abandoned their designs on it or were too weak to pursue them.

The Russians had no problem moving across the Kazakh Steppes where there were no cities or permanently settled areas or any organized military force other than small followings at the disposal of individual tribal leaders. In the settled khanates, however, things were quite different. Here despotic khans and emirs ruled with iron hands and maintained strict social organization and military might. It was against these hotbeds of resistance that Russian efforts were directed beginning in 1855 in an all-out effort to nullify the relatively impotent, but nevertheless harassing, military forces of the native groups who were in the habit of swooping down on the new Russian settlements and carrying off hostages to be sold as slaves in Khiva or Bukhara. Consequently, without too much difficulty, the Russians captured Yangi, now Dzhambul, in 1864; Tashkent in 1865; Khodzhent, now Leninabad, in 1866; Bukhara and Samarkand in 1868; and the last remaining khanates of Khiva in 1873 and Kokand in 1876. Finally, in the early 1880s the Russians succeeded in overrunning Transcaspia and the Merv Oasis after several fierce battles with the Turkmens, who were the most warlike of all the natives of Central Asia.

Suddenly the Russians found themselves in semi-control of this entire great inland empire. Once again they had come into contact with British influence, in India, and in 1888 a frontier was agreed upon that established Afghanistan as a buffer country between Russia and India. Some of the Muslim colonies, such as Bukhara and Khiva, remained nominally independent under the Russian regime until 1920, when finally the Bolsheviks won the civil wars in the area and established Soviet rule.

As in Transcaucasia, the Russian Revolution brought complete chaos to Middle Asia. Actually, what was to follow the 1917 Revolution was portended in 1916 when a great native revolt broke out in Central Asia in response to a Russian imperial decree to call up 500,000 men from among the Central Asian natives to serve as support laborers in the rear of Russian forces engaged on the German front. This was the first time that the Central Asians had been called upon to perform any sort of military duty for the Tsar, and to add insult to injury they were not being asked to actually fight but to dig trenches and do other menial tasks to support the Russian forces. Native wrath was turned largely against the Russian settlers in the area, and full-scale massacres took place on both sides. In addition, it has been estimated that about 300,000 people fled eastward into Chinese territory to escape punitive operations which followed the revolt. The Russian Revolution that followed quickly thereafter was received in Central Asia initially by indifference except for those 3 per cent of the people who were literate and had some idea of what was going on. However, the activities of the Tashkent Soviet, which was set up to administer the general region, and opposition forces in the area made up largely of Russian settlers and dissident loyalist groups from among the higher echelons of previous Tsarist elements, eventually embroiled most of the native groups in disastrous fighting which caused widespread destruction and famine across the entire area. Native resistance finally culminated in a widespread guerrilla movement known as the Basmachi Revolt which lasted for over 5 years, in spite of the fact that by the end of 1920 the whole of the area was pretty well controlled by the Bolsheviks. The Basmachi movement finally collapsed in 1923, and the Central Asian natives resigned themselves to the fact that no material assistance was forthcoming from the outside and no dream of self determi-nation was going to be realized. Obviously, the Soviets had no more intention of relinquishing the territory gained by the Tsars in the nineteenth century than the Tsars themselves had had.

As early as 1920 the Soviets constituted the Kirgiz A.S.S.R., in what is now much of the Kazakh Republic (they were still confusing the Kirgiz and the Kazakhs), and the Turkestan A.S.S.R., which included the rest of Central Asia. Both these A.S.S.R.'s were put under the jurisdiction of the R.S.F.S.R., since that was the only general political entity that existed at the time; the U.S.S.R. was not formed until December 30, 1922. In 1923 and early 1924 the areas controlled by Khiva and Bukhara were constituted as The Peoples Soviet Republic of Khorezm and The Peoples Soviet Republic of Bukhara respectively. (Figure 10–2) In October 1924 the Turkestan, Khorezm, and Bukhara political units were abolished and in their place were established the Uzbek and Turkmen Soviet Socialist Republics, the Tadzhik A.S.S.R., and the Kirgiz and Kara-Kalpak Autonomous Oblasts. When the Stalin Constitution was written in 1936, the Kazakh (Kirgiz) and Tadzhik A.S.S.R.'s and the Kirgiz A.O. were upgraded to the status of S.S.R.'s, and the Kara-Kalpak A.O. was upgraded to an A.S.S.R. Hence by 1936 the five most populous nationality groups in Soviet Middle Asia had been accorded the highest political status possible within the structure of the Soviet Union, and the sixth group had been given the second highest status.

Russian-Chinese Conflict

The Russian drive into Central Asia brought the Russians once more into contact with the Chinese, their long-standing rivals in eastern Siberia and the Far East. The Chinese periodically had exercised nominal control over much of the desert

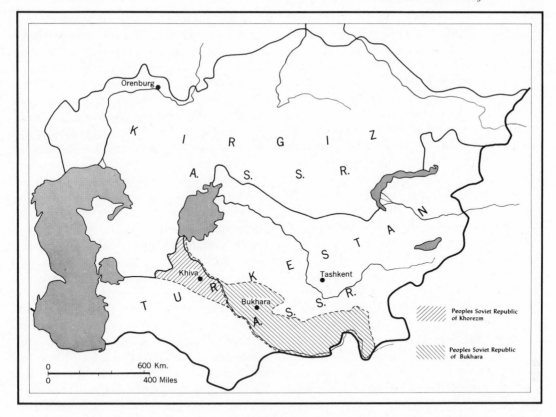

Orenburg

K   I   R   G   I   Z

A.   S.   S.   R.

S

T

Khiva

Tashkent

Bukhara

T   U   R   K   E   S

N

R.

A.   S.   S.   R.

Peoples Soviet Republic
of Khorezm

Peoples Soviet Republic
of Bukhara

0   600 Km.
0   400 Miles

Figure 10–2   The political structure of Middle Asia at the beginning of 1924. After Cherdantsev.

region of Central Asia in spite of the fact that local uprisings largely prevented continuously effective control from the central Chinese government. The Chinese formed only a small minority of the population in the region. Practically all of the population in the area, including the Ili and Dzungarian Districts east of Lake Balkhash in the Tarim Basin, were of Turkic origins, about three quarters of which were made up of so-called Uighurs, Turkic Muslims, who apparently had migrated into the area from the Mongolian Plateau sometime during the eighth or ninth centuries. Kazakhs, Kirgiz, and Uzbeks made up much of the rest. Only about 5 per cent of the population in this district was Chinese, and that was largely made up of the so-called Dungans, Chinese Muslims who felt little if any common bond for the Chinese proper. The small minority of Chinese officials who were located in the area were greatly hated by the national groups. The Chinese had never attempted to settle the area but tried to maintain control in order to exact tribute through local chieftains.

The high point of Chinese influence in this area was reached under the Ching Dynasty in the latter half of the eighteenth century when Dzungaria and Kashgaria were united into the New Dominion, translated as Sinkiang. During this period the khanates of Kokand and Bukhara, as well as many of the Kazakh hordes, submitted to Chinese influence. However, as the Russian drive got under way during the following century it became evident that the corridors of the Ili Valley and the Dzungarian Gate, through which Ghengis Khan and his hordes swept westward in the thirteenth century, were less than one third as far away by camel ride from the out-posts of Russian civilization in south-western Siberia as they were from China proper. Through a series of treaties drawn up between Russia and China be-tween 1860 and 1881, a division of ancient Turkestan was effected between these two great powers. The resultant international boundary divided people of common ethnic, cultural, and religious character-istics. The Kazakh nomads who had wan-dered across the region freely with their flocks and herds in the past suddenly found themselves confronted with an in-ternational boundary. The half million Kazakhs in the Ili-Kazakh District of Sinkiang Province undoubtedly have been the most dynamically rebellious element of the population ever since.

Although the Russian-Chinese boundary set in the late 1800s has not changed sig-nificantly since, the Russians have not abandoned designs upon adjacent parts of Chinese territories. Throughout the first half of the twentieth century the Chinese were experiencing internal difficulties, and the Russians were on the offensive in the area. This offensive was largely an eco-nomic one, although the Russians did not shy away from political advantages when the opportunities presented themselves. Shortly after the establishment of the in-ternational boundary in the 1880s, the Russian government, eager to secure its position against the nomads as well as the Chinese, settled 15,000 crop-cultivating Cossacks in Dzungaria and Ili Districts. The Kazakh nomads were very resentful that their best grass lands had been oc-cupied and that their nomad routes of transhumance from summer to winter pas-tures had been cut. Bloody uprisings were staged against the Russians, and when the Russian Revolution occurred many of the Kazakhs joined the Bolsheviks hoping that their own cause would be benefited. It soon became evident to the Kazakhs that this was not the case, and 100,000 Kazakhs sought asylum in Sinkiang.

It was quite evident that on the eve of World War I Russia had been seriously intending to annex Dzungaria, but the chaos of war, and internal difficulties within China, allowed Sinkiang to live for several years as a semi-independent state under a local Chinese governor. The rela-tive calm ended in 1931 when China sent in a mass migration of thousands of Chinese, and the native Dungans revolted against the local Chinese administration. Turkic-speaking Muslims in the area, in-directly supported by the British, pro-claimed a Republic of East Turkestan. The local Chinese governor, who had been very pro-Soviet throughout the 1920s, called upon the Soviet Union for assistance to put down the revolt, and it was jointly crushed in 1934. Shortly thereafter the Soviets backed a local coup, and from then on they became the dominant political and economic force in the region. They fol-lowed up their advantage very quickly with the establishment of theaters, libraries, and other institutions which became cen-ters for the dissemination of communist propaganda. An intense Sovietization drive was underway. At the same time Stalin was pursuing an all-out drive for collectivization which was generally play-ing havoc with the Kazakh population on the Soviet side of the boundary. It ap-pears that between 1926 and 1939 the Soviet Kazakhs declined from about 4 mil-lion to around 3 million people. It appears that at least 250,000 Kazakhs moved south and east with their herds and flocks, some going over the mountains into India while others attempted to settle in Chinese ter-ritory.

The pro-Soviet Chinese governor in Sinkiang allowed the Soviets to establish military bases in Sinkiang and to monopo-lize the exports of Sinkiang's raw ma-terials. However, in 1942, when it looked as though the Soviet Union was going to lose World War II to the Germans, the Chinese governor in Sinkiang did an about-face and began a massive purge of the communists in the area. The Soviets began a retaliation after World War II, but in 1949 the Chinese communists came into power and a major Chinese force marched into Sinkiang to occupy the territory. In deference to their "communist brothers," the Soviets pulled out of the region, and the Chinese communists have proved their ability to exercise tight control over the area ever since. Since the Chinese communists have taken over the area, population movements largely have been in the opposite direction; Kazakhs, Uighers, and Dungans have been fleeing westward into the Soviet Union to escape the bloody reprisals of the new Chinese regime. It has been reported that Turkic partisans are operating in Sinkiang from bases across the border in the U.S.S.R. It would appear that a former major general from Sinkiang Province who fled to the Soviet Union in 1963 is commanding a 60,000-man army from a base in Alma-Ata. Also, it appears that a secret school exists in the U.S.S.R. for the training of these partisans, and that mounted Turkic partisans make constant forays into Chinese territory.

Present Population

In 1967 it was estimated that southern Kazakhstan and Middle Asia contained about 23 million people who are a mixture of native groups and others who have moved in, particularly Russians and Ukrainians. The 1959 census is the last report available on the national breakdown of the population in the area. (Table 10–1) The five most populous groups give their names to the five union republics.

The Uzbeks are the largest Turkic group in the Soviet Union and the second largest in the world after the Turks of Turkey. With a total of more than 6 million, they are the fourth most numerous nationality in the Soviet Union. Their name was probably derived from Uzbek,

one of the Khans of the Golden Horde. Originally they occupied the area between the lower Volga and the Aral Sea, but in the sixteenth century they migrated southward and conquered the settled regions of Bukhara, Samarkand, Urgench, and Tashkent. Here they became mixed with earlier settlers, including the ancient Iranian population of Khorezm and Sogd. At present more than 80 per cent of the Uzbeks live in the Uzbek Republic, and the remaining million or so are about equally divided among the other four neighboring republics. There are over 1 million Uzbeks outside of the Soviet Union, primarily in Afghanistan, and a few thousand in the Sinkiang-Uighur Autonomous Region in China.

The Turkic Kazakhs are the sixth most numerous nationality in the Soviet Union, with a total of more than 3,500,000 people. About 80 per cent live in Kazakhstan and the remainder in bordering republics. The origin of the Kazakhs is obscure. The word itself does not appear until about the eleventh century when a general term meaning "riders of the steppe" was used to describe the peoples of the area. During the Soviet period there has been a great effort to collectivize and settle the Kazakh nomads, which has resulted in great fluctuations in the population. It has already

Figure 10–3   Uzbek men drinking their afternoon tea on a carpet-covered raised platform beside a shady irrigation ditch north of Tashkent. Photograph by the author.

Table 10–1   Numbers of People by Nationality by Union Republic, 1959

	Number of People (thousands)	Per Cent of Total		Number of People (thousands)	Per Cent of Total
Uzbek S.S.R.	8,106	100.0	Tadzhik S.S.R.	1,980	100.0
Uzbek	5,038	62.2	Tadzhik	1,051	53.1
Russian	1,091	13.5	Uzbek	454	23.0
Tatar	445	5.5	Russian	263	13.3
Kazakh	335	4.1	Tatar	57	2.9
Tadzhik	311	3.8	Ukrainian	27	1.4
Karakalpak	168	2.1	Kirgiz	26	1.3
Korean	138	1.7	Kazakh	13	0.6
Jew	94	1.2			
Kirgiz	93	1.1	Turkmen S.S.R.	1,516	100.0
Ukrainian	88	1.1	Turkmen	924	60.9
Turkmen	55	0.7	Russian	263	17.3
			Uzbek	125	8.3
Kazakh S.S.R.	9,310	100.0	Kazakh	70	4.6
Kazakh	2,795	30.0	Tatar	30	2.0
Russian	3,974	42.7	Ukrainian	21	1.4
Ukrainian	762	8.2	Armenian	20	1.3
Tatar	192	2.1			
Uzbek	137	1.5	Total, Middle Asia		
Belorussian	107	1.2	and Kazakhstan [a]	22,978	100.0
Korean	74	0.8	Slavic Groups	7,250	31.5
Uigur	60	0.6	Russians	6,215	27.0
Pole	53	0.6	Ukrainians	1,035	4.5
Dungan	10	0.1	Titular Native		
			Groups	12,518	54.5
Kirgiz S.S.R.	2,066	100.0	Uzbeks	5,973	26.0
Kirgiz	837	40.5	Kazakhs	3,233	14.0
Russian	624	30.2	Tadzhiks	1,377	6.0
Uzbek	219	10.6	Turkmen	979	4.3
Ukrainian	137	6.6	Kirgiz	956	4.2
Tatar	56	2.7	Other	3,210	14.0
Kazakh	20	1.0			
Tadzhik	15	0.7			
Uigur	14	0.7			

Source: Narodnoye khozyaystvo SSSR v 1960 gody, pp. 17–20.
[a] Includes all of Kazakhstan.
Note: There are significant numbers of Germans who have not been reported, particularly in the Kazakh, Kirgiz, and Tadzhik Republics.

been mentioned that they showed a decrease of about one fourth between the 1926 and 1939 censuses. Since that time they have been on the increase again. About 500,000 Kazakhs live on the Chinese side of the border in Ili District. The Kazakhs differ somewhat in appearance from the Uzbeks in that they have fuller, rounder faces, broader noses, and yellower skin. The Uzbeks tend more toward a dusky complexion, which belies their relation to the Iranians on the south.

Figure 10–4   The interior of the home of a Kazakh collective farmer. The samovar in the foreground provides hot water for making tea, which is drunk out of bowls. Novosti.

The Turkmen are probably the most distinctive Turkic group in Central Asia. They remained quite aloof from the khanates in the settled river valleys to the east, and today they are characterized by long heads with sharp bony features. Their origin is very obscure, but their language indicates origins from the west rather than from the east. Of the 1,004,000 Turkmen in the U.S.S.R., about 924,000 live in the Turkmen S.S.R. and the remainder in the Uzbek S.S.R. There are around 330,000 in Iran and 270,000 in Afghanistan.

The Tadzhiks are undoubtedly the

Figure 10–5   Turkmen women rug weavers listening to newspaper reading during lunch. Novosti.

oldest ethnic element in Central Asia. They are closely related to the Iranians and Afghanians to the south. Of the 1,397,000 living in the U.S.S.R. in 1959, 1,051,000 were living in the Tadzhik S.S.R., and the rest in the Uzbek and Kirgiz S.S.R.'s. The bulk of the Tadzhiks live outside of the Soviet Union, however. There are about 2,100,000 in Afghanistan. There are also Tadzhiks in northern Iran and in Sinkiang Province of China.

The Kirgiz appear to be closely related to the Kazakhs, but their origin is very obscure. It appears that before the ninth century they were living in the upper reaches of the Yenisey River and migrated from there to their present position in the eastern Tyan Shans. The 1959 census showed 974,000 Kirgiz in the Soviet Union, of whom 837,000 lived in the

Kirgiz S.S.R. The remainder lived in the Uzbek and Tadzhik S.S.R.'s. In addition, there are about 70,000 Kirgiz living in the Sinkiang Province of China. Like the Kazakhs, the Kirgiz have yellow complexions and round facial features.

The Karakalpaks numbered 173,000 in 1959, almost all in the Karakalpak A.S.S.R. in the Uzbek Republic south of the Aral Sea. The Karakalpaks were first mentioned toward the end of the sixteenth century. They appear to be closely related to both the Kazakhs and the Uzbeks, probably more closely to the former.

In addition to these six main Asian nationalities, there are Russians, Ukrainians, Jews, Germans, Poles, Belorussians, Tatars, Koreans, Uighurs, and Dungans. Russians, Ukrainians, and Belorussians have been migrating into the area very

Figure 10–6   Tadzhik men playing chess in a tea garden near Dushanbe. Novosti.

Figure 10-7 The felt-covered yurt *is the summer home of Kirgiz shepherds in the mountain pastures of the Tyan Shans. Novosti.*

rapidly in recent years, and consequently the proportion of the titular nationalities in their respective republics has steadily decreased. This is particularly true in Kazakhstan where in 1959 the Kazakhs made up only 30 per cent of the total population. In fact, they were outnumbered by the Russians alone who constituted 42.7 per cent.

In the capital city of Alma-Ata, one sees scarcely anyone but Russians. With this influx of Russians into certain parts of the area, it is quite possible that some changes in the political setup will be made in the near future.

In the oases of Middle Asia where the native populations are more dominant there is very little connection between the native life in the rural villages and the Russian life in the larger cities. The natives live and work the land much as they did before the Revolution, whereas in the cities the factories are being run as they are in Moscow. Most of the natives still live in adobe huts with thatched roofs. The donkey is the universal beast of burden and the donkey cart the chief means of transport of produce.

The population of Kazakhstan and Middle Asia is distributed very unevenly. In general it is concentrated in areas that afford high potentials for agriculture. Such areas are determined primarily by factors of soil and climate, which in turn are very closely related to topography. A few major centers of population and a considerable number of scattered minor settlements owe their existence to the mining of mineral resources, and this is closely related to the geology of the region.

Figure 10–8   Typical mode of transportation in the native villages outside Alma-Ata. An old Kazakh man rides his donkey pulling a cartload of hay. Photograph by the author.

Physical Characteristics

Topographically and geologically the area is quite varied, ranging from broad alluvial plains lying below sea level through old worn-down mountain and plateau areas to the young rugged mountains along the southeastern border.

The Caspian Basin   In the northwest is the low-lying area surrounding the northern and eastern sides of the Caspian Sea. The northern end is part of the old Caspian Lake bed which lies below sea level and is as flat as a floor. The climate here is strictly desert, and many salt flats and auto precipitating salt lakes exist on the plain. Agriculture here, except for extensive grazing of sheep and camels, is quite impossible. The Ural and Emba Rivers, crossing the area on their way from the meager headwater areas in the Southern Urals and Mugodzhar Mountains, barely flow to the Caspian during low-water stage in late summer. Between the two rivers the flat plain is gently interrupted by the slight rises of innumerable salt domes, which are the bases of the Emba oil fields. These flat salt domes are similar to those along the east Texas and Louisiana Gulf Coasts in the United States. Southward along the eastern shore of

the Caspian, the level plain ends abruptly against the Mangyshlak Peninsula in the Kara Tau, or Black Mountain, which is a fault block plateau or horst with steep cliffs on both sides and is split down the middle by a graben that runs the entire length of the peninsula. Elevation here varies from a high of 1742 feet above sea level to 435 feet below sea level in a down-faulted depression in the southeastern part of the peninsula. Recently this area has become active as a new mining region for oil, manganese, and phosphate.

Farther south, Kara-Bogaz-Gol, or Black Mouth Bay, is bordered on almost all sides be steep cliffs of surrounding plateau surfaces that reach heights of a few hundred to one thousand feet above sea level. The gulf itself lies about 100 feet below sea level. Kara-Bogaz-Gol is almost completely cut off from the main body of the Caspian by sand bars which have grown from either side to within about 600 feet of each other, so that the strait between the Caspian and the gulf is now only 600 feet wide and about 10 feet deep. The gulf averages about 30 feet in depth, and according to the Russians it has a surface level that often falls as much as 12 feet below the level of the Caspian. Thus there is a considerable current which flows from the Caspian into the gulf, and the gulf acts as a final evaporation pan for the Caspian. It has been calculated that between 10 and 20 cubic kilometers of water are evaporated from Kara-Bogaz-Gol annually. The salt content here is understandably very high.

South of Kara-Bogaz-Gol is a peninsula formed by the Krasnovodsk Plateau that rises several hundred feet above the Caspian and again plunges off to the sea in very steep cliffs. The city of Krasnovodsk clings to the base of the cliff on a narrow coastal plain bordering the Caspian. Southeast of the Krasnovodsk Plateau lie several anticlines of thick limestone that are known as the Balkhan Ranges, which reach maximum elevations of a little over 5000 feet. The ranges are

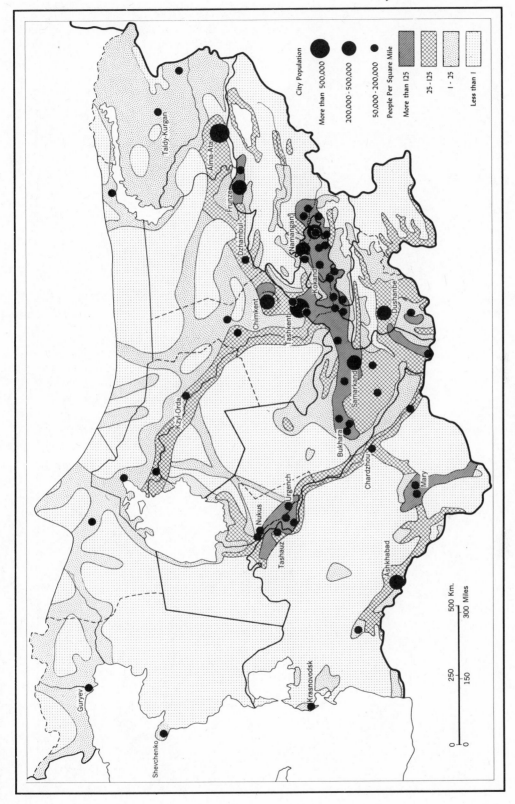

Figure 10–9   Population densities and city sizes. After Cherdantsev.

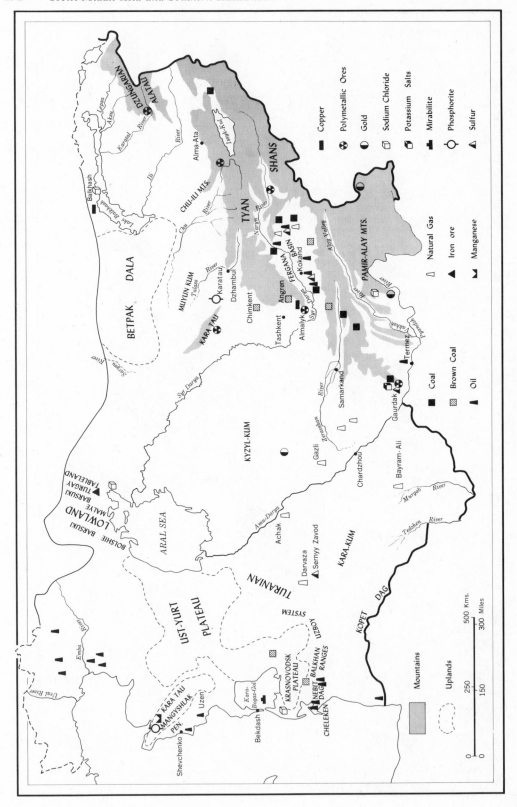

Figure 10-10   The physical landscape and mineral resources.

surrounded by a broad takyr, or salt flat, which represents an old lake bed. The shallow basin was undoubtedly filled with water at one time during the glacial period when a connection existed between the Aral Sea and the Caspian. There are terraces along the slopes of the Balkhans as high as 230 feet above the present surface of the plain. A series of dry stream channels known as the Uzboy System leads through the plain and only a few hundred years ago served as a spillway from the Aral Sea to the Caspian. Nebit-Dag and other low hills rising 150 feet or more above this vast "solonchak" are topographic expressions of dislocated tertiary sediments which yield a considerable quantity of petroleum.

West of Nebit-Dag, or Oil Mountain, lies Cheleken Island, or, since the drop in water level in the Caspian, actually Cheleken Peninsula, another fault block that rises abruptly from the Caspian to elevations of over 300 feet. It has been described as a broken plate, a tertiary, oil-bearing, highly faulted section of sandstone and other deposits underlain by young volcanic magma. Mud volcanoes and petroleum seeps abound and have turned the sand into an asphalt-cemented rock that has split into basaltic-like prisms to form spectacular mesas and buttes. Gases are emitted from some of the mud volcanoes, and gas bubbles constantly rise through the water from the bottom of the Caspian. This sort of activity continues southward to the western end of the Kopet Dag.

This entire coast of the Caspian from the northern end southward all along the eastern side is completely desert, and the landscape is very barren. In spite of the fact that everywhere elevations are relatively low, local relief is considerable, and changes in elevation are abrupt. There are no streams of any note except in the northern end, where the Ural River flows into the Caspian from the Ural Mountains, and the Emba comes in from the northeast off

the Mugodzhar Mountains. The region is little utilized other than the oil-bearing areas of the Emba fields in the north, the Mangyshlak fields in the center, and Nebit-Dag in the south. The few towns that exist along the coast of the Caspian have been established for fishing and trading. All are small and all have acute water supply problems. The largest of these, Krasnovodsk, is supplied with drinking water by tanker across the Caspian from the Kura River in Transcaucasia. Desalting pilot plants have been put into operation at Bekdash, the center of the sodium sulfate industry of Kara-Bogaz-Gol, and at the new oil port of Shevchenko on the Mangyshlak Peninsula. It is said that desalinization processes can produce water for these towns seven times more cheaply than fresh water can be shipped in by tanker from across the Caspian. A second plant of much larger capacity is now being installed at Shevchenko to be powered by a dual-purpose atomic reactor which will provide steam to drive electric turbines as it distills water.

It has been suggested that a 600-mile-long canal be constructed from the lower Amu-Darya to Krasnovodsk utilizing the old Uzboy System, thereby supplying water to Krasnovodsk and providing irrigation water for several million acres of land in the intervening area. But it is quite clear to all who have studied the situation that there simply is not enough water in the Amu-Darya to create such a canal system, and since the death of Stalin no more mention has been made of the project. Perhaps more realistic is a planned extension of the Kara-Kum Canal from Ashkhabad to Krasnovodsk. This canal, which leads off water from the upper Amu-Darya, has already been completed to Ashkhabad.

Between the Caspian and Aral Seas lies the Ust-Yurt Plateau, a dry, flat, barren upland of nearly horizontal sedimentary strata which lies at an elevation of nearly 1000 feet. Its eastern edge plunges in a fault scarp several hundred feet to the Aral Sea at its base. No streams of any significance head in this area, and no water is available to be brought in for irrigation. Hence it is destined to remain an almost unused area.

The Turanian Lowland East of the Ust-Yurt Plateau lies a broad, elongated synclinal trough that stretches in a south-southwest–north-northeast direction from the Kopet Dag along the Iranian border northward into western Siberia. This large plains region is known as the Turanian Lowland, but different sections of it are known by different names.

In its midsection lies the Aral Sea, the fourth largest lake in the world, with a surface area of almost 25,000 square miles. It is a shallow sea, with depths of only 30 to 60 feet throughout much of its extent, and it contains thousands of islands. The name Aral Sea means island sea. The Syr-Darya is building a large delta into the lake in the northeast, and the Amu-Darya is building a large delta from the southern side. Apparently, until only a few hundred years ago the Aral Sea drained southwestward through the Uzboy System into the Caspian; hence the Aral Sea has less than 1 per cent salt. By comparison the southeastern part of the Caspian has about 14 per cent salt. Precipitation in the Aral Sea area totals less than 4 inches per year. If it were not for the surface inflow of the two large rivers fed by the melting snows of the high mountains to the southeast and subsurface seepage of artesian water from fissured aquifers below, the sea would immediately dry up. As it is, the sea seems to be gradually diminishing. The greatest depth, 228 feet, is along the western edge at the base of the fault scarp of the Ust-Yurt Plateau. Hence the basin ends abruptly at a fault scarp on the west, but rises gradually eastward into the sands of the Kyzyl-Kum and Kara-Kum.

North of the Aral Sea the trough is continued as the Turgay Lowland or Turgay Tableland, which extends north of the area under consideration into northern Kazakhstan and southwestern Siberia. The area is a stripped sedimentary plain dotted by mesa and butte remnants of higher strata standing in vertical cliffs above the clay and salt flats occupying much of the basin floor; hence the name Turgay Tableland. Ridges of sand dunes oriented south-southwest–north-northeast occupy parts of the intervening lowlands among the tablelands. The most extensive of these dune areas are the Bolshie, or great, Barsuki, northwest of the Aral Sea, and the Malye, or small, Barsuki, north of the Aral Sea. It is thought that important I.C.B.M. bases have been built in this remote and empty area. South of the Aral Sea the Turanian Lowland continues through the western part of the Kara-Kum, or black sands, desert to the foothills of the Kopet Dag on the Iranian border.

The Eastern Sand-Ridge Deserts and Uplands Southwest of the Amu-Darya lies the Kara-Kum, the most extensive sand desert in Middle Asia. About nine tenths of the area is covered by elongated ridges of sand topped by smaller, shifting barchan dunes of loose sand. Most of it is quite unfit for agriculture. Only the southern margins bordering on the mountains along the south and the northern section near the mouth of the Amu-Darya have rich alluvial soils that are supplied with irrigation water and support a thriving agriculture.

Across the Amu-Darya to the northeast is the Kyzyl-Kum, or Red Sand Desert, which occupies much of the area lying between the Amu-Darya and the Syr-Darya. The Kyzyl-Kum is higher, rockier, and more devoid of sand than is the Kara-Kum, and shows more variety in its relief. Stubby, worn-down outcrops of old Paleozoic formations reach elevations of over 3000 feet in the central and southwestern portions. Like the Kara-Kum, the Kyzyl-Kum is a very dry desert which is little utilized except along the margins where some irrigation water can be derived from either the Syr-Darya or the Amu-Darya.

Northeast of the Syr-Darya is the Kara Tau, or Black Mountain, extending northwestward from the Tyan Shans and overlooking the Muyun Kum to the northeast. The Muyun Kum, or Sandy Desert, is a ridged sand desert similar to the Kara-Kum, but it is much more restricted in area and somewhat higher in elevation. The Muyun Kum is bordered on the west and east by the Talass and Chu Rivers, which head in the Tyan Shans to the south and flow northwestward to end in the sands. The Chu Valley separates the Muyun Kum on the south from the Betpak-Dala to the north.

Betpak-Dala means Cruel, Crafty Steppe. It derives its name, it is thought, from the fact that it is an extensive trackless surface that on hot days abounds in mirages which lead the unwary traveler astray. This dry plateau rises from an elevation of about 450 feet at its southern edge along the Chu River northward to elevations of about 1500 feet where it merges with the higher Kazakh Folded Country north of Lake Balkhash. On the northwest it drops off in an escarpment approximately 150 feet high to the Sarysu River. In its western portion it is composed primarily of horizontal layers of clay and sandstone, predominantly of Tertiary age, but to the east the area is one of melkosopochnik, which is a Russian term designating old worn-down hills composed of granites, syenites, porphyries, diorites, and some sedimentary Paleozoic strata. The Betpak-Dala, or Hungry Steppe, has a cracked-clay and salt-encrusted surface that supports only a sparse vegetation and has very little prospects for development. The area should not be confused with the less extensive Hungry Steppe southwest of Tashkent where an irrigation project has produced the so-called Pakhta Aral, or cotton island, southwest of the Syr-Darya.

Lake Balkhash occupies a large landlocked basin approximately 350 miles long at an elevation of about 1100 feet above sea level. The lake itself has a surface area of approximately 6680 square miles and an average depth of only 20 feet. But terraces along the northern side, rising to elevations approximately 400 feet above the surface of the lake, attest to the fact that the lake was higher at one time and reached as far eastward as the basin of Ebi-Nur in China. Apparently the waters of the lake are of geologically recent origin, since the salt content is quite low. The western end, which is fed by the Ili River, is fresh enough to be used for irrigation and drinking. The lake seems to be in the process of drying up and becoming more salty, however. Large alluvial fans built by small streams flowing northward out of the northern ranges of the Tyan Shans have stretched across the basin of the lake and have cut off segments of its eastern end. These isolated segments are becoming quite salty. A sand bar practically severs the present lake in its midsection, thereby dividing a relatively fresh body of water in the western end, where fresh water is added by the Ili River, from a relatively salty body of water in the eastern end, where the Karatal, Aksu, and Lepsa Rivers are insufficient to counterbalance evaporation. The eastern end serves as the final evaporation pan for the entire lake.

The High Mountains Everywhere on the south and east, Middle Asia is bounded by high, rugged mountains. In the west, bordering on Iran, are the Kopet Dag, or Dry Mountains, a fault-block range which is cut sharply on its northeastern side by a major fault system that runs in a straight line from southeast to northwest along the Transcaspian Railroad through the cities of Ashkhabad and Kizyl-Arvat and continues on northwestward through Nebit-Dag and the Balkhan Mountains to the Caspian. The Kopet Dag reaches elevations of around 7500 feet in the Soviet Union, but the area is so dry that even in their highest elevations the mountains are practically devoid of vegetation. Erosion, in the process of stripping the sedimentary layers down their dip slopes toward the southwest, has produced a series of jagged, overhanging cuesta escarpments facing northeastward overlooking the sandy deserts of the Kara-Kum. The spectacular scenery standing out in bold relief in this dry climate has induced the Soviets to establish the city of Ashkhabad as one of the film-making centers of the Soviet Union. Western-type movies are produced here, utilizing the magnificent backdrop of the Kopet Dag. No streams of any proportions originate in the Kopet Dag, but several small streams provide water for local domestic use and restricted irrigation in areas such as Ashkhabad. Also, wells and underground canal systems constructed centuries ago by the Persians are still utilized to provide limited water supplies.

Eastward from the Kopet Dag rise the Hindu Kush. Although they lie entirely in Afghanistan, they provide the water shed for small streams flowing northward into Soviet Middle Asia. The two largest of these streams, the Murgab and the Tedzhen Rivers, end in the sands of Turkmenistan and form the two oases around the cities of Mary and Tedzhen.

The Hindu Kush rise in eastern Afghanistan to join the Pamir Knot, which straddles the boundaries of Afghanistan, Pakistan, China, and the Soviet Union. On the Soviet Union side, the Pamirs fan out to the west in a series of east-west oriented ranges, known as the Pamir-Alay. These are the highest mountains in the Soviet Union, containing the peaks of Mt. Communism (formerly Mt. Stalin) at an elevation of 24,590 feet and Mt. Lenin at an elevation of 23,363 feet, both in the

Figure 10–11   A relic on the barren high Pamirs, Tadzhik S.S.R. Novosti.

Figure 10–12   The Gissar Range, Tadzhik S.S.R. Novosti.

Tadzhik Republic. In the western ex-
tremities the Pamir-Alay Ranges are
deeply dissected by the headwaters of the
Amu-Darya, especially by the two main
headwater streams, the Vakhsh and the
Pyandzh. Throughout much of its course,
the Pyandzh forms the international
boundary between the Soviet Union and
Afghanistan. The Vakhsh and several
smaller streams flow southwestward
through a gently rolling upland in southwestern Tadzhikistan, and provide irrigation water to transform the steppe
into the primary agricultural area of the
Tadzhik Republic.

The Trans Alay Range forms the northernmost range of the Pamir-Alay Mountains, and northward across the Alay Valley
the Alay Range forms the southernmost
range of an extensive mountain system
known as the Tyan Shans, a Chinese term
meaning Heavenly mountains. The Tyan
Shans stretch all the way from northern

Tadzhikistan, through the Uzbek and
Kirgiz Republics, and through eastern
Kazakhstan east of Lake Balkhash into
China. The individual ranges in this system
are oriented primarily west-east, and generally they are rather widely spaced with
broad steppe-like mountain basins in between. The broadest of these mountain
basins is the Fergana Basin just north of
the Alay Range. This flat-floored alluvial
basin, extending approximately 100 miles
east-west and 10 to 25 miles north-south, is
a major agricultural area of Middle Asia. It
is a steppe area and requires irrigation.

North of the Fergana Basin the main
ranges of the Tyan Shans form a bold escarpment on the north overlooking a string
of important irrigated areas and cities
built on the alluvial fans at their base.
Many small streams flowing northwestward
out of the mountains bring the all-important water to these settlements. Issyk-Kul,
as well as several smaller lakes, lie within

these ranges. The headwaters of the Syr-Darya, particularly the Naryn, head along the southern slope of the ranges and flow the entire length of the Fergana Basin before entering the desert to the northwest. These lakes and streams are fed by melting glaciers during the summer and reach their greatest flow at that time, a fact that is very significant to the agriculture in the area. Most of the precipitation in these mountains comes during the wintertime in the form of snow when cyclonic storms from the Mediterranean and Black Seas penetrate the Middle Asian region. The precipitation in the form of snow is stored until it is needed for irrigation in the summer. Were it not for this natural storage, agriculture in this area would be extremely limited.

The Tyan Shans in general are folded mountain ranges, but faulting has occurred, and some volcanism has broken out along various fault lines. Issyk-Kul, or hot lake, gets its name from the fact that volcanic activity in the immediate surroundings produces warm water in certain portions of the lake. Several fault-block ranges branch out in a general northwesterly direction from the northern side of the main line of the Tyan Shans. The most westerly of these, Kara Tau, has already been mentioned as the divide between the Kyzyl-Kum and the Muyun Kum northeast of the Syr-Darya. Lying in a desert climatic area, the Kara Tau stand out conspicuously although the elevations are no higher than 5700 feet. The dark and somber sedimentary rocks making up the fault block have formed imposing escarpments facing northeast under the erosional process of stripping down the dip slope toward the southwest. Similar to the Kara Tau are the Chu-Ili Mountains, lying between the Chu and the Ili Rivers, extending northwestward from Alma-Ata toward Lake Balkhash. Their highest elevation is a little over 3500 feet.

After a major break where the Ili River flows westward out of China, the Tyan Shans rise once again in the Dzungarian Alatau to elevations of 16,500 feet. As indicated by the name, these mountains also are snow capped year round. The term "Alatau" means "mottled mountains" and comes from the fact that in the summertime from a distance the mountains appear mottled because of patches of snow on their slopes. The Dzungarian Alatau are the northernmost range of the Tyan Shans, and are separated from the Tarbagatay Mountains to the north by the broad Dzungarian Gate east of Lake Balkhash. The Dzungarian Gate has long afforded a low-level route of travel from Sinkiang, China, into Middle Asia and thence to the Middle East and Europe.

North of the Dzungarian Gate, the Tarbagatay Range, rising to 9500 feet, represents the eastern extremity of an extensive area of old, worn-down mountains north of Lake Balkhash. This area, the Kazakh Folded Country, is discussed with northern Kazakhstan in Chapter 11 as are the chains of high mountains that continue northeastward into Siberia.

Hydrology and Soils

Water is the key word in Soviet Middle Asia, as it is in most dry regions of the earth. With water the native population can carry on an extensive irrigation agriculture; without it, they must struggle as best they can with dry-farming procedures in the moister areas and with extensive grazing in the drier areas. As has been pointed out at the beginning of this chapter, the entire plains area of Soviet Middle Asia is dry. Certain areas are moister than others, but none classifies as humid. The streams that originate on the plain flow primarily only as spring freshets when the thin snow cover is melting; many of them dry up completely before the summer is over. All end either in one of the three great interior drainage basins, the Caspian Sea, the Aral Sea, or Lake Balkhash, or in some salt-encrusted playa lake bed. None of the runoff from this area reaches the sea; evaporation eventually accounts for all the precipitation that falls in the area.

Perennial streams are limited primarily to those whose headwaters lie in the high mountains and are fed throughout the summer by the melting snows and glaciers. In the south the two outstanding streams of this nature are the Amu-Darya and the Syr-Darya, the two great rivers of Soviet Middle Asia that flow into the Aral Sea. But many smaller streams flow out of the southern mountains, some of which already have been named. Of these, the most important to irrigation are the Ili and Chu Rivers in the east, the Zeravshan between the Syr-Darya and the Amu-Darya, the Murgab and the Tedzhen in the Turkmen Republic, and the Vakhsh in the Tadzhik Republic.

The Ural River in the northwest does not have much of a water shed in the Southern Urals, but it does find its way to the Caspian all year round. The other stream of significance northeast of the Caspian, the Emba River, heads in the low Mugodzhar Mountains and barely makes it to the sea in late summer.

The inorganic soils of the area are adaptable to a variety of crops wherever irrigation water is available and the surface material is not too sandy or rocky. Large areas of the lower portions of the alluvial fans spreading out from the mountains toward the northern lowlands are deeply covered by loess on which mineral-rich sierozem soils have developed. The loess appears to be material which has been reworked by the wind after it was originally laid down by streams either in the fashion of alluvial fans or in glacio-fluvial deposits during the Pleistocene Period. This is one of the most extensive belts of loess in the world; in places it reaches thicknesses of several hundred feet. The loess stands in vertical cliffs because of its loosely compacted porous nature and is an ideal soil

Figure 10–13   The "fences" around the fields and barnlots near Tashkent are loess walls. Photograph by the author.

for farming and for making adobe walls for houses and fences. Hence it is not difficult to understand why very early civilizations developed in some of these river valleys.

Other than in the loess belt, fine, fertile soils are found in delta areas and in other sections of floodplains of the major rivers. The most extensive area of good river alluvium is near the mouth of the Amu-Darya.

Some of the coarser soils near the heads of alluvial fans are adaptable to vegetable and fruit crops, and are ideally situated with respect to sources of water. The most highly developed area of this type is around Alma-Ata against the very base of the Tyan Shans.

Agriculture

The agriculture of southern Kazakhstan and Soviet Middle Asia can be characterized broadly into three types: (1) extensive grazing throughout much of the area, (2) dry farming of grain in the moister portions of loess-covered foothills of the southern mountains, and (3) intensive irrigation farming of cotton, alfalfa, some grain, and many vegetables and fruits wherever good soil and irrigation water are available.

Figure 10–14   Drying karakul skins. Novosti.

Grazing Some grazing of livestock is carried on nearly everywhere, but it becomes the predominant economy in the drier lowlands and in the high mountains where cultivation is largely impossible. The entire lowland from the Caspian Sea to the eastern end of Lake Balkhash and extending to the southern border of the Turkmen Republic, except for scattered regions of irrigation, is utilized only for grazing. Even grazing is poor throughout the drier areas, in many areas being limited to spring and early summer after the melting snows have produced an abundance of ephemeral vegetation. Thawing and refreezing of winter snow, as well as ice storms, may form a hard crust of ice over the surface of the plains, which makes it impossible for the livestock to reach the grass underneath during prolonged periods in the winter. On the other hand, in the immediate forelands of many of the mountains of the southeast, foehn winds during the winter frequently produce relatively balmy spells of weather with temperatures above freezing, which dispel the snow and provide open grazing through the winter. This is particularly true in the region between the Dzungarian Gate and the eastern end of Lake Balkhash, where a foehn wind, called the "ebe," frequently flows westward down slope from the Sinkiang Basin in China.

Sheep and camels predominate in the lowland deserts. Cattle, sheep, and goats utilize the desert pastures in winter and spring but must be driven to the mountains during the summer. Transhumance is practiced on a grand scale.

The Karakul sheep are admirably suited to desert conditions, having originated in the Karakul, or Black Lake, Oasis at the end of the Zeravshan River. Karakul are black, curly-haired sheep that are raised for the skins of the new-born lambs, which bring very high prices on the world market. They are raised in various places scattered about the desert and in the mountains to some extent, but they are concentrated in the Zeravshan area. The Kara-Kalpak A.S.S.R. south of the Aral Sea owes its name to these sheep. The term "Kara-Kalpak" refers to the large Karakul hat worn by the natives in this area. Today factories in Tashkent and in some of the other cities of Middle Asia are turning out synthetic Karakul cloth.

Camels have been used extensively as beasts of burden in the deserts of Middle Asia, particularly along the caravan route from China to Europe. Such cities as Tashkent and Samarkand were long important as stopover points along the "silk road" between China and Europe, and the camel very early became established as the best means of transport across the Middle Asian deserts. Today camels seem to be

decreasing in importance; they are no longer seen in the vicinity of the larger cities. Cattle and sheep are becoming the predominant animals, for their meat, and the donkey is the chief beast of burden in the cultivated areas of Middle Asia.

A great effort is being made to rely less and less on the native vegetation and more and more on forage and hay crops raised in rotation with cotton and grain. Alfalfa is the chief rotation crop with the cotton in the irrigated areas and produces an abundant supply of forage, being harvested usually about five times per year. Along with this reliance on domestic crops, the Soviets are attempting to settle the nomadic herdsmen and to make farmers out of them. Recently there have been reports that herdsmen from the high mountains are being resettled with their families on irrigated plains to open up new cotton-alfalfa-beef cattle areas.

Although the native vegetation over

Figure 10-15   Saxaul trees in the Kyzyl Kum. Novosti.

much of the desert area is rather poor for grazing, it is very important to the stabilization of the blowing sands. Little of the desert actually is devoid of vegetation, even in the most sandy areas of the Kara-Kum. Besides many species of brushy plants and ephemeral grasses and flowering herbs, there is a stunted tree that appears to be unique to this desert area. This is the Saxaul, a gnarled tree approximately 20 feet high of very heavy, iron-hard wood that burns like charcoal. The Saxaul has two main species: the white, or sand, Saxaul which grows on top of the sand dunes, and the black Saxaul which grows in the alkaline flats between the sand dunes. Maintaining itself practically without water, the Saxaul has been very important both in the stabilization of the sand dunes and as a source of firewood for the nomadic herdsmen. After all, this is a cold region in winter to be weathered in makeshift camps. Lying wide open to cold blasts of Siberian air from the northeast, much of the area averages well below freezing in January. As far south as Tashkent, the January average is only 30°F, and at times the temperature plunges to zero or below. In the past the Saxaul tree has been utilized so extensively for fuel that in certain areas it has been threatened by extinction. There

Figure 10–17   *Women coming with their buckets and yokes to obtain water at the village pump on a state farm north of Alma-Ata. The new rural dwellings of unpainted boards and sheet metal roofs are typical of new single-family dwellings throughout the Soviet Union. Photograph by the author.*

is now an effort to save the Saxaul tree and to reforest certain areas with it to stabilize the drifting sands. Stabilization of the sands becomes especially necessary where canals and railroads are constructed.

Dry Farming   Wheat and some other grains are dry farmed in the moister portions of the loess-covered foothills in the south where precipitation averages between 10 and 15 inches per year. In these areas the rain comes primarily in late winter and early spring, which is quite advantageous for wheat growing. Dry farming of grain has been carried on in the loessial foothills for a long time, but under the virgin lands program additional areas have been opened up.

The loess belt is a dry, hot, dusty place in the summer, and it is not easy to recruit people to settle the new state farms. In the words of Berg, "In summer the towns of Middle Asia may be recognized from a distance by the loessial dust which hangs over them. This dust is a characteristic feature of all the settlements of Middle Asia. Carried by winds and convectional currents, the fine dust rises to a height of at least 6000 meters. Often during the dry period of the year when gales are blowing, the whole sky is covered by a continuous turbid

Figure 10–16   *"Main street" in a village of 5000 people on a new state farm in the loess belt north of Alma-Ata. The building in the left foreground is the village store. Photograph by the author.*

shroud. In general a whitish, foggy atmospheric coloration is very characteristc to the landscape here." The so-called afghanets, a dry, dusty southwest wind, blows from 40 to 70 days per year in the vicinity of Termez on the Afghan border.

Irrigation Agriculture Wherever irrigation water is available, the rich loess soil has been utilized intensively for irrigated crops. Also, some of the more stony soils in the higher parts of the alluvial fans have been irrigated for the growing of fruit trees, grapes, and berries, which do not make heavy demands on the soil. These irrigated areas form a discontinuous belt along the northern slopes of the Tyan Shans all the way from Taldy-Kurgan in the east through Alma-Ata, Frunze, and Dzhambul to Tashkent, and on westward across the Kara-Kum along the northern bases of the Hindu Kush and Kopet Dag.

Irrigation developed the earliest along the River Zeravshan, but the largest continuous area of irrigation today is the Fergana Basin between two prongs of the Tyan Shans. Other extensive areas lie in southwestern Tadzhikistan, utilizing the waters of the Vakhsh and several lesser rivers, and around Tashkent, utilizing the waters of the Chirchik and Angren Rivers before they enter the Syr-Darya. Other extensive regions of irrigation exist along the Amu-Darya and Syr-Darya. The largest of these by far is along the lower Amu-Darya in the so-called Khorezm or Khiva Oasis. A line of oases of lesser size are strung along the Transcaspian Railway from Mary through Tedzhen and Ashkhabad to Kizyl-Arvat. These oases utilize separate small streams flowing northward out of the Hindu Kush and Kopet Dag.

The specialty crop for which the irrigated areas of Middle Asia are best known is, of course, cotton. But many other crops are raised that also utilize the long hot summers and good loess soils. Although the Soviets have forced a continual expansion of cotton acreage in the irrigated

areas at the expense of wheat, a considerable amount of irrigated land is still occupied by grain crops, particularly wheat and rice — the staple food of Middle Asia — and by a great variety of fruits and vegetables. Certain regions are known for their vineyards and wine-making. And recently, sugar beets have been introduced into the area rather heavily. Other specialty crops are raised, such as tobacco and kenaf, a fiber crop for use in making ropes and burlap bags. Not all these crops are scattered throughout the entire region; the physical environment does vary from place to place, and certain regions are conducive to the growing of other crops. Cotton growing is limited to the regions with the longest, hottest growing season, which eliminates it from the northeastern slopes of the Tyan Shans. A brief summary of the main irrigated areas of Middle Asia and characterizations of their crop complexes follows.

Beginning in the east, the first irrigated region is around Taldy-Kurgan, in eastern Kazakhstan just south of the eastern end of Lake Balkhash. (Fig. 10–18) Most of the irrigated acreage here is occupied by grain, primarily wheat and barley, with some rice growing. But the crop for which the area is becoming known is sugar beets, which have been introduced recently by inmigrating Russians and Ukrainians.

Southwestward, along the slopes of the Tyan Shans, is a significant area of irrigated agriculture around the large city of Alma-Ata. Much of this irrigation is carried on in the rather rocky alluvial fans at the very base of the Tyan Shans. Also, the region lies at an elevation of about 2000 feet above sea level, and this together with its expsoure to the north produces a climate that is too cool for cotton. Fruit and vegetable growing are developed to a high degree around Alma-Ata, and the city provides a ready market for such produce. The name Alma-Ata means Father of Apples. Supposedly this area is where apples originated. There are many apple

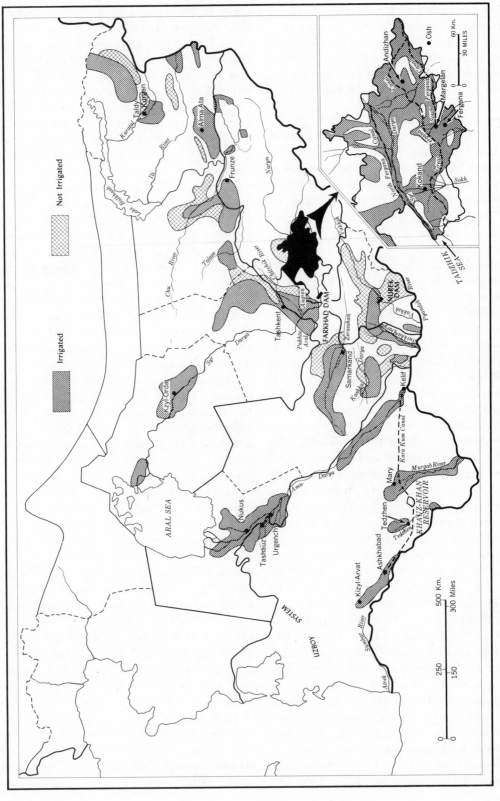

Figure 10–18   Cultivated land.

orchards on the collective farms surrounding the city. Some rice is grown northwest of Alma-Ata near the mouth of the Ili River.

Moving westward, the next important river valley is the Chu, which stretches northwestward from the city of Frunze, the capital of the Kirgiz Republic. About 90 per cent of the irrigated acreage in the Chu Valley is planted to grain crops, particularly winter wheat and barley, but the Valley is better known for its sugar beets. Like the Taldy-Kurgan area farther east, sugar beets have been introduced recently into the Chu Valley by Russian and Ukrainian settlers. The Chu Valley is now the most important sugar beet raising area in Middle Asia and has been dubbed Sugar Beet Valley.

Westward from the Chu Valley across the Muyun-Kum is a small river along the eastern base of the Kara Tau. This is the Talass River, and its valley is the beginning of the cotton belt. The Talass is not a large stream and the irrigated area it supports is not extensive. The chief crop here is cotton, but some grain and sugar beets are grown near the city of Dzhambul. Also, a little rice is grown in this area.

Except in some mountain spurs along the western end of the Tyan Shans, the cotton belt continues unbroken from the Talass River Valley westward down the Chirchik and Arys Rivers to the Syr-Darya. Along the Syr-Darya, irrigated agriculture stretches both upstream and downstream for a long distance. The broadest area of irrigation is in the middle section from the small town of Turkestan southeastward to Tashkent and then eastward into the broad Fergana Basin. Throughout this entire region cotton reigns supreme, but other crops are raised, particularly alfalfa as a rotation crop with the cotton. In the Fergana Basin a considerable amount of irrigated wheat and barley are grown, and in both this area and in the vicinity of Tashkent, rice is grown. Around the larger cities vegetables and fruits of all types are grown for the urban markets. Grapes for wine are grown throughout the area. Such specialty crops as kenaf are being introduced. Mulberry trees have been grown for centuries along the irrigation canals and provide the basis for a silk industry.

Since the mid 1950s, the large Pakhta Aral (Cotton Island) has been created in the Golodnaya Steppe (Hungry Steppe) southwest of Tashkent by irrigating a large continuous area of previously flat, dry land by bringing in water from the Syr-Darya from nearby dam projects. Downstream on the Syr-Darya in a long strip of irrigated land centered on Kzyl-Orda, and again near the delta of the Syr-Darya, are extensive areas of rice growing.

A separate area of irrigation lies along the Zeravshan River, which flows westward out of the Tyan Shans across the southern Kyzyl-Kum toward the Amu-Darya. The Zeravshan has already been mentioned as the location of the earliest river civilization in Middle Asia. For a distance of about 200 miles along the Zeravshan irrigated cotton extends in an almost unbroken belt 10 to 25 miles wide. In its middle and eastern portions this belt is flanked on either side by unirrigated wheat and barley. The irrigated strip extends westward beyond Bukhara to the region of Karakul, which has been mentioned before as the origin of the Karakul sheep. Although this area along the Zeravshan is heavily concentrated on cotton and wheat, other crops, such as rice, tobacco, and certain fiber crops are raised, as well as grapes and other fruits and vegetables for the local market. The irrigated acreage is being considerably extended by use of water brought to the lower Zeravshan area from the Amu-Darya via the newly constructed Amu-Karakul and Amu-Bukhara Canals.

Several extensive areas of irrigated agriculture exist along the Amu-Darya and some of its tributary valleys. In the upstream portions of the river system lies the irrigated region in southwestern Tadzhikistan on the low plateau which is

Figure 10–19   The "Great Uzbek Road" through the "Gate of Tamerlane" on the Zeravshan River near Samarkand. Novosti.

crossed by the Vakhsh River and other tributaries of the Amu-Darya. Long staple cotton and grain are the chief crops in this area. Some rice is grown for local consumption. Adjacent to this area on the west is the region in the very southernmost part of the Uzbek Republic that is watered by the Surkhan-Darya, the Kashka-Darya, and some other minor streams. The Surkhan-Darya Valley grows considerable irrigated cotton, and a small area of cotton exists in the Kashka-Darya Valley. The Kashka-Darya Valley also grows a con-

siderable amount of irrigated grain. Specialty crops such as rice, tobacco, grapes, and so forth are scattered throughout the region. A new canal from the Amu-Darya is providing water to triple the irrigated area in Kashka-Darya Oblast.

The irrigated region along the Amu-Darya extends downstream past the city of Chardzhou, where it ends in the sand, and no more agriculture is found until near the city of Urgench on the lower portion of the river. Downstream from Urgench, except for the swampy, reed-covered delta, the river plain supports an extensive area of irrigated agriculture whose origin dates back to ancient times. This is the famous Khiva Oasis, which at the present time is divided between Khorezm Oblast and the Kara-Kalpak A.S.S.R. within the Uzbek Republic and Tashauz Oblast in the Turkmen Republic. This area is hot and dry with excellent soils that have been deposited by repeated floodings of the river through the ages. The region probably is more highly concentrated on cotton growing than any of the other areas mentioned. Alfalfa serves as the rotation crop. The area is also one of the major rice-growing regions of Middle Asia.

The remaining areas of irrigation lie along the northern bases of the Hindu Kush and Kopet Dag on the southern border of the Turkmen Republic. The largest of these are the Murgab River Valley, with its chief city of Mary, in the east; the Tedzhen River Valley, with its major town of Tedzhen, in the middle; and the area around Ashkhabad, the capital city of the Turkmen Republic, in the west, which is fed by several minor streams. Cotton is grown in all three areas, but it is predominant in the Murgab River Valley. The Tedzhen River Valley is predominantly irrigated grain, and the Ashkhabad region is a mixture of cotton and grain.

One other very small valley that the Russians sometimes mention as having potentialities for citrus growing lies along the Sumbar River which flows through the western end of the Kopet Dag into the Atrek River and finally into the Caspian Sea. This region is a very limited area of irrigated agriculture and does not have enough water or level land to become a major producing area in the future; but it has very mild winters, being protected by the Kopet Dag from the cold air to the north, and the Russians frequently have pointed out that this area is one region in Middle Asia where citrus crops might be grown. At present, what little land is irrigated is put in orchards and vegetable gardens.

Water Construction Projects

It bears repeating that water is the lifeblood of Middle Asia. Because rain does not fall in adequate amounts on the plain, many man-made constructions have had to be devised to distribute the water from the mountains where it falls to the plains where it is needed for agriculture. Some of these man-made constructions date back to the ancient civilizations that occupied the area before the time of Christ, but the Soviets are adding many more of their own. In general the ancient constructions dealt with the smaller streams or the more easily controlled lower portions of the bigger streams, because the inhabitants did not have the technology to harness the very large rivers at the most strategic points where they issue forth from the mountains. Such rivers as the Zeravshan were ideal for the agricultural practices of the ancients, but the Soviets are greatly expanding the irrigated area of Middle Asia by constructing large dams in the gorges where the major streams, such as the Amu-Darya and the Syr-Darya, leave the mountains and enter the plains. Most of these dams and reservoirs are for the purpose of irrigation, but some of them also have power stations, and a few facilitate river navigation. In general, however, river navigation in Middle Asia is insignificant because of shallow water and the shifting nature of the channels in the sands.

The Fergana Basin   The first major water construction project in Middle Asia under the Soviet regime was the so-called Great Fergana Canal, which was completed in 1939. Until this time the

Fergana Basin was rather poorly utilized, with water being tapped only from minor streams to irrigate local areas, primarily along the southern side of the basin. A myriad of small streams flowing down the northern slopes of the Alay Range into the southern portion of the Fergana Basin have built a string of alluvial fans sloping northward into the Basin and afford ideal conditions for gravity-flow irrigation. Many of these small streams have been utilized for centuries because they were easy to control, but the large Syr-Darya which flows the full length of the Basin was not used. During the first two five-year plans the Soviets initiated a large project to tap the waters of the Syr-Darya and to irrigate much more of the floor of the Fergana Basin. The Great Fergana Canal project became one of the three big construction projects in the country, along with the Dnieper Dam and Magnitogorsk, which were held up as symbols of new national strength to capture the imaginations of young volunteers to work on the projects during their spare time and on weekends without pay. The main canal system is about 200 miles long and completely encircles the Fergana Basin. Many feeder canals distribute the water over much of the Basin floor. Only the lowest central portion of the Basin still is not utilized, because it is too sandy and salty for cultivation. At the present time, more than 800,000 hectares are under irrigation. Water supply in the Fergana Basin is still being improved. The Namangan irrigation canal is under construction in the north side of

Figure 10–20   Orchards, fields, and rice paddies in the Fergana Valley. Novosti.

the basin parallel to the older Great Fergana Canal. It will improve water supply to 20,000 hectares and irrigate an additional 30,000 hectares.

In 1943 construction began on the large Farkhad Dam opposite the city of Bekabad (Begovat) at the western mouth of the Fergana Basin where the noisy Syr-Darya rushes through a gorge in the Mogol Tau on its way to the Hungry Steppe to the west. The Farkhad Dam was constructed primarily to provide hydroelectricity to the many industries that are being located in Middle Asia, particularly to a variety of chemical and synthetic industries being established there. It also provides more water for irrigation to expand the Pakhta Aral or Cotton Island in the Hungry Steppe.

There is a romantic legend behind the naming of the Farkhad Dam. According to Uzbek lore, a capricious princess once lived on the high cliff that overlooks the dam site. She agreed to give her hand in marriage to the one of her many suitors who performed the greatest deed. Being in sympathy with the poor people who were in dire need of irrigation water, she announced that she would marry the man who could bring water to the Hungry Steppe. One cunning young nobleman ordered the steppes to be covered with mats of chi grass. When the sun rose in the morning its glare from the chi grass looked very much like the reflection from a water surface. The princess agreed to marry the hero on the spot. Meanwhile (and here the legend takes on a definite Soviet slant), a simple hero of the common people had brought water to the steppes by his honest toil. (The legend does not explain exactly how he did this by his honest toil.) But it was too late, the princess already had married the deceiver. Farkhad, as the honest peasant was called, learning of the trickery, threw his heavy ketmen, a hoe-like spade, into the air, which fell on his head and split his skull. An opera has been written about this unfortunate but noble Uzbek peasant. Now Farkhad is bringing water to the desert.

Just upstream from the Farkhad Reservoir on the Syr-Darya the Kayrak-Kum "hydro-knot," with its Druzhba Narodov (Friendship of Nations) hydroelectric station, was completed in 1957 to form a reservoir known as the Tadzhik Sea, 70 kilometers long within the neck of Tadzhikistan that extends into the western end of the Fergana Basin. The reservoir feeds twelve networks of irrigation canals, which are still being extended, to bring extra water to 400,000 hectares of arid lands, 300,000 of which lie in the Golodnaya (Hungry) Steppe west of the Fergana Basin in the Uzbek Republic. The Sangar pumping station on the Kayrak-Kum Reservoir began operations in 1959 to lift water 56 meters to irrigate the Sangar region in northern Tadzhikistan. This region will be fully reclaimed after the construction of 250 kilometers of canals and 860 installations. These new canals will connect with the western end of the Great Fergana Canal. The Kayrak-Kum hydroelectric plant has a capacity of 126,000 kilowatts.

Water for the Pakhta Aral was further increased in 1964 when the Chardara Dam and hydroelectric station (100,000 kilowatts) came into being on the Syr-Darya at the downstream side of the Hungry Steppe. A 150-mile canal under construction along the left bank of the Syr-Darya will add 200,000 hectares of new rice lands in the early 1970s.

The development of the huge irrigation district of the Pakhta Aral, with its various reservoir and canal systems, prompted the transfer of territory from the Kazakh S.S.R. to the Uzbek S.S.R. in 1963 and the establishment of the new Syr-Darya Oblast within the Uzbek Republic, which is essentially coextensive with the irrigation district. This action took parcels of land from Tashkent and Samarkand Oblasts of the Uzbek S.S.R. and from Chimkent Oblast in the Kazakh S.S.R. and placed them under the jurisdiction of one political unit to facilitate development and management of the irrigation district.

Between 1957 and 1959 the Kokand hydro-knot was constructed at the head of the large alluvial fan on which Kokand sits to collect water from all the distributary channels of the Sokh River to provide for the irrigation of an additional 60,000 hectares of land in the south-central part of the Fergana Basin. A silt basin above the knot catches the coarse, rocky alluvium before it clogs the canals feeding irrigation water both right and left from the hydro-knot.

The Kara-Kum Canal   The largest irrigation project recently completed is the Kara-Kum Canal, which leads water from the Amu-Darya at Kelif westward through the oases at Mary and Tedzhen to Ashkh-

abad. It has brought water to the entire area of thirsty southern Turkmenistan, which until recently was supplied only in local areas by small streams. The Canal was completed to Ashkhabad in 1962. There are long-range plans to extend the Canal to Krasnovodsk on the Caspian. Whether or not this is possible is a question. This is a major undertaking involving the building of a canal through 650 kilometers or more of shifting sands, which during any windstorm may destroy the work already completed. Apparently the Soviets have solved the problems of wind and sand and are successfully bringing additional water to hundreds of thousands of hectares of land in this region, but not without expensive special installations.

The Amu-Darya carries 250 million cubic meters of silt and sand per year and 8 million cubic meters enter the canal.

Figure 10–21   The Kara-Kum Canal cuts through the sand dunes near Mary. Novosti.

This is why the canal starts in the form of three wide branches. A quarter of the sediment remains in these branches, and seventeen excavating pumps continually remove it. The rest settles in the Kelif Lakes, so that after the last of them the canal is clear. The Kelif Lakes are a series of eight stagnant lakes connected by shallow channels that occupy the Kelif Uzboy, the bed of an old tributary of the Amu-Darya, which has been all but swallowed up by the shifting sands of the Kara-Kum. Three of the lakes have already ceased to exist since the canal has brought extra silt to them. Now that the Amu-Darya water has returned to the Kelif Uzboy, life has reappeared on the lakes, which are overgrown with reeds and water plants and swarm with birds. The water plants are a serious problem to the canal; tractors are employed to pull the weeds from the bed of the canal, and special floating cutting machines are used. Because this is very expensive, the Russians are planning to import a species of fish from China to feed on the water plants.

Only one third of the Amu-Darya waters that enter the canal reach the Murgab Oasis at Mary; the rest is lost in evaporation and filtration or is used for irrigation. To supplement the water from the canal, the Sagr-Yazy Reservoir was constructed on the Murgab River in 1953.

The Tedzhen River carries 90 per cent of its annual flow in the spring when the rains come and the snow begins to melt in the mountains. To remedy the shortage of irrigation water in summer, the Tedzhen Reservoir was constructed in 1950. But it is too small, and already it is clogged with sand and silt. Subsequently two other reservoirs have been constructed on the Tedzhen.

A large reservoir, the Khauz Khan, is being built on the Kara-Kum Canal between the Murgab and Tedzhen Rivers to reconcile the even flow in the canal throughout the year with the peak spring and summer usage in the irrigation sys-

tems. The winter flow of the canal can be stored in the reservoir until it is needed for irrigation in spring and summer. Also, the reservoir will store the overflow of water from the Tedzhen River whose reservoirs still are unable fully to control its floods in excessively rainy seasons. A hydro-knot above the first Tedzhen reservoir will direct the excess flow during spring into the Khauz Khan Reservoir. Thus the entire flow of the canal and the Tedzhen River can be used for irrigation. The Khauz Khan Reservoir is to be completed in 1970 with a capacity of 1.3 billion cubic meters.

The Great Turkmen Canal   A still larger project that has been talked about, but which seems to be unrealistic, is the Great Turkmen Canal. As proposed, it would lead off from the Amu-Darya near its mouth at the city of Nukus southwestward, utilizing the old Uzboy System, to carry water all the way to Krasnovodsk on the shores of the Caspian. This would involve building a canal some 680 miles long with branch canals totaling more than 750 miles. According to the Soviets, such a system would enable over 3 million acres of land to be irrigated, and there also would be provisions for hydroelectric stations along the canals and for some navigation. As has been amply pointed out by various authors, the Amu-Darya simply does not have enough water for such a project, particularly in light of the irrigation water that is being led off upstream by the Kara-Kum Canal. In 1951 the Soviets announced with much fanfare that they were starting construction of the canal, but in 1953 after the death of Stalin all such talk ceased. Apparently the Soviets decided that the project was not feasible.

The Caspian Sea Problem   One of the main reasons for wanting to bring Amu-Darya water into the Caspian was to maintain the level of the Caspian, which since 1929 has dropped 2.5 meters to its lowest level in 350 years. A continued drop of similar magnitude will lay bare much of the northern end of the sea bed, which now is covered by water to an average depth of only 5.4 meters. The falling water level and accompanying recession of the shore line has greatly affected shipping facilities, the fishing industry, and the sodium sulfate industry in Kara-Bogaz-Gol, all of which are of national significance. The Caspian each year carries a major part of the maritime traffic of the U.S.S.R., chiefly in the form of petroleum, and provides 90 per cent of the world's sturgeon catch, 95 per cent of the world's black caviar, and about 100,000 seals, not to mention other types of fish.

Since 1929 the delta of the Volga has extended outward into the Sea by more than 30 kilometers, the eastern part of the delta has become "dead," and only one navigable channel remains in the western part of the delta. During the same time the annual fish catch in the Caspian dropped from 510,000 tons to 190,000 tons. Extraction of sodium sulfate from Kara-Bogaz-Gol has been threatened by lack of water.

Several elaborate schemes have been devised to restore and stabilize the water level of the Caspian, all of which show more promise than that of bringing in water from the Amu-Darya. At the All-Union Conference on the Caspian Sea Problem on April 11, 1960, the Pechora-Vychegda River Diversion Project was discussed again, and discussion was begun on possible regulatory measures in the Caspian Sea itself. It was pointed out that the drop in the level of the Caspian since 1929 was due primarily to two factors: a warming, drying climate, and man-made dams and reservoirs on the Volga River, which supplies 78 per cent of the Caspian water. Loss of Volga River water through irrigation and evaporation from large reservoir surfaces before it enters the Caspian obviously is considerable. The construction of a large reservoir in northeastern

European Russia joining headwaters of the Pechora, Vychegda, and Kama Rivers would allow approximately 41 cubic kilometers additional water to flow down the Volga annually, an amount equal to approximately one sixth the present flow of the Volga. This not only would help to stabilize the level of the Caspian, it would increase the water flowing through the turbines of the hydroelectric power stations along the Volga, thereby increasing their electrical output. It has been pointed out that the Pechora-Vychegda Diversion Project would cost about one half the cost of the Kuybyshev Dam and power station and that the additional flow in the Volga produced by it would increase the aggregate electrical output of all the Volga power stations by an amount equal to the present output of the Kuybyshev station. Hence the electricity derived from the project alone would justify the project economically.

A grand scheme to regulate the water level of the Caspian locally has been proposed to supplement the addition of northern water. It provides for a series of dams across the northern Caspian, totalling 460 kilometers in length with an average height of 6.5 meters, which would separate the shallow northern end from the rest of the Caspian and would allow the water level in the north to be maintained about 2.5 meters above that in the south. It is stated that several fringe benefits would accrue from this project, such as generation of power along the dam and exposure of more oil-bearing strata by an additional drop of water in the south. This is indeed a grandiose scheme; such a dam would be very expensive.

A third cause for the drop in the water level has since been put forth by a well-known seismologist, who pointed out that a slight rise in the Caspian Sea level during 1956–1958 was not accompanied by a significant increase in discharge of tributary streams and therefore must have been a result of crustal movements in the sea floor. Perhaps there was a temporary reversal in the general subsidence of the deep basin in the southern half of the Caspian, which according to recent geophysical investigations is undergoing rather intensive subsidence at an average rate of about 16 millimeters per year. This could account for much of the fall in the Caspian Sea level during the last four decades. It has been noticed that activity of mud volcanoes along the southeastern shore of the Caspian varies radically and that increased activity is generally associated with sharp drops in water level, whereas periods of quiescence generally are accompanied by rises in the water level. If tectonic movements in the Caspian Sea area are the primary cause of fluctuations in the water level, then all man's efforts to stabilize the water level might be in vain.

One Russian scientist has argued that there is no need for attempting to stabilize the water level at even the present level of the Caspian. He points out that the dropping water level continually is exposing more farm land in the North Caspian Lowland, which could become very productive if irrigated by water to be brought down the Volga from the Pechora and Vychegda. He contends that this extra water could be put to much better use through irrigation of crops than through maintaining the level of the Caspian. He says that these additional crops would far outweigh the fish loss, which largely has not been due to the falling sea level anyway, but to pollution from oil leakages from wells and refineries, to seismic prospecting, and to mismanagement in the fish industry. He points out that already very little sodium sulfate is taken from Kara-Bogaz-Gol; that it is now mined from the floor of the Caspian itself. Hence there is no need to keep up the water supply of Kara-Bogaz-Gol. In fact, there is no easier way to reduce the evaporation of about 20 cubic kilometers of water annually than

by causing the gulf to dry up. Also, he points out the very obvious fact that all shipping, fishing, and industrial installations along the shores of the Caspian have constantly relocated their facilities to adjust to the lowering levels, and a rise to former levels would not solve their problems, but would simply cause them all to relocate once more.

Hence the Caspian Sea Problem is still being debated. It now looks as though the Pechora-Vychegda Diversion Project has been shelved for good, because of concern about detrimental effects that the large reservoir might have in the European northeast.

Other Amu-Darya Projects The Amu-Darya remains the largest and least used river in Soviet Middle Asia, but the Soviets are rapidly putting to use as much of its flow as possible. In 1959 construction began on the Amu-Karakul Canal which starts on the Amu-Darya above the railroad bridge at Chardzhou and extends 54 kilometers in a northeasterly direction across the Kyzyl-Kum to Karakul, the oasis at the end of the Zeravshan River. Completed in May 1962, it brings Amu-Darya water to the lower Zeravshan River which does not have enough water to irrigate all the rich loess land that stretches from Samarkand through Bukhara to Karakul.

In 1963 construction began on the 160-kilometer Amu-Bukhara Canal which utilizes the enlarged first 20 kilometers of the Amu-Karakul Canal and then branches eastward to take Amu-Darya water all the way to the Tudakul and Kuyu-Mazar reservoirs northeast of Bukhara. The water has to be pumped to a height of 48 meters and can then be led by gravity flow from the reservoirs into the irrigation ditches. The first stage of the project, which was completed in 1965, improves the water supply on 100,000 hectares of cotton land in the Bukhara oasis. Work on the second stage began in 1969. This will improve

72,000 more hectares and add 15,000 new hectares of cotton cultivation. A projected third stage will extend the canal across the Zeravshan to a new area northeast of Bukhara.

In 1964 work began on the Amu-Darya-Karshi Canal which by 1970 is to bring water from the Amu-Darya near Kerki 200 kilometers through the Karshi Steppe to the city of Karshi in the Kashka-Darya valley. The initiation of this project coincided with the reestablishment of Kashka-Darya Oblast in southeastern Uzbekistan. This area previously had been merged with Surkhan-Darya Oblast in 1960. Water from the Amu-Darya will be pumped up 150 meters to a reservoir from which water will be led by gravity flow through the canal which roughly parallels the Kerki-Karshi Railroad. By 1970 it is hoped to expand irrigated area in the basin of the Kashka-Darya from 100,000 hectares to 300,000 hectares and to establish the region as a leading producer of long-staple cotton.

South Surkhan Project   Immediately adjacent to the Kashka-Darya Basin is the Surkhan-Darya Basin. An earth dam 32 meters high was built across the Surkhan-Darya during the period 1960–1962, eventually to provide irrigation water for 180,-000 hectares in the lower part of the valley just upstream from where the river enters the Amu-Darya at Termez. This is one of the warmest spots in the Soviet Union. It thus affords the possibility of high cotton yields and second cropping after the cotton harvest. Thus the project has been deemed worthwhile in spite of the necessity of flushing the generally saline soils.

The Vakhsh Basin   Continuing eastward across the Tadzhik boundary lies the Vakhsh River and other headwater streams of the Amu-Darya which flow from north to south across the long-staple cotton lands of the Yavan-Obi-Kiik Massif in southwestern Tadzhikistan. Several water construction projects exist in this region,

but by far the largest project is the high Nurek Dam on the Vakhsh just southeast of the capital city of Dushanbe. This project has been under construction for nearly a decade and is to be completed sometime in the early 1970s. The dam is 1 kilometer long and 300 meters high. The ultimate capacity of the hydroelectric plant is 2,700,000 kilowatts, which makes it by far the largest in Soviet Middle Asia. Part of the electricity is to be utilized in the Regar aluminum plant which is being constructed in the area to make use of kaolin overburden of the Angren coal beds in the Fergana Basin, as well as a major caustic-chlorine chemical complex that is to be built in the area. These industries will also derive power from natural gas which is to be brought to Dushanbe by pipeline from Afghanistan.

The Nurek Reservoir will provide some water for irrigation, which will be supplemented by water from a reservoir created in 1968 by a directed explosion that created a 50-meter-high rock and earth dam at Postakan on the Vakhsh 30 kilometers downstream from Nurek. This diversion project is sending water westward via a 5-mile tunnel through the Karatau mountain range to the irrigated cotton lands of the Yavan Valley.

Other Projects   Besides the major water projects just mentioned, there are many projects that have been either initiated or improved during the Soviet period which involve other portions of the Amu and Syr-Darya, as well as many other streams. Examples are the large stone dam, Tas-Buget, on the middle Syr-Darya near Kzyl-Orda; the Katta Kurgan Canal along the River Zeravshan; the complex irrigation works in the Khiva Oasis along the lower Amu-Darya; and the many projects involving the Ili, the Chu, and other streams flowing northward out of the Tyan Shans, and the tributaries of the Amu-Darya in southwestern Tadzhikistan.

In the Tashkent area, complex works on the Chirchik and Angren Rivers, tributaries of the Syr-Darya, provide water for irrigation and domestic use. Since 1932 sixteen small power stations with an aggregate capacity of 330,000 kilowatts have been built on the Chirchik River alone. Now a much larger project is being completed on the Chirchik at Charvak gorge 70 kilometers northeast of Tashkent. The generating capacity will be 600,000 kilowatts, and the Charvak Reservoir will expand irrigation and serve recreation needs for the large city of Tashkent. An access railroad and a highway have been built to facilitate its use.

In the mountains south of the large city of Alma-Ata, numerous glacial-fed streams join to form the Alma-Atinka River, which in turn creates the Big Alma-Atinka Lake at an elevation of some 2500 meters. Nine hydroelectric plants are to be constructed to utilize the water flowing down the northern slopes of the mountains from this high lake.

Electric Power

In spite of all these hydro projects, little hydroelectricity is produced in Middle Asia. The highly fluctuating stream flows and high silt contents are not conducive to efficient power generation, and maximum use of water for irrigation is incompatible with the proper operation of power plants. In general, even the more notable hydroelectric stations are far overshadowed by thermal plants, and this situation is intensifying as the new abundant gas resources are put to use in huge new thermal electric stations. For instance, the renowned Farkhad Dam has a power plant with a capacity of only 126,000 kilowatts, whereas the Tashkent power plant fueled by natural gas from Dzharkak in Bukhara Oblast will have an ultimate capacity of 1.92 million kilowatts. The Angren coal-fed plant has a capacity of 600,000 kilowatts, and the gas-fueled plant at the new chemical center of Navoy has a capacity of 450,000 kilowatts. The largest gas-fueled power plant in the Uzbek Republic will be the Syrdarya station, near the Farkhad hydropower plant in Bekabad, which is now being constructed to have an ultimate capacity of 4.4 million kilowatts. It is planned that by 1970 Uzbek electricity will be generated 70 per cent by natural gas, 13 per cent by coal, and only 16 per cent by water.

Mineral Resources

Besides the unusual resources for agriculture, southern Kazakhstan and Middle Asia have some minerals that are used to supplement those of the rest of the Soviet Union. The sedimentary basins of the Caspian and Turanian Lowlands contain considerable deposits of petroleum, natural gas, various salts, and sulfur, and the Tyan Shans contain a variety of metallic ores. A brief summary of the major mineral deposits follows, but minor quantities of other elements exist.

Oil Oil has been produced for over 50 years at the Emba oil fields in the Kazakh Republic along the northern shore of the Caspian and in the vicinity of Nebit Dag south of Kara-Bogaz-Gol in the Turkmen Republic. Also, minor quantities of oil have been produced in the Fergana Valley. These three areas of oil have all been minor producers whose production has held steady or increased slowly through the years. But now a major revolution in the oil industry is taking place in some new areas within Soviet Middle Asia. The largest of these developments is on the Mangyshlak Peninsula in the Kazakh S.S.R. where oil was first struck in August 1961 at Zhetybay in the southern part of the Peninsula and shortly thereafter at Uzen farther northeast. (Fig. 10–10) By 1965 the Uzen fields were producing

300,000 tons of oil which were being piped westward to the new Caspian port of Shevchenko for shipment by tanker across the Caspian and up the Volga. Shevchenko was founded as Aktau in 1959 as a workers' settlement to serve the new oil-producing area. In 1963 it was raised to the status of a city, and in July 1964 it was renamed Shevchenko to commemorate the centennial of the great Ukrainian poet, Taras Shevchenko, who was exiled to this area during the nineteenth century. The potential production of this area is so great that a special railroad was completed in June 1964 from Makat, on the Guryev-Kandagach Railroad southwest 640 kilometers to Shevchenko and Uzen. (Fig. 10–26) This allows some of the Uzen oil to move by rail to the Guryev refinery on the north shore of the Caspian, which has been serving the Emba oil fields for years. Construction is now underway to complete by 1970 a 1760-kilometer pipeline from the Mangyshlak fields to the Volga refining center of Kuybyshev. Thus a region which less than a decade ago was a barren isolated wasteland has suddenly been tied by sea, rail, and pipeline to the heart of the country. In 1966 oil production on Mangyshlak was 1.4 million tons. This increased to 3.7 million in 1967, and is planned to be 5.5 million in 1968. The planned oil production for all of Kazakhstan in 1968 is 7.5 million tons. Thus the new fields of Mangyshlak have quickly outstripped the production of the old Emba fields. By 1970 crude oil output on Mangyshlak is to be between 12 and 15 million tons.

Oil production is also being increased significantly in the Turkmen Republic. The annual average production from 1959 to 1965 was 6,982,000 tons, whereas during the period 1956–1958 it had been only 3,793,000 tons. By 1966 annual production had risen to 10,672,000 tons. Plans call for production of 11.8 million tons in 1967, 15 million in 1970, and as much as 40 million in 1980. Much of this increase has been made possible in the Nebit-Dag

area by deeper drilling and discovery of new fields in older horizons. Also, offshore operations are now being carried out from a causeway that juts out about one half of a kilometer into the Caspian from Cheleken Peninsula.

Gas Equally as important as the oil developments are the findings of large natural-gas deposits in the Uzbek and Turkmen republics. Reserves rivaling those of the North Caucasus and Ukraine have been found at Gazli and other points in the Uzbek Desert around Bukhara and at Achak, Darvaza, and Bayram-Ali in the Turkmen Republic. (Fig. 10–10) By 1963 a pipeline was carrying Gazli gas over 2000 kilometers to Chelyabinsk in the Urals. In 1965 a second line was completed from Gazli to Sverdlovsk in the Urals. By 1966 the Gazli fields were producing more than 22 billion cubic meters of gas, almost 18 billion of which were piped to the Urals. The rest was piped eastward to serve the larger cities along the northern base of the Tyan Shans and in the Fergana Valley. The new city of Navoy has been established in the area of the Gazli fields. It has a thermal electric station and a mineral fertilizer plant to make use of some of the natural gas. It is planned for an ultimate population of 50,000.

In 1967 the first of three 40-inch pipelines was completed from Middle Asia to Moscow where it connects with pipe going on to Leningrad and the Baltic Republics. This line collects gas from the Achak field in northeast Turkmenia on the west side of the Amu-Darya and the Gazli field in western Uzbekistan east of the Amu-Darya. The other two lines will also get gas from the Darvaza and Bayram-Ali fields. Together, the three pipes will carry about 30 billion cubic meters of gas per year to European Russia.

The Achak gas field was discovered only in 1966, and by the end of that year it had produced 51 million cubic meters of gas. The goal for 1970 is for the Turkmen

Republic to produce 12 to 15 billion cubic meters. By 1980 this is to rise to 86 billion.

Coal and Ferrous Metals A number of small coal deposits occur in the Fergana Basin and the surrounding mountains. Some deposits contain hard coal, but the major producer at present is the Angren brown coal deposit in the western part of the Fergana Basin. Here has been built the largest underground gasification plant in the country. Since supplies are limited and quality is low, coal mined in Middle Asia serves only part of the local needs and must be supplemented by coal from the Karaganda fields in northern Kazakhstan and from the Kuznetsk Basin in western Siberia.

So far, no significant iron mining has been developed in Middle Asia and southern Kazakhstan. It appears that perhaps the only possibilities for development are the recently discovered low-grade ore deposits in the Turgay Lowland just north of the Aral Sea. These ores conceivably might be utilized along with Karaganda coal to establish an iron and steel industry somewhere along the lower Syr-Darya, but no definite plans have been formulated.

A manganese deposit supposedly was opened up on the Mangyshlak Peninsula during World War II to compensate partially for the loss to the Germans of Nikopol in Ukraine, but no mention has been made of this development since the war. Manganese has also been mined at the Dzhezdy deposit near Dzhezkazgan, and apparently this operation is now being revived.

Nonferrous Metals In the past mining in Middle Asia has been best developed in the nonferrous metals. Copper has been mined for a long time at the major deposit near Balkhash on the northern shore of Lake Balkhash and at the minor deposit near Almalyk in the Tyan Shans southeast of Tashkent. Lead and zinc mines in the Karatau and other spurs of the Tyan Shans supply smelters in the city of Chimkent. Recently a molybdenum and tungsten combine has been added at Chirchik. Although the magnitude of mining operations in Middle Asia and southern Kazakhstan for each type of metal is surpassed by mining operations in the Urals or in northern Kazakhstan, nevertheless mining in Middle Asia is a significant part of the local economy.

Nonmetallic Minerals Important deposits of nonmetallic minerals scattered about Middle Asia now are being developed as a strong base for new chemical industries. Particularly important are deposits of various mineral salts, phosphate, and sulfur. Sodium chloride is derived from widespread surface deposits associated with the Caspian Sea, the Aral Sea, and Lake Balkhash, as well as with scattered playa lake beds in the Turanian Lowland. Sodium sulfate, mirabilite, or Glauber's salt, important in the pharmaceutical indistries for the manufacture of

Figure 10–22   Open pit copper mine at Kounrad near Balkhash. Novosti.

such things as Epsom salts, is gathered in large quantities from the waters of Kara-Bogaz-Gol.

Important phosphate deposits exist on the Mangyshlak Peninsula and at Karatau north of Dzhambul. Phosphate from the Karatau deposits, combined with sulfuric acid from scattered sulfur deposits, is being used to produce mineral fertilizers, animal feed supplements, and detergents at processing plants in Dzhambul, Chimkent, Chardzhou, Kokand, and Samarkand. There is now an all-out drive to make this production wholly self-sustaining for the Middle Asian and Kazakh republics, so that long hauls of apatite from the Kola Peninsula can be discontinued. Recently, new open-pit mines have been initiated in the Karatau Mountains, and the original mining center of Chulak Tau has been raised to the status of city and renamed Karatau. In 1967 total phosphate production in this area amounted to about 5 million tons. An important deposit of native sulfur is located at Gaurdak, near Termez on the Afghan border, and production there is being expanded to serve the needs of Central Asian superphosphate and other chemical plants. Large nitrogenous fertilizer plants have been established in such cities as Fergana and Chirchik to make use of by-product gases of oil refining, natural gases, and abundant electric power.

These mineral deposits, along with agricultural produce, have laid the basis for some industrialization of Middle Asia and for the rapid development of certain urban areas.

Water Supply

It appears that the greatest problem confronting continued development will be water supply. Already this has become critical in many areas. Practically all of the oil and gas drilling areas are in extremely dry desert regions devoid of surface streams. Water is derived largely from deep wells, but it is barely sufficient for drinking and industrial purposes, and in some cases, not even for that. About 5 million cubic meters of distilled Caspian Sea water are now being used annually, but fresh water is still being supplied to some of the drilling areas in western Turkmenia from Baku via Caspian tanker and by transshipment to tanker trucks which distribute the water to the workers' camps. This is a cumbersome and expensive method of obtaining water. Geological exploration parties in the central Kara-Kum have even been supplied with drinking water by air from Ashkhabad. Atomic-powered desalinization plants are being established in some specialized, permanent, isolated centers such as Shevchenko on the Mangyshlak Peninsula, Tyuratam on the Syr-Darya near the Aral Sea, and Sary Shagan just west of the southwestern tip of Lake Balkhash.

Industries and Cities

Industry is coming to Middle Asia in the form of diversified light industries in the larger cities, mainly in the Republic capitals, to serve the growing market, and metallurgical industries in new or rapidly expanding old towns located near important mineral resources. The industries in the larger cities are designed to turn out finished products for the local markets and are concentrated on machine-building, textiles, and food industries. Tashkent, the capital of the Uzbek Republic, and Alma-Ata, the capital of the Kazakh Republic, have grown rapidly under the impetus of such industries. On the other side, Begovat is a good example of a new small city that has developed because of its function as a mining and metallurgical center to serve the industrial needs of Middle Asia. Perhaps the industries of Middle Asia can be summarized best by a discussion of the major cities.

Tashkent The metropolis of Middle Asia is Tashkent. With a population in 1967 of 1,239,000, it is fourth in size in the Soviet Union. Tashkent has served an important historical role since the seventh century as the main stopover point in Middle Asia for the caravan routes between China and Europe. It has shared with Samarkand and Bukhara the function of the seat of the governmental control over Moslem Middle Asia. In 1865 the Russians took over the area and established a new town outside the old Moslem center. Since that time, and particularly during the Soviet regime, the new city of Tashkent has grown and engulfed the old city, and in the process of transformation many of the old adobe huts have been torn down and replaced by brick and concrete-section apartment buildings. But many new individual homes are being economically built, by Uzbeks, of adobe bricks made from extensive loess deposits.

Today Tashkent is a thriving, bustling city of streetcars and taxis peopled by Russians and Ukrainians as well as by Uzbeks. It sits in the heart of a rich cotton-growing area at a strategic position on the northwest corner of the Tyan Shans around which all transportation routes must funnel. It has been selected

Figure 10–24 An Uzbek woman and boy resting beside an ariq in Tashkent. Photograph by the author.

by the Soviets as the primary manufacturing city of Middle Asia, and machine-building industries and textile industries have been developed to the highest degree. Thus it serves more than the function of political capital of the Uzbek Republic, it is the commercial capital of the entire Middle Asian area.

Tashkent sits at a rather low altitude, 1610 feet, and has long, hot, dry summers. Its annual rainfall is only 14.6 inches, and practically all of it comes during the winter months, with March and April having maximum rainfall. Thus it has a Mediterranean-type rainfall regime, with cyclonic storms moving in from the Mediterranean area during the wintertime, but its temperature range of 50°F between January and July reflects its continental location. January averages 30°F, and there are nights during the winter when temperatures plunge below zero. Since the growing season is hot and dry, irrigation is necessary for all agriculture, as well as the growing of trees and lawns in Tashkent. Small ariqs or water-distributing ditches gurgle along both sides of every street in the city. Often the ditch is a cemented trench from 1 to 2 feet wide and of about equal depth running between the sidewalk and the street, but sometimes it is

Figure 10–23 Large cranes swing prefabricated reinforced concrete slabs into place to be bolted together to form new apartment houses on the outskirts of Tashkent. Photograph by the author.

simply a shallow channel in the earth that is allowed to wander at will alongside the footpaths.

Although factories and apartment buildings have been built in Tashkent, many of the Uzbek residents have maintained much of their old way of life. The native bazaar is still a main feature of the commercial life of the city, as it is in most Middle Asian cities. Farmers bring their produce to the market early in the morning and spend the day selling their own vegetables and fruits. As long as the farmer does not hire someone else to sell his produce for him, private retailing is not considered to be capitalistic. The labor forces in the larger factories are made up largely of Russians and Ukrainians who have moved into the area. Thus there is a considerable racial and social split between the society manning the larger factories and the society carrying on agriculture and much of the retail trade.

Specifications are now being worked out for an earthquake-proof subway, 20 kilometers in length and containing thirteen stations. Disastrous earthquakes in 1966 caused heavy losses in Tashkent, and reminded the citizens of their precarious position along the base of the tectonically unstable Tyan Shans.

Alma-Ata   Second in size among the cities of Soviet Middle Asia is Alma-Ata, the capital of the Kazakh Republic, which in 1967 had a population of 652,000. Unlike Tashkent, Alma-Ata is a newcomer to Middle Asia, and is a Russian, not a native, city. It was founded in 1854 as the Russian fort of Zailisk, which was renamed Vernyy in 1885, and only recently has it been selected as the capital of the new Kazakh Republic. Its name was changed to Alma-Ata in 1921. In 1926 its population was only 45,000. Its rapid growth has taken place largely since it became the capital. Its present form reflects the rather chaotic growth that has taken place. Temporary structures have been thrown up in a hurry to keep up with the influx of population.

The town does not have the look of a metropolitan center as does Tashkent, but nevertheless it is becoming a large city, and it has certain natural advantages over Tashkent. It lies at a somewhat higher elevation than does Tashkent, being nestled directly within the foothills of the Tyan Shans, whereas Tashkent sits out on the desert 50 miles or more from the mountains. Thus Alma-Ata is cooler than Tashkent, has a magnificent backdrop of mountain scenery, and is better watered by the many little rushing torrents which criss-cross the alluvial fan surfaces on their way from the snow-capped mountains in the south to the desert surrounding Lake Balkhash in the north. Many gurgling irrigation ditches run along all the streets, and a great tree-planting campaign has been carried out along the streets and in the parks of the city. The residents of Alma-Ata proudly announce that there are ten trees for every person in the city. In most cases, the trees have been planted very close together, within 4 or 5 feet of one another; consequently they are small and scraggly. Walking through a park is often more like beating one's way through a thicket than strolling beneath stately trees. Nevertheless, now there is deep shade where previously the sun beat down on a dry and rocky landscape; so the citizens contend with a measure of truth that they have transformed a barren area into one of pleasant greenery. Russians far outnumber the native Kazakhs in Alma-Ata, and native faces are not seen in the factories. Like Tashkent, Alma-Ata has a widely diversified industrial base, with machine building being of first importance.

Frunze   Third in size is Frunze, the capital of the Kirgiz Republic, with a population of 396,000. Frunze sits on the northern slopes of the Tyan Shans among the headwaters of the Chu River. It thus lies within a rich agricultural area specializing in grains and sugar beets. Its industries are concentrated on machine building, textiles, and food processing. It was founded in 1878 as the Russian fortress of Pishpek, and was renamed Frunze in 1926 after the famous Bolshevik leader who was born there. At present, Frunze is the fastest growing city in the Soviet Union.

Dushanbe   Fourth in size in Middle Asia is Dushanbe, the capital of the Tadzhik Republic, which in 1967 had a population of 333,000. Dushanbe exemplifies the rapid growth of a native village after it became the seat of government for a newly established republic. From 1927 until 1961 it was known as Stalinabad, but with the further downgrading of Stalin in 1961 it reverted to its old Tadzhik name. The city sits on the southern side of the Zeravshan Range of the Tyan Shans on the upper portions of the plateau in southwestern Tadzhikistan. It serves as the governmental and commercial center for a relatively rich cotton-growing region, and cotton textiles are its primary industry. Machine building and food industries also are important. It is destined to benefit industrially from the nearby Nurek hydroelectric project and from natural gas which is being piped in from Afghanistan.

Samarkand   Fifth in size is Samarkand, with a population of 248,000. Samarkand is situated on the Zeravshan River, which was the cradle of civilization in Middle Asia. The modern city sits on hills of thick loess deposits which cover the remains of many former cities dating back as far as 3000 B.C. During the fourteenth and fifteenth centuries Samarkand served as the center of Tamerlane's far-flung empire, which at times encompassed all the territory from eastern China to the Volga. During this time, many magnificent mosques were built to commemorate important individuals. Ruins of these beautiful mosques still dominate the urban scene, their blue tiles sparkling in the desert sun. Some of the mosques are now being reconstructed out of bricks made from the

Figure 10–25   The Tomb of Tamerlane in Samarkand. Photograph by the author.

loess clay in the same manner as were the originals. Archeologic excavations are unearthing predecessor cities.

In 1868 the Russians established a new town next to Samarkand which has grown and gradually engulfed the old city. It might be said that Samarkand at present is a small-sized Tashkent that lags behind Tashkent in transformation by a period of 10 or 15 years. Samarkand still has the native aspects to a much greater degree than does Tashkent, but as fast as it can be accomplished the native quarters are being torn down and apartment buildings constructed. Some light industries have come to Samarkand, particularly the textile industries.

In 1964 the fabled city was threatened with extinction by flood from a rapidly rising lake that formed behind a huge landslide that had blocked the upper Zeravshan. Only frantic efforts which succeeded in cutting a diversion channel saved the city from certain destruction.

Ashkhabad   Sixth in size is Ashkhabad, the capital of the Turkmen Republic, with a population of 238,000. It was founded in 1881 as a Russian fortress and was known as Poltoratsk from 1919 to 1947. Ashkhabad sits on the major fault zone at the northern base of the Kopet Dag on the southern edge of the Kara-Kum. In 1948 it was virtually destroyed by earthquake. It is in a remote and barren desert area with only a limited amount of irrigation agriculture developed around it. If it were not for its function as the capital city of the Turkmen Republic, Ashkhabad would not have prospered significantly, since it is away from the main activity in Middle Asia. It is connected with the port of Krasnovodsk on the Caspian and with the major cities of Middle Asia to the east by the Trans-Caspian Railroad. If it were not for this single lifeline, it would be isolated indeed. Its function as one of the main film-making centers in the Soviet Union already has been mentioned. Also, it has some textile and machine-building industries.

As was the case in Transcaucasia and in the Baltic and Belorussian Republics of the northwest, it can be seen clearly here in Middle Asia that the function as a governmental seat is of prime importance to the development of a town. Among the six largest cities in Middle Asia, five are the capitals of the five republics. Only Samarkand does not serve that function at the present time. Samarkand, of course, got its start as the center of early civilization and later benefited greatly as the governmental seat of a loosely constructed empire, so in a sense it too might be considered to have grown because of its governmental function.

Other Cities   A number of cities having populations between 50,000 and 225,000 serve as regional centers of commerce and industry and as processiag centers of local produce. Many of these are situated in agricultural areas where raw materials for textile and food industries are available. Others are located near mineral resources. They are concentrated either in the Fergana Valley or along the northern slopes of the Tyan Shans. The rest of the area, that is, the deserts and the high mountains, is almost devoid of urban settlement.

Along the base of the Tyan Shans lies a string of cities besides the three capitals already mentioned, chief among which are Chimkent, with a population of 219,000; Dzhambul, with a population of 158,000, and Chirchik, with a population of 100,-000. These three cities lying within 200 miles of one another on the northwestern corner of the Tyan Shans are industrial centers concentrating on chemical industries and nonferrous metallurgy. Chimkent is reported to have the largest lead smelter in all of Eurasia. Dzhambul recently has become the main superphosphate manufacturing center for the agricultural regions of Middle Asia, utilizing the phosphate deposits at Karatau just northwest of Dzhambul. The lead, zinc, copper, and other ores used in the smelters of these cities partially are derived locally from the Tyan Shans and Karatau and partially are shipped in from the Kazakh Folded Country and the Altay Mountains in the north. Chirchik, on the Chirchik River just northeast of Tashkent, produces chemical fertilizers and agricultural machinery for the farmlands of Middle Asia.

A considerable number of cities of intermediate size lie within the Fergana Basin. Many of these are old cities that have served as cultural and commercial centers of a rich agricultural area for centuries; in large part that is their function today. Their industries are largely based on the processing of local cotton, silk, and a variety of foods. Also, at the town of Fergana, some oil refining has been carried on for 50 or more years utilizing the small local reserves of petroleum. The main cities are Andizhan, with a population of 169,000; Namangan, with a population of 158,000; the famous old Moslem center of Kokand, with a population of 131,000; Fergana, with a population of 93,000; Leninabad, with a population of 100,000; Margelan, with a population of 89,000; and Osh, with a population of 119,000. Most of these cities lie within the Uzbek Republic, although the Fergana Basin is politically divided among the Uzbek, the Kirgiz, and the Tadzhik Republics on the basis of the distribution of ethnic groups. The endeavor to keep nationality groups on the correct sides of the boundaries coupled with the endeavor to include the mountain watershed areas with the corresponding parts of the basin to which they supply water has made for an intricate boundary delineation in the area. Leninabad lies within the Tadzhik Republic, and it is one of the principal Middle Asian centers for cotton and silk textile industries.

The leading cotton textile centers in Middle Asia are Tashkent, Leninabad, Dushanbe, Fergana, and Ashkhabad; the leading silk textile centers are Leninabad, Osh, Margelan, Dushanbe, and Ashkhabad. Leading wool textile centers are Alma-Ata, Frunze, and Dushanbe.

A few other scattered cities might be mentioned because of significant functions as regional centers or as industrial centers. At the western entrance to the Fergana Basin, where the Syr-Darya cuts a deep and narrow gorge through a low range of hills, stands the new city of Bekabad (Begovat), which, like Rustavi in Transcaucasia, has been established by the Soviets as a steel center to serve an outlying area of the Soviet Union. The town now has 59,000 people, most of whom are connected with the steel works, which eventually is to produce enough steel to serve the Middle Asian Region. The present steel plant was constructed in 1944. So far, all the steel has been produced from scrap or from pig iron shipped from the Kuznetsk Basin. Coal is derived partially from Karaganda and partially from local supplies in the Fergana Basin.

Along the three great rivers of Soviet Middle Asia—that is, the Amu-Darya, the Syr-Darya, and the Zeravshan—are located several cities besides those already mentioned. These cities serve as centers of important agricultural areas concentrating primarily on cotton. Where the Trans-

Caspian Railroad crosses the Amu-Darya stands the city of Chardzhou, with a 1967 population of 88,000. Chardzhou serves as an important transshipping point between the railroad and the river as well as an important collection point for cotton. Downstream on the Amu-Darya, near the delta in the extensive irrigated cotton-growing area of the Khiva Oasis, are the cities of Urgench, with a population of 65,000; Nukus, with a population of 56,000; and Tashauz, with a population of 60,000. Along the middle Syr-Darya in an important rice-growing area is the town of Kzyl-Orda, with a population of 91,000. For a short time Kzyl-Orda served as the capital city of the former Kirgiz A.S.S.R. Near the western end of the Zeravshan River stands the ancient city of Bukhara with a present population of 102,000. It is the center of an important irrigated cotton-growing area and the Karakul sheep-grazing region.

On the north end of the Caspian Sea, at the mouth of the Ural River, is the oil refining town of Guryev, which in 1967 had a population of 101,000. It serves as the center of the Emba oil fields, and an oil pipeline leads northeastward from Guryev to Orsk at the southern end of the Urals. Guryev also is an important fishing center. Far to the south on the eastern shore of the Caspian, near the oil fields of Nebit Dag, stands the town of Krasnovodsk, which is the third important oil-refining town of Middle Asia. It also serves as an important fishing port and as the western terminus of the Trans-Caspian Railroad. The three cities, Guryev, Krasnovodsk, and Fergana, serve as the oil-refining centers in the three respective oil-producing areas of Middle Asia and southern Kazakhstan.

Transportation and Trade

In this far-flung area of isolated settlements transportation lines become of utmost importance, and in this arid region the burden falls even more heavily on the railroads than it does in the rest of the Soviet Union.

The streams by and large are unsuitable for navigation. The major streams head in high mountains where rapids and gorges prevent traffic, and when they issue forth on the dry, sandy plains they spread out, become shallow, and divide into many separate, shifting channels with extremely fluctuating levels of flow during different times of the year. There is local navigation on the Amu-Darya, but this stream leads nowhere at either end. A bit of navigation may be carried on during high-water stage in early summer on the Ural River between the Caspian and the Urals, and small boats ply the Ili River south of Lake Balkhash. Other than this, stream navigation largely is lacking.

Soviet policy since the beginning of the five-year plans has brought about both a great increase in the production and consumption of Middle Asia and southern Kazakhstan and a strict specialization of crops raised in the area. Both factors have thrown an increasingly heavy burden on the railroads. The fact that these heavily populated irrigated areas are separated from other populous areas of the Soviet Union by wide expanses of steppe and desert, together with the increasing specialization of the agriculture, has brought about some of the longest rail hauls in the Soviet Union. Although the Middle Asian Republics now produce more than 90 per cent of the country's raw cotton, the Central Industrial Region around Moscow still produces more than 70 per cent of the country's cotton textiles. Hence much of the raw cotton of the country must be shipped more than 2000 miles to be processed. Also, with the intense specialization on cotton in Middle Asia grain must be shipped into the area all the way from northern Kazakhstan and western Siberia and from even more removed areas such as the Trans Volga and the Caucasus.

An increasing demand for lumber products associated with the great buildup of industries and cities in Middle Asia has greatly increased long hauls of lumber from western and eastern Siberia as well as from the Volga and Urals areas. The industrialization of Middle Asia has brought about an increasingly heavy movement of coal and petroleum products between different regions within Kazakhstan and the Middle Asian Republics. A large volume of trade with regions outside the area has been generated by the total absence of pig-iron production in the Middle Asian Republics and the inadequate assortment of locally produced, rolled-steel products. The Begovat plant imports large quantities of pig iron from the Kuznetsk Basin and, in turn, exports steel ingots to the steel plant at Temir-Tau near Karaganda. At the same time, Middle Asian industries are forced to import considerable quantities of rolled-steel products from different portions of the country.

Before the turn of the century, when the interregional trade of the area largely was undeveloped and the bulk of the irrigated acreage was occupied by wheat and other food crops for local consumption, the camel caravan served as the main means of transportation of the small quantities of high-cost goods that were exchanged over long distances. Since that time, interregional trade has increased a hundredfold, and railroad lines have been constructed. The railroads now carry more than 90 per cent of the total freight. Until 1906 the Transcaspian Railroad, connecting the towns along the foothills of the southern mountains between Krasnovodsk and Tashkent, was the only railroad in the area, and its only connection with the rest of the country was by ferry across the Caspian from Krasnovodsk to Baku. This railroad served primarily to bring in oil from Baku to fuel-deficient Middle Asia and to export raw cotton from Middle Asia westward across the Caspian to European Russia. At this time the Turkmen oil

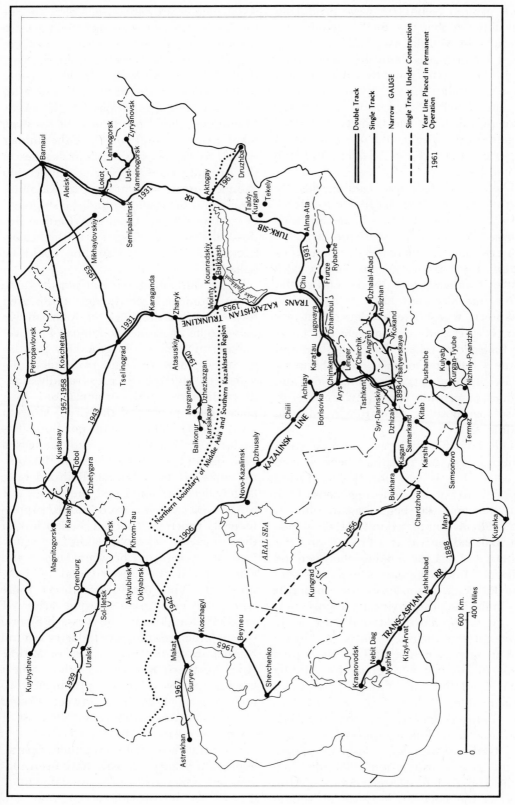

Figure 10–26   The development of the transportation system. Updated from Taaffe.

fields around Nebit Dag were producing very little so that the small need for oil products in Middle Asia had to be provided for primarily from the Caucasus oil fields. Also, at this time, the cotton export trade in Middle Asia was not very flourishing, and much of the cotton textiles that were produced in the Central Industrial Region were produced from raw cotton imported from Egypt, India, and the United States.

Then in 1906 a line leading directly northwestward from Tashkent to Orenburg was completed. This linked up with railroads leading to the west and provided a direct route for increasing shipments of cotton northwestward and grain and lumber southeastward. By the end of the 1920s this Kazalinsk Line, as it came to be known, was so overburdened that new efforts were made to complete the Turk-Sib Railroad to relieve the congestion and at the same time to make possible an increase of shipments of cotton, grain, and lumber to provide for an even more intense specialization of cotton growing in Middle Asia.

The Turk-Sib Railroad, running from Semipalatinsk to Arys, had been started in 1912, but it was abandoned during World War I and the ensuing chaos of the civil war and was begun again only in 1927. Finally completed in 1931, the Turk-Sib Railroad provided a link around the eastern end of Lake Balkhash between the cities of Middle Asia and the Trans-Siberian Railroad in southwestern Siberia. It was built specifically to induce a movement of raw cotton northeastward into newly developing industrial centers in Siberia and to bring about a shift in the supply areas of lumber and grain for Middle Asia. Until this time much of the grain consumed in Middle Asia was raised in the Trans-Volga region, the northern Caucasus and Transcaucasia, the Urals, and Ukraine, with only about one tenth of the grain consumption of Middle Asia being supplied by western Siberia. Also, most of the lumber consumed in Middle Asia came from either the Volga area or the Urals. It was hoped that the Turk-Sib Railroad would induce a change in these supply areas so that western Siberia, particularly the Kulunda Steppe, would supply much of the grain needs of Middle Asia and the slopes of the Altay Mountains and the plains of western Siberia would supply much of the lumber needs. By developing textile industries in the growing cities of Siberia, raw cotton shipment northwestward on the Kazalinsk Line could be reduced, and the shipment of cotton textiles from the Central Industrial Region to Siberia over the heavily burdened Trans-Siberian line could be halted.

These shifts in interregional trade came about agonizingly slowly, and it appeared for a time that the Turk-Sib Railroad was going to be an economic failure. The production of lumber did gradually pick up in Siberia, however, and the lumber demands of Middle Asia grew rapidly as industrialization and urbanization took place. The opening of the virgin lands in southwestern Siberia and northern Kazakhstan since 1954 has greatly increased grain production in that area, so that now the aims of the Turk-Sib Railroad have largely been accomplished, and a new line to the west of it has been built to supplement its function. In 1953 the last link of the so-called Trans-Kazakhstan Trunk Line was completed between Mointy and Chu around the western end of Lake Balkhash. This provides a direct route from the new grain-growing areas of northern Kazakhstan and western Siberia through the area of heavy industry around Karaganda to the major cities of Middle Asia. Northern Kazakhstan, whose wheat acreage increased from approximately 10 million acres in 1953 to between 45 and 50 million acres in 1956, now fills most of the wheat needs of Middle Asia.

Since the early 1930s a number of paralleling and branch rail lines have been constructed either to link major cities more directly or to provide access into new mining and industrial areas. In 1956 a rail line paralleling the Amu-Darya was completed from its junction with the Transcaspian line at Chardzhou to Kungrad near the mouth of the river. This provided the first big leg of a second direct all-rail link between Middle Asia and European Russia. In the mid 1960s the completion of a rail line from Guryev through Beyneu to the new oil port of Shevchenko on the Mangyshlak Peninsula provided another leg, and the completion of the Guryev-Astrakhan Line in 1967 provided still a third. The last, rather difficult, leg is now being built across the Ust Yurt Plateau between Beyneu and Kungrad.

The construction of many of these lines, including the first one, the Transcaspian, which was constructed in record time under the impetus of war against the Turkmen uprisings, was accomplished in the face of overwhelming natural hazards in the form of shifting sands and lack of water. Accounts of their construction provide interesting reading. Around 1960, much publicity was given to the Aktogay-Sinkiang-Lanchow Railroad, which had been completed from the Turk-Sib Railroad at Aktogay to provide a new direct link between the U.S.S.R. and China through the Dzungarian Gate east of Lake Balkhash. The Soviets celebrated the completion of their section of the line by the establishment of the new town of Druzhba, or Friendship, where the railroad was to cross the Soviet-Chinese border. Since the cooling of relations between the two countries no more has been said about this rail line. It has been reported that the Chinese completed their portion of the line westward to Urumchi, but nothing seems to be under construction now to complete the link between Urumchi and Druzhba.

Prospects

The old civilizations of Central Asia that have fallen within the Soviet sphere seem finally to have submitted to a state of passive acquiescence as the Russians and other Slavic groups steadily flood the area to establish industries and build cities and transportation lines. Although the older elements of the native populations still remain quite aloof from the economic and social revolution that is taking place in the cities within their midst, the young people are being educated in Soviet schools and the brighter of these students are being assimilated into the inevitable stream of events. No one can dispute the fact that material life is now much better than it was, and it is generally better on the Soviet side of the border than it is among related groups across the international boundaries in the Middle Eastern countries. Little wonder, then, that present generations have lost sight of former fierce struggles against the Tsar and against the Bolsheviks, civil war, and collectivization. It appears that the Muslim cultures under the Soviets are doomed to extinction. What roles the Middle Asian peoples ultimately will play within the Soviet framework is still uncertain. High birth rates generally are increasing their proportions within the total population, but in their own republics they are being diluted by heavy in-migrations of Russians and other Slavs.

Economically, Soviet Middle Asia will continue to become more integrated with the total Soviet economy, and should play a larger role as its natural gas, oil, and other mineral deposits are fully exploited. It will continue to have a virtual monopoly on raw-cotton production, and absolutely all agricultural production will continue to expand as more and larger river construction projects provide for the irrigation of more land.

Reading List

MIDDLE ASIA — GENERAL

Allworth, Edward, ed., *Central Asia: A Century of Russian Rule,* Columbia University Press, New York, 1967, 549 pp.

Bacon, Elizabeth E., *Central Asians Under Russian Rule,* Cornell University Press, Ithaca, New York, 1966, 273 pp.

Burke, Albert, *A Political Economic Survey of Soviet Central Asia,* Ph.D. Dissertation, University of Pennsylvania, 1959.

Caroe, Olaf, *Soviet Empire: The Turks of Central Asia and Stalinism,* St. Martin's Press, New York, 1967, 2nd ed., 308 pp.

Central Asian Review, Central Asian Research Center, 66 Kings Road, London SW 3; various issues.

Field, Neil C., "Amu-Darya: a Study in Resource Geography," *Geographical Review,* 1954, pp. 528–542.

Hostler, Charles Warren, *Turkism and the Soviets,* Praeger, New York, 1957, 244 pp.

Jackson, W. A. Douglas, *Russo-Chinese Borderlands,* Van Nostrand, Princeton, 1968, 2nd ed., 156 pp.

Kunin, V. N., *Karakumskie zapisky* (Karakum notes), Moscow, 1952, 263 pp. (in Russian).

Lewis, Robert A., "Early Irrigation in West Turkestan," *Annals of the Association of American Geographers,* September 1966, pp. 467–491.

———, "The Irrigation Potential of Soviet Central Asia," *Annals of the Association of American Geographers,* March 1962, pp. 99–114.

Murzaev, E., *Srednyaya Aziya: fiziko-geograficheskaya kharakteristika* (Middle Asia: physical-geographical characteristics), Akademiya Nauk SSSR, Institut Geografiya, Moscow, 1958, 647 pp. (in Russian).

Nove, Alec and Newth, J. A., *The Soviet Middle East,* Praeger, New York, 1967, 160 pp.

Ocherki prirody Kara-Kumov (Studies of the natural habitat of the Kara-Kum Desert), Akademiya Nauk, Institut Geografiya, 1955, 405 pp. (in Russian).

Pavlenko, V. F., "The Transport-Geography Situation and Inter-regional Links of Central Asia," *Soviet Geography: Review and Translation,* November 1963, pp. 27–33.

Pierce, Richard A., *Russian Central Asia 1867–1917: A Study in Colonial Rule,* Russian and East European Study Series, University of California Press, 1960, 306 pp.

Schuyler, Eugene, *Turkistan* (edited by Geoffrey Wheeler), Praeger, New York, 1966, 303 pp.

Semenov-Tian-Shanskii, P. P., *Putishestviye v Tian-Shan* (Expedition to the Tyan Shan), Moscow, 1958, 277 pp. (in Russian).

Sinitsyn, V. M., *Tsentralnaya Aziya* (Central Asia), Moscow, 1959, 455 pp. (in Russian).

Soviet Geography: Review and Translation, June 1968; almost the entire issue is devoted to Soviet Middle Asia.

Taaffe, Robert, *Rail Transportation and the Economic Development of Soviet Central Asia,* Department of Geography Research Paper No. 64, University of Chicago, 1960, 186 pp.

———, "Transportaiton and Regional Specialization: The Example of Soviet Central Asia," *Annals of the Association of American Geographers,* March 1962, pp. 80–98.

Wheeler, Geoffrey, *The Modern History of Soviet Central Asia,* Praeger, New York, 1964, 272 pp.

———, *The Peoples of Soviet Central Asia,* The Bodley Head, London, 1966, 126 pp.

———, *Racial Problems in Soviet Moslem Asia,* Oxford University Press, London, 1962, 67 pp.

CASPIAN SEA

Bobrov, S. N., "The Transformation of the Caspian Sea," *Soviet Geography: Review and Translation,* September 1961, pp. 47–59.

Geller, S. Yu., "On the Question of Regulating the Level of the Caspian Sea," *Soviet Geography: Review and Translation,* January 1962, pp. 59–66.

Problemy Kaspiyskogo morya (Problems of the Caspian Sea), U.S.S.R. Academy of Sciences, Moscow, 1959 (in Russian).

Rikhter, V. G., "Vertical Movements of the Earth Crust and the Fluctuations in the Level of the Caspian Sea," *Soviet Geography: Review and Translation,* September 1961, pp. 59–64.

Taskin, George A., "The Falling Level of the Caspian Sea in Relation to Soviet Economy," *Geographical Review,* October 1954, pp. 508–527.

KAZAKH S.S.R.

Alampiev, P., *Soviet Kazakhstan,* Foreign Languages Publishing House, Moscow, 1958, 186 pp.

Buyanovsky, M. S., "Balkhash-Ili, A Potential Major Industrial Complex," *Soviet Geog-*

raphy: *Review and Translation,* October 1965, pp. 3–15.

TURKMEN S.S.R.

Freikin, Z. G., *Turkmenskaya SSR* (Turkmen SSR), Moscow, 1957, 450 pp. (in Russian).

Skosyrev, Petr G., *Turkmenistan,* Moscow, 1955, 293 pp. (in Russian).

———, *Soviet Turkmenistan,* Foreign Languages Publishing House, Moscow, 1956, 231 pp.

UZBEK S.S.R.

Atlas Uzbekskoy SSR (Atlas of the Uzbek SSR), Tashkent, 1963, 53 pp. (in Russian).

Uzbekskaya SSR (Uzbek SSR), Tashkent Universitet geograficheskii facultet, Moscow, 1956, 470 pp. (in Russian).

Uzbekskaya SSR: ekonomiko-geograficheskie ocherki (Uzbek SSR: economic-geographic studies), Akademiya Nauk Uzbekskoi SSR, Tashkent, 1963, 483 pp. (in Russian).

Vitkovich, Victor, *A Tour of Soviet Uzbekistan,* Foreign Languages Publishing House, Moscow, 1954, 246 pp.

TADZHIK S.S.R.

Luknitsky, Pavel, *Soviet Tadjikistan,* Foreign Languages Publishing House, Moscow, 1954, 254 pp.

———, *Tadjikistan* (Tadzhikistan), Moscow, 1957, 494 pp. (in Russian).

Tadjikskaya SSR (Tadzhik SSR), Akademiya Nauk Tadjikskoi SSR, Moscow, 1956, 227 pp. (in Russian).

KIRGIZ S.S.R.

Albitskaya, Kaleriya A., *Kirgizskaya SSR* (Kirgiz SSR), Moscow, 1958, 59 pp. (in Russian).

Kolbin, L., *Kirgizskaya SSR* (Kirgiz SSR), Moscow, 1960, 46 pp. (in Russian).

Riazantsev, Sergei N., *Kirgizskaya SSR; ekonomiko-geograficheskaya kharakteristika* (Kirgiz SSR; economic-geographic character), Moscow, 1960, 483 pp. (in Russian).

Western Siberia and Northern Kazakhstan

Region	Area (sq mile)	Population	People (sq mile)	% Urban
Western Siberia	978,700	13,264,000	14	
Kurgan Oblast	27,700	1,082,000	39	39
Tyumen Oblast	560,000	1,341,000	2	47
Khanty-Mansi N.O.	215,000	250,000	1	68
Yamal-Nenets N.O.	293,000	73,000	0.2	44
Omsk Oblast	54,700	1,823,000	33	51
Novosibirsk Oblast	69,600	2,469,000	35	62
Tomsk Oblast	127,000	785,000	6	58
Kemerovo Oblast	37,300	3,017,000	81	82
Altay Kray	102,400	2,747,000	27	42
Gorno-Altay A.O.	36,200	169,000	5	22
Northern Kazakhstan	563,200	7,833,000	14	
Uralsk Oblast	59,000	502,000	9	28
Aktyubinsk Oblast (Northern [a])	62,000	545,000	9	43
Kustanay Oblast	77,000	996,000	13	36
North Kazakhstan Oblast	16,000	558,000	35	35
Kokchetav Oblast	30,800	613,000	20	30
Tselinograd Oblast	60,600	893,000	15	47
Pavlodar Oblast	49,800	678,000	14	44
Karaganda Oblast (Northern [a])	100,000	1,518,000	15	81
Semipalatinsk Oblast	70,000	676,000	10	43
East Kazakhstan Oblast	38,000	854,000	22	58
Total	1,541,000	21,097,000		

[a] Estimated areas of parts of Aktyubinsk and Karaganda Oblasts that are included in northern Kazakhstan. Population figures for these two oblasts are total population figures for the oblasts, since the excluded southern parts are only sparsely populated.

11

Western Siberia and Northern Kazakhstan

The deserts surrounding the Caspian, the Aral Sea, and Lake Balkhash give way in northern Kazakhstan and southwestern Siberia to landscapes that are influenced by a moister, cooler climate that has favored the growth of steppe grasses and the development of chernozem and chestnut soils. A homogeneity of climate, soils, and agricultural land use unites the northern tier of oblasts in Kazakhstan with the adjacent strip of land in southwestern Siberia to form a single geographical region. Recent urbanization and the construction of paralleling rail lines linking up with the Trans-Siberian Railroad have united the area still further. Since 1954 northern Kazakhstan has been flooded by Russians, Ukrainians, and Germans to man the state farms created by the plowing of virgin land, and this has made the area still more like the Siberian area immediately across the republic boundary. Northern Kazakhstan now has many more Russians than Kazakhs. (Table 11–1) In 1960 the creation of Tselinnyy Kray out of the five northern oblasts of Kazakhstan seemed to recognize this part of Kazakhstan as something different from the rest of the Republic, and it led certain observers to predict that this was a move to groom the area for splitting off from the Kazakh S.S.R. and joining with the adjacent Rus-

sian Republic, where it more logically belonged ethnically. But now Tselinnyy Kray has been disbanded and the area has reverted simply to oblast subdivision exactly as it was before.

Along with this core area of continuously populated land will be considered the vast expanse of western Siberia to the north and spottily settled central Kazakhstan to the south, because these regions do not logically fall within any other regions, and they do not warrant separate consideration. Thus western Siberia and the northern half of Kazakhstan will be considered as a single unit, even though in the Russian geographical literature the

Table 11–1   Ethnic Groups in the Virgin Lands of Northern Kazakhstan, in Per Cent of Total

Year	Kazakhs	Russians	Ukrainians	Germans
1897	79.2	10.3	3.5	
1926	40.1	26.5	27.0	
1959	19.0	46.2	14.0	12.1

Source: *Soviet Geography: Review and Translation,* April 1962, p. 37.
Note: Approximately twenty-five ethnic groups are represented in northern Kazakhstan among peoples who have moved into the virgin lands from all parts of the Soviet Union.

Figure 11–1   Western Siberia and Northern Kazakhstan.

two are generally treated separately because of the political boundary. In partial
deference to tradition, the eastern boundary of the region shall be arbitrarily set as
the western boundary of Krasnoyarsk
Kray just west of the Yenisey River, although the obvious topographic break occurs within Krasnoyarsk Kray east of the
river. The Altay Mountains in the southeast are a part of the general mountain
belt that continues through eastern Siberia

and the Far East all the way to the Pacific.
But in all Russian texts these mountains
are considered an integral part of western
Siberia, and so they will be treated here.
The economy of the all-important Kuznetsk Basin within their flanks at present
is much more oriented toward the west
than the east, so inclusion of this area with
the west makes sense.

In its entirety, western Siberia and
northern Kazakhstan is an area of 1.5 mil-

lion square miles that contains slightly more than 21 million people.

The Physical Landscape

Topography The landforms of the northern half of Kazakhstan consist in the east and the west of broad rolling uplands, the stumps of old, worn-down mountains that are divided in the middle by a syn-

clinal lowland that opens up to the north onto the broad plain of western Siberia.

The upland in the west is the Mugodzhar Mountains, a southern extension of the Urals, whose ranges fan out in northern Aktyubinsk Oblast at elevations of around 2000 feet. In eastern Kazakhstan north of Lake Balkhash and the Betpak-Dala lies a much more extensive upland known as the Kazakh Folded Country. This also is an old, worn-down mountain area which

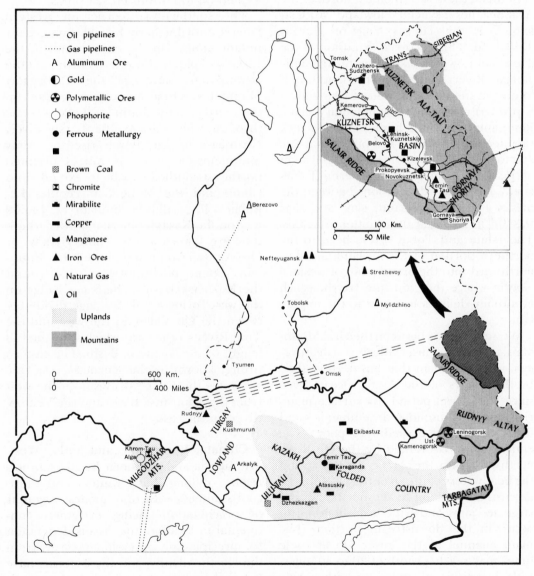

Figure 11–2 Landforms and minerals.

at present consists of low, short ranges of Paleozoic sedimentary formations and many separate hill groups of granite, syenite, porphyry, etc. The ranges in the central portion of the area are oriented primarily northwest-southeast and reach their highest elevation at 4800 feet. The general elevation of the area is considerably lower, however, and the relief everywhere is subdued. The Ulu-Tau, a separate segment of the upland at its western extremity, reach elevations of 3700 feet.

Between these two uplands, north of the Aral Sea, lies a synclinal lowland variously known as the Turgay Vale or Turgay Tableland. This northern extension of the Turanian Lowland takes its name from the Turgay River, which flows the length of it to end in the south in a playa lake bed. It is primarily a stripped sedimentary plain. Remnants of resistant higher layers of rock cap steep-sided mesas and buttes that rise 300 to 600 feet above the general elevation of the sandy plain. Hence, the term "Tableland." Elongated depressions between the mesas are filled by sand, clay, and salts washed in by small, intermittent streams. The Ishim and Tobol Rivers head in the northern portion of the lowland and flow northward into the broad plain of western Siberia where they join the Irtysh, which eventually delivers its water to the mighty Ob.

Western Siberia between the Ural Mountains and the Yenisey River is a featureless, low-lying plain that has been washed by the waters of the Arctic Ocean, even since the glacial period. Its surface materials are unconsolidated sediments, and the drainage is exceedingly poor. The entire region is drained by the Ob River northward into the Arctic. In the spring the headwaters of the river thaw before the downstream section to the north, causing large ice jams and wide-scale flooding to occur in the downstream portion. The main channel of the lower Ob at these times may reach a width of 20 to 30 miles, with hundreds of miles on either side

being flooded to some degree. Large sections of the plain are constantly waterlogged. Standing water occurs over broad regions such as the Vasyuganye Swamp in the south between the Irtysh and Ob Rivers. The southernmost portion of the plain in southwestern Siberia and northern Kazakhstan is dotted by thousands of lakes and intermittently dry lake beds that are formed where deflation hollows intersect the ground-water table. Many of these lakes are auto-precipitating salt lakes located on top of buried salt plugs.

The southeastern corner of western Siberia and northern Kazakhstan is truly mountainous. On the eastern end of the Kazakh Folded Country north of the Dzungarian Gate rise the Tarbagatay Mountains. These mountains descend on the north to the basin of Lake Zaysan, through which drains the Irtysh River. Northeast of the Irtysh rise the Altay Mountains, a series of ranges oriented northwest-southeast, which extend into China and the Mongolian Peoples Republic. The Altay culminate at 14,600 feet on the Kazakh-Siberian border where they are known as the Rudnyy Altay, or Ore Altay. Two prongs of the Altay Mountains extend northwestward to surround the Kuznetsk Basin. The Salair Ridge on the west forms a low drainage divide between the Ob Valley to the west and the Tom River to the east, which runs the full length of the Kuznetsk Basin. The eastern prong, known as the Kuznetsk Ala-Tau, separates the Kuznetsk Basin on the west from the Minusinsk Basin and the Yenisey River on the east.

Climate, Vegetation, and Soils   Western Siberia and northern Kazakhstan is a region of long, hard winters and short, cool summers with only modest amounts of precipitation. Being extremely continental in location, the area is dependent for precipitation on cyclonic storms from the North Atlantic, and these storms have traveled over much land before they reach the region east of the Urals. In winter particularly the storms are relatively ineffectual, because the great Siberian High dominates the area and shunts them off to the northeast around the northern end of the Urals where they die along the Arctic fringes of western Siberia. The storms that come into Middle Asia from the Mediterranean during the winter find the northeasterly path blocked by the Siberian High and die against the slopes of the Middle Asian mountains.

Cyclones that affect the area most frequently in winter are generated in the southern plain of the European part of the Soviet Union north of the Black Sea and follow a northeasterly course across the Southern Urals into western Siberia. Many of these storms become rejuvenated in the region of the Ob Gulf and induce an increase of snowfall in the Middle Yenisey Region. This, together with constantly subfreezing temperatures, produces an extensive area of some of the heaviest snow accumulation in the country. For 200 miles on either side of the Yenisey River average annual maximum snow depths are in excess of 80 centimeters (32 inches). Snow lies on the ground approximately 150 days of the year in northern Kazakhstan and more than 250 days along the Arctic fringe of western Siberia. But such quantities of this cold, dry snow would melt into only 3 or 4 inches of water. Thus wintertime precipitation is rather meager even in the snowiest region, and the western part of the Ob Basin has considerably less snow than the eastern part.

Winter temperatures hover around 0°F. Even in the southern portion of the region, at Semipalatinsk, January temperatures average only 3° above zero, and throughout much of western Siberia January temperatures average below zero. Such winter temperatures correspond to those in central Canada.

During the summer, a broad, shallow low-pressure area lies over much of interior Asia. Thus it is a bit easier for Atlantic air to penetrate the region at this time. Cyclonic storms generally are weaker than they are during the winter, however, so they still do not affect the area appreciably. Local convection combined with weak frontal uplift at this time of year causes precipitation through thunderstorm activity and produces a decided summer maximum of precipitation over the entire region.

Annual precipitation decreases from between 15 and 20 inches in the lower Ob Basin to only 6 to 8 inches in central Kazakhstan. In addition, the longer, warmer summers in the south increase evaporation losses, so that the effects of diminished precipitation are magnified. Coolness and shortness of the growing season limits agriculture primarily to the zone south of 57 degrees latitude. As one moves southward, the increasing length and warmth of the summers increase agricultural possibilities, but the diminishing moisture decreases them. Hence optimum conditions for agriculture do not exist anywhere; one simply must choose as happy a median as is possible between cold and drought. This median lies along the boundary between Siberia and Kazakhstan in a strip of land 200 to 300 miles wide, which in general straddles the 55th parallel.

This zone of optimum climate is also a zone of rich chernozem and chestnut soils which have developed under a steppe grass vegetation. This zone is the eastern extension of the so-called Black Earth Belt which starts as a wide belt in the western Ukraine and continues east-northeastward in a narrowing belt across the Middle Volga and the Southern Urals. To the north of this belt lies the unbroken northern coniferous forest, the taiga, which gives way to the tundra north of the Arctic Circle. Much of this forest and tundra land is swampy and the soils are badly leached, acidic podzols. The northern third of the west Siberian Lowland is underlain by permafrost, which further hampers drainage.

The change from grassland steppes in the south to the taiga of the north is so rapid that the northern limit of agriculture is not subject to much movement. No belt of mixed forests occurs between the steppes and the taiga as it does in European Russia. In southern Siberia the southern limit of the coniferous forest faces the open steppes broken only here and there by clumps of birch and aspen in sheltered valleys. South of the Black Earth Belt the grasses thin and the soils become coarser and sometimes saline as the steppes give way to the semidesert in central Kazakhstan.

Hydrology   The Ob River system drains practically all the area under discussion. The Irtysh and its two main tributaries, the Ishim and the Tobol, drain north-central Kazakhstan northward through western Siberia to the Arctic via the lower Ob. Short streams heading in the Kazakh Folded Country flow outward in all directions to end in salty lakes and playa lake beds, their entire volumes consumed by evaporation. The Turgay River flows southward through the Turgay Lowland and also ends in a salt flat. In the extreme west, the Emba and Ural Rivers flow through portions of Aktyubinsk and Uralsk Oblasts to empty into the Caspian.

Of these streams, only the Irtysh, fed by its mountain headwaters in China and by large Lake Zaysan, maintains a steady flow through the summer. The other streams are freshets in spring when the snow and ground are thawing, but they have very low water in late summer. Hence the possibilities of irrigation and navigation are strictly limited. In the Kazakh Folded Country the only river of significance is the Nura, which during its short course of only about 100 miles flows through the heavily industrialized area at Karaganda. A reservoir has been constructed on the Nura to supply the domestic, mining, and industrial needs of Karaganda.

Several construction works are under way on the Irtysh River system to produce hydroelectricity and to improve navigation. In 1953 the completion of the Ust-Kamenogorsk Dam, built in a narrow gorge, raised the water level 40 meters and backed up the water about 80 kilometers to create the so-called Small Irtysh Sea. Upstream from Ust-Kamenogorsk, near the mouth of the Bukhtarma River, the Bukhtarma Dam was completed in 1960. One of the highest dams in the Soviet Union, it has raised the water level 67 meters and backed water up the Irtysh 600 kilometers to create the Large Irtysh Sea, which engulfed Lake Zaysan and raised its water level 6 meters. The Reservoir has a surface area of 5000 square kilometers and holds more water than the Tsimlyansk, Rybinsk, Uglich, Moscow, and Dnieproges Reservoirs combined. The power plant has a capacity of 675,000 kilowatts. Navigation is made possible by a lock of four chambers. Construction of a third dam is planned on the Irtysh downstream from Ust-Kamenogorsk. More recently a dam 20 miles south of Pavlodar provides water for the newly constructed Irtysh-Karaganda Canal to supply water to the water-deficient areas of growing industry in central Kazakhstan. The canal, which leads off water from the Irtysh 30 kilometers south of Pavlodar, was completed to the coal-mining center of Ekibastuz in 1967. Work is continuing on the section that will run past the future copper mines of Bozshakul, and then will turn southwest to follow the Shiderty River to Karaganda. The total length of the canal will be 500 kilometers. Twenty-three pumping stations will raise the water to an elevation of 520 meters at the divide between the headwaters of the Shiderty and the Karaganda area. The canal will be 40 meters wide at the top and 4 to 7 meters deep. In addition to supplying water to industrial and mining areas, it will allow the irrigation of 37,000 hectares of land which are to be cultivated to supply vegetables, potatoes, and fruit to the developing urban markets.

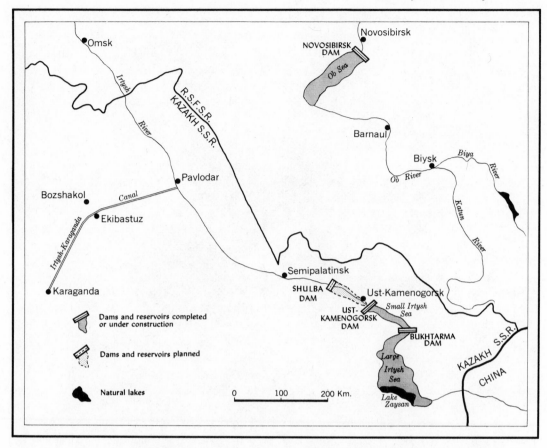

Figure 11–3 Construction projects on the Irtysh and Ob rivers.

A series of hydroelectric plants are planned for the Ob River. The first to be completed was the Novosibirsk plant with a capacity of 400,000 kilowatts. Its reservoir, the Ob Sea, is about 240 kilometers long and in places is 20 kilometers wide. The Kamen plant, 240 kilometers upstream from Novosibirsk, will raise the water level 25 meters and produce a reservoir that will stretch upstream 70 kilometers above the city of Barnaul. The reservoir, with a surface area of 4500 square kilometers, will be one of the largest in the country. It will provide irrigation for more than 2 million hectares of dry land in the Kulunda Steppe and neighboring Kazakhstan. Also, it will prevent the annual spring flooding in the Ob Valley.

The power plant is to have a capacity of 630,000 kilowatts.

A huge dam, the Nizhne-Ob, has been projected for construction near the Arctic Circle about 10 miles from the city of Salekhard on the lower Ob. As proposed, a long, low dam would raise the water level upstream as far as the junction with the Irtysh and produce an enormous reservoir 90,000 square kilometers in area with a capacity equal to three times the annual flow of the entire Ob River system. No construction date has been set. Whether or not this is a feasible or logical project remains to be seen. So much controversy has been raised over the probable changes in the local environment such a body of water would create that probably the proj-

Figure 11-4   Blasting the Irtysh-Karaganda Canal. Novosti.

ect will never be undertaken. The recent discovery of large oil and gas deposits in the area to be flooded is a further deterrent to the project.

In western Kazakhstan construction began in 1957 on the large Ural-Kushum irrigation network. An abandoned bed of the Kushum River, tributary to the Ural River, was widened to serve as the central canal for the system. It will carry a stream of water 50 meters wide and 5 meters deep. When completed, the system will allow for the irrigation of considerable territory in western Kazakhstan.

Agriculture

The zone of chernozem and chestnut soils 300 to 400 kilometers wide in northern Kazakhstan and southwestern Siberia has a cool, subhumid to semiarid climate that is ideal for the growing of spring wheat, and this is the principal crop in the area. Barley also is grown extensively, and there are scattered fields of sunflowers and hemp. Hay crops and corn for silage form the basis for considerable livestock feeding. Along the northern fringes of the agricultural zone where the soils become acidic and the drainage poor, flax growing and dairying are of prime importance. Towns along the Trans-Siberian Railroad, which runs the length of this strip, reflect the agricultural economy with their grain elevators, flour mills, creameries, and cheese factories. Such features dotting the landscape give the area an appearance of a combination of Wisconsin and North Dakota. Sugar beets have been introduced

into the area, particularly into the most southern portion around Barnaul, and sugar-processing plants have been added to the urban scene.

The steppe lands of southwestern Siberia are usually divided into three parts which are given traditional regional names, although these parts do not vary from one another enough to warrant much subdivision. West of the Irtysh River the area

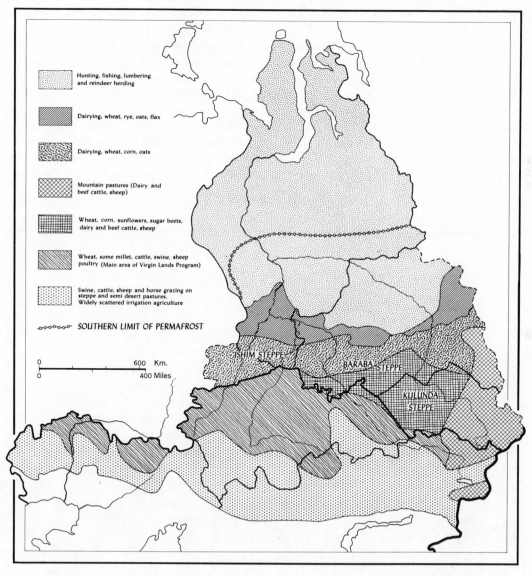

Figure 11–5   Land use in Western Siberia and Northern Kazakhstan. Adapted from Atlas selskogo khozyaystva, SSSR.

is known as the Ishim Steppe after the Ishim River which drains the region. Between the Irtysh and the Ob Rivers, between the large cities of Omsk and Novosibirsk, lies the Baraba Steppe, and in the southeast, nestled within the western slopes of the Altay Mountains, centered on the city of Barnaul, lies the rich Kulunda Steppe. The Kulunda Steppe lies farthest south and has the best soils and the mildest climate of the three regions, and it is here that Ukrainian immigrants have introduced the growing of sugar beets.

Grain growing has been pushing steadily southward into the dry grazing lands of Kazakhstan under the virgin lands program initiated in 1954. Spring wheat now is being grown on 100 million acres of newly broken steppe lands which receive no more than 8 to 16 inches of precipitation per year. This virgin-lands area of northern Kazakhstan and adjacent western

Siberia, extending westward across the Southern Urals to the Middle Volga is larger than the total wheat acreage of the United States, Canada, and Australia combined. It normally produces 50 to 60 per cent of the Soviet wheat, and thus has displaced Ukraine and Central Black Earth Region as the chief wheat-producing area of the Soviet Union. The expansion of wheat into this area has allowed the more richly endowed areas of Ukraine and Central Black Earth Region to be taken out of wheat and to be put into heavier producing crops such as corn.

Wheat growing in the virgin lands is on a grand scale, and is a gamble with the weather. Low yields per acre are compensated for by planting millions and millions of acres. The Soviets recognize that inevitable crop failures will be experienced perhaps half of the time in this region due to drought, but over a period of years they believe that the endeavor is worth the ef-

Figure 11–6   Wheat field in northern Kazakhstan. Novosti.

Figure 11-7   Two-stage wheat harvesting in Western Siberia. Novosti.

fort. Also, some agroclimatologists have pointed out that climatically the new wheat areas in the virgin lands complement the old wheat areas in Ukraine. Rarely does drought occur in both places the same year; in fact, when one area is dry, the other most likely will have above-normal precipitation. This is not pure happenstance. Ukraine and western Siberia are separated by a distance approximately equal to one half of a wavelength of the circulation of the upper troposphere. Therefore it is to be expected that they would experience opposite types of weather. Thus the virgin lands program has been justified on the assumption that insurance is being provided that somewhere in the Soviet Union there will be a good wheat crop every year. On the other hand, some agricultural specialists fear that a huge dust bowl is being created. During the growing season southwest and west winds commonly sweep this area with velocities up to 30 meters per second. Tselinograd, in the midst of the new lands, experiences dust storms 53 days per year.

During recent years wheat yields in the area have been dropping consistently, apparently due primarily to constant monoculture and lack of fallowing. Nevertheless large state farms that have been carved out of the open steppe now have an air of permanency about them.

At first, young single people were recruited to work on these virgin lands, and they lived in tents and in other temporary dwellings. Most of these Komsomols, Young Communist League members, have in one way or another found their way back to more civilized areas, however, and the virgin lands today are being built up with permanent dwellings in big rural villages peopled by families. There is a constant striving to make the economy of these areas more well rounded than simply wheat growing, so there is a great drive to recruit people to develop animal husbandry, dairying, poultry raising, vegetable and fruit growing, and so forth. An example of one of many letters appearing in daily newspapers appealing for volunteers to come to the virgin lands follows. It has been extracted from *Komsomolskaya Pravda*, the Young Communist League newspaper, dated February 4, 1959, and is entitled, "COME TO US, GIRLS.—The Virgin Lands Await Young Enthusiasts. Akmolinsk Province, Kazakhstan—Dear friends.

"In the fall of 1958 young men and women from all the fraternal republics came to Kazakhstan. They saw how the virgin steppe has been transformed by the will of the Party and how much wheat the new Young Communist League Lands are producing.

"The highly fertile virgin lands must give even more bounteously of their riches in the new seven-year period.

"Girls are working gloriously along with the men on the virgin lands. They have taken the initial adversities in stride; like everyone else, they have slept in tents on which the rain was pouring down and have struggled fearlessly through snowstorms. Together with the men they have made adobe huts, built the first houses, plowed the virgin land, and sown, raised, and harvested grain.

"The names of the patriotic young women who left comfortable homes in order to develop the virgin steppe with their own hands, shunning no kind of work, and—all obstacles notwithstanding—to bring cleanliness, comfort, and order even to earth adobes and tents are pronounced with profound respect in the virgin-land regions. Among those who have been awarded orders and medals are tractor drivers, tractor-drawn implement operators, and the glorious brigade housekeepers who also do the combine operators' laundry and prepare borshch for our wonderful fellows.

"The other day the collective of the Zhanyspaisky State Farm nominated Masha Petukhova, a young tractor driver of the third brigade, as its candidate for deputy to the Republic Supreme Soviet. She had lived in Moscow and had worked as a radio operator at Vnukovo Airport.

On the virgin lands, she became an implement operator, finished a course in tractor driving, and is now a wonderful equipment operator and an authoritative and respected person.

"Marina Pashkova was among the first to settle on the Young Communist League State Farm. Implement operator, tractor driver, then truck driver—as you read this letter, Y.C.L. member Marina Pashkova is probably driving her truck over snow-covered steppes and making her way through snowdrifts to deliver food and mail on schedule. Maria Shchurova is a mason, plasterer and stove tender—in other words, a jack-of-all-trades—on the Victory State Farm. People listen to Maria and learn from her, and she deserves the Merit Badge she has been awarded.

"Hundreds of patriotic young women, who have grown up on the virgin lands and passed through a unique school of life there, have been accepted into the ranks of the Communist Party. Quite a number of young men and women have also found personal happiness on the virgin lands. Durable and solid families have been established there and children have been born.

"Our new settlements are growing and virgin-land farms are developing rapidly, but it is becoming more and more apparent that there are still very few girls here. There are brigades without a single girl; there are whole state farms where you can say 'one, two' and you will have counted all the girls. The livestock sectors need dairymaids and calf, pig, and poultry tenders. Tens of millions of chickens, geese, and ducks could be raised on the virgin lands; it is only a matter of girls to tend them, but they cannot be found in broad daylight with a torch.

"We need literate girls with initiative, who can master several trades. We still have few children's institutions and almost no laundries and tailoring shops. Once the Young Communist League girls marry they are obliged to become housewives and to waste precious time cooking, washing, sewing, and milking cows. We want to improve living conditions, trade, and public catering, but it cannot be done here without the solicitous hands of girls.

"Dear friends. You well understand that the present and the future of the new farms depends on the strengthening of the cadres of young people. Permanent women workers are very much needed here. And what is the situation now? Each year tens of thousands of wonderful fellows arrive here from the equipment operators' schools and from military service, but—and this is no secret—many of them are forced to leave because they cannot establish families here.

"Girls represent a great force on the virgin lands. The presence in a brigade of intelligent and glorious girls who deserve real respect noticeably affects cultural behavior and labor productivity. Brigade life thus becomes richer and brighter and acquires more content. Incidentally, when young women came here at the end of last summer to help with the harvest, many fellows began to wash more thoroughly, shave more often, and keep a closer watch on their appearance. The very presence of girls ennobles the life of the distant steppe brigades.

"We are telling you about this frankly, and we hope that you will understand us correctly. Loyalty, candor, and maidenly pride are esteemed on the virgin lands.

"In the name of the girls of the Order of Lenin virgin-land state and collective farms of Akmolinsk Province, we address to you, dear friends, an ardent appeal to come to the Y.C.L. virgin lands, one of the militant sectors of communist construction. Here you will receive help in acquiring a specialty. You will meet solicitous friends, male and female, and work on the virgin lands will become the finest school of life. The virgin lands await enthusiastic, patriotic young women!

"We do not want to offend anyone, but we must say frankly that namby-pambies and adventure-seekers had better stay at home. The virgin lands need enthusiasts who will come here to advance our agriculture and animal husbandry, to build extensively. We wish to say to parents, and especially to mothers, that they should not interfere and should not be afraid to let their daughters go to the virgin lands. Believe us, dear mammas, here they will come to know the real, the great joy of labor.

"Dear friends! Last year the 13th Y.C.L. Congress called on girls to go to the virgin-land regions, to help make homes on the Y.C.L. lands. Now, on the threshold of the new seven-year period, your help is especially needed. Come, dear friends, to do great deeds; come here, best of all, for the spring of the seven-year plan.

(Signed) "In the name of the girls of the virgin-land state farms and collective farms of Akmolinsk Province: Raisa Fedorova, cook for the fourth brigade at the Samara State Grain Farm and auditor of a course in tractor driving; Tamara Moiseyeva, poultry tender at the Akmolinsk State Grain Farm; Galina Kravchenko, plasterer at the Victory State Grain Farm; etc."

One can deduce from such letters that life on these state farms still is in its pioneering stage! Nevertheless, between 1953 and 1956 the area sown to wheat in Kazakhstan alone expanded from 4,638,000 hectares to 18,318,000 hectares. By 1961 wheat acreage in the entire virgin lands area amounted to 40,000,000 hectares.

Mineral Resources and Related Developments

Northern Kazakhstan and western Siberia are especially richly endowed with mineral resources. Coal, oil, gas, and ferrous and nonferrous metals are found in some of the largest deposits in the Soviet Union. Already significant industrialization has developed because of these minerals, and discovery and development continue at a rapid rate.

Coal   Two of the major coal fields of the Soviet Union, as well as other minor coal fields, are located in this area. The Kuznetsk Coal Basin, located along the Tom River, between two northwestern prongs of the Altay Mountains in western Siberia, is the second producing coal basin in the Soviet Union, after the Donets Basin in Ukraine. It produces about 15 per cent of all the country's coal, as compared to about 35 per cent in the Donets Basin, 12 per cent in the Urals, and 9 per cent in the Moscow Basin. It produces about 30 per cent of the country's coking coal. Its reserves are much larger and somewhat higher in quality than are those of the Donets Basin. In the Soviet Union, its reserves are surpassed only by those of the Tunguskan and Lena coal fields in eastern Siberia, neither of which has a significant production. The Kemerovo part of the field has forty working seams, ranging from 2 to 50 meters thick, with an aggregate thickness of 70 meters. About 85 per cent of the coal produced at present is produced by shaft mines in steeply pitching seams in the southern part of the Basin. Farther north the seams are thinner, more nearly horizontal, closer to the surface, and can be exploited by open-pit mines.

Shipments of coal from the Kuznetsk Basin travel farther than they do from any other coal basin in the country. About 40 per cent of the coal produced in the Kuznetsk Basin is used in western Siberia; the rest is shipped to the Urals, the Central Industrial Region, the Volga region, Kazakhstan, and Middle Asia.

The Kuznetsk Basin has been operative on a limited scale for more than a century, but it underwent a major expansion in the early 1930s with the establishment of the Magnitogorsk-Kuznetsk Combine, which project established steel mills both at the iron mines of Magnitogorsk in the Southern Urals and at the coal mines of the Kuznetsk Basin. This allowed for coal to move westward on the Trans-Siberian Railroad and iron ore to move eastward, so that empty railroad cars would not be returned in one direction. Under this impetus, the Kuznetsk Basin soon became the second most important producing coal basin in the Soviet Union.

The Kuznetsk Basin still supplies most of the coal to the industries of the fuel-impoverished Urals, in spite of the inroads of Karaganda coal from Kazakhstan, which is only a little more than half as far away from the Urals as is the Kuznetsk Basin. During the early postwar years there were definite statements made by the Russians to the effect that Karaganda would soon replace Kuznetsk as the coal supplier of the Urals and the Volga Bend area. However, production at Karaganda has lagged, and as yet there has been no reduction in the absolute amount of Kuznetsk coal shipped to the Urals. The Karaganda coal has proved to have such a high ash content that it has to be mixed with Kuznetsk coal in blast furnaces and steel mills at a ratio of about 3 parts Kuznetsk coal to 1 part Karaganda coal. Therefore it is obvious that Kuznetsk will continue to be the major coal supplier to the Urals.

Also, as people continue to move into Siberia and as industries continue to grow, the demand for steel will continue to rise so that the steel plants in the Kuznetsk Basin will demand more and more of the local coal. After the establishment of the Magnitogorsk-Kuznetsk Combine, considerable quantities of iron ore were discovered in the mountains bounding the Kuznetsk Basin on the south and in the Minusinsk Basin to the east. By the mid 1950s the steel mills of the Kuznetsk Basin were almost wholly supplied with iron ore from local sources. Most recently, large new deposits of iron ore in western Siberia and northern Kazakhstan assure the continued expansion of steel production in the Kuznetsk Basin on an independent basis.

The Karaganda coal fields in the central part of the Kazakh Folded Country rival the Donets and Pechora Basins in quantity of reserves. More than twenty working seams ranging in thickness from 1 to 8.5 meters lie in nearly horizontal positions at depths between 50 and 300 meters. Most of the coal is produced by shaft mines.

The Karaganda coals are hampered by ash contents of more than 22 per cent, which limits their usage in the steel industry. This explains why coal from the Kuznetsk Basin continues to move in large quantities to the Urals and to Middle Asia, even though it must travel almost twice as far as the Karaganda coal. Karaganda normally produces about 5 per cent of the nation's coal and thus ranks sixth among the coal-producing areas of the country. But it is third in the production of coking coal. About 45 per cent of the Karaganda coal goes to the Urals, 40 per cent to Kazakhstan and Middle Asia, and the rest to the Volga region and the Central Industrial Region.

Since World War II a new coal deposit in the Kazakh Folded Country has been opened at Ekibastuz about 75 miles southwest of Pavlodar. It is located in a small synclinal basin 25 kilometers long by 9 kilometers wide. At the edges of the syncline the coal outcrops at the surface, but in the middle it reaches depths of 350 to 400 meters below the surface. Four continuous seams of complex structure have a total thickness of up to 160 meters. The coals, with 34 to 45 per cent ash content, are hard to clean and are used mainly in large power stations at Omsk and Pavlodar and in the Urals. Ekibastuz coal is also to be used in the large new Yermak power station which began operation in late 1968 and is to have an ultimate capacity of 2,400,000 kilowatts. Three large open-pit mines are in operation. Ekibastuz now is producing about one fourth as much coal as Karaganda.

Other coal fields in the region are the Kushmurun brown coal field in the Turgay Lowland in Kustanay Oblast, the Mamyt deposit in Aktyubinsk Oblast, and the western part of the elongated Kansk-Achinsk deposits in the eastern part of Kemerovo Oblast. Development was begun in the Kushmurun coal field in 1957, but the operation was abandoned after it was found that the over-burden was water logged and drainage would require excessive expenditures.

Iron Ore and Alloys Until recently, northern Kazakhstan and western Siberia appeared to be one of the iron-poor regions of the country. When the Urals-Kuznetsk Combine was begun in the early 1930s, all the iron ore that was used in the Kuznetsk steel mills was shipped in from Magnitogorsk. Now the area appears to be one of the richest regions of iron ore in the country.

During the 1940s and early 1950s, small deposits of iron ore were exploited in the southern rim of the Kuznetsk Basin in the so-called Gornaya Shoriya area and in the vicinity of Abakan in the Minusinsk Basin to the east. A railroad was completed between Novokuznetsk and Abakan to provide for the utilization of these eastern ores and also to lay the way for expansion of iron mining into the Khakass Autonomous Oblast in the mountains of southern Krasnoyarsk Kray. These operations made the Kuznetsk iron and steel plants essentially self-sufficient of Magnitogorsk ore and brought about the dissolution of the Urals-Kuznetsk Combine. Although Kuznetsk coal continued to move westward to the Urals, little iron ore moved eastward to Kuznetsk. The second iron and steel center in this general area, which was being built among the Karaganda coal fields in north central Kazakhstan, was projected to use iron ore from the nearby Atasu deposit southwest of Karaganda.

None of these iron-ore deposits were large in reserves, however, and the Soviets were building their iron and steel plants very cautiously, with a worried eye to the future when these ores would run out. But since 1955, seemingly unlimited quantities of low-grade iron ores have been located in the Turgay Lowlands of Kustanay Oblast, along the eastern flanks of the Southern and Middle Urals, and, most recently, in the Bakchar area just northwest of the Kuznetsk Basin in Tomsk Oblast. All of these ores are low grade, but most of them lie near the surface and can be mined inexpensively by open-pit methods and made usable by processing through huge concentrators and pelletizers which convert ore as low as 16 per cent iron into readily usable pellets containing 55 to 65 per cent iron and correct ratios of coke, manganese, and fluxing materials. The largest mining operation of these low-grade ores so far has taken place in the so-called Sokolov-Sarbay and Lisakov deposits in Kustanay Oblast, where the mining center of Rudnyy increased its population from 37,000 in 1959 to 89,000 in 1967. A large concentrator and three pelletizer machines at Rudnyy have the capacity to turn out more than 2.5 million tons of pellets per year. In 1965, 62 million tons of raw ore was processed in this area. The dressed ores are being shipped to Magnitogorsk, Chelyabinsk, and Nizhniy Tagil in the Urals and to the plants in the Kuznetsk Basin. The large Bakchar deposit in Tomsk Oblast was discovered only in the late 1960s and will not be explored thoroughly until sometime in the early 1970s.

The envisioned usage of these large quantities of ore has induced the Soviets confidently to expand old iron and steel plants and build new ones in the west Siberian-Kazakhstan region. The largest construction during the past decade has

been the West Siberian Iron and Steel Plant situated at Antonovo about 19 miles northeast of Novokuznetsk on the right bank of the Tom River. The first coke-making facilities were completed in 1963 and the first blast furnace went into operation in July 1964. A second identical blast furnace, of 2000-cubic-meters capacity, went into operation in 1967. Each of these furnaces has an annual capacity of about 1 million tons of pig iron. At the present time two more blast furnaces, of the 2700-cubic-meters size, are now being constructed, which by 1970 are to raise the plant's pig-iron capacity to 5.5 million tons. In addition, rolling mills and a wire mill have been established at the West Siberian Plant. Facilities have also been expanded at the older plant in Novokuznetsk.

In Kazakhstan, at Karaganda, the large new iron and steel plant which the Soviets have been half-heartedly constructing in the northwest suburb of Temir-Tau finally seems to be nearing completion. Although construction was started in 1956 with a good deal of fanfare, construction lagged and completion dates were postponed again and again as it appeared that the Soviets were somewhat wary of going through with initial plans. But the opening of the new iron-ore deposits in Kustanay Oblast seems to have given the construction a definite spurt. The first blast furnace was opened in 1960 and the first open-hearth steel shop in 1964. Steel production at Karaganda jumped from 400,000 tons in 1964 to 1 million tons in 1965 as production from the new plant was added to that of a small steel plant developed during World War II. By 1966 it had risen to 1.3 million tons. Hot- and cold-rolling mills have also been added at Karaganda. When the big plant was first projected, plans called for an ultimate capacity equal to that of Magnitogorsk, but this has since been scaled down to 4.5 million tons. The Karaganda coals have not turned out to be as useful as was first anticipated, and more emphasis is now being placed on the production of steel in the west for expanded industries in the smaller cities of the European part of the country where most of the population lives. Also, the establishment of the second large plant in the Kuznetsk Basin somewhat saturates the market for steel east of the Urals.

In addition to the two large full-cycle iron and steel plants in the Novokuznetsk area, there is a smaller steel plant at Guryevsk in the Kuznetsk Basin and there are steel mills at Novosibirsk northwest of the Basin.

In the western part of Kazakhstan, the new metallurgical center of Novotroitsk uses naturally alloyed nickel-chrome iron ore to produce high-grade steels. In the same general area Soviet chrome production is concentrated at Khrom-Tau.

Nonferrous Metals Before ferrous metallurgy was developed in northern Kazakhstan and western Siberia, the Kazakh Folded Country and the Altay Mountains were already known for their production of nonferrous metals. This production is being greatly expanded with the continued discovery of Deposits of ores. So far, copper, lead, and zinc have been the important minerals, but aluminum has recently joined the group.

It is now estimated that Kazakhstan possesses roughly half of the reserves of copper, lead, and zinc in the Soviet Union. Copper is found mainly in three large deposits, the newly discovered Dzhezkazgan deposit in the western part of the Kazakh Folded Country, which reportedly is the second largest deposit in the world, the Rudnyy Altay deposits near Leninogorsk, and the Balkhash deposits mentioned in Chapter 10 as belonging to southern Kazakhstan.

Lead and zinc deposits are found mainly in two areas in association with one another: the Rudnyy Altay around Leninogorsk and in the Tyan Shans near Chimkent, as was mentioned in Chapter 10.

Other scattered deposits exist in southern Kazakhstan. In northern Kazakhstan a primary lead smelter has been operating at Leninogorsk since 1927. This was modernized in 1940, and a zinc refinery was added in 1966 after abundant hydroelectric power became available from the Ust-Kamenogorsk and Bukhtarma Dams. Zinc refineries were also opened in Ust-Kamenogorsk in 1947 and 1955, and a lead smelter was opened there in 1952. A zinc refinery has been operating for years at Belovo in the Kuznetsk Basin, initially using ore from the Salair Ridge to the west and employing a distillation process based on local coke. Now the Salair ore is largely depleted, and the Belovo plant must ship in ore.

The aluminum industry is expanding into Kazakhstan and western Siberia as new bauxite deposits are being opened in northern and southern Kazakhstan. The most promising deposit seems to be the Arkalyk bauxite in the Turgay Lowland, which apparently rivals the Krasnaya-Shapochka deposits in the Urals. This ore is supplying a new alumina plant which began operating in Pavlodar in 1964. Aluminum production is scheduled to begin at Pavlodar at a later date when the plant becomes fully integrated. Electricity will be supplied to the Pavlodar plant from thermal generators using Ekibastuz coal.

Tin has been reported along the upper Irtysh River in eastern Kazakhstan, and deposits of tungsten and molybdenum have been reported north of Lake Balkhash and in the Rudnyy Altay. Silver and gold exist in the complex ores of the Rudnyy Altay. Recently, a major gold lode has been opened up at Auezov in the mountains of eastern Kazakhstan 70 miles southeast of Semipalatinsk which, along with some other lode operations in Central Asia and Transcaucasia, promises to shift gold production westward from the traditionally dominant placer deposits of eastern Siberia. In 1964 a titanium-magnesium plant in a new suburb of Ust-Kamenogorsk began processing carnallite from Solikamsk in the Urals and titanium concentrates from Ukraine. In 1965 asbestos production began at Dzhetygara in northwestern Kazakhstan, second in importance to the Ural deposits.

Oil and Gas

The most exciting development that is taking place at the present time in western Siberia is the rapid opening of recently discovered huge deposits of oil and natural gas in Tyumen and Tomsk Oblasts. Major producing centers of oil are Nefteyugansk, Surgut, Megion, and Nizhnevartovskiy in Tyumen Oblast and Strezhevoy in Tomsk Oblast. The Tyumen

fields began shipments of crude oil by barge to the Omsk refinery at the opening of the navigation season in June 1964. About 200,000 tons of oil were moved by river barge along the Ob and Irtysh Rivers to the Omsk refinery that year. Production increased to 1 million tons in 1965, and a pipeline was completed from Shaim to Tyumen. Oil output rose to 3 million tons in 1966 and 6 million tons in 1967. In 1967 a 40-inch crude-oil pipeline more than 600 miles long was completed from Nefteyugansk (formerly Ust-Balyk) to Omsk. Also, a railroad was completed from Tyumen to Tobolsk and is being extended to Surgut, the center of the Ob oil fields. Thus the new oil boom finally brought a railroad to the old town of Tobolsk, which at one time was the leading urban center of all of Siberia. Oil pro-

Figure 11–8   Typical landscape of new oil regions in Tyumen Oblast. Novosti.

duction in western Siberia is to increase rapidly to 25 million tons in 1970, which then will be about 7 per cent of the total U.S.S.R. production.

Natural gas fields have been opened up further down the Ob, particularly around Berezovo and Igrim in Tyumen Oblast. The fields apparently extend under wide areas of the West Siberian Lowland southeastward into Tomsk Oblast and northward along the Ob estuary and then eastward along the Arctic coast into the lower Taz River Valley, all in Tyumen Oblast. On January 1, 1968 these west Siberian fields were estimated to have 3.85 trillion cubic meters of reserves, which equalled one half of the 7.75 trillion cubic meters of recoverable reserves for the entire Soviet Union. In comparison, the present principal gas-producing areas of the Soviet Union, Ukraine, the north Caucasus, and Uzbekistan, each are estimated to have from 0.6 to 0.7 trillion cubic meters of reserves. The new Siberian fields are to play a major part in the continued rapid expansion of gas production in the Soviet Union, which by 1980 is scheduled to increase to more than four times the production of 1968.

About the only delay in the expansion of production in this region is the necessity to lay large pipelines to market areas. In 1966 a 40-inch pipeline was completed from Igrim in the Berezovo fields to Serov in the north central Urals where it was to link up with gas pipelines coming northward from Sverdlovsk carrying gas from the Middle Asian fields. Eventually these lines are to be linked westward through Perm to the Volga-Urals area from which gas can be carried westward to the Central Industrial Region and the European Northwest. At the present time construction is under way on large-diameter gas pipelines which will carry gas from the lower Ob and Taz gas fields around Novyy Port and Tazovskiy southwestward across the northern end of the Urals through the Ukhta gas-producing area in northeastern European Russia

to Cherepovets at the northern end of the Rybinsk Reservoir, where connections will be made with other pipelines feeding the center and the western part of the European U.S.S.R. Some of this gas will also be transmitted further west to the satellite countries in Eastern Europe.

In Tomsk Oblast natural-gas deposits have been discovered recently in the area of the Vasyugan River, a left-bank tributary of the Ob. This is the closest reserve of gas to the Kuznetsk Basin. A gas pipeline is scheduled to be laid in the early 1970s from the Vasyugan fields to the Kuznetsk Basin. The transmitted gas will be accompanied by large amounts of liquid hydrocarbons that are to provide the raw materials for a proposed petrochemical plant somewhere southwest of Tomsk. Farther west a petrochemicals complex has been operating at Omsk for over a decade, and a new plastics plant is to be built using petrochemicals from the local oil refinery and the local synthetic rubber factory.

Settlement and Economic Development

When Yermak led his small band of Cossacks across the Urals in 1583 to capture the Tatar town of Sibir, the vast area lying between the Urals and the Pacific was essentially unoccupied except for a few thousand widely scattered so-called Paleo-Asiatics who busied themselves with reindeer herding, hunting, and fishing. Thus the Russians met very little resistance in their eastward sweep to the Pacific, which took place in the short span of approximately 50 years. The original Russian adventurers went into the area primarily in quest of furs, and the first establishments of towns were nothing more than forts and trading posts to facilitate the collection of furs from native hunters. During the seventeenth and eighteenth centuries, however, many of these fur-trading centers in western Siberia grew into centers for agricultural settlement, and many new villages were established to accommodate the influx of Russian farmers. By the end of the nineteenth century southwestern Siberia and northern Kazakhstan presented the aspect of a continuously settled area with a population that was predominantly rural.

The coming of the Trans-Siberian Railroad in the 1890s connected the elongated string of settlements with the more populous west, and initiated urbanization. Wherever the railroad crossed a major river a new town was established to handle the commerce. These river-rail towns grew with the railroad and soon surpassed the old regional centers that lay off the main rail line. Flour milling, textiles, and lumbering industries soon developed in the new towns. Later metallurgical industries became predominant as mining developed in the Kuznetsk Basin and in northern Kazakhstan, and rail lines, hooking up with the Trans-Siberian Railroad, spread out both north and south.

The Trans-Siberian Railroad between the Urals and the Kuznetsk Basin is no longer a single line. Paralleling branches cross the Urals at Sverdlovsk, Chelyabinsk, and Magnitogorsk. The line from Magnitogorsk crosses northern Kazakhstan east-southeastward straight to Karaganda to provide a direct line for coal transport from Karaganda to the Southern Urals. North-south main lines and many spur lines link together the entire area. Oil is being piped into Omsk from the Bashkir Republic west of the Urals, and more recently from the west Siberian fields, to run new oil refineries and provide the bases for chemical and other industries.

Although the recent influx of farmers under the virgin- and idle-lands program has temporarily prolonged the rural aspects of the region, cities are growing rapidly, and new bases for industry are constantly being established. The main industries of the area are the metallurgical industries, based on local mining; machine-building industries to serve local agriculture, industry, and the railroad; textiles to utilize wool produced locally and cotton shipped in on the Turk-Sib Railroad from Middle Asia to satisfy local markets; food industries to mill the flour, process the meat and dairy products, and refine the sugar of the local farms; and now chemical industries, utilizing oil from Bashkiria to supply needed synthetics and plastics.

The forest resource, although not the best, has always provided the basis for some industry in a number of centers, none of which have been of all-union importance. However, some increased activity in forestry is now taking place as railroads are being extended into the area, some of which are being built specifically to open up new timber areas, whereas others incidentally are making new timber stands accessible in areas through which they are being laid to the new oil and gas fields. The 250-mile Ivdel-Ob River Railroad, with its eastern terminus south of Narykary on the Ob River, and the 120-mile railroad from Tavda to Sotnik on the Konda River have been built specifically to open up these forest regions for exploitation. The Tyumen-Surgut Railroad is being built to serve Surgut, which is to become the commercial center of the west Siberian oil fields, and the 180-mile Arctic Railroad from Salekhard to Nadym has been projected to serve the new natural-gas fields in that area. Construction on this railroad was begun in the late 1940s using forced labor, and it initially was planned to go all the way from Salekhard to Igarka. But the project was abandoned until the new gas finds added the needed impetus to rehabilitate it. Present plans include a long bridge across the very broad Lower Ob at Salekhard, but it is still uncertain whether all this construction cost can be justified.

Four major lumber centers are planned: in the Ivdel-Serov district on the east side of the Urals, the lower Ob, the upper Konda, and the Sosva River. The largest of these will be the lower Ob, which ultimately is to process 6 million cubic meters of timber per year in the manufacture of pulp and paperboard, sawn lumber, plywood, and fiberboard. The plant is to form the basis for a town of 50,000 people. In Tomsk Oblast, a new wood-processing complex is being established at Asino northeast of Tomsk. A railroad is being extended into virgin timber stands northwestward ultimately to hook up with the Tyumen-Surgut Railroad at Surgut. Farther south, new forest resources have been made more accessible in the upper reaches of the Ob by the Omsk-Barnaul Railroad which was completed in 1962 to provide an alternate route for heavy traffic between the Kuznetsk Basin and the west.

Cities

Novosibirsk Chief among the new rail-river towns, and now largest in all of Siberia, is Novosibirsk, at the important rail crossing of the Ob River. Founded in 1903 as Novonikolayevsk, it was renamed Novosibirsk (New Siberia) in 1926. By 1967 it had grown to a population of 1,064,000.

The industries of Novosibirsk are varied, and their importance is shared by that of commerce. The city acts as the metropolis for the whole of western Siberia, and it is the regional center for the heavily industrialized Kuznetsk Basin, although the city itself is not located within the Basin. Novosibirsk has often been called the Chicago of Siberia. Diversified machine construction and metal working are the primary industries in Novosibirsk, but there are also important heavy metallurgical industries, chemical industries, and food industries. A specialized suburb, Akademgorodok (Academic town), recently has become famous as an experiment in isolated, concentrated living of top-level research personnel.

Omsk The second largest city in Siberia might be called the sister city of Novosibirsk, since it sits on the same plain in a similar location on a terrace along the right bank of a stream where it is crossed by the Trans-Siberian Railroad. Novosibirsk occupies the rail crossing of the Ob River; Omsk the rail crossing of the Irtysh. Omsk, with a 1967 population of 774,000, is one of the most rapidly growing cities in all of Siberia. Like Novosibirsk, Omsk owes its origin to its strategic location on major transport lines within a rich agricultural plain. But also like Novosibirsk, Omsk long since has outgrown its function as the trading center of an agricultural region and has become a great industrial city. At present the industries of Omsk are concentrated approximately one half on machine construction and metal working, one fourth on chemicals, and one fourth on food industries. Omsk is destined to become the primary oil-refining and chemical center of Siberia, utilizing oil brought in by five pipelines from the Volga-Urals oil fields, and one pipeline from the Surgut oil fields in western Siberia. The synthetic rubber and plastics plants have already been mentioned.

Karaganda Third in size, with a population of 498,000, is the new city of Karaganda, sitting in the important coal mining area in the Kazakh Folded Country. Karaganda is the chief center of heavy industry of Kazakhstan, and since its founding in 1926 it has been the most rapidly growing city of the Republic. Although the coal mining and the steel production have not proceeded as rapidly as had been hoped, Karaganda is destined to continue its growth and to dominate the heavy-industry scene in Kazakhstan. A small steel plant with a capacity of 250,000 tons has operated in Karaganda since 1945. In July 1960 the first blast furnace of an integrated iron and steel plant finally opened. This new plant is located in the suburban city of Temir Tau, or Iron Mountain, northwest of Karaganda. It receives its coal from the local

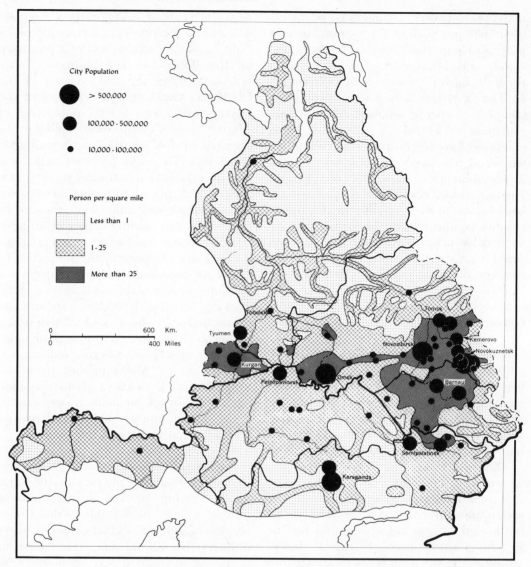

Figure 11–9   Population densities and city sizes. After Cherdantsev.

mines and Kuznetsk and iron ore from Atasu to the southwest and Rudnyy in Kustanay Oblast. Karaganda lies in a somewhat barren landscape on the southern edge of the virgin lands. It gets its water supply from the small Nura River, which flows northwestward through the Kazakh Folded Country. The Nura is not much of a stream, but its water is to be supplemented by the Irtysh-Karaganda Canal.

Cities of the Kuznetsk Basin   Fourth in size now is Novokuznetsk, the main steel center of the Kuznetsk Basin, which grew from nothing in 1930 to 493,000 in 1967. Known as Stalinsk from 1932 to 1961, the city was founded as a new steel center during the first five-year plan across the Tom River from the old town of Kuznetsk. It soon engulfed the old town.

At present about one third of the industry of Novokuznetsk is concentrated on heavy metallurgy. Its other industries are chemicals, based on coking gases, machine construction and metal working, and light metallurgy, particularly aluminum.

The Kuznetsk Basin now has the greatest concentration of large cities in any area east of the Urals. Prokopyevsk, just northwest of Novokuznetsk, is concentrated on metal working and chemicals and has grown rapidly to a population of 290,000 in 1967. Farther northwest is Kemerovo, the oblast center for the Kuznetsk Basin, with a population of 364,000. Kemerovo originally was the largest city in the Kuznetsk Basin, but it has not been growing as rapidly as Novokuznetsk. Kemerovo is primarily a coal-mining town, and its industries are heavily concentrated on chemicals from the coking industry. It also has machine construction and metal working, as well as construction-material industries.

Four other cities, each with more than 100,000 population, lie in the Kuznetsk Basin. These are Leninsk-Kuznetskiy, with a population of 138,000; Kiselevsk, with a population of 138,000; Anzhero-Sudzhensk, with a population of 116,000; and Belovo, with a population of 116,000. These are all coal-mining towns that usually have some metal-working and chemical industries as well as construction-material industries, food industries, and so forth. Belovo is known particularly for its zinc-processing plant. Anzhero-Sudzhensk lies on the main line of the Trans-Siberian Railroad between Novosibirsk and Krasnoyarsk, whereas the other cities lie on a branch line to the south; hence part of its growth has been derived from its favorable location with respect to transport lines.

Cities of the Kulunda Steppe Fifth in size in western Siberia and northern Kazakhstan is Barnaul, population 407,000, the commercial and governmental center of Altay Kray in the rich farm lands of the Kulunda Steppe. Founded in 1771, its name was adopted from a Kazakh term meaning "good pastures." Like Omsk and Novosibirsk, Barnaul has outgrown its function as the center of a rich agricultural region and is rapidly becoming an industrial city. It sits at the junction of the South Siberian Railroad coming in from the southwest from Pavlodar and Tselinograd, the northern extension of the Turk-Sib Railroad coming in from the south from Semipalatinsk, and the new Omsk-Barnaul line coming in from the northwest. These railroads join at Barnaul on the left bank of the Ob River, and a single rail line crosses the river and continues eastward to the Kuznetsk Basin. Barnaul long has been an important center for cotton textiles, utilizing raw cotton shipped in from Middle Asia over the Turk-Sib Railroad to supply cheap cotton goods to the markets in southwestern Siberia. It now has a major synthetic fiber factory. It also has machine-building, wood-working, and food industries.

Two other significant cities in the Kulunda Steppe are Biysk, with a population of 181,000, and Rubtsovsk, with a population of 142,000. They both are regional centers of rich farming districts. Rubtsovsk is known particularly for its manufacture of agricultural machinery.

Regional Centers of the Farming Belt of Northern Kazakhstan and Southwestern Siberia Seven cities in the rich farm lands of northern Kazakhstan and southwestern Siberia have populations between 115,000 and 215,000. In order of size they are Kurgan, Semipalatinsk, Tselinograd, Petropavlovsk, Pavlodar, Aktyubinsk, and Kustanay. They serve the region as rail centers, grain-storage centers, food processing centers, etc. All are administrative centers of their respective oblasts. Many have agricultural machine-building industries; Kurgan and Tselinograd particularly are important in this respect. Pavlodar is being developed into an industrial city with new oil refineries planned. A new alumina

Figure 11–10   A rayon factory in Barnaul. Novosti.

plant converts the bauxite from Arkalyk 640 miles to the southwest.

Until 1961 Tselinograd was named Akmolinsk. It was the administrative seat of the now defunct Tselinnyy Kray in the virgin lands of northern Kazakhstan. The word "tselina" means "virgin soil." "Akmolinsk" means "white tomb," a term that was considered inappropriate for this thriving area.

Old Towns of Western Siberia The old university town of Tomsk, located near the mouth of the Tom River north of the Trans-Siberian Railroad, is seventh in size in western Siberia and northern Kazakhstan, with a population of 324,000. It is one of the older towns in Siberia, having been founded in 1604, and together with Tobolsk and Tyumen farther west, it dominated urban life in Siberia for a couple of centuries. But when the Trans-Siberian Railroad was laid south of all these cities during 1892–1904, new towns established at major river crossings such as Omsk and Novosibirsk rapidly outgrew the older cities. Tomsk sits on a rail spur about 75 miles north of the Trans-Siberian Railroad. It has diversified industries with some concentration on machine building and wood working. It is the site of the first university in Siberia and long has been known as the cultural center of south-western Siberia.

Tyumen, the oldest city in Siberia, was founded in 1585 on the site of the old Tatar city of Sibir, which had been captured 2 years earlier by Yermak and his band. Tyumen is near the mouth of the Tura River where it joins the Tobol at the western head of navigation on the Ob-Irtysh River system. Although the major rivers of Siberia flow northward, it was their east-west flowing portions that were important during the early days of east-ward penetration into Siberia, so the fact that Tyumen occupied the westernmost point of navigation made it a very strategically located city. Later it was the eastern terminus of the old Perm to Tyumen Railroad, and as such served as the main entrepot into Siberia until it was replaced by Chelyabinsk when the Trans-Siberian Railroad was established to the south. With the building of the northern branch of the Trans-Siberian Railroad from Sverdlovsk to Omsk, Tyumen gained a position on a major rail line. However, its main function remained only as an important river-rail transfer point for lumber and grain, and it never regained its former importance until recently when it became the supply base for the vast northern oil region. It is now receiving crude oil by pipe from the west Siberian fields to the north. In 1967 Tyumen had a population of 240,000. Its industries are concentrated on machine building, wood working, and chemicals.

Tobolsk, 47,000 population, sitting at the mouth of the Tobol River where it joins the Irtysh, was once a mighty fur-collecting city and until 1824 served as the administrative center of western Siberia. But after it was by-passed by the Trans-Siberian Railroad, without even a spur line to serve it, it functioned only as a river port and lumbering center of local significance. Finally in 1967 it became connected to the outside world as the rail line was built through from Tyumen to the new oil center of Surgut.

Cities of the Rudnyy Altay The mining and smelting towns of Ust-Kamenogorsk and Leninogorsk in the Rudnyy Altay already have been mentioned in conjunction with the production of lead, zinc, and associated metals. In 1959 Ust-Kamenogorsk had a population of 212,000 and Leninogorsk had a population of 70,000.

Prospects

Western Siberia and Northern Kazakhstan is a treasure house of mineral resources. With the new, large discoveries of oil, gas, and iron ore, the region is destined to continue its industrial growth. But it is also destined to remain a major exporter of these bulk commodities as mining activities expand much more rapidly than does the population of the region. Population spurts induced by agricultural settlement at the turn of the century, industrialization during World War II, and the opening of the virgin lands in the 1950s seem to have tapered off, and, in fact, since the political thaw of 1957 there has been net out-migration from certain areas as formerly exiled persons were rehabilitated and allowed to return westward to former homelands. With the seeming current shift in government policy of moving resources to people rather than people to resources, it can be predicted that, in the future, population in western Siberia and northern Kazakhstan will grow by only a moderate rate, due primarily to natural increase, whereas mining and heavy industries will continue to expand rapidly. The fluid fuels and electricity can easily be transported westward to markets as their production is greatly expanded in this region. With much of its energy resources and minerals being shipped to other parts of the country, this region will probably retain its predominantly rural aspect.

Reading List

Alampiev, P., *Soviet Kazakhstan,* Foreign Languages Publishing House, Moscow, 1958, 186 pp.

Atlas Tselinnogo Kraya (Atlas of Tselinny Kray), Moscow, 1964, 49 pp. (in Russian).

Davitaya, F. F., ed., *Agroklimaticheskiye i vodnyye resursy rayonov osvoyeniya tselinnykh i zalezhnykh zemel* (Agro-climatic and water resources in the regions of the reclamation of the virgin and idle lands), Leningrad, 1955, 464 pp. (in Russian).

Durgin, Frank A., Jr., "The Virgin Lands Programme 1954–1960," *Soviet Studies,* 1962, pp. 255–280.

Hajdu, Peter, *The Samoyed Peoples and Languages,* Indiana University Publications, Uralic and Altaic Series, Bloomington, 1963, Vol. 14, 114 pp.

Holzman, Franklyn D., "Soviet Ural-Kuznetsk Combine: A Study in Investment Criteria and Industrialization Policies," *The Quarterly Journal of Economics,* August 1957, pp. 368–405.

Hooson, D. J. M., *A New Soviet Heartland?* Van Nostrand, Princeton, 1964, 132 pp.

————, "A New Soviet Heartland?" *The Geographical Journal,* March 1964, pp. 19–29.

Jackson, W. A. Douglas, "The Virgin and Idle Lands of Western Siberia and Northern Kazakhstan: A Geographical Appraisal," *Geographical Review,* January 1956, pp. 1–19.

————, "The Virgin and Idle Lands Program Reappraised," *Annals of the Association of American Geographers,* March 1962, pp. 69–79.

Karsten, A. A., "The Virgin Lands Kray and its Prospects of Development," *Soviet Geography: Review and Translation,* May 1963, pp. 37–46.

Krypton, C., *The Northern Sea Route and the Economy of the Soviet North,* Methuen, London, 1956.

Levin, M. G., and Potapov, L. P., eds., *The Peoples of Siberia,* University of Chicago Press, 1964, 948 pp. (translated from the Russian edition published by U.S.S.R. Academy of Sciences in 1956).

Lonsdale, R. E., "Siberian Industry before 1917: The Example of Tomsk Guberniya," *Annals of the Association of American Geographers,* December 1963, pp. 479–493.

Pomus, M. I., *Zapadnaya Sibir* (Western Siberia), Moscow, 1956.

Treadgold, Donald L., *The Great Siberian Migration,* Princeton University Press, 1957, 278 pp.

Tselinyy Kray; kratkie ocherki o prirode, naselenii i khosyaystve (Tselinyy Kray; short study of nature, population, and economy), Akademiya Nauk Kazakhskoy SSR, Alma-Ata, 1962, 188 pp.

Vendrov, S. L., "A Forecast of Changes in Natural Conditions in the Northern Ob Basin in Case of Construction of the Lower Ob Hydro Project," *Soviet Geography: Review and Translation,* December 1965, pp. 3–18.

Eastern Siberia and the Far East

	Area (sq mile)	Popu- lation	People (sq mile)	% Urban
Eastern Siberia	2,207,800	7,921,000	3.6	
Krasnoyarsk Kray	327,000	2,925,000	8.9	60
Khakass A.O.	24,200	462,000	19.1	61
Evenki N.O.	291,000	12,999	0.04	33
Taymyr N.O.	336,000	36,000	0.1	64
Tuva A.O.	66,500	217,000	3.3	37
Irkutsk Oblast	300,000	2,267,000	7.6	70
Ust-Orda Buryat N.O.	8,400	154,000	18.3	18
Buryat A.S.S.R.	137,000	780,000	5.7	44
Chita Oblast	168,000	1,092,000	6.5	57
Aga Buryat N.O.	7,400	62,000	8.4	10
Yakut A.S.S.R.	1,210,000	646,000	0.5	56
Far East	1,215,900	5,175,000	4.3	
Amur Oblast	141,500	781,000	5.5	62
Khabarovsk Kray	322,000	1,317,000	4.1	80
Jewish A.O.	14,100	174,000	12.3	70
Maritime Kray	66,400	1,641,000	24.7	73
Magadan Oblast	468,000	327,000	0.7	87
Chukchi N.O.	288,667	89,000	0.3	78
Kamchatka Oblast	184,000	472,000	2.6	44
Koryak N.O.	118,333	37,000	0.3	32
Sakhalin Oblast	34,000	637,000	18.7	82
Total	3,423,700	13,096,000		

12

Eastern Siberia and the Far East

The belt of continuously settled land in northern Kazakhstan and southwestern Siberia ends abruptly against the northwestern spurs of the Altay Mountains surrounding the Kuznetsk Basin, and thus ends the continuously populated area of the Soviet Union. In the remaining 2000 miles to the Pacific, mountains break the string of settlements along the Trans-Siberian Railroad into isolated pockets of population located in steppe-like intermountain basins. Wherever the topography and climate are such that agriculture and urban development are possible, some settlement has taken place, but the development has been nothing like that in southwestern Siberia where a broad open plain has provided a continuous strip of rich soil and tolerable climate for both agricultural and urban settlement.

The vast expanse of territory east of the Kuznetsk Basin is known as eastern Siberia and the Soviet Far East. This region contains an area of more than 3,400,000 square miles, is larger than the United States of America, and comprises almost 45 per cent of the total area of the Soviet Union. Yet it contains only some 13 million people, so that culturally and economically it is no more significant to the country than are many of the much smaller regions already considered. Hence it does not warrant division into several regions, even though the area is great, the topography is varied, and culturally the southern strip is much different from the empty wastes of the rest of the region.

The western boundary of eastern Siberia is set conveniently along the western boundary of Krasnoyarsk Kray, although this falls a short distance west of the Yenisey River and includes within the area a narrow strip of the West Siberian Lowland. The boundary between eastern Siberia and the Far East is defined by the Soviets as the drainage divide between the Arctic and the Pacific. This is modified somewhat to fit the boundaries of the political units in the area. Thus the political breakdown of eastern Siberia and the Far East is as shown on the summary page at the beginning of the chapter. In general these political units are quite large, and, as was the case in western Siberia, many of them are elongated north-south, with a rather populous fringe in the south being connected to a long expanse of relatively empty land stretching toward the Arctic. This is particularly true of Krasnoyarsk Kray, which stretches from the southern borders of the country to the Arctic shores. Thus, as was done with western Siberia, discussion will focus on the south, but at the same time it will be

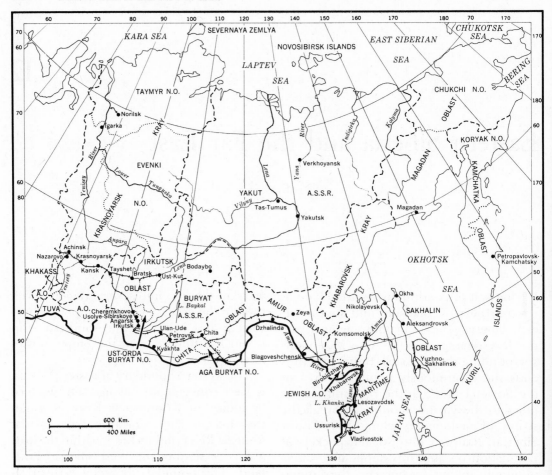

Figure 12–1   Eastern Siberia and the Far East.

kept in mind that a much larger expanse of land is attached to the north, about which there is little to say at present.

History and Settlement

The Russian sweep across Siberia to the Pacific that took place primarily during the first half of the seventeenth century met little resistance from indigenous peoples, who numbered only a few thousand and consisted of reindeer-herding and fur-trapping nomads. The mode of Russian settlement was the erection of a far-flung string of "ostrogs," combination forts and trading posts, which were set up to garrison military personnel to exercise control over the surrounding countryside and to provide fur-collection points for Russian traders who were eager to exchange small items of Russian manufacture with the natives for valuable furs. It was in the quest of furs, then, that the Russians extended themselves into this seemingly endless wilderness and endured untold hardships in isolated outposts separated from the populated parts of European Russia by thousands of miles of trackless forests, swamps, and tundra. The land provided little incentive for agricultural settlements of a permanent nature, and this first wave of occupants was little interested in the land as such. There were too few Cossacks sprinkled sparsely across the territory to do more than exercise nominal control over it, and economic opportunities lay more in exacting tribute from the natives in the form of furs than in the hard personal labor of farming. Therefore the initial penetration of the seventeenth century left little imprint on much of eastern Siberia and the Far East, and the history of intensive colonization of this region really begins in the second half of the nineteenth century.

The initial wave of Russian migration across Siberia happened to coincide with one of the strongest and most organized periods in the modern history of China under the Manchus. Immediately after the Russians had subdued the Buryats and established Irkutsk in 1661, they were challenged by the Manchu Dynasty in the Amur Valley, and in 1689 the Chinese forced the Treaty of Nerchinsk upon the Russians which prevented them from navi-

gating the Amur and established the boundary between the Russian and Manchu Empires along the Argun River and the Stanovoy Mountains far to the north. Further east the line was never precisely determined. But at the first signs of Manchu weakness, which appeared in the 1840s, Russia prepared for further expansion at the expense of China.

The Russians had already gained some foothold further west, where as early as 1691 the northern Mongols had requested protection from the Manchu Emperor. The Russians were quick to seize on the opportunity to establish relations with these people, and in the Treaty of Kyakhta in 1727 Russian traders were permitted to cross Mongolia. There was little activity in this region up to 1850, however. The opium wars of 1840–1842 clearly demonstrated the Manchu weakness, and Russia, in violation of the Treaty of Nerchinsk, in 1850 sent out an expedition to explore the

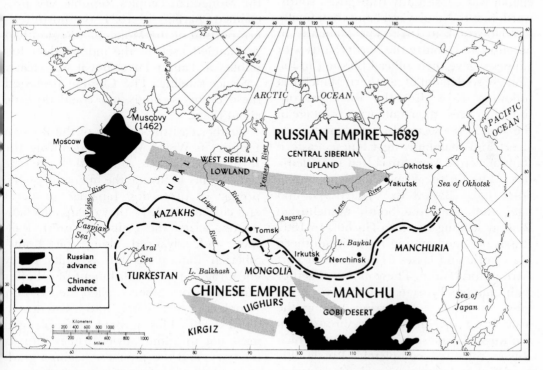

Figure 12–2   Zone of contact of Russian and Chinese Empires as of 1689. Adapted from Jackson, Russo-Chinese Borderlands, *1st ed., 1962, p. 29.*

Amur Region and to establish the Russian post of Nikolayevsk at the mouth of the Amur River. A Transbaykal army was soon organized, and military posts were established all the way to the Pacific coast and even on Sakhalin Island.

Unable to resist, the Chinese were compelled to negotiate, which resulted in the Treaty of Argun in 1858 — a new boundary was established along the Amur from the mouth of the Argun to the Pacific. This agreement placed the territory south of the Amur and east of the Ussuri under joint occupation, but two years later the Treaty of Peking placed the entire territory east of the Ussuri under Russian control. Other agreements between Russia and China during the same year gave Russia trade rights in Outer Mongolia, and a period of Russian economic influence in this region ensued.

In the Pacific the main Russian naval base which had first been established in the far north at Petropavlovsk on Kamchatka was consistently transposed southward, first to Nikolayevsk, and then finally to Vladivostok in 1872. The Manchus, in an effort to colonize the borderlands with Chinese, gave their official blessing to the Chinese settlement of northern Manchuria following 1878. But the Russians continued to press their military advantage in the area. They secured permission to construct and maintain the Chinese Eastern Railway across Manchuria that provided a direct link for the Trans-Siberian running from Lake Baykal to Vladivostok, and later they built the South Manchurian Railway leading south to Harbin. In 1897 Russia obtained mining rights in southern Manchuria and leases to the ports of Port Arthur and Dairen. These moves, together with ominous Russian penetration (in the guise of lumber concessions) along the Yalu River in North Korea, brought on the Russo-Japanese War of 1905 in which Russia collapsed completely. Russia surrendered to Japan the South Manchurian

Railway, along with Port Arthur and access to the mineral resources of southern Manchuria, as well as the southern half of Sakhalin, which had become Russian by treaty in 1875 in return for Japanese title to the Kuril Islands.

Thus the Russian takeover of lands which had been established as Chinese by the Treaty of Nerchinsk was decisively halted by Japan, and Russian attention along the southern border was diverted further westward. In 1911 the Outer Mongols petitioned the Russian Tsar for aid in throwing off the Chinese yoke, and in the same year a revolution in Peking established the Chinese Republic. In the following years Outer Mongolia was recognized as a province of China, but Russia was to have free trading rights in the area. In 1919, after the Russian Revolution, the Chinese president cancelled these agreements and Chinese troops moved into the Mongolian Region, but in 1921 the Red Army occupied Urga, and in 1924 the Mongolian Peoples Republic was proclaimed. Earlier, in 1921, the northwestern portion of the Mongolian Region had proclaimed itself as the independent Republic of Tannu-Tuva, but it was clearly a Soviet satellite. The Chinese protested these events strongly but could do little about them.

Further east the collapse of the Russian Empire in World War I and during the Russian Revolution afforded Japan the opportunity to invade the mainland on the pretext of protecting Japanese property and citizens. In 1918 they occupied Vladivostok, seized the Chinese Eastern Railway, and advanced along the Trans-Siberian Railway as far as Chita. They encouraged the establishment of a buffer state in eastern Siberia called the Far East Republic, which came into existence in April 1920. This puppet state pledged itself not to admit Soviet armies into its territory, and the Japanese began a gradual withdrawal of troops under pressure from the English-speaking powers. However, immediately after all Japanese troops were off the mainland, in November 1922 the Republic voted itself into the Russian Soviet Federated Socialist Republic, which was the only recognizable Russian political entity at that time. During the following year the Buryats east of Lake Baykal were appeased by the Russians by the establishment of the Buryat-Mongol A.S.S.R.

For a time the Russians again had the use of the Chinese Eastern Railway, but it was finally sold to Japan in 1935 after the Japanese had occupied Manchuria and established the puppet state of Manchukuo. Within the next few years, World War II reversed opportunities once more, and the Soviets, just before the end of the Pacific war in 1945, entered the war against Japan with the understanding from the United States and Britain that they were again to have the dominant influence in Manchuria and control of the ports of Port Arthur and Dairen. This, in fact, took place, but the ascension of the Chinese communists in 1949, which seemed to take the Russian communists by surprise, ended the looting of Manchurian heavy industry by the Soviets and eventually induced the Soviet Union to return to China much of the equipment that had been ripped out of the factories in Manchuria. It also induced the Soviets to relinquish any claims on the Chinese Eastern Railway and the ports of Port Arthur and Dairen. As in Sinkiang, at long last Manchuria appeared to be irrevocably oriented toward China.

Located between Manchuria and Central Asia, the Mongolian Peoples Republic became firmly established as a semi-independent political buffer between the Soviet Union and China. The nationalist government of China in 1946 had begrudgingly recognized this independence after a plebiscite in the Mongolian Peoples Republic had voted almost 100 per cent for independence. Since the Soviets were in complete control anyway, this was all rather meaningless, although in later years it has provided the opportunity for the communist Chinese to reopen relations with the Mongols and allowed for active trade and economic development to be carried on by Chinese workers in the Mongolian Republic. Nevertheless Mongolia remains more oriented toward the Soviet Union than toward China. In 1947 it adopted 5-year economic plans of the Soviet type and in 1949 amended its constitution to closely conform to the Soviet one. The Cyrillic alphabet was even introduced to replace the traditional Mongol script. In 1949 the Soviets constructed a railroad south from the Trans-Siberian to Ulan Bator, which by 1956 had been extended to Peking. This affords the most direct railway between Moscow and Peking.

In 1944, during World War II, Tannu-Tuva was quietly made a part of the Soviet Union and was established as the Tuva Autonomous Oblast directly under the jurisdiction of the R.S.F.S.R. Later it was raised to the status of A.S.S.R.

During the 1950s it appeared that at last some rapprochement, uneasy though it might be, had finally been established between the two great powers of Russia and China through the mechanism of "fraternal" communist governments. But since 1960 a great rift has developed between the two countries, as it has become clear that ancient rivalries and differences in race and customs have proved to be much more potent factors in the formation of national aspirations than is the more abstract factor of governmental form. It is now quite clear that the Chinese have never accepted the boundary imposed upon them by the Treaty of Peking in 1860, and they are pronouncing stronger and stronger claims to various pieces of land stretching all the way from Central Asia and western Mongolia to the entire territories of the Amur Region and Maritime Kray. Thus it appears that Russo-

Chinese rivalry in the Far East is a long way from being ended.

Russian Settlement

Beginning in 1840 a gold rush brought a flurry of prospectors to the Yenisey region and south central portions of Prebaykalia and Zabaykalia, which produced a settlement form typical of exploitive occupance — isolated shacks and small villages scattered helter-skelter in river valleys where the prospectors were washing their placer deposits for the coveted gold. Since 1930 and especially since 1955 these old prospectors' settlements have given way to more permanent agricultural settlements and construction sites associated with some of the grandiose water-power projects that are being developed in the area. Many of the old villages are being inundated by the huge reservoirs created by the large dams on the streams, and, in general, rural villages are being amalgamated into larger settlements. As placer deposits have been worked out in the past, individual prospectors have given way to huge dredging operations that rework the gravel of the major streams over the entire width of flood plains for many miles parallel to the streams.

The first modern settlers penetrated into the Far East from Transbaykalia in 1855. These were largely discharged Cossacks, who were later joined by Cossacks from the Urals and as far west as Ukraine, generally under forced agreements, in return for which they were given relatively large sections of land which extended far beyond their immediate use. Later this small stream of Cossacks and peasants along the overland route was joined by a much larger arrival in the Ussuri Region of Ukrainians brought in by the long sea route through the Suez and Singapore Straits. This mass movement by sea was stimulated by peasant poverty and sur-

vival of serfdom in the west, and it reached its culmination in 1883–1886 when 12,700 persons arrived from Chernigov Guberniya, 3200 from Poltava, and others from Kharkov, Voronezh, and Kursk Guberniyas and Kuban Oblast. There were a number of reasons why so many people came from the Ukrainian and north Caucasian Steppe Regions. First, it was felt that residents of the wooded steppe would make the most successful pioneers in the similar conditions of the Maritime Region of the Far East. Also, the requirement that each family have at least 600 rubles upon arrival after having paid for its own voyage limited the movement primarily to medium-sized landowners who could sell their land in the west to accrue the necessary capital to make the move. This virtually ruled out movement from guberniyas in which land was primarily communally owned.

The maritime traffic dwindled to nothing after 1900 with the completion of the Trans-Siberian, Chinese Eastern, and Ussuri railroads. Individual peasant families encroached upon the large communal land holdings of the original Cossack villages, and a new kind of settlement of more intensive agriculture finally evolved. The principal regions of agricultural settlement became the Zeya-Bureya prairie and the southern Ussuri-Khanka Lowland.

Climate, Vegetation, and Soil

Although a major landform break occurs between east and west along the Yenisey River, the east-west zones of climate, vegetation, and soil that were distinguished in western Siberia and northeastern Europe continue unbroken to the Pacific. What generalizations were made about climate in the West Siberian Lowland can be emphasized in eastern Siberia and the Soviet Far East. In winter the Siberian High Pressure Cell, usually centered south of Lake Baykal, occupies the entire region except the extreme northwest, which is influenced by the eastern protrusion of the Icelandic Low, and greatly rules out the possibility of intrusion of maritime air. Cyclonic storms from the Baltic and the Mediterranean are shunted off to the north and to the south to die either along the Arctic coast or the Middle Asian mountains. The northwest winds blowing out of the eastern side of the Siberian High across the Pacific coast consistently prevent the entrance of maritime air from the Pacific, even along the very coastal sections of the Far East. Hence the winters are cold everywhere. In the interior, under the dominance of the high-pressure cell, they tend to be clear and calm, but along the edges of the continent steep pressure gradients produce strong winds, and the weather is bitter indeed. Verkhoyansk, in the upper Yana River Valley east of the Lena, has long been known as the "cold pole" of the world. January temperatures here average −56°F, and temperatures as low as −90°F have been recorded. To the east, in the valley of the Indigirka River, Oymyakon has recorded an even lower minimum temperature of −96°F.

Winter temperatures naturally increase toward the south, but even along the southern border of eastern Siberia, Chita averages −14°F in January. This compares to central Canada. Even in the most southerly part of Maritime Kray along the Pacific coast, Vladivostok averages only 6°F in January. At similar latitudes on the eastern coast of the United States, Boston averages 27°F in January. Hence, in winter, the Pacific coast of the Soviet Far East is much more continental in character than is the east coast of the United States. The explanation is that the consistency of the Siberian High causes the continental polar air of Siberia to be completely dominant even over the coast of the country in wintertime. January temperatures in Vladivostok are more similar to those in Winnipeg, Canada, than they are to anything along the eastern coast of North America.

Since eastern Siberia and the Far East are dominated in winter by high atmospheric pressure, precipitation is at a minimum. Most of the area receives less than 4 inches of precipitation between November and March, and much of it receives less than 2 inches. This may mean between 2 and 4 feet of snow, which, when accumulated and drifted throughout the winter, makes the precipitation appear heavier than it really is. The snow cover reaches its greatest depth, more than 80 centimeters, in the Middle Yenisey Valley.

During the summer the area is covered by a broad, shallow low-pressure atmospheric system, which allows some penetration of air into the region. Between April and October weak cyclonic activity, coupled with local convective activity, produces between 4 and 12 inches of precipitation over much of the region. With the cool temperatures that prevail, this moisture is enough to make the climate humid.

During middle and late summer the Pacific monsoon sets in with some force in the Soviet Far East and penetrates up the Amur Valley occasionally as far as Lake Baykal. The inland intrusion of marine air is abetted by easterly winds in the northeast quadrants of cyclonic storms that form along the Mongolian front, which is active at this time of year. Maritime Kray particularly is affected; the Pacific slopes of the Sikhote-Alin receive upwards of 40 inches of rainfall. During this time the maritime air modifies the weather along a narrow strip of coast as far north as the northern shore of the Sea of Okhotsk and Kamchatka Peninsula. Cold ocean currents flowing southward along the Asian coasts of the Okhotsk and Japan Seas, coupled with the sea breezes in summer, maintain very cool temperatures along the immediate coast and produce thick persistent fogs similar to those in the San Francisco Bay area across the Pacific during the same time of year. During the months of June and July, some of the Asian coast experiences more than 20 days of dense fog. This is the case also on parts of Sakhalin Island and Kamchatka.

The same locational factors that make for very cold temperatures in the wintertime in interior Siberia make for relatively warm temperatures for this latitude in the summertime. Stagnant air in interior valleys, which during the winter experiences extreme temperature inversions and cold surface temperatures, during the summer experiences rapid increases in surface temperatures due to local radiational exchanges of heat in the absence of advection. Verkhoyansk, which in January averages 56°F below zero, in July averages 60°F above zero. There have been daytime temperatures in July of nearly 100°F; hence the absolute range is nearly 200 degrees. Eastern Siberia thus has the questionable distinction of having the greatest temperature ranges on earth. In one of the

settled basins in southern Siberia, Chita averages 66°F in July. This is comparable to northern Michigan in the United States.

The Pacific coast of the Soviet Far East in the summertime is influenced more by maritime air than is the Atlantic coast of the United States. During the winter Vladivostok averages much colder than similar latitudes along the eastern coast of North America because of its dominance by continental air; during the summer it also averages considerably cooler than comparable latitudes along the east coast of North America because of the marine influence. In August, the warmest month, Vladivostok averages 69°F. At a comparable latitude, Boston, Massachusetts, in July averages 72°F.

The subarctic climatic zone and the taiga vegetation zone expand in width in eastern Siberia and the Far East to engulf most of the area between the Arctic and the mountains along the southern border. The

Figure 12–3   Forest-tundra and reindeer in Yakutia. Novosti.

steppe lands, which are so important to the economy of southwestern Siberia and northern Kazakhstan are pinched out between the forest and the southern mountains east of the Kuznetsk Basin, except for isolated mountain basins that occur along the Trans-Siberian Railroad. The arctic fringes of the area, as well as higher elevations throughout the mountainous portions of the region, particularly in the mountains east of the Lena River, lie beyond the tree line and bear only a poor tundra vegetation. Much of the tundra and the taiga are underlain by permafrost, even as far south as Outer Mongolia. This induces a forest predominantly of larch, instead of pine and fir as is typical of western Siberia. The larch spreads its shallow root system over the permafrost and can survive in the thin layer of top soil that thaws during the summer. The podzol and tundra soils that prevail throughout the region are universally poor and drainage is a major problem. The percolation of water from the thawed top soil is largely prevented by the underlying permafrost.

The lowlands of the southern portion of the Soviet Far East that are affected by the monsoons are something apart from the rest of the area. The climate is humid continental with cool summers, the vegetation is predominantly a broad-leaf deciduous forest, and the soils, though still podzolic, in general are better than they are throughout much of the region. This area, together with the steppe basins along the Trans-Siberian Railroad, contains the best soils, the mildest climate, and the greatest agricultural development of eastern Siberia and the Far East.

Geology and Topography

Although the climate, vegetation, and soil zones stretch unbroken from the Urals to the Pacific, east of the Yenisey, and again east of the Lena River, definite geological and topographic breaks divide Siberia into three distinct regions. The first, the West Siberian Lowland, has already been discussed in Chapter 11.

Central Siberian Uplands   The second region, between the Yenisey and the Lena Rivers, variously known as the Central Siberian Uplands, the Tunguskan Plateau, the Anabar Shield, and so forth, is a roughly dissected upland of complex rock structure which here and there rises into subdued mountains. The area is highest in its northwestern portion where the Putoran Mountains rise to elevations of more than 6000 feet above sea level. Elevations are generally below 3000 feet, but the relief is considerable, some of the streams having cut almost canyon-like valleys below the surface of the upland. Much of this extensive area of land represents a geologically stable block of complex crystalline rocks that has resisted tectonic movement as younger mountains have been built to the south and east. Extensive sections of the upland are overlain by more recent sedimentary materials, and in places large lava flows that have emitted from recent fault lines reach thicknesses of more than 1000 feet.

Different sections of the upland are known by different names which correspond to the names of the main rivers flowing through them. Thus in the southeast are the Patom Plateau, the Vitim Plateau, and the Aldan Plateau, all named after rivers that are tributaries to the Lena. In the southwest is the Tunguskan Plateau, named after the three main right bank tributaries of the Yenisey, the Lower Tunguska, the Stony Tunguska, and the Upper Tunguska, which drains the large Lake Baykal and is also known as the Angara River. Other parts of the upland have other regional names.

The natural environment of the Central Siberian Uplands is so harsh that there has been little development in the area. Only along the broad flood plain of the Lena River where it is joined by its two main

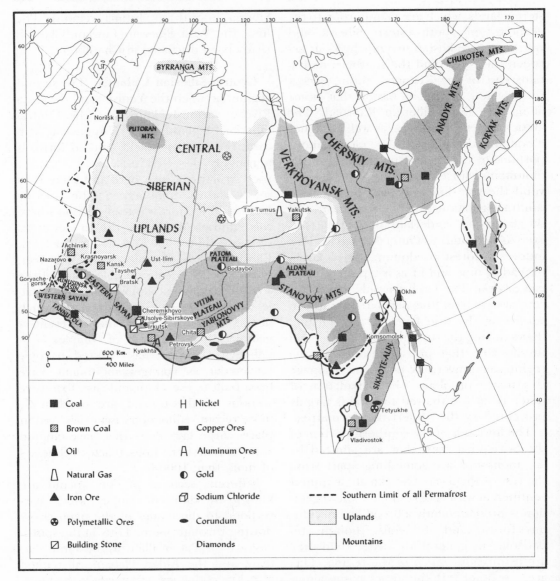

Figure 12–4   Landforms and minerals.

tributaries, the Aldan and the Vilyuy, has agriculture been attempted. The settlement of Yakutsk in the Lena-Aldan-Vilyuy Lowland is famous for its Arctic agriculture, and it is by far the largest agricultural settlement this far poleward in the world.

East of the Lena   East of the Lena River the landscape changes from one of low uplands to one of mountains and river val-

leys. The Verkhoyansk, Cherskiy, and Kolyma Ranges, with elevations in the vicinity of 10,000 feet, are separated by the valleys of the Yana, Indigirka, and Kolyma Rivers, which flow northward into the Arctic. The Anadyr Range, on the Chukotsk Peninsula in the easternmost part of the country, and the Koryak Range, to the south where the Kamchatka Peninsula joins the mainland, reach elevations of more than 6000 feet. Having contained mountain glaciers during the Pleistocene and lying well above the tree line at present, all these mountains exhibit definite alpine features.

Kamchatka and the Kurils The Kamchatka Peninsula is a mountainous piece of land which belongs more to the volcanic island arcs of the Pacific than to the more subdued older mountains of the mainland. It is essentially a double line of volcanic peaks, many of which are active. The highest of these, Mt. Klyuchevskaya, with an elevation of more than 15,000 feet, is one of the great symmetrical volcanic cones of the world. The volcanoes of Kamchatka

spew out dust and ashes so continuously that in places the snow is covered to a depth great enough to prevent the use of sleds. The Russians speak of these places as "nonslip" areas.

The Kamchatkan Peninsula is so remote from the main centers of population in Russia that in the minds of Russian schoolboys it has become associated with the back seats of the school room. At the beginning of each school term there is some jostling for position among the more ornery boys to see who is going to get to sit in "Kamchatka."

The volcanic peaks of Kamchatka continue southwestward in an arc of small

Figure 12–5 Avachinsk Volcano, Kamchatka. Novosti.

islands, the Kurils, which join Kamchatka and Hokkaido with an underwater ridge to complete the encirclement of the Sea of Okhotsk. Since World War II the Kurils and the southern half of Sakhalin Island have reverted from the Japanese to the Russians, and the Sea of Okhotsk has become a Soviet sea.

The Southern Mountains and Basins
South of the Central Siberian Uplands and the mountains and valleys of the northeast, along the southern borders of the Soviet Union all the way from the Kuznetsk Basin to the Pacific, are rugged mountain ranges of varying ages and orientations, broken here and there by basins and valleys. In the west, the Minusinsk Basin along the upper Yenisey is bordered on the south and the northeast respectively by the Western and Eastern Sayans. The Sayans are fairly old mountains with intermediate altitudes similar to those of the Altay in the west, which separate the Minusinsk Basin from the Kuznetsk Basin. The Western Sayans, which are oriented nearly west-east, separate the Minusinsk Basin to the north from the basin occupied by the Tuva A.S.S.R. to the south along the upper Yenisey.

The Eastern Sayans are oriented northwest-southeast between the Yenisey River on the west and its main right-bank tributary, the Angara River, on the east and north. They reach their highest elevation at approximately 11,500 feet, and then continue eastward to Lake Baykal in a lower series of generally north-south oriented ranges lying between the tributaries of the Angara River. As Lake Baykal is approached, the mountains take on a fault block form.

Lake Baykal lies in a fault graben and is bounded by exceedingly steep slopes on all sides. The precipitous cliffs of the deeply dissected mountain spurs around the south end of the lake delayed the completion of the Trans-Siberian Railroad for more than 10 years. During this period,

trains were ferried across the lake in summer and tracks were laid across the ice in winter. Finally, the line was completed around the southern end, clinging to the sheer cliff faces and utilizing more than fifty tunnels and intervening high trestles.

Approximately 1 mile deep, Lake Baykal is credited with having the greatest volume of water of any lake in the world. In fact, it is said to contain 10 per cent of all the fresh water resources of the earth. Its name derives from the fact that it contains 1800 species of animal and vegetable life, 1000 of which are unique to the area. It is drained from the southwestern corner by the Angara River through the Yenisey to the Arctic. Hence the water in the lake is fresh. The lake freezes over from December to May, but the water flowing down the Angara has such a steep gradient and high speed that the river itself does not freeze. The Lena River heads very near the lake on the western side, but, as is so often true with fault grabens, the highest land lies along the immediate rim of the depression, and thus the Lena does not tap the lake. The Selenga River, coming into the southeastern side of the lake from the Mongolian Peoples Republic, is the main stream flowing into the lake.

Around Lake Baykal the mountains and basins become exceedingly complex; it is laborious to separate one from another and to attach names individually. Generally the regional name assigned to the area lying between the Yenisey and Lake Baykal is simply Prebaykalye; the area lying to the east of Lake Baykal and extending to the eastern edge of Chita Oblast is known as Transbaykalya. Thus Lake Baykal, in the minds of the Russians, is a landmark by which the territories around it are designated, either as those lying on the near side of the lake, that is, nearest to populated parts of Russia, or those on the far side of the lake.

East of Lake Baykal the Yablonovyy Range, oriented southwest-northeast, separates the basin around Ulan-Ude in the

Buryat A.S.S.R. on the west from the basin surrounding Chita on the east. Other mountains continue northeastward between the tributaries of the Amur River to the south and the Lena River to the north, and form the drainage divide that separates eastern Siberia from the Far East. South of these ranges, the Argun River flows northeastward out of the Mongolian Peoples Republic to form the boundary between the Soviet Union and Manchuria for a distance of about 400 miles before it is joined by the Shilka in Chita Oblast to form the Amur. The Amur continues along the border of Manchuria for another 600 miles before it is joined by the Ussuri at Khabarovsk, where it turns abruptly northward to empty into the Tatar Strait near the northern end of Sakhalin Island.

A continuous strip of lowland follows the Amur all the way to the Pacific. This lowland is constricted everywhere, but it widens womewhat wherever a tributary comes in from the north to join the Amur. Three broader segments of the plain stand out in their development. One is the Zeya-Bureya Lowland around the city of Blagoveshchensk where the Zeya and Bureya Rivers come in from the northeast to join the Amur. The second is the Jewish Autonomous Oblast, nestled in the southward bend of the river where the small Bira and Bidzhan Rivers come in from the north to join the Amur. The capital city of the oblast, Birobidzhan, takes its name from these two small streams. The third and largest and most significant lowland is the Ussuri-Khanka Lowland in Maritime Kray where the Ussuri River flows northward to join the Amur at Khabarovsk. The large Lake Khanka occupies part of this lowland. Although this lowland continues northeastward along the lower Amur to Nikolayevsk at its mouth, the segment north of Khabarovsk, except for the city of Komsomolsk, is sparsely settled forest land. East of the Ussuri-Khanka Lowland lie the low, heavily forested Sikhote-Alin Mountains.

Across the narrow Tatar Strait, mountains rise once again to form the long island of Sakhalin. A double range of low mountains, rising to heights of approximately 6000 feet, is split down the middle by a valley that runs the length of the island. The cool, moist, foggy climate has fostered the growth of fairly good stands of forest, except in the low, marshy northwestern part of the island, which is tundra. Summers are cooler and foggier along the east coast than along the west, but the damp air drifts westward across the northern end of the island where the mountains descend to a hilly plain. Sakhalin's original settlement was augmented by its being used as a penal colony by the Russian Tsars.

Agriculture

The Minusinsk Basin, the Tuva A.S.S.R., the Irkutsk Basin along the Angara west of Lake Baykal, the basin of the Buryat A.S.S.R., and the basin around Chita are all steppe basins with subhumid and semi-arid climates that have been conducive to good grass growth and development of chernozem and chestnut soils that are quite adaptable to cultivation. Many of the areas are still being used as extensive grazing lands for sheep and beef cattle; native herders carry on life much as they did before the Soviet Era. The Russians are eager to plow up these grazing lands and plant them to wheat and, in some cases, to sugar beets, but so far the conversion from grazing to cultivation has been slow. The Russians would also like to settle the seminomadic herders and made sedentary farmers out of them. The last strongholds of native life are in the Tuva and Buryat A.S.S.R.'s. As Russian settlement progresses in these areas, they also are evolving from their predominantly pastoral economies.

East of Chita Oblast, the moister lowlands of the Lower Amur River Valley, with their monsoonal influences, afford

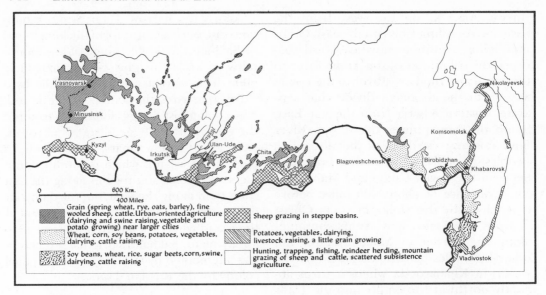

Figure 12–6   Land use in eastern Siberia and the Far East. Adapted from Atlas selskogo khozyaystva SSSR.

possibilities for a variety of agricultural crops. Drainage is the big problem in these areas, but paradoxically supplementary irrigation may be necessary for some crops in spring and early summer.

The rainfall regime in summer is almost exactly wrong, since the monsoon flow of air from the Pacific is not really at its peak until midsummer. Spring and early summer may be positively dry when mois-

Figure 12–7   Sheep being driven to mountain pastures in the Buryat A.S.S.R. east of Lake Baykal. Novosti.

Figure 12–8   Air view of virgin wheat land in Buryat A.S.S.R. Novosti.

ture is most needed for the rapid growth period of the crops, and late summer and fall may be very wet when the crops are being harvested. Nevertheless, the Zeya-Bureya Lowland, the Jewish A.O., and the Ussuri-Khanka Lowland hold the most promise for agriculture in eastern Siberia and the Far East.

The Ussuri-Khanka Lowland in particular has been adapted to a variety of crops. Russian and Ukranian farmers from the west have met up with Chinese and Korean farmers from the south. Thus the settlement in the Ussuri-Khanka Lowland is a mixture of western and oriental, and so is the crop complex. Wheat, sugar beets, potatoes, and a great variety of fruits, vegetables, and melons mix with such oriental crops as rice, soy beans, millet, and grain sorghums. This is the primary soy bean growing region of the Soviet Union. Chinese and Korean farmers have even developed some terrace agriculture with paddy fields. The majority of the people in the area are Russians and Ukrainians, however; many of the towns, with bungalows of whitewashed adobe walls and blue shuttered windows, appear to have come straight from Ukraine. The transplanted Ukrainian farmers claim that even the dust is Ukrainian.

Other than these major areas, scattered agricultural settlements have been established along many sheltered river valleys of middle and northern Siberia, the Far East, Sakhalin Island, and Kamchatka. These agricultural settlements in general have been made in conjunction with mining, lumbering, fishing, or hunting enterprises to support the people of the local areas. They thus are limited in size and produce a few hardy grains and vegetables under very restricted environmental conditions. Among these settlements the most noted is Yakutsk in the Lena-Aldan-Vilyuy Lowland where the Russians over a period of many years have developed strains of wheat, barley, and rye that in some cases mature within 60 days after planting. Most of the strains of these grains that have been introduced into the Fairbanks area of Alaska have come from Yakutsk. These grains do not bear heavily, but transportation being what it is in Siberia, the cost of bringing food into the scattered settlements of the area from better farming lands would no doubt be excessive. Because of low productivity, subsistence farming permits only a low standard of living. During the three centuries or more that Yakutsk has existed, little change in the pioneer outlook of the area has taken place. The buildings of Yakutsk are of rough-hewn logs, and the streets are mud.

With all the effort that has been expended for the development of agriculture, the area east of Lake Baykal still is less than one third self-sufficient in foodstuffs. The rest must be shipped long distances from the west.

Resources and Industries

From a glance at the figures on urbanization in the summary table at the beginning of this chapter, it is quite obvious that the Soviet Far East, and to some extent eastern Siberia also, has been settled primarily for reasons other than agricultural. In these remote areas of sparse population the cities stand out as conspicuous nodes of settlement separated by wide expanses of almost unoccupied virgin territory. The resources that have induced and sustained this nodal form of settlement are minerals, timber, water power, and fish and furs. Industries based on these resources, coupled with the functions of transport and trade, explain the existence of most of the cities.

As might be expected in an area as large and geologically varied as Siberia and the Soviet Far East, there is potential for a great variety of mineral resources. Geological surveys are still inadequate, but better estimates of the quantity and quality of old deposits are being made and new minerals are constantly being discovered.

The Mineral Fuels The most important mineral in Siberia and the Far East today is coal, and it may well retain this position in the future for the reserves are large. Some 70 per cent of the total coal reserves of the Soviet Union lie in this area. Coal has already been the basis for some industrial growth, and it promises to be the basis for a considerable expansion of future industries. The East Siberian fields now produce about 7 per cent of the Soviet Union's coal, and the Far Eastern fields produce about 4 per cent. About two thirds of the coal produced in eastern Siberia comes from the Cheremkhovo deposit near Irkutsk. The coal in this deposit lies in flat seams 1 to 8 meters in thickness, and more than half of it is mined by open-pit methods. Since they are not of good coking quality, these coals are used for chemical processing, as fuel for large power stations, and on the railroad.

Other important coal-producing basins in eastern Siberia are the Kansk-Achinsk, the Minusinsk, and those in the Buryat A.S.S.R. The Kansk-Achinsk coal field forms a wide band running parallel and adjacent to the Trans-Siberian Railroad for a distance of more than 700 kilometers in Krasnoyarsk Kray and eastern Kemerovo Oblast. Thirty almost flat seams lie at depths of no more than 200 meters. Brown coals predominate except in one deposit which contains hard coal. Forty per cent of the country's brown coal deposits are located in this field. Open-pit mines are being developed to produce low-grade coals for local heating and power industries. The Nazarovo thermoelectric station south of Achinsk is one of the largest in the country.

The Minusinsk coal field contains smaller deposits of higher-grade coals that are mined by shaft methods. The Minusinsk coal is used primarily for power production.

In the Buryat A.S.S.R. and in Chita Oblast deposits of brown coal are being used to power local industry and on local sections of the Trans-Siberian Railroad.

In the Far East, important producing coal fields are the Bureya coal field, situated in the upper reaches of the Bureya River 300 kilometers north of the Trans-Siberian Railroad, and scattered coal fields in Maritime Kray and on Sakhalin Island. The Bureya coal is used locally for industry, power generation, and the railroad. Much of the coal is of coking quality and may become important in the Amurstal iron and steel industry to be established in the city of Komsomolsk. The Sakhalin coals are largely hard coals of coking quality, but at present they are used only for local heating, power generation, and ships.

These producing fields along the southern margins of eastern Siberia and the Far East represent only a minor portion of the total coal reserves of the region. Over 90 per cent of the reserves lie in the huge deposits of the Tunguskan, Yakutsk, and Lena fields to the north. Much of these large coal reserves are high-grade coking coals, but they probably will not be intensively utilized in the foreseeable future since they are removed from the population of the region. None of these deposits is now producing enough coal to warrant formation of a kombinat to administer the mining. The most promising among them for immediate development are the south Yakutsk coal fields which may lie far enough south to be used to supplement the Bureya coal in the Far Eastern iron and steel industries that are planned.

Besides coal, there are some deposits of oil and gas in the area. The oil fields of northern Sakhalin have been supplying about 1 per cent of the Soviet Union's oil for the last 40 years, and it appears that they will continue to do so. These oil fields were developed in the 1920s largely by the Japanese on leased land after the Russo-Japanese War of 1905 had given the Japanese the southern half of the island. After the Japanese had leased the oil rights of much of the area around the city of Okha in the north and had developed wells there, the Russians developed what was left of their area. Now, of course, the Soviets control the entire operation, as well as the entire island of Sakhalin.

At present the Soviets are expanding production into a new field about 15 miles north of Okha, and a second pipeline has been laid from Okha across the 20-foot-deep Tatar Strait to Nikolayevsk at the mouth of the Amur River and up the Amur to Komsomolsk where an oil refinery has been built. The Sakhalin oil serves most of the needs of the Soviet Far East and also provides exports to Japan and Cuba.

Mention has been made in the past of the possibilities of oil in the Lena-Vilyuy Lowland and along certain segments of the alluvial coast of the Arctic. Apparently no large reserves of oil have yet been discovered in these areas, however, and eastern Siberia is to be served with oil largely by pipeline from the Volga-Ural oil fields 2500 miles to the west. In September 1964 a pipeline was completed from the Tuymazy oil fields in Bashkiria to Angarsk, where a refinery had gone into operation in 1960 using crude oil hauled in by rail tank cars. An oil refinery has also been planned for Krasnoyarsk, and there has been talk of extending the pipeline to the Pacific to provide oil exports to Far Eastern countries, especially Japan. With the opening of the West Siberian fields, it can be expected that West Siberian oil will rapidly replace Volga-Urals oil in the refineries of Siberia.

Apparently, a significant deposit of natural gas has been discovered in the Lena-Vilyuy Lowland at Tas-Tumus northwest of Yakutsk. A pipeline has been laid from Tas-Tumus to Yakutsk to utilize this deposit.

Water Power The large volume of water in the rivers of eastern Siberia, coupled with the steep gradients in their mountain headwaters, gives the region the highest water-power potential of any area in the Soviet Union. Together, eastern Siberia and the Far East are accredited with 55 per cent of the water-power potential of the U.S.S.R. The Yenisey-Angara River system alone has a hydroelectric potential of at least 30 million kilowatts. The outlet for Lake Baykal, the Yenisey, has the largest and steadiest flow of any river in the country.

The Irkutsk plant on the Angara was completed in 1958 with a capacity of 660,-000 kilowatts. An earthen dam 2363 meters long backed up the water 70 kilometers to Lake Baykal. Downstream on the Angara, the Bratsk plant, which had been under construction for a number of years, began limited operation in October 1961. By 1968 its capacity had been expanded to 4.1 million kilowatts. And 500-kilovolt

transmission lines carry electricity southeast to Irkutsk and west to Krasnoyarsk to supply power to the aluminum plant in Krasnoyarsk, pending completion of the Krasnoyarsk hydro plant.

A concrete dam 127 meters high has created the Bratsk Sea, more than 500 kilometers long, reaching upstream to the Irkutsk Dam. The reservoir, with a capacity of 180 billion cubic meters of water, can store more water than all the reservoirs on the Volga River combined. The ultimate capacity of the power plant is now planned to be in the vicinity of 5,000,000 kilowatts. The annual output of the power plant will be considerably greater than that of Kuybyshev and Volgograd together, since the flow of the Angara is very consistent throughout the year. The Bratsk and Irkutsk Reservoirs have made it possible for ships to sail from Lake Baykal down the Yenisey to the Arctic Ocean. Two other large plants, the Ust-Ilim and the Boguchany, each with capacities of 3 to 4 million kilowatts, are scheduled to be completed on the Angara downstream from Bratsk. Railroads are being extended to both of these sites to facilitate construction.

On the Yenisey itself, construction was begun on the Krasnoyarsk plant in 1955. By 1967 the first two 500,000-kilowatt generators had been installed. A total of twelve such generators are planned, which will give the plant an ultimate capacity of 6 million kilowatts. The dam, over 100 meters high, has been constructed at Divnogorsk 20 kilometers west of the city of Krasnoyarsk where the river is squeezed within a gorge 800 meters wide. The dam has raised the water 100 meters and backed it up 300 to 400 kilometers, thus creating one of the largest reservoirs in the world. Elevators are used to raise and lower ships over the dam.

On the upper Yenisey the Sayan hydro station is now under construction for completion in the mid 1970s. Next on the list is the so-called Yenisey plant, which

Figure 12–9   Construction of the Bratsk Dam, as of 1959. Novosti.

317

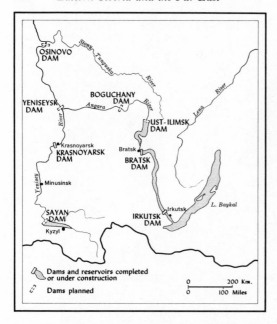

Figure 12–10   Construction projects on the Yenisey and Angara rivers.

is planned for construction downstream from Krasnoyarsk, with a power capacity of 6 million kilowatts. A high dam will raise the water to a level that might allow for the long-cherished plan of Soviet engineers to join tributaries of the Yenisey and the Ob Rivers. Long-range plans call for the building of at least eleven plants on the Yenisey-Angara River system which will have a combined electrical capacity of up to 30 million kilowatts.

Smaller plants have been built on some of the other Siberian rivers, such as the Vilyuy hydro station which was opened in 1967 at Chernyshevskiy, northwest of Mirnyy, to supply power to the diamond-mining district. An atomic power plant is also scheduled for northeastern Siberia to service new gold-mining districts.

A grand scheme has been drawn up for controlling the floods and at the same time exploiting the water-power resources of the Amur River system. As many as seventy power stations of various sizes and capacities have been proposed for the

Amur River and its tributaries. Two plants of immediate importance, since they would bring under control the waters of the unpredictable Amur, are the Zeya plant, to be constructed about 6 kilometers above the city of Zeya on the Zeya River, and the Dzhalindskaya plant, to be built near the town of Dzhalinda about 700 kilometers above Blagoveshchensk on the Amur River. As planned, the Dzhalindskaya plant will have a dam 80 meters high, which will help in eliminating the floods on the Amur caused by the summer monsoons. The Zeya plant calls for a dam 100 meters high. The power station at each dam would have a capacity in the neighborhood of 1,000,000 kilowatts. The Chinese part of the project to control the Amur provides for the construction of ten hydroelectric plants on the Sungari River, one plant of which already is operative. Of this entire Amur scheme, only the Zeya station is actually under construction, and scheduled for completion in the mid 1970s. Strained relations between the Soviets and the Chinese seem to have shelved the other projects indefinitely.

The large power plants of the Angara-Yenisey system will provide abundant electric power for aluminum, wood chemicals, and synthetic plants in the cities of Krasnoyarsk, Angarsk, Bratsk, and other locations now under construction. Also they will greatly enhance the electrification of the Trans-Siberian Railroad, which now has been accomplished all the way from Moscow to Irkutsk. The electrification of the Trans-Siberian Railroad will increase the freight-carrying capacity of the most densely traveled railroad in the world and will eliminate a large portion of the previous coal movement on the railroad, one third of which was for the consumption of the steam engines themselves.

If all the hydroelectric plants now planned for the Yenisey-Angara system are completed, there will be a great surplus of electric power in the area. One Soviet planner has calculated that to utilize fully the electricity produced by the Bratsk hydroelectric plant by the methods in which electricity is now being used in the area, 3,120,000 workers would have to be moved into the area. Obviously, such a transposition of people would be very expensive in terms of housing and other services, which is why large power-con-suming industries, such as aluminum reduction plants, are being built. The same planner points out that even to utilize much of the electricity produced by the Bratsk plant in large aluminum plants, 28,000 workers have had to be settled in the area. With construction projects lag-ging as they are, the settlement of even this number of workers has been a Herculean task. Thus we might suspect that many of the planned construction projects will be a long time in material-izing. For the time being, much of the electricity produced at Bratsk is being transmitted westward more than 1000 miles over high-voltage transmission lines. When the Soviets perfect long-distance high-voltage direct-current lines, Yenisey hydropower will be transmitted all the way to European U.S.S.R.

Iron and Steel At present there are only two small steel plants east of Lake Baykal. These are located at Petrovsk, just east of the lake and at Komsomolsk on the Lower Amur River. Both of the steel plants depend on imported pig iron from the west, but it is hoped that eventually full-cycle plants can be established here utiliz-ing iron ore deposits in eastern Siberia and the Far East. Adequate coal to operate such plants exists in the Bureya, south Yakutsk, and Sakhalin fields. The present Komso-molsk steel plant, with a capacity of 300,-000 tons, supplies only 35 to 40 per cent of the present regional needs, and the steel consumption of the Far East is expected to rise shortly to 7 or 8 million tons.

The location of a so-called third metal-lurgical base in the Kazakhstan-Siberian-Far Eastern area has been under discussion since World War II. Actually the term is rather meaningless since it implies a series of widely scattered locations of iron and steel plants, some in Kazakhstan, some in Siberia, and some in the Soviet Far East. Construction of the first important plant of this series was to be scheduled for the small town of Tayshet, a railroad junction about 250 miles east of Krasnoyarsk. This small settlement was decided on after much debate because of its strategic position among several deposits of iron ore and coal at the major fork of the railroad where the Trans-Siberian turns southeast towards Irkutsk and the Tayshet-Lena rail line heads northeastward to Ust-Kut. The Tayshet plant was originally scheduled to be completed during the seven-year plan, with the first output of pig iron to be pro-duced in 1965. Its iron ore base was to be the Angara-Ilimsk deposit east of Tayshet near the junction of the Ilim and Angara Rivers. At first the Kuznetsk Basin was to have supplied the coke and coal, but later local coal was to be used. Immediately fol-lowing the construction of the Tayshet plant, a new major plant was to be con-structed at Krasnoyarsk utilizing the same iron and coal deposits.

Farther east, plans were made for the construction of an iron and steel plant in the Aldan area in southern Yakutia, where rich deposits of iron ore and coking coal have been found in some abundance and in close proximity to one another. How-ever, one Soviet planner pointed out that before steel plants could be constructed in this empty area, people, houses, transport facilities, food supplies, and so forth would have to be established.

Now it appears that all of these ambitions have been abandoned, at least for the immediate future. Soviet policy has shifted emphasis to expansion of steel capacity in the European part of the country. It ap-pears that the new West Siberian plant in the Kuznetsk Basin will have to supply the steel needs of the east for many years to come.

Aluminum   One of the big developments in mining and industry that is now taking place in eastern Siberia is in the production of aluminum. Aluminum plants have been established in Krasnoyarsk, Bratsk, and Shelekhov (near Irkutsk) to utilize the huge production of hydroelectric power which is running ahead of the need for electricity in this region. To serve these aluminum plants, an alumina plant is being constructed at Achinsk, which will use nephelite ore from Belogorsk (Kiya Shaltyr) about 150 kilometers to the southwest. There is also nephelite at Goryachegorsk, nearer to Achinsk, but its quality is inferior to the more recently discovered ores at Belogorsk. For some reason, completion of the Achinsk plant has been delayed repeatedly and the Siberian aluminum plants have been dependent on alumina shipped in from the old Kamensk plant in the Urals and the newer Pavlodar plant in Kazakhstan, which in 1967 produced 18 per cent of the country's alumina. In the same year, the three East Siberian aluminum plants produced 48 per cent of the country's aluminum.

The Krasnoyarsk aluminum plant, which reportedly is the largest in the world, spreads over an area of 172 hectares of land and has a capacity of 400,000 tons. This compares with a 335,000-ton capacity at the Alcan plant at Arvida, Quebec, which before was rated as the largest in the world. The Krasnoyarsk plant obtains electric power from the Bratsk dam and the huge 6,000,000-kilowatt hydroelectric station now partially completed on the Yenisey River near Krasnoyarsk. Also it obtains some power from the 1,200,000-kilowatt coal-fueled thermal station at Nazarovo south of Achinsk.

The Shelekhov aluminum plant began operation in 1961 utilizing power from the 660,000-kilowatt hydroelectric station at Irkutsk on the Angara River. The capacity of the plant has been reported to be in the vicinity of 300,000 tons.

The Anzeb plant near Bratsk went into production in 1966.

Other Minerals   Besides fuels, iron, and aluminum, a variety of other minerals are found in small amounts scattered about eastern Siberia and the Far East. Although no single deposit is of national significance, it is recognized that surveying has been far from sufficient in this region, and that many minerals might exist in a large area of complex rocks such as this is.

One of the major mining areas that has been developed under the Soviets is at Norilsk on the Lower Yenisey where large deposits of copper and nickel have laid the basis for the development of a boom town.

Tin and some lead and zinc have been mined for years in Chita Oblast and around Tetyukhe in Maritime Kray. More recently, tin, in conjunction with tungsten, has been discovered in the far northeastern corner of the country in the Chukotsk Peninsula, and a refining plant reportedly is under construction in this area to process the two metals. Since 1959, tin is also being mined at Solnechnyy, 50 kilometers west-northwest of Komsomolsk.

In 1967 new mercury mines were opened up in the Chukchi National Okrug in the far northeastern part of the region. The workers are supplied by air and, in winter, by sledge trains. Cobalt and asbestos mines have been opened in Tuva A.S.S.R. Recently it has become evident that one of the biggest users of Bratsk hydroelectricity is a large uranium-processing plant at Ust-Vikhoreva, northwest of Bratsk.

Gold is scattered widely throughout eastern Siberia and the Far East; the richest fields occur in the Vitim and Aldan Plateaus south of the Lena River where mining began in 1923. The small city of

Bodaybo in the Vitim Plateau is the central outfitting city for the gold workers. Also, important gold mines have been established in far off Magadan Oblast about 200 miles inland from the northern shore of the Sea of Okhotsk. Huge dredges as high as a three-story house have been shipped in and assembled on the Middle Yenisey and are working the gravels of that stream for placer gold. As far as can be determined, the Soviet Union is second only to South Africa in gold production, and most of the gold comes from eastern Siberia and the Far East.

Perhaps the most exciting development in the mining industry in Siberia recently has been the opening of newly discovered diamond deposits which are scattered widely through the western portion of the Central Siberian Upland. The Russians state simply that these deposits are in no way inferior to those in South Africa. A sizable diamond production would greatly facilitate the machine-tool industry in the Soviet Union, since diamonds are needed in all sorts of cutting instruments. So far mines have been established at Mirnyy, Aykhal, and Udachnyy (Novyy).

Forests Roughly half of the forest reserves of the U.S.S.R lie in eastern Siberia and the Far East. The eastern forests in general are not of the best quality, and as long as better forests are available nearer to the markets of European Russia and western Europe a great expansion of

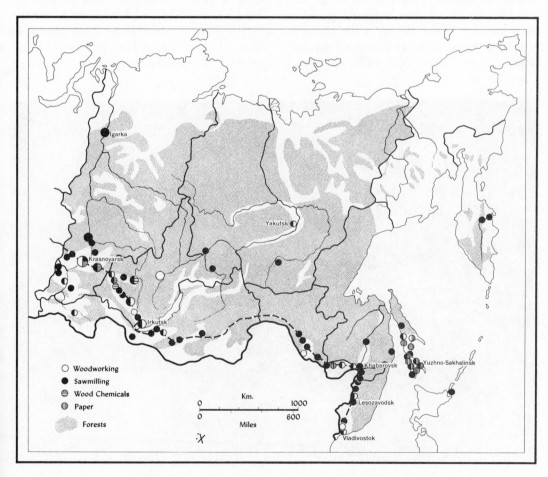

Figure 12–11   Forest cover and lumbering. After Cherdantsev.

lumbering cannot be expected in this area. Eastern Siberia and the Far East normally produce about one sixth of the sawed lumber in the Soviet Union and enough paper to serve the needs of the local area.

The sawmilling industry in eastern Siberia and the Far East is sufficient to serve all local needs, and some lumber is sent down the major streams in summer to be shipped westward via the Northern Sea Route to foreign markets in western Europe. All the major towns along the Trans-Siberian Railroad engage in some sawmilling, and some major centers exist off the railroad along the primary streams. Igarka is just such a sawmilling center established on the Lower Yenisey to ship lumber via the Northern Sea Route to foreign markets.

A string of smaller sawmilling towns exist in the Ussuri-Khanka Lowland in Maritime Kray, located wherever the railroad between Khabarovsk and Vladivostok crosses tributaries of the Ussuri River flowing down the western slopes of the Sikhote-Alin Mountains. The prime forests of Maritime Kray are found on the slopes of the Sikhote-Alin, and timber is floated down the streams to the west. The largest of these sawmilling towns, located where the railroad crosses the Ussuri River itself, is called Lesozavodsk, or sawmill.

Lumbering is one of the major industries on Sakhalin Island, particularly in the better forested southern part of the island. Many pulp and paper factories are located in the towns of southern Sakhalin, particularly in the largest city, Yuzhno-Sakhalinsk, or South Sakhalin.

Two new large wood-processing complexes have been under construction for a number of years at Bratsk and at Amursk, just south of Komsomolsk on the Amur River. Both began operation in 1967. The Bratsk plant processes wood pulp for the production of rayon tire cord

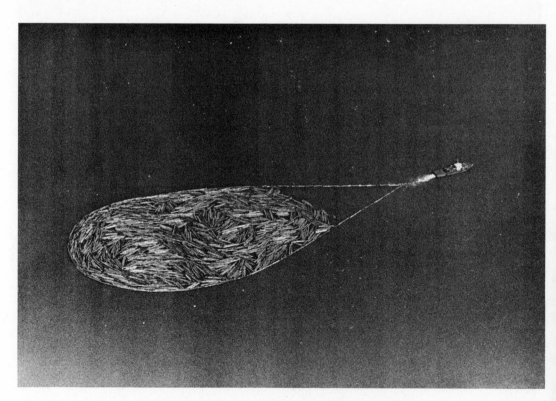

Figure 12–12   Log floating on the Yenisey. Novosti.

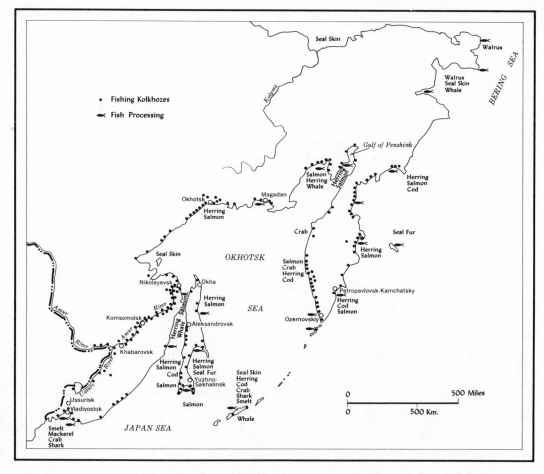

Figure 12–13   Fishing in Far Eastern waters. Adapted from Atlas selskogo khozyaystva SSSR.

and the Amursk plant produces pulp, container board, and fiber board. The Bratsk plant has already caused consternation among conservation-minded people, who reported that 1800 cubic meters of poisonous wastes are being dumped into the Angara River every minute. Earlier it was reported that timber-processing plants along the Selenga River were depositing 79 million tons of waste per year into Lake Baykal.

Fish   Since World War II the total fish catch in the Soviet Union has increased steadily, and the geographical distribution has changed until at present the seas of the Far East yield 30 per cent of the total catch. Together with 2.6 per cent of the total catch contributed by Siberian rivers and lakes, this area becomes the most important fishing ground in the Soviet Union. The main centers of the fishing industry are along the shores of Maritime Kray, especially around Peter the Great Bay in the vicinity of Vladivostok, the southern part of Khabarovsk Kray, particularly around the mouth of the Amur River, and Kamchatka Peninsula and Sakhalin Island.

The Sea of Okhotsk, or hunters' sea, is one of the richest fishing grounds of the country. It is especially known for its salmon, which are caught mainly in either the Lower Amur River, as the fish enter for their annual spawning, or the Gulf of Penzhina next to Kamchatka. The Gulf of

Penzhina, with an average difference of 45 feet between high and low water, has some of the greatest tides in the world. According to the Russians the salmon are so large and so numerous in this area that in shoal water during low tides sea gulls stand on the backs of the salmon and peck at them. The fisheries of Kamchatka account for about 60 per cent of the salmon catch in the U.S.S.R. Another product, one that is world renowned, is the Kamchatka crab, which the Russians claim reaches the size of a washtub! The waters surrounding Kamchatka supply a large percentage of the world's crabs.

Far Eastern waters also are rich in sea animals: whales, walruses, and seals. Whaling ships based in Vladivostok range to the Bering Straits, 3000 miles to the northeast. Seal rookeries are maintained on the Commander Islands. Although minor fishing ports exist in many places along the coast of the mainland, the peninsula of Kamchatka, and the island of Sakhalin, larger ocean-going fleets all are based in Vladivostok and nearby Nakhodka.

Before World War II a large part of the fishing in the Sea of Okhotsk was done by the Japanese who then controlled the southern half of Sakhalin and the Kuril Islands. Now that the Soviet Union controls all these islands, it considers the Sea of Okhotsk to be its own territorial waters, and the Japanese have had difficulty negotiating fishing rights with the Russians.

Furs and Game Animals   It was the quest for furs that originally brought Russian colonizers to Siberia and the Far East, and fur-bearing animals are still a major resource. Furs provide valuable exports as well as major domestic needs for warm clothing. Yakutia is the Soviet Union's leading fur supply area, normally producing about 15 per cent of the annual take by value. The leading types are squirrel, white fox, ermine, muskrat, and hare. The sable, which was nearly extinct at the turn of the century, is now making a come-

back under carefully controlled trapping arrangements. The muskrat, which was introduced from Canada in 1930, rapidly became established in the familiar swampy, wet environment of its new home.

In addition to fur-bearing animals, the expansive wilderness of this region abounds in elk, wild reindeer, and mountain sheep, which provide significant amounts of meat for the local population.

Cities

As in western Siberia, the largest cities in eastern Siberia and the Far East lie in the south where the Trans-Siberian Railroad crosses the major rivers.

Krasnoyarsk   Krasnoyarsk, located at the point where the Trans-Siberian crosses the Yenisey, is the largest city, with a population of 576,000. The city serves important transport functions, is the seat of government for huge Krasnoyarsk Kray, and has a variety of industries, chief among which are the machine-building industries, and metal-working, lumbering, wood-working and paper-milling, textiles, and food industries. Recent innovations to the industries of Krasnoyarsk are an oil refinery and associated chemical plants, a synthetic rubber factory, and a large aluminum plant, which is to utilize electricity from the large hydroelectric plant being constructed on the nearby Yenisey.

Khabarovsk   Second in size is Khabarovsk, founded in 1858 as a fortress at the important junction of the Ussuri, Sungari, and Amur Rivers. With a population of 435,000, Khabarovsk is the metropolis of the Far East. It serves as the governmental seat of extensive Khabarovsk Kray and occupies a strategic position on the rail and water transport systems where the Trans-Siberian Railroad leaves the Amur River to run southward through the Ussuri-Khanka Lowland to Vladivostok. Its varied industries are concentrated somewhat on

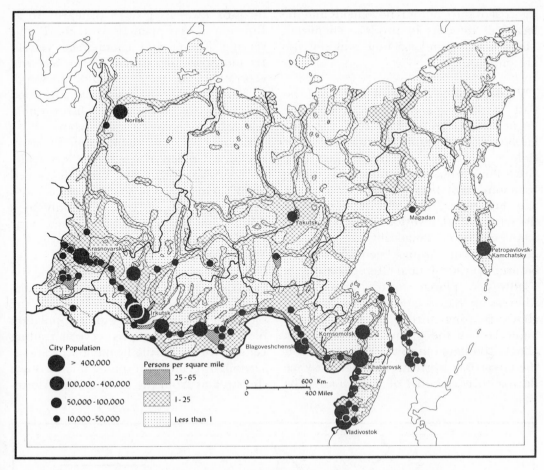

Figure 12–14   Population densities and city sizes. Updated from Cherdantsev.

machine building and metal working, oil refining, chemicals, and lumbering and wood working. It also has some textile and food industries to serve the Far Eastern markets.

Irkutsk   Third in size in eastern Siberia and the Far East is Irkutsk at the mouth of the Irkut River on the upper Angara near Lake Baykal, which in 1967 had a population of 420,000. Irkutsk serves as the metropolis of the rapidly industrializing region west of Lake Baykal. Situated on the Angara River in the midst of the Cheremkhovo coal fields, Irkutsk has become very rich in supplies of energy both from coal and from hydroelectric power generated by the huge dams being

constructed on the Angara. Also an oil pipeline has been laid all the way from the Volga-Urals oil fields and an oil refinery has been constructed in the nearby city of Angarsk. The industries in Irkutsk at present are primarily machine and metalworking industries, lumbering and woodworking industries, food industries, and other diversified industries. A new aluminum plant has been opened in Shelekhov, and with the development of oil refining some growth of the chemical industries might be expected. Other cities of note in the vicinity are Angarsk, with a population of 183,000; Cheremkhovo, with a population of 109,000; and Usolye-Siberskoye, 75,000, so named because of the salt deposits in the region. These cities utilize the coal of the Cheremkhovo fields and the local salt deposits to produce chemicals. Metal working and machine building also are important.

Vladivostok Vladivostok, "Ruler of the East," with a population of 397,000 is the major seaport on the Pacific. Sitting on a knobby granite peninsula at the head of Golden Horn Bay, an arm of Peter the Great Bay, its physical setting and shipping functions have been likened to those of San Francisco. Although topograpically the setting of Vladivostok can be likened to San Francisco, climatically the two are quite different. As has been pointed out before, average January temperatures in Vladivostok plunge to 6°F above zero, whereas in San Francisco they are well above freezing throughout the winter. Snow lies on the ground in Vladivostok almost 100 days out of the year, and Peter the Great Bay is greatly hampered by ice during three months of the winter. Vla-

divostok owes its growth primarily to its function as the main port on the Pacific serving fishing and commercial vessels. Its industries are varied, with some concentration on machine-building, woodworking, and food industries. The food industries are dominated by fish canning and fish processing of many types.

Because of the ice problem in semienclosed Golden Horn Bay, the satellite port of Nakhodka has been developed about 20 miles east of Vladivostok on more open water. It has grown rapidly to a population of 96,000, and each year handles a larger percentage of Soviet Far Eastern trade.

A number of smaller towns lie along the railroad between Vladivostok and Khabarovsk, chief among which is Ussurisk, the old town of Voroshilov, with a population of 124,000. These towns serve as trading centers for the fertile farming area and as sawmilling centers for timber floated down the streams from the Sikhote-Alin Moun-

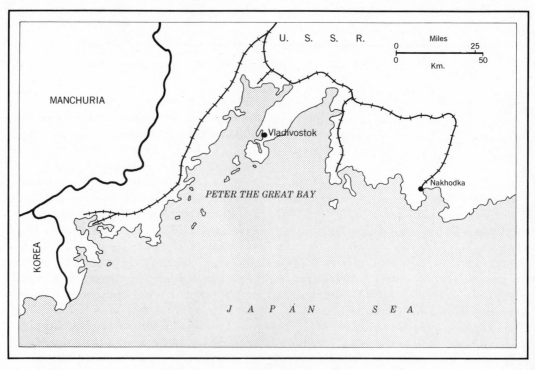

Figure 12–15   Vladivostok and its environs.

tains to the east. Ussurisk looks much like a Ukrainian town with its whitewashed adobe cottages with thatched roofs and blue painted shutters.

Komsomolsk   Komsomolsk-on-Amur, with a population of 209,000, is a new city founded in 1932 in the forests along the Lower Amur to serve as a primary steel center for the Far East. So far, it has only a steel plant and must ship in pig iron and scrap metal for steel production. It is hoped that in the future coal from the Bureya fields to the west and iron ore from Maritime Kray can be utilized to produce pig iron at Komsomolsk. As its name implies, it is a Young Communist League city, and was constructed primarily by young volunteers. It is one of those strange zionistic endeavors staged now and then by the Soviets to excite the imaginations of certain groups of people, but it does not make much sense economically. If a primary steel industry was really needed in the Far East it might better have been placed in the large city of Khabarovsk. Nevertheless, no matter how artificial the setting, under the Soviet system of induced settlement new cities grow rapidly, and Komsomolsk now is third in size in the Far East. Besides its steel industry it has machine and metal-working industries and chemical industries. The chemical industries are based largely on the by-product gases from the oil refinery set up in the city to refine oil brought in by pipeline from northern Sakhalin.

Ulan-Ude and Chita   Ulan-Ude, with a population of 227,000, and Chita, with a population of 203,000, are situated in similar mountain basins east of Lake Baykal and are governmental centers of their respective regions. Ulan-Ude is the capital of the Buryat A.S.S.R., and Chita is the governmental center of Chita Oblast. Commercial and governmental functions are foremost in both cities, but some diversified industries have developed in machine building, wood-working, food industries, etc. The cities also serve important rail service functions on the Trans-Siberian Railroad; Ulan-Ude has the main locomotive repair shops between the Urals and the Pacific.

Norilsk   Norilsk, in the far north near the mouth of the Yenisey River, is a boom town in the wilderness and owes its growth to the copper and nickel mining and smelting that is carried on there. By 1967 Norilsk had grown to a city of 129,000.

Bratsk   The workers' settlement of Bratsk, at the site of the largest hydroelectric development in the U.S.S.R. thus far, is growing rapidly into a city of industries based on wood processing and aluminum. On July 1, 1967 its population was 122,000. By January 1, 1968 this had increased to 170,000 and by 1970 it is expected to be 300,000.

Blagoveshchensk and Birobidzhan   Blagoveshchensk, with a population of 121,000, is the regional center of the Zeya-Bureya Lowland. It lies along the Amur River at the end of a rail spur leading southward from the Trans-Siberian Railroad. Its industries are concentrated on machine building, wood-working, and food industries. Once it was the largest Russian city on the Amur, but it has stagnated since the Trans-Siberian Railroad by-passed it.

Just east of Blagoveshchensk is Birobidzhan, the capital of the Jewish Autonomous Oblast, with a population of 46,000. The Jewish A.O. has not developed as the Soviets had envisioned it would; Jews have not moved into the area in great numbers, and those that have moved in from the west have not taken up farming as they were supposed to have done. Rather they set up the same tailoring shops that they had been running in western Russia, Belorussia, and Ukraine. Thus, in spite of its world renown, Birobidzhan has remained a minor city in size. It has some wood-working and food processing, but it is probably best known for its tailor shops whose products serve much of the clothing needs of the Soviet Far East.

Cities on Sakhalin Island   Yuzhno-Sakhalinsk, near the southern end of Sakhalin Island, with a population of 92,000 is the largest city in Sakhalin Oblast, which includes the Kuril Islands. Other towns of significance on Sakhalin are Aleksandrovsk, 21,000, along the middle of the west coast, and Okha, 30,000, the center of the oil fields in the north. A single highway connects the towns along the west coast, but tides daily inundate the shore and in places cover the highway. Local newspapers publish the times of day during which the highway will be covered by water. Much of the local transportation is by boat.

During much of the last decade, the population of Sakhalin has remained the same. Much of the population is transient in nature, with about the same number arriving and leaving each year. Labor turnover is a problem of first magnitude, as it is throughout much of Siberia and the Far East.

Petropavlovsk and Magadan   Petropavlovsk-Kamchatsky, with a population of 123,000, is the chief city and governmental seat of Kamchatka Oblast. It serves as an important port and fish-processing center. On the coast of the mainland to the northwest is Magadan, with a population of 82,000, which serves as the center of large Magadan Oblast and as the port and regional center for the Kolyma gold fields to the north.

Yakutsk   Yakutsk, on the middle Lena, with a population of 95,000, is another important regional center. It serves as the political and commercial center of the Yakut A.S.S.R., the largest single political unit in the Soviet Union except for the Russian Republic itself, within which it lies. The Yakut A.S.S.R. is even larger than the very extensive Kazakh Republic. Its total population is small, however, and the economy is very limited. The agricultural area within the immediate vicinity of Yakutsk has already been mentioned.

Transportation

The lifeline of Siberia and the Far East is the Trans-Siberian Railroad. Since construction began in 1892, a number of branch lines and paralleling lines have been laid along certain sections, and the entire line has been doubletracked and electrified. It still serves only the southern part of the region, however, and millions of square miles of territory are without adequate transportation facilities. Nevertheless, the railroad, supplemented by the major streams, is the main supplier of Siberia and the Far East. Goods for northern Siberia usually are moved into Siberia by rail and then floated downstream to the north. All this must take place during the summer since the streams are frozen at least half the year.

Much fanfare has been made about the Northern Sea Route, which during 2 or 3 months of summer is kept open from Murmansk on the Kola Peninsula across the Barents, Kara, Laptev, East Siberian, and Chukotsk Seas, and through the Bering Strait into the Pacific. The Northern Sea Route has bases along the Arctic coast near the mouths of the major streams for transshipment between ocean-going vessels and river boats. But the shortness of the navigation season, coupled with the fact that supplies going into Siberia must be shipped upstream rather than down, has rendered the Northern Sea Route of little economic significance to Siberia and the Far East. Its significance lies more in its potential strategic value during wartime, and even that is questionable because of the hazards to navigation. Convoys of ships must be accompanied by ice breakers and aided by airplanes and helicopters, which spot the courses from aloft, a clostly and slow operation.

The Trans-Siberian Railroad originally hooked up with the Chinese Eastern Railway across northern Manchuria, which came under the strong influence of the Russians after the Boxer Rebellion. This provided a direct route to Vladivostok. After the Russo-Japanese War of 1905, when Manchuria was taken over by the Japanese, the Russians were forced to extend the Trans-Siberian Railroad on Soviet territory north of the Amur River all the way to Khabarovsk and then south to Vladivostok. Since that time, until World War II, the Soviets intended to build a second line, the so-called BAM, leading off from Tayshet east of Krasnoyarsk, going north of Lake Baykal, and staying considerably north of the southern boundary, because they feared the disruptive possibilities of the Japanese in Manchuria. This rail line was never built because the Soviets never got around to it. Since World War II, with the removal of the Japanese from Manchuria and with the supposedly friendly Communist regime in China, the Soviets apparently have felt no need for building this second line. There have been plans formulated recently, however, to extend the line from Tayshet to Yakutsk and on to Magadan to better serve the remote areas of the northeast. This projected railroad is known as the BAM-Chulman-Aldan Railroad.

Other branch lines leading off the Trans-Siberian Railroad, such as the Achinsk-Abalakovo Railroad, are being con-

Figure 12–16   Construction of the railroad between Abakan and Tayshet. Novosti.

structed to facilitate mining and industrial development. Service on the Trans-Siberian itself has been improved through electrification and automatic signaling.

Prospects

Eastern Siberia and the Soviet Far East, in spite of Soviet efforts, have remained relatively empty parts of the country remote from the populated ecumene. Previous efforts at a great migration eastward to fill up this land have produced only minor results, primarily in the form of major urban nodes along the Trans-Siberian Railroad, which provide the commercial and political means to exploit some of the mineral, timber, and other resources of the area. But this exploitation has been one primarily of extraction of resources for the use of the people in the European part of the country and has involved long rail movements of bulky commodities. Therefore it has proved to be a rather expensive operation. Population flows eastward largely have ceased, except for localized areas, and in the future it appears that any population increase will probably be due to excess of births over deaths rather than to any net in-migration. In fact, during the last decade in many areas there has been more out-migration than in-migration.

With a tendency to shift more toward cost accounting and profit motives for industrial development, the Soviet government seems to have put into play an unstated policy to slow down or halt the development of large industrial complexes in remote areas of Siberia and the Far East in favor of moving raw materials to new industrial plants in the old populated areas of the west. Hence it appears that the role of Siberia, at least for the immediate future, is to act as a storehouse of certain raw materials that will be provided to the populated part of the country. As far as its own economic develop-

ment is concerned, it will be somewhat limited in scope, primarily to serve its own needs, and will not be intimately integrated with economic activities in other parts of the country.

In fact, the Soviets are now actively planning the economic development of parts of the Soviet Far East as integrated elements in the general economy of the whole Far East, including particularly Japan and to some extent China. The Soviets now see great opportunities for large markets of certain raw materials in industrialized Japan. Wood products and oil seem to be the most obvious items of export. Japan is eager to get these raw materials and has offered to help with the construction of an oil pipeline from Irkutsk to the Pacific to facilitate the export of west Siberian oil. It has also offered to help in the development of certain mineral resources in eastern Siberia, such as the exploitation of aluminum deposits in the Lake Baykal area. There is also a fairly lively trade springing up between the two countries in fish products. The Soviets are exporting flounder, salmon, herring, whale meat, shrimp, and other mollusks to Japan in return for fishing nets, men's shirts, women's blouses, stretch nylon socks, fruit, and other commodities.

Within the mainland, transportation remains the big problem in eastern Siberia and the Far East. Although the Trans-Siberian Railroad effectively links the settlements along the southern fringes of the region, the huge expanses to the north generally are untapped by passable highways. Geological survey parties still find it necessary to travel on the ground primarily via reindeer teams operated by the local Yakuts and Buryats. As late as the early 1960s it was reported that such transport operations supplied as much as 50 per cent of the income for many of the collective farms in the area. In general the high prices paid for reindeer teams and reindeer drivers has served to divert the efforts of the local collective farmers from reindeer raising for meat and hides to reindeer raising for the ephemeral business of providing transportation for itinerant survey parties. Although helicopters and airplanes to some extent are taking up the transportation slack in this vast land, they cannot totally replace land transportation for surveying and mining activities. It appears that the very remoteness and vastness of the region, combined with the very difficult surface conditions of severe climate, marsh, and mountains, will provide such transportation difficulties that the bulk of the area will be relegated forever to the status of a sparsely populated wilderness.

Reading List

Eastern Siberia and the Far East

Armstrong, Terence, *Russian Settlement in the North,* Cambridge University Press, 1965, 224 pp.

———, *The Russians in the Arctic; Aspects of Soviet Exploration and Exploitation in the Far North, 1937–1957,* Methuen, London, 1958, 182 pp.

Atlas Irkutskoy Oblasti (Atlas of Irkutsk Oblast), Moscow, 1962 (in Russian).

Dyakonov, F. V., "Productive Forces and Productive Territorial Complexes in the Northeast of the U.S.S.R.," *Soviet Geography: Review and Translation,* January 1964, pp. 40–52.

Gibson, James R., *Feeding the Russian Fur Trade: Provisionment of the Okhotsk Seaboard and the Kamchatka Peninsula, 1639–1856,* University of Wisconsin Press, 1969, 337 pp.

Gurvich, I. S. and Kuzakov, K. G., *Koryakskii natsionalniy okrug* (The Koryak National Okrug), Moscow, 1960, 302 pp. (in Russian).

Hopkins, Mark W., short articles on various features of Eastern Siberia and Soviet Far East, *Milwaukee Journal,* October 9, 1966, Part 5, p. 1; November 1, 1967,

Part 2, p. 7; January 16, 1968, Part 1, p. 9; and January 18, 1968, Part 1, p. 9.

Jackson, W. A. D., *The Russo-Chinese Border Lands: Zone of Peaceful Contact or Potential Conflict?,* Van Nostrand, Princeton, 2nd ed., 1968, 156 pp.

Kravanja, Milan A., "Soviet Far East Fisheries Expansion," *Commercial Fisheries Review,* November 1964.

Kremnev, A., *Chitinska Oblast* (Chita Oblast), Chita, 1959, 159 pp. (in Russian).

Naymushin, I. and Gindin, A., "Problems of the Angara Series of Hydroelectric Stations," *Soviet Geography: Review and Translation,* June 1960, pp. 61–67.

Parmuzin, Yu. P., "The Zonal Character of the Cold Pole," *Soviet Geography: Review and Translation,* January–February 1960, pp. 40–42.

Pokshishevskiy, V. V., "On the Geography of Pre-Revolutionary Colonization and Migration Processes in the Southern Part of the Soviet Far East," *Soviet Geography: Review and Translation,* April 1963, pp. 17–31.

———, *Zaseleniye Sibiri* (The Settlement of Siberia), Irkutsk, 1951 (in Russian).

Soviet Geography: Review and Translation, February 1968; almost the entire issue deals with eastern Siberia and the Far East.

Staf, Karl, *Yakutia as I Saw It,* Foreign Languages Publishing House, Moscow, 1958, 113 pp.

Thiel, Erich, *The Soviet Far East,* Praeger, 1957, 388 pp.

Treadgold, Donald L., *The Great Siberian Migration,* Princeton University Press, 1957, 278 pp.

Udovenko, B. G., *Dalniy Vostok* (The Far East), Moscow, 1957 (in Russian).

Vorobyev, A. A., "Problems in the Location of Transportation in the Southern Part of Eastern Siberia," *Soviet Geography: Review and Translation,* May 1964, pp. 3–12.

Yegorovo, V. V., "The Economic Effectiveness of the Construction of Pioneering Railroads in Newly Developed Areas (as illustrated by the Lena Railroad)," *Soviet Geography: Review and Translation,* April 1964, pp. 46–55.

Topical Analysis of Cultural and Economic Phenomena

IN THE PRECEDING CHAPTERS the geography of the U.S.S.R. was covered region by region. Within each region all geographical phenomena were considered in their spatial and functional relations to one another. This was necessary for the reader to become familiar with locations, to understand the interplays among phenomena, and to depict distinctive regions as functioning entities.

Now it is necessary to tie the regions together, to consider separate phenomena across the entire country, and to place each region in its correct perspective with regard to each set of phenomena. The geographical aspects of population, agriculture, industry, transport, trade, and foreign relations are taken up in turn. Analyses of their evolution through time and distribution in space are presented. For each phenomenon the significance of separate regions within the U.S.S.R. are noted, and the U.S.S.R. as a whole is considered in context with the rest of the world.

Population, July 1, 1967	Total	Per Cent of Total
U.S.S.R.	235,500,000	100
Urban	129,100,000	55
Rural	106,400,000	45
Women	127,400,000	54.1
Men	108,100,000	45.9

	Average per 1000 People
Birth Rate	17.4
Death Rate	7.6
Growth Rate	9.8
Life Expectancy (years)	men 66, women 74

Note: Since this book went to press, the Soviets released preliminary figures from their 1970 census. A summary of these are given in the appendix at the end of the book.

13

Population, Nationalities, Manpower, and Employment

In many respects the greatest resource, and the greatest problem, of any country is its population. The strength and potential of a given population depends not only on total numbers, but to a large degree on the cultural attainments of that population, the social organization, and the composition with respect to age and sex. The Soviets took an all-union census on January 15, 1959, and since that time they have kept accurate records of births and deaths and have tried to keep track of migrations through records contained in work books that each person must carry in order to get a job in his new location. Thus it is now possible to make much more precise statements about various factors of population in the U.S.S.R. than could ever have been made before the 1959 census. This was the first census since 1939 and the most complete census since 1926. Although accurate records have been kept since 1959 on certain facets of population, in many instances it will be necessary to hark back to the 1959 census, and therefore this date will crop up frequently throughout the chapter. Nationality statistics, for instance, all date from 1959. No information has been released on nationality numbers since that time. Although a new census originally had been planned for January 1969, this was postponed to January 1970. The 1970 census no doubt will turn up some discrepancies in estimates that have been made during the last 11 years, and it should shed considerable new light on developments and movements of nationality groups.

Since the 1959 census there has been an unprecedented flurry of activity by Soviet demographers and other research people, who have written a great deal about the Soviet population and have analyzed it in many different ways. Thus we have a wealth of information to work with which has never been available before. It is obvious that there is a growing concern among Soviet statesmen and scholars about population in general and the labor market in particular. Finally they are beginning to abandon what so far has been a rather tacit assumption that labor is a free good and are beginning to realize that the population is the single most important asset or liability of any country.

Population Dynamics

As of July 1, 1967, the latest date for which information was available at the time of this writing, the Soviet Union had a total population of 235,500,000, which makes it the third most populous nation on earth. During the previous 5 years, the Soviet Union had averaged 19.9 births per 1000 people and 7.2 deaths. The annual growth rate of the population was slightly under 1.5 per cent per year. By comparison in the United States the population was estimated at about 200 million, the birth rate was 20.6 per 1000, and the death rate 9.5. Therefore the growth rate was similar to that of the Soviet Union. The Soviet Union has a slightly lower death rate than does the United States because of a younger age distribution in its population. Neither country has a high birth rate compared to some of the underdeveloped countries of Latin America, Asia, and Africa, but their birth rates are nearly twice those of countries of Western Europe, and they have much lower death rates than do any of the countries with higher birth rates. Thus they are both experiencing a moderate growth rate.

The Soviet population reflects a combination of three major influences during the past half century: industrial-urban development, governmental policies, and disastrous war and civil strife. The demographic response of the communist society of the U.S.S.R. to industrial-urban

development has been very similar to that of the capitalist society of the United States — lower mortality and lower fertility. (Fig. 13–1) In 1920 the birth rate in the U.S.S.R. was around 45 per 1000. By 1959 this had dropped to 25 per 1000, and since then it has dropped steadily to less than 18. Thus economic and social changes brought about by urbanization and industrialization have overridden any policies or decrees that the government might have issued in regard to population fertility. At the same time the death rate has dropped from between 20 and 30 per 1000 to a little over 7 per 1000. The life expectancy thus has risen sharply from about 45 years in 1920 to around 70 years at the present time. In 1967 the life expectancy for men in the Soviet Union was given as 66 years and for women, 74. By comparison, life expectancy in the United States was around 68 for men and 74 for women. Such life expectancies are only exceeded in the Scandinavian countries, the Netherlands, and New Zealand. The rest of the world has considerably shorter life expectancies. (One Soviet wit has said that life really is no longer under the Soviets than it was under the Tsars, it just seems that way.) The drastically reduced death rate in the Soviet Union has been due to a commendable improvement in general sanitary and medical conditions throughout the country and the control of communicable diseases, which often reached epidemic proportions in the past. The Soviet Union now has more doctors per capita than does the United States, and they have instituted an inoculation program for the entire population against communicable diseases of all sorts.

Government policy toward population growth has been described as "blatantly pronatalist." Undoubtedly it has always been the intention of the Soviet leaders to promote rapid population growth. Economic and social realities, however, have often forced governmental actions contrary to the basic purpose, so that the

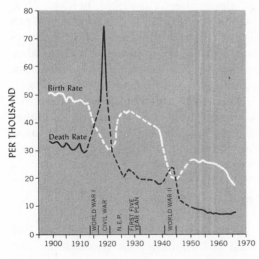

Figure 13–1 Birth and death rates, U.S.S.R., 1897–1967. Updated from French. By permission of St. Antony's College, Oxford.

record during the past 50 years appears to reflect vacillating and indecisive government policies. Programs and practices which tend to encourage child bearing co-exist with programs and practices which tend to discourage it. Although not by design, practices which tend to depress the birth rate are the more numerous and the more effective. At the outset there was conflict between ideology and economic desirability. Lenin contended that one of the basic rights of a citizen was to decide whether a child should be born, and thus he legalized abortion and urged the dissemination of contraceptives. At the same time, his government had a tacit understanding that it was desirable to have a continually increasing population that eventually would spread uniformly across the country.

During much of the Soviet era there has been a program of family allowances to encourage births. In the 1950s this amounted to cash renumerations to families according to numbers of children, as is shown in Table 13–1. As can be easily surmised, this schedule of payments is only a token effort that does little more than compensate for the immediate costs of birth and loss of work time for the mother. A 20-ruble lump sum payment at the birth of the third child would about supply him with his initial layette, and monthly subsidies for subsequent children of 4, 6, 7, etc. rubles would not go very far toward their upkeep. Thus this program has been largely ineffectual, as has been the system of medals and awards given to mothers of large families. The Order of Mother Heroine with a scroll from the Presidium of the Supreme Soviet of the U.S.S.R. goes to women who have had ten children.

Family allowance payments for a family with five children at the time the fifth child is born would average about 12 per cent of the annual wage of the family, and a family having a tenth child would receive payments totaling about 41 per cent of its annual wage. Family allowance payments throughout the Soviet Union amount to only about 0.25 per cent of the national income. If one considers all the various subsidies to families in some other countries, such as aid to families without fathers, hot lunch programs, free maternity hospitalization, and so forth, then such aid in the United States amounts to about 0.29 per cent of the national income, and in certain other countries it is considerably higher. Percentages for most of the West European countries are quite high in this regard. France appears highest with 4.76 per cent. Of course, there are many benefits in the Soviet Union that do not show up in these family allowances. So it is very difficult to compare.

Table 13–1   Schedule of Payments to Mothers of Large Families and to Unmarried Mothers in the U.S.S.R., in New Rubles

	Lump Sum at Birth of Child	Monthly Amount Paid on Behalf of Child	Period of Monthly Payments
A. To mothers of large families			From first to fifth birthday
Number of older living children			
2	20	—	
3	65	4	
4	85	6	
5	100	7	
6	125	10	
7	125	10	
8	175	12.5	
9	175	12.5	
10 or more	250	15	
B. To unmarried mothers			From birth to twelfth birthday
Number of living children			
1	—	5	
2	—	7.5	
3	—	10	

Source: David M. Heer and Judith G. Bryden, "Family Allowances and Fertility in the Soviet Union," *Soviet Studies,* October 1966, p. 155.

On the antinatalist side, the government and other agencies in the Soviet Union have sponsored education on birth control and general hygiene and have made contraceptives readily available in the health dispensaries of factories and farms. A liberal abortion policy was practiced in the 1920s and early 1930s, which at its height in the early 1930s raised the level of abortion to twice that of births. Between 1936 and 1955 a restrictive abortion policy was followed and a strengthening of family ties was attempted after Stalin decided that a generation of delinquents had resulted from previous policies. During this period, however, illegal abortions became so prevalent that the government became alarmed and once more liberalized policy. At present, abortions are legal and free of cost. The recipient has only to show certification that it was performed under safe and sanitary conditions. Sterilization also is legal for health and other reasons. At the present time the annual number of abortions may well be higher than the number of live births. It has been reported that among working women abortions average 41.5 per 1000 per year, whereas among nonworking women they average 10.5. The abortion rate is very high all through eastern Europe. Most of the socialist governments sincerely want to reduce the abortion rate, if for no other reason than economic ones, since they tie up hospital facilities and result in the loss of many hours of work. However, the way of life in these countries has mitigated against these governmental desires.

More important than any governmental policies regarding fertility are the antinatalist effects of an extreme shortage of housing and a high percentage of women in the full-time work force, as well as a broad array of other factors indicative of general standards of living. Per capita housing space has actually decreased during the past decade or so, contrary to plans for a substantial increase.

In addition to government policies and economic and social realities, a series of calamities have left lasting scars on the Soviet population. Only the present generation of young people have been fortunate enough to have largely escaped the repercussions of war, revolution, forced labor, or famine. Between 1913 and 1959, within the same boundaries, the Soviet population increased by only 49 million, or 30 per cent in 46 years. In contrast the population of the United States increased about 80 per cent, growing from 97 million in 1913 to 176 million in 1959. It has been estimated that since 1913, population losses in the U.S.S.R. from war, civil strife, and famine, together with birth deficits and modest emigration, amounted to a staggering total of between 70 and 80 million people. Losses from World War I and subsequent revolutions, civil wars, and famine have been assessed at more than 25 million; losses during 1931 to 1933 due to collectivization of agriculture with its attendant famine have been estimated at over 5 million; and losses associated directly or indirectly with World War II have been placed at 45 million. During the same period the United States profited from heavy immigration and a high birth rate induced by wars on foreign soils. The World War II population losses in the United States amounted to about 300,000 people, almost exclusively military. The 40 to 50 million population deficit caused by World War II in the Soviet Union (a number approximately equal to the total population of France today) includes 25 to 30 million excess deaths brought about by military and other war-related causes and a deficit of approximately 15 million births during the period. It appears that only about one third as many children were born in the Soviet Union during 1943 and 1944 as during 1939 and 1940. Thus the war had almost exactly opposite effects in the Soviet Union, which fought most of the war on its own soil, and in the United States, which fought all of the war on foreign soil.

Whereas the United States is now experiencing bulging enrollments in colleges and increasing fertility due to the maturity of the "war babies," the Soviet Union is experiencing a low point in enrollments and fertility brought about partially by the male deficit during the war.

Immediately after the war in 1945, there were only 74 males for every 100 females in the entire Soviet population. Much of this male deficit existed in the ages most productive for fertility and labor. For instance, in 1950 the war-caused deficit of males affected virtually all the prime reproductive ages. At ages 22–25 there were 12 per cent more females than males; at ages 25–29 there was a female excess of nearly 30 per cent; and at ages 30–34 there was an excess of 37 per cent. If women married men of their own ages only about two thirds to three quarters of the women in the prime reproductive ages could marry even if all men married. The number of unmarried women was probably even higher than these figures imply, since women generally marry men somewhat older than themselves and some men do not marry at all. According to the 1959 census, only about 70 per cent of the women who had been 25–29 years old in 1950, about 60 per cent of those who had been 30–34 years old, and about 55 per cent of those who had been 35–39 years old in 1950 were married in 1959. Thus, the peculiar Soviet psychology with which the world must cope is shaped to a great degree by a preponderance of frustrated old maids. Since 1950 this deficit has risen up the age ladder, so that in 1967 male and female populations were approximately equal up to the age of 30. There were still 19 million more females than males above this age. At age 37 there were about 10 women for every 9 men; at age 41 about 10 women for every 8 men; at age 46 about 10 women for every 6 men; and at age 63 more than 2 women for every man. Thus, as can be seen in Fig. 13–2, the population pyramid for the Soviet Union is warped in two dimensions, age and sex. There is a great deficit of males at higher age levels, and a great constriction of total population in the 16 to 23 age group, which is beginning to produce an echo in the under 5 age group, which largely are the offspring of these reduced war cohorts.

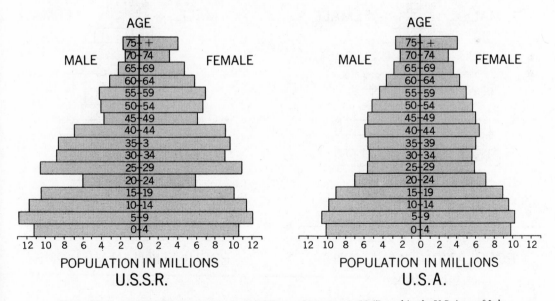

Figure 13–2   Age-sex distributions in the U.S.S.R. as of January 1, 1967, and in the U.S.A. as of July 1, 1966. Data from New Directions in the Soviet Economy *and* Current Population Reports.

If no other catastrophes happen in the Soviet Union, the population pyramid still will not be a normal one until well into the twenty-first century. Males will not catch up with females until the year 2020.

The net result of the demographic forces at work has been a decline in the Soviet birth rate by about one fourth during the past few years and an indication that this decline will continue into the foreseeable future. This has dropped the annual growth rate of the population from around 1.6 to 1.8 per cent during the 1950s to around 1 per cent at the present time, which is slightly lower than that of the United States. If present trends continue, the growth rate might fall as low as 0.5 per cent by the mid 1970s. All indications are that the present trend of decreasing birth rates will continue into the foreseeable future. The deficit of war cohorts alone, which are now constituting much of the reproductive population, would continue this decrease. There are other factors just as important, however. It is clear that urbanization has been a major contributor to declining fertility. In 1965 the birth rate in urban areas was only 16.2 per 1000, whereas in rural areas it was 21. The ratio between rural birth rates and urban birth rates had reached an all-time high of 149 per cent in 1928. Then the ratio declined rapidly through the 1930s and reached an all-time low of only 103 per cent in 1940. After World War II the ratio increased again, until in 1965 the rural rate was 130 per cent of the urban rate. Both the urban and the rural birth rates are now at the lowest that they ever have been, but the rural rate is considerably higher than the urban. This, together with a general exodus of young working people from the farms to the cities, is leaving a farm population consisting of old people and children. (Fig. 13–3) As more and more people become urbanized, birth rates of more people will decline.

Birth rates vary drastically from one

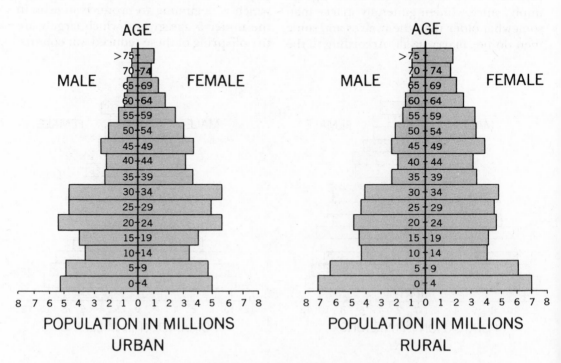

Figure 13–3   Age-sex distributions of urban and rural populations, U.S.S.R., January 15, 1959. Data from Karcz, Soviet and East European Agriculture, p. 299.

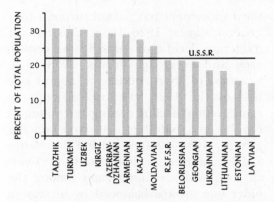

Figure 13–4   Under-ten age group as a percentage of total population, 1959, by republic. After French. By permission of St. Antony's College, Oxford.

part of the Soviet Union to another, not only between urban and rural areas, but also between nationality groups. (Figs. 13–4 and 13–5) In 1967 birth rates in the Soviet Union ranged from 12.0 per 1000 in the Central Region to 35.6 in the Turkmen Republic. Death rates ranged from 5.3 in Kaliningrad Oblast, where there

must have been a great influx of young people, to 10.5 in Estonia. Growth rates ranged from 3.2 in Latvia to 29.0 in the Turkmen Republic. The highest birth rates are in Central Asia and the Caucasus where the populations grew from 30 to 35 per cent between 1959 and 1967. The Kazakh Republic grew 35 per cent in this period, which was the highest for any entire republic. On the other hand, the Russian, Belorussian, Estonian, Latvian, and Ukrainian Republics grew only 8 or 9 per cent. (Table 13–2) Of course migrations entered into the picture somewhat, but by and large these growth rates reflect different rates in births. The areas of very high births are characterized by large proportions of the population in agriculture, low levels of employment in industry, lower education among women, younger ages at which women become physically fertile, younger ages at which women marry, and feudal attitudes regarding the role of women in the family. (Table 13–3) The European part of the

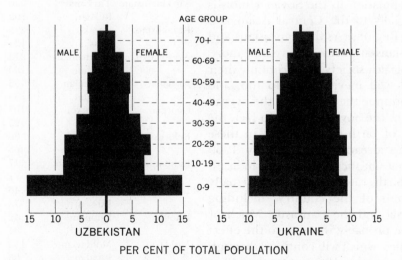

Figure 13–5   Age-sex distributions of the populations in the Ukraine and in Uzbekistan. Courtesy of Michael K. Roof and Population Bulletin. *The age-sex structure of the population varies from one part of the Soviet Union to another. Uzbekistan did not suffer the wartime losses that the Ukraine did and it has a much higher birth rate.*

Table 13–2   Population by Union Republics, January 1, 1967, and Per Cent Increase, 1959–1967

	Population	Per Cent of Increase
U.S.S.R.	234,396,000	12
R.S.F.S.R.	127,312,000	8
Ukraine	45,966,000	9
Belorussia	8,744,000	8
Uzbek	10,896,000	31
Kazakh	12,413,000	35
Georgia	4,611,000	14
Azerbaydzhan	4,802,000	30
Lithuania	3,026,000	11
Moldavia	3,425,000	18
Latvia	2,285,000	9
Kirgiz	2,749,000	33
Tadzhik	2,654,000	33
Armenia	2,253,000	27
Turkmen	1,966,000	29
Estonia	1,294,000	8

Source: Strana Sovetov za 50 let, p. 16.

country is now barely reproducing itself or may even have entered the stage where it is not reproducing itself. The expansion of total population in the Soviet Union is due essentially to the Central Asian and Caucasian Regions. As the Caucasians and Central Asians are drawn more and more into the socialist society and economy their birth rates will inevitably drop too, and this will continue the decline of the overall birth rate in the Soviet Union. In fact, the beginning of birth rate declines in these areas seems already evident. From 1960 to 1965 what statistics are available indicate that the birth rate declined in virtually every region of the country, including Central Asia and the Caucasus. Much of this decline probably was due to the effect of war babies, which will continue through the decade of the 1960s. On the other hand, data broken down by specific ages indicate that birth rates have been in the process of general decline since the beginning of rapid industrialization. This down-

ward movement has passed through four general stages: 1926–1938, a period of moderate decline of some 12 per cent in each and every age group; 1938–1954, a period of sharp decline to almost one half of the 1926 rate overall, with an even greater decline among the youngest (15–19) and oldest (45–49) reproducing groups; 1954–1960, a period of relative stability, showing a slight rise in the overall rate, with declining rates among the older age groups balanced by increasing rates among the younger age groups; 1960–present, a period of renewed decline

Table 13–3   Married Women per 1000 Women in Given Age Groups, by Nationality, by Republic

Republic	Nationality	16–19	20–24	25–29
R.S.F.S.R.	Russian	91	477	757
Ukraine	Ukrainian	96	468	727
Tadzhikistan	Tadzhik	384	869	939
	Russian	86	465	746
Kirgizia	Kirgiz	448	874	916
	Russian	106	530	790
Uzbekistan	Uzbek	323	839	930
	Russian	89	458	743
Turkmenistan	Turkmen	320	894	952
	Russian	102	493	769
Kazakhstan	Kazakh	275	776	904
	Russian	125	551	795
Azerbaidzhan	Azerbaidzhani	272	680	839
	Russian	100	480	761
Armenia	Armenian	166	566	800
	Russian	150	535	789
Georgia	Georgian	107	456	733
	Russian	125	469	700
Belorussia	Belorussian	60	425	710
	Russian	65	476	799
Lithuania	Lithuanian	47	365	654
	Russian	71	479	744
Latvia	Latvian	45	359	645
	Russian	73	476	764
Estonia	Estonian	42	367	668
	Russian	81	496	791
Moldavia	Moldavian	150	572	771
	Russian	93	520	784

Source: Robert A. French, "Recent Population Trends in the USSR," *St. Antony's Papers,* Number 19, *Soviet Affairs,* Number Four, Oxford University Press, 1966, p. 80.

of more than 20 per cent overall, with each age group participating to some degree. The present declining fertility could give rise to an absolute decline in the total labor force beginning sometime in the 1980s.

The Soviet government has always been intent upon obtaining the highest possible percentage of women in the work force. This, of course, has worked against any higher fertility rates. Recent data indicate that the birth rate among women working in the socialist sector of the economy is 14 per cent lower than among those not working regular jobs. Thus the Soviets have always been faced with the choice of maximizing the present labor force (using women of child-bearing age) or preparing for a future labor force (encouraging women to bear children). In the past a rather low proportion of children in the population has been a benefit to the rapid industrialization of the country, since not much of the national product had to be devoted to the raising of children. But now this is catching up with the Soviets, since they have not laid the basis for the future labor force.

If the continued reduced fertility becomes a serious bottleneck to continued expansion of industrial production, the Soviet leaders may have to resort to a reordering of economic priorities and shifts in resource allocations. Soviet demographers have nicely explained the secular decline of fertility rates as a natural effect, attained by family planning, resulting from the situation that under the Soviet regime the cultural levels of the population have been changing more rapidly than the material means made available to the population by economic development. Continuing this line of thought, one might say that the economy of the Soviet Union has now reached a level at which the Soviet leaders could afford to divert more resources to raise the material well-being of the population and thereby induce an increase in births. Experiences in other countries, however, do not point to any

direct correlation between material well-being and fertility. The present way of life in the Soviet Union has developed a prevalent attitude among city dwellers that any more than one or two children in a family will excessively curtail the activities of the parents, and this attitude will probably prevail regardless of standard of living.

The American image of the fertile Russian peasant woman with a large family is a misconception on our part—and her part too, considering the abortion rate in the country. The number of large families has been on the decline since the beginning of the five-year plans. In 1940 the annual number of fifth or higher births in families was over 200,000 in the Soviet Union, whereas in the United States it was 350,000. There are somewhat more large families in rural areas than in urban areas in the Soviet Union, but nationality differences exercise more control on family size than do urban-rural differences. In 1959, for the country as a whole, rural families averaged 3.9 persons, whereas urban families averaged 3.5. Among the fifteen largest nationality groups, Tadzhik families averaged 5.2 persons, whereas Estonian families averaged 3. (Table 13–4) The Kazakhs and Estonians show larger urban families than rural families. This probably attests to the poverty in rural areas of Estonia and to the seminomadic character of the rural Kazakhs who would have difficulty moving around large families. When interpreting statistics on family size, it must be remembered that many families in the Soviet Union involve more than one married couple, and therefore family size has a different connotation than it does in the United States. Statistics show a great paucity of two-person families in the Soviet Union. This could probably be explained by the fact that the housing shortage forces many young married couples to continue living with parents or in dormitories long after they are married.

As a result of the Soviet Union's male

Table 13-4   Average Family Size in the Soviet Union by Nationality and Urban-Rural Residence, January 15, 1959

	Average Family Size			Per Cent Distribution of the Total	Per Cent
Nationality	Total	Urban	Rural	Population	Urban
All nationalities	3.7	3.5	3.9	100.0	48
Tadzhik	5.2	5.1	5.2	0.7	21
Uzbek	5.0	4.9	5.0	2.9	22
Turkmen	5.0	4.7	5.1	0.5	25
Azerbaydzhan	4.8	4.6	4.9	1.4	35
Armenian	4.7	4.4	5.0	1.3	57
Kazakh	4.6	4.7	4.5	1.7	24
Kirgiz	4.5	4.3	4.6	0.7	11
Georgian	4.0	3.8	4.1	1.3	36
Moldavian	3.9	3.6	4.0	1.1	13
Belorussian	3.7	3.4	3.7	3.8	32
Russian	3.6	3.5	3.7	54.6	58
Lithuanian	3.6	3.4	3.6	1.1	35
Ukrainian	3.5	3.3	3.6	17.8	39
Latvian	3.1	3.0	3.2	0.7	48
Estonian	3.0	3.1	3.0	0.5	47

Source: *New Directions in the Soviet Economy*, p. 644.
Note: Because about 10 per cent of the population are members of nationality groups other than those listed, the distribution does not add to the total. Data on average family size for other nationalities are not reported.

deficit, 14.4 million Soviet families out of a total of 50.3 million, or 28.5 per cent, reported female heads in the 1959 census. This is about 3.5 times the ratio of American families headed by women. In the Soviet Union, however, heads of families are often listed according to income. If the wife makes more than the husband does, she is listed as head of the family even if her husband is living with her. Thus the concept of head of family is somewhat different in the Soviet Union than it is in the United States.

Nationalities

We have seen that the Soviet population is distorted in many ways. Women greatly outnumber men, the age distribution is abnormal, and birth rates vary widely from one region to another. Another very important unusual characteristic is the heterogeneous nature of its national makeup. Whereas most states have tended toward national unity, the Russian Empire followed a path in the opposite direction as its expansionism absorbed one peripheral territory after another which was occupied by peoples totally different from the Russians and varying greatly among themselves. Perhaps only India among the other countries of the world can come close to the national complexity of the Soviet Union, but for years it was under the homogenizing influence of an outside power and more recently it has been greatly simplified by its split with Pakistan. The Soviet Union probably stands alone in the number and distinctiveness of its national groups. The so-called nationality problem has been painfully recognized by the Bolsheviks, who have been forced to make many concessions to it in order to gain support for their Sovietization programs. Many fierce struggles ensued between the Red forces and the larger national minorities immediately following the Revolution. More subtle, less violent struggles have been engaged in ever since. The nationality question is not settled yet. The Soviet leaders still do not dare to ignore nationality loyalties in the establishment of political, economic, and educational institutions, though Marxian doctrine is completely opposed to such divisive loyalties. Today there seems to be no imminent revolt festering within any nationality group, but the diversity of nationalities still presents many problems because of unequal levels of cultural development, widely varying ways of life, and a multitude of languages.

The 1959 census identified 108 distinct nationality groups by name and listed "others" totaling 17,000 people. Since no information on nationalities has been supplied since the census, the following discussion represents conditions in 1959. (Table 13–5)

The many peoples of the Soviet Union stem from a long history of migrations and assimilations from all directions across the Eurasian Plain. From time immemorial wave after wave of nomadic peoples swept out of central and eastern Asia westward across the southern plain into eastern and central Europe, there to mingle with existent populations, often to lose their respective identities, and to impart new characteristics to the indigenous peoples. It is impossible to unravel fully the past of most of these groups, but strong physical and cultural differences still remain.

Slavs   The Slavic peoples emerged during the first few centuries of the Christian era in the region between the Carpathians and the Baltic. They suffered successive invasions from Turkic and Mongolian peoples from the east and fought a constant struggle against the Germans and Scandinavians in the northwest. In their flight northward before the Tatar invasion in the thirteenth century they came into contact with ancient settlers of northeastern Europe, the Finno-Ugrians. Thus as the Slavs emerged and became distinguished into separate groups—Great Russians, Ukrainians and Belorussians—they displayed admixtures of mingling groups—Tatars, Finns, Germans, and western Slavs—the Poles and Slavonic-Baltic peoples.

In the Soviet Union today the Russians make up about 55 per cent of the population and their percentage of the total population is slowly increasing. Together with the other two large Slavic groups, the Ukrainians and Belorussians, they make up 76 per cent of the total U.S.S.R. population. They dominate much of the European Plain and all of Siberia and are predominant in many of the cities and new farming areas of Kazakhstan and Middle Asia.

Turkic Groups   The Turkic groups are the next most populous in the Soviet Union and comprise a number of important and populous political units: the Tatar, Bashkir, and Chuvash A.S.S.R.'s in the Volga-Urals area, the Uzbek, Kazakh, Kirgiz, and Turkmen S.S.R.'s in Middle Asia, and the Azerbaydzhan S.S.R. in Transcaucasia. Lesser groups in the Caucasus also are of Turkic origin as are the Yakuts in eastern Siberia and the Khakass and Tuvinians in southern Siberia. All these Turkic groups originated in Central Asia and are strongly Moslem in religion. The Azerbaydzhanis migrated to the Caucasus around the southern end of the Caspian Sea and on the way absorbed many Persian influences into their culture.

Caucasians   The so-called Caucasians have a very old history of location in the Transcaucasian region. The Georgians,

Table 13–5   Ethnic Groups of the U.S.S.R.: Their Populations and Locations, 1959

1. Groups historically associated with European Russia (30)

Russians — 114,588,000

Russian S.F.S.R.	97,845,000	Georgian S.S.R.	438,000
Ukrainian S.S.R.	7,400,000	Moldavian S.S.R.	293,000
Kazakh S.S.R.	4,014,000	Tadzhik S.S.R.	263,000
Uzbek S.S.R.	1,101,000	Turkmen S.S.R.	263,000
Belorussian S.S.R.	729,000	Estonian S.S.R.	260,000
Kirgiz S.S.R.	624,000	Lithuanian S.S.R.	231,000
Latvian S.S.R.	556,000	Armenian S.S.R.	56,000
Azerbaydzhan S.S.R.	515,000		

Ukrainians — 36,981,000

Ukrainian S.S.R.	31,853,000	Georgian S.S.R.	52,000
Russian S.F.S.R.	3,377,000	Latvian S.S.R.	29,000
Kazakh S.S.R.	762,000	Tadzhik S.S.R.	27,000
Moldavian S.S.R.	421,000	Turkmen S.S.R.	21,000
Belorussian S.S.R.	150,000	Lithuanian S.S.R.	18,000
Kirgiz S.S.R.	137,000	Estonian S.S.R.	16,000
Uzbek S.S.R.	88,000		

Belorussians — 7,829,000

Belorussian S.S.R.	6,444,000	Latvian S.S.R.	61,000
Russian S.F.S.R.	845,000	Lithuanian S.S.R.	30,000
Ukrainian S.S.R.	291,000	Estonian S.S.R.	11,000
Kazakh S.S.R.	108,000		

Tatars — 4,969,000

Russian S.F.S.R.	4,077,000	Tadzhik S.S.R.	57,000
Uzbek S.S.R.	445,000	Kirgiz S.S.R.	56,000
Kazakh S.S.R.	192,000	Turkmen S.S.R.	30,000

Lithuanians — 2,326,000

Lithuanian S.S.R.	2,151,000	Latvian S.S.R.	32,000
Russian S.F.S.R.	109,000		

Jews — 2,268,000

Russian S.F.S.R.	875,000	Georgian S.S.R.	52,000
Ukrainian S.S.R.	840,000	Latvian S.S.R.	37,000
Belorussian S.S.R.	150,000	Lithuanian S.S.R.	25,000
Moldavian S.S.R.	95,000	Estonian S.S.R.	5,000
Uzbek S.S.R.	94,000		

Moldavians — 2,214,000

Moldavian S.S.R.	1,887,000	Russian S.F.S.R.	64,000
Ukrainian S.S.R.	239,000		

Germans — 1,619,000

Russian S.F.S.R.	820,000	Tadzhik S.S.R.	33,000
Kazakh S.S.R.	700,000	Uzbek S.S.R.	18,000
Kirgiz S.S.R.	40,000		

Chuvash — 1,470,000

Russian S.F.S.R.	1,436,000

Table 13–5   Ethnic Groups of the U.S.S.R.: Their Populations and Locations, 1959 (Continued)

Latvians — 1,400,000			
Latvian S.S.R.	1,298,000	Russian S.F.S.R.	75,000
Poles — 1,380,000			
Belorussian S.S.R.	539,000	Russian S.F.S.R.	118,000
Ukrainian S.S.R.	363,000	Latvian S.S.R.	60,000
Lithuanian S.S.R.	230,000	Kazakh S.S.R.	53,000
Mordovians — 1,285,000			
Russian S.F.S.R.	1,211,000		
Bashkirs — 983,000			
Russian S.F.S.R.	948,000		
Estonians — 969,000			
Estonian S.S.R.	873,000	Russian S.F.S.R.	79,000
Udmurts — 623,000			
Russian S.F.S.R.	613,000		
Mari — 504,000			
Russian S.F.S.R.	498,000		
Komi and Komi-Permyak — 431,000			
Russian S.F.S.R.	426,000		
Bulgarians — 324,000			
Ukrainian S.S.R.	219,000	Moldavian S.S.R.	62,000
Greeks — 310,000			
Ukrainian S.S.R.	104,000	Russian S.F.S.R.	47,000
Georgian S.S.R.	73,000		
Karelians — 167,000			
Russian S.F.S.R.	164,000		
Hungarians — 155,000			
Ukrainian S.S.R.	149,000		
Gypsies — 132,000			
Russian S.F.S.R.	72,000		
Gagauz — 124,000			
Moldavian S.S.R.	96,000		
Rumanians — 106,000			
Ukrainian S.S.R.	101,000		
Kalmyks — 106,000			
Russian S.F.S.R.	101,000		
Finns — 93,000			
Russian S.F.S.R.	72,000	Estonian S.S.R.	17,000

Veps — 16,000
Karaites — 5900
Saamy (Lapps) — 1800
Izhora — 1100

Table 13-5   *Ethnic Groups of the U.S.S.R.: Their Populations and Locations, 1959 (Continued)*

2. Groups historically associated with the Caucasus (27)

Azerbaydzhanis — 2,929,000

Azerbaydzhan S.S.R.	2,481,000	Armenian S.S.R.	108,000
Georgian S.S.R.	157,000	Russian S.F.S.R.	71,000

Armenians — 2,787,000

Armenian S.S.R.	1,552,000	Russian S.F.S.R.	256,000
Georgian S.S.R.	443,000	Turkmen S.S.R.	20,000
Azerbaydzhan S.S.R.	442,000		

Georgians — 2,650,000

Georgian S.S.R.	2,558,000	Russian S.F.S.R.	58,000

Dagestan ethnic groups — 945,000

Russian S.F.S.R.	795,000
Avars — 268,000	
Lezgins — 223,000	
Azerbaydzhan S.S.R.	98,000
Dargins — 158,000	
Kumyks — 135,000	
Lak — 64,000	
Nogai — 41,000	
Tabasaran — 35,000	
Agul — 8000	
Rutul — 7000	
Tsakhur — 6000	

Chechen — 418,000

Russian S.F.S.R.	261,000	Kirgiz S.S.R.	25,000
Rest mainly in Kazakh S.S.R.			

Osetians — 410,000

Russian S.F.S.R.	248,000	Georgian S.S.R.	141,000

Kabardians — 204,000

Russian S.F.S.R.	201,000

Ingush — 106,000

Russian S.F.S.R.	56,000

Karachay — 81,000

Russian S.F.S.R.	71,000

Adyge — 80,000

Russian S.F.S.R.	79,000

Abkhaz — 74,000

Georgian S.S.R.	71,000

Kurds — 59,000

Armenian S.S.R.	26,000	Georgian S.S.R.	16,000

Balkars — 42,000

Russian S.F.S.R.	35,000

Table 13–5   Ethnic Groups of the U.S.S.R.: Their Populations and Locations,
1959 (Continued)

Cherkess—30,000
Aissor—22,000
Abaza—20,000
Tats—11,000
Udins—3700

3. Groups historically associated with Siberia and the Far East (27)

Koreans—314,000			
Uzbek S.S.R.	139,000	Russian S.F.S.R.	91,000
Kazakh S.S.R.	74,000		
Buryats—253,000			
Russian S.F.S.R.	252,000		
Yakuts—236,000			
Russian S.F.S.R.	235,000		
Tuvinians—100,000			
Russian S.F.S.R.	100,000		
Khakass—57,000			
Russian S.F.S.R.	56,000		

Altaians (Oirots)—45,000
   All in Russian S.F.S.R.

Nentsy (Samoyeds)—25,000	Nivkhi (Gilyaks)—4000
Evenki (Tungus)—24,000	Ulchi—2000
Khanty (Ostyaks)—19,000	Udege (Ude)—1400
Shors—15,000	Eskimos—1100
Chukchi—12,000	Itelmen (Kamchadals)—1100
Eveny (Lamuts)—9000	Ket (Yenisey Ostyaks)—1000
Nanai (Golds)—8000	Orochi—800
Koryaks—6300	Nganasan (Tavghi)—700
Mansi (Voguls)—6000	Tofalar—600
Selkups (Ostyak-Samoyeds)—4000	Yukagir—400
	Aleuts—400

4. Groups historically associated with Middle Asia (8)

Uzbeks—6,004,000			
Uzbek S.S.R.	5,026,000	Kazakh S.S.R.	137,000
Tadzhik S.S.R.	454,000	Turkmen S.S.R.	125,000
Kirgiz S.S.R.	219,000		
Kazakhs—3,581,000			
Kazakh S.S.R.	2,755,000	Turkmen S.S.R.	70,000
Russian S.F.S.R.	383,000	Kirgiz S.S.R.	20,000
Uzbek S.S.R.	335,000	Tadzhik S.S.R.	13,000
Tadzhiks—1,397,000			
Tadzhik S.S.R.	1,051,000	Kirgiz S.S.R.	15,000
Uzbek S.S.R.	312,000		

Table 13–5   Ethnic Groups of the U.S.S.R.: Their Populations and Locations, 1959 (Continued)

Turkmen—1,004,000

Turkmen S.S.R.	924,000	Uzbek	57,000

Kirgiz—974,000

Kirgiz S.S.R.	837,000	Tadzhik S.S.R.	26,000
Uzbek S.S.R.	92,000		

Kara-Kalpaks—173,000

Uzbek S.S.R.	168,000

Uygurs—95,000

Kazakh S.S.R.	60,000	Kirgiz S.S.R.	14,000

Dungans (Chinese Moslems)—21,000

Kazakh S.S.R.	10,000

5. Minor groups historically associated with foreign countries (16)

Turks—35,000	Yugoslavs—5000
Chinese—26,000	Spaniards—2400
Czechs—25,000	Afghans—1900
Iranians—21,000	Mongols—1800
Slovaks—14,700	Italians—1200
Arabs—8000	French—1000
Beluchi—7800	Japanese—1000
Albanians—5000	Vietnamese—800

Source: Soviet Geography: Review and Translation, March 1960, pp. 71–75 and September 1961, pp. 69–70.
Note: Population totals for republics vary somewhat from subsequent figures in *Narodnoe khozyaystvo.*

or Gruzians, and Armenians are the most numerous, but there are many small groups in isolated valleys among the mountains. The Armenians apparently are related to the old Tadzhik population of Iran. They have occupied the volcanic plateau straddling the border between the Soviet Union, Turkey, and Iran for more than 2000 years. During the period 1926 to 1959 some 100,000 Armenians immigrated into the U.S.S.R. from France, England, and the United States in the hope of at last establishing a political state in their national territory. Only about half of the Armenians in the Soviet Union today are located within the territorial limits of the republic bearing their name; other major concentrations are in the neighbor-

Figure 13–6   Ethnic Groups of the U.S.S.R. Adapted from Atlas selskogo khozyaystva SSSR. *The central locations of major nationalities other than Russians are shown on the map by numbers as follows:*
2. Ukrainians, 3. Belorussians, 4. Moldavians, 5. Lithuanians, 6. Latvians, 7. Estonians, 8. Karelians, 9. Komi, 10. Udmurts, 11. Mari, 12. Mordovians, 13. Chuvash, 14. Tatars, 15. Bashkirs, 16. Kalmyks, 17. Karachay, 18. Dagestani Groups, 19. Adyge, 20. Balkars, 21. Kabardinians, 22. Chechen-Ingush, 23. Osetians, 24. Georgians, 25. Adzhars, 26. Abkhaz, 27. Armenians, 28. Azerbaydzhanis, 29. Tadzhiks, 30. Turkmen, 31. Uzbeks, 32. Karakalpaks, 33. Kazakhs, 34. Kirgiz, 35. Tuvinians, 36. Buryats, 37. Yakuts, 38. Jews.

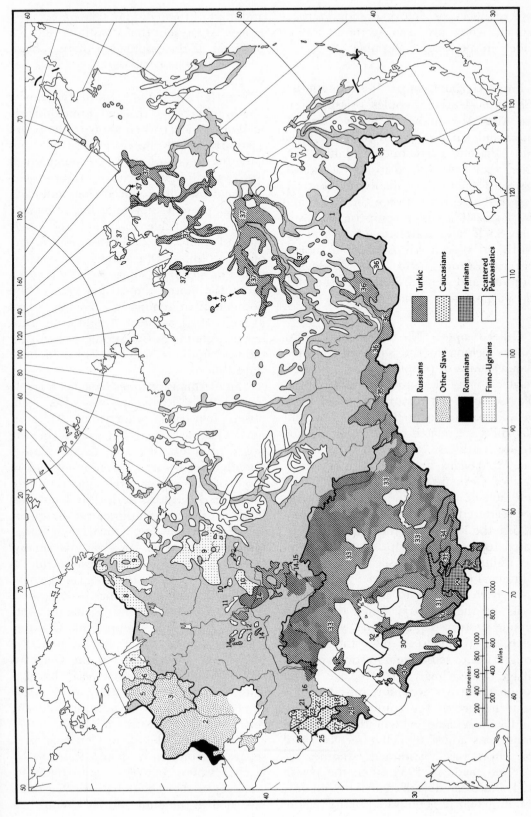

Figure 13–6   See opposite page for descriptive legend.

ing republics of Georgia and Azerbay-dzhan. They are also scattered rather widely in the Russian Republic.

Finno-Ugrian Groups It is thought that the Finno-Ugrian peoples originated in the Altay Mountains of southwestern Siberia and early migrated to Scandinavia and adjacent parts of the Baltic area. Later they were forced to migrate south-eastward again where many of them settled in the region between the Volga and the Urals. They now comprise the Estonian S.S.R. and Karelian A.S.S.R. in the northwest, the Komi A.S.S.R. in northeastern Europe, and the Mordovian, Udmurt, and Mari A.S.S.R.'s in the middle Volga-Ural region.

Other Peoples The Latvians and Lithuanians belong to the so-called Slavonic-Baltic groups of peoples. They are closely related to the Slavs to the south but display some of the features of other Baltic peoples to the north. In Middle Asia the Tadzhiks are related to the Iranians. And in the southwestern part of the country, the Moldavians are of Rumanian stock.

Jews, Germans, and Poles exist in considerable numbers in the Soviet Union, but are scattered throughout various regions. Before the Revolution the Jews were relegated to the so-called pale of settlement in Lithuania, Belorussia, and western Ukraine, but under the Soviet regime they have been allowed to migrate to other parts of the country. Since the Soviet regime destroyed petty trade, which had been the livelihood of Jews, the solution sought was to settle them in compact rural villages. Accordingly, in 1926, five Jewish national districts were organized in the western part of the country, but it immediately became evident that the Jews would not adjust to being farmers, and the effort was abandoned. Another effort was made in 1934 when the Jewish A.O. was created in the Far East, but only about 50,000 Jews migrated to the region,

and most of them did not take up farming either. At present they constitute only 8.8 per cent of the population of the oblast, whereas Russians account for 78.2 per cent.

The Jewish population in the Soviet Union might have reached 5 million early in World War II when many of them fled eastward before the German armies, but later the policy of total extermination in the German-held territory of the Soviet Union drastically reduced their numbers until at present they total less than half that figure. (Table 13–6 and Fig. 13–7) Most of them are still in the western part of the country, where they are concentrated in the larger cities. In Kiev they account for more than 10 per cent of the population, in Leningrad 5.6 per cent, and in Moscow 1.1 per cent. A significant number migrated to Soviet Middle Asia during the war, however, and many of them have stayed there.

The Germans at times have been freely invited into Russia to serve as technicians in various branches of the economy. This was particularly true during the reign of Catherine the Great. Consequently they became rather numerous in some of the larger cities and they also established wealthy agricultural colonies in some of the better agricultural regions. In general they maintained their racial identities and their ties with Germany. Before World War II the greatest concentration was in the Middle Volga area where a Volga German A.S.S.R. had been created. They also existed in considerable numbers in the Black Sea Steppes of Ukraine. During the war the Volga German Republic was abrogated, and the Germans were moved eastward into Siberia, Kazakhstan, and Middle Asia. Many of the Black Sea Germans evacuated westward with the retreating German army in 1943.

The census identified Germans as a separate group only in the Russian Republic, where 820,000 were reported. This represents about half the Germans recorded in the entire Soviet Union. It is

Table 13–6   Ethnic Compositions of Union Republics, 1959

	Number of People	Per Cent of Total		Number of People	Per Cent of Total
R.S.F.S.R.	117,534,000	100.0	Belorussia S.S.R.	8,055,000	100.0
Russian	97,864,000	83.3	Belorussian	6,532,000	81.1
Tatar	4,075,000	3.5	Russian	659,000	8.2
Ukrainian	3,359,000	2.9	Pole	539,000	6.7
Chuvash	1,436,000	1.2	Jew	150,000	1.9
Mordovian	1,211,000	1.0	Ukrainian	133,000	1.7
Bashkir	954,000	0.8			
Jew	875,000	0.7	Uzbek S.S.R.	8,106,000	100.0
Belorussian	844,000	0.7	Uzbek	5,038,000	62.2
German	820,000	0.7	Russian	1,091,000	13.5
Dagestan Peoples	797,000	0.7	Tatar	445,000	5.5
Udmurt	616,000	0.5	Kazakh	335,000	4.1
Mari	498,000	0.4	Tadzhik	311,000	3.8
Komi and Komi-			Kara-Kalpak	168,000	2.1
Permyak	426,000	0.36	Korean	138,000	1.7
Kazakh	382,000	0.3	Jew	94,000	1.2
Armenian	256,000	0.2	Kirgiz	93,000	1.1
Buryat	252,000	0.2	Ukrainian	88,000	1.1
Osetian	248,000	0.2	Turkmen	55,000	0.7
Yakut	236,000	0.2			
Kabardinian	201,000	0.2	Kazakh S.S.R.	9,310,000	100.0
Karelian	164,000	0.1	Kazakh	2,795,000	30.0
Peoples of the North	126,000	0.1	Russian	3,974,000	42.7
Pole	118,000	0.1	Ukrainian	762,000	8.2
Kalmyk	101,000	0.09	Tatar	192,000	2.1
Tuvinian	100,000	0.08	Uzbek	137,000	1.5
Korean	91,000	0.08	Belorussian	107,000	1.2
Adyge	79,000	0.07	Korean	74,000	0.8
Gypsy	72,000	0.06	Uygur	60,000	0.6
Finn	72,000	0.06	Pole	53,000	0.6
Azerbaydzhanian	71,000	0.06	Dungan	10,000	0.1
Moldavian	62,000	0.05			
Georgian	58,000	0.05	Georgia S.S.R.	4,044,000	100.0
Khakass	56,000	0.05	Georgian	2,601,000	64.3
Greek	47,000	0.04	Armenian	443,000	11.0
Altay	45,000	0.04	Russian	408,000	10.1
			Azerbaydzhanian	154,000	3.8
			Osetian	141,000	3.5
Ukraine S.S.R.	41,869,000	100.0	Greek	73,000	1.8
Ukrainian	32,158,000	76.8	Abkhazian	63,000	1.6
Russian	7,091,000	16.9	Ukrainian	52,000	1.3
Jew	840,000	2.0	Jew	52,000	1.3
Pole	363,000	0.9	Kurd	16,000	0.4
Belorussian	291,000	0.7			
Moldavian	242,000	0.6	Azerbaydzhan S.S.R.	3,698,000	100.0
Bulgarian	219,000	0.5	Azerbaydzhanian	2,494,000	67.5
Hungarian	149,000	0.4	Russian	501,000	13.6
Greek	104,000	0.2	Armenian	442,000	12.0
Rumanian	101,000	0.2	Lezghian	98,000	2.7

Table 13–6   Ethnic Compositions of Union Republics, 1959 (Continued)

	Number of People	Per Cent of Total		Number of People	Per Cent of Total
Lithuania S.S.R.	2,711,000	100.0	Tadzhik S.S.R.	1,980,000	100.0
Lithuanian	2,151,000	79.3	Tadzhik	1,051,000	53.1
Russian	231,000	8.5	Uzbek	454,000	23.0
Pole	230,000	8.5	Russian	263,000	13.3
Belorussian	30,000	1.1	Tatar	57,000	2.9
Jew	25,000	0.9	Ukrainian	27,000	1.4
Ukrainian	18,000	0.7	Kirgiz	26,000	1.3
			Kazakh	13,000	0.6
Moldavia S.S.R.	2,885,000	100.0			
Moldavian	1,887,000	65.4	Armenia S.S.R.	1,763,000	100.0
Ukrainian	421,000	14.6	Armenian	1,552,000	88.0
Russian	293,000	10.2	Azerbaydzhanian	108,000	6.1
Gagauz	96,000	3.3	Russian	56,000	3.2
Jew	95,000	3.3	Kurd	26,000	1.5
Bulgarian	62,000	2.1			
			Turkmen S.S.R.	1,516,000	100.0
Latvia S.S.R.	2,093,000	100.0	Turkmen	924,000	60.9
Latvian	1,298,000	62.0	Russian	263,000	17.3
Russian	556,000	26.6	Uzbek	125,000	8.3
Belorussian	62,000	2.9	Kazakh	70,000	4.6
Pole	60,000	2.9	Tatar	30,000	2.0
Jew	37,000	1.7	Ukrainian	21,000	1.4
Lithuanian	32,000	1.5	Armenian	20,000	1.3
Ukrainian	29,000	1.4			
			Estonia S.S.R.	1,197,000	100.0
Kirgiz S.S.R.	2,066,000	100.0	Estonian	893,000	74.6
Kirgiz	837,000	40.5	Russian	240,000	20.1
Russian	624,000	30.2	Finn	17,000	1.4
Uzbek	219,000	10.6	Ukrainian	16,000	1.3
Ukrainian	137,000	6.6	Belorussian	11,000	0.9
Tatar	56,000	2.7	Jew	5,000	0.5
Kazakh	20,000	1.0			
Tadzhik	15,000	0.7			
Uygur	14,000	0.7			

Source: Narodnoe khozyaystvo SSSR v 1960 godu, pp. 17–20.

believed that most of the remaining Germans are in Kazakhstan, because the census did not identify the nationality of 967,000 residents of that republic, which represents more than 10 per cent of its total population. No other group as large was left unidentified in the census. In the thirteen republics outside the R.S.F.S.R. and Kazakhstan, a total of only 466,000 people were not identified by nationality. Some of these other republics have significantly high unidentified numbers, which might signify the presence of Germans, but these numbers are small relative to those in Kazakhstan. A map published in 1962 by the Soviets showing population by native languages shows scattered pockets of German-speaking people along the R.S.F.S.R.-Kazakh border in Kuybyshev, Aktyubinsk, Tselino-

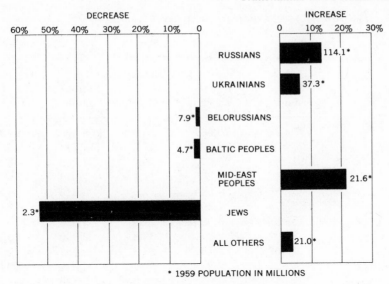

DECREASE

60% 50% 40% 30% 20% 10% 0

INCREASE

0 10% 20% 30%

RUSSIANS   114.1*

UKRAINIANS   37.3*

7.9* BELORUSSIANS

4.7* BALTIC PEOPLES

MID-EAST
PEOPLES   21.6*

2.3* JEWS

ALL OTHERS   21.0*

* 1959 POPULATION IN MILLIONS

*Figure 13–7   Changes in populations of leading nationality groups, 1939–1959.
Courtesy of Michael K. Roof and* Population Bulletin.

grad, Karaganda, Omsk, and Novosibirsk Oblasts. Other pockets appear in the Kirgiz and Uzbek Republics and in the northern Caucasus. The 1959 census cited German as the native language for 1.2 million people.

Many Poles have always been involved in one way or another with the Russian Empire, and subsequently with the Soviet Union. Since the western territories of the Soviet Union changed hands many times among Poland, Russia, and other powers, it is only natural to expect that a great mixture of peoples exist in these areas. Although mass deportations took place after exchange of territories resulting from World War II, the operation was not complete, and Poles are still quite numerous in Belorussia, western Ukraine, and Lithuania. Together with Latvia and the western portions of the Russian Republic, these regions account for almost all the Poles in the Soviet Union.

In Siberia and the Far East exist the Mongol and Paleo-Asiatic groups. The largest Mongol group is in the Buryat A.S.S.R. Some of the old Asiatic groups apparently are related to the American

Indians and the Eskimos. Their origins go so far back that they are indiscernible. Their total numbers are relatively few, and their individuals are scattered widely over remote expanses of sparsely settled territory which often are organized as national okrugs, the most primitive category of the nationality-based political units.

Nationalities and Political Regions

Many of the political administrative regions of the country are based on nationality groups. This is true of the major divisions, the S.S.R.'s, and also the A.S.S.R.'s, the A.O.'s, and the N.O.'s. Political identity was not handed out equitably to all nationality groups, however, and frequently political identity was given where it was not warranted because of expected propaganda values. In certain instances, even the constitution of the U.S.S.R. was violated, whenever the communist leaders found it expedient to do so. According to the constitution, the nationality-based political region can be formed only in an area where the majority of the people are

Table 13–7 Nationality Numbers, 1926, 1939, and 1959

Nationality	1926, in Thousands	1939, in Thousands	Per Cent of Change 1926–1939	1959, in Thousands	Per Cent of Change 1939–1959	Per Cent of Change 1926–1959
All	147,028	170,467	15.9	208,827	22.4	42.0
Russian	77,791	99,020	27.3	114,114	15.2	46.7
Ukrainian	31,195	28,070	−10.0	37,253	33.1	19.5
Belorussian	4,739	5,267	11.2	7,913	50.2	67.2
Uzbek	3,955	4,844	22.5	6,015	24.2	52.2
Tatar [a]	3,478	4,300	23.7	4,968	15.2	42.8
Kazakh	3,968	3,099	−21.9	3,622	16.8	−8.7
Azerbaydzhan	1,707	2,275	33.3	2,940	29.2	72.4
Armenian	1,568	2,152	37.3	2,787	29.7	77.7
Georgian	1,821	2,249	23.5	2,692	19.5	47.8
Lithuanian	43	32	−24.3	2,326	−	−
Jew	2,672	3,020	13.0	2,268	−24.9	−15.1
Moldavian	279	260	−6.8	2,214	−	−
German	1,247	1,424	14.2	1,620	13.7	29.8
Chuvash	1,117	1,368	22.4	1,470	7.3	31.5
Latvian	154	127	−17.7	1,400	−	−
Tadzhik	981	1,229	25.3	1,397	13.7	42.3
Pole	792	627	−20.9	1,380	120.0	74.2
Mordovian	1,340	1,451	8.3	1,285	−11.4	−4.1
Turkmen	764	812	6.3	1,002	23.2	31.2
Bashkir	741	843	13.7	989	17.2	33.4
Estonian	156	142	−8.7	989	−	−
Kirgiz	763	884	15.9	969	9.6	27.1
Dagestani Peoples	669	857	28.1	944	10.2	41.1
Udmurt	504	606	20.1	625	3.1	24.0
Mari	428	481	12.4	504	4.8	17.8
Komi	376	409	8.7	431	5.2	14.6
Chechen	319	408	28.0	419	2.8	31.3
Osetian	272	355	30.2	413	16.4	52.0
Bulgarian	114	113	−0.5	324	186.0	184.0
Korean	172	180	4.9	314	74.2	82.2
Greek	260	286	10.1	309	8.1	18.9
Buryat				253		
Yakut				237		
Kabardino	140	164	17.3	204	24.2	45.7
Karakalpak	146	186	27.0	173	−7.0	18.4
Karelian	248	253	1.8	167	−34.0	−32.6
Hungarian				155		
Gypsies				132		
Peoples of the North				127		
Gagauz				124		
Rumanian				106		
Kalmyk	129	129	3.9	106	−20.8	−17.8
Ingush	74	92	24.3	106	15.3	43.3
Tuvinian				100		
Uighur	43			95		

Table 13–7   Nationality Numbers, 1926, 1939, and 1959 (Continued)

Nationality	1926, in Thousands	1939, in Thousands	Per Cent of Change 1926–1939	1959, in Thousands	Per Cent of Change 1939–1959	Per Cent of Change 1926–1959
Finn	139	143	3.1	93	−35.0	−33.3
Karachay	55	76	37.4	81	6.7	47.2
Adygey	65 *b*	88 *b*	34.8	80	−	−
Abkhaz	57	59	3.5	65	10.2	14.1
Kurd	55	46	−16.1	59	28.2	14.1
Khakas	46	53	15.3	57	7.4	23.8
Altay (Oyrot)	39	48	22.2	45	−6.2	15.3
Balkar	33	43	28.1	42	−2.3	27.3
Turk				35		
Cherkess				30		
Chinese	92 *c*	30	−67.8	26	−13.3	−71.8
Czech	31 *d*	27 *d*	−12.2	25	−	−
Dungan				22		
Assyrian		20		22		
Iranian	44	39	−11.2	21	−46.1	−52.1

Sources: Itogi vsesoyuznoy perepisi naseleniya 1959 goda, SSSR, 1962, pp. 184–188, and Frank Lorimer, *The Population of the Soviet Union,* pp. 138–139.

a 1926 and 1939 figures include other groups in Siberia and Middle Asia.
b Apparently includes Cherkess.
c Includes 81,783 aliens.
d Includes Slovaks.
Dash indicates that comparison is meaningless because of exchanges of territory or inconsistent definitions of groups.

of the titular nationality group. This has not always been the case, even at the time of the initiation of these political units, and it has become even less so in subsequent years with the rapid spread of Russians throughout the country. (Fig. 13–8) Russians are now the principal group in all five of the autonomous oblasts in the R.S.F.S.R. and in all but one of the ten national okrugs. (Table 13–8) In 1959 the Komi-Permyaks were the only people in a national okrug who comprised a majority of the population, and they comprised only 58 per cent. In 1959 Russians outnumbered the titular group in ten of the twenty A.S.S.R.'s. (Table 13–9) In the Abkhaz A.S.S.R., the Abkhazians made up only 15 per cent of the population. Together with the Russians they only totaled 36 per cent. Obviously, a third group was very important. This was the Georgians, within whose republic the Abkhaz A.S.S.R. is situated. The Karelians now make up only 13 per cent of the total population of the Karelian A.S.S.R. Russians make up 63 per cent of the population of the region. For a short time during and after World War II this region was even constituted as the sixteenth union republic. Obviously this was a propagandistic effort to entice the Finns across the border. The republic never had the requisite minimum of 1 million people nor did it come anywhere near to having a majority of the titular group. In 1956, without any fanfare at all, it was simply announced that the Karelo-Finnish Republic was abrogated

Table 13–8   Russians as a Percentage of Total Populations in S.S.R.'s, A.S.S.R.'s, A.O.'s, N.O.'s, and Capitals of S.S.R.'s, 1926 and 1959

	1926			1959			
	Total Population in Thousands	Russians in Thousands	Per Cent Russians	Total Population in Thousands	Russians in Thousands	Per Cent Russians	Increase in Per Cent Russians
U.S.S.R.	147,028	77,791	53	208,827	114,114	54.6	1.6
R.S.F.S.R.	93,395 [a]		78 [a]	117,534	97,864	83.3	5.3
Bashkir A.S.S.R.	2,666		40	3,342	1,418	42.4	2.4
Buryat A.S.S.R.	491		53	673	503	74.6	21.6
Dagestan A.S.S.R.	788		12	1,062	214	20.1	8.1
Kabardino-Balkar A.S.S.R.	204		8	420	163	38.7	30.7
Kalmyk A.S.S.R.	142		11	185	103	55.9	44.9
Karelian A.S.S.R.	270		58	651	413	63.4	5.4
Komi A.S.S.R.	207		7	806	390	48.4	41.4
Mari A.S.S.R.	482		44	648	310	47.8	3.8
Mordovian A.S.S.R.				1,000	591	59.1	
North Osetian A.S.S.R.	152		.7	451	179	39.6	32.6
Tatar A.S.S.R.	2,594		43	2,850	1,252	43.9	0.9
Tuvinian A.S.S.R.				172	69	40.1	
Udmurt A.S.S.R.	756		43	1,337	759	56.8	13.8
Chechen-Ingush A.S.S.R.	385		3	710	348	49.0	46.0
Chuvash A.S.S.R.	894		20	1,098	264	24.0	4.0
Yakut A.S.S.R.	289		10	487	215	44.2	34.2
Adyge A.O.	113		26	285	200	70.4	48.4
Gorno-Altay A.O.	100		52	157	109	69.8	17.8
Jewish A.O.				163	127	78.2	
Karachay-Cherkess A.O.	102		3	278	142	51.0	48.0
Khakass A.O.	89		47	411	314	76.5	29.5
Aga Buryat N.O.				49	24	48.6	
Komi-Permyak N.O.				217	71	32.9	
Koryak N.O.				28	17	60.6	
Nenets N.O.				46	31	68.8	
Taymyr N.O.				33	22	65.3	
Ust-Orda Buryat N.O.				133	75	56.4	
Khanti-Mansi N.O.				124	90	72.5	
Chukotsk N.O.				47	28	60.7	
Evenki N.O.				10	6	57.9	
Yamal-Nenets N.O.				62	28	44.6	
Ukraine S.S.R.	29,018 [b]		9 [b]	41,869	7,091	16.9	7.9
Belorussia S.S.R.	4,983		8	8,055	659	8.2	0.2
Uzbek S.S.R.	4,446		6	8,106	1,091	13.5	7.5
Kara-Kalpak A.S.S.R.	305		2	510	23	4.5	2.5
Kazakh S.S.R.	6,503		20	9,310	3,974	42.7	22.7
Georgian S.S.R.	2,666		4	4,044	408	10.1	6.1
Abkhaz A.S.S.R.	201		6	405	87	21.4	15.4
Adzhar A.S.S.R.	132		8	245	33	13.4	5.4
South Osetian A.O.	87		<1	97	2	2.5	
Azerbaydzhan S.S.R.	2,315		10	3,698	501	13.6	3.6
Nakhichevan A.S.S.R.	105		2	141	3	2.2	0.2
Nagorno-Karabakh A.O.	125		<1	130	2	1.4	
Lithuania S.S.R.				2,711	231	8.5	
Moldavia S.S.R.	572 [c]		9 [c]	2,884	293	10.2	1.2

Table 13–8   Russians as a Percentage of Total Populations in S.S.R.'s, A.S.S.R.'s, A.O.'s, N.O.'s, and Capitals of S.S.R.'s, 1926 and 1959 (Continued)

	1926			1959			
	Total Population in Thousands	Russians in Thousands	Per Cent Russians	Total Population in Thousands	Russians in Thousands	Per Cent Russians	Increase in Per Cent Russians
Latvia S.S.R.				2,093	556	26.6	
Kirgiz S.S.R.	993		12	2,066	624	30.2	18.2
Tadzhik S.S.R.	827		<1	1,980	263	13.3	13
Gorno-Badakhshan A.O.				73	1	1.9	
Armenia S.S.R.	880		2	1,763	56	3.2	1.2
Turkmen S.S.R.	1,001		8	1,516	263	17.3	9.3
Estonia S.S.R.				1,197	240	20.1	
S.S.R. Capitals							
Moscow (R.S.F.S.R.)				5,046		86.6	
Kiev (Ukraine)				1,104		23.0	
Alma-Ata (Kazakh)				456		73.1	
Tashkent (Uzbek)				912		43.9	
Minsk (Belorussia)				509		22.8	
Frunze (Kirgiz)				220		68.6	
Riga (Latvia)				605		39.5	
Baku (Azerbaydzhan)				971		34.7	
Tbilisi (Georgia)				695		18.1	
Kishinev (Moldavia)				216		32.2	
Ashkhabad (Turkmen)				170		50.3	
Dushanbe (Tadzhik)				224		47.7	
Tallin (Estonia)				282		32.2	
Vilnius (Lithuania)				236		29.4	
Yerevan (Armenia)				509		4.4	

Sources: Itogi vsesoyuznoy perepisi naseleniya 1959 goda, SSSR, 1962, pp. 202–208; Frank Lorimer, *The Population of the Soviet Union,* pp. 63–64; and *New Directions in the Soviet Economy,* p. 633. Political units as of 1959.
[a] Excluding Kazakh and Kirgiz A.S.S.R.'s.
[b] 1926 boundaries.
[c] Moldavian A.S.S.R. of 1926.

and that the territory would be reconstituted as the Karelian A.S.S.R. within the R.S.F.S.R. With the stroke of a pen the Soviets committed an act commensurate to the abolishment of one of the states in the United States of America. There are other cases at the union republic level in which the constitution is not adhered to any more. Russians outnumber the Kazakhs in the Kazakh Republic, and the Kirgiz represent only a plurality, not a majority, in their republic.

Some sizable nationality groups such as the Tatars, who number 5 million members, were not given union republic status because they were not on the peripheries of the country. According to the constitution, any union republic has the right to secede from the U.S.S.R. at any time that it desires. Although events have proven the constitution to be a worthless piece of paper, when it suits their convenience the Soviets use the constitution to deny certain things to certain groups of people. In this case it suited the purpose of the central government to use the constitution to

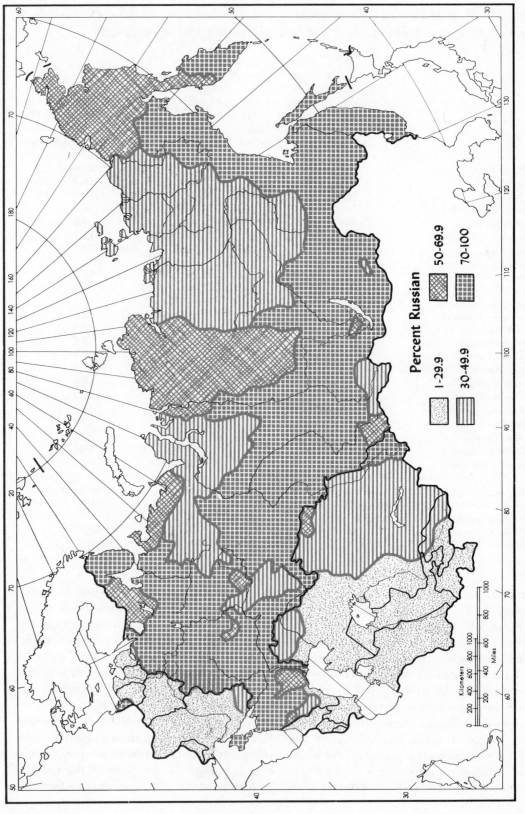

Figure 13–8   Russians as a percentage of total population, by administrative areas, as of January 15, 1959. From James W. Brackett and John W. DePauw in New Directions in the Soviet Economy, p. 635

Percent Russian

1-29.9

30-49.9

50-69.9

70-100

Table 13–9   Russians and Titular Groups in the A.S.S.R.'s, 1926 and 1959

under 1 million people, were accorded union republic status.

A.S.S.R.	Per Cent Russian		Per Cent Titular Groups	
	1926	1959	1926	1959
Abkhaz	6	21	28	15
Adzhar	8	13	54	73
Bashkir	40	42	23	22
Buryat	53	75	44	20
Chechen-Ingush	4	49	71	41
Chuvash	20	24	75	70
Crimean Tatar	42	–	25	–
Dagestan	12	20	65	69
Kabardino-Balkar	8	39	76	53
Kalmyk	11	56	76	35
Karakalpak	2	5	38	31
Karelian	58	63	37	13
Komi	7	48	92	30
Mari	44	48	51	43
Moldavian	9	–	30	–
Mordovian	56	59	37	36
Nakhichevan	2	2	84	90
North Osetian	7	40	84	48
Tatar	43	44	45	47
Tuvinian	–	40	–	57
Udmurt	43	57	52	36
Volga German	20	–	66	–
Yakut	10	44	82	46

Source: Thomas S. Fedor, *The Future Status of the Autonomous Soviet Socialist Republics in the Soviet Federative System,* Master's Thesis, University of Wisconsin—Milwaukee, August 1967, pp. 64a and 66a.

point out that, because of its right to secede, it was only obvious that a union republic would have to lie on the periphery of the U.S.S.R. Therefore the Tatars were accorded only the status of A.S.S.R. So much gerrymandering took place during the establishment of the boundaries, however, that many more Tatars were left outside the A.S.S.R. than were included in it. This was also true of the Mordovians. On the other hand, the Kirgiz, who number

Russification

As can be seen in Table 13–9, between 1926 and 1959 the percentage of Russians in the total population increased in every single A.S.S.R. in the country, whereas the percentage represented by the titular group decreased in fifteen of the twenty A.S.S.R.'s that still existed in 1959. Inevitably Russification goes on incessantly throughout the country. At times this has been actively promoted by the Soviet government. At other times the government has taken a hands-off policy when it appeared that open revolt would flare up. But all the economic and social institutions promote Russification, whether anyone wants them to or not. The process takes place not only by Russians moving into all the national minority areas, but also by the conversion of individuals to the Russian way of life. One of the most potent indicators of Russification of individuals is the consideration of native language. The 1959 census reported for each nationality group more individuals in the group than those who actually spoke the native language. In each case most of the remainder reported Russian as their native language. (Table 13–10) For instance, 12.2 per cent of the Ukrainians reported Russian as their native language and 15.7 per cent of the Belorussians reported Russian as their native language. Even greater percentages were reported by those people who are most scattered and who do not have political identity within the country: the Germans, Poles, and Jews; 24.2 per cent of the Germans reported Russian as their native language, 14.7 per cent of the Poles, and 76.4 per cent of the Jews. Thus it is obvious that among individuals the Jews have become the most Russified. Since in most cases they have not been allowed to practice their own ways of life, the Jews

Table 13–10   Major Nationality Groups and Their Native Languages, 1926 and 1959, in Per Cent of Total, Listed in Order of Total Numbers in 1959

| | 1926, Per Cent Speaking Their Own Language | 1959, Per Cent Speaking | | Change in Per Cent Speaking Own Language 1926–1959 |
		Their Own Language	Russian	
All		94.4	4.9	
Russian	99.7	99.9	99.9	0.2
Ukrainian	87.1	87.8	12.2	0.7
Belorussian	71.9	84.2	15.7	12.3
Uzbek	99.1	98.4	0.5	−0.7
Tatar	98.9	92.0	7.0	−6.9
Kazakh	99.6	98.4	1.2	−1.2
Azerbaydzhan	93.8	97.6	1.2	3.8
Armenian	92.4	89.8	8.3	−2.6
Georgian	96.5	98.7	1.3	2.2
Lithuanian	46.9	98.7	0.7	41.8
Jew	71.9	21.5	76.4	−50.4
Moldavian	92.3	95.3	3.6	3.0
German	94.9	75.0	24.3	−19.9
Chuvash	98.7	90.8	9.0	−7.9
Latvian	78.3	95.0	4.6	16.7
Tadzhik	98.3	98.2	0.6	−0.1
Pole	42.9	45.2	14.7	2.3
Mordovian	94.0	78.1	21.8	−15.9
Turkmen	97.3	98.8	0.7	1.5
Bashkir	53.8	61.9	2.6	8.1
Estonian	88.4	95.3	4.5	6.9
Kirgiz	99.0	98.8	0.3	−0.2
Dagestani Peoples	98.0	96.2	1.6	−1.8
Udmurt	98.9	89.2	10.7	−9.7
Mari	99.3	95.2	4.6	−4.1
Komi	95.5	88.7	11.0	−6.8
Chechen	99.7	98.8	1.0	−0.9
Osetian	97.9	89.1	4.9	−8.8
Bulgarian	92.4	79.3	18.2	−13.1
Korean	98.9	79.3	20.5	−19.6
Greek	72.7	41.4	46.2	−31.3
Buryat	98.1	94.9	5.1	−3.2
Yakut	99.7	97.6	2.4	−2.1
Kabardino	99.3	97.8	1.9	−1.5
Karakalpak	87.5	94.9	0.3	7.4
Karelian	95.5	71.2	28.6	−24.3

Sources: Itogi vsesoyuznoy perepisi naseleniya 1959 goda, SSSR, 1962, pp. 184–186, and Frank Lorimer, *The Population of the Soviet Union*, pp. 55–61.

have been forced to act like the Russians in order to get ahead. Only 45.2 per cent of the Poles reported Polish as their native language; 40.1 per cent reported some language other than Polish or Russian. Undoubtedly, many Poles speak Ukrainian, Belorussian, and Lithuanian, since those are the regions in which the bulk of the Poles live. (Table 13–5)

As can be seen in Table 13–11, generally urban dwellers are much more prone to speak a language other than their national language than are rural dwellers, and younger people are a little more likely to speak an adopted language than are older people.

Belorussia and Ukraine are rather special cases which reflect the relatively easy shift to Russian ways of these closely related Slavic groups. The lowest percentage of Ukrainians speaking Ukrainian is 68.7

per cent for urban men, ages 40–44. There is a wide discrepancy between men and women in this category—76.6 per cent of the urban Ukrainian women, ages 40–44, speak Ukrainian. It is interesting to note that among urban dwellers below the age of 20, somewhat fewer women than men speak Ukrainian, but above the age of 20 many more women than men speak Ukrainian. The biggest discrepancy, however, is between urban and rural—77.2 per cent of all urban Ukrainians speak Ukrainian, whereas 94.5 per cent of all rural Ukrainians speak Ukrainian. In all cases, Ukrainians over 45 years of age speak Ukrainian more than do Ukrainians under 45 years of age. The Belorussians show a distribution similar to that of the Ukrainians. The category showing lowest percentage of Belorussian-speaking persons is urban men, ages 40–44, with only

Table 13–11 Numbers of People Who Consider Their National Language to Be Their Native Language, in Per Cent of Total by Major Nationalities, Sex, Abode, and Age, as of January 15, 1959

| | Urban | | | | Rural | | | |
| | Men | | Women | | Men | | Women | |
Nationality	Ages 10–19	Ages 60–69	Ages 10–19	Ages 60–69	Ages 10–19	Ages 60–69	Ages 10–19	Ages 60–69
Russian	99.8	99.9	99.8	99.9	99.7	99.9	99.7	99.9
Ukrainian	76.3	79.9	75.9	83.4	94.6	95.8	94.9	96.6
Moldavian	87.7	85.5	85.6	87.7	98.4	98.4	98.4	98.7
Belorussian	66.0	53.1	66.2	67.4	94.9	94.1	95.4	96.5
Lithuanian	98.6	97.8	98.7	97.6	98.6	98.7	98.7	98.7
Latvian	97.5	98.3	97.8	99.0	98.6	98.9	98.6	99.2
Estonian	98.8	99.5	98.8	99.4	99.8	99.9	99.9	99.9
Georgian	98.0	99.6	98.0	99.4	99.8	99.96	99.9	99.95
Armenian	82.8	90.4	81.4	92.1	97.3	97.2	96.8	97.9
Azerbaydzhan	95.3	99.4	95.0	99.5	98.4	98.6	98.4	98.7
Kazakh	95.6	99.6	95.7	99.7	98.0	99.7	98.3	99.7
Uzbek	95.9	98.4	95.4	98.6	98.7	99.2	98.7	99.3
Turkmen	96.9	99.9	95.4	99.97	99.9	99.96	99.9	99.97
Kirgiz	96.7	99.0	96.8	99.5	98.3	99.4	98.5	99.6
Tadzhik	95.9	98.6	94.9	99.1	98.3	98.6	98.2	98.9

Source: Itogi vsesoyuznoy perepisi naseleniya 1959 goda, SSSR, 1962, pp. 211–225.

50.9 per cent. Urban women in this age category, on the other hand, are 62.0 per cent Belorussian-speaking. All age categories of urban men are less than 66 per cent Belorussian-speaking and all age categories of urban women, less than 73 per cent. Rural men and women in all age brackets except one are well above 90 per cent Belorussian-speaking.

Practically all Ukrainians and Belorussians who did not report their national languages as their native languages reported Russian as a native language instead. (Table 13–10) This is also true of the Armenians, who rank third among the national groups holding union republic status in percentage of people not reporting their national language as their native tongue. Relatively large numbers of Belorussians, Ukrainians, and Armenians live outside their own republics. Probably second and third generations living in cities outside their republics of origin have become quite Russified. The significant discrepancy between languages used by urban and rural dwellers of almost all national origins suggests that individual cultural achievement in the Soviet Union is almost inevitably accompanied by Russification.

Mass Movements of Nationality Groups

World War II and its aftermath induced many movements of nationalities *en masse,* allegedly for strategic reasons. As the Nazi armies advanced southeastward through Ukraine into the Caucasus, various nationalities, or individuals within these nationalities, put up little resistance to the German advance, or even collaborated with them in the hope that this might lead to freedom from the Soviet Union. The Crimean Tatars were under German occupation for three years, and the Germans overran the territories of other minorities in the North Caucasus beginning in August 1942. Later in 1942 the Soviet counterattack at Stalingrad drove the Germans back, and Soviet security troops then rounded up the minorities in the North Caucasus and the Crimea and transported them eastward into exile. Approximately 1,500,000 German settlers along the Volga River had been exiled earlier, as the Nazi army advanced in 1941. During the war the political identities of the Kalmyks, Chechen-Ingush, Balkars, Karachay, Volga-Germans, and Crimean Tatars were abrogated and the people reportedly were moved eastward. Three years after the death of Stalin, in 1956, Khrushchev announced a general amnesty of these exiled peoples, and the five minorities of the North Caucasus and nearby plains, totaling about 1 million people, were allowed to return home, and their homelands were reinstated politically. Khrushchev denounced Stalin's banishment of the minorities and declared that the Ukrainians also would have been exiled for collaboration with the Germans but there were too many of them — almost 40 million. In 1965 the legal rights of the German minority were restored but their former autonomous republic was not reestablished. Finally, in 1967, the Crimean Tatars were freed of exile restrictions, but they were not allowed to recover their former homeland, the Crimean Peninsula, which is a popular resort area on the Black Sea and is now part of the Ukrainian Republic. The Crimean Tatars, now living mainly in the Uzbek, Kazakh, and Tadzhik Republics, have been encouraged to remain in their present homes. They number about 500,000 people.

Although the more than 1,600,000 Germans now living in the Soviet Union are scattered and do not have any political identity, they have managed to reconstitute themselves as a sturdy cultural community with education and literature in their own language. The German language newspaper *Neues Leben* published in Moscow is disseminated to German groups throughout the country. Unlike Moscow's three other foreign language weeklies, in English, French, and Spanish, the German publication is designed specifically for an ethnic minority within the Soviet Union. A regular column in the paper provides space for readers to ask the whereabouts of lost relatives and reflects the breakup of families during the turmoil of the 1941 deportation. In addition to this central newspaper, the Siberian Germans are served by at least one local German-language paper which is published in Slavgorod in the Altay region. Also radio stations of Alma-Ata and Tselinograd and several other cities in the new settlement areas of western Siberia and northern Kazakhstan regularly broadcast programs in German to the many German exiles who reside in these areas. German-language schools have been restored in some of these new settlement regions, but according to reports this has been a slow and painful process that has had to overcome much bureaucratic inertia.

In addition to the Volga Germans, about 350,000 Black Sea Germans, as well as 200,000 Baltic peoples, fled westward with the retreating German armies and have never returned to the Soviet Union. With the exchange of territories along the western boundary after the war, about 1,800,-000 Poles and Jews were expatriated to Poland and 500,000 Ukrainians, Belorussians, and Lithuanians were moved into the Soviet Union. In general, incoming peoples were scattered eastward through the Soviet Union, and the empty areas left in the west by expatriation were filled with Russians or Russified people from the local nationalities who had spent some time in the interior of the U.S.S.R. Many Baltic peoples have been forced to reside in the eastern areas of the U.S.S.R. and have little contact with their homelands.

The 1,500,000 Germans who found themselves in Kaliningrad Oblast after the northern half of what had been East Prussia was transferred to the Soviet Union were largely expatriated, and 600,000 Russians were moved in. Apparently not all of the Germans in this region have been expatriated to West Germany yet. As late as 1963 the Bonn Government demanded that the Soviet Union repatriate 10,000 people of German origin. The communication acknowledged the repatriation of 14,800 people since the April 1956 agreement signed by the Soviet Union and West Germany, which provided for the repatriation of all persons on Soviet territory who held German nationality on June 21, 1941, the day of the Nazi attack on the Soviet Union. The German note charged, however, that the Soviets were delaying the departure of another 10,000 Germans, probably from Kaliningrad Oblast.

In the Far East, 370,000 Japanese (100 per cent) were resettled from southern Sakhalin and the Kurils. Along the Chinese frontier, "border purifications" have taken place since the late 1930s, and the uneasy alliance between the U.S.S.R. and China has occasionally been broken by sporadic incursions of armed strife. This is particularly true along the Central Asian border between the two countries where local nationalities in Sinkiang and the bordering Soviet area seek independence from both the Soviet Union and China.

Summary of Nationality Question

The multinational character of the Soviet population presents many problems to Soviet leaders. Though the theorists would like to think that a new Soviet man has been created, uniform across the country, the fact is that nationality differences have declined little during the Soviet period. And though the official policy is one of Russification, the Bolsheviks from the very beginning have had to make all sorts of accommodations with the national groups in order to maintain themselves in power. In many instances Soviet action has been to enliven or even manufacture national consciousness in the hope that such awareness would occupy the minds of the national minorites and divert their attentions away from more sensitive political issues. Also, inadvertently, awareness of nationality has been nurtured by such practices as the requirement of internal passports for every Soviet citizen above the age of 16, which among other things identifies him according to nationality.

Equality of peoples is officially promoted, and there is little overt discrimination among individuals in the Soviet Union. Varied levels of development among the different nationality groups, however, have caused the Russians, for instance, to look down somewhat upon the Central Asian nationalities, and at the same time the Baltic peoples frequently look down their noses at the Russians. Many nicknames for various nationality groups have survived from Tsarist days that have connotations similar to those associated with "dago" or "greaser" in the United States. Inter-racial or international marriages are few, and the assimilation of nationalities is slow. In the Middle Asian cities of Tashkent and Samarkand, for example, only 6–7 per cent of the marriages have been between whites and nonwhites. In the Russian city of Leningrad, bordering on other European peoples in the west, international marriages have accounted for only about 17 per cent of the total.

Though there seems to be little tendency toward actual separatism, except perhaps for the Baltic Republics, the rising educational level of the formerly "have not" Soviet nationalities may well feed internal nationalism. The Soviet leaders are very sensitive to nationalistic uprisings outside the Soviet Union, particularly in border areas, and keep a close watch on the effects that such events have among nationality groups in the Soviet Union. The liberalization in Czechoslovakia during the summer of 1968 stirred much excitement in the bordering parts of western Ukraine. It was as much for this reason as for any other that the Soviets were so intent upon squelching the movement in Czechoslovakia.

Inevitably the growing urbanization and industrialization of the Soviet Union draws more and more of the national minorities into the main stream of economic and social life and brings about some sort of amalgamation which tends toward a uniform culture, despite national differences. Many of the national minorities have benefited materially by being part of the Soviet Union, and they are well aware of this. Most of the national groups of Soviet Middle Asia have higher standards of living than similar national groups across the international boundaries to the south. Thus most of these groups feel a vested interest in the Soviet system, even though they feel and resent creeping Russification. The educational system, which is becoming more uniform throughout the country all the time, is, of course, a great leveling factor on the younger generations. Ultimately the universal use of the Russian language will probably be the single most significant Russification factor. In order to get ahead, a young person from a national minority group knows that he must know Russian well and be able to master the technologies that have been instituted by the Russians.

The Bolsheviks will do whatever they can to erase national traditions. True, they often have been forced to backtrack and make concessions, but whenever the opportunity arises they will either do something or not do something which will result in a general trend toward denationalization. One of the best examples of this is the handling of the Jewish population. Although, with few exceptions, the Soviets have not persecuted individual Jews, they have tried to erase the Jewish culture by making it virtually impossible for Jews to follow their religion, train religious leaders, or properly educate their offspring in Jewish traditions.

Population Distribution and Location Change

Population Distribution The population is distributed very unevenly throughout the Soviet Union. The European Plain, which comprises less than one sixth of the total territory of the country, contains 65 per cent of the population, despite a policy promoting movement eastward since the Revolution. Within the European Plain the population is concentrated in the western and central portions where the possibilities for agriculture are most favorable. The population thins out very rapidly north of latitude 58 degrees where the climate becomes too cool and the soils too poor for agriculture, and it thins again east of the Sea of Azov where the climate becomes too dry. East of the Urals, much of Siberia and the Far East, except for a narrow strip along the southern margin, is practically devoid of population.

The continuously populated area of the Soviet Union may be described as a wedge with its broad base at the western border of the country which extends eastward in an ever narrowing belt across the Middle Volga Valley and Southern Ural Mountains into western Siberia. It stretches eastward as a belt about 200 or 300 miles wide along either side of the Trans-Siberian Railroad to the Altay Mountains, after which it continues to the Pacific as isolated spots of settlement in intermontaine basins. (Fig. 13–9)

This wedge of population corresponds very closely in areal extent to the region of mixed forest and steppe vegetation with associated black and chestnut soils, a fact which reflects the influence of agricultural potentialities on original settlement. The nodes of concentrated population within

this wedge are in the heavily industrialized areas: the Central Industrial Region, eastern Ukraine, and the Urals; or in the areas of most favorable agricultural conditions, such as in western Ukraine and Moldavia. In portions of this western region, the rural population density is more than 200 people per square mile.

Two important areas of outlying population are the Caucasus and portions of Middle Asia. Here again it is the agricultural potentialities that have induced the settlement. The summers are long and hot, and, in Transcaucasia, the winters are mild so that crops exotic to the rest of the Soviet Union may be grown. An abundance of irrigation water from the surrounding mountains has made possible ever-expanding areas of intensive agriculture. Hence rural populations in these areas have become quite high. In portions of the Fergana Valley in Uzbekistan the population density is as high as 500 people per square mile. But these two areas are islands of population separated from the main population wedge to the north by deserts and mountains.

Other than these areas of population, there are widely scattered populated points in other areas of the country which generally consist of cities or workers' settlements specifically located to exploit some mineral or forest resource or to construct a major hydroelectric project.

Locational Changes A basic tenet of Soviet policy has been that population should be spread as evenly as possible across the entire territory of the country and that eventually all regions should be equally industrialized and urbanized and all nationality groups should achieve equal levels of cultural attainment. This is a big order in a country where natural conditions have dictated extremely unequal distributions of population and where the nationality makeup is so diverse that levels of attainment reach all the way from very

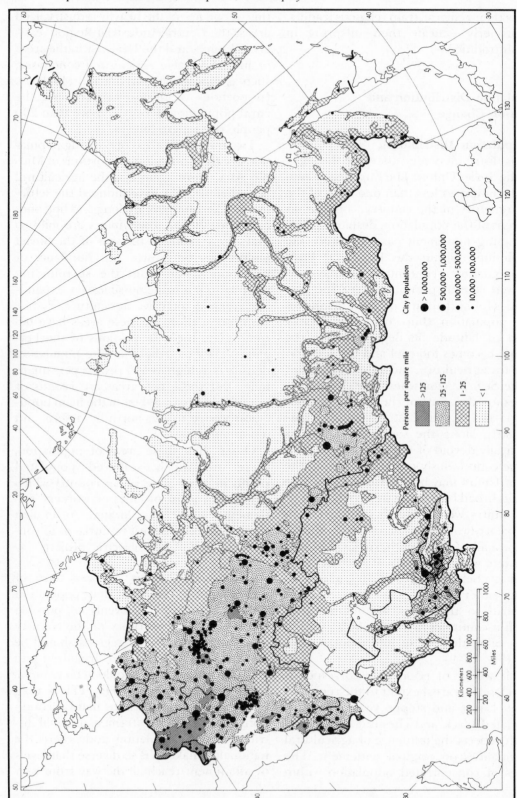
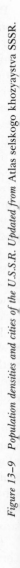

Figure 13–9   Population densities and cities of the U.S.S.R. Updated from Atlas selskogo khozyaystva SSSR.

primitive nomadic groups to highly industrialized and urbanized societies. Superimposed on this general policy of egalitarianism has been a pioneering fervor for the so-called eastward movement. However, both the general spread of population across the territory of the U.S.S.R. and the eastward movement have been greatly tempered, and at times even reversed, by certain economic and cultural realities.

Though the eastward movement has always been regarded as the principal direction of migration before the Revolution, the fact is that during the nineteenth and early twentieth centuries the movement southward into south European Russia and the North Caucasus was quantitatively more important. About 8 million people migrated southward during this period compared with 5 million people who migrated eastward. This southward migration ceased during Soviet times, however, and there was no further net population flow into the steppe belt of European Russia. There appears to have been little movement eastward either during the early part of the Soviet period, but the German invasion in World War II largely produced the territorial shift in population that Soviet policy had not been able to accomplish. Between 1926 and 1939 only about 3 million people had moved to Siberia and the Far East and about 1.7 million to Middle Asia and Kazakhstan. Most of this population shift was in response to new industries established in the east, and most of the new settlers settled in cities. The share of the urban population in the eastern regions during this period rose from 18 to 32 per cent.

Then a great spurt took place in response to the German invasion. Between June 1941 and February 1942, according to railroad statistics, 10.4 million people were evacuated eastward. A second wave later in 1942 raised the total of evacuees to about 20 million by October 1942. Al-

though this was planned to be a temporary shift, many of the people stayed in the Urals, western Siberia, Kazakhstan, and other eastern regions. In 1947 when the last count of evacuated population was made in Irkutsk Oblast, 15 per cent of the original arrivals were still there. And, of course, the masses of nationality groups deported from the North Caucasian, Volga, and Crimean Regions for political reasons were not allowed to return to their homelands until the late 1950s. These migrations, coupled with natural increases in the eastern regions, undevastated by the war, and large war-related losses in the west, produced a population that at the time of the 1959 census showed a 20-year increase taking place almost wholly within regions from the Urals eastward.

If the 20,000,000 people gained by the wartime annexation of the western provinces of Ukraine, Belorussia, Moldavia, Lithuania, Latvia, and Estonia are subtracted from the intercensal (1939 to 1959) increase in population of 38,000,000, the natural increase during the 20-year period within the present boundaries of the U.S.S.R. was 18,000,000 people. This figure corresponds almost precisely to the population gain in the eastern regions (Urals and eastward). The population west of the Urals and north of the Caucasus has remained almost exactly the same; in 1939 the population of this part of the country was listed as 135,530,000 people and in 1959 it was listed as 135,-669,000.

The loss of life and the destruction of property in the west during the war was very severe. The Belorussian Republic in particular lost almost one tenth of its population. On the other hand, the Urals increased their population during the period 1939–1959 by 32 per cent, western Siberia increased by 24 per cent, eastern Siberia by 34 per cent, Kazakhstan by 53 per cent, Middle Asia by 30 per cent, and the Far East by 70 per cent. During the 20-year period, the share of the east in the total population of the country rose from 29 per cent to 35 per cent.

The area bounded by Leningrad-Kirov-Kharkov-Lvov-Leningrad contained 70 per cent of Russia's population a century ago, 50 per cent in 1940, and 40 per cent in 1959. This "old Russia" supplied population first to southeastern Ukraine, North Caucasus, and Middle Volga Steppes, then to the southwest Siberian agricultural lands, and later to the Urals and central Siberia. The Uralo-Baykal industrial area grew largely from migration from old Russia. This new region, which contained only 5 per cent of the country's population a century ago, contained 12 per cent in 1940 and 15 per cent in 1959.

Old Russia lost 7 million people from 1940 to 1955. Within the area only the Central Industrial Region, Latvia, and Estonia gained population. The area completely surrounding the Central Industrial Region (Central Black Earth Region, Volga-Vyatka Region, Valday Region, Belorussia, western Ukraine, Lithuania, and Kaliningrad Oblast) suffered a loss of more than 10 per cent of its population due to intense out-migration. This occurred in areas that were not occupied by the Germans during World War II as well as in areas that were.

During the years 1955–1959 a total population increment in the U.S.S.R. approximately equal to that which occurred during the years 1940–1955 was far more evenly distributed across the country. During this period natural growth was the dominant factor in each region. Only the Valday area and western Belorussia showed a decline. A decrease in the Tyan Shans during this period was coincident with increases in the North Caspian and North Caucasian areas. This reflected the restoration of the Chechen, Ingush, and Kalmyks to their homelands. Migrations into the Subarctic, Middle Volga, and Kazakh and Middle Asian industrial areas continued, but flows to eastern Siberia

and the Far East were no longer evident. These years saw a temporary revival of rural in-migration in western Siberia and northern Kazakhstan to implement the famous virgin lands program.

The period 1959–1962 marked a reversal in many of these migrations, particularly those into Siberia and the Far East. With the proclaimed amnesty of deported peoples in the late 1950s, large numbers of deportees who had lived in the eastern regions for two or three decades were propelled westward by nostalgia to visit the scenes of their childhoods and rejoin relatives and old friends. Many of these people took up permanent residence in the west and swelled already over-populated regions such as the northern Caucasus, western Ukraine, and Moldavia. This westward stream of resettlement was joined in many instances by more recent newcomers to the Siberian scene who had been recruited for jobs in the new industries and farms of Siberia and northern Kazakhstan somewhat against their will through the mechanism of the educational system, which provides free education and stipends to university students, in return for which they are required to work in assigned areas for at least three years after graduation before they can seek employment on their own volition. Many new graduates are sent to the eastern regions to supply much needed manpower there, and they await the first opportunity to move back to the west. Many of them do not serve out their full three-year terms, but one way or another break their contracts and move elsewhere.

Labor mobility and labor turnover in the eastern regions has become a very acute problem for planners and plant managers, a reflection of the fact that voluntary migration had contributed very little to the 35 per cent increase in trans-Ural population between 1939 and 1959.

Much of the present problem stems from the fact that until recently the Soviets regarded manpower much as a free good and were preoccupied with raw materials and the opening up of new lands. Thus they were not aware of the growing crisis in manpower until it was upon them. The result has been that they have been quite unable to control unauthorized migrations and to stabilize the labor force by regions. Theoretically interregional migrations should be organized either through governmental hiring for work in distant areas, planned rural settlements, assignment of college graduates, or organized resettlement as a result of public appeals. The fact is, however, that now individual movements must make up 80–85 per cent of the total migration each year.

The unauthorized and individualistic nature of much of the population movement makes record keeping very difficult, although it is not entirely impossible, since every individual past the age of 16 must carry an internal passport and a work record book which he must present at his new location in order to obtain a job. The migration picture is further obscured by great differences in natural increases of population from region to region. Since rates of natural increase are quite high in Siberia and the Far East, population figures due to these natural increases must be subtracted from sometimes rather high net increases in order to realize that the net migration has been outward, not inward. After taking account of all relative factors, one study indicates that western Siberia experienced a net migratory loss of 230,000 during the period 1959–1963. Another Soviet study revealed that about half of the new arrivals in such new industrial cities of Siberia as Achinsk and Nazarovo departed after three years. Reasons given for repulsion from the eastern regions and new settlements is the general lack of social and cultural amenities. Housing is often a big factor, but just as important is the broad group of services. Many of the new settlers in new areas are young unmarried people who demand adequate recreational

and social facilities in after-work hours. If leisure time lies heavy on their hands, they become malcontent and may even turn to hooliganism (vandalism) or other petty criminal activities for diversion. Since frequently many of these young people have been recruited from among the ranks of malcontents in the west, many of whom already have some sort of police record, their antisocial behavior is only intensified by the boredom of pioneer areas. Such activities create a social atmosphere that is unattractive to the more responsible citizens of the areas, and they too may become disillusioned.

Another fact about the eastern areas that is disturbing to the Soviet leaders is that the chief migrations into the individual regions of western Siberia, eastern Siberia, the Far East, and Kazakhstan take place among these very regions themselves. Most of the movement takes place between regions that are in juxtaposition, and thus there is little net movement from the west to the east. Beween 1956 and 1960 the main regions from which migration took place into western Siberia were the Far East, Kazakhstan, the Urals, and the Volga-Vyatka regions in that order. Into eastern Siberia, migrants came overwhelmingly from the Far East and western Siberia. Hence workers are moving from areas in which they are needed into other areas in which they are needed, and no Union-wide problem is being solved.

For the country as a whole, net migrations can be viewed in Fig. 13–10. Here it can be seen that for the period 1959–1962 the chief area of in-migration was a swath of territory beginning on the eastern shore of the Black Sea and running eastward into Middle Asia and Kazakhstan. The migrations into Middle Asia and Kazakhstan were primarily in response to new opportunities in the industries and farms of those areas, but the heavy migrations to the North Caucasus and adjacent regions were not in response to such a worthy cause. These included re-

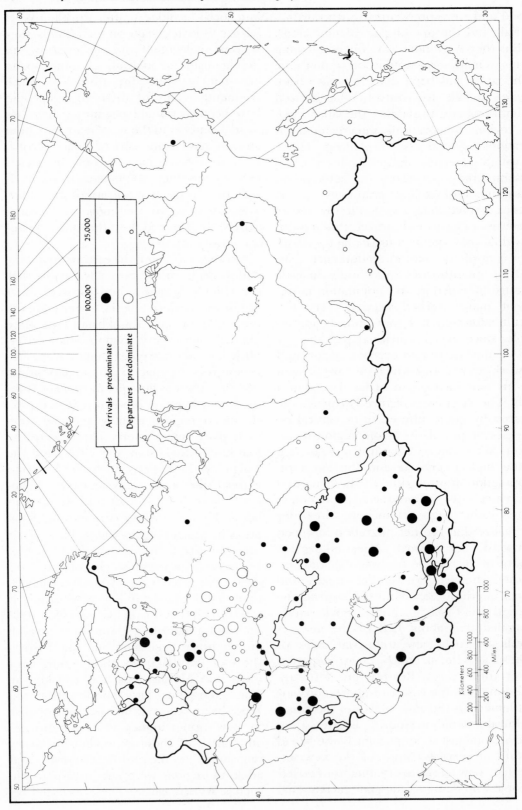

Figure 13–10   Net migration, 1959–1962. From Soviet Geography: Review and Translation, December, 1964, p. 8.

turnees of earlier deported nationalities from these areas as well as many comfort-seekers from other population groups who were crowding into the climatically favorable areas of the south in spite of labor surpluses already there. Many of these newcomers into these labor-surplus regions become absorbed into already established collective farms and other enterprises where they do nothing more than work private plots of ground. Thus they are lost to socialized labor.

Much of the rest of the country during the period shown experienced a net outward migration, except for large urban agglomerations, such as Moscow and Leningrad, and certain regions, such as the Baltic areas and the far north. By far the greatest out-migration took place from the central European Russian area, although this is obscured somewhat by the continued growth of Moscow Oblast, where in-migrants generally took up residence in the intermediate and smaller sized cities surrounding Moscow, since the population of Moscow is being strictly limited. Table 13–12 shows net migration figures for 1962 for each of the major reporting regions of the country. This reveals the continued mobility of the people of the central part of European Russia and the extremely high out-migration for the Volga-Vyatka Region and the Central Chernozem Region. It also indicates the very high outward movement from Belorussia and Transcaucasia and the modest migration losses of the entire Asiatic part of the Russian Republic, particularly the Soviet Far East. Although some reversals have occurred during certain years in some of the eastern regions since 1962, trends generally continue the same. Central Asia is outstanding for its continued excess of in-migration; Moldavia, the Baltic Republics, and Ukraine show surprisingly high in-migrations in recent years. Thus some of the areas already having highest population densities are experiencing some of the highest in-

migrations. Within Ukraine there has been some reordering of population toward the east to the heavy industrial area of the Donets Basin and into the resort areas of the Crimea.

The regions that suffer from a constant manpower shortage are Kazakhstan, Siberia, and the Far East. This in spite of the fact that Kazakhstan is the fastest growing region in the country. (Table 13–2) After the Kazakhs suffered heavy losses because of intense class struggles during the late 1920s and early 1930s, the Republic of Kazakhstan increased its population by more than 50 per cent between 1939 and 1959, whereas the whole U.S.S.R. was increasing by only 9.5 per cent. From 1959 to 1967 Kazakhstan increased another 35

Table 13–12   Interregional Migrations, U.S.S.R., 1962

	Out-migration, Per Cent of U.S.S.R. Total	In-migration, Per Cent of U.S.S.R. Total	Out/In Per Cent
R.S.F.S.R.	69.6	65.9	106
European R.S.F.S.R.	51.2	49.2	104
North	3.5	3.8	91
Northwest	5.3	6.1	86
Center	8.4	7.8	108
Central Chernozem	5.4	3.5	155
Volga-Vyatka	5.9	3.5	167
Volga	6.4	6.8	94
North Caucasus	6.7	7.3	91
Ural	9.6	10.4	93
Asiatic R.S.F.S.R.	18.4	16.7	110
Western Siberia	7.1	6.6	108
Eastern Siberia	6.2	5.9	105
Far East	5.1	4.2	121
Republics outside R.S.F.S.R.	30.4	34.1	89
Ukraine	10.9	12.7	84
Belorussia	3.2	2.2	141
Transcaucasia	2.0	1.4	139
Central Asia	3.7	5.8	64
Kazakhstan	8.4	9.1	93
Moldavia	0.7	1.0	78
Baltic Republics	1.5	1.9	80

Source: V. I. Perevedentsev, "Nekotorye voprosy mezhrayonnogo pereraspredeleniya trudovykh resursov," *Izvestiya Sibirskogo otdeleniya akademii nauk SSSR, seriya obshchestvennykh nauk,* 1964, No. 9, vyp. 3, p. 78.

per cent. An important growth factor here is the high rate of natural increase, almost double that of the U.S.S.R. as a whole. Natural increase accounted for 1.3 million people during the 4½ year period from January 1959 to July 1963, whereas in-migration, primarily of Russians and other Slavs, accounted for about 1 million. Migration to Kazakhstan started even before the Revolution and has continued at a high rate ever since, with some fluctuations due to government programs. The devastation of the Kazakh people themselves during their fierce struggles with the Bolsheviks caused the population in the area to remain relatively constant during the 1920s and much of the 1930s. Around 1944 there probably was a net out-migration because of resettlement back to European Russia after the Nazi armies had been expelled from the areas from which most of these evacuees had come. After the war this trend was quickly reversed, however, and in-migration set in again at a high pace and reached its greatest intensity immediately following 1955 with the opening of the virgin lands. Eventually this influx slowed down because of increasing numbers of departures. In 1955, 44 per cent of the new arrivals settled for good, but in 1963 only 18.5 per cent settled.

In the early 1960s the regions that most actively exported people to Kazakhstan were Altay Kray, Sverdlovsk, Kemerovo, Perm, Novosibirsk, Chelyabinsk, Omsk, Irkutsk, Gorky, and Kirov Oblasts, and Ukraine, Belorussia, and Moldavia. Thus, within the R.S.F.S.R., except for the Volga-Vyatka Region, the main manpower to Kazakhstan came from bordering areas in western Siberia which can ill afford to lose people. The high figures of migration into Kazakhstan from Kemerovo Oblast in the Kuznetsk Basin and Donetsk and Lugansk Oblasts in eastern Ukraine reflect the high need for manpower in the Karaganda coal basin, which is drawing skilled workers away from the older coal-producing areas. The irrational out-migrations from Sibe-

ria and the Far East during the past few years have the Soviet government worried. It has been estimated that the development of this area in the foreseeable future will require the in-migration of from 5 to 15 million people. Yet, with some exceptions, much of the region has suffered a net out-migration since around 1959. In some areas, such as Sakhalin, during certain years out-migration has actually exceeded natural increase, so that the absolute population of the area has declined. (Fig. 13–11) To add to the problems in these eastern areas, the population there has been characterized by a mobility two to three times greater than that in European Russia. An attempt has been made to replace some of the out-migrants from factories in the larger cities with the in-migrants from local rural areas, but in general this has not solved the industrial labor problem, since the local inhabitants have few skills. At the same time it has produced severe dislocations on the farms, since it is usually the brighter and better educated youths who are moving to the cities.

Another rapid postwar migration took place into the European North, particularly into Murmansk Oblast, Karelian A.S.S.R., and Komi A.S.S.R., in connection with the opening up of new mines and forestry. Since many of the migrants into these areas were Russians and other Slavic groups, the nationality balance has greatly shifted as a result of the in-migration.

Another region where the nationality situation has been almost completely changed through migrations is Kaliningrad Oblast, formerly part of East Prussia, which after the war saw the repatriation of practically all of its Germans to Germany and a replacement almost entirely by Russians. Although the in-migration equaled only about half of the out-migration from this area, there does not seem to be a sustained in-migration into the region. In fact during the last few years the migration balance here has been negative. It appears that the desire of

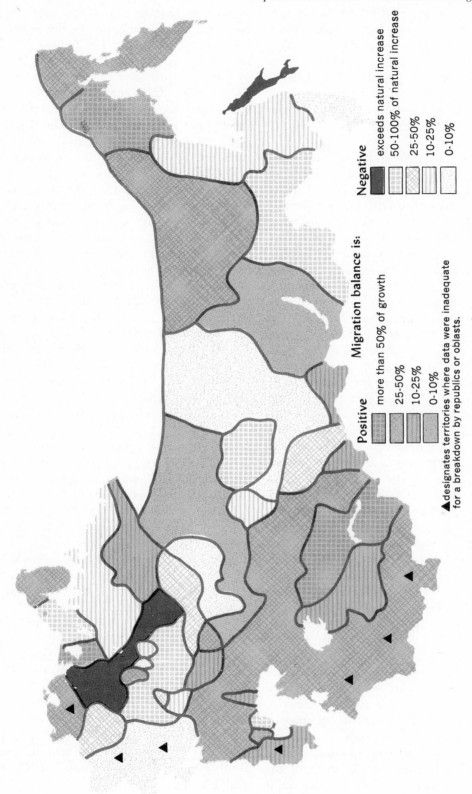

Migration balance is:

Positive

more than 50% of growth

25-50%

10-25%

0-10%

Negative

exceeds natural increase

50-100% of natural increase

25-50%

10-25%

0-10%

▲designates territories where data were inadequate for a breakdown by republics or oblasts.

Figure 13–11 Net migration and natural increase, 1959–1962. From Soviet Geography: Review and Translation, December, 1964, p. 10.

Russians to return to their former homes is stronger than the policies of the Soviet government to populate this area with Russians. Certainly the Soviet government must be eager to populate this area as heavily as possible, since it is the westernmost point of the Soviet Union on the Baltic and hence of high strategic significance.

Russians have taken by far the most active part in migration. This is true even from non-Russian areas. For example, of the migrants who arrived in Novosibirsk in 1959 from Ukraine, 65 per cent were Russians and only 31 per cent were Ukrainians, although, of course, Ukrainians far outnumber Russians in Ukraine. Russians also accounted for 65 per cent of the migrants coming from Transcaucasia, 86 per cent from Middle Asia, 78 per cent from Kazakhstan, and 82 per cent from the Baltic Republics. The Belorussians are quite mobile, and migrants from Belorussia far exceed those from Ukraine even though the population is only about one fifth that of Ukraine. The non-Russian groups in the Volga Region are also quite mobile and make up about one third of the migrants from that area, which is one of the main population-exporting regions of the country. Tatars, while decreasing in number in their own A.S.S.R., between 1939 and 1959 increased in the European North, the Urals, and Siberia. Although the Middle Asian Republics, Transcaucasia, and Moldavia are labor-surplus areas, ethnic factors operate against the migration of most of the national groups from these areas. In general they not only do not move to labor-deficit areas in the rest of the country, but they do not even migrate to the cities in their own regions. While in Russian-populated areas migration to cities takes place largely from nearby rural areas, in the non-Russian republics local rural-to-urban migrations are often negligible. Consequently the share of the indigenous population in the cities tends to decline despite high birth rates and growing rural population in these areas. For example, the share of Uzbeks in the population of Tashkent declined from 37.7 per cent in 1939 to 33.8 per cent in 1959 while the rural population in Uzbekistan was increasing. From 1959 to 1964 the rural population in the Middle Asian Republics increased by more than 13 per cent, whereas the rural population of the U.S.S.R. as a whole declined. This, of course, has aggravated the manpower surpluses in these non-Russian rural areas.

In many of the larger industrial concerns in the bigger cities of the non-Russian Republics one seldom sees workers from the local nationality groups. This is also true on large construction projects. At the Nurek hydroelectric construction project in the Tadzhik Republic in 1964 the labor force consisted of 51.8 per cent Russian, 7.3 per cent Ukrainian, and only 27.8 per cent Tadzhik. In the same republic at the Dushanbe textile mill the labor force consisted of 55.7 per cent Russian, 15.2 per cent Tadzhik, 10.1 per cent Uzbek, 7.4 per cent Tatar, and so forth. The ethnic composition of the labor force in this largest industrial enterprise in the Tadzhik capital was almost identical with the ethnic makeup of the city itself.

Language and customs work against the absorption of local peoples into labor forces. The Tadzhiks have a very poor knowledge of the Russian language, which is a definite drawback when they seek jobs in large industrial enterprises and construction projects organized by Russians in their area. Also early marriages and large families work against Tadzhik women participating in such things as textile production. According to the 1959 census, 394 of every 1000 Tadzhik women between the ages of 16 and 19 were married and 869 of every 1000 between the ages of 20 and 24. These figures compared with 86 per 1000 and 465 per 1000 among Russian women living in Tadzhikistan. (Table 13–3)

On the other hand, Russians are able to move freely into non-Russian cities where the urban citizens speak Russian fluently. Therefore language is no barrier to the migration of Russians into cities in any part of the country, whereas language is a barrier to the movement of indigenous rural populations into the cities and industries of their regions. Some Soviet demographers are now recognizing this problem and are urging that the teaching of Russian must be improved in the rural areas of the non-Russian regions so that local rural-to-urban migration can be promoted. This is a logical solution and, of course, would be of benefit financially to the local inhabitants, but on the other hand it would hasten the process of Russification. It is easy to see how Russification is an inevitable process brought about by economic and social realities.

During recent years the intensity of migration, which has never been anywhere near great enough to distribute population properly to meet the manpower needs of the economy, has tended to decline. Some of this is the natural result of an unwritten change in governmental policy which has abandoned the idea of filling up empty areas with people and equipment. Now the Soviet leaders are more intent on gaining time and more return on investments by expanding production in old developed areas and moving raw materials from the east to the west. This alleviates the necessity of providing all sorts of services to an expanded population in the eastern areas, and the investment capital thus saved can be put to use in the construction of industries in the older areas where the population is already pretty well supplied with services, meager as they may be. At last it appears that the Soviet leaders have abandoned a segment of ideology that has always been in conflict with economic and social realities. Unless the irrational goal to spread population fairly evenly across the country is revived sometime in the future, it appears that no significant change in population distribution is in the offing.

Urbanization

The largest migration in the Soviet Union throughout the entire Soviet period has been the rural-to-urban one. (Fig. 13–12) This has taken place rapidly throughout the country, although it has been more rapid in certain sections than in others. At the time of the Revolution, urban dwellers made up only 18 per cent of the total population of the country. Under the impetus of planned industrialization, the urban share had increased to 33 per cent by 1939 and 48 per cent by 1959. Since the 1959 census the urbanization process has continued, and on January 1, 1967, 55 per cent of the population were estimated to be urban. Thus the Soviet Union is rapidly joining the ranks of developed countries with predominantly urban populations. In comparison in 1960 the United States listed 70 per cent of its population as urban, Britain 80 per cent, West Germany about 80 per cent, and France 60 per cent. There were thirty cities in the U.S.S.R. with

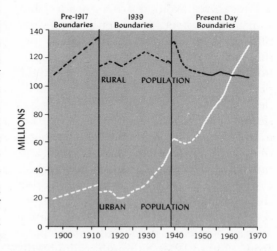

Figure 13–12   Changes in urban and rural population, 1897–1967. Updated from French. By permission of St. Antony's College, Oxford.

populations over 500,000, eight of which had more than 1 million. At the same time the United States had more than fifty urban agglomerations with populations exceeding 500,000, half of which had more than 1 million. If one considers individual cities rather than agglomerations, however, the Soviet Union has surpassed the United States in number of large cities. In 1960 the Soviet Union had 192 cities with populations of more than 100,000 each, totaling a population of 64.8 million people. The United States had 132 such cities with a total population of 51 million. The Soviet Union had thirty cities each with more than 500,000 population totaling 32.1 million people, whereas the United States had twenty-one cities each with more than 500,000 totaling 28.6 million people.

Initially the rural-to-urban migration was promoted in order to man the industries in the new and expanding cities in the Soviet Union. After World War II efforts were redoubled to make use of every available labor source, much of which had to come from the countryside. This was necessitated by the deficit of war babies which was threatening a shrinkage of the labor force around 1960. Changes in the educational system and other precautionary measures avoided a nationwide labor shortage, however, and later in the 7-year plan the government attempted to put the brakes on the rural-to-urban migration to avoid the flooding of cities and the per capita degeneration of housing facilities. Although the move to the cities has slowed somewhat during the last few years, it has continued at a rate much higher than the government has desired and much higher than it had anticipated. From 1959 to 1967 the urban population still increased at a rate of about 3.5 per cent per year. This was a higher annual average increase than had taken place from 1940 to 1959, although undoubtedly World War II greatly disrupted the movement in the early 1940s. If one can take the 1950 population estimate at face value, then the rate of urbanization took place at an average of 5 per cent per year between 1950 and 1959. Hence it appears that the last 8 years have witnessed some slowing in the urbanization process, but not nearly as much as the government had hoped for. One consequence of this has been that urban housing per capita in 1965 was 1.26 square meters below the planned figure for that year. If one realizes that it costs 2.5 billion rubles to increase the per capita urban housing space in the Soviet Union by 0.1 square meter, then one can realize the enormity of the problem of trying to keep up with urban housing in the face of the large rural-to-urban migration.

The Soviet desire generally is to limit the sizes of cities and to close the larger cities to in-migration. They look upon the ultra-large city as an undesirable phenomenon on the landscape and cite disadvantages to the urban dweller such as increases in distances between home and work and between home and places of recreation, deterioration of sanitary conditions, and so forth. They are quite concerned with air pollution over cities and are setting aside broad green belts around the bigger cities, which, among other things, are supposed to purify the air. Nevertheless large cities are continuing to grow in the Soviet Union, and more people are living in larger cities all the time. From 1959 to 1967 all urban settlements increased their total population by 28 per cent. At the same time total population in cities of more than 100,000 increased by 38.9 per cent. Even those cities of more than 500,000 people each increased their total population by 38 per cent. At the other end of the scale, cities of less than 10,000 population decreased their total population by 10 to 20 per cent. Thus it is evident that little cities are growing into big cities, that the number of small cities is decreasing and the total number of people living in small cities is decreasing, whereas the number of big cities is increasing and the total population in big cities is increasing very rapidly. The population increase in the larger cities has been primarily due to in-migration, since in general the birth rate decreases with the size of the city. In most cases migration accounted for 70 to 80 per cent of the growth of the larger cities between 1959 and 1967.

As can be seen in Table 13–13, the most rapid city growth was registered in the republic capitals of Middle Asia. Between 1959 and 1967, Frunze, the capital of the Kirgiz Republic, increased by 80 per cent. The other Middle Asian capitals increased from 40 to 50 per cent. Minsk, the capital of Belorussia, increased by more than 51 per cent. The larger cities of western Siberia increased between 20 and 40 per cent. Even Moscow, where the Soviets are desperately trying to limit in-migration, increased by about 1 per cent per year within consistent boundaries. Expansion of the city limits during the period added another 20 per cent to the population. Present policy to pour large portions of investment capital into new industries in the small- and medium-sized cities of European Russia may initiate changes in urbanization trends which will begin to become evident sometime in the 1970s, but, as has been pointed out by many economists, large industries cannot be located in very small cities, and therefore most rapid growth might be expected to take place in the future in cities of from 10,000 to 100,000 population.

Figure 13–13 shows the regional pattern of growth of larger cities (over 250,000 population in 1959). From 1939 to 1959 the most rapid growth of these cities took place in a belt across the central part of the country from the Volga River to the Yenisey. This reflects government efforts during these two decades to populate the territory on both sides of the Trans-Siberian Railway from Kuybyshev to Krasnoyarsk. It also reflects the rapid eastward mass movement of industries and personnel during World War II. But after 1959 the pattern seems to be almost exactly the opposite. Generally, during the period 1959–1965 European cities grew faster than Asiatic cities and the overall city growth rate in the U.S.S.R. was less than it had been before 1959. Part of the decline in the Volga-Yenisey strip no doubt was related to the political thaw which after 1957 allowed many departees to return to their homelands in the European part of the country. Another factor is the recent shift in governmental policy toward further industrialization of the populous European part of the country. Map 4 (lower right) of Figure 13–13 dramatically shows this shift in urban emphasis from the Asiatic to the European part of the country. With only six exceptions, since 1959 urban growth rates have decreased significantly in Asiatic U.S.S.R. and increased significantly in European U.S.S.R.

The rural-to-urban migration is draining off all of the natural increase and a little more from the farms. This exodus of nearly 1 million persons per year generally consists of 16 to 30 year olds who should be the backbone of the developing force for agriculture. Thus the present migration not only presents a problem to the cities where housing is lacking, but also seriously threatens the effectiveness of the farms. It has been reported that on many collective farms at the present time the average age of the working force is more than 50 years. When it is realized that well over half of the agricultural labor force is women, and that the official retirement age for women in the Soviet Union is 54, it can be understood that much of the labor force on farms is approaching or even over the retirement age. The present rural-to-urban migration is neither planned, anticipated, nor welcomed by the Soviet authorities. However, certain institutions continue to promote it. For instance, young men drafted in the Soviet army and navy from rural villages frequently do not return home after their service but get

Table 13–13   Cities in the U.S.S.R. with Populations over 100,000 in 1967, in Order of 1967 Size, in Thousands

	Jan. 1, 1939	Jan. 15, 1959	Per Cent Change 1939–59	July 1, 1967	Per Cent Change 1959–67
Moscow	4,138	5,046	21	6,507	29
Leningrad (St. Petersburg, Petrograd)	3,385	3,321	−2	3,706	12
Kiev	847	1,104	30	1,413	28
Tashkent	550	912	66	1,239	36
Baku	775	971	25	1,196	23
Kharkov	833	934	12	1,125	20
Gorky (Nizhny Novgorod)	644	942	46	1,120	19
Novosibirsk (Novonikolaevsk)	404	886	119	1,064	20
Kuybyshev (Samara)	390	806	106	992	23
Sverdlovsk (Ekaterinburg)	423	779	84	961	23
Tbilisi	519	695	34	842	21
Donetsk (Stalino)	466	699	50	840	20
Chelyabinsk	273	689	152	836	21
Kazan	398	647	63	821	27
Dnepropetrovsk	527	660	25	816	24
Perm (Molotov)	306	629	106	796	27
Odessa	602	667	11	776	16
Omsk	289	581	101	774	33
Minsk	237	509	115	772	52
Rostov-on-Don	510	600	18	757	26
Volgograd (Stalingrad, Tsaritsyn)	445	592	33	743	25
Saratov	372	581	56	720	24
Ufa	258	547	112	704	29
Riga	355	605	70	680	12
Yerevan	204	509	150	665	31
Alma-Ata (Verny)	222	456	106	652	43
Voronezh	344	448	30	611	36
Zaporozhye	282	435	54	595	37
Krasnoyarsk	190	412	117	576	40
Lvov	340	411	21	512	25
Krivoy Rog	189	388	105	510	31
Karaganda	156	397	154	498	25
Yaroslavl	309	407	32	498	22
Novokuznetsk (Stalinsk)	166	377	127	493	31
Khabarovsk	207	323	56	435	35

Table 13–13   Cities in the U.S.S.R. with Populations over 100,000 in 1967, in Order of 1967 Size, in Thousands (Continued)

	Jan. 1, 1939	Jan. 15, 1959	Per Cent Change 1939–59	July 1, 1967	Per Cent Change 1959–67
Irkutsk	250	366	46	420	15
Makeyevka	242	358	48	414	16
Barnaul	148	305	106	407	33
Ivanovo	285	335	18	407	21
Krasnodar (Ekaterinodar)	193	313	62	407	30
Vladivostok	206	291	41	397	36
Frunze (Pishpek)	93	220	137	396	80
Zhdanov (Mariupol)	222	284	28	385	36
Nizhniy Tagil	160	339	112	377	11
Tula	272	316	16	377	19
Izhevsk	176	285	62	376	32
Astrakhan	254	296	17	368	24
Kemerovo	133	278	109	364	31
Magnitogorsk	146	311	113	357	15
Lugansk (Voroshilovgrad)	215	275	28	352	28
Gorlovka	181	293	61	343	17
Tallin	160	282	76	340	21
Dushanbe (Stalinabad)	83	224	171	333	49
Penza	160	255	60	333	31
Groznyy	172	242	40	331	37
Orenburg (Chkalov)	172	267	56	326	22
Tomsk	145	249	72	324	30
Kalinin (Tver)	216	261	21	318	22
Vilnyus	215	236	10	316	34
Ryazan	95	214	125	311	45
Archangel	251	256	2	310	21
Kirov (Vyatka)	144	252	76	309	23
Kishinev	112	216	93	302	40
Nikolaev	169	226	34	300	33
Ulyanovsk (Simbirsk)	98	206	110	294	43
Prokopyevsk	107	282	163	290	3
Bryansk	174	207	19	288	38
Murmansk	119	222	86	287	29
Kaunas	152	214	41	284	33
Kaliningrad (Koenigsberg)		204		270	32
Kursk	120	205	71	255	24

Table 13–13   Cities in the U.S.S.R. with Populations over 100,000 in 1967, in Order of 1967 Size, in Thousands (Continued)

	Jan. 1, 1939	Jan. 15, 1959	Per Cent Change 1939–59	July 1, 1967	Per Cent Change 1959–67
Lipetsk	67	157	135	253	61
Samarkand	136	196	44	248	27
Taganrog	189	202	7	245	21
Tyumen	79	150	90	240	60
Ashkhabad	127	170	34	238	40
Gomel	139	168	21	237	41
Kherson	97	158	63	235	49
Ulan-Ude	126	175	39	227	30
Dneprodzerzhinsk	148	194	31	224	15
Simferopol	143	186	31	223	20
Chimkent	74	153	106	219	43
Ordzhonikidze (Vladikavkaz)	131	164	26	219	33
Kurgan	53	146	174	215	47
Orsk	66	176	166	215	22
Rybinsk (Shcherbakov)	144	182	26	212	16
Ust-Kamenogorsk	20	150	647	212	41
Tambov	106	172	62	211	23
Vladimir	67	154	130	211	37
Komsomolsk-on-Amur	71	177	150	209	18
Kostroma	121	172	42	209	22
Orel	111	150	36	209	39
Sevastopol	114	148	30	209	41
Shakhty	135	196	46	209	7
Semipalatinsk	110	156	42	204	31
Chita	121	172	42	203	18
Vitebsk	167	148	−11	203	38
Dzerzhinsk	103	164	59	201	23
Smolensk	157	147	−6	196	33
Sochi	62	95	53	188	98
Poltava	128	143	11	184	29
Angarsk		134		183	37
Biysk	80	146	82	181	24
Kaluga	89	134	50	179	34
Cheboksary	31	104	236	178	71
Chernovtsy	106	146	38	178	22
Zlatoust	99	161	62	178	11
Stavropol	85	141	65	177	26
Mogilev	99	122	22	176	44
Tselinograd (Akmolinsk)	32	102	216	176	73
Kirovabad	99	116	17	174	50
Petrozavodsk	70	136	95	171	26
Vologda	95	139	46	170	22
Andizhan	85	130	54	169	30
Syzran	83	149	79	169	13

Table 13–13   Cities in the U.S.S.R. with Populations over 100,000 in 1967, in Order of 1967 Size, in Thousands (Continued)

	Jan. 1, 1939	Jan. 15, 1959	Per Cent Change 1939–59	July 1, 1967	Per Cent Change 1959–67
Kirovograd	100	128	28	168	31
Kopeysk	60	161	167	166	3
Petropavlovsk	92	131	43	166	27
Cherepovets	32	92	185	165	79
Makhachkala	87	119	37	165	39
Podolsk	72	124	71	163	31
Vinnitsa	93	122	31	163	34
Sterlitamak	39	112	188	162	45
Kamensk-Uralskiy	51	141	177	161	14
Novocherkassk	76	95	26	161	69
Kutaisi	78	128	65	159	24
Dzhambul (Aulie-Ata)	64	113	78	158	40
Namangan	80	123	55	158	28
Pavlodar	29	90	216	154	71
Saransk	41	91	123	154	69
Temirtau	5	54	1000	150	178
Togliatti (Stavropol)		61		143	134
Rubtsovsk	38	111	195	142	28
Kramatorsk	94	115	23	141	23
Zhitomir	95	106	11	141	33
Sumy	64	98	53	140	43
Armavir	84	111	33	139	25
Chernigov	69	90	31	139	54
Kadievka	135	180	34	139	−23
Kiselevsk	44	130	196	138	6
Leninsk-Kuznetskiy	83	132	60	138	5
Yoshkar-Ola	27	89	227	137	54
Kremenchug	90	87	−3	136	56
Aktyubinsk	49	97	98	135	39
Berezniki	51	106	107	134	26
Leninakan	68	108	60	133	23
Klaypeda		90		131	46
Kokand	85	105	24	131	25
Kolomna	75	100	33	131	31
Belgorod	34	72	110	129	79
Norilsk	14	109	688	129	18
Cherkassy	52	85	64	128	51
Novomoskovsk (Stalinogorsk, Bobriki)	76	107	40	126	18
Kommunarsk (Voroshilovsk)	55	98	79	124	27
Ussuriysk (Voroshilov)	72	104	45	124	19
Novorossiysk	95	93	−2	123	32
Petropavlovsk-Kamchatskiy	35	86	142	123	43

Table 13–13   Cities in the U.S.S.R. with Populations over 100,000 in 1967, in Order of 1967 Size, in Thousands (Continued)

	Jan. 1, 1939	Jan. 15, 1959	Per Cent Change 1939–59	July 1, 1967	Per Cent Change 1959–67
Uralsk	67	104	54	123	18
Bratsk		51		122	139
Engels	69	91	32	122	35
Miass	38	99	163	122	23
Blagoveshchensk	59	95	61	121	27
Serpukhov	91	106	17	121	14
Severodvinsk	21	79	269	121	53
Bobruysk	84	98	16	120	22
Lisichansk	26	38	46	120	216
Lyubertsy	46	93	101	120	29
Melitopol	76	95	25	119	25
Nalchik	48	88	83	119	35
Osh	33	65	96	119	83
Kerch	104	98	−6	118	20
Kustanay	34	86	158	118	37
Elektrostal	43	97	127	117	21
Orekhovo-Zuevo	99	108	9	117	8
Anzhero-Sudzhensk	69	116	68	116	0
Belovo	43	107	147	116	8
Kovrov	67	99	47	116	17
Volzhskiy		67		114	70
Slavyansk	78	83	6	113	36
Mytishchi	60	99	64	112	12
Pskov	60	81	34	112	38
Grodno	49	73	48	111	52
Nikopol	58	83	44	110	33
Pervouralsk	44	90	104	110	22
Cheremkhovo	56	123	121	109	−11
Novgorod	40	61	53	107	75
Novokuybyshevsk		63		107	70
Novoshakhtinsk	48	104	116	107	3
Maykop	56	82	47	106	29
Serov	65	98	51	104	6
Sumgait	6	52	721	104	100
Konstantinovka	96	89	−7	103	16
Bukhara	50	69	38	102	48
Krasnyy Luch	59	94	58	102	9
Noginsk	81	93	15	102	10
Syktyvkar	24	64	165	102	59
Guryev	41	78	89	101	29
Batumi	70	82	18	100	22
Chirchik	15	66	345	100	52
Leninabad	46	77	70	100	30
Rovno	43	56	31	100	79

Sources: SSSR Administrativno-territorialnoe delenie, 1967, pp. 592–604, and Narodnoye khozyaystvo SSSR v 1959 godu, pp. 35–44.

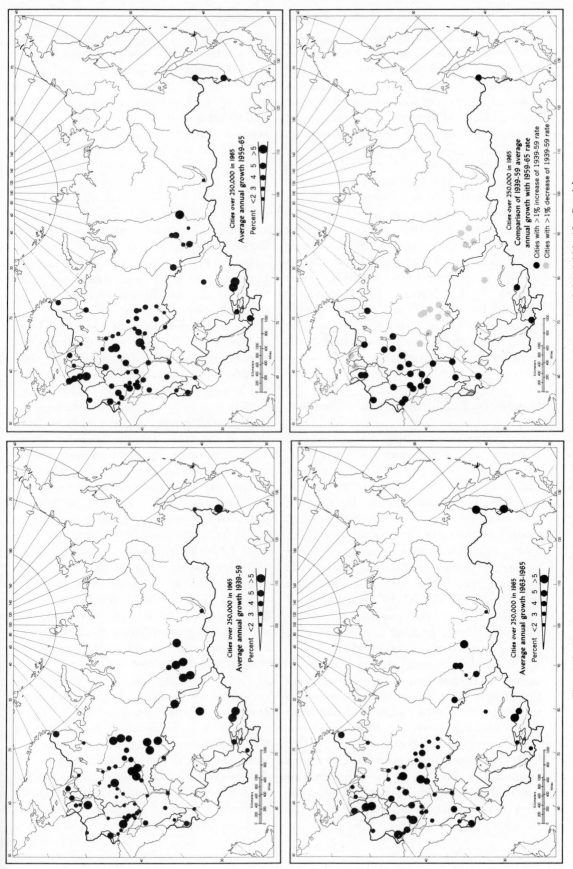

Figure 13–13 *Average annual growth rates of Soviet cities whose 1965 populations exceeded 250,000. After Pettyjohn,*
Leonard, unpublished term paper, Department of Geography, University of Wisconsin—Milwaukee, Spring, 1967.

jobs in cities. Also peasant youths who enter universities, all of which are in the larger cities, tend to remain in cities if they can find jobs there after graduation. Since young people who have been reared in cities lack the know-how to farm, there is no movement in the opposite direction. The Soviet government has tried to use the internal passport and registration system to halt the flow into the cities, but this has been of little success. To take up permanent residence in a city, a Soviet peasant coming in from the country must receive a permit, and in large cities such as Moscow and Leningrad he cannot receive a residence permit until he shows written proof of having a job. In any case he must have his internal passport. Some state and collective farms are now holding passports of the individuals on their farms in order to control movement.

Manpower, Employment, and Education

Since the Soviet Union has a planned economy, the government has the dual responsibility of providing manpower where needed and providing all people with jobs. The peculiarities of the age, sex, and racial character of the population, along with the rather irrational population movements that have been going on in the past few years, make this task a tricky one. Until the mid 1950s, the Soviets were not much worried about the availability of manpower, since the population had always contained a good deal of slack in the form of excess rural population. An attempt to exercise control over the whereabouts of people had been instituted before World War II, but this did not stem so much from labor needs as it did from the traditional Russian desire to know where everybody is all of the time. In 1938 labor booklets were issued to all persons employed in the state sector as a means of controlling hiring and turnover, and a year later some controls were extended to the

collective farms when a minimum number of labor days was established to be earned annually by each collective farmer. There has always been a problem of the availability of people with necessary skills and training, but this has not been directly related to numbers of people. By the mid 1950s, however, it became apparent to the Soviet authorities that much of the slack had been taken up in the unoccupied population, and this, coupled with the prospect of reduced numbers of teenagers entering the labor force due to birth deficits during World War II, induced some sweeping changes in the education, pension, and military structures in order to meet an anticipated shortage of industrial labor.

The legal definition of the labor force in the Soviet Union is able-bodied males between the ages of 16 and 59 and able-bodied women between the ages of 16 and 54. During the period 1951–1955 about 4 million people per year were reaching the legal working age. These had been born during the peak fertility years of 1934–1938. However, this was drastically reduced in subsequent years as the survivors of the war babies became 16 years of age. In 1960 only 1,700,000 youths entered the labor force. Although it was anticipated that the number would increase after 1960, it was apparent that the 1951–1955 level would not be met until 1966. Also World War II had left a great deficit of men in the middle age brackets and great numbers of war invalids. Hence Soviet planning would have to take into account the utilization of many women and considerable numbers of invalid men. (Table 13–14) In the face of all these prospects, the authorities under the leadership of Khrushchev initiated an educational reform, a partial demobilization of the army and navy, and a relaxation of restrictions on the work of pensioners.

The educational system was reoriented in several ways to emphasize the poly-technical nature of the training. General

Table 13–14   Civilian Labor Force by Sector, Socioeconomic Category, and Sex, U.S.S.R., January 15, 1959

Category	Total (in Thousands)	Males (in Thousands)	Percentage Distribution	Females (in Thousands)	Percentage Distribution	Per Cent Females
Total civilian labor force	105,372	48,817	100.0	56,555	100.0	53.7
Agriculture	48,291	18,576	38.1	29,715	52.5	61.5
Collective farmers	31,723	13,731	28.1	17,992	31.8	56.7
Workers and employees	6,611	3,898	8.0	2,713	4.8	41.0
Individual peasants	92	32	0.1	60	0.1	65.2
Private subsidiary sector	9,865	914	1.9	8,951	15.8	90.7
Industry, construction, transportation and communications	36,575	22,423	45.9	14,152	25.0	38.7
Trade, public dining, etc.	5,171	1,993	4.1	3,178	5.6	61.5
Education, science, and public health	9,793	2,864	5.9	6,928	12.3	70.7
Housing, communal economy, administration, financial system	4,660	2,385	4.9	2,275	4.0	48.8
Other branches	882	575	1.2	306	0.5	34.7

Source: Norton T. Dodge and Murray Feshbach, "The Role of Women in Soviet Agriculture," in Jerzy F. Karcz, ed., *Soviet and East European Agriculture*, 1967, p. 268.

schools were replaced with trade schools and "tekhnikums," and many students were classified as "working and rural youths" and allowed to complete secondary education only through evening and correspondence work. Students in the vocational schools were required to work 2 days per week in local enterprises or school workshops, and full-time tekhnikum students were required to work regular 46-hour work weeks in their final third or fourth year of training. In order to infuse secondary graduates into the labor force directly, the majority of young people desiring to go on to higher education were required to work at least 2 years before applying for entrance to a college or university. At the elementary-secondary school levels, an additional year was added to the old 10-year system in order to allow enough time to complete the traditional curriculum and in addition to master the required technical training and the part-time work required.

The military manpower capability of a country, in terms of personnel only, is usually adjudged to be the male population between the ages of 20 and 34. The number in this category reached a maximum in 1961 when, significantly enough, major reductions of the armed forces were announced. It was anticipated that the male population, ages 20–34, would decline to a level about 11 per cent below the 1961 peak by approximately 1968. Thereafter a modest increase could be expected, but the 1961 peak would not be reached even by 1975. In the face of this simple fact, the armed forces in the Soviet Union have been held to 3 million men ever since 1961. The Soviet Union does not have a universal military training, but follows a policy of drafting similar to that used in the United States to meet current military requirements. Beginning in 1965 the period of active military duty was reduced to 1 year for enlisted men who were graduates of higher educational institutions, thereby enabling them to be employed much earlier in the civilian economy and to lengthen their working life.

In February 1964 a new law was adopted regarding the work of pensioners. Under a 1956 regulation, persons receiving pensions had been penalized for working full time. Anyone who had made more than 100 rubles per month before retirement could not draw a pension if he went back to work, no matter what the amount of his new wages. Those who had made less than 100 rubles per month before retirement could earn any amount in their new jobs and receive their pensions of 15 rubles per month. And persons who had retired on a privileged basis under the 1956 law could receive up to 50 per cent of their pensions no matter what they earned. In order to receive any pension men had to work at least 25 years before retirement and women 20 years. According to the new 1964 regulations, there are no limits on the amount of time that can be worked by persons receiving pensions, although there are limits on the branch or sector of the economy in which certain categories of retired personnel may seek employment, and there are also limits on the amount of gross earnings or combined pensions and earnings. Special consideration is given to pensioners who are willing to accept jobs in less desirable sectors of the economy and less desirable regions of the country. There are no limits set for pensioners who find work on collective or state farms, which probably signifies the need in agriculture for people with special skills. All these revisions in the pension regulations were designed to stimulate the reentry of skilled persons into the labor force. Actually there has always been a large proportion of those over retirement age who are

still working. In 1959, 48.5 per cent of the males over 60 years old and 37 per cent of the females over 55 years old were in the labor force. Hence the retirement age does not mean too much. At the other end of the scale, in 1959, 7 per cent of the males and 5.9 per cent of the females between the ages of 10 and 15 were in the labor force. Such child labor is probably most prevalent in the non-Russian nationality areas, particularly on farms.

The rather rapid conversion of collective farms to state farms during the 7-year-plan period, 1959–1965, also injected considerable numbers of people into state employment, since in general the collective farms had had more people living on them than were needed for farm operation. In October 1960 the abolishment of the producers' cooperative system released another 1.4 million people to the state sector of the economy. However, many of the workers in these cooperative artels were war invalids, and the government eventually found it necessary to require certain enterprises to hire up to 2 per cent of their personnel from war invalids. In 1962 it was reported that 2.5 million invalids were in the labor force. Another measure was the organization of volunteers from among persons who had full-time jobs, were full-time students, or were on pensions, who were eager to have a hand in governmental activities and were willing to donate their time and services. In 1962 more than 2 million volunteers were participating in the work of lower-level city and rayon administrations. Most of this work was organized in the areas of trade, cultural activities, and organizational-instructional work. Beginning during the 1962–1963 school year the curriculum in many cases was altered to provide upper classmen in higher educational institutions with the opportunity of holding part-time paying jobs for 6 to 10 months of the year. Also short-term volunteers contributed free labor in the form of building and repairing roads and houses, planting trees, gathering harvests, collecting scrap metal, and so forth. Many students in secondary specialized institutions were utilized in this way. Old laws were brought into play that required collective farmers to put in 4 to 6 days per year in maintaining roads and required military personnel to help harvest crops, unload ships, do construction work, and so forth.

The upshot of all these measures that were taken to meet the anticipated need for labor during the 7-year plan, 1959–1965, was a broad over-fulfillment of the plan for labor, and a return to the problem of seeking out appropriate types of labor with required skills and technical training, rather than concern with sheer numbers. In fact as 1965 approached Soviet planners became very concerned about how to find jobs for the double graduation class that was going to be flooding the labor market in June 1966 when the eleventh year of the elementary-secondary school system was to be abolished and the 10-year system reinstituted. Three million young people were graduated from the tenth and eleventh grades in June 1966. This, on top of the fact that the 7-year plan, which was to have added 11 to 12 million people to the labor force during the period 1959–1965, had in fact added 22.3 million persons. As a result, the greatest change that took place in manpower during the 7-year plan was the government's approach to the manpower problem. At the beginning, with the expectation of a labor shortage, the strategy was to attract as many persons as possible into the socialized economy. By the end of the plan period, however, the emphasis had shifted toward adjusting the labor market and the educational system to absorb large inflows of young persons.

The educational system was reorganized again in August 1964 to begin to take effect in the 1966–1967 school year and to be completed by the 1970–1971 school year. The new educational system consists of primary grades 1–3, secondary grades 4–8, and senior grades 9–10. The first eight grades are supposedly compulsory. Throughout most of the country, most of the children do get 8 years of education at the present time, although there are some exceptions to this in outlying areas. However, many students do not go on through years 9 and 10 because of one reason or another. The new school reform largely reorients the schools away from so much technical training and abolishes the requirement to work 2 years before entering higher education. With the labor crisis past, more persons are being encouraged to enter higher educational institutions, and in spite of the fact that during the 1960s college-age persons decreased in number, enrollments in higher institutions increased rapidly. During the 1959–1960 school year about 2.3 million students were enrolled in higher education, which amounted to about 11 students per 100 persons between the ages of 20 and 24. By 1964 enrollment had risen to 3.6 million and the ratio to 24 per 100. This trend has been continuing since 1964.

Females are still preponderant in the working force. Although the great discrepancy between males and females is moving up the age ladder, and many of the excess females are now beyond the working age, in 1965 there still were 5,800,000 more females than males in the working-age population, which includes a greater span of years for men than for women. At the same time, there were 15,100,000 more women than men above the working age, which includes more years for women than for men. In 1965 females constituted 50.4 per cent of the labor force, which was down from a maximum of 53.7 per cent in 1959. (Table 13–14) Older females are more predominant on the farms than in the cities, and females still make up 54 per cent of the agricultural labor force. Projecting population statistics forward, it appears that the working age population will have more women than men until 1976, after which men will predominate, primarily because men work 5 more years before retirement than women do.

The major problem in manpower has always been and remains the regional and temporal imbalances between need and supply and chronically low labor productivity. In general there still is a labor surplus in most of the small towns and rural areas of the European part of the country, and even in some of the larger cities of the European part, but at the same time there are severe labor shortages throughout much of the Asiatic section of the country, particularly in some of the more rapidly growing new cities with burgeoning industries.

The general exodus from the eastern regions during the past decade has already been mentioned, and the liberalizations on labor mobility have not helped this situation. Although differential wages have been constructed to entice people to outlying areas, the fact is that overall wages are no more than 15 per cent higher than they are in the west, whereas living costs are frequently at least twice as high, and most of the amenities of life simply do not exist in the east. Wages in heavy industries and construction in the east are 130 to 200 per cent those in the west, but average wages in the east are dragged down by wages in light industries and services, which are no higher than those in the west, if as high. In many of the new cities of the east founded specifically around one large industry or one large construction project, there is little work for women and therefore there is actually an excess of certain types of labor existing side-by-side with shortages of skilled labor for heavy industry. Therefore women are glad to find work at any price in these localities, and this drives down the average wage. At the same time, market basket prices are often 175 per cent those in the west, and the cost of community services are two to two and a half times as much. Child-care facilities

and other auxiliary institutions which would facilitate the working of housewives are often lacking. It appears that there probably is not any kind of action that the government can afford to take that will accomplish the movement of 5 to 15 million people eastward into Siberia as was originally hoped. Therefore the government is now in the process of quietly capitulating to reality and reorienting its investment capital to the greater industrialization of small- and medium-sized cities in the European part of the country where the population already is located. Thus they have finally come to the conclusion that it is cheaper to move raw materials to people than it is to move people to raw materials. To move a given labor force to an industry in the eastern regions requires not only the initial costs of moving the people but the much expanded costs of providing these people with all sorts of services including transportation into and out of the area, as well as the establishment of a large number of auxiliary people who in one way or another are necessary for a complete community. Therefore manning a large industrial plant in a new region becomes extremely expensive.

The easiest form of skilled labor that can be shipped into outlying areas is recent graduates who have benefited from the free educational system and who are obligated by law to serve for 3 years wherever the government places them. However, many of these young people have been able to get out of their contracts long before the 3 years are up. The government has softened on this point too and has recently allowed new graduates to look for jobs themselves before being assigned to government-chosen posts. In order to try to stabilize manpower somewhat in these new areas, the authorities have initiated the practice of withholding the diploma from would-be graduates until they have served at least a year in their initial posts. In spite of all this, labor mobility remains quite high in the eastern regions and, in fact, throughout the Soviet Union. At the present time more than 3 per cent of the population of the U.S.S.R. is involved in internal migration each year. And by far the largest percentage of these migrants now move under their own volition without any real sanction from the authorities. Over 90 per cent of the people hired in new jobs during the past decade have been hired "at the gate." This has been unplanned and unorganized; people simply show up at industrial enterprises looking for jobs and are hired on the spot whenever needed.

There is still much inefficiency in all aspects of the Soviet economy, and labor productivity is low by Western standards across the board. Theoretically there are significant pools of inefficiently used and unused labor which still might be exploited, but in actuality it is very difficult to make use of this reserve. Probably the greatest inefficiency exists in agriculture, which still utilizes around 35 per cent of the labor force, as against only about 7 per cent in the United States. (Table 13–15) It is true, as the Soviets point out, that their figures for agricultural labor include such people as construction workers in rural areas, transport workers engaged in transporting agricultural produce, professional people and technicians engaged in all sorts of auxiliary services to farms, and so forth; whereas the United States statistics do not include such auxiliary personnel nor do they include the work of many part-time people, mostly youths who work less than 15 hours per week, or many migrant laborers, who work as wage earners only during part of the year. Nevertheless there is still a great discrepancy between the two countries. Also 700,000 collective farmers in the Soviet Union spend about 250 million man-hours each year trading their produce at collective markets. Thus the lack of a capitalistic retail system induces great inefficiency in the use of collective farmers' time. There is great seasonality in the use of labor on the farms, with a low point in

winter, and even during peak production it appears that much useless busy work is engaged in simply to keep brigades occupied. It has been estimated by the Soviets themselves that only two thirds to three quarters of the total potential working time of able-bodied collective farmers is actually used. And in some of the more densely populated rural areas of the country, such as the North Caucasus and western Ukraine, there are several million able-bodied men living on collective farms who simply are not engaged in any socialized work. They are listed simply as being employed in the "household and subsidiary economy." The recent immigrants into these high rural surplus labor areas generally have been unable to find jobs for themselves, and have settled down with relatives on collective farms and simply engage in intensive work on private plots of ground. This is true also of many of the rural women throughout the country who account for about 90 per cent of the labor on all the private plots. The 1965 relaxation of limitations on the use of private plots is not going to help this situation. In many cases, particularly for women, who can work both in the household and on the private plots, it would not pay for them to shift to full-time labor in the socialized economy. The wages that they could earn would not equal the intangible benefits that they now enjoy in taking care of their own families and at the same time deriving a reasonable cash income from their individual efforts.

Table 13–15   Employment, U.S.S.R. and U.S.A., 1964

	U.S.S.R.	U.S.A.
Total labor force	103,364,000	67,736,000
Nonagricultural	66,765,000	62,975,000
Agricultural	36,598,000	4,761,000

Source: New Directions in the Soviet Economy, p. 786.

This is true also of women everywhere in the economy who do not hold jobs in the socialized sector of the economy. The Soviet authorities have always looked to the households as a large source of potential labor, but on close scrutiny it appears that the possibilities of recruiting labor from this sector of the population are essentially nil. First, women are generally poorly trained; the majority over 45 years of age have had no more than 6 years of schooling, if that. In addition, it has been estimated that the minimum annual wage necessary to induce women to give up the personal care of their children and their individual earnings from their private economy to go into factory work or some other sort of socialized economy would be around 1100 rubles per year. In view of the fact that the average annual money wage received by all workers and employees in the U.S.S.R. is about 1080 rubles, it is quite clear that a conversion of such labor would hardly make sense. In areas where the women are more skilled, most of those who can and will work are probably already working. It is in the Caucasus and Middle Asian Regions that large pools of unemployed women exist, and it is precisely here that they are the least suited for urban jobs. (Table 13–16)

The use of indigenous rural people for industrial labor in nearby towns to reduce long-distance migrations has been tried again and again, but in most of the outlying areas this simply has not worked. Most of the indigenous peoples have been poorly trained and generally are unsuitable for the work desired. And, as has been pointed out before, usually Russians and other Slavic groups have been moved in to form the labor forces on large construction projects and in large factories.

There are far fewer people in households unemployed in the larger cities than in smaller cities in rural areas where job opportunities are less. Moscow and Leningrad have about 6 to 7 per cent of the able-bodied population not participating in the socialized economy, whereas in the U.S.S.R. as a whole it is about 20 per cent, and in Siberia it is 26 per cent. These statistics include quite a few young men who have not found jobs to their liking and who simply have not taken jobs. Many of these are from higher income families, the parents of which are professional people who have succeeded in giving their children a fairly easy life. From this sector of the population often stems a rebellious young group who are quite antisocial in their attitudes and therefore provide a problem for Soviet authorities. One meets a surprising number of such youths in their early twenties on the streets of the larger cities who approach tourists for the purposes of illicit trading of money, clothing, and so forth. When questioned as to their occupation, they reply simply that they do not work. And one gets the feeling from the tones of their voices that they do not ever intend to work.

High labor turnover results in much loss due to time involved between jobs, which over the entire country seems to average about 20 to 30 days per person per year. It has been estimated that in 1964 turnover accounted for a loss of about 85 million man-days, around 1.5 per cent of the total labor that year. The 1940 law restricting voluntary quitting was removed in 1956,

Table 13–16   Percentage of all Women in Employment, by Republic

U.S.S.R.	41.5	Georgia	38.8
R.S.F.S.R.	42.0	Armenia	31.9
Ukraine	43.7	Azerbaydzhan	34.5
Belorussia	48.6	Kazakhstan	30.4
Lithuania	42.6	Uzbekistan	33.9
Latvia	44.4	Kirgizia	34.0
Estonia	44.9	Turkmenistan	32.2
Moldavia	51.1	Tadzhikistan	35.0

Source: Robert A. French, "Recent Population Trends in the USSR," *St. Antony's Papers, Number 19, Soviet Affairs, Number Four,* Oxford University Press, 1966, p. 81.

and immediately thereafter there was a very large turnover in jobs, which has since leveled off somewhat. It is quite clear that, despite Soviet protestations to the contrary, the U.S.S.R. has a labor market in which workers seek the highest possible returns in terms of money and fringe benefits. And often it is the fringe benefits that are the deciding factor, since the basic wages universally are low. It has been the policy of the Soviet government, and still is, that the basic wage will not rise very rapidly as the economy improves, but that fringe benefits will increase greatly. At the present time housing costs practically nothing, certainly no more than 5 per cent of the average income, public transportation in cities is rapidly becoming free of charge, and, of course, health benefits, retirement, and so forth are provided by the government. Thus the basic wage in the Soviet Union is somewhat similar to the wages paid military service men in the United States. This cash is simply pocket money, the necessities of life being supplied by the organization. Therefore there is little that the Soviet authorities can do in the way of wage differentials to induce mass conversions of labor from one sector to another. The necessities of life are generally provided for equally poorly by the Soviet system, whether you work or not. Therefore the job of organizing labor and inducing more efficiency into the system is a very complex one in the Soviet Union. The experimentation carried out during the past few years under the label "Libermanism" may in the long run solve some of the problems of inefficiency in labor, but so far such efforts have been very modest and have been for the most part strangled by traditions of the past which simply cannot incorporate the idea of an enterprise being allowed to work independently under a purely profit motive. Where local autonomy has been imposed from above, local bureaucrats more likely than not have defected the effort.

Prospects for the Future

With the continued industrialization and urbanization in outlying areas of the Soviet Union, the non-Russian nationality groups will inevitably be drawn more and more into the mainstream of the social and economic life of the country, and birth rates will drop in these areas as they have in the Slavic regions. Therefore undoubtedly the average birth rate of the country will continue to fall as it has in the past several decades, and the growth rate of the entire population will continue to decrease. In fact if trends continue, the population could stagnate and undergo absolute decline sometime after 1980. Thus a real labor shortage looms for sometime in the not too distant future. This is well recognized by the Soviet leaders who are actively, but rather quietly, trying to establish measures which will better utilize unused portions of the labor, as stated previously. Gone are the days when a virtually inexhaustible labor supply existed on the farms ready to be moved to the cities as fast as urban housing could take care of it. An annual increase of the nonagricultural labor force as high as even 3 per cent, which is considerably lower than in the past, is simply untenable for any length of time because by approximately 1980 there would be no one left on the farms. Gone are the days also when huge masses of political prisoners could be moved about from labor camp to labor camp to provide labor needed for the construction of new cities and new industries. Although there are still a number of ways in which a Soviet citizen can be sentenced to forced labor in a given area of the country, particularly under the laws passed during the past decade to eliminate antisocial and parasitic elements of society, this is done on a scale that is nowhere comparable to what it was in the days of Stalin when it involved millions of people. Undesirable districts such as Siberia and the Far East no longer have this huge, cheap labor pool to draw upon. Thus the Soviets are going to be faced with a much knottier problem of the management of labor in the future than they have ever had before. One can expect that the simple facts of the population makeup of the country in the future, as in the past, are going to dictate much of the government policy and government action. And as demands of the populace increase for all sorts of consumer goods and amenities, the Soviet leaders are going to be faced with the necessity of more and more diversion of materials and personnel from primary production to services and other such activities. At the present time about 15 per cent of the total labor force is employed in nonmaterial production and in services, if 20 per cent for commerce is excluded. These activities may well absorb 40 per cent of the labor force eventually.

The biggest concession of the Soviet leaders to economic and social realities is the switch to a policy for the immediate future of locating much of the new economic activity in the smaller and medium-sized towns in the European part of the country. When it is realized that the development and population of the eastern regions has always been a basic tenet of the communist doctrine in the Soviet Union, then it can be realized how big this switch in orientation really is. It appears now that Siberia and the Soviet Far East may remain largely unpopulated and will serve the country mainly as storehouses of large amounts of a great variety of mineral resources. These mineral resources will be exploited by minimum numbers of people in the area and shipped to the populous west for processing.

In the face of all their labor problems, the Soviets have continually decreased the length of the work week. During 1956–1960 the work week for most laborers was reduced from 48 to 41 hours. At the end of the period most people in industry worked 7 hours per day for 5 days a week plus 6 hours on Saturday, with Sunday free. Since that time there has been some move toward a 5-day work week with a retention of about 41 hours total work. There has been talk of a 34-hour work week, but such talk has diminished in the past few years. In certain branches of the economy, where hazardous work is involved, a shorter work week already is in effect. The continued reduction of the work week seems to be another basic tenet of the Communist Party, but it is a question as to how soon such benefits will reach diminishing returns. The use of leisure time is already quite a problem in a country where very little exists in the way of private entertainment and recreational facilities. Too much idle time is always a dangerous thing, and in the Soviet Union where housing generally is inadequate, not much leisure time can be spent in the home. Therefore the streets are constantly crowded with milling people who are going nowhere and doing nothing but killing time. There is little opportunity for purposeful activity outside of working hours. This in itself is a tremendous waste of manpower and energy. A great many extracurricular activities have been organized to accomplish useful purposes, such as taking care of children after school hours, working on construction projects of national significance on weekends and holidays, and so forth, but this type of activity, noble as it may be, cannot absorb all the free time of all the people.

Reading List

Aspaturian, Vernon V., "The Non-Russian Nationalities," in Allen Kassof, ed., *Prospects for Soviet Society*, Praeger, New York, 1968, pp. 143–202.

Atlas narodov mira (Atlas of the Peoples of the World), Moscow, 1964, 184 pp. (in Russian); contains good regional maps of the U.S.S.R. at large scales.

Brackett, James W., "Population Dynamics in the U.S.S.R.," report of the Foreign Manpower Research Office, U.S. Bureau of Census.

———, *Projections of the Population of the U.S.S.R.,*

by Age and Sex: 1964–1985, International Population Reports, U.S. Department of Commerce, Bureau of the Census, Washington, 1964, Series P-91, No. 13, 45 pp.

Caroe, Olaf, *Soviet Empire: The Turks of Central Asia and Stalinism,* Macmillan, London, 1967, 2nd ed., 308 pp.

Conquest, Robert, *Soviet Nationalities Policy in Practice,* Praeger, New York, 1967, 160 pp.

———, *The Soviet Deportation of Nationalities,* Macmillan, London, 1960, 203 pp.

Davidovich, V. G., "Satellite Cities and Towns of the U.S.S.R.," *Soviet Geography: Review and Translation,* March 1962, pp. 3–34.

Eason, Warren W., "Population Changes," in Allen Kassof, ed., *Prospects for Soviet Society,* Praeger, New York, 1968, pp. 203–240.

———, "The Soviet Population Today," *Foreign Affairs,* July 1959, pp. 598–606.

———, *Soviet Manpower: The Population and Labor Force of the U.S.S.R.,* PhD Dissertation, Columbia University, 1958.

Fedor, Thomas S., *The Future Status of the Autonomous Soviet Socialist Republics in the Soviet Federative System,* Master's Thesis, University of Wisconsin–Milwaukee, August 1967, 111 pp.

Field, Neil C., "Land Hunger and the Rural Depopulation Problem in the U.S.S.R.," *Annals of the Association of American Geographers,* 1963, pp. 465–478.

French, R. A., "Recent Population Trends in the U.S.S.R.," in Kaser, Michael, ed., *Soviet Affair's No. 4, St. Antony's Papers Number 19,* Oxford University Press, 1966, pp. 68–95.

Geiger, H. Kent, *The Family in Soviet Russia,* Russian Research Center Studies, 56, Harvard University Press, 1968, 381 pp.

Geografiya naseleniya S.S.S.R. (Geography of the Population of the U.S.S.R.), *Voprosy Geografii,* Moscow, 1962, No. 56, 228 pp. (in Russian).

Goldberg, B. Z., *The Jewish Problem in the Soviet Union, An Analysis and Solution,* Crown Publishers, New York, 1961, 374 pp.

Goldhagen, Erich, ed., *Ethnic Minorities in the Soviet Union,* Praeger, New York, 1968, 351 pp.

Goodman, Ann S. and Feshbach, Murray, *Estimates and Projections of Educational Attainment in the U.S.S.R.: 1950–1985,* International Population Reports, U.S.

Department of Commerce, Bureau of the Census, Washington, 1967, Series P-91, No. 16, 23 pp.

Greenbaum, Alfred A., "Soviet Jewry During the Lenin-Stalin Period–I," *Soviet Studies,* April 1965, pp. 406–421.

Hajdu, Peter, *The Samoyed Peoples and Languages,* Indiana University Publications, Bloomington, 1963, Uralic and Altaic Series, Vol. 14, 114 pp.

Harris, Chauncy D., *Cities of the Soviet Union: Studies in their Functions, Size, Density, and Growth,* Association of American Geographers Monograph Series, No. 5, Rand McNally and Company, in press.

———, "City and Region in the Soviet Union," in R. P. Beckinsale and J. M. Houston, *Urbanization and its Problems,* Basil Blackwell, Oxford, 1968, pp. 277–296.

———, "The Cities of the Soviet Union," *Geographical Review,* 1945, pp. 107–121.

———, "Ethnic Groups in Cities of the Soviet Union," *Geographical Review,* 1945, pp. 466–473.

Hayuk, Hlib S., *Changes in the Ethnic Structure and in Regional Distribution of Population in Ukraine, 1897–1959,* M.A. Thesis, University of Wisconsin–Milwaukee, August 1967, 106 pp.

Heer, David M. and Bryden, Judith G., "Family Allowances and Fertility in the Soviet Union," *Soviet Studies,* October 1966, pp. 153–163.

Hooson, David J. M., "The Growth of Cities in Pre-Soviet Russia," in R. P. Beckinsale and J. M. Houston, *Urbanization and its Problems,* Basil Blackwell, Oxford, 1968, pp. 254–276.

Hostler, Charles Warren, *Turkism and the Soviets,* Praeger, New York, 1957, 244 pp.

Hrdlicka, Alex, *The Peoples of the Soviet Union,* Smithsonian Institution War Background Studies, Washington, July 15, 1942, No. 3, 29 pp.

Kantner, John F., "The Population of the Soviet Union," *Comparisons of the United States and Soviet Economies,* Part I, U.S. Government Printing Office, Washington, 1959, pp. 31–71.

Khodzhayev, D. G., "The Planning of the Distribution of Production in Population Centers and Some Problems in Population Geography," in V. V. Pokshishevskiy, D. I. Valentey, and S. A. Kovalev, *Nauchnyye problemy geografii naseleniya,* Moscow University, 1967, pp. 7–19; translated into English in *Soviet Geography: Review and Translation,* October 1967, pp. 619–629.

Kolarz, Walter, *Russia and Her Colonies,* Praeger, New York, 1952, 335 pp.

Konstantinov, O. A., ed., *Geografiya naseleniya v S.S.S.R.: osnovnye problemy* (The Geography of Population in the U.S.S.R.: Principal Problems), Akademiya Nauk, Moscow, 1964, 278 pp. (in Russian).

———, ed., *Geografiya naseleniya i naselennykh punktov S.S.S.R.* (The Geography of Population and of Populated Points in the U.S.S.R.), Leningrad, 1967 (in Russian).

———, "Some Conclusions about the Geography of Cities and the Urban Population of the U.S.S.R. Based on the Results of the 1959 Census," *Soviet Geography: Review and Translation,* September 1960, pp. 59–74.

Krueger, John R., ed., *The Turkic Peoples,* Indiana University Publications, Bloomington, Uralic and Altaic Series, Vol. 32, 440 pp.

Lamont, Corliss, *The Peoples of the Soviet Union,* Harcourt, Brace, New York, 1944, 214 pp.

Leasure, J. William and Lewis, Robert A., "Internal Migration in Russia in the Late Nineteenth Century," *Slavic Review,* September 1968, pp. 375–394.

———, "Internal Migration in the U.S.S.R.: 1897–1926," *Demography,* 1967, IV, No. 2, pp. 479–496.

Levin, M. G. and Potapov, L. P., ed., *The Peoples of Siberia,* The University of Chicago Press, Chicago, 1964, 948 pp.

Lorimer, Frank, *The Population of the Soviet Union: History and Prospects,* League of Nations, Geneva, 1946, 289 pp.

Medlin, William K., "Education," in Allen Kassof, ed., *Prospects for Soviet Society,* Praeger, New York, 1968, pp. 241–262.

Melezin, Abraham, "Trends and Issues in the Soviet Geography of Population," *Annals of the Association of American Geographers,* June 1963, pp. 144–160.

New Directions in the Soviet Economy, Part III, The Human Resources, Studies Prepared for the Subcommittee on Foreign Economic Policy of the Joint Economic Committee of the Congress of the United States, U.S. Government Printing Office, Washington, 1966, pp. 594–871.

Newth, J. A., "Some Trends in the Soviet Population, 1939 to 1956," *Soviet Studies,* January 1959, pp. 252–278.

Perevedentsev, V. I., "The Influence of Ethnic Factors on the Territorial Redistribution of Population," *Izvestiya Akademii Nauk S.S.S.R., seriya geograficheskaya,* 1965, No. 4, pp. 31–39; translated in *Soviet Geography: Review and Translation,* October 1965, pp. 40–50.

Podyachikh, P. G., *Naselenie S.S.S.R.* (Population of the U.S.S.R.), Moscow, 1964, 190 pp. (in Russian).

Pokshishevskiy, V. V., "Prospects of Population Migration in the U.S.S.R.," in *Geografiya naseleniya Vostochnoy Sibiri* (Population Geography of Eastern Siberia), Academy of Sciences, Moscow, 1962; translated in *Soviet Geography: Review and Translation,* January 1963, pp. 13–25.

———, *Geografiya naseleniya v SSSR, Itogi Nauki, geografiya SSSR,* Vypusk 3, Moscow, 1966, 170 pp. (in Russian); this contains a bibliography of 1940 items published by the Soviets about population geography between 1961 and 1965.

———, V. V. Vorobyev, N. Gladysheva Ye, and V. I. Perevedentsev, "On Basic Migration Patterns," *Fourth Congress of the Geographical Society of the U.S.S.R., Economic-Geography Symposium;* translated in *Soviet Geography: Review and Translation,* December 1964, pp. 3–18.

Population Bulletin, Population Reference Bureau, Inc., Washington, D.C., October 1961, Vol. XVII, No. 6.

Prociuk, S. G., "The Manpower Problem in Siberia," *Soviet Studies,* October 1967, pp. 190–210.

Rakowska-Harmstone, Teresa, *Russia and Nationalism in Central Asia: The Case of Tadzhikistan,* The Johns Hopkins Press, Baltimore, 1969, 352 pp.

Reed, Ritchie H., *Estimates and Projections of the Labor Force and Civilian Employment in the U.S.S.R.: 1950–1975,* International Population Reports, U.S. Department of Commerce, Bureau of the Census, Washington, 1967, Series P-91, No. 15, 39 pp.

Roof, Michael, "Soviet Population Trends," *Eugenics Quarterly,* September 1961, Vol. 8, No. 3, pp. 123–134.

——— and Leedy, Frederick, "Population Redistribution in the Soviet Union, 1939–1956," *Geographical Review,* 1959, Vol. 49, pp. 208–221.

Schlesinger, Rudolf, *The Nationalities Problem and Soviet Administration,* Routledge and Kegan-Paul, London, 1956, 299 pp.

Semenov-Tian-Shansky, Benjamin, "Russia: Territory and Population: A Perspective on the 1926 Census," *Geographical Review,* 1928, pp. 616–640.

Shimkin, Demitri, "Demographic Changes and Socio-Economic Forces within the Soviet Union, 1939–1959," *Population Trends in Eastern Europe, the U.S.S.R., and Mainland China,* Milbank Memorial Fund, 1960, pp. 224–262.

Soviet Geography: Review and Translation, October 1968; entire issue is devoted to settlement. Entire issue of April 1968 is devoted to population migration.

S.S.S.R.: Administrativno-territorialnoe delenie soyuznykh respublik (The U.S.S.R.: Adminis-trative-territorial divisions by union republics), Moscow, July 1, 1967, 655 pp. (in Russian); this annual statistical handbook lists all administrative subdivisions, city sizes, etc.

Ts SU S.S.S.R., Itogi vsesoyuznoy perepisi naseleniya 1959 goda (Results of the All-Union Census of Population in 1959), Gosstatizdat, Moscow, 1962–1963, 15 volumes (in Russian).

Wädekin, Karl-Eugen, "Internal Migration and the Flight from the Land in the U.S.S.R., 1939–1959," *Soviet Studies,* October 1966, pp. 131–152.

Wheeler, Geoffrey, *The Peoples of Soviet Central Asia,* The Bodley Head, London, 1966, 126 pp.

———, *The Modern History of Soviet Central Asia,* Praeger, New York, 1964, 272 pp.

———, *Racial Problems in Soviet Muslim Asia,* Oxford University Press, London, 1962, 67 pp.

14

Agriculture

General Production and Consumption Levels

The Soviet Union is one of the world's leading agricultural countries. It regularly sows about one third of the world's wheat land and produces more than one fourth of the world's wheat supply. It produces nearly one half of the world's rye, one third of the world's sugar beets, three fourths of the world's flax, one half of the world's sunflowers, and one third of the world's potatoes. In all these crops, as well as in barley, it is the world's leading producer. The Soviets claim now to have surpassed the United States in butter and milk production, and they are bending every effort to surpass the United States in the production of meat and eggs. Yet there seems to be a chronic food shortage, and the agricultural crisis has been a perennial one. The Soviet Union with a sixth of the land area of the earth and one fifteenth of the earth's population has had a hard time feeding itself. More than seven times as many farmers in the Soviet Union cultivating about 70 per cent more land raise approximately 75 per cent as much agricultural produce as farmers in the United States do. This 75 per cent must feed 35 million more people than are in the United States.

Although the per capita caloric intake in the Soviet Union is approximately equal to that in the United States, the Soviets diet is poorly balanced. It is heavy on starches and low on meat, eggs, fresh fruits and vegetables, and to some extent vegetable oils and fats. And these ills will probably plague the Soviets for years to come, despite government efforts to overtake the United States. Khrushchev's boasts during the mid 1950s of surpassing the United States in per capita livestock products around 1965 are not being voiced anymore. The 1966 meat production in the Soviet Union was no larger a percentage of the contemporary United States' meat production than was the 1913 production. In 1913 the Soviet Union produced 47.6 per cent as much meat as the United States, and in 1966 it produced 47.4 per cent as much. Soviet egg production shows a similar ratio. Tables 14–1 through 14–5 present some comparisons between the U.S.S.R. and the United States of basic agricultural resources, development, and production. Table 14–6 compares basic components of the Soviet diet with those of some other leading countries.

Total agricultural output in the Soviet Union increased just enough between 1926 and 1953 to maintain per capita output at approximately the same level. The per capita availability of grains in 1953 was approximately what it was in 1926. Potatoes, sugar, and cotton increased substantially, and there was a small improvement in eggs, but there were fewer vegetables, less meat and milk, less wool and flax fiber, and less sunflower seed, the major source of vegetable oil. Roughly speaking, the index of net agricultural output on a per capita basis was slightly lower in 1950 to 1953 than in 1928. The situation has improved significantly since 1953, however. (Table 14–7)

During the period 1925–1958 the index of farm output for both the United States and the Soviet Union increased by roughly 58 per cent. This, while the United States was trying to curtail production. (The agricultural problems of the two countries are almost diametrically opposed. The Soviet Union is straining to feed itself, whereas the United States is trying to control production in order to avoid glutting the market.)

Reasons for Production Lag The natural environment over much of the country sets severe limits on agriculture; cold and drought limit cultivation to little

Table 14–1   Agricultural Resources, U.S.S.R. and U.S.A.

Item	Year	Unit	United States	Soviet Union	U.S.S.R. as Percentage of U.S.A.
Population, July 1	1966	Millions	196.9	233.2	118
Civilian labor force	1966	Millions	86.3	118.4	137
Annual average employment	1966	Millions	72.9	110.0	151
Annual average employment in agriculture	1966	Millions	5.2	39.8	765
Farm share of total employment (annual average)	1966	Per cent	7.1	36.2	510
Sown cropland	1966	Millions of acres	298	511	171
Sown cropland per capita	1966	Acres	1.5	2.2	147
Tractors on farms, Jan. 1	1967	Thousands	4,815	1,660	34
Motor trucks on farms, Jan. 1	1967	Thousands	3,100	1,017	33
Grain combines on farms, Jan. 1	1967	Thousands	880	531	60
Agricultural consumption of electricity	1966	Billions of kilowatt-hours	29.1	23.2	80
Use of commercial fertilizer in terms of principal plant nutrients:					
Total	1966	1,000 short tons	12,445	7,707	62
Per acre of sown area	1966	Pounds	84	30	36

Source: Soviet Economic Performance: 1966–1967, p. 31.

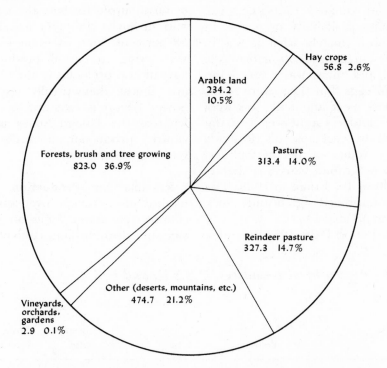

Figure 14–1   Land use in the U.S.S.R., in millions of hectares and per cents of total. Adapted from Atlas selskogo khozyaystva SSSR, *p. 90.*

Table 14–2   Farm Numbers, Sizes, and Workers, U.S.S.R. and U.S.A., 1966

			Soviet Union	
Item	Unit	U.S. Farms	Collective Farms	State Farms
Total	Number	3,239,000	36,493	12,196
Land area per farm	Acres	351	31,425	120,632
Sown area per farm	Acres	92	6,919	18,038
Workers per farm	Number	1.6	417	651
Land area per worker	Acres	219	75	185
Sown area per worker	Acres	58	17	28

Source: Soviet Economic Performance: 1966–1967, p. 32.

Table 14–3 Crop Acreages, Yields, and Production, U.S.S.R. and U.S.A., 1966

	Area				Yields			Production		
	Thousands of Acres		U.S.S.R. as % of U.S.A.	Unit	Per Acre		U.S.S.R. as % of U.S.A.	1000 Short Tons		U.S.S.R. as % of U.S.A.
	U.S.S.R.	U.S.A.			U.S.S.R.	U.S.A.		U.S.S.R.	U.S.A.	
Corn, grain	7,907	56,933	14	bu.	33.9	72.3	47	7,490	115,300	7
Wheat	172,970	49,867	347	bu.	18.1	26.3	69	93,695	39,333	238
Rye	33,606	1,275	2,636	bu.	14.1	21.8	65	13,230	771	1,701
Oats	17,791	17,861	100	bu.	29.0	44.9	65	8,260	12,820	64
Barley	47,937	10,205	470	bu.	23.0	38.5	60	26,480	9,430	280
Sorghum grain in United States; pulses in U.S.S.R.	14,579	12,813	114	bu.	15.9	55.8	28	231,812 [a]	714,992 [a]	32
Rice	598	1,967	30	lb.	2,354	4,322	54	704	4,251	17
Cotton	6,079	9,552	64	lb.	738	480	154	9,341 [b]	9,575 [b]	98
Soybeans for beans	2,088	36,546	6	bu.	10.5	25.4	41	657	27,854	2
Sunflowers	12,355	73	16,924	lb.	1,008	894	113	6,228	33	18,873
Flax	3,459	2,576	134							
Sugar beets	9,390	1,161	809	short ton	8.7	17.5	50	81,570	20,342	401
Sugarcane, for sugar and seed		625		short ton		39.2			24,515	
Tobacco	348	977	36	lb.	1,161	1,933	60	202	944	21
Potatoes	20,756	1,464	1,418	100 lb.	84	210	40	87,203	15,345	568
Vegetables	3,459	3,421	101	short ton		5.7	100	19,731	19,650	100
Fruits (including citrus), grapes, berries, and nuts	6,323	3,046	208	short ton				8,603	22,370	38
Citrus	20	932	2							
Hay	79,072	65,140	121	short ton	0.67	1.86	36	53,350	121,027	44

Source: Adapted from *Soviet Economic Performance: 1966–1967*, pp. 32–33.

[a] 1000 bushels.

[b] 1000 bales.

Table 14–4   Livestock Numbers

Livestock	Year [a]	United States (Million Head)	Soviet Union (Million Head)	U.S.S.R. as Percentage of U.S.A.
All cattle	1967	108.5	97.1	89
Cows	1967	49.8 [b]	41.2 [c]	83
Hogs	1967	51.0	58.0	114
Sheep	1967	23.7	135.5	572
Poultry	1966	399.9 [d]	490.5	123

Source: Soviet Economic Performance: 1966–1967, p. 34.

[a] Beginning of year.

[b] Cows, 2 years and older, included in cattle.

[c] All cows included in cattle.

[d] Chickens and turkeys only, excluding commercial broilers.

more than 10 per cent of the total area. In general, where the area is humid the temperatures are cold, and where the temperatures are warm the area is dry. It is estimated that practically all of even the producing area needs climatic amelioration of one sort of another; 3 million square miles of the country require additional water, and 1 million square miles require drainage.

It is the in-between areas of climate—the subhumid and semiarid—that carry the bulk of the agriculture. Throughout these areas the soil is generally good. In fact the Soviet Union contains one of the largest areas of high-grade soil in the

Table 14–5   Production of Livestock Commodities, 1966, in Millions of Pounds

Commodity	United States	Soviet Union	U.S.S.R. as Percentage of U.S.A.
Beef and veal	20,604	8,245	40
Pork	11,328	7,440	66
Mutton, lamb, and goat	650	1,587	244
Poultry meat	7,596	1,764	23
Lard	1,932	1,800	93
Tallow and grease	5,026	530	11
Margarine and shortening	5,291	1,321	25
Milk (cows)	120,230	147,990	123
Butter	1,128	2,297	204
Eggs	66.4 [a]	31.7 [a]	48
Wool	250	818	327

Source: Soviet Economic Performance: 1966–1967, p. 34.

[a] Billion.

Table 14–6   Basic Components of the Diet in the U.S.S.R. and Other Leading Countries

	Annual per Capita Consumption in Kilograms				
	United States, 1962	United Kingdom, 1962– 63	France, 1960– 61	West Germany, 1962– 63	U.S.S.R., 1963– 64
Grains and pulses (as flour)	65	87	106	82	175
Potatoes	47	94	194	128	125
Sugar (refined)	41	47	29	30	27
Meat and poultry	97	77	74	61	30
Eggs	19	15	11	13	4
Fats	21	23	17	26	9

Source: New Directions in the Soviet Economy, p. 471.

world. But even under the most favorable environmental conditions crop yields have always been low compared to much less favorably endowed areas, such as western Europe. Table 14–3 compares yields of some leading crops in the Soviet Union and in the United States.

The greatest limitation to agricultural production is not the physical drawbacks of the country, but the economic and political organization. Not only are yields low per acre, but they are also low per farmer. Labor used per unit of output in the Soviet Union ranges from 160 per cent of the United States level for cotton on state farms to 1630 per cent for the production of hogs on collective farms. (Table 14–8) Such low labor productivity stems from an almost total lack of incentives for farmers, combined with an un-

Table 14–7   Per Capita Net Output of Major Agricultural Products, Soviet Union (Kilograms per Annum)

	1926–1929	1950–1953	1955–1958	1966–1967
Grains	241.4	247.9	297.6	554.0
Potatoes	102.1	172.8	163.2	388.5
Vegetables	49.8	41.2	56.4	80.1
Sugar beets	52.0	118.0	187.5	342.0
Sunflower seeds	12.2	10.8	18.1	25.1
Milk	176.2	144.8	200.9	311.0
Meat	32.7	27.5	34.8	41.7
Eggs	64.2	68.0	95.1	–
Cotton	4.9	19.7	20.8	–
Wool	1.12	1.06	1.34	1.63
Flax fiber	1.86	1.18	2.09	1.73 [a]

Source: Computed from *Comparisons of the United States and Soviet Economies,* Part I, p. 210, and *Soviet Economic Performance: 1966–1967,* pp. 28–29.
[a] 1961–1965 average.

warranted amount of governmental interference in local decision-making, which has largely wrecked any attempts at rational crop rotations or proper regional specializations, and from time to time has plunged the country into agricultural malpractices on a grand scale. Examples include attempts to grow dry-land cotton in southern Ukraine and Lower Volga Regions, which have too-short growing seasons for such a crop, and the attempt to become self-sufficient in rubber by wide plantings of dandelion-like plants such as kok-sagyz, which until after World War II occupied thousands of acres of prime agricultural land without any beneficial effects. Such experimentations, together with erroneous Lysenkoan ideas regarding plant adaptations to environment and capricious governmental requirements without adequate notice, have kept the peasants in a confused state and made them leery of depending upon the decisions of the government or the research establishment in the Soviet Union. Therefore agricultural practices have not progressed as they should have; Soviet agriculture has been characterized by poor use of fertilizers and farming techniques, inadequate capital investments, and an over-reliance on an abundance of unskilled labor.

Until recently the general assumption in the Soviet Union was that there was an unlimited supply of agricultural labor and land, and that total production could be continually expanded by opening up new land to cultivation and employing more farmers. Money investments in agriculture were held to a minimum, while major emphasis was given to industrialization, and excess labor was used in agriculture in lieu of capital expenditures. Much hand labor is still used in many phases of agriculture. Plowing and sowing of grain are mechanized, but some harvesting and almost all of the drying and cleaning of grain are still done by hand. Almost all potato growing is done by hand, and much cotton is still picked by hand. All of this manual labor is little rewarded monetarily. The general practice has been to divide a residual amount of the income from the farms at the end of the year among farmers according to the work days they have put in. After various governmental procurements have been satisfied, there has been little left to divide, and thus farmers often find themselves with essentially zero annual income. Hence it is little wonder that they do not work very efficiently. Only since 1953 have the Soviets seen fit to allot significant amounts of time and money to alleviate some of these difficulties in agriculture.

The ability to increase production when proper emphasis is placed on it has already been demonstrated to a certain extent in the production of industrial crops. Whereas during the period 1928 to 1957 livestock products increased 65 per cent and food crops increased 52 per cent, industrial crops increased 232 per cent. Their share in net agricultural output rose from 7.7 to 15.5 per cent, whereas the portion of total sown area occupied by them declined from 7.7 to 6.1 per cent. A policy of self-sufficiency in such items as cotton and sugar has fostered the scientific growth of these

Table 14–8   Labor Used per Centner of Output, U.S.S.R. and United States

Man-Hours

	Collective Farms, U.S.S.R.	State Farms, U.S.S.R.	United States
Grain	7.3	1.8	1.0
Potatoes	5.1	4.2	1.0
Sugar beets	3.1	2.1	0.5
Cotton	42.8	29.8	18.8
Milk	14.7	9.9	4.7
Beef	112.0	52.0	7.9
Pork	103.0	43.0	6.3

Source: Comparisons of the United States and Soviet Economies, Part I, p. 215.

crops; other crops have been left to traditional devices. Heavy fertilization, irrigation, and drainage have been the most important means for intensifying production. Also grand climatic amelioration schemes involving the construction of large reservoirs of water and the planting of thousands of miles of windbreaks are being experimented with in the drier, better soil regions of the country.

As long as marketing facilities are inadequate a certain degree of crisis is going to remain in the food supply of the country no matter what the production on the farms. Poor transportation is a prime factor in agricultural inefficiencies and in the structure of the agricultural economy. For instance, lack of all-weather farm-to-market roads largely has determined the development of the butter industry instead of a full development of the use of whole milk. Refrigeration equipment is very limited in the Soviet Union. Much of the meat slaughtered in state packing houses is immediately canned. Much of the fresh meat supply depends on the free markets, though the sales of meat by private individuals make up only a small portion of total meat sales.

Economic and Social Organization

It is generally agreed that the lack of capital investments, the inflexible social order, and the disparity between prices and costs have been the chief restraints on Soviet agricultural performance. Overpopulation on the farms and net incomes of almost zero have stymied any incentive that the farmers might inherently have had for improving production. In the dialectical jargon of the Marxist, the farmers in the Soviet Union have been the exploited and the city dwellers the exploiters. This has even been stated as a basic principle by some Soviet economists. Stalin himself said that agriculture provides the Soviet state, bent on indus-

trialization, with "something like a tribute." Until recently as much as possible was extracted from agriculture and as little as possible was put into it.

Agriculture, like the rest of the economy, was in a sorry state during the period of "War Communism" following the Revolution. A substantial recovery was made under an essentially capitalistic system during the period of the New Economic Policy (NEP) in the 1920s, but then a collectivization drive was launched in 1929 to organize the peasantry to comply more closely with communist doctrine and to insure adequate food procurements for the cities. With temporary retrenchments to meet emergencies, the socialization of agriculture has continued and increased in intensity down to the present time, until now practically no independent farmers remain.

The Socialized Sector The socialization took two forms, and in each case minor degrees of private enterprise were allowed in order to appease the peasants and to assure them enough foodstuffs for their own sustenance. The two forms of farm organization are state farms or sovkhozes (state economy) and collective farms or kolkhozes (collective economy). In general the collective farms were organized in the better farming areas that were already densely settled by farmers. Initially they greatly outnumbered the state farms and accounted for the bulk of the agricultural produce. State farms largely were organized in outlying areas of sparse settlement or newly opened land where vested interests in the area were small or nonexistent.

Until recently the collective farmers have worked on their collective farms without wages and have shared the produce of the farm according to the number of work days they have put in. Workers on the state farms, on the other hand, have been salaried workers working on state-owned land. The land of the collective farms ultimately belongs to the state also, but the collective farmers, many of whom originally held title to the land, hold a perpetual lease on the land. In general the collective farmers still are living in their villages of huts that they have always lived in, whereas on many of the state farms individual and multiple dwellings have been built for the workers. Often one collective farm will comprise several old villages, in which the peasants live, and new farm buildings which have been built at focal points about the farm. The buildings and facilities in one part of the farm may be concentrated on dairying, in another part on truck gardening, and so forth. Khrushchev's so-called agrogorods, or agricultural cities composed of apartment houses for farmers, appear to be a long time in the future, building construction and demand being what they are in the cities.

The collective farms have been the most exploited part of the economy. State procurements of produce at practically no price, state purchases at not much better prices, and large payments in kind to the Machine Tractor Stations (MTS) for services rendered have left very little produce to divide among the peasants. It has been calculated that up until 1958 the average income on collective farms was equivalent to about $60 per year, and there was a great disparity between good and bad farms. Some collectives yielded their farmers practically nothing. Had it not been for foodstuffs and some cash income derived from their private plots, many collective farmers could not have existed at all. Workers on state farms at least had a guaranteed wage, and until recently enjoyed a considerably higher standard of living than did collective farmers.

The Private Sector A minimal amount of private enterprise has persisted in agriculture in three forms: (1) the private plots of the collective farmers, (2) the private plots of employees and workers on collective and state farms and in some factories, and (3) individual farms. The third category has practically ceased to exist since 1950. Only about 14,000 hectares, or less than one hundredth of 1 per cent of the total cultivated land, is in uncollectivized farms in remote areas where settlement is so sparse and production so limited that it would not pay to collectivize.

Although the private plots of all collective farmers and workers and employees have never amounted to much more than 5 per cent of the total sown area in the country, the production from these plots has represented a much larger fraction of total agricultural production, particularly livestock products, and the plots have been all-important to the sustenance of the collective farmers. (Tables 14–9 and 14–10) It has been estimated that in 1966 private plots produced one third of the agricultural output of the country on less than 3 per cent of the agricultural land. Much more effort has been expended on these plots than on similar areas of the collectivized land, and much higher yields have been attained. (Table 14–11) Also the plots have yielded higher returns for labor input. It has been estimated that until 1958 the incomes of collective farmers from the collectivized sections of farms and from their own plots were about equal. However, the average collective farmer spent two thirds of his time working on the collectivized land and only one third of his time on his own plot. Therefore the labor on his plot was twice as remunerative as the labor on the collective. Hence it made more sense to work on the plot than on the collectivized section of the farm. Thus there was a constant tendency for extra effort to be expended on the plot at the expense of the collective farm work, which led to a further deterioration of production on the collectivized acreage of the farm. Until recently individual collective farmers derived 60 to 75 per cent

Table 14–9   Sown Areas, Total and Private Sector, in Thousands of Hectares and Per Cents

	1950	1959	1965
Total	146,302	196,319	209,100
Private sector	9,375 (6.41%)	7,238 (3.69%)	
Private plots of collective farmers	5,904 (4.04%)	5,312 (2.71%)⎫	
Plots of workers and employees	1,563 (1.07%)	1,912 (0.97%)⎬ 6,600 (3.15%)	
Uncollectivized farms	1,908 (1.30%)	14 (0.01%)⎭	

Sources: Newth, "Soviet Agriculture: The Private Sector, 1950–1959," p. 161, and *Narodnoye Khozyaystvo SSSR v 1965 g.,* p. 288.

of their total cash income from their private plots, in addition to feeding themselves.

Most of these private plots are no more than a half acre or an acre per family, but with constant care a great deal of produce can be raised on that amount of land. The private plots are sown primarily to heavily producing food crops, potatoes, vegetables, and fruit, and to livestock feed, maize and fodder. (Table 14–12) A certain amount of cattle, hogs, and an unlimited

Table 14–10   Output of Private Sector and Percentage of Total

Crop	1950 1000 Tons	1950 Per Cent of Total	1959 1000 Tons	1959 Per Cent of Total	1966, Per Cent of Total
Potatoes	65,248	73.6	54,959	63.5	64
Vegetables	4,068	43.5	6,774	45.9	42
Ripe maize	2,139	32.2	1,323	23.4	
Roots (fodder)	2,761	33.9	2,141	20.5	
Sunflowers	83	4.6	140	4.5	
Rye	1,878	10.5	501	3.0	
Millet	144	8.4	38	2.9	
Barley	541	8.5	259	2.6	
Pulses	183	8.9	29	1.5	
Hay	1,142	1.8	892	1.1	
Oats	363	2.8	39	0.3	
Wheat	423	1.4	98	0.1	

Sources: Newth, "Soviet Agriculture: The Private Sector, 1950–1959," p. 167, and Clarke, "Soviet Agricultural Reforms Since Khrushchev," p. 169.

Table 14–11   Average Yields of Crops, 1950–1959, Public and Private, in Centners per Hectare

	Public	Private
Fully ripe maize	13.84	18.45
Potatoes	61.5	119.9
Vegetables	70.6	147.4

Source: Newth, "Soviet Agriculture: The Private Sector, 1950–1959," pp. 163–165.

number of poultry can be maintained by an individual household. In 1967 the private plots produced almost 40 per cent of the meat and milk of the country and 65 per cent of the eggs; in the past they had produced even larger percentages of the total. (Table 14–13) In the 1940s the private sector held about half of the country's livestock. This decreased to about 30 per cent during Khrushchev's reign, largely due to his urging that the kolkhozniki turn over their livestock to the kolkhozes. (Table 14–14) Almost half the land devoted to potatoes, vegetables, and fruits is in these private plots. (Table 14–15) Yields of potatoes and vegetables from the private plots are nearly twice as high as they are from the collectivized areas. In 1959 the private sector of agriculture produced 63.5 per cent of the potatoes of the country and 45.9 per cent of the vegetables. It had produced almost three fourths of the potatoes in 1950. Much of the introduction of corn for dry

Table 14–12   Percentages of Private Plots Under Various Crops, 1965

Cereals	16
Industrial crops	1
Potatoes and vegetables	59
Fodder	6
Fruits and berries	18

Source: Lovell, "The Role of Private Subsidiary Farming During the Soviet Seven-Year Plan, 1959–65," p. 54.

Table 14–13   Meat, Milk, and Egg Production

	Total	Public	Private
Meat (dead weight, millions of tons)			
1947	2.5	0.9	1.6
1954	6.3	2.7	3.6
1960	8.7	5.1	3.6
Milk (millions of tons)			
1947	30.2	5.1	25.1
1954	38.2	13.5	24.7
1960	61.7	32.6	29.1
Eggs (billions)			
1947	4.9	0.4	4.5
1954	17.2	2.2	15.0
1960	27.4	5.3	22.1

Source: Newth, "Soviet Agriculture: The Private Sector, 1950–1959 — Animal Husbandry," pp. 431–432.

grain has been effected on the private plots; in 1959 the private sector produced almost one quarter of the ripe maize.

Until 1954 sales on the free (kolkhoz) markets in the cities exceeded the total cash income of collective farms. This has now been reduced to about one third of the total farm income. A much smaller portion of the produce from private plots enters the retail trade than does produce from public lands. In 1959, 19 per cent of the crops and 23 per cent of the livestock products of the private sector were sold, whereas 59 per cent of the crops and 72 per cent of the livestock products of the public sector were sold. (Table 14–16) It appears that a significant portion of the Soviet population is providing its own foodstuffs with only a minor interest in supplying the market. The output of private producers has increased substantially in recent years, and they are consuming the increase themselves. According to the 1959 census, nearly 10 million people (dependents of kolkhozniki and workers) were engaged in this activity. Add to this

Table 14-14   Livestock Holdings (January 1), in Millions

	Cows	Other Cattle	Pigs	Sheep	Goats	Horses
1947						
Total	23.0	24.0	8.7	57.7	11.6	10.9
Public	4.6	14.1	4.0	40.4	5.1	8.4
Private	18.4	9.9	4.7	17.3	6.5	2.5
1954						
Total	25.2	30.6	33.3	99.8	15.7	15.3
Public	10.1	22.0	17.8	84.8	4.2	14.8
Private	15.1	8.6	15.5	15.0	11.5	0.5
1961						
Total	34.8	41.0	58.7	133.0	7.3	9.9
Public	18.4	33.6	42.2	104.3	1.3	n.a.
Private	16.4	7.4	16.5	28.7	6.0	n.a.

Source: Newth, "Soviet Agriculture: The Private Sector, 1950–1959 — Animal Husbandry," pp. 430–431.

Note: At the end of 1965, private plots accounted for 30 per cent of all cattle, 31 per cent of swine, 21 per cent of sheep, and 84 per cent of goats. Lovell, p. 55.

full-time workers and kolkhozniki who grew produce and reared livestock in their spare time, and the total number of persons involved must be very large.

Machine Tractor Stations   Until 1958 the Machine Tractor Station was an integral part of the agricultural scene. Collective farms owned practically no agricultural machinery and were totally dependent on Machine Tractor Stations for heavy field work. A typical Machine Tractor Station had a crew of tractor drivers, implement operators, mechanics, agronomists, and zoo-technicians who did the field work, serviced the machinery, and advised on problems of agronomy and animal husbandry for four or five collective farms. Thus the economy of the collective farms was tied very closely to that of the Machine Tractor Station. A considerable proportion of the produce of each farm went to the Machine Tractor Station at the end of each harvest to pay for work done. Also the Machine Tractor Station was usually a focal point for governmental activities to disseminate

Table 14-15   Private Sector as Percentage of All Land Devoted to Particular Crops, 1959

Potatoes	50
Vegetables	32
Fruit, etc.	9
Total of three groups	45

Source: Newth, "Soviet Agriculture: The Private Sector, 1950–1959," p. 163.

Table 14-16   Percentage of Public Sector in Total Commercial Production, 1953 and 1959

	1953	1959	1965
Total	80	85	87
Crops	86	89	90
Livestock	68	82	84

Sources: Newth, "Soviet Agriculture: The Private Sector, 1950–1959," p. 170, and Lovell, "The Role of Private Subsidiary Farming During the Soviet Seven-Year Plan, 1959–65," p. 63.

information and propaganda in the rural areas. It was thus a governmental control point in the countryside.

The Machine Tractor Station gradually outlived its usefulness as a political arm in the countryside, and economically it had become a stumbling block to the expansion of production. Differences of opinion often arose between the "two bosses on the land," the collective farm management and the MTS personnel, and field work would not get done or it would not get done at the proper time. Therefore in 1958 the abolishment of Machine Tractor Stations began, and much of the machinery was sold to the collective farms for them to operate themselves.

Long-Term Goals in Agricultural Organization   The state farm has always been considered a superior organization to the collective farm, and the long-term goal is to convert all farmers into agricultural workers, similar to factory workers, working for wages on state-owned land. The collective farm was simply a compromise measure to meet expediencies, and it was considered transitory from the first. The fact that it has persisted this long is somewhat of a surprise. Now that the economy has improved and the peasants have been more adequately indoctrinated into the Soviet system, it might be expected that there will be a gradual likening of the two types of farms. The process has already been initiated by the sale of machinery to the collective farms, which allows their operation to be much more similar to that of the state farms than it was previously. Also some collective farms have begun to carry out the 1966 directives of the Communist Party to guarantee a minimum wage to collective farmers and to pay them monthly rather than yearly, following the harvest. This again brings the collective operation nearer to the state farm.

The abolishment of the Machine Tractor Station, a state institution, was first looked on by some American analysts as a retreat from state control and a move toward a more collective economy. It can also be interpreted, however, as a move to gradually convert collective farms into state farms. In fact, some conversion took place along with the sale of machinery in areas where it was necessary for the national government to loan substantial sums of money to the collectives so they could buy equipment. Some wholesale conversions of collective to state farms also have taken place in the western part of the country where the collective economy had broken down during the German occupation and in the new lands of northern Kazakhstan and western Siberia. In 1957 in northern Kazakhstan 833 collective farms were merged into 188 state farms. Some conversion of collective to state farms has also taken place in the irrigated cotton-growing regions of Middle Asia in cases where the need for new capital investment by the state has been large.

In 1950 collective farms had accounted for 87.5 per cent of the total area under grains, state farms had accounted for only 9 per cent, and private plots for 3.5 per cent. By 1964, however, collective farms accounted for only 50.7 per cent of the grain land, state farms for 48.5 per cent, and private plots for 0.8 per cent. This rapid change in the relative amounts of grain land between collective and state farms is due largely to the opening up of the virgin lands after 1954 in the spring-wheat areas of northern Kazakhstan and western Siberia. In this new region, state farms controlled more than 90 per cent of the cultivated land, whereas in the winter-wheat regions of the western part of the country the state farms controlled only about 30 per cent of the land. In southwestern Ukraine and Moldavia state farms controlled less than 7 per cent. The share of state grain procurements supplied by state farms has increased from about 12 per cent in 1953 to approximately 50 per cent at the present time.

Much of the conversion from collective to state farms took place during the 7-year plan from 1959 to 1965. However, 8500 farms had been converted before this period, 5730 of these in the peak year of 1957. In 1959, 2074 farms were converted; in 1960, 5068 farms; in 1961, 2906 farms; in 1962, 402 farms; in 1963, 271 farms; and in 1964, 902 farms. With the adoption of new plans for agriculture in March 1965, Brezhnev announced a moratorium on such conversions, but recent data have shown that in 1965 a total of 1336 collective farms were eliminated and 1564 state farms were created. This process seems to have continued in 1966, with 515 new state farms created and about 400 collective farms abolished, although conflicting statistics confuse the picture in this case.

Khrushchev had a positive policy to amalgamate collective farms into larger units, to convert collective farms into state farms, and gradually to reduce and eliminate private plots. Much of this policy was predicated on the assumption that in the very near future the collective and state farm functions would become so similar that there would be little to distinguish them, and that the collectivized sector of agricultural production would become so efficient and remunerative that the individual farmers would no longer find it desirable to work their private plots. Between 1958 and 1965, however, as agricultural production stagnated the picture grew increasingly more pessimistic, and after Khrushchev's ouster in 1964 his successors immediately set about reversing some of the organizational trends in agriculture in an attempt to revive lapsing production. It is not clear yet whether or not the practice of conversion of collective farms to state farms has ceased, and whether the government intends for this new policy to be a permanent arrangement or simply a temporary retreat from a practice that seemed to be detrimental to pro-

duction. Inevitably as new areas are opened up for cultivation and as old areas are reorganized under drainage and irrigation systems, the state will continue to establish new farms along the lines of sovkhozes instead of kolkhozes. The advance of agricultural technology and the reorganization of poorly producing lands into reclamation projects sponsored and financed by the central government leads to the continual expansion of the state farm system at the expense of the collective farm system.

Another recent development which has placed greater reliance on state farms is the designation of a number of state farms, first near Moscow and subsequently near other large cities, to specialize in growing potatoes and vegetables cheaply to lower their costs to city consumers. If these experiments prove successful, they will operate to the disadvantage of collectives, which derive an important share of their incomes from selling these products at high prices on the free markets in the cities.

The Soviet government has already justified the conversion of collectives to state farms by illustrating that labor productivity has been higher on state farms than on collectives. However, the fact that state farm workers had to be paid set wages generally caused agricultural production on the state farms to be more costly than on the collective farms where farmers were living largely a noncash subsistence, deriving their livelihood from their own private plots plus what small amounts of cash and kind they received from the collective effort. Also the higher labor productivity on the state farms was to a large extent due to greater mechanization, for which the equipment was very costly. Thus again the collective farms, with their labor-intensive production, have cost the state less than the state farms have. Table 14–17 illustrates that agricultural production throughout the U.S.S.R. in 1964 was about 14 per cent more expensive on state farms than on collective farms, considering the actual payments in money and kind that collective farmers were paid. Even if the state farms were to be compared with collective farms using labor costs remunerated at the same norms as on the state farms, production costs would still be about 4 per cent higher on the state farms. Only in the better farming regions of the country, such as Ukraine, Transcaucasia, and Middle Asia, do state farms seem to produce at less cost than

Table 14-17 Regional Production Costs for Grain (Excluding Maize) on Kolkhozy and Sovkhozy, 1964, in Rubles

Economic Region	Kolkhozy [a]		Sovkhozy, Production Cost per Metric Ton
	Production Cost "A" per Metric Ton	Production Cost "B" per Metric Ton	
Russian Federation (R.S.F.S.R.)	43	47	48
North-West	116	144	176
Center	70	85	95
Volga-Vyatka	75	90	99
Central Chernozem	35	37	36
Volga	37	40	35
Northern Caucasus	31	32	27
Urals	44	49	51
Western Siberia	44	44	55
Eastern Siberia	44	47	60
Far East	74	76	100
Ukraine	37	39	30
Donets-Dnieper	33	34	28
South-West	44	47	51
South	31	33	26
Moldavia	69	69	77
Kazakhstan	41	41	54
Other regions			
Belorussia	85	99	127
Baltic	84	83	101
Transcaucasia	81	82	80
Central Asia	65	65	57
U.S.S.R.	44	48	50

Source: The Economics of the Soviet Wheat Industry, p. 80.
[a] Production costs for kolkhozy, including: "A," estimated labor costs for kolkhozniki by actual payments in money and kind; and "B," estimated labor costs for kolkhozniki by norms paid for work on sovkhozy.

collective farms. It must be realized, however, that in these better farming areas, state farms are not very numerous, and those that exist are largely recently organized farms near large cities for urban supply purposes, and they apparently are operating quite efficiently. In poorer agricultural areas where production costs are much higher, state farms generally are at a disadvantage. In general, the higher the costs, the greater the discrepancy between state farm and collective farm costs.

When comparing the costs shown in Table 14-17, it must be kept in mind that these represent only current costs such as wages, seed, fertilizers, and, to a certain extent, equipment. The initial costs for buildings and other fixed stock for the establishment of state farms have been written off as state expenditures and have not been charged to the farm operation over a normal depreciation period. Thus the state has heavily subsidized the state farms. If one considers the costs of fixed capital as well as current expenditures there is ample evidence to conclude that practically all state farms have operated at a loss during almost every year of their existence. Thus it would appear that the continuing conversion of collective farms to state farms is economically irrational and that the process has always been ideologically motivated. Such ideological purpose stems not only from Marxian doctrine, which abhors any form of individual vested interest, but also from ingrained Russian desires to exercise central control over everybody and everything.

Throughout the collectivization drive there has been a general trend to merge collective farms into fewer and larger farms. The number of collective farms reached a peak in 1935 with approximately 245,000. In 1940 this was reduced to 237,000. After a weak collectivization effort in the western regions newly annexed during the war, the number of collectives increased to 252,000 for a short period, but in 1950 within 1 year the number of collectives was reduced by more than half to 121,000. Since then there has been a continual drive for merger and conversion to state farms until at the end of 1966 there were only 36,493 collective farms in the country. The average size of collective farms has been brought nearer to that of state farms. (Table 14–2)

Both the state farms and the collective farms seem to be unwieldy organizations that are much too large to operate efficiently. Their operation is generally beyond the ability of run-of-the-mill farm chairmen, who by and large have not been the sharpest individuals. The position of farm chairman is largely a thankless job which has not attracted top personnel. The Soviet farm units are much larger than any commercially organized units in other parts of the world, let alone the privately operated farms that are common to the rest of Europe and North America. Thus it would seem that gigantomania in agriculture, as well as in other branches of the economy, has been detrimental to the Soviet effort. Soviet agriculture has evolved as a curious mixture of very small-scale, intensive, personalized agriculture on the private plots, alongside giant collective and state farms with their over-abundant labor forces where the man-land relationship has become completely impersonalized.

The private plots too were looked upon initially as transitory features on the landscape which were temporarily necessary politically to appease the kolkhozniki and economically to sustain their existence without cost to the state. Official policy regarding the private plots has vacillated throughout the Soviet period, sometimes allowing expansion of plots and livestock holdings, at other times cracking down severely on private enterprise. From 1954 through 1964 Khrushchev carried on an active program of reduction of plot sizes and prevailed upon the better nature of the kolkhozniki to turn over their livestock to the collective sector of the economy.

During this decade the share of the private plots in total cultivated acreage of the country diminished from about 5 per cent to around 3 per cent. In March 1965, however, Khrushchev's successors reversed this trend and liberalized plot sizes, private livestock holdings, and usage of collective farm fodder for private livestock feeding. Thus it appears that the private plot is here to stay for the foreseeable future, along with the two forms of farm organization.

Rather than competing with the collective sector, the private plots have proved to be a complementary operation which has allowed the state to derive the maximum produce from the collective sector. Since farmers have been practically self-sustaining on their private plots, a large percentage of the total crop raised by the collective sector could be available for state procurements to be distributed to the urban population. Without the private plots, a major share of the collective produce no doubt would have been consumed on the farms. Thus the private sector has proved to be a necessary condition for the survival of the socialized sector.

The private plot has also served some other functions. Through the feeding of private livestock, it has been a necessary vehicle for the conversion of inedible payments in kind from the socialized sector of agriculture to the individual kolkhozniki. Without the private plots, the farmers would have had no way to utilize payments in hay and other coarse feeds. The plot has also served to absorb excess labor which has always existed on the farms. This is particularly true of women, elderly and disabled people, and youths who are not engaged in the socialized economy. A great number of women have spent their full time on housekeeping and cultivation of their private plots, and women have made up over 90 per cent of the labor expended on the private plots. Most recently, the plots have provided a livelihood for recent farm immigrants into labor-surplus areas, such as the North Caucasus, western Ukraine, and Moldavia, where returnees from Siberia and other eastern parts of the country have been pouring into already heavily settled regions in unprecedented numbers. The collective economy has been unable to absorb such newcomers, and they have found work and income only by operating their own little private plots of land. There are indications that on some farms in these regions at least 50 per cent of the population is deriving its livelihood from nothing but the private plots. Thus again we witness the curious semi-independent development of Orientally intensive agriculture utilizing great amounts of hand labor on small plots of ground in a country that has promulgated large farms and extensive agriculture on the grandest scale ever known to man.

All through the Soviet period the private sector of agriculture has occupied about one third of all the farm labor, and since 1958 it has risen to more than 40 per cent. In 1963, for instance, it was reported that of all man-days worked in agriculture, the private sector occupied 42 per cent, collec-

Table 14–18 Farm Employment by Sector of Economy, 1932–1963, in Percentages of Total Man-Days

| | | | Socialized Sector | |
| | | | Collec- | |
Year	Total	Private Sector	tive Farms	State Farms
1932	100	39	52	8
1937	100	33	62	5
1940	100	36	59	4
1945	100	38	57	5
1950	100	36	59	5
1953	100	37	56	6
1958	100	36	53	11
1963	100	42	39	19

Source: Karcz, *Soviet and East European Agriculture,* p. 192.

tive farms 39 per cent, and state farms 19 per cent. (Table 14–18) At the present time, the status of the private plot seems once again to be on the rise, and it appears that the private sector of agriculture will not diminish significantly until the socialized sector becomes so remunerative that it pays collective farmers more to work on the collective land than on their own private plots. Such a situation would seem almost impossible to attain, if past performance is any indicator.

Events Since 1953

Until the death of Stalin in 1953, little was done for agriculture to optimize production or to better the life of the peasants. As much as possible was taken from the agricultural sector of the economy to support the industrialization drive, and only enough was put into the agricultural effort to keep production from breaking down completely. But after the death of Stalin, Khrushchev, who had a much greater knowledge of and greater interest in agriculture than Stalin ever did, rapidly inaugurated several programs designed to get agriculture out of the doldrums. Much of this reform was politically motivated, since Khrushchev realized that a sudden boost in the agricultural economy would endear him to a large segment of the population. For his own purposes, it was necessary to realize quick gains through spectacular measures that attracted much attention. The quickest way to realize a substantial gain in overall production was to open up new land. Khrushchev was not the originator of this bright idea, since the opening of new lands had long been a panacea for Soviet leaders, and Russian rulers before them. Khrushchev, however, was astute enough about agricultural potentials to realize that the type of land that could be plowed up most quickly with the least cost was the so-called virgin and idle lands in the dry steppe areas east of the Volga which were flat, treeless, fine soil areas that could be converted to cultivation with little preparation other than plowing. Within 4 years, 40 million hectares of land, largely in northern Kazakhstan and western Siberia, were put into cultivation, primarily for spring wheat. This is an area greater than the total arable land of France, West Germany, and the United Kingdom combined. By 1961 additional scattered areas, some as far south as the mountain foothills of Middle Asia and as far east as Maritime Kray, expanded the total cultivated land of the U.S.S.R. by 47 million hectares, or 30 per cent over what it had been in 1953. (Table 14–19)

Although all the virgin lands in northern Kazakhstan and western Siberia suffer from cool, short, droughty growing seasons that frequently become cold and rainy during the harvest, the total production of grain in the U.S.S.R. was significantly increased by their cultivation, particularly immediately following 1953. (Table 14–20) The Soviets realized that they were gambling against the weather and that they were making up for small yields per acre by cultivating millions of acres, but government leaders considered the project worth the risk. Besides, certain climatologists had pointed out that these new grain lands are separated from the old grain land of Ukraine by a distance that is just about equal to half a wave length of the standing waves of the upper atmosphere which broadly control seasonal weather. This would mean that on the average the new grain lands and the old grain lands would have complementary types of weather. If there is drought in Ukraine, one might well expect excessive moisture in the virgin lands, and vice versa. Records over the past 60 years tend to corroborate this theory. Thus the virgin lands program has been justified partially on the basis that it provides the insurance that somewhere in the country there will always be a decent grain crop.

The second spectacular innovation that Khrushchev set into motion was the corn-growing program. This was made possible largely by the opening up of the virgin lands which allowed some of the best lands in the west to be vacated by wheat and turned into corn. Khrushchev looked upon the growing of corn as the answer to the meat problem in the country. He personally pointed out the advantages of corn as a heavy producer of fodder and exhorted the collective and state farms to expand their corn areas from around 4 million hectares in 1953 to 28 million hectares in 1960. This expansion, in fact, took place and reached a peak in 1962 when 37 million hectares were planted to corn. Only 7 million hectares were planted for ripe grain corn, however; the rest were harvested as silage and green fodder in various stages of maturity. (Table 14–21 and Fig. 14–2)

Along with these spectacular changes in types of agricultural production, an attempt was made to instigate a number of measures that were calculated to offer incentives to farmers to produce. Most of the different types of state procurements were consolidated into one type of purchase, and prices for these purchases

Table 14–19 Cropland, 1953 and 1961, in Hectares

Region	1953	1961	Per Cent Increase
U.S.S.R.	157,200,000	204,600,000	30
Kazakhstan	9,700,000	28,600,000	195
Tselinny Kray [a]	5,100,000	18,300,000	260
R.S.F.S.R.	38,900,000	55,500,000	40
Lower Volga	8,300,000	10,800,000	30
Urals	13,900,000	18,200,000	31
Orenburg Oblast	4,200,000	5,500,000	31
West Siberia	13,800,000	17,700,000	28
Omsk Oblast	2,800,000	4,800,000	71
Altay Kray	4,600,000	7,400,000	61
East Siberia and Far East	5,300,000	8,800,000	66

Source: Laird, *Soviet Agriculture: The Permanent Crisis*, p. 30.
[a] No longer existent.

Table 14–20 Soviet Wheat Production, Area, and Yields, 1953–1966

Description	1953	1954	1955	1956	1957	1958	1959	1960	1961	1962	1963	1964	1965	1966
Production (million bushels)														
Total	1,517	1,558	1,738	2,476	2,136	2,814	2,539	2,363	2,443	2,601	1,827	2,735	2,191	3,700
Spring	785	896	822	1,932	1,133	1,727	1,575	1,688	1,378	1,485	1,046	1,770	1,018	
Winter	727	662	907	548	1,001	1,083	973	669	1,072	1,119	775	964	1,172	
Area (million acres)														
Total	119	122	149	153	171	165	156	149	156	167	160	169	174	173
Spring	75	83	104	121	125	120	113	120	113	122	119	122	124	
Winter	44	39	45	32	46	45	43	30	43	45	40	47	49	
Yields (bushels per acre)														
Total	12.7	12.8	11.6	16.2	12.5	17.1	16.4	15.8	15.6	15.6	11.5	16.2	12.7	22.4
Spring	10.4	10.7	7.9	13.9	9.1	14.5	14.0	14.2	12.2	12.2	8.8	14.8	8.2	17.9
Winter	16.5	17.1	20.1	17.8	21.9	24.1	22.6	22.5	25.2	25.0	19.2	20.6	24.0	30.2

Sources: The Economics of the Soviet Wheat Industry, p. 9, and Strana Sovetov za 50 let, pp. 128–129 and 132–133.

Table 14–21 Maize Area and Yields, 1953–1964, in Million Hectares and Quintals per Hectare

Maize Type	1953	1956	1958	1962	1964
Area					
Grain fully ripe	3.84	6.60	4.40	7.01	5.11
Milk wax grain	—	2.69	3.73	7.18	
Silage	—	5.98	5.89⎫	22.90⎫	22.30
Green fodder	—	8.66	5.70⎭		
Total maize	3.84	23.93	19.72	37.10	27.41
Yields					
Grain fully ripe	10.60	15.00	23.25	22.07	26.08
Milk wax grain	—	9.66	17.40	11.13⎫	109.60
Silage and green fodder	—	38.59	125.88	85.11⎭	
Average all maize	10.60	28.83	82.46	58.86	94.05

Source: The Economics of the Soviet Wheat Industry, p. 76.

were raised to what was considered to be a correct level that would allow farms to actually make a profit and pay their farmers a decent wage which was not too far below the going industrial wage of the country. In 1958 the Machine Tractor Stations were abolished and much of the machinery was sold to the collective farms. This was intended to give the collective farms more decision-making power and flexibility in operation. Other increased inputs in the agricultural sector included the expansion of fertilizer and machinery production, loans to collective farms, and

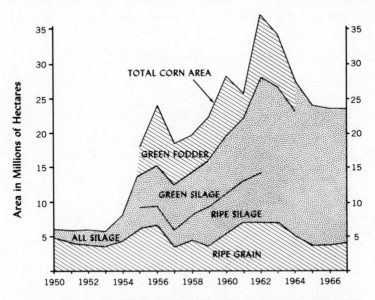

Figure 14–2 Area sown to corn, classified by utilization, U.S.S.R., 1950–1967. From Anderson, Jeremy, "A Historical-Geographical Perspective on Khrushchev's corn program," in Karcz, Soviet and East European Agriculture, p. 115. Reprinted by permission of the Regents of the University of California. Professor Anderson graciously supplied data to update original figure.

increased capital investments. (Table 14–22)

It will have to be conceded that these measures initially gave a great boost to overall production, and they certainly were politically effective in consolidating Khrushchev in his position of power. From 1953 to 1958 total agricultural production increased about 50 per cent, crop production increased about 40 per cent, and livestock production increased about 43 per cent. (Fig. 14–3) The initial successes caused Khrushchev to make wild boasts about overtaking the United States in all sorts of livestock products by 1970, however, and he became so overconfident that he began pulling back on inputs into agriculture and returned to traditional regressive measures that were designed to extract as much from agriculture as possible. Retail prices of consumer goods to peasants were structured to absorb any increase in wages that they might have realized. The sale of machinery from the MTS to the collective farms was made at very high prices calculated to absorb any extra funds that the farms had managed to accumulate, and in fact were calculated to force many farms to either amalgamate or actually to convert to state farms. And the expanded production of mineral fertilizers was largely effected by diverting some of the investment capital allotted for farms to the chemical industries to produce the mineral fertilizers. Thus by 1958 it became quite apparent that the price raises were not correct or adequate to allow farms to produce at a profit, and that a slowdown in production was setting in which was going to cause real problems in the immediate future. In fact this tapering off would have been apparent after 1956 had not 1958 been such a favorable year in weather conditions that a new high in crop production was reached that year. The weather was not as favorable in 1959, however, and crop production plunged by about 12 per cent. Crop production continued near this lower level for the next 4 years and then reached a low in 1963 due to disastrous droughts throughout much of the country.

The 1963 low was the lowest crop production since 1954. In the meantime consumption had risen considerably, and the world witnessed the Soviet Union turning

Table 14–22   Trends in Inputs and Incentives, 1953–1965

	1953 = 100, 1958	1958 = 100						
	1958	1959	1960	1961	1962	1963	1964	1965
Sown area	124	100	104	105	110	112	109	106
Chemical fertilizer	159	105	107	110	126	146	202	265
Deliveries of machinery								
Tractors	207	92	100	118	131	152	n.a.	n.a.
Trucks	148	75	65	68	81	67	n.a.	n.a.
Grain combines	158	82	88	108	122	123	n.a.	n.a.
Productive investment								
State	266	89	108	131	148	184	(212)	(249)
Collective farms	239	126	111	112	121	125	n.a.	n.a.
Employment in man-days	112	97	93	93	91	(88)	n.a.	n.a.
Output per man-day	135	104	111	115	118	n.a.	n.a.	n.a.
Procurement prices	192	101	101	103	112	n.a.	n.a.	n.a.
Money income of collective								
farms	266	104	101	103	115	121	n.a.	n.a.

Source: Karcz, Soviet and East European Agriculture, p. 320.

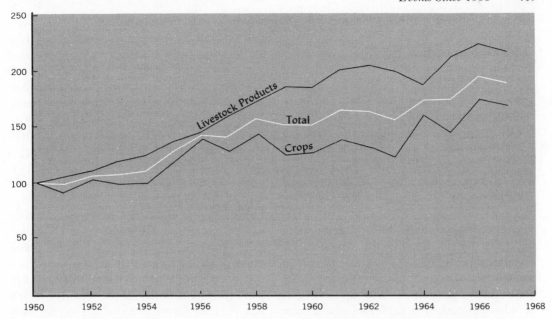

Figure 14–3 Trends in net agricultural production, U.S.S.R., 1950–1967. (1950 = 100.) Data from New Directions in the Soviet Economy, *p. 346 and* Soviet Economic Performance: 1966–67, *p. 28.*

from a wheat-exporting country to a major wheat-importing country. Although the bumper crop of 1964 somewhat alleviated the situation, it did not make up for previous deficits, and in the following year, which was dry again, the Soviet Union was forced to continue wheat imports and to make arrangements for long-term supplies of wheat from such places as Canada, Australia, the United States, and Argentina, in anticipation of future needs. During the winter of 1963–1964 the Soviet Union imported about 11 million metric tons of wheat, in the winter of 1964–1965 about 3 million tons, and in the winter of 1965–1966 about 9 million tons.

The production of livestock products continued to increase after 1958, albeit at a reduced rate, until 1962 when the mediocre crops of the previous 4 years began to have telling effects on livestock herds. The drastic crop failure of 1963 forced this process at an increasing rate because many livestock had to be slaughtered since not enough feed was available for the 1963–1964 winter. Thus the pro-

duction of livestock products reached a minimum in 1964 at the same time that a new crop record was being set.

The same measures that had caused praise to be heaped upon Khrushchev in 1954 and 1955 began to bring severe criticism to him only 3 years later, and by 1964 the crisis in agriculture was one of the major factors that led to his downfall. Although his government had planned a 70 per cent overall increase in agricultural production for the 7-year plan, 1959–1965, this period in fact was able to effect only about a 10 per cent increase, and certain years fluctuated dangerously low. The virgin lands program had not lived up to expectations. During the decade 1953–1963, instead of the anticipated 2 years of excellent harvest, 4 average, and 4 below average, Tselinny Kray in northern Kazakhstan experienced 1 excellent harvest in 1956, 4 average harvests, and 5 unsatisfactory harvests or failures, with the last year being particularly bad. (Table 14–23) Monoculture and lack of fallowing had taken their toll. Spring wheat annually occupied at least three quarters of the cultivated land in the area, and wheat yields decreased drastically throughout the decade. Some years barely produced the amount of wheat that had to be planted, 1.8 quintals per hectare. Since about 10 million acres of good winter-wheat land in Ukraine had been closed out, the country had become about 60 per cent dependent upon the spring-wheat areas of the virgin lands. The result was that although bumper crops for all grains were realized in 1962, 1964, and 1966, which were considerably higher than the total grain yield in 1958, wheat production never again reached the 1958 level, and in 1963 wheat production was only 65 per cent of 1958. Since the Soviet diet is made up so largely of wheat bread, it is understandable how the reduced wheat production could plunge the country into a crisis even though overall grain production was on the increase.

The corn program ran into many snags also. Only about 20 per cent of the corn planted has been able to mature into ripe grain in the cool short summers that exist even in the southern part of the country. Corn cut for silage and green fodder has often been in such an immature stage that it has had little food value, and the indiscriminate sowing of corn for such purposes throughout many unsuitable regions in the country appears to have had little beneficial effect on total agriculture. In fact the reporting of green-fodder production in many regions probably means no more than a rather expensive green

manure, the immature corn having been plowed under rather than harvested. The grain corn, by and large, displaced some of the best winter wheat in the south central Ukraine, Moldavia, and North Caucasus Regions. Where attempts have been made to grow corn and winter wheat in rotation, farmers have run into conflicting desires to leave the corn in the field as long as possible in the fall in order for it to ripen and on the other hand to harvest it early enough to plant the next year's wheat crop before winter sets in. Delay in planting winter wheat has often led to much winter kill, since the wheat has not been given enough time to establish itself before hard freezes set in. This has led to much spottiness in wheat fields in the spring, which has forced farmers to make a decision about whether to plow up the wheat and put it into some other crop or to wait and hope for the best. Either way, some loss is sustained. The partial winter kill of winter wheat, whose sowing has been delayed by the harvesting of corn the previous year, has probably contributed heavily to the decline of winter-wheat yields, which between 1961 and 1964 fell by 23 per cent in the U.S.S.R. Since the peak corn sowings in 1962, corn acreage has been reduced by about 30 per cent, which signifies a swing back to the more traditional small grains in areas where corn is ill-suited. Although corn normally will produce more heavily than any other grain and requires less seed than most grains, the fact remains that most of the Soviet Union is very ill-suited for this crop.

Table 14–23   Grain Growing in Tselinny Kray, 1953–1963

	1953	1954	1955	1956	1957	1958	1959	1960	1961	1962	1963
Grain area (million hectares)	3.9	5.0	11.2	15.6	16.1	15.9	14.9	15.1	16.0	17.0	16.0
Grain output, revised estimates (million tons)	—	4.2	2.8	14.5	6.0	12.1	11.3	10.5	8.7	8.6	4.4
Yields, adjusted (quintals per hectare)	—	8.4	2.5	9.3	3.7	7.5	7.6	6.9	5.4	5.1	2.8

Source: Laird, *Soviet Agriculture: The Permanent Crisis,* p. 34.

Table 14–24   Areas Sown to Grain, 1913–1965, in Millions of Acres

Crop	1913 [a]	1928 [b]	1940 [c]	1953 [d]	1963 [e]	Increase (+) or Decrease (−) 1953–1963	1965	Increase (+) or Decrease (−) 1963–1965
Wheat	82.4	69.2	100.7	120.7	161.5	+40.8	173.3	+11.8
Spring	61.7	53.7	65.0	76.2	120.5	+44.3	124.4	+3.9
Winter	20.7	15.5	35.7	44.5	41.0	−3.5	48.9	+7.9
Rye	70.5	60.2	57.7	50.7	37.5	−13.2	39.5	+1.8
Barley	31.7	17.2	26.2	24.0	51.0	+27.0	45.2	−5.8
Oats	47.7	43.0	50.5	38.2	14.2	−24.0	16.3	+2.1
Maize [f]	5.5	11.0	9.0	8.7	85.5	+76.8	57.9	−27.6
Millet	8.7	14.2	15.0	10.2	10.0	−0.2	8.2	−1.8
Buckwheat	5.5	7.2	5.0	6.5	4.5	−2.0	4.4	−0.1
Rice	0.7	0.5	0.5	0.3	0.3	nil	0.5	+0.2
Total all grains	252.7	222.5	264.6	259.3	364.5	+105.2	345.3	−19.2

Sources: The Economics of the Soviet Wheat Industry, p. 21, and *Narodnoye Khozyaystvo SSSR v 1965 g.*, p. 284.

[a] Prerevolutionary year.

[b] Interwar year.

[c] Eve of U.S.S.R.'s entry into World War II.

[d] Last Stalinist year.

[e] Although 1963 was generally a very bad year for Soviet grain production, the grain acreage was down only 4 per cent from the 379.6 million acres of 1962.

[f] The 1963 and 1965 figures are for all maize—lactic stage, silage, and green fodder—as well as for grain. The acreage under maize for fully ripe grain in 1963 was 17.5 million acres; in 1965 it was 7.9 million acres.

Some other detrimental results of Khrushchev's program were the great reductions in the areas of fallow from 24 million hectares in 1958 to 5.3 million in 1963, in annual and perennial grasses from over 30 million hectares to less than two thirds that amount, and in some of the coarse grains. Khrushchev continually criticized the growing of oats, and during the decade 1953–1963 he caused oat acreages to be decreased from 38.2 million acres to 14.2 million. Rye also decreased during the decade from 50.7 million acres to 37.5. Oats is a high protein cereal which is a very good feed grain for most livestock; it is well adapted to growth in cool, moist areas, in which the Soviet Union abounds; and it provides an excellent cover crop for the establishment of clover and alfalfa, which are the main hay crops in the Soviet Union. Therefore its great reduction in acreage in the Soviet Union is undoubtedly a mistake. Since 1963 there seems to have been some reversal in this trend. (Table 14–24).

Khrushchev's successors denounced his opportunistic measures and slowdown of investments in agriculture, and at an all-party plenum in March 1965 Brezhnev announced a new program in agriculture that was planned to cure most of the existent ills. Prices paid for crops by the state were again raised to a level that would allow most of the farms to make a profit. A guaranteed wage for the collective farmers was instituted, and monthly payments of wages in cash and kind were substituted for annual payments to kolkhozniki, who previously had been remunerated only at the end of the harvest season when the residual income of the farm, if any, was parcelled out to individuals according to accumulated work days. Debts to the state for purchases of machinery and fertilizers in past years were liquidated for many of the poorer farms, and a promise was made that there would be no more attempts to convert collective farms to state farms, although there is some evidence to the contrary since the statement was made. Restrictions over the private subsidiary plots were removed, numbers of private livestock were increased, and feed from the collective sector was made available to private livestock holders. In 1966 another decree established pensions for collective farmers.

The income of state farm workers was also improved. The state farm had often served as the transition stage for collective farmers who ultimately moved into industry. Since in the past state farmers generally fared somewhat better than collective farmers, there tended to be a movement from collective farm to state farm, where a guaranteed wage was assured. As industry was paying considerably higher wages than state farms, often the collective farmers moved on through the state farm to the cities. As long as there was an excess of labor on the farms, this movement was of no particular concern to the government, and in fact might have been desired. But now that the farm labor supply is tightening up, particularly in semiskilled labor, there has been some attempt to reorder wages so that farmers with needed skills will be retained on the state farms. Even so, it appears that state farm wages in 1965 were only about 71 per cent of industrial wages. It is difficult to estimate collective farm wages, but given the fact that in 1965 the collective farmer was paid for a day's labor at a rate of about 90 per cent that of a state farm laborer, and that the average collective farmer worked only about two thirds as many days during the year as a state farmer did, then one can estimate that the yearly wage income of the collective farmer from the socialized sector amounts to about 60 per cent of the income of the state farm worker and about 44 per cent of the income of the industrial worker. One must realize, however, that the socialized sector is only one source of

income for the collective farmer, and in many instances not the main source. Officials of Ryazan Oblast in 1964 reported that the average kolkhoz family in Ryazan Oblast derived 28 per cent of its income from the collective sector of the farm, 55 per cent from the personal plot, and 17 per cent from outside work. Thus it would appear that kolkhoz families might have the wherewithal to earn just as high or even higher incomes than do their state farm and industrial brothers. At the same time, they have a good deal more freedom in choosing the type of work they are going to do and how much they are going to work.

The new regime has also restated the principle of greater autonomy for decision making on the farms, and in fact has stated that most of the farms will go on the system of khozraschet—the individual farm would choose to grow the crops and produce that which would yield the most profit. However, local bureaucrats have exhibited a fantastic amount of inertia in instituting any such reforms. It simply is not within the grasp of the Russian mentality to allow much local decision making. Undoubtedly the collective farms will be plagued with "petty tutelage" from government bureaucrats for a long time to come, as they always have been in the past, a practice which, incidentally, has always been completely illegal according to the original charters extended to the kolkhozes by the central government.

The 1965 plenum also provided for increased inputs of various kinds into agriculture. Greatly expanded production of mineral fertilizers and machinery was to be supplied to farms at reasonable prices. And at least twice as much electricity was to be made available. This would not only greatly improve efficiency and production but would also alter the way of life of the peasants. Until 1953 peasant households actually were prohibited from using state-supplied electricity. What little electricity was used domestically on the collective farms had to be generated by self-constructed power plants with capacities of 30 to 50 kilowatts, most of which were using high-cost fuels, which caused collective farm managers to generate electricity only at certain times. Therefore it might be said that before 1953 most kolkhoz households simply were not supplied with electricity. Since that time this aspect of rural life has improved considerably.

The present Soviet leaders are calling for the reestablishment of cottage industries to make use of unused labor on the farms. There is also an unstated policy to establish light industries in nearby towns within short enough distances from the farms so that young people particularly can be trucked to work every day and brought back home to live in their original village dwellings. This alleviates the necessity of moving industrial workers into the larger cities and providing housing for them there. This practice is contrary to stated policy, but nevertheless it is becoming quite evident in the countryside. It appears that an increasing number of persons living on collective farms are not engaged in the work of the farms. This may alleviate surplus-labor problems on the farms, but on the other hand it poses a financial problem to the farms since they are called upon to provide housing and social services to people who are not contributing to the farm income. Scattered statements in the Soviet press indicate that this is becoming a problem to be grappled with. Probably some sort of charge will have to be made to people who are living on farms but working outside of them. Here then is an emerging problem in the Soviet Union that is inversely related to that of the suburban-dwelling, city-working individual in the United States.

Whether these new measures by the Soviet government will give the needed stimulus to agriculture is still too early to be determined. There was a significant rise in overall agricultural production between 1965 and 1966, for which Brezhnev took credit because of his new program. However, 1966 was a very good year in regard to weather conditions, and when production fell somewhat in 1967 Brezhnev turned to the relatively poor weather as the cause. Thus when the weather is good the Soviet leaders exalt their organizational reforms, and when the weather is bad they blame the weather.

The present government realizes that probably the only way to increase overall production from now on is to increase yields per acre in the better parts of the country. New land, by and large, is no longer available for the opening. One of the major ways that the Soviets intend to improve yields per acre is through land and climate melioration, primarily through irrigation and drainage. The current 5-year plan, 1966–1970, calls for irrigation of 3 million additional hectares of land and drainage of 6 million. This is more land melioration than has been done during the past 20 years. It would increase irrigated acreage by about 50 per cent, and drained acreage would practically double.

The *Atlas of Agriculture of the Soviet Union* shows that in 1957 a total of 7,210,000 hectares were under irrigation and 6 million hectares were under drainage. (Fig. 14–4) The main irrigated areas, of course, are found in the dry southern parts of the country where generally abundant heat supplies are available. Therefore these regions show some of the highest yields in the country. In many cases these valuable acres have been turned over to specialty crops which cannot be grown elsewhere, such as cotton. It has been calculated by leading Soviet authorities that irrigated land might be increased by about ten times ultimately, but further expansion would run into continually greater problems as sources of water become more difficult to exploit and soils show greater tendencies toward secondary salinization. The present irrigation program shows in-

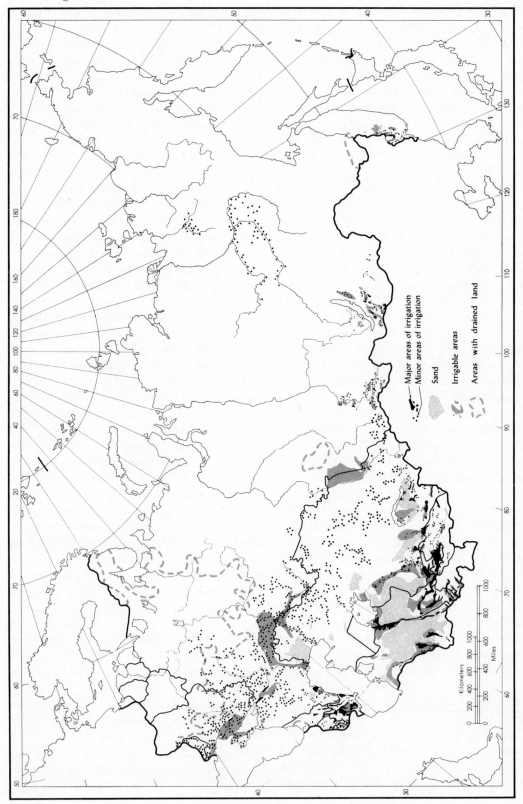

Figure 14–4 Irrigation and drainage in the U.S.S.R. From Atlas selskogo khozyaystva SSSR, pp. 98–99.

tentions to carry on more supplemental irrigation in some of the more humid parts of the country and to irrigate crops, such as grains, which so far have been largely unirrigated.

The drained lands of the Soviet Union largely lie north of the irrigated lands, particularly in the northwestern part of European U.S.S.R. where recent glaciation has caused so much deranged drainage. In general these lands do not yield as much per acre as the irrigated lands, but drainage projects often are more easily effected than are irrigation projects; they do not entail grandiose construction projects or large initial outlays of capital. Therefore the present trend is for more drainage than irrigation. One of the reasons for this is that the Soviets would like to insure themselves from the vagaries of drought as much as possible, and therefore they would like to locate more of their farming in the traditional old non-chernozem agricultural areas of European Russia.

Crop and Livestock Distributions

General Pattern With few exceptions, the Soviet Union is humid north of a line starting at approximately the city of Lvov in western Ukraine and extending east-northeastward in an irregular line to the vicinity of Ufa in the western Urals, from where it continues eastward in a nearly straight line at about 56 degrees north latitude. And it is definitely dry south of a line which begins in the eastern part of the North Caucasus, swings northward around the Caspian Sea approximately through the cities of Volgograd and Uralsk, and then extends eastward to the Chinese border in an irregular line which criss-crosses the parallel of 50 degrees north latitude. Between these two lines exists a strip of land approximately 350 miles wide, extending from the western border of the country in western Ukraine and Moldavia eastward to the Yenisey

River in central Siberia, where the climate is transitional from humid to dry, the original vegetation was tall grasses, and the soils are of high fertility. This is the so-called chernozem or black-earth belt. It is within this belt of prime soils and sub-humid to semiarid climate that much of the agriculture of the Soviet Union is found. (Fig. 14–5) Wheat, sugar beets, corn, sunflowers, and a great variety of other crops are grown here.

To the north of this belt the climate is humid and cool, the soils are of a podzol character, drainage is often poor, and the crops are primarily potatoes, flax, hardy grains, and vegetables. South of the black-earth belt in the deserts of the Caspian Lowland and Middle Asia cultivation is limited to isolated patches of grain growing without irrigation wherever the precipitation is above normal for the region or to areas of intensive irrigated agriculture wherever water can be derived from the melting snows and glaciers in the high mountains. The chief crop throughout the irrigated areas of Soviet Middle Asia is cotton, but a great variety of fruits and vegetables are grown, as well as considerable quantities of alfalfa, grain, and sugar beets. In Transcaucasia, the crop complexes are split between east and west, with the dry eastern portion of the region resembling the deserts of Middle Asia with their irrigated fields of cotton and alfalfa and the humid west being an area of subtropical crops such as citrus, tea, and tobacco.

Agriculture in eastern Siberia is almost absent except for patches of cultivation in the steppe-like mountain basins along the southern fringes of the region on either side of the Trans-Siberian Railroad. These mountain basins still are utilized primarily for sheep and cattle grazing, but some wheat is grown. The cultivated acreage increases again as one approaches Amur Oblast and Maritime Kray in the Soviet Far East where the summer monsoon from the Pacific provides favorable conditions

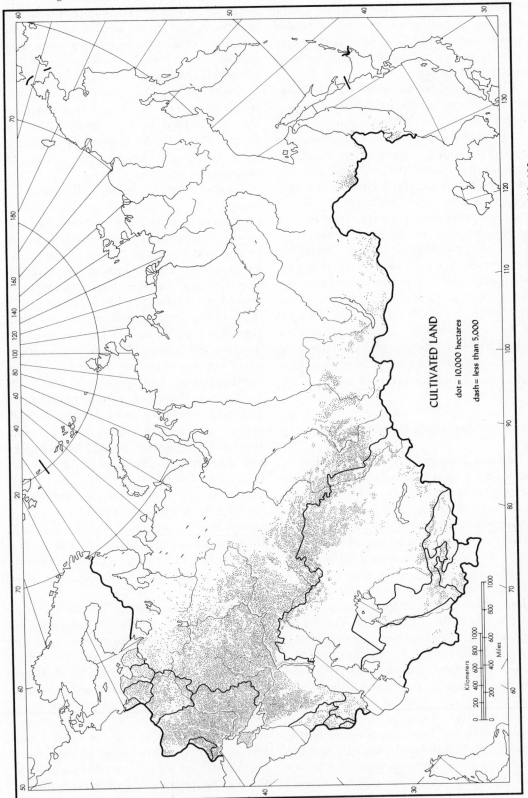

Figure 14–5 Cultivated Land in the U.S.S.R. From Atlas selskogo khozyaystva SSSR, *pp. 102–103.*

for a variety of crops. Western and Oriental types of agriculture meet here to produce a complex of wheat, sugar beets, sunflowers, soy beans, rice, and a variety of fruits, vegetables, and melons.

It must be realized that various crops often are competing with one another for their optimum soil and climatic conditions in the same areas, and hence a choice has to be made as to which crop is going to be grown in the area that is most conducive to its growth and which crop will have to take second best as far as its growth environment is concerned. For instance, grains largely have been pushed out of the irrigated areas of Middle Asia in favor of cotton, which yields more value per acre and which cannot be grown in other regions of the country, as grains can be. Within the last decade probably the greatest competition between crops has been taking place in the prime agricultural areas of Ukraine, the Central Black Earth Region, and the Kuban District in the North Caucasus. Here the introduction of corn as a heavily producing grain and fodder crop for livestock and, to some extent, sugar beets have displaced much wheat, which in turn has had to move to drier and drier regions. Thus the opening of the virgin lands in northern Kazakhstan and southwestern Siberia partially has been due to the introduction of corn into the better farming areas of the European Plain. Heavy yields of wheat in Ukraine and European Russia have been sacrificed for the growing of corn in that area, and to compensate for the reduction of wheat production in this area, the Soviets have resorted to extensive cultivation of this crop in a less favorably endowed area with reduced production per acre. Hence a grain such as wheat is often found growing in an area not optimal for it.

Although the government is very concerned about what crops are raised where and the relative total productions of different types of crops, it has never made much of an attempt to structure prices so as to bring about the desired crop distributions. Prices paid for different crops do not make much sense in terms of cost of production, and the distribution of crops does not reflect relative profits. As can be seen in Table 14–25, in 1962 collective farms in the northwestern part of the country were actually losing money by growing grain. So were Transcaucasia and Central Asia, areas where crop specialization theoretically was being promoted strongly but actually was being stymied by strict procurement plans that required most of the farms in these areas to deliver certain amounts of grain as well as specialty crops. To alleviate this situation, Brezhnev in 1965 proposed a plan of differential prices by regions so that low-yielding areas and high-cost regions could show a profit. Table 14–26, using production costs and yields for 1964 and regional procurement prices proposed by Brezhnev in 1965, shows net incomes that could be expected by major grain-growing regions according to the new plan. Although the data for 1962 are computed on the basis of all grains and the hypothetical data for 1965 are based on wheat only, Tables 14–25 and 14–26 are fairly comparable since maize has been excluded from all data, and therefore wheat makes up more than 55 per cent of all the grain data considered in 1962. It can be seen that the proposed regional price differentials would tend to penalize some of the most profitable grain-growing regions, particularly Moldavia, which in 1962 showed the highest ruble return per acre for grain growing and in 1965 stood last in this respect, showing hardly any profit. On the other hand, the Baltic Region, which showed the largest losses in 1962, would show the highest profits in 1965. Under regional price differentials, the objective to expand wheat into the non-chernozem belt undoubtedly would be accomplished, but at a fantastic cost to the overall economy of the country.

As can be seen in Table 14–27, widely

varying profits are realized in the same area from different crops. Grains, which occupy the most acreage in Ukraine, actually realize the lowest net income. This is because of the relatively low yields per acre and modest prices per ton. Vegetables, which yield about eight times as much weight per acre as grains do and command a somewhat higher procurement price per ton, show the greatest gross income per acre of any crop, but the production cost per acre is also very high, and therefore the net income per acre is rather low. The highest prices are paid for sunflower seeds, but yields per acre are relatively low. Since the production cost per acre for sunflower seeds is the lowest for all crops, the net income is moderate. Sugar beets show the heaviest yields, but procurement prices are lowest per ton of any of the crops, and production costs are moderate, so the net incomes are not the

highest. Potatoes show the highest net income. If collective farmers had had their way in Ukraine in 1964 they would no doubt have planted everything to potatoes. But since the agriculture of Ukraine reflects central planning which puts Ukraine in proper perspective with the rest of the country, Ukraine is called upon to produce mostly grain and sunflowers, which cannot be grown further north to any great extent. Potatoes, although they are a major crop in Ukraine, are grown more heavily in the north where climate limits agriculture to fewer choices. Thus central planning has effected some rationality in crop distributions, but only through decree, rather than through proper pricing, which could have brought about the desired results in a painless manner.

The fact that Soviet farmers, like all farmers, are responsive to profits, has been proven occasionally when prices have

Table 14–25   Actual Relative Regional Net Income for Grains on Kolkhozy in the U.S.S.R. for 1962, in Rubles

Region	Production Cost per Ton[a]	Procurement Price per Ton[b]	Yield per Acre	Production Cost per Acre	Gross Income per Acre	Net Income per Acre[c]
Ukraine	33.0	65.0	0.72	23.8	46.8	+23.0
Kazakhstan	40.0	65.0	0.26	10.4	16.9	+6.5
Russian Federation	35.0	65.0	0.44	15.4	28.6	+13.2
Moldavia	40.0	65.0	0.93	37.2	60.4	+23.4
Belorussia	79.0	65.0	0.28	22.1	18.2	−3.9
Baltic	105.0	65.0	0.34	35.7	22.1	−13.6
Transcaucasia	76.0	65.0	0.43	32.7	28.0	−4.7
Central Asia	74.0	65.0	0.31	22.9	20.1	−2.8
U.S.S.R.	37.0	65.0	0.44	16.3	28.6	+12.3

Source: The Economics of the Soviet Wheat Industry, p. 53. Maize is excluded from all columns.

[a] Includes actual payments in money and kind to the kolkhozniki.

[b] Average grain price; some regions could be 10 to 20 per cent higher on a sliding scale of regional moisture content and yield variations.

[c] Income minus cost.

Table 14–26   Hypothetical Relative Regional Net Income for Wheat on Kolkhozy in the U.S.S.R. for 1965, in Rubles

Region	Production Cost per Ton [a]	Procurement Price per Ton		Yield per Acre [b]	Production Cost per Acre	Gross Income per Acre		Net Income per Acre [c]	
		Within Quota	Over Quota			Within Quota	Over Quota	Within Quota	Over Quota
Ukraine	37.0	76.0	114.0	0.68	25.2	51.7	77.5	+26.5	+52.3
Kazakhstan	41.0	80.0	120.0	0.40	16.4	32.0	48.0	+15.6	+31.6
Russian Federation	43.0	86.0	129.0	0.42	18.1	36.1	54.2	+18.0	+36.1
Moldavia	69.0	76.0	114.0	0.36	24.8	27.4	41.0	+2.6	+16.2
Belorussia	85.0	130.0	195.0	0.36	30.6	46.8	70.2	+16.2	+39.6
Baltic	84.0	130.0	195.0	0.52	43.7	67.6	101.4	+23.9	+57.7
Transcaucasia	81.0	90.0	135.0	0.40	32.4	36.0	54.0	+3.6	+21.6
Central Asia [d]	65.0	85.0	127.5	0.35	22.8	29.7	44.6	+6.9	+21.8
U.S.S.R.	44.0	76.0 to 130.0	114.0 to 195.0	0.44	19.4	27.4 to 67.6	41.0 to 101.4	+2.6 to +26.5	+16.2 to +57.7

Source: The Economics of the Soviet Wheat Industry, p. 53.

[a] Production costs for grain in 1964 excluding maize; as such, wheat production is over 55 per cent of grains production.

[b] Actual wheat yields for 1964.

[c] Income minus cost.

[d] The 1965 wheat prices are for Kirgizstan, which is the most important Central Asiatic wheat producer.

been increased suddenly to stimulate crash programs for the widespread growing of certain new crops. In fact in certain instances the government has been embarrassed by the "successes" of such measures which have brought on immediate over-productions of the favored crops. Thus it would appear that the Soviet leaders would do well to make a thorough study of relative costs and profits of different types of crops and adjust procurement prices accordingly to effect the balances of crops that they want. Rather than ruling by decree, they could then painlessly manipulate by rational price systems.

The final footnote of Table 14–27 shows that in 1964 collective farms in Ukraine were losing money on all livestock products except wool. It is little wonder that the government was having trouble inducing farmers to feed their grains, which they

were growing at some profit, to livestock, from which they would ultimately realize losses. This also would tend to explain the very low labor productivity in livestock raising. It can readily be seen in Fig. 14–6 that numbers of livestock have fluctuated drastically all through the Soviet period. Although data are lacking for the years 1913–1928, it is generally known that livestock suffered heavily after 1916 during the periods of Civil War and War Communism and then recovered during the New Economic Policy until in 1928 they were more numerous than they had been before the Revolution. Livestock numbers plunged to record lows in 1933 and 1934 due to unwarranted slaughtering during forced collectivization. They recovered steadily up to the beginning of World War II, although there still were less livestock in 1941 than there had been in 1928. All livestock suffered some during World War

Table 14–27   Relative Net Income for Grains and Other Crops on Kolkhozy in Ukraine, 1964, in Rubles

Crop	Production Cost per Ton [a]	Procurement Price per Ton [b]	Yield per Acre	Production Cost per Acre	Gross Income per Acre	Net Income per Acre [c]
Grain [d]	37.0	65.0	0.62	22.9	40.3	+17.4
Sunflower seeds	29.0	181.0	0.61	17.7	110.4	+92.7
Sugar beets	16.0	28.7	9.68 [e]	154.9	277.8	+122.9
Potatoes	34.0	71.0	4.04	137.4	286.9	+149.5
Vegetables	66.0	75.2	4.80	316.7	360.9	+44.2
Wheat [f]						
1963 price	37.0	75.6	0.68	25.2	51.4	+26.2
1965 price within quota	37.0	76.0	0.68	25.2	51.7	+26.5
1965 price over quota	37.0	114.0	0.68	25.2	77.5	+52.3

Source: The Economics of the Soviet Wheat Industry, p. 54.
[a] Includes actual payments in money and kind to the kolkhozniki.
[b] Prices for 1963.
[c] Income minus cost.
[d] Excludes maize.
[e] Yield of sugar beets for cattle feed is 5.16; on this basis net income per acre is +65.6 rubles. Previously the price for sugar beets was 23 rubles a ton and on this basis net income was +67.7 rubles per acre.
[f] Production costs are for grain, 1964; yields for wheat, 1964. Normally in Ukraine wheat comprises over 50 per cent of grain output, excluding maize.
Note: In the Ukrainian livestock sector in 1964 the net income on a ton of milk was −31.2 rubles, on a ton of beef −176 rubles, on a ton of pork −295 rubles, on a kilo of wool +0.58 rubles, and on 1000 eggs −18.0 rubles.

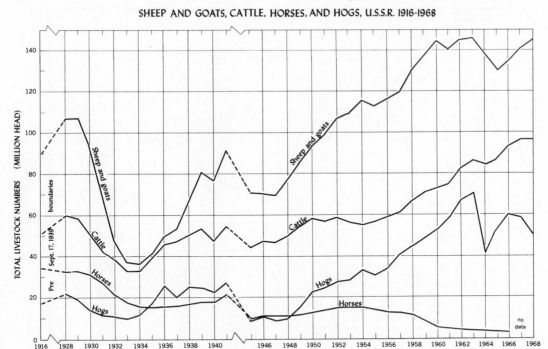

Figure 14–6   Numbers of sheep and goats, cattle, horses, and hogs, U.S.S.R., 1916–1968. Data from Comparisons of the United States and Soviet Economies, *p. 230,* Soviet Geography: Review and Translation, *March 1962, p. 85,* Soviet Economic Performance: 1966–67, *p. 29, and* Strana Sovetov za 50 let, *pp. 152–153.*

II, but recovered quickly after the war. Although there seems to be a sustained drive on now to build up cattle herds, particularly dairy cattle, other livestock are still not showing consistent growth, and hogs have never fully recovered after dropping more than 40 per cent in 1 year between 1963 and 1964 when heavy slaughtering was necessitated by lack of grain following the disastrous droughts of the summer of 1963. Horses continue to decline as farms become more and more mechanized.

Under present price and cost structures and other governmental policies, farms in different regions of the country realize widely varying profits. As can be seen in Fig. 14-7, the Kuban Region in Krasnodar Kray is considerably more fortunate than any other farming region in the country. Net incomes per hectare of farm land range from an index of 100 there to 15 in western Siberia, and probably less in some outlying areas. Among the large areas not mapped, only portions of Transcaucasia and the irrigated areas of Middle Asia would show significant incomes. Specialty crops in some of these southern areas might yield higher incomes per acre than are obtained in Krasnodar Kray. Obviously the Soviets have a long way to go to make farming equally profitable throughout the cultivated regions of the country.

In general it can be said that the policies that largely determine the relative distributions of individual crops in the Soviet Union are as follows: (1) a more heavily yielding crop will displace a less yielding crop in areas that have favorable growth conditions for both; (2) a specialty crop such as cotton or citrus that has very restricted tolerances for climate and soil conditions will displace other crops with wider tolerances in areas of its optimum

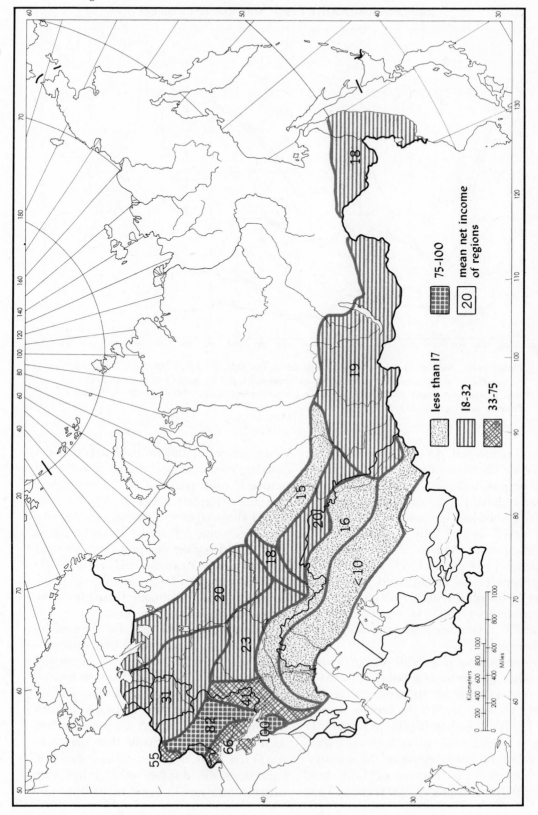

Figure 14-7   Net incomes of collective farms per hectare of farm land (Krasnodar Kray = 100). From Zvorykin, K. V. and Lebedev, P. N., "The Tasks of Rational Utilization of Land Resources," Soviet Geography: Review and Translation, March, 1968, pp. 160–161.

growth conditions, even though its value yields per acre may be no higher than those of the other crops; (3) the desire for national and regional autarchy in most types of production has induced the experimentation with and commercial growth of a variety of crops that might more economically be imported from another country or another part of the U.S.S.R. Examples are the rather extensive cultivation over a considerable number of years of kok-sagyz and other rubber-producing plants, even though the effort never proved to be very successful; the present great push to produce corn for grain and silage in practically all regions of the country in spite of unfavorable climatic and soil conditions in many regions; and the dispersal of sugar beet production into many outlying regions of the country, some of which do not have favorable environments for sugar beets.

Since 1953 the Soviets have launched a drive to overtake the United States in per capita production of meat, milk, butter, and eggs. This means that a large number of livestock and poultry of all types have been introduced into all regions of the country, and in many cases regions that previously had concentrated primarily on a cash grain crop now have adopted a more rounded agricultural economy, with livestock as the main source of cash income. The livestock economy of the country has at the same time been changed from one of extensive seminomadic herding of cattle and sheep to one of a more sedentary raising of cattle, sheep, hogs, and poultry fed primarily on fodder and grain within feedlots in the main grain-growing areas. The dairy industry, for instance, has shifted considerably from western Russia to Ukraine. With these generalizations in mind, we can better understand the distribution of crops and animals shown in Figs. 14–8 through 14–28, maps adapted from the *Atlas of Agriculture of the U.S.S.R.*

Distributions of Individual Crops   The greatest concentration of all grain growing is in the southern part of the European Plain where the level of production is the highest. But wheat growing is no longer concentrated in this area. It has constantly been pushed eastward as corn has been expanded in Ukraine and the North Caucasus. The greatest concentration of wheat growing is now in northern Kazakhstan and southwestern Siberia, and most of this is spring wheat because the winters generally are too severe for winter wheat. Throughout much of this eastern area spring wheat occupies one half to three quarters of the cultivated area, whereas in Ukraine and the North Caucasus wheat occupies no more than 20 to 40 per cent of the sown area. Most of the wheat raised on the European Plain is winter wheat, because it is possible to raise winter wheat there, and because winter wheat yields more heavily and has a higher quality than spring wheat. Both winter and spring wheat are scattered throughout the moister areas of the foothill belt of Middle Asia.

Corn is grown most heavily in Ukraine and the Kuban District where in many cases it occupies more than 30 per cent of the sown area. Much of the corn in these areas is grown for grain, although much is grown for fodder and silage, whereas farther north in a rather wide belt in European Russia and extending into Siberia, most of the corn is grown for silage or green fodder for dairy cattle. Corn produces most heavily in central and western Ukraine and in the Kuban District in Krasnodar Kray. Hence corn is grown mainly in the areas with the most favorable environmental conditions. Actually, optimum environmental conditions for corn do not exist in the Soviet Union, which is why corn was not grown extensively until Khrushchev decreed that it would be. In the humid north the summers are too short and cool, and the south with its

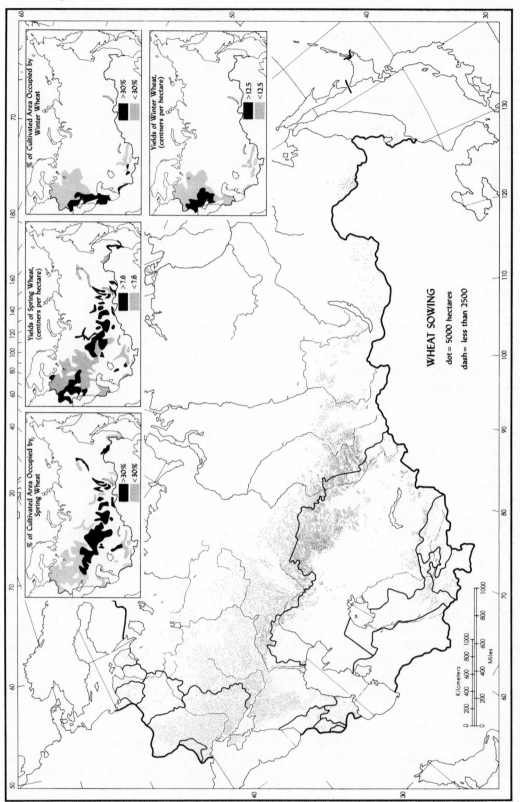

Figure 14–8 Wheat sowing.

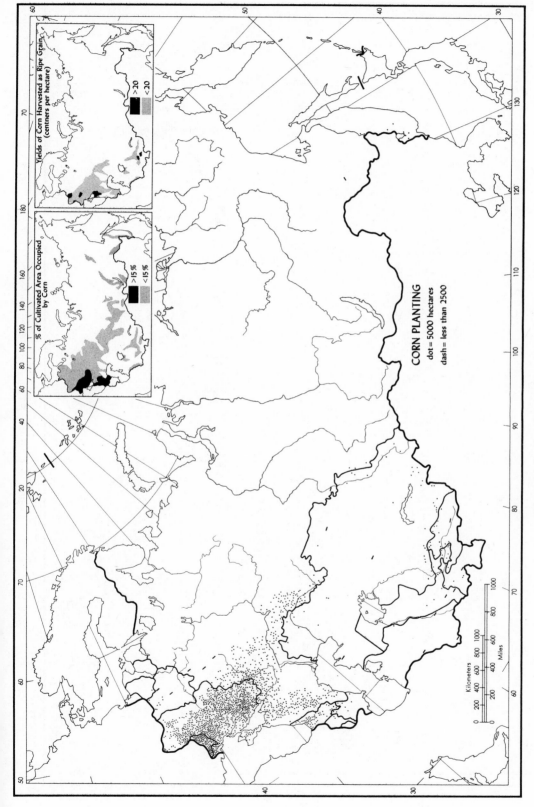

CORN PLANTING

dot = 5000 hectares

dash= less than 2500

Yields of Corn Harvested as Ripe Grain
(centners per hectare)

> 20

< 20

% of Cultivated Area Occupied
by Corn

>15%

<15%

Figure 14–9   Corn harvested in ripe or wax stage.

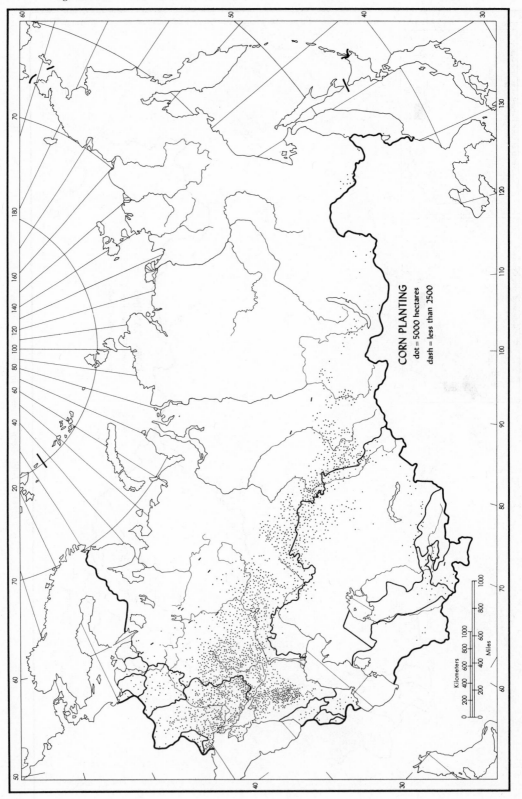

CORN PLANTING
dot = 5000 hectares
dash = less than 2500

Figure 14–10   Corn used for silage and green fodder.

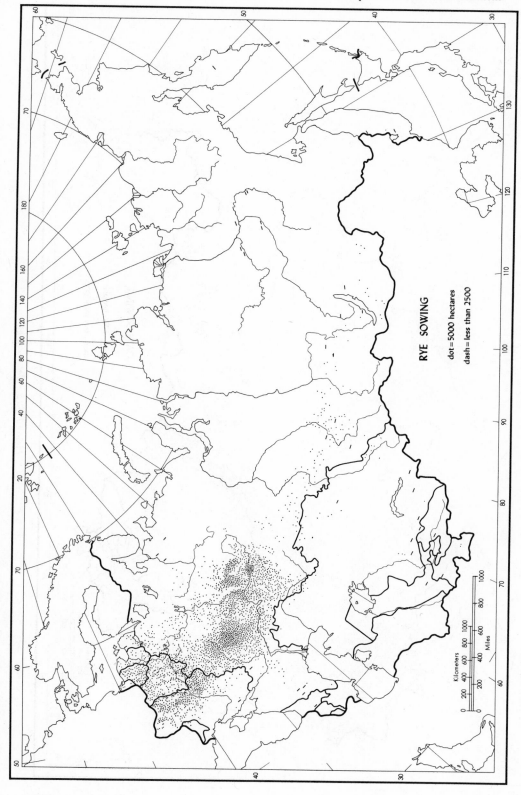

RYE SOWING

dot = 5000 hectares

dash = less than 2500

Figure 14–11　Rye sowing.

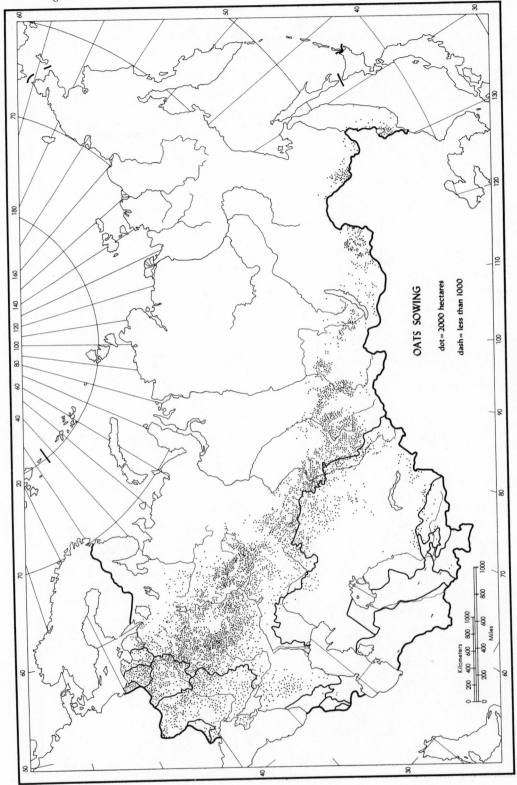

OATS SOWING

dot = 2000 hectares

dash = less than 1000

Figure 14–12   Oats sowing.

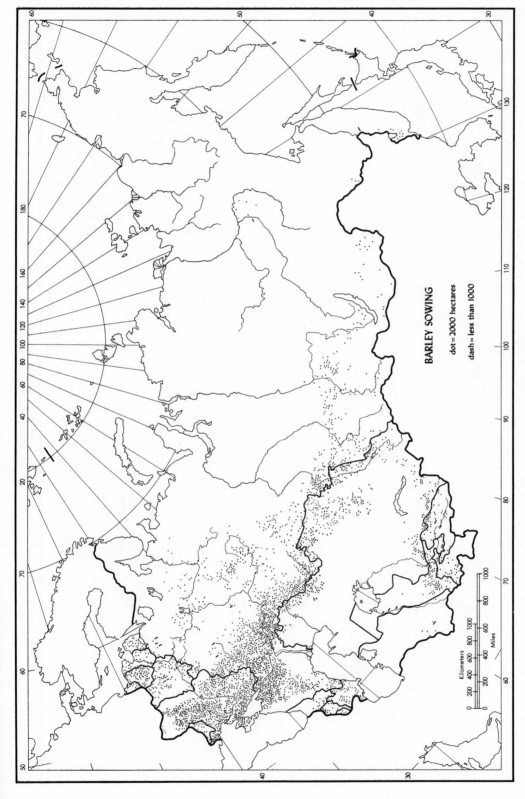

BARLEY SOWING

dot = 2000 hectares

dash = less than 1000

Figure 14–13   Barley sowing.

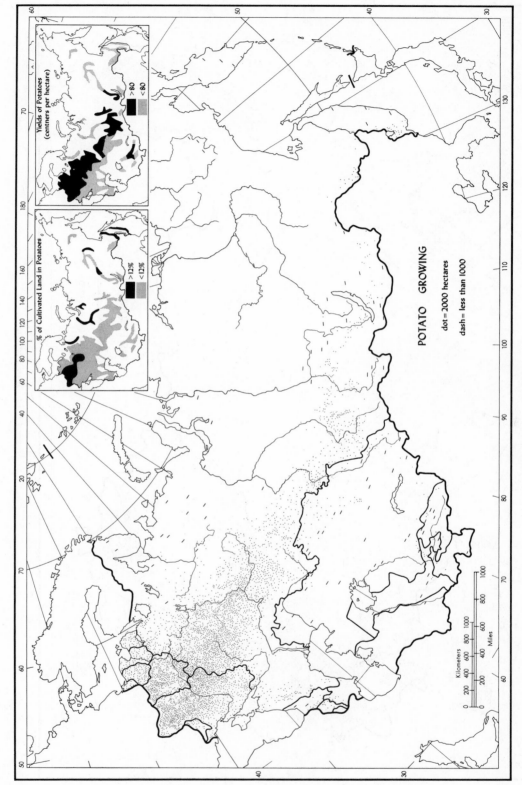

POTATO GROWING

dot = 2000 hectares

dash = less than 1000

% of Cultivated Land in Potatoes

> 12%

< 12%

Yields of Potatoes
(centners per hectare)

> 80

< 80

Figure 14–14   Potato growing.

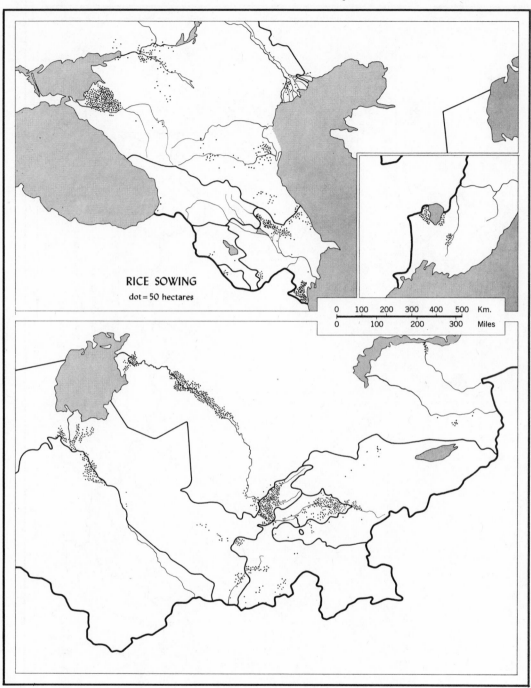

RICE SOWING

dot = 50 hectares

Figure 14–15   Rice sowing.

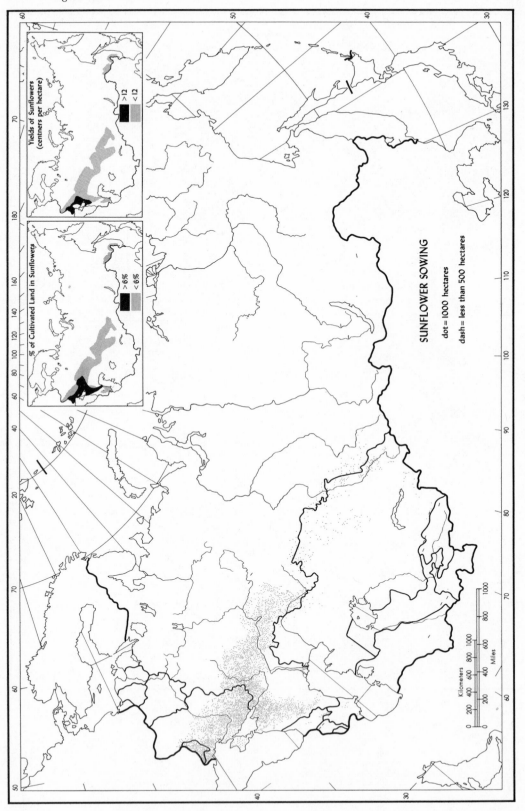

SUNFLOWER SOWING

dot = 1000 hectares

dash = less than 500 hectares

Yields of Sunflowers
(centners per hectare)

> 12
< 12

% of Cultivated Land in Sunflowers

> 6%
< 6%

Figure 14–16 Sunflower sowing.

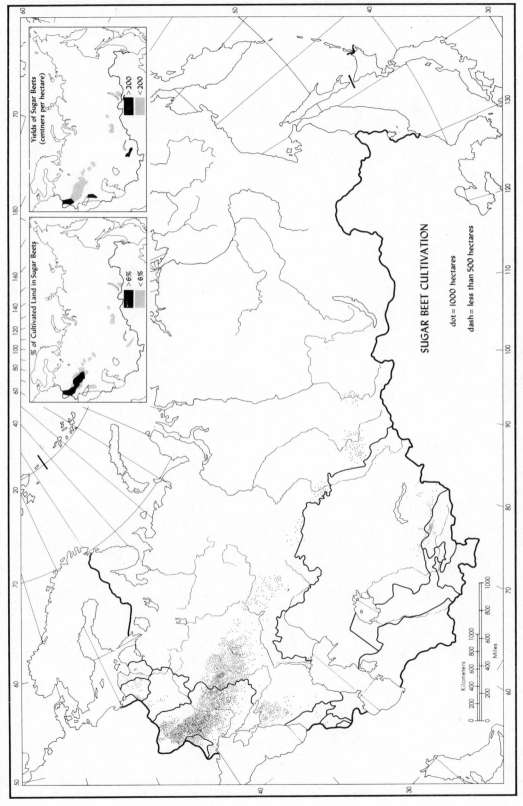

SUGAR BEET CULTIVATION

dot = 1000 hectares

dash = less than 500 hectares

Yields of Sugar Beets
(centners per hectare)

> 200

< 200

% of Cultivated Land in Sugar Beets

> 6%

< 6%

Figure 14–17 Sugar beet cultivation.

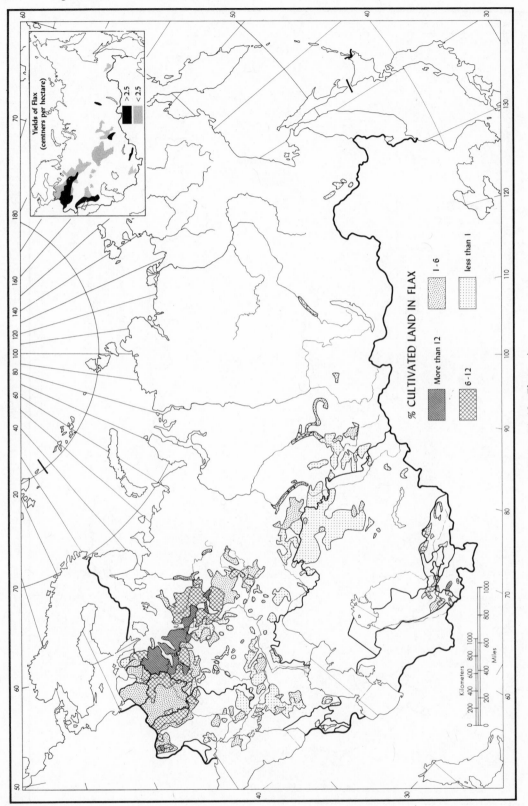

Figure 14-18 Flax sowing.

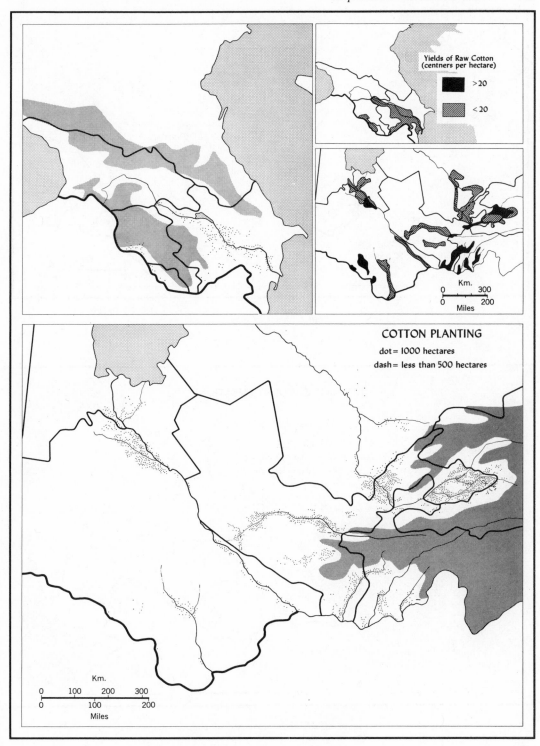

Figure 14–19   Cotton planting.

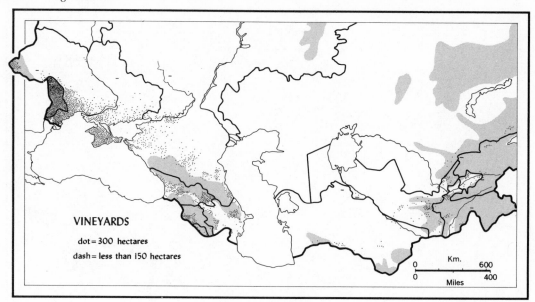

Figure 14–20   Vineyards.

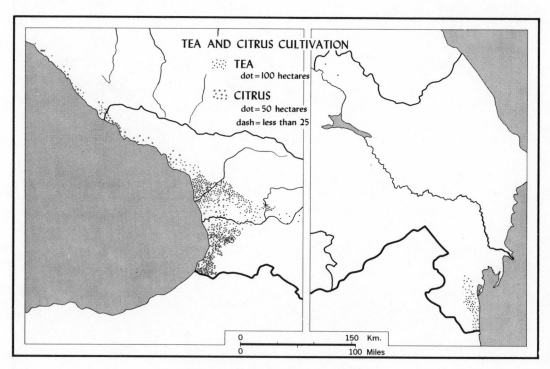

Figure 14–21   Tea and citrus cultivation.

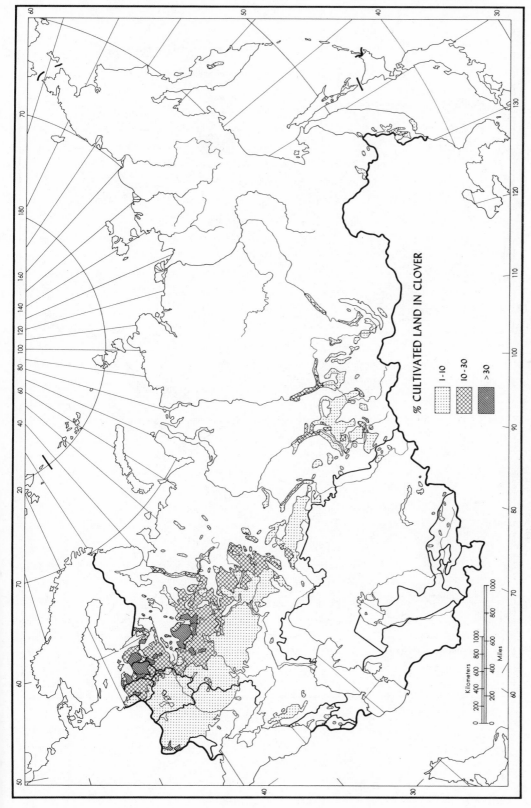

% CULTIVATED LAND IN CLOVER

1-10

10-30

>30

Figure 14–22   Per cent of cultivated land in clover.

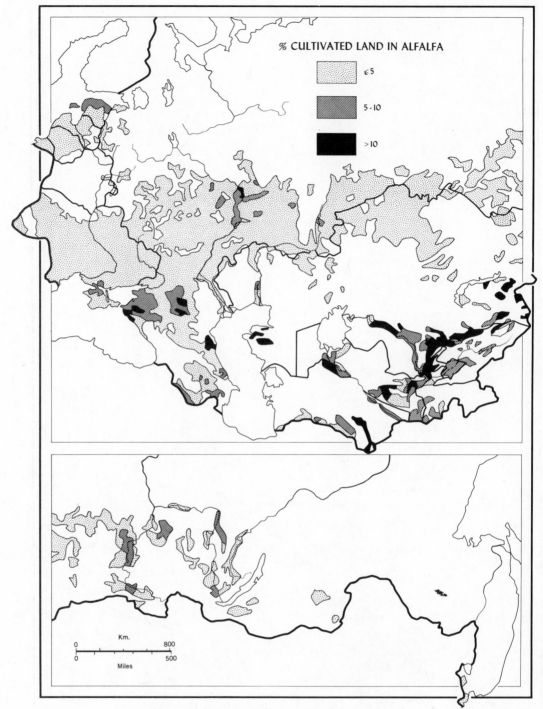

% CULTIVATED LAND IN ALFALFA

≤ 5

5 - 10

> 10

Figure 14–23   Per cent of cultivated land in alfalfa.

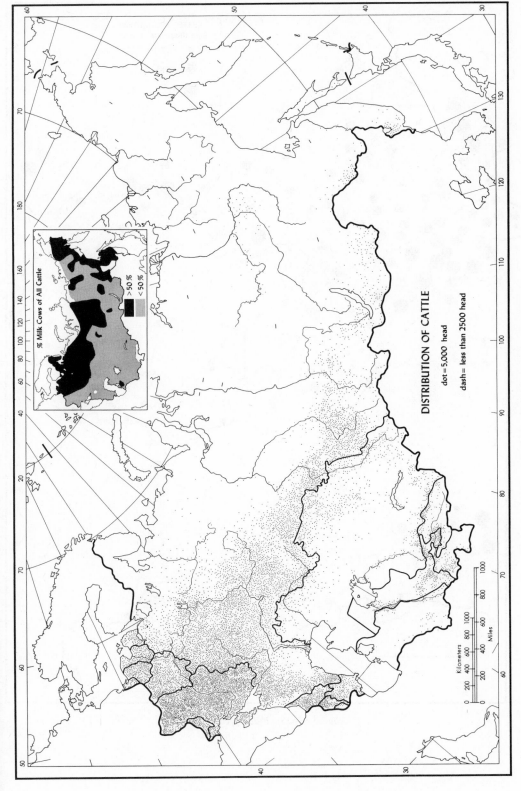

DISTRIBUTION OF CATTLE

dot=5,000 head

dash= less than 2500 head

% Milk Cows of All Cattle

>50 %

<50 %

Figure 14-24 *Distribution of cattle.*

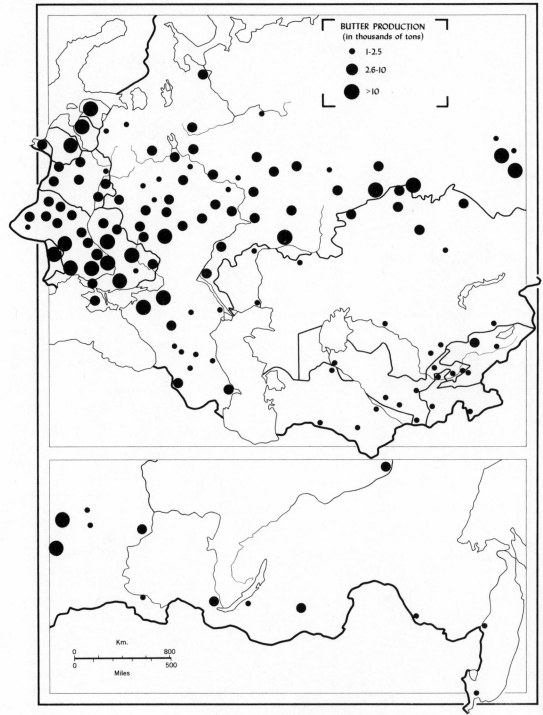

Figure 14–25   Butter production.

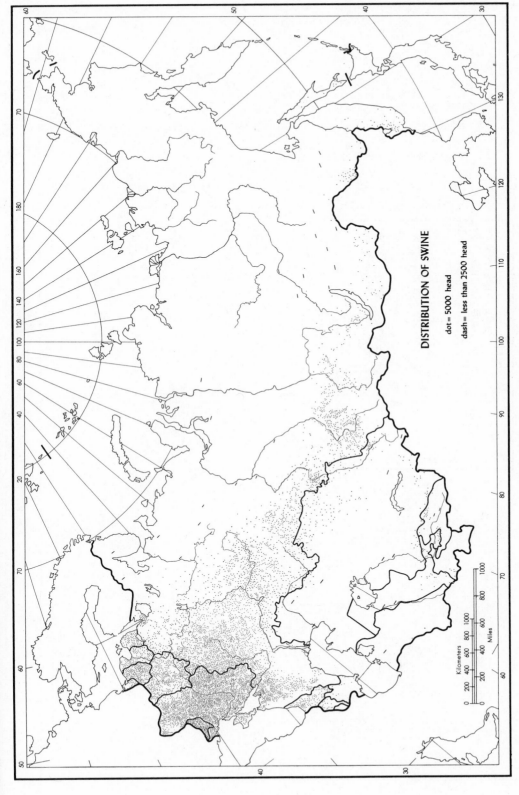

DISTRIBUTION OF SWINE

dot = 5000 head

dash= less than 2500 head

Figure 14-26 Distribution of swine.

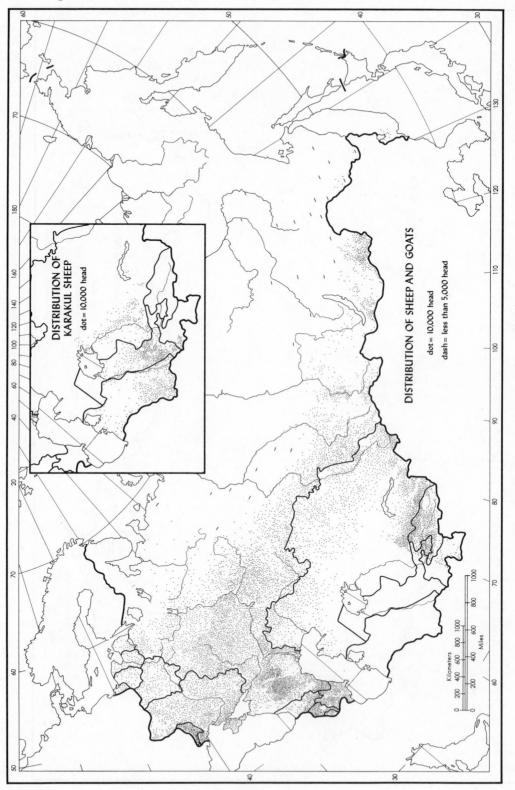

Figure 14–27   Distribution of sheep and goats and karakul sheep.

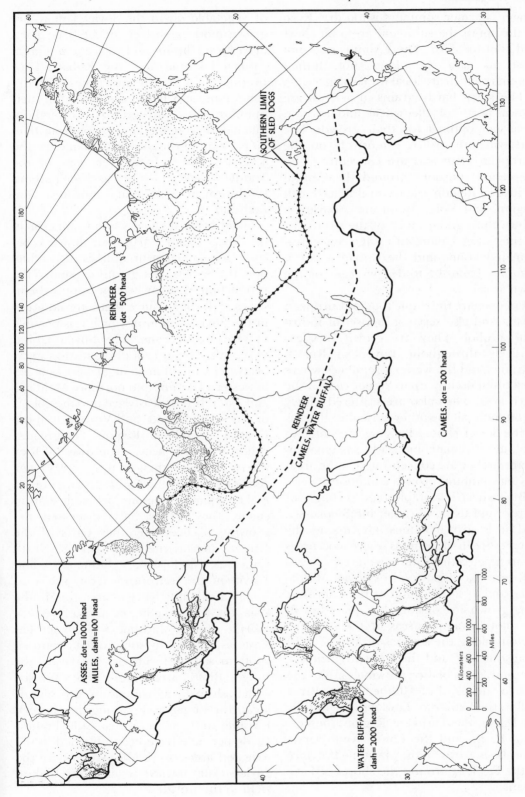

SOUTHERN LIMIT OF SLED DOGS

REINDEER, dot = 500 head

REINDEER, CAMELS, WATER BUFFALO

CAMELS, dot = 200 head

ASSES, dot = 1000 head
MULES, dash = 100 head

WATER BUFFALO, dash = 2000 head

Kilometers
Miles

Figure 14-28   Distributions of camels, asses, mules, water buffalo, reindeer, and sled dogs.

longer, warmer summers is too dry. Even in the south the summers are a bit short and cool for corn. There simply does not exist an area with long, hot, humid summers which are ideal for corn growing.

The small hardy grains in general are grown north of the wheat and corn in areas not optimal for their growth. Rye and oats are grown extensively on the European Plain and are concentrated in the central portions around the Central Industrial Region, the Central Black Earth Region, and Volga Bend area. Barley is grown throughout much of the sown area of the Soviet Union with some concentration in Ukraine and the Kuban where it occupies from 10 to 15 per cent of the sown area.

Potatoes are the staple food of European Russia and also serve as a base for industrial alcohol. They are grown very extensively throughout European Russia, Ukraine, and the western republics where they often occupy up to 20 per cent of the sown area. They also are scattered widely throughout all the other agricultural areas of the Soviet Union. Potatoes are suited to cool, moist climate and acidic soil environment, so they are concentrated in the areas having optimum growth conditions.

Buckwheat is a staple food throughout European Russia, Ukraine, and Belorussia, and it is grown extensively among the other crops in these areas where it occupies up to 8 per cent of the sown area.

Rice is the basic food of Soviet Middle Asia, and to some extent of the Caucasus. It is grown in considerable quantities in the more swampy areas of the irrigated regions along the streams of Middle Asia, Transcaucasia, and the Kuban. Particular concentrations of rice growing exist in the Kuban delta, the Middle Kura River Valley, the Lenkoran Lowland, the Middle Syr-Darya, the Tashkent Region, the Fergana Basin, and the Lower Amu-Darya. Rice also is grown in the Maritime Province of the Far East around the shores of Lake Khanka.

Sunflowers, which are the main source of vegetable oil in the Soviet Union, are grown most extensively in the drier parts of western Ukraine and adjacent Moldavia, eastern Ukraine, and the Kuban. They produce most heavily under these hot, dry conditions, and hence are located in their optimum areas for growth. Throughout much of this region they occupy from 10 to 15 per cent of the sown area. They are also scattered rather extensively east of the Middle Volga and into the drier parts of southwestern Siberia and northern Kazakhstan.

Sugar beets are a very important crop in the Soviet Union. With their desire to become self-sufficient in all lines of production, the Soviets have greatly expanded the production of sugar beets to supply themselves with sugar, since there are no areas in the Soviet Union in which it is possible to grow sugar cane. The Soviet Union raises over 40 per cent of the world's sugar beets. The traditional sugar-beet belt lies in western Ukraine and northern Moldavia and extends northeastward into the oblasts of Kursk, Belgorod, and Voronezh in the Central Black Earth Region. The greatest concentration of beets is southwest of Kiev where in places they occupy over 12 per cent of the cultivated area. In an effort to make separate regions self-sufficient in sugar, the Soviets have dispersed the growing of beets to other parts of the Union, such as the Kuban in the North Caucasus, Belorussia, Lithuania, and Latvia in the European West, the Chu Valley and Taldy-Kurgan areas in Middle Asia, the Kulunda Steppe in southwestern Siberia, and in Maritime Kray in the Far East, as well as in some other scattered spots in southern Siberia, the Urals, the Volga Bend area, and Transcaucasia. Although natural conditions are almost ideal for sugar-beet raising in western Ukraine and in the Kuban, the highest yields per acre have been obtained in the irrigated areas of Middle Asia, where the Soviets claim to have attained the highest yield in the world.

Soy beans might well be adapted to extensive areas of the warm and semiarid U.S.S.R., where they would compete with sunflowers, wheat, and corn, and this might be some solution to the need for vegetable oils in the country. They have been introduced in significant amounts only in the Far East, however, particularly in the Khanka-Ussuri Lowland and the Zeya-Bureya Lowland. Other beans and peas for human consumption are raised extensively, with concentrations in western Ukraine and Moldavia and in the eastern part of the Central Black Earth Region and the Volga Bend area.

Flax is a traditional crop of Russia; the Soviet Union produces about 78 per cent of the world's supply. It is admirably suited to the cool, moist, poorly drained northern part of the European Plain where it is grown extensively in conjunction with potato growing and dairying. It reaches its greatest concentration northwest of Moscow where it occupies about 12 per cent of the sown area. Fiber flax yields most heavily in this region and southwestward in Belorussia and northern Ukraine. Flax for linseed oil is raised in scattered areas of the dry south, along the Lower Don and North Caucasus and in the steppes of northern Kazakhstan and southwestern Siberia, as well as in scattered regions of eastern Ukraine and Middle Asia.

The other important fiber crop, cotton, is grown exclusively in the irrigated areas of Middle Asia and Transcaucasia. It is most concentrated in the Fergana Basin, the "Pakhta Aral," the Tashkent Region, the Zeravshan Valley, and the Lower Amu-Darya. It produces most heavily in the Fergana Basin, southwestern Tadzhikistan, and the Tedzhen Oasis. Since 1913 Soviet cotton output has increased by more than eight times until now it is approximately equal to that of the United States. The sown area has more than tripled and yields have more than doubled.

Mulberry trees grown along the canal systems of most of the irrigated areas of Middle Asia and Transcaucasia provide the basis for the silk industry in those areas.

Some kenaf and jute are grown in a few areas of irrigation in Middle Asia and the Transcaucasus. The largest area is near Tashkent. A considerable acreage of hemp, raised primarily for its oilseed, is grown in central Ukraine, the Central Black Earth Region, and the area west of the Volga Bend. Some is now being raised in irrigated areas in the North Caucasus.

Truck gardens and orchards are widely distributed throughout the warmer parts of the Soviet Union, particularly in Ukraine and Moldavia, in the Caucasus, and in Middle Asia. The amount and quality of production still are not nearly what is to be desired, and marketing facilities are very primitive. Grapes are one of the major fruit crops; they are used both for eating and for wine making. The major grape-growing region in the country is in Moldavia and adjacent parts of Ukraine including the Crimean Peninsula. Moldavia might be called the Champagne of the Soviet Union. Grape growing also is well developed in Transcaucasia and in the irrigated areas of Middle Asia. Such table fruits as apples, peaches, pears, plums, cherries, apricots, and so forth are grown widely throughout the Union wherever it is possible. In much of the European south, young plantings of fifteen to twenty rows of apple trees line most of the roads in back of broad shelter belts, thus augmenting the shelter belts and ultimately serving the dual purposes of wind protection and fruit production. The growing of citrus fruits is limited to the foothills surrounding the Colchis Lowland in Georgia, particularly around Batumi, and to a very small area in the Lenkoran Lowland. Tea growing is limited to the same two areas.

Fodder Crops With the increased emphasis on livestock raising, the expansion of the acreages of forage and silage crops has become very necessary. These needs are satisfied mostly by clover, alfalfa, and green corn. Clover and alfalfa make good rotation crops for grain, both being legumes, and they have largely replaced the fallowing phase of the rotation cycle of earlier days. This provides a greatly increased amount of forage for livestock, and also is better for the soil than fallowing. In general clover is raised in the more humid parts of the agricultural area, whereas alfalfa is raised in the drier south. Alfalfa is highly tolerant of saline soil conditions and hence is ideal in semiarid and arid regions. Alfalfa is raised in the irrigated areas in rotation with cotton, not only to restore nitrogen to the soil but also to remove excessive salts which tend to accumulate under prolonged irrigation.

Livestock   The country's livestock are concentrated in the better farming areas, particularly in Ukraine and adjacent regions. Cattle and swine especially are concentrated in these areas; sheep and goats are scattered more widely with some concentrations in Moldavia, the Caucasus, and the Middle Asian mountains. The production of wool is especially important in the Caucasus and in the mountains and deserts of Middle Asia. Cattle make up more than 50 per cent by weight of all livestock in the U.S.S.R. More and more, cattle raising is being conducted in feed lots using harvested feed and fodder. Nomadic herding is fading out of the picture. Although transhumance is still practiced in the southern mountains, families no longer move with the herders.

Although the northern areas such as Vologda Oblast have become known as the dairy regions of the Soviet Union, more milk and butter are now produced in the grain-growing regions farther south. However, dairying occupies a larger part of the total farming economy in the north than it does in the south. Throughout much of the northern part of European Russia, milk cows make up more than 60 per cent of the cattle population. This reflects the much greater emphasis on milk than on beef at present. In fact much of the beef of the Soviet Union is derived from dairy stock rather than from beef stock. Veal is

one of the chief entrees found in Soviet restaurants, indicating the great number of bull calves of dairy stock which are sold for meat soon after birth.

Poultry raising is also being greatly expanded in the Soviet Union, for, like swine, poultry are scavengers and can be raised on table scraps and other waste materials. Poultry are scattered throughout all the farming regions of the country but are heavily concentrated in Ukraine and the adjoining areas of Moldavia and the Kuban. A small, separate region of concentration surrounds the Moscow area. Most of the poultry are kept on private plots by individual farmers.

Although the age of the tractor supposedly arrived in Russia early in the Soviet period, many draft animals are still kept on the farms. Horses are raised extensively throughout European Russia and the steppe lands of northern Kazakhstan and southwestern Siberia as well as in the Caucasus and Middle Asia. Also some oxen are still used. Bulls not slaughtered for veal are castrated and put to work at the age of 10 months, and cows are often worked after they are no longer useful for milk. The large Siemmenphal and Holstein breeds are admirably suited for tri-purpose duty: milk, meat, and work. Asses and mules are used extensively in Ukraine, the Caucasus, and Middle Asia. The principal means for conveying produce to market in Middle Asia is the donkey standing no more than 3 feet or so in height pulling a cart whose wheels are considerably greater in diameter than the height of the donkey. The camel is widely distributed as a beast of burden throughout the deserts of Middle Asia, in the North Caspian Lowland, and in the dry Kura River Valley of Transcaucasia. Water buffalo are used in the moister areas of Transcaucasia, and reindeer are used extensively in the north, both for draft animals and for meat.

Interchanges of Agricultural Products   The fact that there are some sharp crop

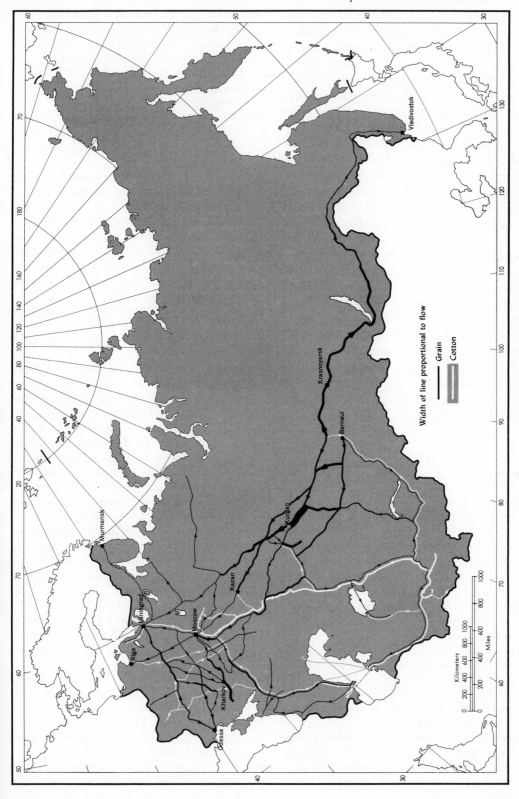

Figure 14–29   Movements of grain and cotton.

differentiations from one part of the country to another necessitates considerable movements of produce from growing to consuming areas. Grain flows northward from Ukraine and the North Caucasus to the central and northwestern parts of European Russia, and heavy grain flows move out of southwestern Siberia and northern Kazakhstan westward to the Urals and European Russia, eastward along the Trans-Siberian Railroad to eastern Siberia and the Far East, and southward into Middle Asia. A heavy cotton flow moves northwestward from Middle Asia to the Central Industrial Region and a lighter flow moves from Transcaucasia to the center. Flax moves generally northeastward from the flax-growing areas of the European West, the Central Black Earth Region, and Ukraine to the Central Industrial Region and other processing centers of European Russia. Minor flows of these products, as well as flows of livestock products and vegetable oil products, move from producing areas to outlying areas of consumption.

Reading List

Anderson, Jeremy, "Fodder and Livestock Production in the Ukraine: A Case Study of Soviet Agricultural Policy," *The East Lakes Geographer*, October 1967, pp. 29–46.

Atlas selskogo khozyaystva S.S.S.R. (Atlas of Agriculture of the U.S.S.R.), Moscow, 1960, 208 pp. (in Russian).

Bone, Robert M., "Soviet Tea Cultivation," *Annals of the Association of American Geographers*, June 1963, pp. 161–173.

Bush, Keith, "The Question of Khozraschet," *Bulletin of the Institute for the Study of the U.S.S.R.*, June 1967, pp. 18–27.

Clarke, Roger A., "Soviet Agricultural Reforms Since Khrushchev," *Soviet Studies*, October 1968, pp. 159–178.

Comparisons of the United States and Soviet Economies, Subcommittee on Economic Statistics, Joint Economic Committee, Congress of the United States, Washington, 1959, Part I, pp. 201–318.

Davitaya, F. F., "A Natural Transmission Belt for the Year-Round Supply of Fresh Farm Products," *Soviet Geography: Review and Translation*, February 1963, pp. 25–31.

De Pauw, John W., "The Private Sector in Soviet Agriculture," *Slavic Review*, March 1969, pp. 63–71.

The Economics of the Soviet Wheat Industry, Bureau of Agricultural Economics, Commodity Research Report No. 1, Australia, December 1966, 82 pp.

Field, Neil C., "Land Hunger and the Rural Depopulation Problem in the U.S.S.R.," *Annals of the Association of American Geographers*, December 1963, pp. 465–478.

———, "Environmental Quality and Land Productivity: A Comparison of the Agricultural Land Base of the U.S.S.R. and North America," *Canadian Geographer*, January 1968, pp. 1–14.

French, R. A., "The Reclamation of Swamps in Pre-Revolutionary Russia," *Institute of British Geographers Publication No. 34*, 1964, pp. 175–188.

Gerasimov, I. P., "Reducing the Dependence of Soviet Agriculture on Natural Elements to a Minimum," *Soviet Geography: Review and Translation*, February 1963, pp. 3–11.

Jackson, W. A. Douglas, "Durum Wheat and the Expansion of Dry Farming in the Soviet Union," *Annals of the Association of American Geographers*, 1956, pp. 405–410.

———, "The Russian Non-Chernozem Wheat Base," *Annals of the Association of American Geographers*, June 1959, pp. 97–109.

Jasny, Naum, *The Socialized Agriculture of the U.S.S.R.; Plans and Performance*, Stanford University Press, Stanford, 1949, 837 pp.

Jensen, Robert G., "Soviet Subtropical Agriculture: A Microcosm," *Geographical Review*, April 1964, pp. 185–202.

———, "Regionalization and Price Zonation in Soviet Agricultural Planning," *Annals of the Association of American Geographers*, June 1969, pp. 324–347.

Kabysh, S., "An Unsolved Problem," *Bulletin of the Institute for the Study of the U.S.S.R.*, April 1968, pp. 33–38.

Kahan, Arcadius, "Agriculture," in Allen Kassof, *Prospects for Soviet Society*, Praeger, New York, 1968, pp. 263–290.

Kalvoda, Joseph, "Soviet Agricultural Reform and the Future of Collective Farms," *The Russian Review*, October 1960, pp. 384–395.

Karcz, Jerzy F., "The New Soviet Agricultural Programme," *Soviet Studies,* October 1965, pp. 129–161.

———, ed., *Soviet and East European Agriculture,* University of California Press, Berkeley, 1967, 445 pp.

Krylov, Constantine, "The Sovkhoz Dilemma," *Bulletin of the Institute for the Study of the U.S.S.R.,* June 1967, pp. 15–18.

Kucherov, Samuel, "The Future of the Soviet Collective Farm," *American Slavic and East European Review,* April 1960, pp. 180–201.

Laird, Roy D., "Soviet Goals for 1965 and the Problems of Agriculture," *Slavic Review,* October 1961, pp. 454–464.

———, ed., *Soviet Agricultural and Peasant Affairs,* University of Kansas Press, Lawrence, 1963, 335 pp.

——— and Crowley, Edward L., eds., *Soviet Agriculture: The Permanent Crisis,* Praeger, New York, 1965, 209 pp.

Lovell, C. A. Knox, "The Role of Private Subsidiary Farming during the Soviet Seven-Year Plan, 1959–65," *Soviet Studies,* July 1968, pp. 46–66.

New Directions in the Soviet Economy, Studies Prepared for the Subcommittee on Foreign Economic Policy of the Joint Economic Committee, Congress of the United States, Washington, 1966, Part II-B, Section 3, pp. 339–493.

Newth, J. A., "Soviet Agriculture: The Private Sector, 1950–1959," *Soviet Studies,* October 1961, pp. 160–171 and April 1962, pp. 414–432.

Nove, Alec, "Soviet Agriculture Marks Time," *Foreign Affairs,* July 1962, pp. 576–594.

Sapozhnikova, S. A. and Shashko, D. I., "Agroclimatic Conditions of the Distribution and Specialization of Agriculture," *Soviet Geography: Review and Translation,* November 1960, pp. 20–34.

Schlesinger, Rudolf, "The New Structure of Soviet Agriculture," *Soviet Studies,* January 1959, pp. 228–251.

Soviet Economic Performance: 1966–1967, Materials Prepared for the Subcommittee on Foreign Economic Policy of the Joint Economic Committee, Congress of the United States, Washington, 1968, pp. 30–36.

Soviet Geography: Review and Translation, March 1968; the entire issue is devoted to articles by Russian authors concerning land evaluation and regional pricing. Compiled and introduced by Robert G. Jensen.

Stolte, Stefan C., "Facts and Figures on Communist Agriculture," *Bulletin of the Institute for the Study of the U.S.S.R.,* February 1967, pp. 17–22.

Strauss, Erich, *Soviet Agriculture in Perspective,* Praeger, New York, 1969, 328 pp.

United States Department of Agriculture, *Livestock in the Soviet Union,* 1961, 84 pp.

Volin, Lazar, "The Russian Peasant: From Emancipation to Kolkhoz," in Cyril E. Black, *The Transformation of Russian Society,* Harvard University Press, Cambridge, 1960, pp. 292–311.

———, "Soviet Agriculture; A Continuing Problem," *Current History,* November 1961, pp. 286–291.

———, *A Survey of Soviet Russian Agriculture,* United States Department of Agriculture Monograph 5, 1951.

Zvorykin, K. V. and Lebedev, P. N., "The Tasks of Rational Utilization of Land Resources," *Soviet Geography: Review and Translation,* March 1968, pp. 154–161.

15

Industry

Economic Indices

Gross National Product Since the beginning of the 5-year plans in 1929 the Soviets have been plowing the bulk of their production back into capital investments to provide the basis for future production, and hence their gross national product has shown a commendable growth rate through the years. By 1966 it had reached an estimated total of 357 billion dollars, which was almost half that of the leading producer, the United States, and 2.5 times that of the third producer, West Germany.

(Table 15–1) In terms of per capita production, however, it still ranks behind West Germany, France, and the United Kingdom, as well as the United States. Per capita production in the U.S.S.R. in 1966 was only slightly more than 40 per cent that in the U.S.A. Thus the Soviets still have a long way to go before they overtake the leading producer.

Since 1961 the Soviet economy relative to that of the United States seems to have plateaued at a level of about 48 per cent that of the U.S.A. (Table 15–2) What's more, except for minor annual fluctua-

Table 15–1   Gross National Products, U.S.S.R. and Selected Market Economies, 1966

Country	Ranked by GNP (Billions of Dollars)	Country	Ranked by per Capita (Dollars)
United States	743	United States	3,777
U.S.S.R.	357	Germany	2,382
Germany	142	France	2,217
Japan	134	United Kingdom	2,047
United Kingdom	113	U.S.S.R.	1,532
France	110	Italy	1,408
Italy	73	Japan	1,352

Source: Soviet Economic Performance: 1966–67, p. 16.

Table 15–2   Gross National Products, U.S.S.R. and U.S.A., in Terms of Market Prices in Billions of 1966 U.S. Dollars

	1950	1955	1958	1961	1965	1966	1967 [a]
United States	414	508	519	575	711	743	762
U.S.S.R.	132	185	229	272	330	357	372
Difference	282	323	290	303	381	386	390
U.S.S.R. GNP as a percentage of United States GNP	31.9	36.4	44.1	47.3	46.4	48.0	48.8

Source: Soviet Economic Performance: 1966–67, p. 16.
[a] Preliminary.

tions, since 1950 the absolute gap between the two economies has been widening. Therefore one can hardly say that during the past two decades the Soviet Union has been gradually catching up with the United States, even if it has improved its position relatively. The difference between relative and absolute comparisons here is analogous to the famous old algebra problems in high school textbooks which were based on changing age ratios through the years that gave the impression that a son's age would eventually catch up with his father's, which, of course, is an absurdity. Since much more of the gross national product in the Soviet Union is utilized in capital investments and defense budgets than in the United States, the dollar gap between the two economies shown in Table 15–2 is even wider in terms of consumer welfare but somewhat narrower in military potential.

Although the Soviet gross national product has been increasing at a rather rapid rate, the growth is not unparalleled during equivalent growth stages in other countries, and in fact it is considerably exceeded by that of Japan at the present time. Between 1962 and 1967 the annual growth rate of the gross national product averaged 5.8 per cent in the U.S.S.R. and 9.5 per cent in Japan. In general the growth rate has been declining in the Soviet Union during the first half of the 1960s over what it had been in the mid 1950s. Much of this decline was due to the stagnation in agriculture

after 1958, although there also was some decline in the growth rate of industry. Whereas industry grew at an annual rate of approximately 10 per cent during the 1950s, during the first half of the 1960s it grew at an annual rate of about 7.5 per cent.

Such a growth rate is still highly respectable, but some other indices show cause for alarm. Although labor productivity grew at a consistent rate during the period 1940–1962, capital productivity declined almost throughout the entire period. Thus as time has gone on the Soviets have been getting less returns on the large amounts of investment that they have been putting into various sectors of the economy. Since the Soviets have been relying heavily on large capital inputs (almost three times as high as those of the United States) to sustain a high rate of growth, the declining productivity of this capital is of major concern. Between 1940 and 1962 Soviet inputs per dollar's worth of gross national product, as a percentage of equivalent United States inputs, changed as follows: labor input, from 395 per cent to 314 per cent; gross fixed business capital stock, from around 50 per cent to more than 100 per cent; mineral fuels input, from 67 per cent to around 90 per cent; input of basic metals, from 96 per cent to 160 per cent; input of freight transportation, from 129 per cent to 209 per cent; and input of electrical energy, from 71 per cent to 83 per cent. Thus labor was the only Soviet input that improved relative to the United States. But labor productivity in the Soviet Union still remains very low compared to that in the United States. In 1962 a dollar's worth of Soviet gross national product required about 3.14 times as much labor input as in the United States, whereas it required about the same amount of fixed business capital. Thus Soviet production is still very labor intensive, utilizing excessive amounts of labor to conserve on capital investment, fuels, and electrical energy.

The lag in Soviet factor productivity can be explained to some extent by the technological lag. It has been estimated that the technological level of the Soviet economy in 1962 was on a par with that in the United States sometime between 1939 and 1947. During the period from World War II to 1962, technological progress in the United States resulted in an increase in labor productivity of about 50 per cent and of capital productivity of about 20 per cent. Thus it appears that if the Soviet technology were to catch up completely with that of the United States, about 20 per cent of the gap in overall productivity would be closed, but this would leave a residual gap which must be attributed to poorer resource endowment of the Soviet

economy, particularly in agriculture, and poorer utilization of the resources on hand.

Industry Capital investment has been more concentrated in mining, manufacturing, and construction in the Soviet Union than in any of the other leading producing countries. This was especially true during the rapid industrialization period of the early 5-year plans between 1928 and 1936, and it is still true to some extent today. (Table 15–3) There is a particularly large discrepancy in this respect between the U.S.S.R. and the U.S.A. It is obvious that the U.S.A. has developed both its industry and its agriculture to the point where only minimum amounts of capital investments are necessary to sustain required production levels, while the bulk of capital investment can go into housing and other consumer goods and services. Since the Soviet Union still has not come very close to satisfying its demands for agricultural and industrial products, the primary effort is still expended to develop these sectors of the economy to the utmost without much regard for potential limitations that might be imposed by lack of consumer demand. In spite of these high capital inputs, industry still accounts for a smaller percentage of the gross national product in

Table 15–3   Comparative Compositions of Capital Investments, in Per Cents of Total

Country	Period	Agriculture	Mining, Manufacturing, Construction	Utilities	Transportation, Communications	Housing	Other	Total
U.S.S.R.	1959–64	15.8	34.0	4.2	9.7	19.9	16.5	100
United States	1958–63	4.7	19.2	7.4	7.8	30.8	30.0	100
France	1958–63	6.2	29.6	9.2	14.3	25.0	15.6	100
West Germany	1958–63	6.0	30.4	4.9	14.3	22.3	22.1	100
Italy	1958–63	10.7	25.6	5.3	16.1	26.6	15.8	100
United Kingdom	1958–63	5.3	28.8	11.2	11.3	18.3	25.1	100

Source: New Directions in the Soviet Economy, p. 118.

Table 15–4   Comparison of Gross Domestic Products by Originating Sectors, in Per Cents of Total

Country	Year	Agri-culture	Industry	Con-struc-tion	Transpor-tation, Commu-nications	Com-merce	Services	Total
U.S.S.R.	1964	25.2	33.9	9.2	9.7	5.3	16.5	100
France	1963	8.7	39.9	7.7	5.0	13.4	25.2	100
West Germany	1963	5.2	45.0	7.6	6.2	13.4	22.0	100
Italy	1963	15.2	36.0	7.9	6.9	9.1	24.9	100
United Kingdom	1963	3.7	40.1	6.5	8.2	11.9	29.7	100
Japan	1963	13.5	34.5	7.1	7.2	16.2	21.5	100
United States	1963	4.1	32.3	5.0	6.0	16.2	36.0	100

Source: New Directions in the Soviet Economy, p. 110.

the U.S.S.R. than in any other leading country, except the United States, which is notorious for its high percentage of gross national product in the form of services. (Table 15–4) Among the countries shown, the U.S.S.R. still has the highest percentage of its gross national product in agriculture, even though this category dropped 10 percentage points between 1950 and 1964. The Soviet Union also has the highest percentage in transportation, which attests to the extremely long distances that goods must be hauled in that large country. Of the seven countries shown, the U.S.S.R. has the least per-centage of its total labor force in industry, and the greatest in agriculture and transportation. (Table 15–5)

Among different types of industries, capital stock is greatest in such things as electrical power production, coal, ferrous metals, machinery of various kinds, and food industries. Except for 1 or 2 years, during the entire Soviet period more capital has been poured into producers' industries than consumers' industries, and consequently the value of goods manufactured for the use of other producers has generally considerably exceeded that of goods manufactured for the use of indi-

Table 15–5   Comparison of Distributions of Employment by Economic Sector, in Per Cents of Total

Country	Year	Agri-culture	Industry	Con-struc-tion	Trans-porta-tion, Commu-nications	Com-merce	Services Civil-ian	Services Mili-tary	Total
U.S.S.R.	1964	36.5	24.4	5.0	7.5	5.4	18.1	3.1	100
France	1962	19.8	30.0	8.3	5.5	13.3	18.4	4.7	100
West Germany	1962	13.3	53.7		31.6			1.4	100
Italy	1962	27.4	46.2		24.7			2.0	100
United Kingdom	1962	4.0	40.4	6.8	6.8	16.1	24.1	1.8	100
Japan	1962	29.9	25.0	5.9	5.3	18.5	15.3	0.0	100
United States	1962	8.2	25.6	6.0	4.8	24.1	27.3	4.0	100

Source: New Directions in the Soviet Economy, p. 111.

vidual consumers. This has provided a rapidly expanding base for further production but has been rather hard on consumers while the industry is being built up. Personal sacrifice has been made by the past few generations in order to benefit future generations. It has been estimated that although total industrial output in the Soviet Union between 1913 and 1955 multiplied between five and six times, the output of machinery and equipment multiplied about sixteen times, that of intermediate industrial products about nine times, and consumer goods only three times. Although consumer-goods production has picked up somewhat since then, it is evident that the emphasis is still on producer goods.

Among individual industries, between 1960 and 1967 the industries that increased their production the most were the electric-power industry, petroleum products and natural gas, and civilian machinery, including electronics. The last category is very difficult to separate from military equipment, which, besides munitions, might include a great deal of the equipment manufactured for the use of the means of production. Also the category is inflated by the electronics industry which during recent years has been the single most rapidly expanding industry. In 1960 civilian machinery and electronics produced almost one quarter of all value added in manufacture. Together with soft goods and processed foods, total consumer production comprised about 44.8 per cent of the total value added by manufacture that year. Industrial production materials made up the other 55.2 per cent. (Table 15–6) Among the industrial materials, coal still made up the greatest amount of value added by manufacture, followed by forest products, ferrous metals, and construction materials.

Growth rates of individual industries have fluctuated up and down rather drastically annually. (Table 15–7) This is especially true of processed foods, which,

of course, depend upon agricultural production, which in turn depends upon the vicissitudes of the weather. If one evens out the year-to-year fluctuations, there appears to be a general trend downward in growth in most industries. This is especially true in the rapidly growing industries of electrical power, chemicals, construction materials, petroleum products and natural gas, and ferrous metals. In most of these basic industries the Soviet Union still considerably trails the United States in total production, so that one might assume that tapering growth rates have come about through no desire of the Soviets. (Table 15–8) In terms of per capita production the Soviet Union would compare even less favorably and, in fact, would show in most cases much lower production than the leading countries of western Europe and Japan.

As was true of the gross national product, industry has experienced a declining growth rate since about 1958. As can be seen in Table 15–9, total industrial output grew at an average annual rate of about 10.6 per cent between 1950 and 1958; between 1958 and 1961 it grew at an annual rate of about 8.6 per cent; and between 1961 and 1964 at an annual rate of 7.3 per cent. Since 1965 the growth rate seems to be recovering. At the present time the industrial output of the Soviet Union appears to be about two thirds that of the United States.

Among the obvious causes for the decline of industrial production in the early 1960s were: (1) the reorganization of industrial administration along regional lines, which was begun in 1957 and abandoned in the fall of 1965. The late 1950s and early 1960s was a period of experimentation to find if a regional organization rather than a ministerial one would provide industrial plants and local areas with enough incentives and freedom of choice to rejuvenate industrial growth, which had begun to stagnate, allegedly because of an overly structured central administration which was no longer able to cope with the scale of the industrial plant. Ministerial autarky gave way to regional autarky, however, the industrial supply system for key materials became very confused, and the ability of the center to force the introduction of new technology was seriously hampered. Therefore Khrushchev's experimentation with regional administration in the final analysis did not work, and in the meantime it induced uncertainty and chaos into the economic system. (2) The Soviet military and space program was significantly expanded after 1958, and this absorbed a great deal of investment capital as well as a significant number of the best scientists, engineers, and managers from the civilian sector. (3) During this very period the quality of the labor force was diluted by the coming of age of the "thin" generation born during the war and by the following remedies for this problem. During the period 1958–1964 civilian nonagricultural employment increased 14.8 million, whereas the working age population (15–64) increased by only 6.2 million. The difference was made up of 0.5 million decrease in the armed services, 2.5 million decrease in agricultural employment, and 5.6 million decrease in nonworkers. Undoubtedly the 8.1 million people gained from the agricultural sector and the nonemployed sector were of substandard quality. The reorganization of secondary and higher education during this period to allow for the incorporation of teenagers into the work force also tended to lower the quality of labor, since many of these teenagers proved to be very poor workers. (4) The high-priority industries of chemicals, oil and gas, and complex machinery were in a period of transition to the introduction of new technologies and the production of more sophisticated products. Many of these new industrial plants were strange to the Soviet scene, and therefore Soviet workers and technicians were unfamiliar with the processes that were demanded. This was particularly true in many of the chemical plants where crash programs of investments retarded other projects and did not allow time for the development and production of machinery to equip such plants.

In addition to the preceding four causes for industrial slowdown, which were somewhat unique to the 1958–1965 period, there were the old bugaboos of confused bureaucracy, improper incentives, and irrational prices whose effects became intensified as the economy grew more and more unwieldy. One of the main problems all along has been that rewards have been handed out for relative rather than absolute performance. Thus a smart plant manager aims for low plan targets and attempts to limit overfulfillment so that planners will not be afforded an excuse for raising future targets. There is an associated reluctance to innovate or to introduce new technology or equipment, for such actions involve risks and uncertainties in the short run and increased norms in the long run if the innovations prove to be successful. It is to any plant manager's advantage under such a system to understate his production potential so that he can be sure to fulfill or overfulfill his present goals in such a way that he will accrue the most personal benefit. Until 1965 the output targets were geared almost completely to quantity of product, very often in terms of weight as the unit of measure. Therefore firms naturally attempted to produce heavy goods and to disregard needs of consumers, adhering strictly to original planned targets. This resulted in the glutting of warehouses with unsellable materials which were often already obsolete or unwanted by consumers.

All of the foregoing chronic illnesses of Soviet industry can be summed up as follows: when an intricately functioning system is guided by an inflexible set of rather arbitrary rules, individuals "work the rules" to their advantage and lose

Table 15–6 U.S.S.R.: Indices of Civilian Industrial Production, 1960–1967

	1960 Value Added Weights (Per Cent)	1960	1961	1962	1963	1964	1965	1966	1967[a]
Industrial materials	55.2	100	106.2	114.1	121.6	130.3	140.1	149.5	159.8
Electrical power	4.7	100	112.1	126.5	140.7	156.4	172.2	185.3	200.3
Coal	11.9	100	100.0	102.4	105.4	109.7	114.5	116.7	118.8
Petroleum products and natural gas	3.7	100	112.3	127.4	142.3	154.2	169.2	184.8	201.7
Ferrous metals	8.1	100	109.2	118.5	126.6	136.8	146.6	160.0	170.4
Nonferrous metals	4.0	100	108.9	118.5	128.0	137.8	149.6	162.7	178.4
Forest products	10.2	100	101.3	105.2	111.2	116.4	118.4	120.9	128.6
Paper products	0.9	100	106.0	113.4	119.7	128.7	145.2	160.7	172.0
Construction materials	7.2	100	110.8	120.3	126.6	134.7	147.4	161.9	174.9
Chemicals	4.5	100	108.2	119.9	128.5	144.5	167.7	182.8	200.2

Civilian machinery, including electronics[b]	23.5	100	110.9	125.8	140.4	155.5	170.8	187.0	205.7
Nondurable consumer goods	21.3	100	105.4	110.4	112.0	117.2	126.1	132.7	141.0
Soft goods	12.4	100	103.3	107.5	109.8	114.4	117.1	125.8	134.3
Processed foods	8.9	100	108.4	114.6	115.0	121.0	138.5	142.0	150.3
Aggregate civilian industrial production	100.0	100	107.2	116.1	124.0	133.4	144.3	154.7	166.6

Source: Soviet Economic Performance: 1966–67, p. 22.

[a] Preliminary.

[b] Machinery uniquely military in character (for example, munitions) is excluded from the index shown in the table.

Table 15–7 U.S.S.R.: Annual Rates of Growth in Industrial Production, 1960–1967, in Per Cent

	1960	1961	1962	1963	1964	1965	1966	1967
Industrial materials	7.8	6.2	7.4	6.5	7.2	7.6	6.7	6.9
Electrical power	10.2	12.1	12.8	11.2	11.2	10.0	7.6	8.1
Coal	2.2	0.0	2.4	3.0	4.0	4.4	1.9	1.8
Petroleum products and natural gas	13.9	12.3	13.5	11.6	8.4	9.7	9.2	9.1
Ferrous metals	8.9	9.2	8.5	6.8	8.0	7.2	9.1	6.5
Nonferrous metals	9.1	8.9	8.8	8.0	7.7	8.6	8.8	9.6
Forest products	1.0	1.3	3.9	5.7	4.7	1.7	2.1	6.4
Paper products	4.5	6.0	7.0	5.6	7.5	12.8	10.7	7.0
Construction materials	15.3	10.8	8.6	5.3	6.4	9.4	9.9	8.0
Chemicals	19.8	8.2	10.8	7.2	12.4	16.1	9.0	9.5
Civilian machinery, including electronics	11.3	10.9	13.4	11.7	10.8	9.8	9.5	10.0
Nondurable consumer goods	4.3	5.4	4.8	1.4	4.7	7.6	5.2	6.3
Soft goods	5.8	3.3	4.1	2.2	4.2	2.3	7.4	6.7
Processed foods	2.2	8.3	5.7	0.4	5.3	14.5	2.6	5.8
Aggregate civilian industrial production	7.8	7.2	8.3	6.8	7.6	8.2	7.2	7.7

Source: Soviet Economic Performance: 1966–67, p. 23.

Table 15–8   Production of Individual Industrial Items, U.S.S.R. and Other Leading Producers, 1967

Industry	Unit	U.S.S.R.	U.S.A.	United Kingdom	France	West Germany	Italy	Japan
Electrical energy	Billion kilowatt hours							
Total Production		589	1,384	208	117	180	98	240
For Industry		402	615	100	76	114	57	144
Petroleum	Million tons	288	435	–	–	–	–	–
Natural Gas	Billion cubic meters	159	514	17	10	8	10	9
Coal	Million tons							
Total		556	511	175	51	209	2.5	48
Hard (other than lignite)		415	507	175	48	112	0.4	48
Iron ore	Million tons	168	92 [a]	14 [a]	56 [a]	7 [a]	1 [a]	2 [a]
Pig iron	Million tons	75	78	15	16	28	7	40
Steel	Million tons	102	118	24	20	37	16	62
Sulfuric acid and monohydrates	Million tons	10	27	3	3	4	4	6
Synthetic fibers	Thousand tons	511	1,700	395 [a]	234 [a]	455 [a]	321 [a]	954 [a]
Plastics	Thousand tons	1,112	6,192 [a]	–	–	–	–	–
Mineral fertilizers, in pure nutrients	Million tons	9.4	13.7	1.2	4.0	4.7	1.7	2.4
Cement	Million tons	85	67	18	25	32	26	44
Wood products	Million cubic meters	384	334 [a]	4 [a]	45 [a]	28 [a]	17 [a]	72 [a]
Tractors	Thousands	405	331 [a]	217 [a]	65 [a]	100 [a]	66 [a]	21 [a]
Passenger cars	Thousands	251	8,598 [a]	–	–	–	–	–
Trucks and buses	Thousands	477	1,731 [a]	–	–	–	–	–
Refrigerators	Thousands	2,697	4,685 [a]	–	–	–	–	–
Washing machines	Thousands	4,300	4,408 [a]	–	–	–	–	–
Television sets	Thousands	5,000	12,402 [a]	–	–	–	–	–
Cotton cloth	Million square meters	6,438	8,400	700	1,200	1,000	1,000	2,900
Wool cloth	Million running meters	427	230	200	125	100	150	250
Silk and synthetic cloth	Million running meters	1,080	3,600	549 [a]	291 [a]	470 [a]	300 [a]	3,163 [a]
Leather shoes	Million pairs	561	615	184 [a]	174 [a]	156 [a]	150 [a]	–
Meat	Million tons	11.4	22.3	2.7 [b]	4.4 [b]	3.6 [b]	1.5 [b]	–
Milk	Million tons	79	54	13 [a]	28 [a]	21 [a]	9 [a]	3 [a]

Sources: S.S.S.R. v Tsifrakh v 1967 godu, pp. 34–37, and *Soviet Economic Performance: 1966–67*, pp. 24–25.

[a] 1966.

[b] 1965.

Table 15–9   Average Annual Rates of Growth in Soviet Industry, 1950–1964, in Per Cent

	1950–1958	1958–1961	1961–1964
Output	10.6	8.6	7.3
Employment	4.2	4.6	3.1
Man-hours	3.1	−0.1	3.4
Man-hour productivity	7.2	8.7	3.8
Capital stock	11.3	11.5	11.1
Capital productivity	−0.7	−2.6	−3.4
Combined inputs (man-hours and capital)	5.3	3.0	5.5
Combined factor productivity	5.0	5.4	1.7

Source: Herbert S. Levine, "Industry," in Kassof, *Prospects for Soviet Society,* p. 298.

sight of the original reasons for the rules or the good of the total economy.

Although central planning undoubtedly had its place during the early period of industrialization in the Soviet Union, the Soviet economy now has obviously grown beyond the point at which any central planning agency can totally comprehend and adequately anticipate the needs of individual industries and enterprises. In fact one Soviet economist made the statement in the mid 1960s that if present trends in the planning force continued, by 1980 the entire Soviet labor force would be required for planning and administration! Such realizations have led the Soviet leaders to contemplate new administrative arrangements that could better cope with the geometrically expanding complexities of industrial management. For a while they envisioned a gigantic computer system into which could be fed the multitudes of minute details on every industry in the country and from which could be extracted proper planning relations which would ensure each industrial plant of its

correct mix of manufacturers for the year and assure it proper supplies at proper times. It was eventually realized, however, that the Soviet economy was far too large and too complex to be handled in such a manner, and in September 1965 the decision was made to embark on a modified form of what has become known as Libermanism.

Libermanism alludes to a proposed reform in the realm of plan implementation which aims to improve the incentive system and to enable industrial firms to accomplish better what central planners have been ordering them to do. Much of this scheme was proposed by an economics professor named Liberman from Kharkov University, although he was not the originator of much of the idea. He suggested that directives handed down to industrial plants be concerned with only three targets: volume and assortment of output, delivery schedules, and utilization levels of major input materials. To implement these directives, he suggested that remuneration to industrial workers and plant managers be computed in terms of profitability, measured as the difference between value of sales and cost divided by fixed and working capital. In addition he suggested that the reward schedule be extended for a significant period of time so that plant managers would not have the tendency to hold down production one year in fear of having their production targets raised the following year. Taking into account value of sales rather than value of output would lead a firm to be aware of the needs of the customers, and taking account of costs of production would encourage a firm to economize on uses of materials and labor. Relating profit to capital would induce a firm to economize on initial capital outlays and discourage it from ordering unneeded capital investments from the government. In essence, the plan was devised to eliminate "petty tutelage" from governmental agencies and create an incentive mechanism which would make the benefits to the individual coincide with the benefits to the national economy.

The September 1965 party directive tempered the Liberman proposals somewhat and drew some compromises between the profitability scheme and traditional procedures. Volume of sales became the primary criterion of success, although profitability was given some attention. At any rate, gross output indicators as major obligatory targets were discarded. The plant manager's freedom to handle labor questions (hiring and firing) and acquisition of supplies and to make midyear changes in the production mix was greatly expanded, although the centralized system of supply and assignment of wage funds was retained. A charge on state capital was established. And finally the regional form of economic administration was abandoned and the branch line ministerial type of control was reestablished.

These reforms undoubtedly will improve the industrial supply system, promote the development of new technology, and act to improve the balance between production and consumption. It is too early yet to evaluate fully the practical results of such measures, but the Soviets did report that in 1967 total industrial production grew by 10 per cent, which is a step back in the right direction from the low growth they had recorded the previous year of about 7 per cent.

Any real success of the modified Liberman system will depend heavily on the meaningfulness of the price system. Without a rational price structure that will take into account proper relations involving costs of production as well as central desires to manipulate the production mix, any attempt at decentralization of command and grass-roots decision making will largely come to naught. The Soviets still do not seem to grasp the basic tenets of price setting. For instance, although interest is now being charged on capital, this is to be deducted from profits, not added to costs. Thus such interest payments will not be reflected directly

in prices. In addition, once prices are set in the Soviet Union they tend to become very inflexible. So far the Soviets have not displayed any ability to be able to adjust prices quickly to changing market conditions, and this undoubtedly will continue to be a serious road block to the achievement of desired manipulations and adjustments of production.

Since the September 1965 directive, there seems to have been a shift toward a greater emphasis on personal consumption as one of the basic goals of economic life of the country. A recent Soviet study revealed that real per capita consumption in the Soviet Union was substantially lower than that in East Germany or Czechoslovakia and somewhat lower than in Hungary and Poland, and of course much lower than that in the West. Now that the total economy has grown to the point where it can afford some luxuries, undoubtedly there will be a rapidly rising demand for all sorts of consumer goods.

Industrial Development and Location

At the time of the Bolshevik Revolution in 1917, Russia was not a totally undeveloped country. Industrialization had begun in Russia as early as the reign of Peter the Great during the first quarter of the eighteenth century when he used his governmental influence to employ domestic and foreign capital to establish certain basic industries in European Russia and the Urals. Half a century later Catherine the Great facilitated the practice of the Russian nobility to move excess labor off their large land holdings and to employ them in newly established factories and mines of the Urals and elsewhere. During the latter part of the eighteenth century Russia became the world's largest producer of pig iron and in fact exported it to England. Although this initial spurt in industrialization was allowed to lapse for about a century while western Europe was undergoing a rapid industrial revolution, the thread was picked up again around 1880 when an industrialization drive got underway that by 1890 had turned into a real industrial revolution under the able direction of Minister of Finance Witte. The most significant regional development that took place at this time was eastern Ukraine where the Donets Coal Basin was opened up and the iron and steel industry was established. Although these industrial efforts suffered temporary setbacks by incipient revolutions during the first decade of the twentieth century, particularly the uprising of 1905, which prompted repressive measures from the Tsar that were not conducive to optimum economic development, industrialization did continue at a growth rate of more than 5 per cent per year until the beginning of World War I. This is a faster growth rate than the overall annual average from the Revolution onward to about 1960. This comparison has led some observers to conclude that Russia would be further ahead now had the Soviet system never been initiated; they say that the growth rate that has been achieved has not been because of the Soviet system but in spite of it. However, one obviously cannot average industrial growth throughout the entire Soviet period because it was so broken up by strife — two world wars, the Revolution, and at least two periods of civil war. Industrial output dropped by at least 90 per cent between 1913 and 1920.

After much of the political and military upheaval had ended in 1920 Lenin initiated the new economic policy (NEP) to rehabilitate the economy of the country. From about 1921 through 1928 much of the industrial management was turned back to many of the original owners to operate on a semicapitalistic basis in order to effect a rapid improvement in economic conditions. Although the central government retained control of the "upper heights" in the form of banks and all financial arrangements, the economy was much more free to operate on its own than

it had been during the previous period from 1917 through 1920 under so-called War Communism when people and goods were moved about by central command and money exchange was a rather insignificant part of the economic process. Under the private initiative allowed during the 1920s, the economy largely was reestablished to the level that it had been in 1913 by the time that the 5-year plans were initiated in 1928. Only after this period of reconstruction did Stalin institute his famous 5-year plans which were conceived to reestablish complete central control and to effect a rapid industrialization at the expense of agriculture and consumer welfare.

Thus the Soviets did not start from scratch in their industrialization drive; they inherited a considerable industrial plant from the Tsarist Empire. And although much of the physical stock was destroyed or damaged in the subsequent wars and civil strife, they nevertheless had a certain fund of knowhow in the country as a residual of an industrial society that had existed, rudimentary as it might have seemed in comparison to the countries of western Europe or the United States. The initial period of industrialization during the 1930s was also enhanced in the Soviet Union by the fact that much of the Western world was plunged in an economic depression and was eager to sell whatever it could to any country that would buy it. Thus the Soviet Union was able to import significant quantities of prototype equipment and skilled technical knowhow at relatively low costs. Also the fact that the Western world was so far ahead of them in industrial technology allowed the Soviets to quickly borrow and adapt whatever advanced technologies were necessary in their belated buildup. Therefore although the Soviet Union never quite caught up in industrial technology with the countries of the West it was able to keep only one jump behind them through very little effort of its own. The fact that it could practically overnight beg, borrow, or steal and adapt to its own needs the advanced technology of the West, which had been developed painfully and expensively over long periods of time through research and practical experience, both saved the Soviet Union a tremendous amount of capital outlay for its own research and development needs and allowed it to advance technologically much more quickly than any other country had been able to do previously.

During this period of the 1930s, as well as during the first decade after World War II, the Soviet industrial drive was of such an unsophisticated nature that it was neither hampered by the need for domestic development of new technology at the input end of the cycle nor by delicate balances of supply and demand at the output end of the cycle. The Soviets merely had to plug in existent technologies in their simplest forms and produce and produce and produce in sectors that would show the fastest short-run gains, without much attention paid to balances between different sectors or to the danger of glutting the market, because everything was needed in as big quantities as possible.

From 1928 to 1937 all civilian industrial production in the Soviet Union increased at an annual average rate of about 11 per cent. During this time production goods grew at an average annual rate of about 15 per cent, whereas consumer goods grew at only about 5.5 per cent. Machinery alone grew at a phenomenal rate of more than 26 per cent. However, this auspicious beginning of Soviet industry was interrupted by the necessity to prepare for World War II, and the war itself devastated much of the European part of the country which contained more than 60 per cent of the total industrial plant. Therefore the Soviets essentially had to start anew after the war to reconstruct the industries of the old centers around Moscow, Leningrad, and eastern Ukraine, as well as other parts of the European territory, utilizing the newly built up industries of the Urals and Siberia to carry on during the interim period.

Thus the period from about 1937, when the young Soviet Union began to gird its defenses for the Hitlerite onslaught, until around 1948, when the Soviet Union had essentially regained its prewar industrial level, cannot be considered as a normal growth period during which any net gain in industrial production was achieved. From 1948 through the first half of the 1950s Soviet industrialization proceeded at a high pace spurred onward by extreme needs for all sorts of industrial goods and guided by the simple principle of producing to the utmost. During the late 1950s industrial expansion began to slow down as needs became less acute and the economy became much more complex, so that guidelines more subtle and more varied than bulk production had to be brought into play to effect correct mixes of industrial goods, proper work incentives, and the introduction of new technologies in the rapidly changing structure of the total industrial effort.

Industrial Location At the time of the Revolution much of the industrial production of Russia was concentrated in the European part of the country. The Central Industrial Region accounted for more than 80 per cent of the textile industry, and Ukraine and adjacent parts of the Donets Basin in the Russian Republic accounted for over 90 per cent of the coal production, almost all of the iron-ore production, and nearly 75 per cent of the pig-iron production. Almost all the rest of the ferrous metallurgy was located no farther east than the Ural Mountains. The machine-building industries were almost entirely located in the European part of the country.

The communist ideology adopted by the Soviets did not approve of such an unequal distribution of development. Lenin's government immediately proclaimed a doctrine which stated that the economy should develop according to the following precepts: (1) there should be a rapid industrialization, (2) economic activity should be distributed as evenly as possible throughout the country, (3) the economy should stimulate the development of backward nationalities and areas, (4) production should take place close to raw materials and markets in order to minimize transport, and (5) specialized production should be promoted in regions that possess uniquely favorable conditions for such development in terms of either natural resources, transport facilities, skilled labor, or historic precedence. In practice it has been found that some of these objectives are largely mutually exclusive. Shortage of capital and emphasis on speed of industrialization have led to the construction of giant industrial enterprises in old centers of production at the expense of industrial dispersal. Also it became apparent that in order to establish new industrial plants in the eastern part of the country, the old industries in the west would first have to be strengthened because they were going to have to supply much of the materials to build up the east. But the biggest hindrance to industrial dispersal into empty areas eventually proved to be the reluctance of the people themselves to move into these outlying regions where the necessities of life were barely adequate and cultural amenities by and large did not exist. As far as the use of industrial development to stimulate the cultural advancement of backward nationalities was concerned, it soon became evident that most of the non-Slavic groups of peoples in the country were largely unadaptable to factory life, and therefore what new industries were established in such areas as Central Asia generally had to be manned almost 100 per cent by Russians, Ukrainians, and Belorussians. The establishment of industries in new regions, then, was going to entail movements of great numbers of laborers and the establishment in these new regions of homes, shops, schools, transportation facilities, and all other material means of life to which the Slavic peoples from European U.S.S.R. were accustomed. The Soviets soon learned the principle that it is much more expensive to move about people and supply them with their material needs than it is to move bulk quantities of raw materials to industries in old established centers. Consequently little had been accomplished in regard to the heralded "eastward movement" before the onset of World War II.

Within three months after the German attack in June 1941, however, more than 1360 major industrial enterprises, mainly of military significance, were moved from European Russia and Ukraine into the eastern regions of the country. Entire plants and equipment were loaded onto trains of flat cars, and then the factory personnel would climb on top and the whole enterprise would be relocated. About 455 such enterprises were relocated in the Urals, 210 in western Siberia, and 250 in Middle Asia and Kazakhstan. Before the Germans were finally repulsed, they had occupied and largely devastated an area that before the war had housed 40 per cent of the total population of the Soviet Union and had produced 62 per cent of the coal, 68 per cent of the pig iron, 58 per cent of the steel, and 60 per cent of the aluminum. In addition the German advance had threatened the primary oil-producing area of the Caucasus. During this time the eastern regions experienced a rapid growth, and the Urals eventually produced 40 per cent of all the war industrial materials. Between 1940 and 1943 the output of industrial production in western Siberia increased 3.4 times. In 1945 the Urals and the Kuznetsk Basin produced 75 per cent of the country's pig iron, steel, and rolled-steel products. These hastily relocated industries remained in the eastern regions after the war, and new industries were added to them. World War II thus brought about the industrial relocation that Soviet policy before the war had been unable to do. This new pattern of industrial location has been maintained down to the present, although the outstandingly large industrial relative importance of the eastern regions during World War II has settled back down to proportions more in keeping with the population distribution. With the rehabilitation of the heavy industries of Ukraine the share of the eastern regions in the iron and steel industry by 1960 had decreased back down to around 43 per cent of the country's total. However, this was still considerably higher than it had been in 1940 before the war when it had accounted for only about 30 per cent of the country's iron and steel products. Thus it might be said that the war effected about a 13 per cent relative increase in the eastern regions in the heavy metallurgical industries.

Although industrial plants are still being expanded and added to in the eastern regions, relatively these areas seem to be on the decline since 1960. In 1966 the Urals and areas to the east produced 37.7 per cent of the pig iron, 40.3 per cent of the steel, and 40 per cent of the rolled steel of the country. In each category this was more than a 3 per cent relative decrease from 1960. Thus it is obvious that in spite of the expansion of the Magnitogorsk, Novokuznetsk, and Karaganda steel mills in the east, there was an even more rapid expansion in the west in such places as Krivoy Rog, Lipetsk, and the various industrial centers of the Donets Basin. This is true in other industries as well. As has been stated before, there is an unwritten policy now being applied by the Soviet government to locate much of the new industry in the small and medium-sized cities of the west where excess labor exists. The eighth 5-year plan (1966–1970) slated 70 per cent of new industrial development capital to go to small and medium-sized towns in the European part of the country. Although this shift in capital investment has not made its effects

felt yet, after 1970 there should be an acceleration in the improvement of the relative industrial position of the west as compared to the east.

In spite of the renewed emphasis on industries in old established areas, there are new industrial areas emerging, primarily in response to the development of huge resources of energy. (Fig. 15–1) The tremendous expansion of the petroleum industry and associated petro-chemicals in the Volga-Urals area since World War II has suddenly jumped this area into the fastest growing industrial region in the country. This has been aided by the completion in the 1950s and 1960s of the large hydroelectric plants on the Volga, and it has also been aided by its intermediate location in relation to the Urals, the Central Industrial Region, and eastern Ukraine. With so much traffic crisscrossing the area between these three primary industrial centers, it was only a matter of time before the Middle Volga Region would develop anyway, but the discovery of large quantities of oil and the development of hydroelectricity has greatly speeded up the process and has made this region a freight originating area as well as a transit area. The concurrent Soviet emphasis on the build-up of the chemical industries and the shifting of these industries to oil and gas products as the resource base has further speeded development here.

In eastern Siberia, between the headwaters of the Yenisey and Lake Baykal, lies another emerging region of urbanization and industrialization based primarily on large energy resources. In this case water power is the most obvious element, but important coal fields are producing here also. The dams built and being built on the Angara and Upper Yenisey Rivers have suddenly catapulted this area into an energy-surplus region which has induced the establishment of several high-energy-consuming industries such as aluminum and wood processing.

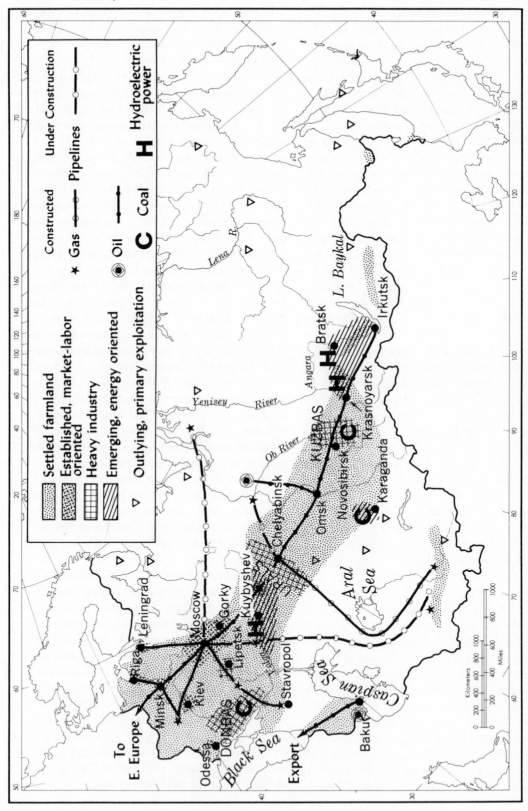

Figure 15–1 Distribution of industry in the U.S.S.R. Adapted from Hooson, David, "Industrial Growth: Where Next," Survey, October 1965, p. 113. Note that except for some scattered mining activity, industrial settlement merely forms intensified nodes within agricultural settlement and therefore does not alter the overall pattern of population distribution, which was determined initially by agricultural activity.

The further discovery of huge new deposits of oil and gas has initiated what will eventually become large mining developments in such regions as the swamps of western Siberia and the deserts of Middle Asia, but these regions cannot be expected ever to become populated and industrialized.

While regional shifts of major proportions in the production of fuels and electricity have induced the emergence of some new industrial areas, at the same time the shift in emphasis away from coal to these new energy sources has freed the total economy from the heavy dependence on resource-oriented industries and has therefore enhanced the possibilities of the further expansion of market-oriented industries in old heavily populated centers. Oil and gas pipelines and high-voltage electrical transmission lines are making it possible for these energy sources to be provided rather inexpensively anywhere in the country, and logically the most heavily populated areas are attracting the nets of pipes and wires which supply the new technology being established in chemical, metallurgical, and machine industries. More and more the total industry of the country is becoming market-oriented rather than resource-oriented, largely as a result of these fluid energy sources. The position of Moscow as the primary industrial center is being strengthened even more as it becomes the hub of a huge radiating network of pipelines bringing in gas from Central Asia, the North Caucasus, Ukraine, and western Siberia and oil from the Volga-Urals.

Obviously the present phase of industrial growth seems to be guided by governmental conservatism which strives to maximize short-run returns through the expansion of established reliable centers of production. In the long run, there may be a return to an effort to build up industries and resources in the east if the total economy becomes so affluent that government policies become optimistic and expansive and promote the investment of large amounts of capital in outlying areas without the assurance of profitable returns. But the east probably never again will be the beneficiary of the fear of military invasion that produced the brisk build-up before and during World War II. On the one hand a continuing pioneering spirit and the discovery of huge new resources in outlying areas will entice some development into these regions, but the emerging era of oil, gas, and electricity, along with growing governmental realization of people as skilled workers and consumers, throw the advantages to the European core of the country. Perhaps the Middle Volga region best blends elements of the conservative and the adventurous which eventually might show it to be the best located region within the entire national context. But one cannot foresee all the changes in political and technological advances that could eventually greatly alter the present regional distribution. The Soviet Union is so large in area that the Soviets are afforded much room for maneuvering before things become too crowded and the pattern forever set.

The Mineral Fuels

The mineral fuels are still the primary bases for industry. The Soviet Union, having the second largest industrial output in the world, naturally has great demands for fuel. The Soviet Union now uses more coal than the United States does, about half as much oil, and nearly one third as much natural gas. Fortunately for the Soviets the U.S.S.R. contains large reserves of all three of these items. The Soviets now claim to have more than half the total geological reserves of coal on earth, about one third of the geological reserves of natural gas, and more oil reserves than any other country. Since large areas of the Soviet Union are still inadequately explored, ultimate reserves are hard to esti-

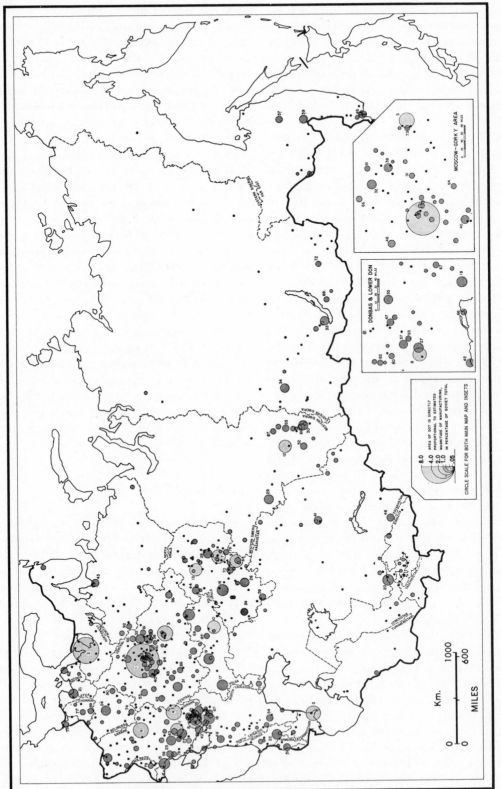

Figure 15–2   See following page for descriptive legend.

mate, but it has been predicted on the basis of suitable sedimentary structures that the U.S.S.R. should eventually produce about 68 per cent more oil than the United States and 40 per cent more natural gas. The discovery of natural gas in the Soviet Union has only just begun; it was not until 1955 that the Soviets started a serious drive for the increased production and use of natural gas.

Although the total reserves of all three mineral fuels seem to be quite adequate for any foreseeable needs in the Soviet Union, the regional distributions of these reserves are far from ideal. Large reserves lie in remote, sparsely populated, inclement areas. This has prompted the development of lesser reserves when they can be found nearer to population and industrial concentrations and long hauls of bulky commodities when resources cannot be found in juxtaposition with markets. Thus there are often great discrepancies between distributions of reserves and production and between distributions of production and consumption. (Tables 15–10 and 15–11) Although the Asiatic part of the country has been credited with at least 91 per cent of all power resources, during the decade 1955–1965 fuel production rose 150 per cent in the European part of the country and only 80 per cent in the

Table 15–10 Distribution of Soviet Natural Power Reserves, in Per Cents of Total

	European U.S.S.R. and Urals	Asiatic U.S.S.R.
All power resources	8.9	91.1
Coal	6.6	93.4
Natural gas	42.9	57.1 [a]
Hydroelectric power	19.8	80.2

Source: Vvedensky, "The Soviet Fuel and Power Industry," p. 19.

[a] Asiatic U.S.S.R. now has a considerably greater share of total gas resources, since the discovery of huge reserves in western Siberia and Middle Asia.

Asiatic part. Among producing and consuming regions, the Volga is the greatest exporter of fuel and the Central Industrial Region the greatest importer.

As the Soviet Union has industrialized and fuel and power consumption has expanded rapidly, an ever-growing portion of total fuel and power production has been utilized by industry, construction, transportation, and agriculture at the expense of domestic and municipal uses. (Table 15–12) Although most urban dwell-

Figure 15–2 Industrial outputs of cities in the U.S.S.R. A list of the 93 foremost industrial cities with their percentages of total U.S.S.R. production follows. Numbers correspond to those on map. 1. Moscow, 8.20; 2. Leningrad, 4.90; 3. Gorky, 1.65; 4. Kharkov, 1.65; 5. Baku, 1.60; 6. Kiev, 1.60; 7. Sverdlovsk, 1.45; 8. Donetsk, 1.30; 9. Chelyabinsk, 1.25; 10. Kuybyshev, 1.25; 11. Dnepropetrovsk, 1.10; 12. Novosibirsk, 1.10; 13. Perm, 1.10; 14. Kazan, 0.95; 15. Odessa, 0.95; 16. Ufa, 0.95; 17. Volgograd, 0.90; 18. Rostov, 0.85; 19. Saratov, 0.80; 20. Tashkent, 0.80; 21. Riga, 0.75; 22. Tbilisi, 0.75; 23. Zaporozhye, 0.75; 24. Minsk, 0.70; 25. Krivoy Rog, 0.65; 26. Magnitogorsk, 0.65; 27. Makeyevka, 0.65; 28. Nizhniy Tagil, 0.65; 29. Omsk, 0.65; 30. Novokuznetsk, 0.65; 31. Voronezh, 0.65; 32. Yaroslavl, 0.65; 33. Irkutsk, 0.60; 34. Krasnoyarsk, 0.60; 35. Lugansk, 0.60; 36. Lvov, 0.60; 37. Gorlovka, 0.55; 38. Ivanovo, 0.55; 39. Khabarovsk, 0.55; 40. Tula, 0.55; 41. Karaganda, 0.50; 42. Zhdanov, 0.50; 43. Archangel, 0.45; 44. Izhevsk, 0.45; 45. Vladivostok, 0.45; 46. Alma-Ata, 0.40; 47. Kadiyevka, 0.40; 48. Kalinin, 0.40; 49. Krasnodar, 0.40; 50. Orenburg, 0.40; 51. Yerevan, 0.40; 52. Barnaul, 0.35; 53. Bryansk, 0.35; 54. Grozny, 0.35; 55. Kemerovo, 0.35; 56. Kirov, 0.35; 57. Komsomolsk, 0.35; 58. Nilolayev, 0.35; 59. Orsk, 0.35; 60. Penza, 0.35; 61. Prokopyevsk, 0.35; 62. Tallin, 0.35; 63. Dneprodzerzhinsk, 0.30; 64. Kopeysk, 0.30; 65. Kursk, 0.30; 66. Rybinsk, 0.30; 67. Shakhty, 0.30; 68. Taganrog, 0.30; 69. Ulyanovsk, 0.30; 70. Zlatoust, 0.30; 71. Astrakhan, 0.25; 72. Chita, 0.25; 73. Dzerzhinsk, 0.25; 74. Gomel, 0.25; 75. Kaliningrad, 0.25; 76. Kamensk-Uralskiy, 0.25; 77. Kaunas, 0.25; 78. Kherson, 0.25; 79. Kishinev, 0.25; 80. Konstantinovka, 0.25; 81. Kostroma, 0.25; 82. Kramatorsk, 0.25; 83. Lipetsk, 0.25; 84. Ryazan, 0.25; 85. Syzran, 0.25; 86. Tambov, 0.25; 87. Tomsk, 0.25; 88. Ulan-Ude, 0.25; 89. Vilnyus, 0.25; 90. Vitebsk, 0.25; 91. Vladimir, 0.25; 92. Vologda, 0.25; 93. Yenakievo, 0.25. From Lonsdale, Richard E. and Thompson, John H., "A Map of the U.S.S.R.'s Manufacturing Economic Geography, January 1960, facing p. 36.

ings and rural villages are now provided with electricity and some urban dwellings are being supplied with natural gas, by far the greater share of all fuels and power is utilized to expand the means of production. It will be a long time before all homes in the country are adequately supplied with electricity and all forms of fuel.

The attempt to provide new housing with modern utilities and sewer services has been one of the factors dictating the type of new housing construction. The Soviets are aiming at central-supply systems for heat and hot water and country-wide networks for electricity, petroleum, and gas. They claim that already more than one third of all steam heat and hot water supplied to dwellings is generated

Table 15–11 Regional Distributions of Primary Fuel Production and Consumption, 1960, in Millions of Tons of Conventional Fuel

Region	Production	Consumption	Surplus (+) or Deficit(−)
Northwest and European North	24.0	43.7	−19.7
Center	32.4	102.7	−70.3
Volga	117.6	39.1	+78.5
North Caucasus	62.9	30.1	+32.8
Urals	83.7	104.6	−20.9
Western Siberia	76.7	41.1	+35.6
Eastern Siberia	26.5	30.8	−4.3
Far East	16.4	18.6	−2.2
Ukraine	168.2	143.1	+25.1
West	5.5	12.2	−6.7
Transcaucasia	34.4	18.0	+16.4
Middle Asia	15.6	15.4	+0.2
Kazakhstan	25.1	29.5	−4.4
Belorussia	3.8	10.3	−6.5
Moldavia	0.0	2.6	−2.6
Total	692.8	641.8	+51.0

Source: Campbell, *The Economics of Soviet Oil and Gas,* p. 13.

Table 15–12 Changing Energy Consumption in the Soviet Economy, by Sector, in Per Cents of Total

	1930	1950	1960
Industry and construction	28.2	49.2	53.0
Transportation	1.8	5.7	12.0
Housing and municipal services	69.6	43.2	32.0
City	13.3	19.5	18.0
Rural	56.3	23.7	14.0
Agricultural production	0.4	1.9	3.0

Source: Campbell, *The Economics of Soviet Oil and Gas,* p. 7.

by large unified systems. Under such arrangements, they argue, it would be too expensive to build single-dwelling houses. If the rural areas want modern conveniences, central heating, and sewer services, they must go to apartment living.

So far coal is still the primary fuel in the Soviet Union, but since 1955 its expansion rate has been outdistanced by oil and gas about ten to one. (Table 15–13) Due to an underestimation of oil and gas reserves, the official policy from 1932 to 1953 was to limit the production of oil and gas and to concentrate on coal production. In 1950 the share of coal in total fuel production had risen to 73 per cent and that of oil and gas had dropped to less than 20 per cent. But in 1957 a new 15-year plan for fuels was launched which completely reversed the policy. By 1967 coal accounted for only about 42 per cent of total mineral fuel production and oil and gas rose to about 57.5 per cent. By 1970 the thermal effect of oil alone is to exceed that of coal, and gas is to be more than half as important as coal. Such a fuel ratio is much closer to that of the United States, a fuel ratio that one might expect to be geared to a highly industrialized economy. Since huge new gas reserves have been discovered, even since the goals in Table 15–13 were formulated, gas production

Table 15–13   Soviet Fuel and Energy Production, 1928–1980, in Million Tons of Conventional Fuel

	1928	1940	1945	1955	1965	1966	1967	Plan 1970	Plan 1980
Total energy	54.8	241	188	492	1,016	1,100		1,371	2,950
Coal	29.8	141	115	311	420	426	432	487	850
Oil	16.6	44.5	27.8	101	347	379	411	500	1,000
Gas	0.4	4.4	4.2	11.4	151	170	186	271	850
Peat	2.1	13.6	9.2	20.8	22.0	26.8	24.2	34.3	[b]
Shale		0.6	0.4	3.3	7.5	7.5	7.6	9.8	50 [b]
Firewood [a]	5.7	34.1	28.4	32.4	32.0	31.9	31.9	32.0	[b]
Hydropower	0.2	3.3	3.0	12.3	35.5	59.4		36.0 [c]	200 [d]

Sources: Campbell, *The Economics of Soviet Oil and Gas,* pp. 4–5, *Strana Sovetov za 50 let,* pp. 65 and 68, and *SSSR v tsifrakh v 1967 godu,* p. 55.

[a] Excludes wood gathered by individuals, which in 1928 might have amounted to five times that reported by the lumbering industry. In later years the ratio probably decreased to about 2:1.

[b] Firewood and peat are included with shale.

[c] Plan appears obsolete.

[d] Includes atomic energy.

might become even more significant than the table indicates.

The change in policy on fuel balance has been brought about by economic considerations which only recently have begun to play a major role in Soviet planning. It has been found that for the U.S.S.R. as a whole the cost of production of oil is one fourth that of coal in equivalent heat units. Oil also presents a two-fold advantage in transport considerations: (1) pipelines have relieved the heavily overburdened railroads, and (2) the conversion of railroad locomotives to Diesel and electric traction has greatly reduced the relative needs for long coal hauls and has increased the efficiency and power of the locomotives. Now electric and Diesel locomotives handle more than 85 per cent of all rail traffic, as compared with 26 per cent in 1958. Oil and gas are playing much greater roles in the fuel consumption of thermal-electric stations, in steel furnaces, and in cement kilns. Also the development of oil and gas industries is providing a broad new base for the rapid development of all aspects of

the chemical industry. And lastly, adequate development of the oil and gas industries will make the Soviet Union more defensively viable.

The Coal Industry   The Soviet Union has enough coal reserves to last about 20,000 years at the present rate of consumption. Although three fourths of these reserves lie in eastern Siberia and the Far East, deposits are scattered widely throughout the Soviet Union. (Fig. 15–3 and Tables 15–14 and 15–15) Since transportation is a major part of the cost to consumers, development has taken place as near as possible to markets, and the most productive fields are not necessarily those that are richest in deposits. (Fig. 15–4 and Table 15–16) The most productive fields are the Donets, the Kuznetsk, the Urals, the Moscow, the eastern Siberian fields, and Karaganda. In 1967 the Donets Basin still produced almost 35 per cent of the country's coal and more than half of the country's coking coal. Although by percentage this is a reduction from pre- Soviet

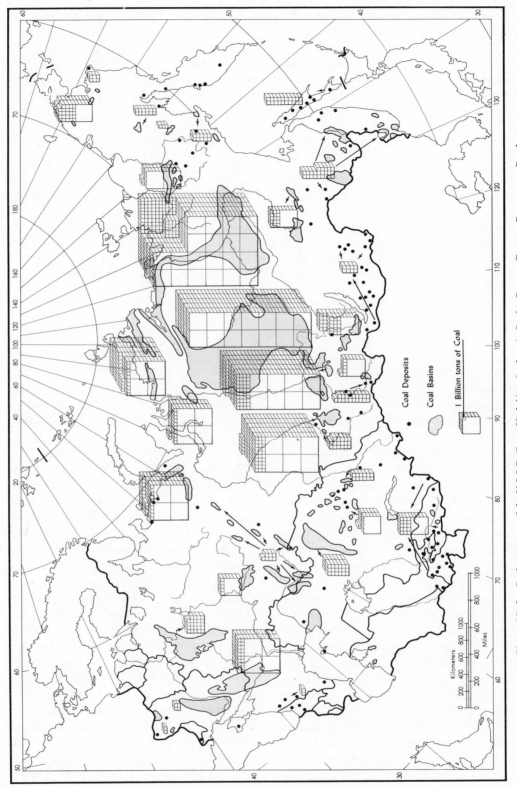

Figure 15–3 Coal resources of the U.S.S.R. From Hodgkins, Jordan A., Soviet Power: Energy Resources, Production and Potential, 1961. By permission of Prentice-Hall, Inc.

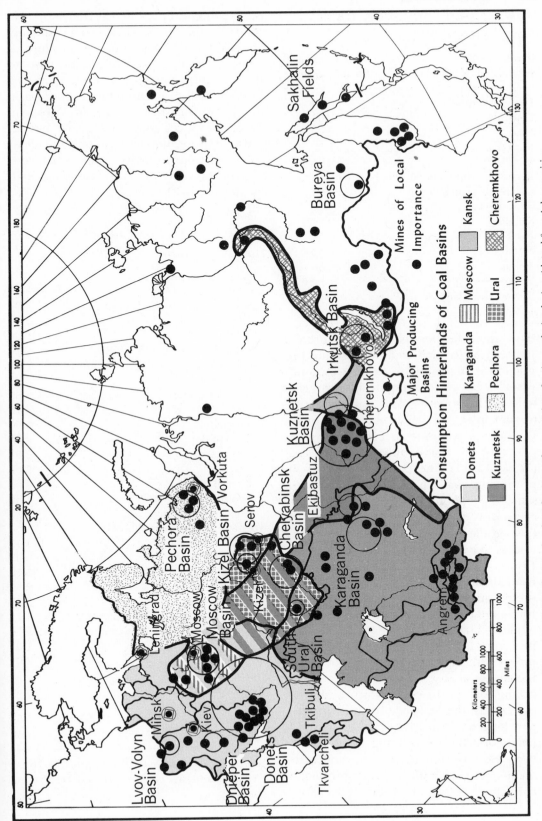

Figure 15–4 Distribution of coal production and consumption of major producing basins. Adapted from Atlas razvitiya khozyaystva i kultury SSSR, p. 26.

Table 15–14   Mineable Reserves of Coal by Regions

Traditionally Established Regions	Per Cent of Mineable Reserves
European Russia	6.52
Caucasia	0.01
Urals	0.09
Kazakhstan	1.58
Middle Asia	0.49
Arctic and Subarctic Siberia	60.52
South Siberian Belt	27.61
Transbaykal	0.09
Sakhalin	0.21
Far East	0.50
North East	2.38
Totals	100.00

Source: Hodgkins, *Soviet Power,* p. 28.

days when the Donets Basin produced almost all of Russia's coal, its absolute production is higher than it ever was, and it is still by far the most important producing field in the country. And apparently it is to remain so; the 1980 plan calls for the Donbass to continue to produce over 50 per cent of the country's coking coal. (Table 15–17) The order of rank of the producing coal basins has remained the same throughout the Soviet period and apparently is to remain the same in the foreseeable future. Thus the heavy producers have been and will remain the Donets, Kuznetsk, Urals, Moscow, Cheremkhovo, and Karaganda Basins. Of these, only the Donets, Kuznetsk, and Karaganda fields produce coal of coking quality. The Karaganda coals are hampered by high ash content and must be mixed with higher grade coals for heavy metallurgical use. Thus much of the coking coal for the country is produced by two basins, the Donets and the Kuznetsk, and long hauls are required to serve the needs of many consuming areas. Of the two, Kuznetsk has the greater and better quality reserves and the lower production costs, but because of its remote location it

is not as highly developed as Donets. (Table 15–18) Although Kuznetsk coal costs only about 60 per cent as much to produce as Donets coal does, transportation costs to the European part of the country raise its price by 250 per cent. The Pechora Basin in the northeastern corner of European Russia produces good coking coal, but because of its location it serves only the needs of the European North and Northwest. Production costs there are almost as high as they are in Donets.

Table 15–15   Proven Coal Reserves by Basins, in Billions of Metric Tons

Basins and Deposits	
European part of the U.S.S.R.	74.91
Donets Basin	57.16
Ukraine S.S.R.	49.00
Rostov Oblast, R.S.F.S.R.	8.16
Lvov-Volyn coal-bearing region	1.65
Dnieper Basin	3.05
Moscow Basin	8.89
Pechora Basin	4.10
Caucasus	0.56
Tkibuli deposits	0.29
Tkvarcheli deposits	0.07
Urals	5.00
Kizel Basin	0.61
South Urals Basin	1.56
Chelyabinsk Basin	1.37
Western and Eastern Siberia (southern part) [a]	114.49
Kuznetsk Basin	0.07
Kansk-Achinsk Basin	35.00
Minusinsk Basin	2.31
Irkutsk Basin	5.17
Eastern Siberia (northern part) [a]	4.11
Transbaykal, Far East, Sakhalin	8.74
Bureya Basin	1.63
Sakhalin deposits	2.01
Kazakhstan	28.99
Karaganda Basin	10.30
Ekibastuz deposit	9.11
Middle Asia	3.55
Angren deposits	1.52

Source: Hodgkins, *Soviet Power,* pp. 158–162.

[a] Siberia contains large unproven reserves of coal.

Table 15–16   Coal Production by Regions, 1950–1968, in Millions of Tons

	1950	1966	1967	1968	Plan 1980
U.S.S.R.		586(143)	595(148)	594(155)	1200(290)
R.S.F.S.R.	160	329(51)	334(55)	330(58.5)	
European		92			
Urals		58			
Siberia and					
Far East		179			
Kuznetsk Basin			104		
Ukraine S.S.R.	78	196(76)	199(77)	200(78.3)	
Donets Basin					
(including					
Rostov Oblast)			205		
Kazakh S.S.R.	17	48(13)	51(14)	53(15.9)	
Karaganda Basin			33		
Uzbek S.S.R.	1.5	4.4			
Kirgiz S.S.R.	1.8	3.9			
Tadzhik S.S.R.	0.5	0.9			
Georgian S.S.R.	1.7	2.6	2.4(1.8)	2.3	

Sources: Soviet Geography: Review and Translation, March 1968, pp. 223–224 and April 1969, p. 210, *Strana Sovetov za 50 let,* pp. 307–335; and Rodgers, "Coking Coal Supply," p. 114.

Note: Figures in parentheses are for coking coal.

The big coal consuming regions are eastern Ukraine, the Urals, and the Central Industrial Region. Of these only Ukraine produces all its own coal needs. Although the Urals fields, particularly the Kizel field, supply more than half the coal needs of the Urals, coking coal must be imported from Kuznetsk and Karaganda. The Central Industrial Region derives half its coal locally from the Moscow Basin, but all this coal is low grade and suitable only for electrical generation and heating. Higher grade coals must be brought in from Donets, Kuznetsk, Kizel, and Karaganda. The Donets Basin supplies the bulk of the imported coal for the Central Industrial Region.

All this movement of coal puts a tremendous burden on the railroads, which transport more than 90 per cent of the coal moved. Coal and coke constitute about 20 per cent of all railroad freight traffic.

Fourteen million tons of coal mined east of the Urals are transported annually to the European part of the country. It is hoped that this can be eliminated by the greater production of hydroelectricity in European Russia, by the development of the gas industry which in the future is to supply much of the fuel needs of the

Table 15–17   Coking Coal Production by Field, 1913–1980, in Per Cents of Total

	1913	1940	1958	1961	Plan 1965	Plan 1980
Donets	100	74.7	57.7	58.4	53.7	50.1
Kuznetsk		19.9	27.2	26.9	26.3	31.1
Karaganda		3.1	7.0	7.2	12.6	11.3
Pechora			2.8	3.5	4.4	4.9
Kizel		2.3	2.4	2.0	1.3	
Georgia			2.5	1.9	1.7	

Source: Rodgers, "Coking Coal Supply," pp. 116 and 146.

Table 15–18 Proved Coking Coal Reserves of the U.S.S.R. by Fields, 1958, in Per Cents of Total

Fields currently mined	78.9
Donets	22.2
Kuznetsk	34.2
Karaganda	10.9
Pechora	8.3
Kizel	2.1
Tkibuli	0.8
Tkvarcheli	0.2
Norilsk	0.2
Possible new fields	21.1
Bureya	6.3
Sayan Partizan (Kansk-Achinsk)	4.1
Novo-Metelkinsk (Cheremkhovo)	3.6
Ulukhemsk (Tuvinsk)	2.2
South Yakutsk	2.0
Fan Yagnobsk (Tadzhik S.S.R.)	1.2
Sakhalin	0.9
Suchan (Maritime Kray)	0.5
Bukachachinsk (Chita Oblast)	0.2
Uzgensk (Kirgiz S.S.R.)	0.1

Source: Rodgers, "Coking Coal Supply," p. 117. *Note:* The huge coal fields of northcentral Siberia might have large reserves of coking coal, but none of these have been proved.

Central Industrial Region, and by increasing coal output in the European part of the country.

Coal used by railroad locomotives is another burden on the railroads, since the coal has to be hauled as it is used. The railroads have always been one of the greatest users of coal; until 1957 they accounted for more than 20 per cent of coal consumption in the country. Since then, with conversion from steam engines to Diesel and electric, coal consumption has been greatly reduced. It was planned that in 1965 the railroads would consume no more than 1.2 per cent of the country's coal production. In 1958 the greatest coal consumers were thermal electric stations which used almost one third of the country's coal production and which generated about three fourths of the country's electricity. (Table 15–19)

Coal mining in the east is more economical than it is in the west. The capital expenditure per ton increase of coal output in eastern Siberia on the average is about 40 per cent and in the Kuzbass about 67 per cent of that in the Donbass. The production cost per ton of Kuzbass coal is approximately 40 per cent below that of the Donbass coal, primarily because of thicker seams of coal in the east which in some cases lie nearer to the surface so that open-pit mining can be utilized. On the average the coal seams in the Kuznetsk Basin are six times as thick as those in the Donbass. Large open-pit mines are being introduced wherever possible, since productivity in open pits is four to six times higher and costs are 3.5 times lower than in shaft mines. Mines can be brought into production four to six times faster by open-pit methods. Some of the better fields, however, are not adaptable to open-pit mining because of the depth of the seams. In the Donets Basin 95 per cent of the mining is shaft mining. The percentage of coal mined in the entire U.S.S.R. by open-pit methods jumped rapidly after the war from around 4 per cent in 1940 to almost 25 per cent in 1966.

Underground gasification of coal had its inception in 1935 in the Moscow and Donets Coal Basins. The German invasion interrupted this development, but underground gasification plants have been built at other coal fields as well as in the Moscow and Donets fields since the war. Apparently this method of coal utilization has met with some success in supplying gas to thermal electric stations; however, this type of utilization is only a minor part of the total coal consumption of the country.

Oil One of the most spectacular and significant recent developments in industry in the Soviet Union is the rapid expansion of the oil and natural gas industries. Russia and the Soviet Union has always been a major oil producer, and at the turn of the century it was the leading producer in the world. But during the 1930s the industry had not expanded as rapidly as most other industries, and the German invasion during World War II caused an absolute decline in production. Since 1945, and particularly since 1953, production has increased at a rate of more than 20 per cent annually. In 1968 the Soviet Union produced 309 million metric tons of crude petroleum; this compared to 435 produced by the United States in 1967. By 1980 the Soviets hope to be producing 700 million metric tons.

The rapid expansion of production has been accompanied by a major geographical shift in the primary producing areas of oil. Whereas in 1940 the Caucasus produced 87 per cent of the country's oil, by 1960 the newer Volga-Urals fields produced 70 per cent, and their share increased to 72 per cent in 1965. At the same time there has been almost an exact reversal in the proved reserves of the two regions; in 1940 the Caucasus were credited with 80 per cent of the country's reserves and the Volga-Urals fields were credited with 16 per cent; in 1955 the Caucasus were credited with 15 per cent and the Volga-Urals with 81 per cent.

The Baku fields, the traditional leaders of Russian production, were surpassed in

production first by the Bashkir fields in 1954, then by the Tatar fields in 1956, and by Kuybyshev Oblast in 1959. Thus three separate political regions within the Volga-Urals fields—the Bashkir A.S.S.R., the Tatar A.S.S.R., and Kuybyshev Oblast—individually have surpassed the Baku production. In addition, Perm and Volgograd Oblasts are also significant producers in this area. The Tatar A.S.S.R. is the leading producer in the country at present and is to remain so in the immediate future, with the Bashkir A.S.S.R. and Kuybyshev Oblast close behind. (Fig. 15–5)

The Baku fields suffered an absolute decline during World War II, but since that time production has been slowly rising, largely due to deeper drilling and drilling in the water of the Caspian offshore, until it has essentially regained its 1941 level. The old North Caucasian oil fields are now experiencing a spurt in production as new fields have been opened up in the Chechen-Ingush and Dagestan A.S.S.R.'s and Krasnodar and Stavropol Krays. The new Chechen-Ingush fields around the old oil city of Grozny seem to be particularly promising. (Table 15–20) New fields have also been opened in the Chernigov District of the Donets-Dnieper

Table 15–19 Coal Consumers

Consuming Branch of the Economy	Per Cent of Total		
	1954	1958	1965 (Plan)
Railroad transport	22.96	17.3	1.2
Ferrous metallurgy (Power and coke-chemical)	21.38	–	–
Including coke burned	(15.00)	15.5	21.1
Electrostations	18.53	32.8	41.1
Machine building	6.02	–	–
Coal industry	4.69	–	–
Domestic uses	–	13.1	18.3
Other industries and agriculture	–	21.3	18.3
All other branches of the economy	26.42	–	–
Total	100.0	100.0	100.0

Source: Hodgkins, *Soviet Power,* p. 41.

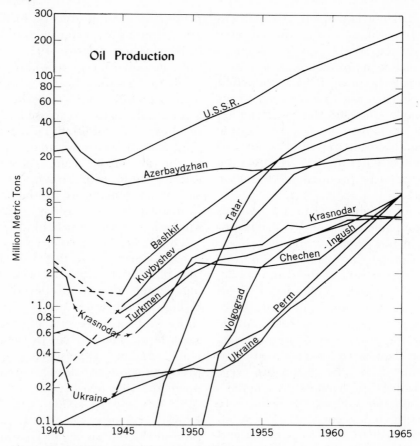

Figure 15–5   Oil production by regions in the U.S.S.R., 1940–1965. After Lydolph and Shabad, p. 466 and Campbell, p. 124.

Upland to augment the old producing areas of the North Carpathian foothills in western Ukraine, and a renewed expansion is taking place in the Nebit Dag area of the Turkmen Republic. The old producing areas of the Emba fields in the North Caspian Lowland, the scattered deposits of the Fergana Valley, and northern Sakhalin Island in the Far East are continuing to produce consistent but small shares of the country's total oil.

The most exciting development in the oil industry during the 1960s has been the discovery and initial development of two new oil areas, the first a rather concentrated region on the Mangyshlak Peninsula on the eastern shore of the Caspian in the Kazakh Republic, the second a broad area of great promise in western

Siberia. Producing wells at present in western Siberia lie along the middle course of the Ob River in Tyumen and Tomsk Oblasts, but eventually production might spread to much of the Ob Basin and total reserves might surpass even those of the Volga-Urals. The entire West Siberian Lowland is a flat sedimentary floor which is geologically correct for oil deposits. Production began in three different areas in Tyumen Oblast in 1964, and output quickly rose to 12 million tons in 1968. A 650-mile, 40-inch pipeline has been built to the Omsk refinery where Tyumen crude oil can be fed into the master east-west pipeline system that extends all the way from Angarsk, near Lake Baykal, in the east to Poland, East Germany, Czechoslovakia, and Hungary in the west. The oil development has also sparked the construction of an important railroad branch from Tyumen through Tobolsk to Surgut. In the Mangyshlak area, a short pipeline has been built from the producing fields westward to the new Caspian port of Shevchenko from whence crude oil can be moved by tanker to any of the refineries along the Caspian-Volga waterway. Also crude oil is moved northwestward along a new railroad to the Guryev refinery on the north shore of the Caspian. A 1100-mile pipeline is under construction from Mangyshlak to the refining complex of the Kuybyshev area on the Middle Volga. It was completed to Guryev in early 1969. A third new development of minor proportions is taking place in southeast Belorussia where oil was struck in the middle 1960s near the town of Rechitsa.

The great expansion and geographical shifts of oil production have brought about major changes in transport facilities and refining complexes. No longer is the Caspian-Volga waterway the main artery of oil movement. The Volga-Urals fields have established a new east-west axis of movement by pipeline, and more recent

Table 15–20   Soviet Crude Oil Production by Regions, 1937–1980, in Millions of Tons

Region	1937	1945	1955	1965	1966	1967	1968	Plan 1970	Plan 1980
U.S.S.R.	28.5	19.4	70.8	243	265	288	309	350	700
Volga-Ural	1.0	2.8	41.2	174	186				
Tatar A.S.S.R.	0.0	–	14.6	76.4					
Bashkir A.S.S.R.	1.0	1.3	14.2	43.9					
Kuybyshev Oblast	–	1.0	7.2	33.4					
Volgograd Oblast	0.0		2.3	6.2					
Saratov Oblast	0.0		1.9	1.3					
Orenburg Oblast	0.0		0.5	2.6					
Perm Oblast	–	0.2	0.6	9.7		13.0		17–18	
Komi A.S.S.R.	0.4		0.6	2.2					
Western Siberia	0.0	0.0	0.0	1.0	3.0	6.0	12	20–25	
North Caucasus	4.3		6.5	20.7	23.6				
Krasnodar Kray	1.4	0.7	3.9	6.2					
Chechen-Ingush A.S.S.R.	2.7	0.9	2.1	9.0			16		
Dagestan A.S.S.R.	0.2	0.6	0.5	1.0					
Stavropol Kray	0.0			4.6					
Sakhalin	0.4		1.0	2.4					
Azerbaydzhan S.S.R.	21.4	11.5	15.3	21.5	21.7	21.6	21.1		
Georgian S.S.R.	–	–	–	–					
Turkmen S.S.R.	0.5	0.6	3.1	9.6	10.7	11.9	12.9		
Kazakh S.S.R.	0.5	0.8	1.4	2.0	3.1	5.6	7.4		
Mangyshlak	0.0	0.0	0.0		1.4	3.7	5.5	12–15	
Fergana Valley	0.4	0.5	1.1	2.1			1.9		
Ukraine S.S.R.		0.2	0.5	7.6	9.3	11.0	12.1		
Belorussia S.S.R.	0.0	0.0	0.0	–		0.8	1.7		

Sources: Campbell, *The Economics of Soviet Oil and Gas,* pp. 5 and 124; *Strana Sovetov za 50 let,* p. 69; and *Soviet Geography: Review and Translation,* March 1968, pp. 223–224; December 1967, p. 803; January 1968, p. 74; May 1968, p. 426; and April 1969, p. 210.
—means less than 50,000 tons. Blank space means no report.

developments to the north and the south are feeding oil, through branch lines, into this system. Large new refineries generally are being established at the market ends of these pipes, and products pipelines are then being built to distribute the refined materials outward in radial patterns from the refinery centers. So the country is becoming a rat's nest of collecting and distributing pipelines and refineries. (Fig. 15–6) By January 1, 1968, 32,200 kilometers of oil pipelines had been built. By comparison, in 1967 the U.S.A. had 321,900 kilometers of oil pipelines. The Soviet pipeline system is still a long way from being adequate to handle the amount of oil being produced. Railroads still carried almost 40 per cent of all tons originated in 1966, which in absolute terms was almost six times the oil carried on railroads in 1950. (Table 15–21) But the Soviets are bending every effort to match pipeline construction to the burgeoning oil production, and they are continually developing larger and larger pipe. They now have four plants capable of producing 40-inch pipe, at Zhdanov, Novomoskovsk, and Khartsyzsk in Ukraine and Chelyabinsk in the Urals. The Chelyabinsk plant has been converted to produce 48-inch pipe, and plans are being made for the production of 58- and 100-inch pipe.

By far the greatest pipeline system is the one running east and west from the Volga-Urals oil fields, which still produce 70 per cent of the country's crude oil. Construction started shortly after World War II, and the first short segment connected the oil center of Tuymazy in the Bashkir A.S.S.R. with the Ufa refining complex in 1947. The first crude oil pipeline eastward reached Omsk in 1955 at the same time that the first oil refinery there opened. By 1959 the pipeline had been extended to Novosibirsk and by 1964 a total of 2500 miles to Angarsk, near Irkutsk. The Angarsk refinery had gone into operation in 1960, receiving crude oil by rail pending completion of the Trans-Siberian pipeline. In the meantime, two crude lines and two products lines had been completed between Ufa and Omsk; one of each was extended to Novosibirsk. Omsk has become the primary refining center in Siberia, and the new pipeline coming in from the north will enhance its position greatly as the west Siberian fields come into full production.

Two main trunklines lead westward from the Volga-Urals fields. Construction began on the so-called Druzhba (Friend-

Table 15–21   Transport of Oil and Products, by Carrier, 1950 and 1966

	Million Tons		Billion Ton-Kilometers		Average Length of Haul, Kilometers
	1950	1966	1950	1966	1966
Pipelines	15.3	247.7	4.9	165.0	666
Crude oil	12.7	225.6			
Products	2.6	22.1			
Railroads	43.2	240.2	52.2	301.9	1,257
Crude oil only	14.1		12.0		
River	11.9	26.9	12.0	30.5	1,516
Sea	15.8	59.9	11.9	231.0	3,856
Total	86.2	574.7	80.8	728.4	

Source: Campbell, *The Economics of Soviet Oil and Gas*, p. 142.

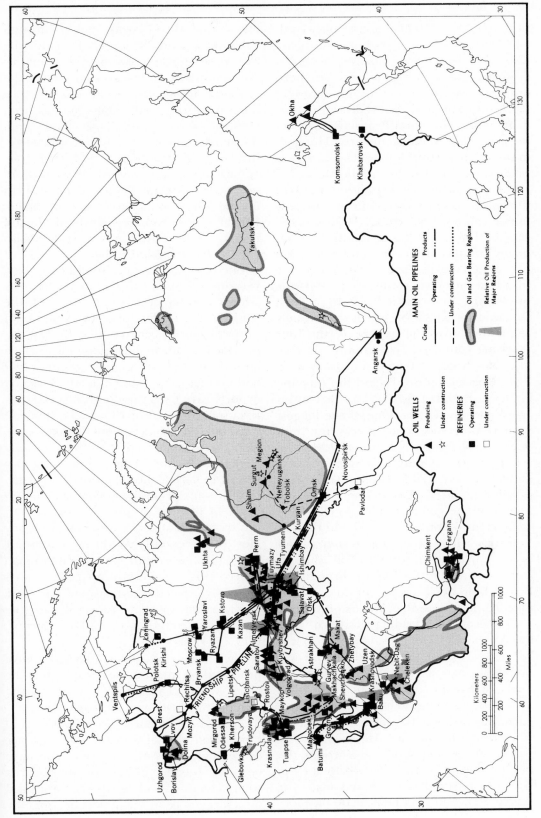

Figure 15–6 Distribution of the oil industry. Updated from Atlas razvitiya khozyaystva i kultury SSSR, p. 24.

491

ship) pipeline in 1959 to carry Volga-Urals oil 2500 miles across southern European Russia to Mozyr in Belorussia where it bifurcates into northern and southern branches which extend to refineries at Plock, Poland and Schwedt, East Germany in the north and Bratislava, Czechoslovakia and Szaszhalombatta, Hungary in the south. A temporary rail terminal was established at Brody in northwestern Ukraine to begin feeding oil into the East European system, sections of which became operative between October 1961 and December 1963. The Soviet trunk line was finally completed in 1964 and since then has carried Volga-Urals oil directly to the four East European countries. In 1967 the Friendship line carried 17–18 million metric tons of crude oil, which was virtually all of the Soviet oil exports to the four receiving countries. In addition a branch line has been extended northwestward from Unecha, on the Friendship pipeline in Bryansk Oblast, to Polotsk, Belorussia and Ventspils, Latvia. One of the biggest refineries in the country was put into operation at Polotsk in February 1963 with an initial throughput capacity of about 6 million tons of crude oil per year. This greatly enhanced the fuel-poor western region of the country. The pipeline was completed to Polotsk in 1965 and then to Ventspils where a marine terminal had been established in 1968 to transship oil from pipe to ship for export through the Baltic. Now work has begun on a second pipeline parallel to the Friendship system.

The second line leading westward from the Volga-Urals fields carries oil to refineries at Gorky and Yaroslavl, and will eventually extend to the new large refinery at Kirishi southeast of Leningrad, as well as to Leningrad itself. A branch line runs southwestward from Gorky to serve refineries in Ryazan and Moscow.

The recent modest oil boom around the old producing center of Grozny in the North Caucasus has prompted plans for the construction of a new crude oil pipeline from the Grozny fields through Tikhoretsk and Rostov-on-Don to the Donets Basin where two new oil refineries are planned. Construction on one of the refineries began in Lisichansk in 1968. In the Far East, a second pipeline has been constructed across the Tatar Strait from the north Sakhalin fields to mainland refineries at Komsomolsk and Khabarovsk. A new oil field has been developed in northern Sakhalin about 15 miles north of the old producing center of Okha. Sakhalin now supplies much of the oil needs of the Soviet Far East and also exports to Japan and Cuba.

The Soviet Union has found oil to be a very useful item of export which has afforded entry into some areas of the world where trade offers otherwise would probably have been rebuffed. It has also provided a negotiable commodity which has substituted for money where rubles had no real value. Consequently Soviet oil exports have risen rapidly from a negative level (net imports) in 1950 to 78.8 million tons in 1967. Since 1960 exports have taken between 25 and 28 per cent of total Soviet production. This is something of a return to earlier days, before 1930, when the Russians generally exported about 30 per cent of their oil production, but now the quantities involved are much larger. Most of the exports go to the Communist Bloc and western Europe, although Japan is becoming a major buyer. Crude exports generally exceed products exports by a considerable margin, especially to the communist countries of eastern Europe. (Fig. 15–7)

The newer oil fields generally have produced oil much more cheaply than the older fields. (Table 15–22) Costs in the Volga-Urals fields run approximately half those of the national average, and costs in some small old fields of the Caucasus are exceedingly high. Also recovery rates have been much better in the Volga-Urals area where contour flooding has been practiced on a large scale in the almost horizontally lying strata. Comparative costs have not been established yet in the west Siberian fields, but the simple geological structure should be conducive to very efficient methods, although the remoteness of the area and the harshness of the climate might add somewhat to costs.

Natural Gas The production and consumption of large quantities of natural gas in the Soviet Union is a much more recent development than is the oil industry. Only since 1955 has there been a significant production of natural gas. Until this time gas was not recognized as one of the primary fuels; much of the by-product gases of oil production were flared off at the fields,

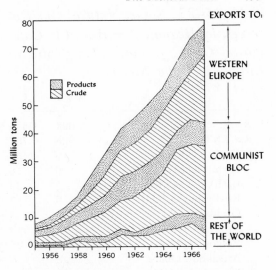

Figure 15–7   *Soviet oil exports by area and type, 1955–1967. After Campbell,* Soviet Oil and Gas, *Johns Hopkins Press, p. 227. Professor Campbell supplied data for the additional years 1966 and 1967.*

Table 15–22   Cost of Oil Extraction by Regions, 1950 and 1963, in Rubles per Ton

	1950	1963
U.S.S.R. average	6.24	3.04
Volga-Ural		1.77
Tatar A.S.S.R.	3.39	1.40
Bashkir A.S.S.R.	2.97	2.31
Kuybyshev Oblast	2.68	1.52
Volgograd Oblast	9.62	1.67
Perm Oblast		2.37
Orenburg Oblast		3.95
Saratov Oblast		3.68
North Caucasus		4.53
Krasnodar Kray	4.70	5.75
Chechen-Ingush A.S.S.R.	5.64	4.35
Dagestan A.S.S.R.	9.81	8.91
Stavropol Kray		2.10
Komi A.S.S.R.		6.38
Sakhalin	15.24	10.18
Azerbaydzhan	6.85	7.81
Georgia	53.37	28.60
Kazakhstan	11.21	10.24
Turkmenia	5.30	4.44
Fergana Valley	3.50	8.38
Ukraine	23.70	3.16

Source: Campbell, *The Economics of Soviet Oil and Gas,* p. 139. The new fields of the Mangyshlak Peninsula and western Siberia might prove to have the lowest costs yet.

and the Soviets were largely unaware of the great deposits of natural gas that existed in their country. During the last 15 years all this has changed. Large deposits of natural gas have been discovered in Stavropol and Krasnodar Krays in the North Caucasus, in Transcaucasia near Baku, in eastern and western Ukraine, in the Middle Asian desert, and, most recently, in western Siberia. Other deposits exist in the Volga-Urals area, in the Komi A.S.S.R. in northeastern European Russia, and in the Lena-Vilyuy Lowland in eastern Siberia. Table 15–23 shows the distribution of proved reserves only, as of January 1, 1966. Since then, the confirmation of large gas deposits in western Siberia and new deposits in Middle Asia have boosted Soviet estimates of total proved recoverable reserves to 7.75 trillion cubic meters. Of this total, Tyumen Oblast, in western Siberia, alone is credited with 3.85 trillion cubic meters. This compares with reserves of 0.6 to 0.7 trillion in each of the three major producing areas: Ukraine, North Caucasus, and Uzbekistan. In 1968 the Soviets estimated their ultimate gas reserves to be 67 trillion cubic meters, which represented

Table 15–23   Soviet Natural Gas Reserves, by Region, A + B and C Categories Only, January 1, 1966, in Billions of Cubic Meters

	A + B	C
U.S.S.R.	2,021	1,545
R.S.F.S.R.	928	767
Komi A.S.S.R.	9	30
Perm Oblast	6	18
Bashkir A.S.S.R.	5	26
Kuybyshev A.S.S.R.	6	5
Orenburg Oblast	16	9
Saratov Oblast	41	29
Volgograd Oblast	68	22
Astrakhan Oblast	2	0
Kalmyk A.S.S.R.	21	26
Rostov Oblast	0	4
Krasnodar Kray	379	86
Stavropol Kray	192	43
Chechen-Ingush A.S.S.R.	6	3
Dagestan A.S.S.R.	10	33
Western Siberia	149	306
Eastern Siberia	8	90
Sakhalin	11	38
Ukraine S.S.R.	448	207
Azerbaydzhan S.S.R.	27	27
Kazakh S.S.R.	4	88
Turkmen S.S.R.	125	251
Uzbek S.S.R.	484	182
Tadzhik S.S.R.	1	12
Kirgiz S.S.R.	4	10

Source: Campbell, *The Economics of Soviet Oil and Gas,* p. 200.

about one third of total world reserves. By comparison, in 1960 the United States' ultimate reserves were estimated at 48 trillion cubic meters.

Soviet gas production increased from only 10.4 billion cubic meters in 1955 to 171 billion in 1968, and it is scheduled to rise to 700 billion by 1980. By comparison, production in the U.S.A. in 1967 was 514 billion. (Table 15–24) By 1980 the energy equivalent of gas production in the Soviet Union is to be equal that of coal and almost as important as oil. (Table 15–13) At present, gas is produced mainly around Krasnodar and Stavropol in the North Caucasus, around Shebelinka in eastern Ukraine, Dashava in western Ukraine, and Gazli in the Uzbek Republic of Middle Asia. (Table 15–25) Undoubtedly production will continue to expand rapidly in these main areas, especially in Middle Asia where large new deposits are being opened up in eastern Turkmenia even before the Gazli fields come into full production just across the Amu-Darya. In addition the huge west Siberian fields are beginning to enter the production picture and might become predominant sometime during the 1970s. Smaller producers lie around Saratov on the Middle Volga, Ukhta in the European northeast, Karadag southwest of Baku, Nebit Dag in western Turkmenia, Tas-Tumus northwest of Yakutsk, and Okha in northern Sakhalin, as well as in conjunction with oil wells in such fields as the Volga-Urals. Since the big consumers are industry and electrical stations (Table 15–26), much of the gas is consumed in the three established industrial regions— eastern Ukraine, Center, and Urals—and in the newly emerging industries of the Middle Volga where petro-chemicals are becoming very important. (Table 15–25) Since the Center and the Urals produce no gas, heavy consumption in these areas has induced the construction of multi-trunk lines of gas pipes from the North Caucasus and Middle Asia to these areas. (Fig. 15–8) The development of these fields has been completely dependent upon the construction of the pipelines. The first two pipelines between the Caucasus and the Center were completed in the early 1960s; since then a third line has been constructed, and a line has been extended to Leningrad. The Shebelinka field in eastern Ukraine is fortuitously located to utilize these lines. The first pipeline between Middle Asia and the Urals was completed in 1963. This consists of a 40-inch-diameter pipe over 1200 miles in length. In 1965 a second similar line was completed parallel to the first. In 1967 the first of three pipelines was

Table 15–24   Gas Output, Soviet Union 1955–1980, and United States 1967, in Billions of Cubic Meters

	1955	1965	1967	1968	Plan 1970	Plan 1980	U.S.A., 1967
Gas well	5.9	111.2	138.6		200–210		
Oil well	3.1	16.5	18.9				
Manufactured	1.4	1.7	1.7				
Total	10.4	129.4	159.2	171	225–240	700	514

Sources: Campbell, *The Economics of Soviet Oil and Gas,* p. 196; *SSSR v Tsifrakh v 1967 godu,* pp. 34–35; *Soviet Geography: Review and Translation,* May 1968, p. 425, and April 1969, p. 210; and Theodore Shabad, personal communication.

Table 15–25   Regional Distribution of Natural Gas Production and Consumption, in Billion Cubic Meters

	1965 Consumption (All Natural Gas)	1965 Production (Gas-well Gas Only)	1966 Total Production	1967 Total Production	1968 Total Production
U.S.S.R.	127	111.2	143	159 [a]	171
European R.S.F.S.R.			64.5	66.3	
North		1.0			
Northwest	6.2	0			
West	4.1	0			
Estonia (shale)			0.5		
Center	30.2	0			
Volga	14.4	7.3			
North Caucasus	11.7	43.8			42.0
Urals	14.4	1.5	4.5	4.1	
Siberia	} 0.6	} negligible	1.2	5.6	
Far East					
Ukraine	31.5	37.6	43.6	47.4	50.9
Transcaucasia	7.6	3.1			
Azerbaydzhan			6.2	5.8	5.0
Middle Asia	5.7	16.4			
Uzbek S.S.R.			22.6	26.6	29.0
Turkmen S.S.R.			1.3	2.2	4.3
Kirgiz S.S.R.			0.02		
Kazakh S.S.R.			0.05		

Sources: Campbell, *The Economics of Soviet Oil and Gas,* p. 202; *Soviet Geography: Review and Translation,* March 1968, p. 223, and April 1969, p. 210; and *Strana Sovetov za 50 let,* pp. 307–337.
[a] All gas.

Table 15–26   Soviet Consumption of Gas by Sector of Economy, 1966, in Billions of Cubic Meters

Total	143.54
Household-municipal	15.95
Industry	80.62
Chemicals	6.32
Metallurgy	22.52
Cement	8.00
Machinery and metal-working	15.21
Construction and	
construction materials	6.50
Electric stations	40.65
Transport	0.82
Agriculture	0.46
Own needs and losses	4.24
Export	0.80

Source: Campbell, *The Economics of Soviet Oil and Gas,* p. 214.

completed between Middle Asia and the Center. This is a 40-inch pipe over 1600 miles in length. It is capable of transmitting 10.5 billion cubic meters of gas per year. A second line now under construction uses 48-inch pipe. Some of the Middle Asian gas now joins North Caucasian gas at Moscow to move all the way to Leningrad where it moves westward with the reversed gas flow on the old double 20-inch Kohtla-Jarve pipeline which was built originally to carry shale gas eastward from Kohtla-Jarve to Leningrad. Two pipelines, of larger diameter still, are being built across the northern end of the Urals to bring west Siberian gas to the European Center. One uses pipe 48 and 56 inches in diameter, and the other is to be entirely 100 inches in diameter. Much of the 56-inch pipe is being manufactured at the new industrial center of Volzhskiy across the river from Volgograd, whereas the 48-inch pipe comes primarily from Chelyabinsk in the Urals. Connecting lines distribute gas from these main suppliers to much of European U.S.S.R. and some is being exported to Poland. There are plans for

gas exports to other east European satellites, as well as to Sweden. Gas could be taken from pipeline terminals in Leningrad and Kaliningrad by tanker under pressure in liquid form to supply much of the Baltic area.

The gas supply is very important to the western regions, which previously relied on such fuels as peat and firewood. It is greatly enhancing the establishment of industries and electric-generating stations. In the Caucasus and Middle Asia, local pipeline systems are providing much needed fuel to the major cities and industries and relieving the necessity of constructing some high-cost hydroelectric plants that had been planned before the discovery of gas. The gas supply in Transcaucasia is to be augmented by a pipeline from northern Iran which will feed gas into the Karadag field southwest of Baku, which is rapidly being exhausted. Also gas is being brought into Transcaucasia from the North Caucasian fields via a pipeline that was laid in 1964 completely across the Great Caucasus following the route of the Georgian Military Highway. In Middle Asia, gas is to be brought into the Tadzhik Republic by pipe from Afghanistan.

Since 1958 the Soviets have expanded their gas pipeline network from 9500 kilometers to 52,800 kilometers at the beginning of 1968. This compares to 420,000 kilometers in the U.S.A. in 1967. Much of the Soviet network is of considerably larger diameter than that in the United States. Table 15–27 compares the two countries as of 1963. Since then the Soviets have been going to larger and larger pipes.

Shale   The mining of oil shale has persisted in the Soviet Union in spite of the growth of the oil and gas industries and the fact that the production of oil from shale is much more expensive than it is from petroleum. In 1965 shale still accounted for 0.75 per cent of the energy consumed in the U.S.S.R. Although the

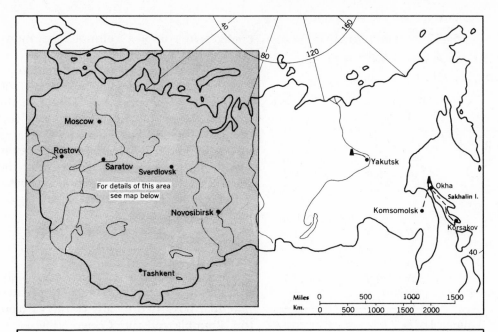

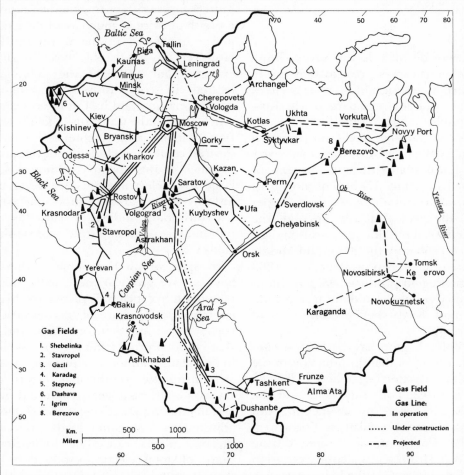

Gas Fields

1. Shebelinka
2. Stavropol
3. Gazli
4. Karadag
5. Stepnoy
6. Dashava
7. Igrim
8. Berezovo

Gas Field

Gas Line:

In operation

Under construction

Projected

Figure 15–8   Gas fields and gas pipelines. After Campbell, Soviet Oil and Gas, *Johns Hopkins Press, p. 205.*

Table 15–27 Comparative Gas Pipeline Sizes, U.S.S.R. and U.S.A., January 1, 1963

	Pipe Diameter (Inches)	Per Cent of Total
U.S.S.R.		
	<15	25.6
	16.7–20.8	26.4
	28.3–40.0	48.0
U.S.A.		
	<10	30.5
	10.1–15.0	11.6
	15.1–20.0	18.3
	20.1–25.0	14.3
	25.1–30.0	22.7
	>30	2.7

Source: Campbell, The Economics of Soviet Oil and Gas, p. 208.

resources of oil shale in the Soviet Union are nowhere near as great as they are in the United States, significant reserves exist in Estonia and adjacent parts of the Russian Republic, in the Middle Volga area, in northeastern Europe, in the northeastern Siberian platform west of the Lena River, and in Kazakhstan east and northeast of Lake Balkash. (Fig. 15–9) The northeast Siberian area contains more than 70 per cent of the geological reserves, but the oil content of the Baltic reserves is higher, and since 1956 only the Baltic and Middle Volga areas have been producing. In 1963 the Baltic Region produced 85 per cent of the country's oil shale, and the area around Syzran and Kuybyshev produced about 15 per cent.

The Volga Region has the longest continuous record of shale production in the U.S.S.R.; production began here in the late 1920s. By 1932 both the Baltic and the Volga Regions were in production, with the major share centered in the Volga area. With the acquisition of Estonia during World War II there was a large expansion in the shale industry in the Baltic area. Apparently the Baltic is the only region that engages in complex refining operations; apparently all the shale in the Volga area is burned in power-generating stations.

Although the Baltic shales yield about 60 gallons of oil per ton, the highest in the world, shale is still considered a local fuel because of its low-energy content per unit of weight, and it is not shipped over extensive distances. Its production is most important to the Estonian Republic, where it generates much of the electricity.

Electric Power

The U.S.S.R. has 12 per cent of the world's water-power potential, the greatest potential possessed by any country except the Republic of the Congo. These resources are sufficient to generate annually more than twice as much as all the electric power generated in the world in 1957. However, it is not feasible to realize all this energy. Four fifths of the potential is located in comparatively undeveloped Asiatic territory and half of the remaining one fifth is in the Caucasus (Table 15–28). Inaccessibility and remoteness from industrial centers preclude the development of much of this resource, although some large hydroelectric plants are being built in fairly remote areas to supply large electric-consuming industries such as aluminum, magnesium, nitrate, and synthetic rubber.

In spite of all the publicity that the Soviets have given to the construction of mammoth hydroelectric plants, the hydroelectric capacity share of total electric capacity is still less than one fifth, and the share of total production is even less, since hydro plants cannot be run near capacity as consistently as thermal plants can. Hydro plants are adversely affected by ice and fluctuating water stages and cannot be adjusted to fluctuating loads as well as thermal plants can. The hydroelectric share of total electric production rose steadily from only 1.7 per cent in 1913 to 19.7 per cent in 1958 as bigger and bigger

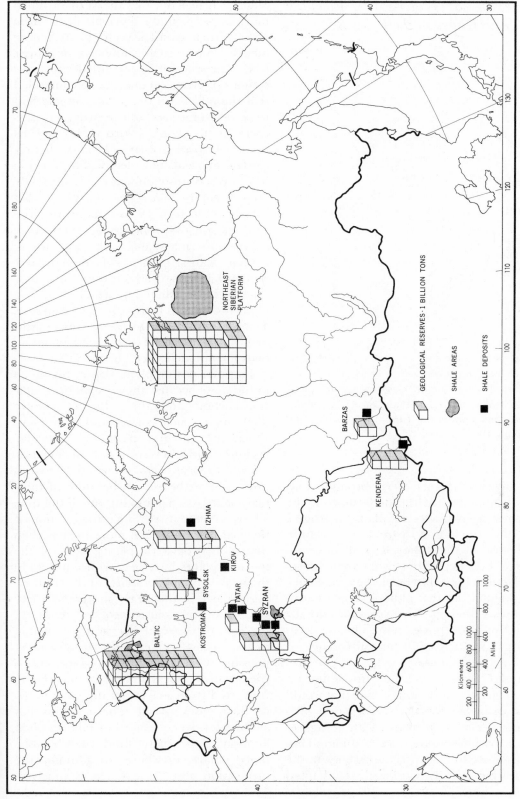

Figure 15–9   Geological reserves of shale. After Hodgkins, Jordan A., Soviet Power: Energy Resources, Production, and Potential, 1961. By permission of Prentice-Hall, Inc.

Table 15–28   Water-Power Potential of Major Rivers in the U.S.S.R.

River	Million Kilowatts
Lena	18.4
Yenisey	18.2
Angara	9.9
Amur	6.4
Indigirka	6.2
Volga	6.2
Naryn	5.9
Pyandzh	5.8
Ob	5.7
Amu-Darya	3.8
Irtysh	3.2
Dnieper	2.8
Syr-Darya	2.0
Kura	2.0
Zeya	1.9
Bureya	1.7
Pechora	1.6
Kama	1.5
Sulai	1.2
Rioni	1.0

Sources: Petrov, Victor, *Geography of the Soviet Union: Electric Power,* p. 4, and *Soviet Geography: Review and Translation,* June 1960, p. 38, and January 1969, p. 40.

hydroelectric plants were brought into production. But at the dedication of the Kuybyshev hydroelectric plant on August 10, 1958 (the largest hydroelectric plant in the world at that time), Khrushchev concluded his speech by saying that henceforth emphasis would be on thermal plants. He pointed out that although such hydro plants as that at Kuybyshev eventually would produce power more cheaply than thermal plants would, the construction of the 2,300,000-kilowatt Kuybyshev plant required 7 years, which tied up capital investments over a period of time that would have provided for the construction of a number of thermal plants with an aggregate capacity of more than 12 million kilowatts. Since time was of the essence in the Soviet race to catch up with the United

States, Khrushchev said that it made much more sense to build thermal plants from which returns could be realized much more quickly. Since such things as improved labor productivity depended on new sources of electrical energy, he contended that the effects on the total economy had to be taken into account in order to assess correctly the choice, hydro versus thermal power. Accordingly, since 1958 the hydroelectric share of total electrical production has wavered unsteadily downward to only 16 per cent in 1965. The Soviets boast that they have perfected and standardized the construction of prefabricated reinforced-concrete thermal plants to the point where a plant with a capacity of more than 1 million kilowatts can be brought into production in less than 1 year. The building of each dam and hydro plant, of course, is a unique problem which requires months or even years of surveying and planning before construction can begin.

Thermal power plants are never much in the news because they are all of similar construction and they do not involve phenomena, such as river and mountains, which are integral parts of particular regions, and therefore are of intrinsic interest to local residents as well as to outsiders. Nevertheless the building of thermal plants has been going on all the time all over the country. Since the location of thermal plants is much more flexible than that of hydroelectric plants, most of the thermal plants have been concentrated in the heavily populated parts of the country, particularly in the heavy industrial areas, since industry still consumes about 65 per cent of the total electrical production in the Soviet Union. With the great expansion of the oil and natural gas industries, many thermal power plants are being converted from coal to natural gas and by-product gases of oil refining. This has allowed for even greater flexibility of plant location, since these fluid fuels can be piped almost anywhere. In addition, the production costs of gas are as much as twelve times less than that of coal, and this together with reduced costs of transportation and plant construction, as well as greater efficiency of boiler units, has greatly improved the costs of electrical production in thermal plants as compared to those in hydro plants. The opening of cheaply operating open-pit coal mines in such areas as Siberia and Kazakhstan has also lowered the costs of thermal electric production. Another innovation has been the underground gasification of coal in which coal is burned underground without mining and the gases given off are used to generate steam to turn the turbines in thermal electric plants. Underground gasification of coal is being utilized in several different parts of the country, particularly in some of the large brown coal deposits near large concentrations of industry, such as the Moscow Basin. Finally, economies of scale are being utilized in thermal plants just as they are in hydroelectric plants, and capacities of well over 1 million kilowatts are now quite common for thermal plants as well as for hydroelectric plants. (Tables 15–29 and 15–30) In both cases, capacities which were unheard of a few years ago are now ordinary, and new plants continually dwarf old plants. The largest thermal power complex now under construction is at the new town of Volgorechensk, 25 miles southeast of Kostroma, on the right bank of the Volga River, which is to have an ultimate capacity of 5.2 million kilowatts.

Water-power projects often have significance to the regions in which they are located other than those of power generation. The construction of large dams to create large reservoirs on rivers completely alters the natural settings of the surrounding areas and often necessitates the moving of old villages out of the reservoir areas, and provides the basis for the new workers' settlements. Navigation, irrigation, and recreational facilities may be important adjuncts of the electrical function. Some of the larger reservoirs may even alter the climate significantly along their shores.

Thus there is some reason for the attention that some of these projects have received which may seem excessive judged from their power outputs alone. Such mighty rivers as the Volga and the Dnieper in Europe have been completely altered into stairways of huge reservoirs. And high dams on rivers such as the Angara, Yenisey, Ob, and Irtysh in Asia have transformed the aspects and economies of these remote areas.

In most cases, large new thermal plants are being constructed even in the areas with greatest development of hydroelectricity. This is necessary in order to even out the production of electricity during periods of low water stage or ice and to meet peak load capacities which occur at certain times of day. In line with the Soviets' constant striving to make projects multipurpose, the steam generated by thermal electric plants in many instances after it has turned the electrical turbines is fed into centralized heating systems to heat homes and industries. It has been reported that at the present time 25 per cent of the power stations in the Moscow area are utilized in this way and heat 50 per cent of the apartments in the city. This has effected a 20 per cent saving. It is planned that by 1980 thermal electric plants will produce 50 per cent of all the heat consumed in the country.

Another source of electrical energy that the Soviets hope to make great use of is atomic power. It would be particularly useful to supply large amounts of electrical energy to large industrial plants located in sparsely populated regions remote from conventional sources of power, since it would not necessitate the transport of bulky fuels. The Russians were the first in the world to complete an experimental nuclear-power station for public use in 1954. This was the 5000-kilowatt experimental station at Obninsk southwest of Moscow. Since then Soviet interest in atomic power for civilian purposes has lagged somewhat behind that in the West,

Table 15–29   Data on Selected Hydroelectric Projects

Dam	Height in Meters	Length in Meters	Reservoir Area in Square Kilometers	Ultimate Power Capacity in Kilowatts	Date Construction Started	Date Production Started
Volga River						
Volgograd	48	6,000	3,500	2,563,000	1950	1958
Kuybyshev	80	4,400	6,500	2,300,000	1950	1955
Cheboksary				1,400,000	1969(?)	1974(?)
Saratov	13			1,290,000	1956	1967
Gorky				520,000	1947	1955
Rybinsk				330,000	1936	1941
Ivankovo				300,000	1932	1937
Uglich				110,000	1935	1940
Kama River						
Lower Kama				1,080,000	1963	
Votkinsk				1,000,000	1954	1961
Kama (Perm)				504,000	1939	1954
Dnieper River						
Dnieproges (Zaporozhye)	50	700		650,600	1927	1932 [a]
Kakhovka	20			343,200	1951	1955
Kremenchug				686,400	1954	1959
Dneprodzerzhinsk				350,000	1956	1963
Kiev				370,000	1961	1964
Kanev				420,000	1963	
Western Dvina River						
Plavinas				825,000	1961	1965
Ob River						
Novosibirsk	25		4,500	400,000	1957	1959
Kamen				630,000	Proposed	
Irtysh River						
Bukhtarma	90		5,000	675,000	1953	1960
Ust-Kamenogorsk				330,000	1939	1952
Yenisey River						
Sayan				6,500,000	Before 1969	1975
Yenisey	139			6,000,000	Proposed	
Krasnoyarsk	130	1,100		6,000,000	1956	1967
Angara River						
Bratsk	100		5,000	5,000,000	1956	1961
Ust-Ilimsk				4,500,000	1962	1972
Irkutsk		2,363		660,000	1950	1956
Zeya River						
Zeya				1,470,000	1964	1975
Vilyuy River						
Vilyuy				312,000	1964	1967
Vakhsh River						
Nurek				2,700,000	1961	After 1970

Sources: Data are from scattered Soviet sources; Shabad "News Notes" in various issues of *Soviet Geography: Review and Translation;* Michel and Klain, p. 208; and personal communication from Theodore Shabad.
[a] Destroyed during World War II and reconstructed in 1949.

but this is apparently changing now. The first large Soviet atomic-power plant went into operation in 1958 somewhere in Siberia to provide electrical power for the production of plutonium for use in nuclear weapons. Its capacity has been reported as 600,000 kilowatts. The first major civilian installation went into operation in 1964 at Beloyarskiy east of Sverdlovsk in the Urals. Its initial capacity of 100,000 kilowatts has since been raised to 300,000. Later in the same year a 210,000-kilowatt plant went into operation at Novovoronezhskiy on the Don River south of Voronezh. Since then the plant has been expanded, and sometime in the early 1970s it is supposed to reach its ultimate capacity of 1.5 million kilowatts, which will make it the Soviet Union's largest atomic-power plant. Reactors of 440,000-kilowatt capacity are now being used in new installations. Two of these are to be installed in a new atomic-power station under construction in the Kola Peninsula south of Murmansk, and two more are to be installed in a plant near Yerevan in Armenia. Other Soviet atomic-power projects are the 50,000-kilowatt reactor at Melekess in the Middle Volga Valley; the dual-purpose power-producing and desalting reactor with an electric capacity of 350,000 kilowatts which is under construction at Shevchenko, the center of the arid Mangyshlak oil field on the east coast of the Caspian; and the 48,000-kilowatt reactor under construction at Bilibino, the gold-mining center of the far northeastern part of Siberia.

The production of hydroelectric energy has increased rapidly in the Soviet Union from only about 2 billion kilowatt hours

Table 15–30   Major Thermal Electric Stations in the U.S.S.R.

Region	Plant	Fuel	Ultimate Capacity in Million Kilowatts	Date Construction Started	Date Production Started
Northwest	Pribaltik	Shale gas	1.6		Before 1962
	Lithuania	Gas	1.2		1962
Center	Konakovo	Gas	2.4		About 1965
	Cherepets		1.2		
	Volgorechensk	Gas and oil	5.2	1965	1969
	Kashira	Moscow brown coal	2.0		1922
Volga	Zainsk		1.2		1963
Dnieper Bend	Krivoy Rog		2.4		1964–65
	Pridneprovsk		2.4		
	Novodneprovsk	Donets coal	3.6		
Kharkov	Zmiyev		1.2		
Donbass	Slavyansk		1.1		
	Lugansk		1.5		
	Starobeshevo		2.3		
Lower Don	Novocherkassk		2.4		1964–65
Urals	Verkhne Tagil		1.0		
	Troitsk	Coal	2.0		1960
	Yuzhnouralsk		1.0		
	Sverdlovsk	Gas and coal	3.0	After 1963	
	Chelyabinsk		3.0	After 1963	
Transcaucasia	Ali Bayramli	Gas	1.2		1967(?)
Pavlodar	Yermak		2.4		1964–65
Krasnoyarsk	Nazarovo		1.4		
Kuzbass	Belovo		1.5		
	Tomusinsk		1.3		
Middle Asia	Tashkent	Gas	1.92		1963
	Angren	Coal	0.6		1957
	Navoy	Gas	0.45		1961
	Syrdarya	Gas	4.4	Under construction	

Sources: Shabad "News Notes" of various issues of *Soviet Geography: Review and Translation,* and Michel and Klain, p. 214.

in 1913 to 589 billion in 1967. This makes it by far the second most important producer of electrical energy in the world after the United States, which in 1967 produced 1384 billion kilowatt hours. (Table 15–8) On a per capita basis, of course, the Soviet Union still lags behind many countries. The Soviets are eager to continue their expansion, not only because they need the electricity in their industries, farms, transportation systems, and homes, but also because electrification has a special meaning to the Soviets. This dates back to Lenin who early after the Revolution formulated the equation "communism equals Soviet power plus electrification of the whole country." Although as technologies have changed during the past 50 years electricity has progressively occupied a less central position, the Russian peasant lived so long in darkness without the aid of electrically run conveniences that he has never lost the desire to have as much electrical power at his disposal as he can possibly use. Therefore undoubtedly the electrical industry will continue to expand at an exceedingly rapid rate. During the past decade or more, electrical machinery has been expanding at a rate of more than 20 per cent per year, which is by far the highest rate of growth of any sector of industry. This sort of zeal will also undoubtedly continue to induce the Soviets to construct large hydroelectric projects in remote areas of the country and to harness mighty rivers even though economically the projects might not be justifiable. Since the demise of Khrushchev, there seems to have been some swing back toward hydroelectric construction, and many large plants which originally had been planned for such rivers as the Yenisey and the Angara are now being carried through. However, many other plans for hydroelectric construction on such rivers as the Amur seem to have been dropped for good. Therefore it seems that the zeal for hydroelectric construction has been tempered somewhat by economic considerations.

The regional distribution of Soviet production of electrical energy reveals the heavy uses of industry. (Table 15–31) The Ukraine, Urals, and Central Industrial regions are outstanding in this respect. The Volga Region is also a high producer, because of the tremendous generating capacity of the hydroelectric plants along the river and the new gas and oil powered plants in the Volga-Urals area. However, a great deal of this energy is transmitted westward to the Center or eastward to the Urals. It is unfortunate that so much of the hydroelectric potential of the Soviet Union lies in the sparsely

Table 15–31   Soviet Production of Electric Energy, by Regions, in Million Kilowatt-Hours

Million Kilowatt-Hours	1965	1968
U.S.S.R.	506.7	638
R.S.F.S.R.	332.8	411
Northwest	25.2	
Central	48.9	
Volga-Vyatka	12.0	
Central Chernozem	8.7	
Volga	56.0	
North Caucasus	17.7	
Ural	75.7	
Western Siberia	34.9	
Eastern Siberia	43.1	
Far East	9.3	
Ukraine S.S.R.	94.6	116.5
Belorussia S.S.R.	8.4	12.2
Lithuanian S.S.R.	3.9 ⎫	
Latvian S.S.R.	1.5 ⎬	17.8
Estonian S.S.R.	7.1 ⎭	
Moldavian S.S.R.	3.1	6.8
Georgian S.S.R.	6.0 ⎫	
Armenian S.S.R.	2.9 ⎬	23.8
Azerbaydzhan S.S.R.	10.4 ⎭	
Kazakh S.S.R.	19.2	27.6
Uzbek S.S.R.	11.5 ⎫	
Turkmen S.S.R.	1.4 ⎪	
Kirgiz S.S.R.	2.3 ⎬	22.2
Tadzhik S.S.R.	1.6 ⎭	

Sources: Narodnoye khozyaystvo SSSR v 1965 g., p. 170; Narodnoye khozyaystvo R.S.F.S.R. v 1965 g., p. 82; and Soviet Geography: Review and Translation, April 1969, p. 212.

populated east, but the utilization of large amounts of electricity produced by huge hydroelectric plants in Siberia might be made feasible by very high voltage transmission lines which connect these plants with the populous European part of the country. The Soviets are experimenting with direct-current lines with voltages as high as 800,000 volts to transmit electricity over very long distances, which seems to be possible with low line losses as long as power is not taken off for uses along the line. An 800-kilovolt power-transmission line now connects the Volgograd power plant with markets in the Donets Basin. This is a short preliminary line which is to provide the experience for the building of much longer lines between Siberia and the European Center. Such construction is to take place sometime in the early 1970s when lines with voltages as high as 1500 kilovolts might be put into operation.

Much of European Russia has already been integrated into one grid system, and another grid has been established in south-central Siberia. In the near future the Soviets plan to connect these grids by high-voltage lines to bring about an integrated grid throughout the entire country. If such efforts prove to be economically successful, they might provide a second boost to the construction of large hydroelectric plants in remote parts of the country. Some plans have even been made to integrate certain parts of the Soviet electrical grid with those in the east European satellites. Already some electricity is being sold to Poland from Belorussia and to Czechoslovakia, Hungary, and Rumania from western Ukraine. A transmission line is under construction from the big thermal electric station at Pridnestrovsk, Moldavia, to Bulgaria.

Ferrous Metallurgy

Historical Development Ferrous metallurgy in Russia originated around Tula in the early part of the seventeenth century when the smelting of small deposits of local iron ore was begun with the utilization of charcoal from the surrounding forests. During the reign of Peter the Great in the first part of the eighteenth century a considerably greater development of ferrous metallurgy took place in the Urals where rich deposits of iron ore were opened up and the smelting again was done with charcoal from the local forests. The Urals quickly became the main metallurgical base of Russia and remained so for nearly two centuries until they were surpassed by eastern Ukraine with the technological shift in iron smelting from charcoal to coke.

For a time the Urals were the foremost metallurgical area in the world. In 1767 the Urals produced 56,000 tons of pig iron, which was twice as much as was then produced in England. Russia even exported iron to England at this time. But during the early part of the nineteenth century when western Europe underwent the Industrial Revolution Russia lost the lead in iron production. In 1860 England produced 3,980,000 tons of pig iron, France produced 967,000 and Russia produced only 336,000.

During the 1860s construction of metallurgical plants began in eastern Ukraine to utilize the rich coal deposits in the Donets Basin and the rich iron ore deposits of Krivoy Rog west of the Dnieper. Rapid development took place after 1880, and by 1900 Ukraine had replaced the Urals as the main metallurgical base of Russia. In 1913 Ukraine produced 75 per cent of the iron ore of the country, 69 per cent of the pig iron, and 57 per cent of the steel, whereas the Urals produced only about 21 per cent of both pig iron and steel.

A revitalization of the steel industry in the Urals was begun late in the first 5-year plan with the opening of the iron ore mines at Magnitogorsk and the establishment of the Urals-Kuznetsk Combine in 1932. With relocation of plants from the west during World War II the steel industry in the Urals took a great spurt forward.

By 1956 the Urals were producing nearly 36 per cent of the country's pig iron and 36 per cent of its crude steel. Since then these percentages have declined as the industry has dispersed somewhat and emphasis has shifted back to the European part of the country.

The Soviet Iron and Steel Industry Compared to Other Producers Since World War II the production of iron and steel in the Soviet Union has been increasing at more than 10 per cent per year. At the same time in the United States and most west European countries production has been rising unsteadily and faltering with general economic conditions. In 1958 the U.S.S.R. became the world's largest producer of iron ore as production in the United States went into a slump from which it has never recovered. In 1967 the Soviet Union produced almost twice as much as the United States and more than three times as much as France. (Table 15–8) The United States imports a good deal of iron ore, however, whereas the Soviet Union is entirely self-sufficient. Therefore the production of pig iron and steel in the United States is still a little higher than it is in the Soviet Union. But the Soviet Union is quickly closing the gap as it continues to expand its production as rapidly as possible, whereas market saturation in the United States and west European countries keeps production far below capacity.

Distribution of the Iron and Steel Industry in the Soviet Union * The economic factors that have primarily determined the location of iron and steel plants in the Soviet Union, as in any country, are proximity to markets, coal, iron ore, and to a lesser extent, sources of manganese, limestone, and water. Transportation costs relative to the costs of raw

* Much of the data on regional breakdowns of resources and production were originally compiled by Nyla Albrecht Dereszynski.

materials have also been instrumental. The two main sources of coking coal production are the Donets Basin in eastern Ukraine and the Kuznetsk Basin in western Siberia. Secondary producers are Karaganda in northern Kazakhstan and Pechora in northeast European Russia. (Fig. 15–4) Iron ore resources are scattered abundantly across the Soviet Union, but the most important deposits are concentrated in eastern Ukraine, the Central Black Earth Region, and the Urals and adjacent parts of western Siberia and northern Kazakhstan. (Fig. 15–10 and Table 15–32) Manganese is concentrated in eastern Ukraine and Transcaucasia, whereas limestone is rather readily available to all centers of development. So far, water supply probably has not been a limiting factor, although it has been something of a problem for large steel plants located in dryish areas, such as Magnitogorsk and Karaganda. Apparently water supply has come into play in considerations regarding the precise locations of new steel plants in the region of the Kursk Magnetic Anomaly in European Russia. Markets, of course, are heavily concentrated in the west, particularly in the Central Industrial Region, Ukraine, and the Volga Valley.

Conditions for the production of pig iron are most ideal in eastern Ukraine, where the large Krivoy Rog iron ore deposits of the Dnieper Bend area lie only 200 miles to the west of the most highly developed Donets Coal Basin. In addition, one of the two largest manganese deposits is located at Nikopol on the Dnieper River between t'⸱ iron and the coal, and high-grade deposits of limestone for fluxing are located south of Donets and ⸜on the Crimean Peninsula. Thus the greatest iron and steel production has developed in the larger cities of the Donets Basin and the Dnieper Bend area, as well as in two cities along the coast of the Sea of Azov. In 1968 Ukraine still produced 56 per cent of the country's iron ore, 49 per cent of the country's pig iron, and 41

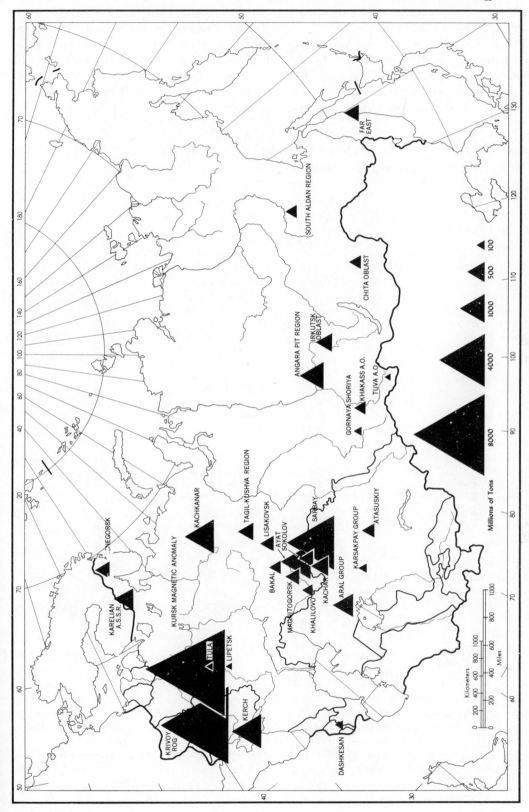

Figure 15–10   Iron ore deposits in the U.S.S.R. Data from Cherdantsev and Braun and Pokrovskiy.

per cent of the country's crude steel. (Tables 15–33, 15–34, and 15–35)

These percentages are not as high as they had been in 1928 when the Donets Basin produced about three quarters of all the pig iron production in the Soviet Union. At that time the Urals were still producing pig iron using charcoal from the local forests as fuel. With transportation costs what they were at the time relative to the costs of ores and coal, it would have been economically prohibitive to expand production in the Urals and simultaneously shift to the new technology using

Table 15–32   Iron Ore Resources by Regions, January 1, 1958, in Millions of Tons and Per Cent of Iron Content

Place	Amount	Per Cent of Iron Content (Average)	Place	Amount	Per Cent of Iron Content (Average)
1. South	3,440	39.5	2. Siberia	1,042	39.9
Krivoy Rog	3,080	39.9	Beds gravitated		
Rich ore	960	57.2	towards Kuznetsk		
Iron quartzites	1,310	34.5	and west Siberian		
Iron quartzites	810	37.8	plants:	198	40.2
Kerch Basin	360	37.3	Gornaya Shoriya	73	44.6
Brown ore	140	37.5	Khakass	76	38.9
Snuff-colored ore	220	37.2	Altay	35	38.5
2. Caucasus	33	39.9	Ampalyksk	14	32.8
3. Center	26.75	42.9	Angaro-Pit	325	40.2
K.M.A.	2,640	42.9	Angaro-Ilim	195	37.2
Rich ore	1,120	59.2	Aldan	164	44.1
Iron quartzites	1,110	35.4	Priargunsk	132	37.8
Iron quartzites	410	41.3	Others	28	38.6
Other beds	35	41.8	3. Far East	114	38.1
4. Northwest	355	30.2	4. Kazakh S.S.R.	1,972	40.3
Iron quartzites	230	33.2	Central Kazakhstan	186	50.0
Magnetites	65	31.5	Kustanay Basin	1,588	40.0
Titano-magnetites	60	23.0	Magnetite ore	663	45.6
Total West	6,503	39.7	Oolitic ore	925	36.5
			Pri-Aral beds and		
1. Urals	915	23.0	others	198	38.9
North	20	44.2	5. Central Asia	10	48.4
Tagilo-Kushvinsk	114	37.1	Total East	4,053	34.0
Alapayevsk	12	38.3			
Kachkanar	447	16.8	Total U.S.S.R.	10,556	37.3
Bakal	115	35.7			
Magnitogorsk	105	50.2			
Bashkir A.S.S.R.	38	41.3			
Orsk-Khalilovo	37	32.8			
Others	27	36.7			

Source: G. A. Braun and M. A. Pokrovskiy, *Razvitie zhelezorudnoy promyshlennosti SSSR v 1959–1965 godakh,* Moscow, 1960, pp. 37–39. The figures represent extractable reserves of industrial category only. More recent sources indicate that many ore deposits have considerably larger reserves than are shown in this table. This is particularly true for the Krivoy Rog and Kursk deposits which have been estimated to have proven reserves of as much as 30 billion metric tons and 65 billion metric tons respectively, and additional potential reserves of 20 billion and 100 billion metric tons.

Table 15–33 *Iron Ore Production in the U.S.S.R. by Regions, 1913– 1970, Selected Years, in Thousands of Metric Tons*

Basin	1913	1928	1940	1945	1958	1968	Plan 1970 [a]
U.S.S.R.	9,214	6,133	29,866	15,864	88,816	177,000	224,400
Ukraine	6,868	4,722	19,127	3,819	49,826	99,200	103,280
Krivoy Rog	6,386	4,671	17,820	3,819	46,808		83,000
Kerch	482	51	1,307		3,018		20,280
Transcaucasia (Dashkesan)					1,223	1,430	1,490
Center	561	308	1,106	469	1,736		11,340
Kursk M.A.					281		
Lipetsk	262	188	494	200	841		1,000
Tula	195	108	594	260	614		980
Other	104	12	18	9			
Northwest	3				1,697		5,890
Olenegorsk					1,697		3,470
Kovdor							1,920
Pudozhgorsk							500
Urals	1,778	1,094	8,082	10,759	27,294	27,000 [b]	40,900
Bogoslov		105	103	215	678		540
First northern base					277		
Maslov and Samsk				57	218		
Tagilo-Kushva	230	341	1,143	2,407	5,521		6,300
Blagodat	74	78	373	822	1,787		2,200
Vysokaya			745	1,585	3,054		2,530
Lebyazhinsk	156	263	25		680		740
Alapayevsk	97	120	70	106	410		500
Pervouralsk			84	150	371		490
Zlatoust (Kusinsk)			320	264	729		
Akhtensk					217		600
Bakal	269	386	430	1,271	4,387		5,890
Magnitogorsk			5,593	6,155	13,300		9,830
Orsk-Khalilovo			162		836		4,870
Beloretsk	242	89	128	134	351		
Kachkanar							11,150
Bashkir			128				460
Western Siberia	2		493	815	3,904		6,645
Kuznetsk area			493	815	3,904		2,710
Eastern Siberia	1	9		2	1,112		23,470
Abakan					1,111		1,620
Petrovsk-Zabaykalskiy	1	9		2	1		
Nizhne-Angarsk							3,400
Rudnogorsk							2,300
Sivaglinsk							1,080
Far East							1,380
Kazakh S.S.R.					2,009	17,600	32,740
Atasu (Karazhal)					729		3,500
Kustanay Oblast							26,000
Sokolov-Sarbay					1,113		9,970
Kachar							1,940

Sources: Grigorii A. Braun, *Zhelezorudnaya baza chernoy metallurgii SSSR,* 1960, pp. 260–263, 274–281, 285; Naum Jasny, "Prospects of the Soviet Iron and Steel Industry," *Soviet Studies,* January 1963, pp. 275–294; *Narodnoye khozyaystvo SSSR v 1961 godu,* Moskva, 1962, p. 196, and *v 1962 godu,* 1963; p. 149; *Promyshlennost SSSR,* 1957, Moskva, p. 116, and 1964, p. 162; *Steel in the Soviet Union,* American Iron and Steel Institute, New York, 1959, p. 28: and *Soviet Geography: Review and Translation,* March 1968, p. 222, and April 1969, p. 209. Production figures are totals of rich ore and ore concentrates, usually averaging about 60 per cent iron content.

[a] Plan made in 1958. Subsequent production figures indicate that in most cases these goals are too high.
[b] 1967.

Table 15–34   Pig Iron Production in the U.S.S.R. by Regions, 1913–1968, Selected Years, in Thousands of Metric Tons

	1913	1928	1940	1945	1955	1968
U.S.S.R.	4,216	3,282	14,902	8,803	33,310	78,800
Ukraine S.S.R.	2,893	2,361	9,642	1,647	16,607	38,600
Center [a]	200	190	1,010	476	1,908	8,800 [b]
Georgia S.S.R.					436	860
Urals	902	692	2,714	5,113	11,872	21,100 [b]
Western Siberia		5.6	1,536	1,567	2,400	5,600 [b]
Kazakh S.S.R.						1,720

Sources: Breiterman, *Ekonomicheskaya geografiya SSSR*, p. 215; Clark, *The Economics of Soviet Steel*, pp. 231 and 240; M. V. Fedorovskiy, *Chornaya metallurgiya Ukraini*, Kiev, 1960, p. 168; A. T. Khrushchev and I. V. Nikolskiy, *Razvitie i razmeshchenie promyshlennosti i transporta SSSR v semiletke*, Moscow, 1960, p. 17; V. B. Khlebnikov, *Sovetskaya chernaya metallurgiya v 1959–1965*, Moscow, 1960, pp. 62 and 63; Jasny, "Prospects of the Soviet Iron and Steel Industry," pp. 275–294; Livshits, *Razmeshcheniye chernoy metallurgii SSSR*, pp. 162, 171, 175, and 176; *Narodnoye khozyaystvo SSSR v 1962 godu*, p. 147; *Promyshlennost SSSR*, 1957, p. 112, and 1964, pp. 170–171; Lazar Roitburd, *Soviet Iron and Steel Industry*, Moscow, 1956, pp. 15, 26, 33, and 65; Stepanov, *Geografiya tyazheloy promyshlennosti SSSR*, p. 54; and *Soviet Geography: Review and Translation*, March 1968, p. 221, and April 1969, p. 209.
[a] Tula and Lipetsk until 1955. Tula, Lipetsk, and Cherepovets after 1955.
[b] 1967.

coal as a fuel. The cost of transporting coal from Kuznetsk would have been more than equal to the price of coal in the Donets Basin. In addition, the products of the steel industry in the Urals would have had to be shipped considerably farther to markets than those from the Donets Basin. Nevertheless, the Soviets proceeded to establish the Urals-Kuznetsk Combine after 1928, and made it economically feasible by arbitrarily establishing what at that time was a fantastically low rate for the rail transportation of iron ore and coal between the two large steel plants built at Magnitogorsk and Stalinsk. By building steel plants at both ends of the raw materials shuttle, it was intended that a transportation saving would be effected by utilizing the freight cars in both directions, shipping coal westward and iron ore eastward. However, these transport advantages were somewhat offset by the tying up of capital investments over a period of several years in the construction of two large steel plants instead of one, and also by the prospect of an overabundance of steel-producing capacity in the eastern regions, which, if operated to full capacity, would have to look for markets in the west, thereby necessitating other long rail hauls of products.

It was the advent of World War II, and the German occupation of much of Ukraine, that eventually justified the Urals-Kuznetsk Combine and revealed it as being absolutely vital to the survival of the country. After the war, the preferential rail rates in western Siberia were not reestablished, but by this time raw materials costs had risen so much relative to railway freight costs that the steel economy in the Urals and in the Kuznetsk Basin had become economically viable. Since 1928, while freight rates have increased about 2.5 times, the price of iron ore has risen about 7 times, pig iron 8 times, and coke 12.5 times. Thus the cheaper production of coking coal in the Kuznetsk Basin as compared to the Donets Basin has more than offset the rail costs of greater distances between the Kuznetsk and the Urals than between the Donets Basin and the Krivoy Rog iron ore. In addition, a rapidly rising market in the east during the war years and the following decade has partially alleviated the need of the eastern regions to ship their iron products westward to market. Therefore the iron and steel industries of the Urals and the Kuznetsk Basin are on a fully competitive basis with Ukraine, and in fact are generally cheaper producers than Ukraine is at the present time.

Cheaper mining costs for coal and iron ore in the eastern regions have largely offset the distance factor. With the location of raw materials thus somewhat neutralized across the country, it appears that

Table 15–35   Crude Steel Production in the U.S.S.R. by Regions, 1913–1968, Selected Years, in Thousands of Metric Tons

	1913	1928	1940	1945	1955	1968
U.S.S.R.	4,307	4,251	18,317	12,252	45,271	107,000
Ukraine S.S.R.	2,442	2,409	8,938	1,374	16,935	44,200
Rostov Oblast	288	90	501	212	931	
Center	288	378	1,485	1,129	2,605	
North (Cherepovets)				2.5	13.3	
Northwest (Leningrad)	169	190	555	162	878	
Belorussia S.S.R.			5.2		53	
Latvia S.S.R.	76		28	3.4	76	300 [a]
Lithuania S.S.R.					0.5	
Estonia S.S.R.					3.4	
Povolzhye	147	172	912	251	1,521	
Georgia S.S.R.			0.2	0.4	582	1,450
Armenia S.S.R.					0.1	
Azerbaydzhan S.S.R.		11	24	23	371	770
Urals	898	995	3,924	6,494	16,381	31,100 [b]
Western Siberia		6.3	1,870	2,408	3,857	6,800 [b]
Kazakh S.S.R.				4.6	235	1,370
Uzbek S.S.R.			11	21	211	400 [a]
Kirgiz S.S.R.					0.3	
Eastern Siberia			63	113	320	
Far East				55	250	

Sources: Breiterman, *Ekonomicheskaya geografiya SSSR,* p. 215; Clark, *The Economics of Soviet Steel,* pp. 231 and 241; Fedorovskiy, *Chornaya metallurgiya Ukraini,* Jasny, "Prospects of the Soviet Iron and Steel Industry," p. 275; Khlebnikov, *Sovetskaya chernaya metallurgiya v 1959–1965,* pp. 62 and 63; Livshits, *Razmeshcheniye chernoy metallurgii SSSR,* pp. 162, 171, 175, and 176; *Narodnoe khozyaystvo SSSR v 1961 godu,* p. 197, and *v 1962 godu,* p. 148; *Promyshlennost SSSR,* 1957, p. 112, and 1964, pp. 170–171; and *Soviet Geography: Review and Translation,* March 1968. p. 221, and April 1969, p. 209.
[a] 1966.
[b] 1967 data. Includes all of Siberia and Far East.

in the future market location will play a more decisive role in the location of iron and steel plants. The balance seems to be tipping toward the west again as metal-using industries are being expanded in old populated centers. This, together with the development of new iron deposits, has stimulated the expansion of steel plants in most of the old producing centers of Ukraine and Central Russia.

The market factor has also induced the Soviets to develop small-scale steel industries in outlying areas wherever iron ore and coking coal can be brought together. Most outstanding in this respect is the pig iron production at Cherepovets in the north and at Rustavi in Transcaucasia. Cherepovets is perhaps the only case remaining where distance might act prohibitively if strict cost accounting were adhered to. The iron ore of the Kola Peninsula and the coking coal of Vorkuta lie 3500 kilometers apart in severe climatic areas that make for high mining costs. These high-cost minerals are assembled in the steel plant at Cherepovets, which is approximately 500 kilometers away from its main markets in Leningrad. These distance factors between raw materials and plant, and plant and market, undoubtedly make the Cherepovets operation the most costly in the country. Nevertheless, the Soviets have expanded capacity at Cherepovets to make it one of the largest plants in the country, and they have opened up a new iron-mining district in the Kola Peninsula to maintain an adequate supply of raw materials. In 1969 the opening of the fourth blast furnace boosted annual pig iron capacity to 4.8 million tons. Perhaps when the Volga-Baltic waterway becomes fully operative transportation costs for the assemblage of materials at Cherepovets can be reduced by a greater utilization of water transport.

The Rustavi operation in Transcaucasia is a fairly economic one, being based on local iron ore and coking coal and serving a local market. But it is a very small operation. In 1967 the Georgian Republic produced about 1.5 per cent of the country's crude steel. (Table 15–35)

Some steel is produced in other outlying plants where pig iron production is impossible because of lack of raw materials. Examples are the Bekabad plant in Middle Asia and Komsomolsk in the Far East. (Fig. 15–11) These plants produce steel from pig iron shipped in from other areas, or metal scrap. This is true also of many plants scattered about the more populous centers of European Russia. Steel plants are considerably less tied to raw materials than are pig iron plants, and therefore the steel industry is more dispersed than is pig iron production. (Compare Tables 15–34 and 15–35.) Dispersion is even more characteristic of rolled-steel products. (Table 15–36) Such industries are generally more market oriented than are pig iron and crude steel industries. Considerable discrepancies still exist, however, between the areal distribution of the production of rolled-steel products and the consumption of these products. (Table 15–37) Obviously the Center and the Volga Regions, with their great amounts of machine-building industries and minor amounts of steel production, utilize much more steel than is produced locally, whereas Ukraine and the Urals are outstanding as suppliers of steel to the rest of the country. These two major industrial areas, together with the Kuznetsk Basin, supply all the surplus steel that is produced in the country, whereas all other regions are forced to ship in steel. It is obvious that in spite of efforts to establish small steel industries in outlying districts such as Middle Asia, the Far East, and the West, these areas still are ill supplied and their industries demand inshipments of steel products which entail long rail hauls.

Recent Developments and Prospects for the Future

The better grade ores of Krivoy Rog and Magnitogorsk have largely run out, and

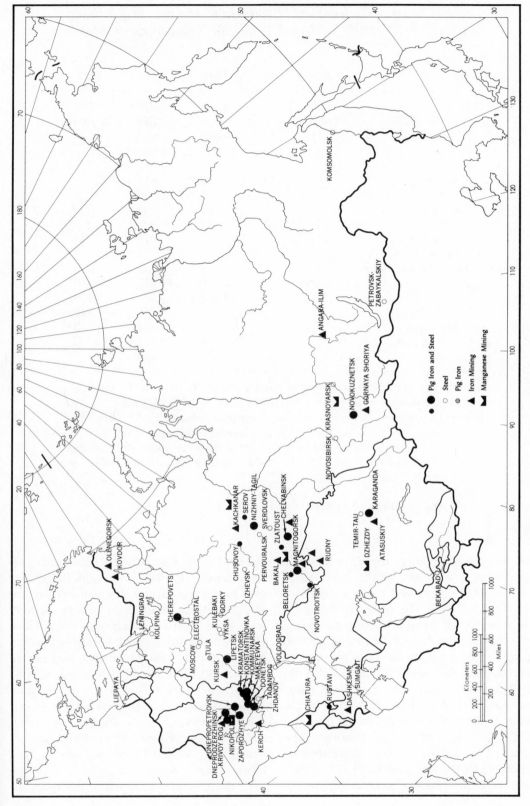

Figure 15–11   Iron and steel industry.

Table 15–36   Rolled-Steel Production in the U.S.S.R. by Regions, 1913–1967, Selected Years, in Thousands of Metric Tons

Region	1913	1928	1940	1955	1967
U.S.S.R.	3,509	3,433	13,113	35,339	70,500
Ukraine S.S.R.	2,087	1,995	6,520	13,610	30,600
Rostov Oblast	221	28	333	693	
Center	203	290	944	1,597	
North				0.7	
Northwest	217	99	488	817	
Belorussia S.S.R.			4.1	31	
Latvia S.S.R.			24	103	300 [a]
Povolzhye	123	127	584	903	
Georgia S.S.R.				578	1,170
Armenia S.S.R.				1.9	
Azerbaydzhan S.S.R.		6.9	8.5	23	700
Urals	659	882	2,816	12,577	20,000 [a]
Western Siberia		5.4	1,370	3,549	5,900 [b]
Kazakh S.S.R.				235	1,340
Uzbek S.S.R.				142	300 [a]
Eastern Siberia			23	321	
Far East				158	

Sources: Bannyy, *Ekonomika chernoy metallurgii SSSR,* p. 107; Khlebnikov, *Sovetskaya chernaya metallurgiya v 1959–1965,* pp. 62–63; Khrushchev and Nikolskiy. *Razvitie i razmeshchenie promyshlennosti i transporta SSSR v semiletke,* pp. 16 and 17; Livshits, *Razmeshchenie chernoy metallurgii SSSR,* p. 162; *Narodnoe khozyaystvo SSSR v 1962 godu,* p. 148; *Promyshlennost SSSR,* 1957, pp. 106 and 114, and 1964, pp. 170–171; and *Soviet Geography: Review and Translation,* March 1968, p. 221.

[a] 1966.

[b] 1966 data. Includes all of Siberia and the Far East.

the Soviets have gone to the wide-scale development of lower grade ores which have to be concentrated for blast furnace use. (Table 15–38) In order to maintain costs of ore at approximately the same level, the Soviets have switched more and more to open-pit methods of mining in near-surface deposits. (Table 15–39) By 1970 it is planned that more than three quarters of all the iron ore mined in the Soviet Union will be mined by the open-pit method and 80 per cent of this ore will be enriched by the use of huge concentrators which crush the ore and wash it to eliminate large quantities of gangue before it is shipped long distances to blast furnaces. Fortunately for the Soviets, as the richer ores have run out, new discoveries of seemingly limitless deposits of low-grade iron ores have been found close to the surface along an extensive north-south belt in the Eastern Urals, western Siberia, and northern Kazakhstan, as well as in areas peripheral to the Krivoy Rog Basin in Ukraine. In addition, the Soviets have largely solved the problem of water-logged overlying strata in the Kursk Magnetic Anomaly which has allowed them to open up that large rich ore deposit.

In the east Urals region, it has been re-

Table 15–37   The Distribution of the Production and Consumption of Rolled Steel in the U.S.S.R., by Major Regions, 1955, in Millions of Tons

Region	Production	Consumption	Surplus or Deficit
U.S.S.R.	35.3	33.8	+1.5
Ukraine S.S.R. and Rostov Oblast	14.3	7.8	+6.5
Center	1.6	6.7	−5.1
Northwest	0.8	1.4	−0.6
West	0.1	1.1	−1.0
Povolzhye	0.9	4.9	−4.0
Transcaucasia	0.6	0.6	0.0
Urals	12.6	5.7	+6.9
Western Siberia	3.5	2.4	+1.1
Kazakhstan and Middle Asia	0.4	1.0	−0.6
Eastern Siberia	0.3	0.5	−0.2
Far East	0.2	0.4	−0.2
Other	−	1.3	−1.3

Source: Complied from data presented in Table 15–36 and in Livshits, *Razmeshchenie chernoy metallurgii SSSR,* p. 302.

ported that 38 different deposits of iron ore have been discovered in the Turgay Lowland in Kustanay Oblast in Kazakhstan. Beneficiating plants have already been built and production has started at Sokolov-Sarbay, and Lisakov is under construction. The development of these ores, just as it appeared that supplies for the Urals and the Kuznetsk Basin were in danger of running out, has prompted the expansion of the Magnitogorsk plant to approximately double its original capacity, to about 12 million tons per year; the construction of the so-called West Siberian Plant at Novokuznetsk with an ultimate capacity of 5.5 million tons per year; and the completion of the Karaganda plant whose construction had been lagging for more than a decade.* The West Siberian Plant, situated at Antonovo, on the right bank of the Tom River just northeast of Novokuznetsk, opened its first blast furnace in July 1964. Like the older Kuznetsk plant at Novokuznetsk, it uses iron ore from nearby mines in the Gornaya-Shoriya area and from Zheleznogorsk east of Bratsk.

A similar development of low-grade ore is taking place in the Kachkanar deposit in the Northern Urals where 16 per cent ore is being concentrated and converted into naturally alloyed iron-vanadium concentrate to supply new oxygen converters at Nizhniy-Tagil, Chelyabinsk, and Chusovoy. Further north deep shaft mines have been sunk into the north Peschanka iron ore basin to replace several small deposits that in the past have supplied the Serov iron and steel industry. In the Southern Urals a large blast furnace has been established at Novotroitsk to utilize the naturally alloyed nickel-chrome-iron ore from the nearby Khalilovo mines.

With the shift of emphasis back toward the west, the Soviets have expanded many of the old plants in Ukraine and Central Russia. Outstanding among these is the development of the nation's second largest plant at Krivoy Rog which is to have an ultimate capacity of about 8 million tons of pig iron per year. This construction has coincided with the development of a series of huge concentrating plants to process iron quartzites with a metal content of about 35 per cent which make up a large part of the Krivoy Rog reserves. In 1966 about half of the Krivoy Rog ore was concentrated before it was shipped to blast furnaces. South of the Krivoy Rog Basin, the high-grade Belozerka iron ore deposit was discovered in the middle 1950s on the left bank of the Dnieper about 45 miles south-southwest of Zaporozhye. Operations began here in October 1967 around the new mining town of Dneprorudnoye which was founded in 1963 on the south shore of the Kakhovka Reservoir.

In the Central Black Earth Region mining of high-grade ore deposits began at the town of Gubkin in 1959 and at Zheleznogorsk in 1960 to supply the large new iron

* These compare to capacities of 8 million tons at Gary, Ind., and 6 million tons at Sparrows Point, Md.

Table 15–38 The Amount of Iron Ore Which Has Undergone Enrichment and Its Per Cent of Total Iron Ore Production, by Regions, 1940–1970, Selected Years

Regions and Principal Deposits	1940 Amount in 1000 Tons	Per Cent	1955 Amount in 1000 Tons	Per Cent	1960(Plan) Amount in 1000 Tons	Per Cent	1970(Plan) Amount in 1000 Tons	Per Cent
Western Regions of the U.S.S.R.								
Southern Region	1,850	9.4	8,117	18.8	23,880	36.0	102,550	68.7
Krivoy Rog	0	0	4,267	10.9	17,980	29.8	67,550	59.1
Transcaucasia	–	–	1,150	100	1,810	100	2,400	100
Central Region	0	0	550	26.4	2,220	41.7	8,880	59.2
Kursk Magnetic Anomaly	–	–	550	100	2,220	59.7	7,700	60.1
Northwest Region	–	–	1,190	100	4,440	100	13,550	100
Total for Western Regions	1,850	8.9	11,007	23.1	32,350	41.5	127,380	70.7
Eastern Regions of the U.S.S.R.								
Urals Region	3,462	33.8	25,399	71.5	32,270	78.5	93,660	90.9
Magnitogorsk Kombinat	607	10.4	10,682	69.6	13,490	80.8	14,200	97.3
Western Siberia Region	477	77.0	3,070	62.8	6,880	97.2	5,950	96.7
Eastern Siberia Region	–	–	–	–	1,950	99.7	30,275	81.6
Far East Region	–	–	–	–	–	–	2,270	100
Kazakh S.S.R.	–	–	0	0	5,150	73.6	48,460	90.3
Karaganda Oblast	–	–	0	0	5,150		44,860	–
Kustanay Oblast	–	–	–	–	0		3,600	43.3
Total for Eastern Regions	3,939	36.2	28,469	70.1	46,250	80.9	180,615	89.3
Total, U.S.S.R.	5,789	18.3	39,476	44.8	78,600	58.2	307,995	80.5

Source: Braun, Zhelezorudnaya baza chernoy metallurgii SSSR, pp. 196–197.

Table 15–39 Amounts of Iron Ore Mined by the Open-Pit Method and Per Cents of Total Amounts, by Regions of the U.S.S.R., 1940–1970, Selected Years

Regions and Principal Deposits	1940		1955		1960 (Plan)		1970 (Plan)	
	Amount 1000 Tons	Per Cent	Amount 1000 Tons	Per Cent	Amount 1000 Tons	Per Cent	Amount 1000 Tons	Per Cent
Western Regions of the U.S.S.R.								
Krivoy Rog Basin	0	0	2,990	7.6	15,100	25.0	57,300	50.2
Kerch Basin	1,850	100	3,850	100	5,900	100	35,000	100
Transcaucasia	–	–	1,150	100	1,810	100	2,400	100
Central Region	150	13.5	310	14.9	1,920	36.1	5,700	38.1
Kursk Magnetic Anomaly	–	–	0	0	1,500	40.4	5,100	39.8
Northwest Region	–	–	1,190	100	4,440	100	13,550	100
Total for Western Regions	2,000	9.6	9,490	20.0	29,170	37.4	113,950	63.2
Eastern Regions of the U.S.S.R.								
Urals	9,460	92.3	33,203	88.5	33,480	81.2	94,490	91.0
Tagilo-Kushvinsk Region	2,245	90.2	7,659	78.5	6,200	56.8	4,000	41.4
Bakal Iron Ore Administration	440	100	3,533	85.5	4,200	87.5	3,400	56.6
Western Siberia	320	51.7	1,200	24.6	1,100	15.5	500	8.1
Eastern Siberia	–	–	4	100	1,955	100	33,720	90.8
Far East	–	–	–	–	–	–	2,270	100
Kazakh S.S.R.	–	–	237	100	7,010	100	50,450	93.9
Karaganda Oblast	–	–	–	–	1,200	100	6,000	72.3
Kustanay Oblast	–	–	237	100	5,810	100	44,450	98.0
Total for Eastern Regions	9,780	89.9	34,644	81.0	43,545	76.0	181,430	89.4
Total, U.S.S.R.	11,780	37.2	44,134	48.9	72,715	53.8	295,380	77.1

Source: Braun, Zhelezorudnaya baza chernoy metallurgii SSSR, pp. 191–192.

517

and steel plants under development at the old steel centers of Lipetsk and Tula. At the present time large concentrators are being constructed at both of these sites to utilize 30 per cent iron quartzites which make up one of the largest deposits in the Soviet Union. In fact, it is now speculated that the total reserves of the Kursk Magnetic Anomaly exceed those of the Krivoy Rog Basin. These ores are admirably located to serve the needs of the heavily populated Central Industrial Region and to supply ore concentrates to the east European satellites, thereby alleviating the burden on the Krivoy Rog Basin. By 1980 it is planned that the Kursk Magnetic Anomaly will be providing 135 million metric tons of ore concentrate, which is 50 per cent more than the Krivoy Rog Basin was producing in 1967. The Lipetsk iron and steel plant is being enlarged into one of the largest in the country, and in addition fairly precise plans have been worked out for a completely new plant to be located somewhere within the Kursk Magnetic Anomaly that will exceed in capacity the Magnitogorsk mill. It is also planned that a city with a population of around 350,000 will be located next to the plant. Eventually, it would seem logical that ore from the Kursk Magnetic Anomaly would move northward to Cherepovets to replace higher cost ores coming down from the Kola Peninsula. At the moment, however, nothing has been said about that, and the Soviets are going ahead with the expansion of the Olenegorsk operation in the Kola Peninsula with the completion of a large concentrator, and the opening of a new mine at Kovdor to the southwest.

Ferroalloys The Soviet Union is well supplied with most of the ferroalloys, particularly the most important of them, manganese, which is a necessary ingredient of all types of steel. Both of the world's largest deposits of manganese lie in the Soviet Union, one at Nikopol on the Dnieper in Ukraine, and the other at Chiatura in the Colchis Lowland of Georgia. These two deposits alone account for about two thirds of the world's production. For years Chiatura was the major producer, but as the high-grade Georgian ores became depleted in the late 1950s production at Chiatura declined from 3.05 million metric tons in 1960 to 1.7 million tons in 1968. Consequently the Soviets have relied increasingly on lower-grade ores, which are much more abundant in the Nikopol deposit. The establishment of large concentrators in that area have facilitated the increase of manganese production in the Nikopol Basin from 2.7 million tons in 1960 to 4.7 million tons in 1968. A few hundred thousand tons are produced by small mines in the Urals, Siberia, and Kazakhstan. Until the late 1940s the Soviet Union was a major supplier of manganese to the United States, but since then the United States has had to look elsewhere. Of its annual production of 7–8 million tons, the Soviet Union now exports about 1 million tons, mainly to its east European allies and selected west European countries.

Nickel and chromium are scattered up and down the Urals, with some of the most significant deposits having only recently been discovered in the southern Urals in the Orsk-Khalilovo area. Besides the production in the Urals, nickel is produced on the Kola Peninsula and at Norilsk along the Lower Yenisey where a boom town of more than 150,000 people has sprung up in the Arctic tundra. The Soviet Union annually is the second most important producer of nickel in the world, after Canada, producing about one sixth of the world's nickel, and it accounts for about one third of the world's production of chromium. It still ships about 200,000 tons of chromium per year to the United States, which purchases approximately one third of all Soviet chromium exports.

Titanium also is scattered rather widely in the Urals. Since the late 1950s alluvial placers in Ukraine have become the major source of titanium. The largest deposit of molybdenum in the country is in the North Caucasus in the Kabardino-Balkar A.S.S.R. Lesser deposits of molybdenum, as well as deposits of tungsten, are scattered through the mountains of Middle Asia, southern Siberia, and the Far East. Recently impressive deposits of tungsten and molybdenum have been discovered in Kazakhstan primarily in the Tyan Shans, north of Lake Balkhash, and in the Rudnyy Altay. Important deposits of tungsten also exist in the Urals. The Soviet Union is regularly the third largest producer of tungsten in the world after China and the United States, producing about one ninth of the world's supply.

Nonferrous Metallurgy

Soviet data on the production of nonferrous metals are the most conspicuous omission in the handbooks of statistics released since 1956. For some reason the Soviets have not reported many data on total productions for various nonferrous metals and they have not reported any data on regional distributions of production. Enough information has been gleaned from scattered sources, however, to make some generalizations.

It appears that the Soviet Union is well supplied with virtually all the nonferrous metals needed by a modern industrial economy. These metals are located primarily in old crystalline rock areas in Kazakhstan, the Urals, and the Kola Peninsula and in pockets among the younger more rugged mountains of the Caucasus, Middle Asia, western Siberia, the Transbaykal area and Maritime Kray in the Far East. So far the Urals have been outstanding in their production of nonferrous metals, but Kazakhstan seems to have the potential to be the prime producer of many of these metals, and the Urals are becoming more important for the production of iron. In general, the

nonferrous ores in Kazakhstan are found in the Mugodzhar Mountains in the northwest, the Kazakh Folded Country in the center, the Rudnyy Altay in the east, and in the Tyan Shans in the south. Most recently, important bauxite ores have been discovered in the Turgay Lowland in northcentral Kazakhstan.

Copper The Russian area has had a long history of copper production. It has been reported that as early as 1700 Russia accounted for 3000 tons of the total world output of 15,000 tons, and around 1750 Russia exported copper. In 1913 Russia produced 33,700 tons and imported 7900. This decreased during World War I and it did not pick up again until 1928. Although no precise figures have been given, estimates put U.S.S.R. copper production in 1964 at 770,000 tons, which compares to a production of 1,247,000 in the United States during that year. Apparently the Soviets are producing enough copper to supply themselves and in addition are exporting some to their east European satellites. Soviet sources claim that the U.S.S.R. now has more known reserves of copper than any other country in the world.

Initially most of the known reserves were in a north-south belt along the Eastern Urals, but as new discoveries have been made it has become apparent that copper deposits occur in many regions of the country, and three or four large deposits in the Kazakh S.S.R. might total more reserves than those in the Urals. Around 1960 it was estimated that the Kazakh Republic probably contained more than half of the U.S.S.R. copper reserves, but now it appears that vast new deposits have been discovered in Chita Oblast east of Lake Baykal which might have reserves equal to or greater than those of either Kazakhstan or the Urals. In addition, significant copper deposits are located in Transcaucasia, the North Caucasus, eastern Uzbekistan, the Kola Peninsula, and northcentral Siberia around Norilsk. (Fig. 15–12)

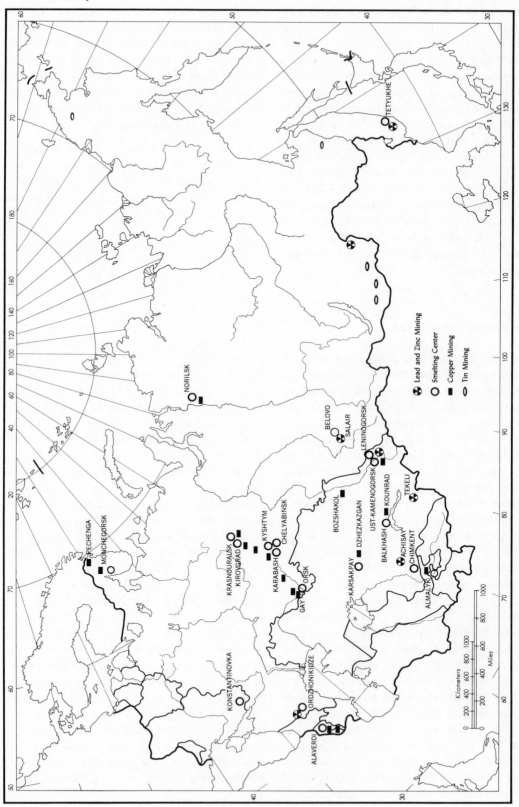

Figure 15–12   Copper, lead, zinc, and tin mining and smelting.

The Urals are still first in copper production in the country. Early development was concentrated around the cities of Krasnouralsk, Karabash, Kyshtym, and several other smaller towns in the middle Urals, but since 1960 emphasis has shifted southward to a large new deposit at Gay which has a 10 per cent copper content, the highest in the country. A large new smelter has been established at the new town of Mednogorsk just west of Gay. Copper-smelting plants have been undergoing expansion throughout the Urals, and some of the plants in the Central Urals are now bringing in ores from the southern Urals and from Dzhezkazgan in central Kazakhstan.

The copper reserves at Dzhezkazgan are reportedly the largest proven reserves of copper in the U.S.S.R. They exist in 16 separate deposits, many of which have fairly high copper content and lie near or at the surface and therefore afford cheap exploitation by open-pit methods. The deposits at Dzhezkazgan have only recently been exploited, and until a new smelter was built at Karsakpay the ores were shipped to older smelters at Balkhash on the northern coast of Lake Balkhash and to smelters in the Urals.

The Balkhash smelter has been in operation for a number of years, utilizing copper ore from the large open-pit mine at Kounrad just to the east. The Kounrad ores are huge deposits of copper porphory which contain only 0.4–1.5 per cent copper, but the ores are concentrated in small areas and are cheaply extracted by open-pit methods and cheaply processed. They also yield molybdenum and some other rare metals. A similar deposit has recently been discovered near Bozshakul in northeastern Kazakhstan. Large copper porphory deposits have also been discovered at Almalyk 80 kilometers south of Tashkent in the western foothills of the Tyan Shans. These ores are being exploited by a polymetallic combine that was built during the early 1960s.

Armenia has been a traditional copper producer. Its copper reserves are now estimated at about 35 million tons which constitute about 10 per cent of the known reserves of the U.S.S.R. The major deposit is at Alaverdi, where a copper-chemical combine is in operation. Other deposits exist in southeastern Armenia. A copper combine has been established at Kafan in eastern Armenia to ship copper concentrates by rail to the smelter in Alaverdi. This ore also contains molybdenum, and copper-molybdenum combines are being constructed in Agarak and Kadzharan in eastern Armenia. Copper is also produced in conjunction with nickel at Monchegorsk and Pechenga in the Kola Peninsula and at Norilsk in central Siberia.

At present there is considerable discrepancy between the distribution of copper ores and the distribution of smelters. In 1965 the eastern regions accounted for 88 per cent of all U.S.S.R. copper production. Much of the consumption, of course, was in the European part of the country where rapid electrification and expansion of machine building tremendously increased the demand for copper products. Undoubtedly the bulk of production will remain in the Urals and Kazakhstan, with secondary concentrations in Armenia, Uzbekistan, and the Kola Peninsula.

The Almalyk copper smelter in 1963 began turning out metallic molybdenum and tungsten as by-products, and since that time the Uzbek Republic has become the leading producer of these two important metals.

Lead and Zinc Lead and zinc are often found in the same ore, commonly in association with other metals such as gold, silver, and copper. The Soviet Union appears to be well supplied with lead and zinc. It is regularly the second producer of lead in the world after the United States, producing about one eighth of the world's supply, and second after the United States in the production of zinc with about one tenth of the world's production.

The Kazakh Republic apparently contains about one half the lead and zinc deposits of the Soviet Union. These deposits occur primarily in the Altay Region around Leninogorsk and in the Tyan Shans in the vicinity of Chimkent. Other important producing centers are in the vicinity of Ordzhonikidze in the Osetian A.S.S.R. in the northern Caucasus and at Tetyukhe in the Sikhote-Alin Mountains in Maritime Kray in the Far East. Primary lead-producing plants in the Soviet Union are at Chimkent, which reportedly is the largest smelter in all of Eurasia, at Leninogorsk, at Ordzhonikidze, and at Tetyukhe.

Zinc is produced in all these areas and also in the Urals and in the Salair Ridge west of the Kuznetsk Basin. The zinc ore of the Urals is found in combination with copper, but at all other places it is found in combination with lead. The lead smelters are located near the ore, but zinc processing is concentrated in regions of abundant cheap electric power. The first zinc plant was established in Ordzhonikidze to utilize hydroelectric power produced by dams on headwaters of the Terek River. It has been reported that before World War II Ordzhonikidze produced about 37 per cent of the zinc in the U.S.S.R. Then two plants were established at Konstantinovka in the Donets Basin and at Belovo in the Kuznetsk Basin to utilize cheap thermal electric power in these coal basins. Later, plants were constructed at Chelyabinsk, utilizing electric power generated by steam using the low-grade lignite, and at Ust-Kamenogorsk in the Rudnyy Altay, utilizing hydroelectric power.

Aluminum The large-scale production and use of aluminum is a relatively recent development in the Soviet Union. Before World War II its use was limited and imports supplied much of what was needed. During and since the war production in the Soviet Union has probably jumped at least twenty times until now the Soviet Union apparently is the third largest producer in the world after the United States and Canada, producing about one sixth of the world's supply. In 1965 its production was estimated at more than 1,000,000 tons, which is apparently more than adequate for the present needs of the Soviet Union, since about one fifth of it was exported. The recent expansion of production has been accompanied by the surveying and opening of many new deposits of various aluminum ores: bauxite, alunite, nephelite, and sillimanite. The Soviet Union has been a pioneer in the utilization of ores other than bauxite, and is still experimenting with the processing of certain ores, which is delaying completion of some new alumina plants.

Aluminum production started in the Soviet Union in 1932 at Volkov east of Leningrad to utilize bauxite mined nearby at Boksitogorsk and hydroelectricity produced by the new power plant on the Volkov River. Shortly thereafter another aluminum plant was established at the Dnieper Dam, and alumina, an intermediate product, was shipped from Boksitogorsk to the Dnieper for final processing. The production of aluminum is a two-stage process, the first of which usually is carried on near the mines where the ore is smelted into alumina. The reduction process from alumina to aluminum requires large amounts of electricity and usually is done near large and cheap sources of electricity. The intermediate product, alumina, is often shipped over considerable distances to areas of abundant electricity and to markets for conversion into the final product, aluminum.

The plants at Volkov and Zaporozhye largely were destroyed during World War II, and the deposits of bauxite at Boksitogorsk were rapidly running out anyway. Since the war, both plants have been reconstructed and enlarged, and the bauxite of Boksitogorsk is supplemented about 80 per cent by nephelite from the Kola

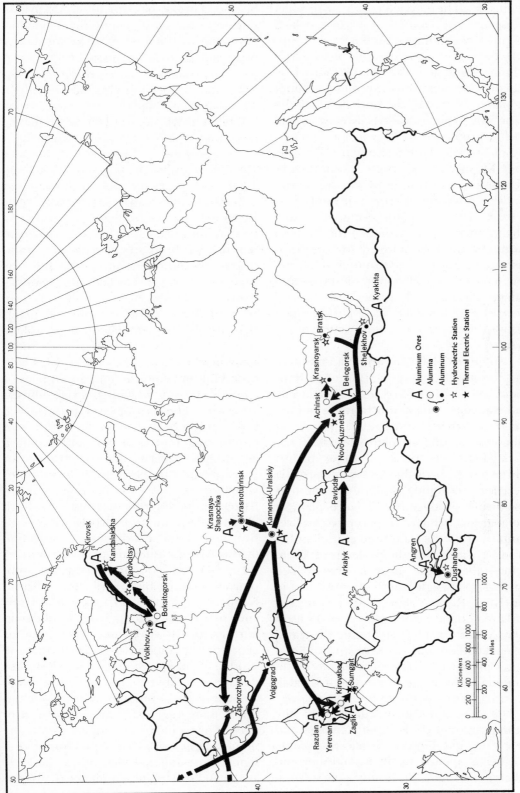

Figure 15-13   Aluminum resources and production. Compiled from Shabad, Theodore, The Soviet Aluminum Industry, American Metal Market, New York, October 1958, and other scattered sources.

Peninsula. The nephelite is a by-product of apatite ores mined at Kirovsk which originally was dumped on the waste heaps.

In the meantime operations in the Urals eclipsed those at Volkov and Zaporozhye. Bauxite ores were discovered in a number of places in the Urals, but the chief deposit was the so-called Krasnaya-Shapochka group north of Serov. Large smelting plants were built at Kamensk-Uralskiy and Krasnoturinsk. Both alumina and aluminum are produced at Kamensk-Uralskiy, utilizing electricity produced by a thermal power plant using low-grade Chelyabinsk coal, but some of the alumina produced there is shipped to Transcaucasia to be transformed to aluminum using cheap hydroelectric power of the Sevan-Zanga Cascade at Yerevan and thermal electricity at Sumgait. It is also shipped eastward to new aluminum plants in Siberia.

Two newer plants in the Kola Peninsula and the Karelian areas started operations about 1955. These are the Kandalaksha and Nadvoitsy plants which utilize nephelite from Kirovsk and bauxite from Boksitogorsk. Abundant hydroelectricity has dictated the locations of these plants. Three dams across the Niva River provide electricity to Kandalaksha. Aluminum is also being produced in a large plant at Volgograd, which apparently utilizes alumina from the Urals and abundant hydroelectricity from the Volgograd Dam.

Recently alunite deposits have been opened up at Zaglik south of Kirovabad in the Kura River Valley of Transcaucasia and an alumina plant began operations in 1966 at Kirovabad. The alumina is transformed to aluminum at Yerevan and Sumgait. Construction is now under way on an alumina plant at the new town of Razdan in Armenia to process local nephelite ores.

The geographical distribution of the aluminum industry is rapidly changing as new ores and huge hydroelectric plants are being opened up in Kazakhstan and Siberia. The most promising ores seem to be the Turgay bauxite near Arkalyk in northern Kazakhstan and the Belogorsk nephelite in the Kuznetsk Alatau. Other ores exist at nearby Goryachegorsk, and Krasnooktyabrskiy in northern Kazakhstan, in southern Kazakhstan, and in Transbaykalia. (Fig. 15–13)

The Arkalyk deposit is now supplying an alumina plant in Pavlodar which went into commercial production in November 1964 after a pilot plant between 1962 and 1964 had perfected the technology of processing the high silica bauxite. The Belogorsk nephelite will be processed in a new alumina plant at Achinsk, whose opening date has been greatly delayed by difficulties encountered in processing the Belogorsk ore. Eventually the Achinsk plant is to be the principal alumina supplier to the huge new aluminum plants that are now in production at Novokuznetsk, Krasnoyarsk, Bratsk, and Shelekhov near Irkutsk. These new plants have been built in response to large supplies of cheap electricity which would go unused otherwise. The Krasnoyarsk plant, which is the largest of its kind in the world, went into operation in June 1964 and is to have an ultimate capacity of 400,000 tons per year sometime in the early 1970s. Another very large plant began operation near the Anzeb railroad station in a western suburb of the new famous hydroelectric city of Bratsk in 1966. Pending the completion of the Achinsk alumina plant, all four of these Siberian aluminum plants are shipping in alumina by rail all the way from Kamensk and Krasnoturinsk in the Urals and, to a lesser extent, from Pavlodar in northeastern Kazakhstan. This is a rather expensive operation. It is obvious that the sudden overexpansion of electrical production in Siberia has pulled a large amount of the aluminum industry out into this remote region before adequate supplies of ore could be developed. Eventually things might work themselves out to present a more rational picture economically as the Achinsk plant eliminates the necessity of bringing in Urals alumina and the Pavlodar plant is developed into a complete alumina-aluminum operation. In the meantime the eastward shift of aluminum production has run far ahead of the eastward shift of alumina production. It has been reported that in 1967 aluminum plants in Siberia accounted for 48 per cent of the total U.S.S.R. production, whereas the only operating alumina plant in the eastern regions, at Pavlodar, produced 18 per cent of the country's alumina.

One other prospect for aluminum production lies in the far south in the Tadzhik Republic where completion of the high Nurek Dam on the Vakhsh River presents the prospect of an over-abundance of electricity in the near future. In 1964 detailed plans were laid for the Regar aluminum plant to be built in the Dushanbe area to process ore to be derived from the coal-mining operation at Angren. The plant is now under construction.

Other Minerals The Soviet Union has developed what appears to be an adequate supply of uranium for its nuclear energy and weapons programs since 1950. Before then it was heavily dependent on some of its east European satellites. Main Soviet producing areas lie in the Tyan Shan Mountains of Middle Asia. Uranium is also recovered from some of the Krivoy Rog iron operation around the town of Zheltyye Vody (yellow water) in Ukraine and from the oil shale operation in Estonia.

Titanium and magnesium are now being produced at Ust-Kamenogorsk in eastern Kazakhstan, as well as in Ukraine. Asbestos is produced in old mines in the Urals and at a new mine in the Tuva A.S.S.R. Total Soviet production in 1964 was more than 1 million tons, which was a good share of world production. A new mercury mine opened in the Chukchi N.O. of far northeastern U.S.S.R. in 1967 adds to older production in the Donets Basin of Ukraine and in the Kirgiz S.S.R. Tin min-

ing has been started at Solnechnyy, a new town 35 miles west-northwest of Komsomolsk-on-Amur. This might eventually alleviate some of the present Soviet dependence on China and Southeast Asia for tin.

The Soviet Union is probably the world's second largest producer of gold, after South Africa. This has proved to be a very handy commodity to facilitate foreign trade within the limits of self-imposed bilateral arrangements and precisely structured world trading relations where the ruble has no real value. Main production at present occurs in eastern Siberia and the Far East, but older mines still produce in the Urals and other mountain areas, and newly discovered lode deposits are becoming important in Kazakhstan. In many cases, silver occurs in association with the gold.

Many other minerals are found in the huge expanse of the Soviet territory. The Soviet Union is probably the best mineral endowed country in the world.

Chemical Industries

During the last decade the greatest increase in capital investment in all industries has been in the chemical industries. This was in response to a serious lag in this important sector of industry. A rapid expansion of this field was needed not only to supply the needs of other industries but also to partially solve the demand for more and better consumer products made out of plastics and synthetics which are so common in Western markets.

The Soviets do not publish detailed statistics on most of their chemical industries; but it would be difficult to assess the total chemical production and to compare it with that of other countries anyway, because the raw materials, processes, and products are so varied. The major categories of finished products are mineral fertilizers, synthetic rubber, artificial and synthetic fibers, plastics, paints and dyes, soaps and detergents, insecticides and weed killers, pharmaceuticals, and various products for use in industries, such as chemicals for use in oil refining and metallurgy. The chief intermediate substances for the production of these products are sulfuric acid, nitric acid, hydrochloric acid, ammonia, soda ash, caustic soda, chemical pulp, and various polymers. The basic raw materials for these intermediate products are natural gas and oil by-product gases, petroleum, coal tars and gases, sulfur and pyrites, phosphorite and apatites, potassium salts, sodium chloride and sodium sulfate, wood waste, and various vegetable products, such as potato and grain alcohol.

Some idea of the relative world position of the U.S.S.R. in chemicals can be gained from a comparison of productions of the intermediate products by leading countries for which data are available. Of these intermediate products perhaps the most important to the entire chemical complex is sulfuric acid. Large quantities are used in the production of rayon; in the metallurgical processing of copper, cobalt, nickel, platinum, and silver; in the production of galvanizing elements; in the production of oil products; in the processing of starches and sugar; in the production of dyes; in the tanning of hides; and for many other uses. In the production of sulfuric acid the Soviet Union is now second in the world but it still produces only 37 per cent as much as the United States, which is not much of a relative gain since 1960. (Table 15-8)

Soda is the second most important chemical material. Calcined soda, or soda ash, is used in the production of a great array of chemical products and also in the production of soap, glass, textiles, leather, paper, and many other things. Caustic soda is used in the production of such things as artificial fibers and organic dyes. The U.S.S.R. now produces about 60 per cent as much soda ash as the U.S.A. does and only 20 per cent as much caustic

soda. In the chemical applications of pulp the U.S.S.R. with its great supply of wood lags behind Canada and Sweden and is only slightly ahead of Finland.

Sulfuric acid in the Soviet Union is produced from pyrites (45 per cent), native sulfur (25 per cent), smelter gases (24 per cent), and oil refinery hydrogen sulfide (6 per cent). The three main plants producing sulfuric acid in the U.S.S.R. are at Konstantinovka in the Donets Basin, at Leningrad, and at Voskresensk south of Moscow, all of which produce it as a by-product from coking and metallurgical industries. But there are many other plants producing sulfuric acid from various sources. Many sulfur deposits occur in the republics of Middle Asia and along the foothills of the Carpathians, and pyrites are scattered abundantly through the Urals and, to some extent, along the Middle Volga. Gypsum deposits are found primarily in the Southern Urals, the Caucasus, and the Carpathians, with lesser deposits near Kuybyshev and Kerch and in the North Caspian Lowland. Ammonium sulfate production for the mineral fertilizer industries is concentrated in the heavy industry towns of the Donets-Dnieper Bend area, in all of the heavily industrialized cities of the Middle and Southern Urals, and at Novokuznetsk in the Kuznetsk Basin. (Fig. 15-14)

Soda is produced primarily from sodium chloride and Glauber's salt. The two main plants producing soda in the Soviet Union are at Slavyansk in the Donets Basin and at Berezniki on the Upper Kama River, which utilize the rich underground deposits of rock salt at Artemovsk and at Solikamsk respectively. A new soda works has been established at the city of Sterlitamak, south of Ufa, since World War II to utilize the salt deposits at Iletsk. Other soda works of lesser size utilize the surface deposits of sodium chloride and Glauber's salt at Lakes Baskunchak and Elton in the North Caspian Lowland, of Kara-Bogaz-Gol, of Aralsulfat, and of the Kulunda

Steppe in the vicinity of Tavolzhan, as well as underground deposits in the Carpathian foothills.

So far, most chemical industries have been connected with the coking and metallurgical industries in Ukraine, the Urals, and the Kuznetsk Basin and in the manufacturing and marketing complexes of the Moscow and Leningrad areas. It can be assumed that construction of new plants will continue in these areas and also that new plants will be constructed in new areas, mainly those of gas production and of oil production and refining. This will allow for the use of the most valuable and cheapest raw materials; gases from oil extracting and refining, natural gas, and products of the coke-chemical industry. The largest quantities of these raw ma-

terials are in eastern and western Ukraine, central European Russia, the Urals, the Kuznetsk Basin, the Caucasus, and in Middle Asia near Bukhara. The new network of pipelines will facilitate the utilization of oil and gas products outside of the areas of their production, thus allowing for new chemical complexes to be located in such places as Omsk and Krasnoyarsk in Siberia; Moscow, Leningrad, Novgorod and Novomoskovsk in European Russia; and Volzhskiy and Togliatti on the Volga.

Besides the plants located near oil and gas, coal, or large industrial complexes, there are chemical enterprises located near special sources of raw materials. Several of these represent some of the oldest chemical combines in the country. Examples are the Apatite Mining and

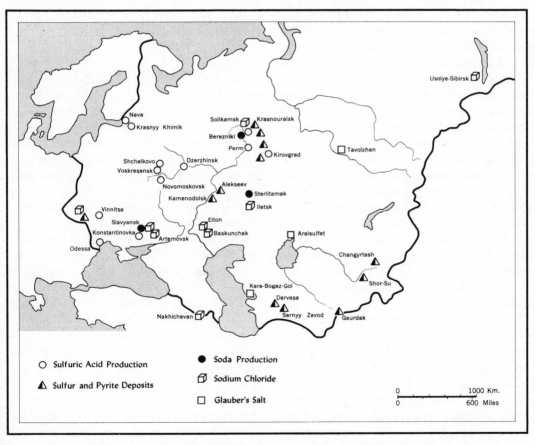

Figure 15–14   The production of sulfuric acid and soda. After Shabad and Lydolph.

Chemical Combine in the Kola Peninsula, the Berezniki and Solikamsk potassium combines, nitrogen and superphosphate plants in the Urals, and the Artemovsk and Baskunchak sodium chloride works in the Donets Basin and the North Caspian Lowland.

Mineral Fertilizers   The mineral fertilizers — phosphates, potash, and nitrogen — are based on apatite and phosphorite deposits, potassium salts, sulfur and pyrites for the production of superphosphates, and coking and oil refinery gases for nitrogen synthesis. The Soviet Union is well endowed with these necessary resources; the Soviets claim now to hold first place in the world in deposits of potassium salts and natural sulfur and to own one third of the phosphate reserves in the world. They intend to put these enormous resources to use immediately to offset the effects of a long history of notoriously poor use of mineral fertilizers. Until recently supplies have been so short that mineral fertilizers have been applied primarily only to cotton, sugar beets, tea, and some other industrial crops. Although production has expanded rapidly during the last 15 years, total mineral fertilizer production in the U.S.S.R. is still less than 70 per cent that of the U.S.A., and it must supply the needs of a considerably greater arable acreage. The production of mineral fertilizers is concentrated in European Russia, Ukraine, the Baltic Republics, the Urals, Transcaucasia, Middle Asia, and southwestern Siberia near sources of raw materials and in areas where the fertilizers are most needed. (Fig. 15–15)

Superphosphate plants treat phosphate with sulfuric acid, and thus are located near sources of both phosphate and the means of producing sulfuric acid. The principal source of phosphate is the apatite of the Kola Peninsula at Kirovsk, which supplies all superphosphate plants in European Russia. The second main source of phosphate is the phosphorite mine at Karatau (Chulak-Tau) near Dzhambul in southern Kazakhstan.

Potash production is more limited in amount and in areal extent than is the production of phosphate. The principal sources of potassium salts are the old mines at Solikamsk in the Urals, with factories at Solikamsk and Berezniki, and at the newly opened deposit at Soligorsk in Belorussia. When fully developed, the Soligorsk area is to supply 40 per cent of the country's needs. Potash is also mined at Stebnik and at Kalush in western Ukraine.

The location of nitrogen fertilizer plants is dictated by the source of hydrogen, which combines with nitrogen from the air to produce ammonia. Most of the hydrogen of the country is derived as a byproduct from coking and metallurgical industries or from the utilization of lowgrade coals, such as the Moscow lignite, and more recently from natural gas (60 per cent in 1965).

Synthetic Rubber   The Soviet Union embarked on an all-out program of synthetic rubber production in 1932, considerably earlier than did either Germany or the United States. The Russians largely were responsible for the early advances in the technology of synthetic rubber production, but they have lost this lead to the United States. The Soviet Union now produces no more than half as much synthetic rubber as the United States does. Since the U.S.S.R. relies much more heavily on synthetic rubber than the United States, it can be deduced that the U.S.S.R. consumes much less total rubber than the United States. About two thirds of Soviet rubber is synthetic.

The early Soviet synthetic rubber factories were located in or near the potatogrowing zone in central European Russia since the basic raw material was ethyl alcohol derived primarily from potatoes. The first pilot plant was established in Leningrad in 1931, and the first industrial synthetic rubber plant was opened at Yaroslavl in 1932 to supply the local tire factory. A second rubber plant was completed the same year at Voronezh and a third in 1933 at Yefremov. A fourth was opened somewhat later at Kazan. All these factories were located close to principal rubber consumers—the tire plants of Moscow, Yaroslavl, and Voronezh—which in turn served the automotive factories at Moscow, Yaroslavl, and Gorky. The synthetic rubber factories were also situated favorably with respect to the rubber footwear industry which was concentrated in central European Russia and Leningrad.

In Armenia abundant limestone resources and cheap hydroelectric power were used to produce calcium carbide and acetylene, the raw materials for polychloroprene rubber at a plant established at Yerevan in 1940. This neoprene rubber was a special type with adhesive qualities and resistance to crude oil and refined products which was used widely in the petroleum industry at Baku and for conveyor belts and cable coverings.

During World War II many of the synthetic rubber plants of European Russia were either damaged or evacuated, but after the war they were restored. Since 1955 these rubber plants have all been converted to the use of gas and oil by-products,

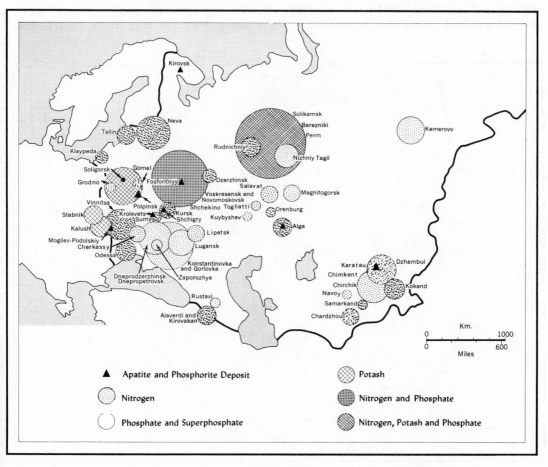

Figure 15–15   The relative production of mineral fertilizers. Nitrate and phosphate plants are now distributed so thickly across the European part of the country that it is impossible to show all of them.

thereby releasing large quantities of potatoes and grain for uses other than the making of ethyl alcohol.

The first synthetic rubber plant to be situated near an oil-refining center opened in 1957 at Sumgait north of Baku. It supplies general purpose rubber to the Baku tire plant which opened in 1959 and to the Yerevan tire plant which opened in the early 1940s. Other synthetic rubber plants based on oil refinery by-products opened in 1963 and 1964 at Sterlitamak, near the oil fields of the Bashkir Republic on the western slopes of the Urals, at Togliatti (Stavropol) on the Volga near the Kuybyshev oil-refining complex, at Volzhskiy near Volgograd, and at Omsk in western Siberia. A synthetic rubber plant that opened at Krasnoyarsk in 1956 is based on alcohol derived from the hydrolysis of wood, and a plant at Temir-Tau near Karaganda uses monomers from the Volga-Urals petrochemical industry. The carbide-acetylene process is also being used at a new plant opened in 1968 at Usolye near Irkutsk to produce special-purpose chloroprene. Its raw materials are local limestone and salt deposits. As oil and gas pipelines have brought the new raw materials to many cities, synthetic rubber and tire production has dispersed considerably. (Fig. 15–16)

The plastics and synthetic fiber industries are being expanded rapidly in many of the larger manufacturing centers, particularly in those supplied by gas and oil pipelines. New towns, or greatly expanded old towns, that have been constructed expressly as chemical centers for a variety of plastic and synthetic products are such

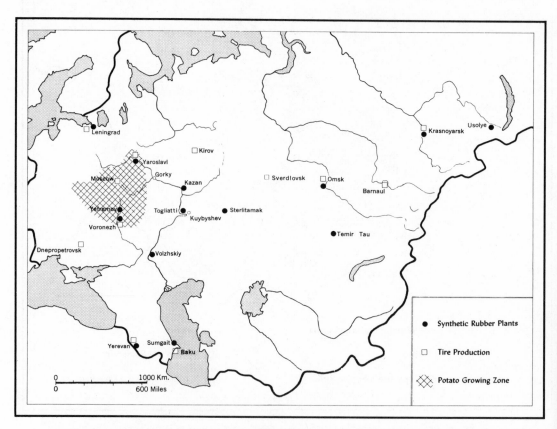

Figure 15–16   The production of synthetic rubber and tires. From Atlas razvitiya khozyaystva i kultury SSSR, *p. 41 and various "News Notes,"* Soviet Geography: Review and Translation.

rapidly growing cities as Novomoskovsk, Volzhskiy, and Togliatti.

Machine-Building Industries

Machine building is the foundation of technical progress and development of a modern economy. The Soviets claim to have increased the machine-building and metal-fabricating industries since the Revolution by more than 500 times to make them the second largest machine industries in the world after the United States and the fastest growing sector of industry in the U.S.S.R. One third of the industrial workers and one fourth of the industrial fixed capital of the U.S.S.R. are in these industries. Although the Soviet Union does not produce a great abundance of many of the consumer items, such as automobiles, that are so common to everyday living in the West, it cannot be disputed that the Soviets have worked wonders in their machine-building industries, bringing about a change from a backward economy that largely lacked a machine-building industry to one capable of producing earth satellites, atomic reactors, and some of the most modern jet airplanes in the world.

Machine building began in Tsarist Russia in the Central Industrial Region, in St. Petersburg, and in Ukraine. Many of the machine-building industries are still concentrated in these regions, but a considerable dispersal of industry has taken place to outlying areas, either to utilize raw materials in those regions or to serve markets. Some of these newer areas are growing at much faster rates than the older areas. It has been estimated that the eastern regions including the Urals now produce one third of Soviet machines.

Moscow and Leningrad largely have served as the proving grounds for prototypes of new industrial production, and thereby they have controlled the direction of many of the machine-building industries and have retained virtual monopolies on certain items. For instance Leningrad produces almost all the large turbines for hydroelectric installations being constructed about the country. Power-generating equipment and the production of precision machines, equipment, and tools are the outstanding industries in Leningrad.

The Central Industrial Region contains large machine-building centers with a wide range of diversified machine building. It is difficult to name a branch of machine building and metal fabrication that has not been created in Moscow. The region contains 80 per cent of the automotive industry of the country, including the manufacture of cars, trucks, and buses, as well as all of their accessories, primarily in Gorky, Moscow, and Yaroslavl.

After the Central Industrial Region, the second largest machine-building complex has been created in Ukraine. It specializes in machines requiring large amounts of steel, such as metallurgical, mining, and chemical equipment, Diesel locomotives, railroad cars and tank cars, tractors, agricultural machinery, metal-cutting machine tools, and building and road machines.

The Urals have become the third largest machine-building region in the country. They contain dozens of large machine-building plants manufacturing machinery and equipment for industry, agriculture, transportation, and construction. The Uralmash machine-building plant in Sverdlovsk is known throughout the country for its manufacture of metallurgical, petroleum-extracting, chemical, coal, and mining equipment. About 75 per cent of the pig iron produced in the U.S.S.R. is smelted in blast furnaces equipped by Uralmash. Rolling equipment bearing its trademark turns out one fourth of the rolled-steel products in the country. Eighty per cent of all the ferrous and nonferrous ores are processed in crushers and grinders manufactured by this plant. The Chelyabinsk tractor plant is one of the largest in the country, and one of the largest railroad car plants is in Nizhniy Tagil. In 1944 an automobile assembly plant was established at Miass in the Urals.

A new large region of machine manufacture has emerged in the cities along the Volga. The Volgograd tractor plant, the Syzran combine plant, the Kuybyshev electric milking machine plant, as well as petroleum equipment plants, ship yards, automobile assembly plants, and many plants concerned with the aircraft industry dominate this region. Some of the older machine industries in this area are turning out business machines, typewriters, watches, and so forth.

Western Siberia is one of the most rapidly growing regions for machine-building industries in the country. The cities of Novosibirsk, Omsk, Kemerovo, Barnaul, and others have grown rapidly, primarily under the impetus of the machine-building industries. These industries grew especially during World War II when many plants were relocated from European Russia. Novosibirsk turns out farm machinery, electric generators and motors, Diesel-electric equipment, electric saws, coal-mining equipment, structural steel for bridges and the mining industry, pumps, drilling equipment, river vessels, telephones, bearings, and various instruments. Tool making and machine tool plants turn out forge and press machine tools, and measuring and cutting tools. Omsk produces electrical goods, motors, machine tools, foundry equipment, farm machinery, equipment for transportation and the leather, wool, meat, and dairy industries, precision tools, and spare parts for tractors.

Distribution of Some Machine Industries Before the Revolution about 80 per cent of the machine tools were manufactured in the Center and the Northwest, but now only about 30 per cent are manufactured in the Center and 4.4 per cent in the Northwest. Machine tools are now manufactured in regions that formerly had no machine tool plants. Twelve per cent of the present production is in Ukraine, about 10 per cent in Belorussia, more than 10 per cent in the Urals, about 9 per cent in the North Caucasus, and more than 7 per cent in the Volga Region.

The railroad locomotive industry inherited old plants from Tsarist Russia in the cities of Kolomna, Gorky, Bryansk, and Kharkov. Since then locomotive works have been constructed in Kaluga and Lyudinovo in the Center, Lugansk and Novocherkassk in the Donets Basin, Tbilisi in Georgia, and Kambarka on the Kama River. In addition, locomotive-repair shops exist in many cities along main railroad routes. By the time of the Revolution there were fifteen railroad car building works in Russia, the largest of which were in Kolomna, St. Petersburg, Sormovo (Gorky), Bryansk, and Revel (Tallin). Since then large plants turning out railroad rolling stock have been constructed at Tagil in the Urals, at Dneprodzerzhinsk and Kremenchug in Ukraine, at Engels on the Volga, at Barnaul in the Altay region, and in several other cities. The largest railroad car works in the country at present is the Tagil works in the Urals.

The output of automobiles in the Soviet Union is much less than that in the United States, and the lack of highways will probably keep it that way for a long time to come. In 1967 the Soviet Union produced only 728,000 vehicles of which 477,000 were trucks and buses. Only 251,000 passenger cars were produced. By contrast, in 1966 the United States produced 10,329,000 motor vehicles of which 8,598,000 were passenger cars. (Table 15–8) The Soviet industry has shown only a modest increase since 1958. From the beginning, the main centers of the automobile industry have been Gorky, Moscow, and Yaroslavl. Gorky had the first large plant in the country and is the main manufacturer of automobiles to this day. Since World War II new plants have been established at Zavolzhye and Bryansk in central European Russia; at Ulyanovsk on the Volga; at Saransk in the Mordovian A.S.S.R.; at Miass and Izhevsk in the Urals; at Kutaisi in Georgia; at Dnepropetrovsk, Zaporozhye, Kremenchug, and Melitopol in Ukraine; at Minsk in Belorussia; and at Petropavlovsk in Kazakhstan. In addition, buses are manufactured in Riga, Lvov, Odessa, Engels, Kurgan, and two small cities in the Central Industrial Region. Huge construction trucks are assembled at Zhodino just east of Minsk.

Two large factories in Moscow turn out the well-known ZIL and Moskvich cars. The ZIL car used to be known as the ZIS car before the death of Stalin. The letters ZIS stood for Zavod Imeni Stalin, which means "the plant named after Stalin." After his death the car was renamed ZIL in honor of an ex-manager of the plant. Gorky contains several automobile plants manufacturing the large limosine named the Chaika (seagull), as well as light passenger cars such as the Pobeda and the Volga. Most of the taxis in the Soviet Union are Volga or Moskvich cars. Gorky also manufactures trucks, and the Yaroslavl plant manufactures heavy trucks. The Minsk plant specializes in trucks and highway tractors, and the Kutaisi plant in trucks and dump trucks. The Miass plant in the Urals manufactures a 10-ton cargo truck called the Ural which can negotiate any road condition. The Kremenchug plant is to start production of a powerful truck called the Dnieper.

A newer model passenger car, the Zaporozhets, went into production in 1960 at the Zaporozhye plant. It is a small four-passenger car with four cylinders having 20 to 25 horsepower and an air-cooled engine located in the back.

In 1966 Italy's Fiat Company agreed to build a plant that by 1970 is to produce about 700,000 Fiats per year. The plant is now being completed at Togliatti on the Volga near Kuybyshev, the old town of Stavropol which was renamed after the Italian communist leader.

Shipbuilding during Tsarist days was located in St. Petersburg on the Baltic, and at Sevastopol and Nikolayev on the Black Sea. New shipyards have been built at Murmansk on the Kola Peninsula and at Komsomolsk in the Far East as well as at Kherson on the Black Sea. The river fleet is supplied by shipyards at Gorky, Rybinsk, Krasnoarmeysk, and Astrakhan on the Volga River, Perm on the Kama, Kiev on the Dnieper, Tyumen on the Tura River, and several small shipyards located on the Ob, the Yenisey, and the Amur Rivers. The Sormovo shipyards in Gorky have been experimenting with an ultramodern hydrofoil rocket-type ship, which is a cigar-shaped, jet-like ship capable of carrying 150 passengers at speeds of up to 100 kilometers per hour. These so-called meteor ships were to start regular runs between Gorky and Kuybyshev on the Volga River in 1960. In these boats the distance between the two cities can be covered in 14 hours, whereas a regular Diesel ship takes 3 days.

Very little information is available on the aircraft industry in the Soviet Union, although it is obvious that it has developed to a high degree. Apparently airplane factories are concentrated in the Central Industrial Region, Ukraine, the Volga Region, and the Urals. There is some evidence that the aircraft industry is dispersed throughout all industrial regions of the Soviet Union.

Agricultural machine building takes place primarily in the richest agricultural regions where the bulky machines can be delivered without too much transportation. Ukraine is perhaps the region of the most concentrated agricultural machine building. Plants are located in Kirovograd, Kharkov, Zaporozhye, Kherson, Odessa, and other cities. The largest single agricultural machinery plant in the country, Rosselmash, is in Rostov just east of Ukraine. Similar plants exist in the North Caucasus and in the Central Black Earth Region. New plants have been established in western Siberia, particularly at Kurgan, Omsk, Rubtsovsk, and Tselinograd, to serve the agriculture in that area. A new plant has been constructed at Pavlodar to help meet the needs for farm machinery in the newly plowed virgin lands.

Tractors are manufactured primarily at Volgograd, Chelyabinsk, Kharkov, and recently, at Rubtsovsk, Vladimir, and Lipetsk. Potato harvesters are built at Tula, flax harvesters at Bezhetsk in Kalinin Oblast, cotton pickers at Tashkent, and corn pickers at Zaporozhye.

Textile Industries

The textile industries are some of the oldest industries in Russia. They initiated the industrialization of the Center and still are one of the more important groups of industries in that area. Although their value of output in the Central Industrial Region has been surpassed by that of the machine-building industries, and in some cities by that of the chemical industries, a greater percentage of their value is represented by labor. Hence their importance to the region in terms of number of workers engaged is more important than the money value might indicate. All the textile industries are still heavily concentrated in the Central Industrial Region, although the concentration is not quite as great as it was before the Revolution. (Table 2–2) In 1965 the Center produced 73 per cent of the country's cotton cloth, 54 per cent of the wool, 64 per cent of the linen, and 67 per cent of the silk and synthetic fibers.

Many new plants have been constructed during the Soviet period both in areas where the raw materials are produced and in areas of growing markets. Thus in 1935 large cotton mills were built in Tashkent in the heart of the cotton-growing region of Middle Asia and at Barnaul in the Kulunda Steppe of southwestern Siberia. Barnaul receives raw cotton from Middle Asia over the Turk-Sib Railroad and produces cotton textiles for the growing markets in southwestern Siberia. During World War II new cotton mills were constructed at Dushanbe in the cotton-growing region of southwestern Tadzhikistan and at Chelyabinsk and Ufa in the Urals. Since the war new mills have been constructed at Kansk in eastern Siberia, at Chimkent in Middle Asia, at Gori in Transcaucasia, at Cheboksary and Kamyshin along the Volga, and at Kherson on the Black Sea coast of Ukraine. In 1965 the chief cotton-growing republic, Uzbekistan, produced 3.6 per cent of the country's cotton cloth.

In the Central Industrial Region the cotton textile industry continues to be heavily concentrated in Ivanovo and surrounding cities along the Volga northeast of Moscow and in Moscow and its suburban cities. In 1913 the textile industry in this region depended for nearly 50 per cent of its raw cotton on areas outside of Russia, primarily Egypt. By 1933 the Soviet Union had expanded cotton growing in Middle Asia and Transcaucasia to the point where it served 97 per cent of its own needs, and this has continued to the present.

Fine wool materials traditionally have been centered around Moscow and Leningrad, and coarse woolens have been manufactured in the Volga area. During and since World War II new factories have been built in Minsk and other cities in the west and in the sheep-producing areas in the mountains of Middle Asia, Siberia, and the Caucasus. Chardzhou and Alma-Ata are important woolen centers in Middle Asia, Ulan-Ude is important in eastern Siberia, and Tbilisi is the most important center in Transcaucasia.

Linen is produced primarily in the Center and the Northwest where the flax is grown. Kostroma traditionally has been the leader in linen production, and other cities in the Volga Region northeast of Moscow are important.

The traditional centers of the silk industry are in Middle Asia and Transcaucasia where silk worms are grown, utilizing mulberry trees that are planted along irrigation canals. However, silk statistics are far overshadowed by statistics on synthetic fibers, with which silk is included, so the regional distribution of silk is obscured. Apparently natural silk accounts for only about one sixteenth of what is reported as silk in the Soviet Union at present. The most important producers in the Central Industrial Region are Kalinin and Moscow, but what they produce is probably all rayon. Rayon factories also have been established in Ukraine, in the Central Black Earth Region, and in Krasnoyarsk in eastern Siberia.

Hemp is an old crop in Russia, and jute is a newcomer. The largest hemp-jute industry originally was concentrated in port cities since it provided the shipping industries with rope. Smaller factories have been built in the hemp-growing regions of Belorussia, Smolensk, Orel, Bryansk, and Kirovograd Oblasts, and the Mordovian A.S.S.R. Before the Revolution all jute was imported. Now some is grown in Middle Asia, particularly around Tashkent. The first jute factory was constructed in Tashkent in 1952. Several jute factories are planned for the Tadzhik Republic.

The Soviets seem to be a technological step behind the United States and western Europe in synthetic fiber manufacture. While the Soviets are expanding rayon production, the more developed countries are moving ahead with a great variety of finer products. Also the relative volume of synthetic fabrics has not reached the proportion that it has in the West. It appears that synthetics make up no more than 15 per cent of total cloth production in the Soviet Union, whereas in the United States it is more than 25 per cent.

Food Industries

The main branches of the food industry are flour milling, sugar processing, meat processing, canning, vegetable-oil produc-

tion, and fishing. Flour milling has grown with grain production in the regions of the Center, the South, the Volga, the Southern Urals, southwestern Siberia, northern Kazakhstan, the Far East, and Middle Asia.

The sugar industry in the Soviet Union is based on the sugar beet crop which until recently was produced almost entirely in Ukraine and the Central Black Earth Region. In 1965, 61 per cent of the sugar production in the U.S.S.R. was still in Ukraine and 14 per cent in the Central Black Earth Region. (Table 15–40) Considerable expansion has taken place in Moldavia, the Baltic Republics, Belorussia, the Chu Valley of the Kirgiz S.S.R., and the Taldy-Kurgan area in southeastern Kazakhstan. New regions of sugar production are the Kuban in the North Caucasus, the Kulunda Steppe in southwestern Siberia, and the Ussuri-Khanka Lowland in the Far East. The Soviet Union is now the largest sugar producer in the world. (Table 15–41) In addition to domestically grown sugar beets, the Soviet Union processes large quantities of raw cane sugar imported from Cuba.

Meat processing is centered in the rich farming areas of the country. In 1965 Ukraine processed 21 per cent of the country's meat, the central regions 15 per cent, the North Caucasus 9 per cent, western Siberia 8 per cent, and the Urals 8 per cent. The largest meat combines are located in Moscow, Leningrad, Baku, and Semipalatinsk. In 1967 the Soviet Union processed 11,400,000 metric tons of meat; this compared to 22,300,000 in the United States.

Since there is so little refrigeration equipment in the Soviet Union, the canning industry has become the mainstay of the food industries. Much of the meat produced in slaughter houses is immediately canned, and the fresh meat supply depends primarily on the Kolkhoz markets where the farmers bring newly slaughtered meat each day. The canned goods industry has grown rapidly in the

Table 15–40   Food Production, by Major Producing Regions, 1965, in Thousands of Tons

	Sugar	Meat	Vegetable Oil
U.S.S.R.	11,037	5,245	2,770
R.S.F.S.R.	3,087	2,830	1,186
Northwest		196	20
Center	177	447	30
Volga-Vyatka	17	120	21
Central Chernozem	1,551	228	266
Voronezh Oblast	476		144
Volga *a*	228	439	162
North Caucasus	991	483	599
Krasnodar Kray	956		351
Urals		322	20
Western Siberia	56	326	30
Eastern Siberia	2	194	0
Far East	65	50	38
Ukraine	6,686	1,107	872
Moldavia	345	80	133
Baltic Republics	354	301	28
Belorussia	128	232	26
Transcaucasia	93	83	40
Middle Asia	174	202	428
Kirgiz Republic	174		
Kazakh S.S.R.	171	411	58

Sources: Narodnoye khozyaystvo SSSR v 1965 g., pp. 241–242 and 245, and *Narodnoye khozyaystvo RSFSR v 1965 g.,* pp. 158–160 and 163–165.
a Includes the Bashkir A.S.S.R.

Soviet Union along with urbanization and public catering. Canned vegetables are mostly prepared in the steppe regions of Ukraine and North Caucasus, canned

Table 15–41   Sugar Production, by Leading Countries, 1966, in Metric Tons

U.S.S.R.	9,019,000
Cuba	4,867,000
Brazil	3,852,000
U.S.A.	3,667,000
India	3,633,000
Australia	2,447,000
Communist China	2,400,000
Mexico	2,252,000

Source: United Nations Statistical Yearbook, 1967, pp. 238–239.

meat in Kazakhstan, canned fruit in Transcaucasia, North Caucasus, Crimea, Moldavia, and other southern regions, and much fish canning is carried on in all regions of fishing.

In the Soviet Union vegetable oil is produced 40 per cent from sunflower seeds and 16 per cent from cotton seeds. Other oil sources are soy beans, arachis, flax seed, hemp seed, castor seed, mustard seed, and tung nuts. Ukraine, North Caucasus, and Middle Asia are the leading producers, the first two primarily from sunflowers and Middle Asia mainly from cotton.

Fish   In 1913 Russia caught about a million tons of fish of which two thirds came from the Caspian Sea, about 10 per cent from Far Eastern waters, 7 per cent from the Black and Azov Seas, and about 6 per cent from the European North. The 1966 catch was more than five times as large as the 1913 catch, and the geographical distribution of the catch had changed considerably. In 1966 the Soviet catch was 5,349,000 tons, which ranked it third in the world, after Peru and Japan. (Table 15–42) Communist China claims to have surpassed the Soviet fish catch, which would make the Soviet Union fourth in the world. However, the Chinese have not released any statistics on their fishing industry. The Atlantic Ocean now produces about 50 per cent of the total Soviet catch, and Murmansk is the home port for about half of all the Soviet fishing ships, although it apparently accounts for less than 25 per cent of the total tonnage. (Table 15–43) The Far East whaling ships are much greater in size. The Soviet Union ranks second in the world in whaling after Japan. (Table 15–44)

The largest fish-processing plants are at Murmansk on the Barents Sea, Archangel on the White Sea, Astrakhan and Guryev on the Caspian, Zhdanov on the Sea of Azov, and Vladivostok in the Far East. Perhaps the best fishing grounds are in the Barents Sea and the White Sea. Herring, haddock, halibut, cod, sea perch, and salmon are the main fish caught in these waters. The Caspian is especially famous for its sturgeon from which is obtained the Russian black caviar. The Sea of Azov also is a very rich fishing ground, particularly around the estuaries of the Don and

Table 15–42 Fish Catch in Leading Countries, 1966, in Metric Tons

World	56,800,000
Peru	8,789,000
Japan	7,077,400
U.S.S.R.	5,349,000
Norway	2,849,400
U.S.A.	2,514,600

Source: United Nations Statistical Yearbook, 1967, pp. 151–152.

Table 15–43 Soviet Fish Catch by Water Area, 1964, in Per Cents of Total

Far East	32.2
Northeast Atlantic	20.9
Northwest Atlantic	12.7
East-central and southeast Atlantic	15.2
Azov and Black Seas	4.7
Caspian Sea	8.4
Aral Sea	0.7
Other	5.2

Source: Atlas razvitiya khozyaystva i kultury S.S.S.R., p. 15.

Kuban Rivers. Many fish migrate into the Sea of Azov through the narrow Kerch Straits in spring to spawn and in the fall they reverse their movements back to the Black Sea. The Far East is especially known for its salmon and crab. Sixty per cent of the salmon catch in the U.S.S.R. comes from the shores of Kamchatka. The eastern waters also are rich in flounder, smelt, herring, mackerel, cod, and sea animals — whales, walruses, and seals. Some of the new Soviet floating factories used for whaling in the Antarctic during the southern hemisphere summer return to Vladivostok and are used to catch white whales in the Sea of Okhotsk during the northern hemisphere summer.

Table 15–44 Numbers of Whales Caught, 1965–1966

World	57,891
Japan	21,856
U.S.S.R.	21,313
Norway	4,897
South Africa	4,148

Source: United Nations Statistical Yearbook, 1967, p. 153.

Note: World whaling has fallen considerably since 1960–1961 and has been fluctuating drastically with respect to country. In 1953–1954 Norway was the leading country with 15,320 whales.

The fishing industry is very important to the food supply of the Soviet Union, regularly contributing from one fourth to one third of the meat supply of the country. Since the meat supply is still far below demand in the Soviet Union, the fishing effort is being extended in every way possible. Much fish is now being produced in small ponds, which seem to be an integral part of every farm in the Soviet Union. Most collective and state farms in the more humid parts of the country have fish quotas as well as crop and livestock quotas and regularly report fish tonnages along with other annual production statistics. At the other end of the scale, the Soviets are pushing farther out into the oceans of the world in search of new deep sea fishing areas. During the past decade they have expanded their fishing fleet into one of the largest and most modern fleets in the world. In addition to building ships of their own, they have been making large purchases from Poland, West Germany, East Germany, Japan, Sweden, Denmark, Great Britain, Finland, Belgium, France, and the Netherlands. Huge Soviet trawlers and factory ships are now a common sight off the east, west, and south coasts of North America, off the east coast of Patagonia in South America, and off the southwest coast of Africa, as well as in more traditional waters in the Mediterranean, along northern Norway, and so forth. The intensity of Soviet fishing has prompted most countries to enact a 12-mile limit on territorial waters, rather than the previous 3 miles, and the Peruvians have extended their territorial rights 200 miles to sea in the rich fishing area off their west coast in the cool Humboldt Current. In order to institute logical controls on Soviet fishing that otherwise would have depleted permanently stocks of certain species of fish in the North Atlantic, the United States has had to make concessions to the Soviets which allow them to come within the 12-mile limit off the coasts of Long Island and New Jersey.

Lumbering, Wood Working, and Paper Milling

The Soviet Union traditionally has been a great lumbering country, and wood has been the primary construction material throughout the history of old Russia and the Soviet Union. Until recently the buildings of even the largest cities of the country were built primarily of wood. Fires were a constant hazard. The great Moscow fires that have occurred all through history are legendary. Now the building industry is switching heavily to reinforced concrete and other materials, but the uses for wood still continue to increase.

About 30 per cent of the territory of the U.S.S.R. is covered by forests. This represents about 20 per cent of the world's forest lands, and, even more important, about one third of the world's utilized forest area and growing stock. The Soviet Union has consistently led the world in the production of forest products. In 1966 the Soviet Union produced a total of 373.4 million cubic meters of round wood, which was 50 million more than its nearest competitor, the United States, and more than three times as much as the third ranking country, Canada. (Table 15–45) The Soviet production represented more than 18 per cent of total world production.

Table 15–45   Roundwood Production in Leading Countries, 1966, in Millions of Cubic Meters

	Coniferous	Broad Leaved	Total
World	993.0	1056.0	2049.0
U.S.S.R.	307.0	66.4	373.4
U.S.A.	230.4	93.5	323.9
Canada	103.7	10.4	114.1
Sweden	40.7	7.7	48.4
Finland	28.6	13.0	41.6

Source: United Nations Statistical Yearbook, 1967, pp. 148–149.

There are certain drawbacks to the Soviet forest resource. Much of it is not of the highest quality, and it is very unevenly distributed across the country, with the greatest resources in the areas of least population. Much of Siberia and the Far East, except for the northern tundra fringe, has at least 40 per cent of its territory covered by forest, whereas Kazakhstan and Middle Asia, except for the southern mountains, are practically devoid of any trees whatsoever. (Fig. 15–17) By far the largest percentage of trees in Siberia, as well as in many other poorly drained areas of the country, are larch, whose spreading root system enables it to survive over permafrost and in partially flooded areas. The larch wood is not the best for lumber production, and the logs are heavy and tend to sink in water, which makes log floating difficult in many of the Siberian rivers. Needle-leaf trees of all types make up almost three quarters of the total forest resource, whereas broad-leaf trees make up only a little more than one quarter. (Table 15–46) Thus broad-leaf hardwood makes up only about 17 per cent of the total wood production in the U.S.S.R., whereas in the U.S.A. it makes up about 29 per cent. (Table 15–45)

Some of the more heavily populated parts of European Russia are still surprisingly forested. The Central Industrial Region still has 36 per cent of its total area covered by forests, as does the western portion of the Russian Republic, as well as much of Belorussia and the Baltic Republics. But these forests in the old populated parts of the country have been cut over repeatedly and therefore are of little value as timber producers. Nevertheless they still produce disproportionate shares of a variety of other types of wood products, because they are so handy to markets.

The highest grade forests are in northern European Russia in portions of Archangel and Vologda Oblasts and the Karelian A.S.S.R. in the west, in Kirov Oblast of the Volga-Vyatka Region, and in Perm and Sverdlovsk Oblasts in the Urals. There is also good quality timber in southcentral Siberia in Tomsk and Irkutsk Oblasts and the southern portion of Krasnoyarsk Kray. During the past decade production has shifted more and more to these prime areas as an effort has been made to spare the over-cutting in the central part of European Russia which up until 1955 was the largest producing region in the country. (Inset, Fig. 15–17) This territorial shift in logging activity has necessitated longer and longer rail hauls, which now average more than 1500 kilometers. This has added quite a burden to the heavily loaded railroads which still carry about two thirds of all forest shipments. Although log floating is very important in such rivers as the Northern Dvina in Archangel Oblast, in most cases the rivers do not serve the needs of domestic flows of wood very well. In the forest areas most of the rivers flow north to the Arctic, not to domestic markets, and even in European Russia most of the wood used domestically must move by rail.

The transportation problem still keeps logging activity nearer to markets than would be ideal for the correct utilization of the total timber resource. Some of the best forests in the northern and eastern parts of the country are made up largely of

Table 15–46   Forest Resources, by Types of Tree, in Per Cents of Total

Needle leaf	72.7
Larch	38.4
Scotch pine	15.7
Spruce	11.8
Stone pine and other coniferous	6.8
Broad leaf	27.3
Birch	12.3
Other hardwood	5.0
Other softwoods	3.2
Other woody species, willow, and brush	6.8

Source: Atlas razvitiya khozyaystva i kultury, p. 14.

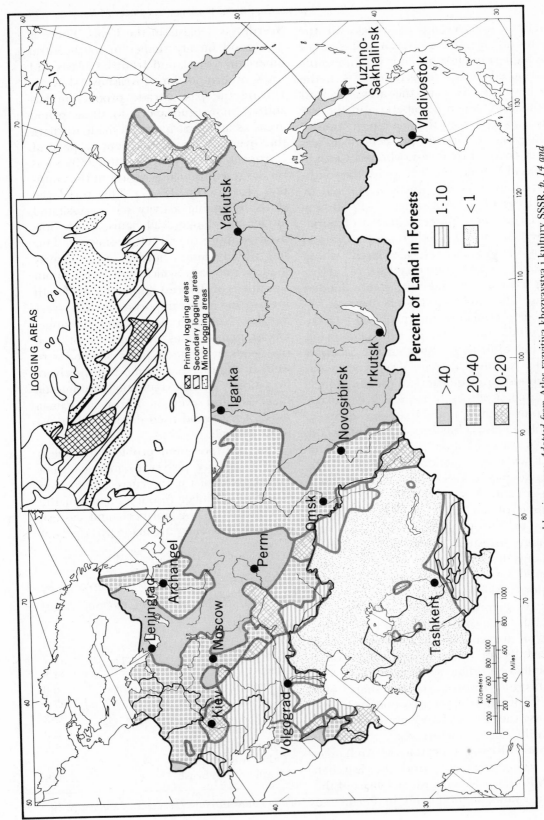

Percent of Land in Forests

>40

20-40

10-20

1-10

<1

LOGGING AREAS

Primary logging areas
Secondary logging areas
Minor logging areas

Yuzhno-Sakhalinsk
Vladivostok
Yakutsk
Igarka
Novosibirsk
Irkutsk
Omsk
Perm
Archangel
Leningrad
Moscow
Kiev
Volgograd
Tashkent

Kilometers
0 200 400 600 800 1000
Miles
0 200 400 600 800 1000

Figure 15–17 Forest cover and logging areas. Adapted from Atlas razvitiya khozyaystva i kultury SSSR, p. 14 and Bone, "The Soviet Forest Resource," Canadian Geographer, 1966, p. 106.

over-mature trees which remain unused, whereas over-cutting continues along the southern fringes of the forest in European Russia next to the heavy markets. Production is better adapted to resource than it was a few years ago, however. At the present time, Archangel Oblast is first in the production of commercial timber, followed by Irkutsk, Sverdlovsk, and Perm Oblasts, Krasnoyarsk Kray, and the Karelian A.S.S.R. (Table 15–47) In terms of total timber production, Sverdlovsk Oblast is first and Perm Oblast third, which makes the western slopes of the Urals the greatest producing area in the country. This area is also very high in paper production, with Perm Oblast leading any other single political unit by a considerable margin. (Table 15–47) The Kama River Valley in general is the leading paper-producing area in the country.

Much of the railroad traffic of wood products consists of raw timber which is shipped southwestward out of the forest region for processing. Therefore there is a large territorial discrepancy between distribution of wood industries and logging. At least 60 per cent of all sawn wood is produced in consuming centers, most of which lie in the Central Industrial Region, eastern and western Ukraine, the Baltic Republics, and intervening territories. As revealed by the 1959 census, the numbers of people employed in timber processing form a pattern across the country very similar to that of total population. Cities that are outstanding are Moscow, Leningrad, Kiev, Riga, Volgograd, Kuybyshev, Saratov, and some other of the larger cities in the European part of the country; Perm and Sverdlovsk in the Urals; Novosibirsk, Krasnoyarsk, and Irkutsk in Siberia; and Khabarovsk in the Far East. The city most outstanding in this respect in the entire country is Archangel, which, of course, is the main port for lumber export. To a lesser degree other ports, such as Igarka on the Lower Yenisey, and Sovetskaya Gavan and Vladivostok in the

Far East, are distinguished for similar reasons. In addition, certain new centers, such as Bratsk, are becoming very important.

The export of timber has always been very important to the Soviet Union's economy. This was true in Russian Empire days as well. The Soviet Union is second only to Canada as an exporter of sawed coniferous timber. In 1964 the Soviet Union exported 1,642,600 standards, or about 7,660,000 cubic meters, which was about 3.5 per cent of total production. The main importers of Soviet timber are Great Britain, Hungary, West Germany, the Benelux countries, and France. In 1965 Japan became a significant importer of Soviet sawed and round coniferous timber, and the ports of Vladivostok and Nakhodka have been expanded recently, which seems to indicate an increasing trade in that direction.

The main timber ports of the Soviet Union lie along the Arctic, the Baltic, and the Pacific. In the Arctic region, Archangel is outstanding, although other ports on the White Sea account for some of the exports. In 1965, 35 trips of timber ships were made out of Archangel carrying a gross tonnage of 132,342 metric tons. The smaller ports of Onega, Mezen, Kovda, and Pechora together accounted for 9 trips with a total tonnage of about 15,000 tons. Farther east, Igarka, a port built on the lower Yenisey exclusively for timber exports along the Northern Sea Route, had 16 timber trips in 1965 with a total tonnage of 67,499, or roughly half that of Archangel. It is planned to considerably expand the operation at Igarka in the near future to utilize some of the untapped forest resources of central Siberia. The port is also being supplied by railroad lines leading out from the city into the forests. On the Baltic, the port of Leningrad accounts for about 90 per cent of all Soviet sawn timber exported through the Baltic. Also important are Riga, Ventspils, Vyborg, and Tallin. In the Far East, Vladivostok and Nakhodka dominate the scene,

Table 15–47   Production of Timber and Paper by Primary Regions, 1965

	Total Timber in Cubic Meters	Commercial Timber in Cubic Meters	Paper in 1000 Tons
U.S.S.R.	378,113	273,595	3,231
R.S.F.S.R.	345,324	251,885	2,659
Northwest Region	93,073	73,115	1,008
Archangel Oblast	26,383	21,550	148
Vologda Oblast	15,144	11,250	114
Leningrad Oblast	6,409	4,252	
Karelian A.S.S.R.	19,348	16,652	465
Komi A.S.S.R.	18,338	14,669	
Kaliningrad Oblast			113
Central Region	29,661	18,059	128
Kalinin Oblast	5,295	3,066	
Kostroma Oblast	9,778	6,577	
Volga-Vyatka Region	31,724	22,224	387
Gorky Oblast	7,943	5,416	275
Kirov Oblast	18,870	13,610	
Central Chernozem Region	1,275	953	8
Volga Region	13,028	7,404	44
North Caucasus	4,469	2,877	26
Ural Region	62,041	45,233	681
Perm Oblast	24,957	19,469	613
Sverdlovsk Oblast	26,867	19,569	
Western Siberia	29,517	20,768	2
Tomsk Oblast	8,723	6,310	
Tyumen Oblast	8,261	5,867	
Eastern Siberia	57,108	44,461	94
Krasnoyarsk Kray	21,899	17,196	94
Irkutsk Oblast	24,522	19,790	
Buryat A.S.S.R.	5,848	4,260	
Far East	22,922	16,465	167
Maritime Kray	4,573	3,396	
Khabarovsk Kray	7,414	5,870	
Sakhalin Oblast			158
Ukraine	12,529	9,704	166
Southwest Region	11,560	9,028	
Moldavia	184	79	
Baltic Region	9,879	5,400	265
Belorussia	7,183	4,884	90
Transcaucasia	1,337	708	34
Middle Asia	144	29	17
Kazakh S.S.R.	2,039	1,232	

Sources: *Narodnoye khozyaystvo SSSR v 1965 g.*, pp. 208–209 and 213, and *Narodnoye khozyaystvo RSFSR v 1965 g.*, pp. 108–111 and 119.

while a number of smaller ports in southern Sakhalin handle considerable amounts of local lumber.

The Soviets are still pretty wasteful in the use of their timber resource as well as in the utilization of cut wood, and often their wood-cutting operations have paid little attention to conservation of water sheds. This is particularly true on heavily populated collective farms in the forest zone of the European part of the country where individual collective farmers find it most convenient to continue to cut trees for firewood and other purposes as near to their villages as possible, which are usually down in the river valleys along the steeper slopes of the river breaks. A recent forest survey in central European Russia and Ukraine revealed that in general river banks have lighter forest covers than do whole territories of corresponding oblasts. This is a surprising reversal of what might be expected under natural growing conditions in relatively drought-ridden areas. One would expect the thicker forests to be along the larger streams near constant supplies of moisture. Repeated cutting, however, has laid these steeper slopes bare to erosion. It has also essentially destroyed

what could be a renewable resource if it were managed properly.

A tremendous amount of wood is still cut for firewood. Although firewood now makes up only about 4 per cent of total fuel requirements, this still represents about one quarter of all the timber cut, or around 100 million cubic meters of wood per year. There is little hope of effecting any significant absolute decrease in this usage as long as peasants are not supplied with better sources of fuel and are forced to be self-reliant to keep themselves warm during the long winters.

Although wood processing is improving rapidly, the percentage of total cut wood that undergoes chemical processing is far lower in the Soviet Union than it is in the United States. The uses of scrap materials for plywood, paper, cardboard, fiber board, and so forth are still in their infancy in the Soviet Union. Therefore the Soviets have been faced with the need for increased cutting of timber each year, whereas countries such as the United States have been able to increase production of finished wood products while reducing their logging activities.

Table 15–48 Types of Production in Soviet Manufacturing Centers

Center	Type of Manufacturing Activity
Alma-Ata	General food products, wool, wood working, general fabricated metal products, general machinery, general chemicals and allied products, and fertilizers.
Archangel	Fish, lumber, ship building, wood chemicals.
Ashkhabad	Food products, textile products and clothing, burlap, machinery, chemicals and allied products.
Astrakhan	Fish, fruit, ship building.
Baku	Food products, textile products and clothing, petroleum, fabricated metal products, machinery, petroleum refining.
Barnaul	Grain milling, cotton, fabricated metal products, machinery.
Bratsk	Hydroelectricity, aluminum, wood processing.
Bryansk	Food products, meat, phosphate, machinery, farm machinery, transportation equipment, railroad equipment, cement.
Chelyabinsk	Iron and steel, fabricated metal products, machinery, tractors and farm machinery, metal-working machinery, aircraft and parts, industrial chemicals and allied products.

Table 15–48　Types of Production in Soviet Manufacturing Centers (Continued)

Center	Type of Manufacturing Activity
Chita	Meat, leather products, lumber and wood products, lignite, fabricated metal products, railroad equipment.
Dneprodzerzhinsk	Iron and steel, railroad equipment, industrial chemicals and allied products.
Dnepropetrovsk	Food products, textile products and clothing, iron and steel, fabricated metal products, machinery.
Donetsk	Coal mining, iron and steel, metal working, machinery, chemicals.
Dushanbe	Meat, leather products, cotton, silk, general fabricated metal products, farm machinery.
Dzerzhinsk	Grain milling, peat, general chemicals and allied products.
Frunze	Grain milling, meat, fruit, wool, general fabricated metal products, farm machinery.
Gorky	Food products, general fabricated metal products, general machinery, metal-working machinery, electrical machinery and equipment, motor vehicles, aircraft and parts.
Gorlovka	Coal, general fabricated metal products, general machinery, ceramics.
Groznyy	Meat, fish, beverage, petroleum, metal-working machinery, petroleum refining.
Irkutsk	Food products, lumber, general fabricated metal products, general machinery, construction and mining machinery, motor vehicles, hydro generating electric power, oil refining, aluminum.
Ivanovo	Meat, cotton, general machinery.
Izhevsk	Meat, wood working, iron and steel, farm machinery.
Kalinin	Food products, general textile products and clothing, general fabricated metal products, general transportation equipment, general chemicals and allied products.
Kaliningrad	General food products, wood working, paper, general machinery, ship building.
Karaganda	General food products, coal, general machinery, construction and mining machinery, iron and steel.
Kaunas	General food products, general textile products and clothing, peat, general fabricated metal products, general chemicals and allied products, rubber products.
Kazan	Leather products, textile products and clothing, general machinery, farm machinery, railroad equipment, aircraft and parts, general chemicals and allied products, vegetable and animal oils, general rubber products.
Kemerovo	Coal, general fabricated metal products, general machinery, industrial chemicals.
Khabarovsk	General food products, lumber, general fabricated metal products, farm machinery, motor vehicles, ship building, aircraft and parts, petroleum refining.
Kharkov	General fabricated metal products, engines and turbines, tractors and farm machinery, construction and mining machinery, metal-working machinery, electrical machinery and equipment, railroad equipment, motorcycles and bicycles.
Kiev	General food products, general textile products and clothing, general fabricated metal products, farm machinery, metal-working machinery, electrical machinery and equipment, railroad equipment, ship

Table 15–48   Types of Production in Soviet Manufacturing Centers *(Continued)*

Center	Type of Manufacturing Activity
	building, aircraft and parts, motorcycles and bicycles, chemicals and allied products, rubber products.
Kirov	Meat, wood working, general fabricated metal products, general machinery.
Kishinev	General food products, leather products, textile products and clothing, general fabricated metal products, cement.
Komsomolsk-on-Amur	General food products, lumber, steel, general fabricated metal products, general machinery, ship building, aircraft and parts.
Kostroma	General food products, leather products, linen, lumber, general fabricated metal products, general machinery.
Krasnodar	General food products, wool, general machinery, electrical machinery and equipment, petroleum refining.
Krasnoyarsk	General food products, lumber, general fabricated metal products, farm machinery, construction and mining machinery, railroad equipment, stone, clay and glass products, oil refining, aluminum.
Krivoy Rog	Iron mining, iron and steel.
Kursk	General food products, wood working, tractors and farm machinery, electrical machinery and equipment, chemicals and allied products.
Kuybyshev	General food products, general fabricated metal products, general machinery, farm machinery, petroleum refining.
Leningrad	General food products, textile products and clothing, iron and steel, general fabricated metal products, general machinery, engines and turbines, metal-working machinery, electrical machinery and equipment, general transportation equipment, general instruments, chemicals and allied products, printing and publishing.
Lipetsk	Iron mining, iron and steel, tractors and farm machinery.
Lugansk	General fabricated metal products, general machinery, construction and mining machinery, railroad equipment, ceramics.
Lvov	General food products, textile products and clothing, general fabricated metal products, electrical machinery and equipment, petroleum refining, glass products.
Magnitogorsk	Iron mining, iron and steel, general fabricated metal products, general machinery, industrial chemicals.
Makeyevka	Coal, iron and steel.
Minsk	General food products, textile products and clothing, general fabricated metal products, farm machinery, electrical machinery and equipment, motor vehicles.
Moscow	General food products, textile products and clothing, wood working, general fabricated metal products, general machinery, motor vehicles, railroad equipment, aircraft and parts, chemicals and allied products, printing and publishing.
Murmansk	Fish, burlap, wood working, general machinery, ship building.
Nikolayev	General food products, textile products and clothing, general machinery, ship building.
Nizhniy Tagil	Meat, iron mining, iron and steel, general transportation equipment, industrial chemicals.
Novokuznetsk	Coal, iron and steel, aluminum, general fabricated metal products, general machinery, railroad equipment, industrial chemicals.
Novosibirsk	Grain milling, textile products and clothing, iron and steel, general

Table 15–48   Types of Production in Soviet Manufacturing Centers (Continued)

Center	Type of Manufacturing Activity
	fabricated metal products, farm machinery, general chemicals and allied products, vegetable and animal oils, oil refining.
Odessa	General food products, grain milling, textile products and clothing, farm machinery, metal-working machinery, ship building, chemicals and allied products, petroleum refining.
Omsk	Grain milling, meat, wool, general fabricated metal products, farm machinery, railroad equipment, chemicals and allied products, oil refining.
Ordzhonikhidze	Fruit, metal industries, general machinery, hydro generating electric power.
Orenburg	Grain milling, meat, leather products, general fabricated metal products, general machinery, engines and turbines.
Orsk	Meat, iron mining, nickel mining, metal industries, general machinery, railroad equipment, petroleum refining.
Penza	General food products, paper, general fabricated metal products, general transportation equipment.
Perm	General food products, copper, general fabricated metal products, general machinery, engines and turbines, general transportation equipment, aircraft and parts, industrial chemicals, hydro generating electric power.
Prokopyevsk	Grain milling, coal, general fabricated metal products.
Riga	General food products, general textile products and clothing, general fabricated metal products, general machinery, electrical machinery and equipment, railroad equipment, ship building, general chemicals and allied products, stone, clay and glass products.
Rostov-on-Don	General food products, general tobacco products, leather products, tractors and farm machinery, metal-working machinery, ship building, aircraft and parts.
Ryazan	Meat, fruit, general fabricated metal products, general transportation equipment, railroad equipment, oil refining.
Rybinsk	Grain milling, lumber, general machinery, ship building, hydro generating electric power.
Saratov	General food products, general machinery, petroleum refining.
Shakhty	Leather products, general textile products and clothing, coal, thermal generating electric power.
Simferopol	General food products, general tobacco products, general machinery.
Smolensk	Meat, dairy, linen, wood working, general fabricated metal products, general machinery.
Sverdlovsk	General food products, iron and steel, copper, general fabricated metal products, engines and turbines, construction and mining machinery, metal-working machinery, electrical machinery and equipment, industrial chemicals.
Syzran	General food products, oil shale, tractors and farm machinery, railroad equipment, glass products, petroleum refining.
Taganrog	Iron and steel, general machinery, tractors and farm machinery.
Tallin	Grain milling, fish, general textile products and clothing, wood working, electrical machinery and equipment, ship building.
Tambov	General food products, general machinery, electrical machinery and equipment, railroad equipment, aircraft and parts, industrial chemicals, wood chemicals.

Table 15–48 Types of Production in Soviet Manufacturing Centers (Continued)

Center	Type of Manufacturing Activity
Tashkent	General food products, leather products, cotton, general fabricated metal products, general machinery, farm machinery.
Tbilisi	General food products, leather products, wool, silk, general machinery, general chemicals and allied products.
Tomsk	General food products, wood working, general fabricated metal products, electrical machinery and equipment.
Tula	Lignite, iron and steel, general fabricated metal products, general machinery, farm machinery, general instruments.
Ufa	General food products, cotton, wood working, general fabricated metal products, engines and turbines, farm machinery, electrical machinery and equipment, petroleum refining.
Ulan-Ude	Grain milling, meat, wool, general fabricated metal products, general transportation equipment, glass products.
Ulyanovsk	General food products, lumber, general machinery, motor vehicles.
Vilnyus	General food products, wood working, general fabricating metal products, farm machinery, metal-working machinery, electrical machinery and equipment, fertilizers.
Vladimir	Cotton, general fabricated metal products, farm machinery, general instruments, general chemicals and allied products.
Vladivostok	Grain milling, fish, lumber, general fabricated metal products, construction and mining machinery, ship building.
Volgograd	General food products, lumber, iron and steel, tractors and farm machinery, petroleum refining, aluminum.
Volzhskiy	Chemicals, synethics, steel pipe.
Voronezh	General food products, general machinery, railroad equipment, general rubber products, ceramics.
Yerevan	General food products, general tobacco products, leather products, wool, general machinery, general chemicals and allied products.
Zaporozhye	Iron and steel, aluminum, general fabricated metal products, farm machinery, chemicals and allied products, hydro generating electric power, motor vehicles.
Zhdanov	Fish, graphite, iron and steel, general machinery, ship building.

Source: Updated from Richard E. Lonsdale, and John H. Thompson, "A Map of the U.S.S.R.'s Manufacturing," *Economic Geography,* January 1960, pp. 44–50.

Reading List

GENERAL

Bornstein, Morris, "A Comparison of Soviet and United States National Product," *Comparisons of the United States and Soviet Economies,* Part II, pp. 377–395.

Hodgman, Donald R., *Soviet Industrial Production, 1928–1951,* Harvard University Press, Cambridge, 1954, 241 pp.

Hooson, David, "Industrial Growth: Where Next?" *Survey,* October 1965, pp. 111–124.

Hoyt, John Stanley, *An Investigation of the Economies of Soviet Locational Doctrine, Policy, and Practice, with Special Emphasis on Heavy Industry,* University Microfilms, Ann Arbor, 1959.

Jerschkowsky, Oleg and Lewins, Leon, "Basic Data on the Economy of U.S.S.R.," *Overseas Business Reports,* U.S. Department of Commerce, April 1966, 27 pp.

Krengel, Rolf, "Soviet, American, and West

German Basic Industries: A Comparison," *Soviet Studies,* October 1960, pp. 113–125.

Levine, Herbert S., "Industry," in Allen Kassof, *Prospects for Soviet Society,* Praeger, New York, 1968, pp. 291–317.

Lonsdale, Richard E., "Siberian Industry Before 1917: The Example of Tomsk Guberniya," *Annals of the Association of American Geographers,* December 1963, pp. 479–493.

——— and Thompson, John H., "A Map of the U.S.S.R.'s Manufacturing," *Economic Geography,* January 1960, pp. 36–52.

New Directions in the Soviet Economy, Studies Prepared for the Subcommittee on Foreign Economic Policy of the Joint Economic Committee, Congress of the United States, Washington, 1966, Part II-A, pp. 99–337.

Nove, Alec, "The Industrial Planning System Reforms in Prospect," *Soviet Studies,* July 1962, pp. 1–15.

Nutter, G. Warren, *The Growth of Industrial Production in the Soviet Union,* Princeton University Press, Princeton, N.J., 1962, 733 pp.

———, "The Structure and Growth of Soviet Industry: A Comparison with the United States," *Comparison of the United States and Soviet Economies,* Part I, pp. 95–120.

Petrov, Victor P., *Geography of the Soviet Union, Part IV, Soviet Industry,* Washington, 1960, 90 pp.

Prociuk, Stephan G., "The Territorial Pattern of Industrialization in the U.S.S.R.," *Soviet Studies,* July 1961, pp. 69–95.

Promyshlennost SSSR (Industry of the U.S.S.R.), Moscow, 1957, 447 pp., and 1964, 495 pp. (in Russian).

Quarterly Economic Review, various issues.

Shabad, Theodore, *Basic Industrial Resources of the U.S.S.R.,* Columbia University Press, New York, 1969, 393 pp.

———, "The Resources of a Nation," in Harrison E. Salisbury, ed., *The Soviet Union: The Fifty Years,* Harcourt, Brace, and World, New York, 1967, pp. 222–240.

———, "Soviet Economic Regions," *Soviet Geography: Review and Translation,* November 1963, pp. 58–61.

Shimkin, Demitri B., *Minerals: A Key to Soviet Power,* Harvard University Press, Cambridge, 1953.

Soviet Economic Performance: 1966–67, Materials Prepared for the Subcommittee on Foreign Economic Policy of the Joint Economic Committee, Congress of the United States, Washington, May 1968, pp. 1–29.

Stolte, Stefan C., "Features of Soviet-Bloc Economic Development," *Bulletin of the Institute for the Study of the U.S.S.R.,* May 1968, pp. 3–13.

———, "Economic Developments in the Soviet Bloc," *Bulletin of the Institute for the Study of the U.S.S.R.,* October 1967, pp. 29–35.

MINERAL FUELS

Buyanovskiy, M. S., "On the Questions of the Prospects of Development of the Pechora Coal Basin," *Soviet Geography: Review and Translation,* March 1960, pp. 9–20.

Campbell, Robert W., *The Economics of Soviet Oil and Gas,* Johns Hopkins Press, Baltimore, 1968, 279 pp.

Gazovyye resursy SSSR (Gas Resources of the U.S.S.R.), Moscow, 1959, 350 pp. (in Russian).

Hassmann, Heinrich, *Oil in the Soviet Union,* translated by Alfred M. Leeston and published by Princeton University Press, Princeton, N.J., 1953, 173 pp.

Hodgkins, Jordan A., *Soviet Power: Energy Resources, Production and Potential,* Prentice-Hall, Englewood Cliffs, N.J., 1961, 190 pp.

Lydolph, Paul E. and Shabad, Theodore, "The Oil and Gas Industries in the U.S.S.R.," *Annals of the Association of American Geographers,* December 1960, pp. 461–486.

Rodgers, Allan, "Coking Coal Supply: Its Role in the Expansion of the Soviet Steel Industry," *Economic Geography,* April 1964, pp. 113–150.

Shimkin, Demitri B., *The Soviet Mineral Fuels Industries, 1928–1958: A Statistical Survey,* International Population Statistics Reports, United States Bureau of the Census, 1962, Series P-90, No. 19, 183 pp.

Sudoplatov, A., *Coal Industry of the U.S.S.R.,* Foreign Languages Publishing House, Moscow, 1959, 155 pp.

Vvedensky, G. A., "The Soviet Fuel and Power Industry," *Bulletin of the Institute for the Study of the U.S.S.R.,* January 1968, pp. 18–25.

ELECTRIC POWER

Michel, Aloys A. and Klain, Stephen A., "Current Problems of the Soviet Electric Power

Industry," *Economic Geography,* July 1964, pp. 206–220.

Petrov, Victor P., *Geography of the Soviet Union, Part IV-B, Electric Power,* Victor P. Kamkin, Inc., Washington, 1959, 70 pp.

IRON AND STEEL

Akademiya Nauk SSSR, *Zhelezorudnaya baza chernoy metallurgii SSSR* (The iron ore base of the heavy metallurgy of the U.S.S.R.), Moscow, 1957, 566 pp. (in Russian).

———, *Voprosy razrabotki mestorozhdeniy Kurskoy Magnitnoy Anomalii* (Problems of extracting the deposits of the Kursk Magnetic Anomaly), Moscow, 1961, 307 pp. (in Russian).

American Steel and Iron Ore Mining Delegation to the Soviet Union, *Steel in the Soviet Union,* American Iron and Steel Institute, 1959, 376 pp.

Bannyy, N. P., et al., *Ekonomika chernoy metallurgii SSSR* (The economics of heavy metallurgy in the U.S.S.R.), Moscow, 1960, 566 pp. (in Russian).

Bardin, I. P., *Magnititovye rudy Kustanayskoy oblasti i puti ikh ispolzovaniya* (Magnetic ores of Kustanay Oblast and ways of utilizing them), Akademiya Nauk SSSR, Moscow, 1958, 489 pp. (in Russian).

———, *Metallurgy of the U.S.S.R., 1919–1957,* translated by Joint Publications Research Service, 1961.

———, *Zhelezorudnye mestorozhdeniya Tsentralnogo Kazakhstana i puti ikh ispolzovaniya* (Iron ore deposits of Central Kazakhstan and ways of utilizing them), Akademiya Nauk SSSR, Moscow, 1960, 856 pp. (in Russian).

Belevtseva, Y. N., *Geologicheskoe stroyeniye i zheleznyye rudy Krivorozhskogo Basseyna* (Geological structure and iron ore of the Krivoy Rog Basin), Moscow, 1957 (in Russian).

Braun, G. A., *Zhelezorudnaya baza chernoy metallurgii SSSR* (The iron ore base of heavy metallurgy in the U.S.S.R.), Moscow, 1960 (in Russian).

Burstein, Abraham C., *The Iron and Steel Industry in Pre-Revolutionary Russia,* Ph. D. Dissertation, New School for Social Research, 1963.

Clark, Mills Gardner, *The Economics of Soviet Steel,* Harvard University Press, Cambridge, 1956, 400 pp.

———, "Economics and Technology: The Case of Soviet Steel," in Nicolas Spulber, ed., *Study of the Soviet Economy: Direction and Impact of Soviet Growth, Teaching, and Research in Soviet Economics,* Russian and East European Series, Indiana University Publications, Vol. 25, pp. 17–31.

———, "Magnitogorsk: A Soviet Iron and Steel Plant in the Southern Urals," in Thoman and Patton, eds., *Focus on Geographic Activity,* New York, 1964, pp. 128–134.

Granick, David, *Soviet Metal-Fabricating and Economic Development: Practice Versus Policy,* University of Wisconsin Press, Madison, 1967, 367 pp.

Holloway, Robert J., *The Development of the Russian Iron and Steel Industry,* Stanford, 1952, 59 pp.

Holzman, F. D., "Soviet Ural-Kuznetsk Combine: A Study in Investment Criteria and Industrialization Policies," *Quarterly Journal of Economics,* 1957, pp. 368–405.

Jasny, Naum, "Prospects of the Soviet Iron and Steel Industry," *Soviet Studies,* January 1963, pp. 275–294.

Khlebnikov, Viktor B., *Sovetskaya chernaya metallurgiya v 1959–1965 gg* (Soviet heavy metallurgy in 1959–1965), Gosplanizdat, Moscow, 1960, 242 pp. (in Russian).

Livshits, R. S., *Razmeshchenie chernoy metallurgii SSSR* (The distribution of heavy metallurgy in the U.S.S.R.), Moscow, 1958, 371 pp. (in Russian).

Metallurgy in the U.S.S.R., 1917–1957, various authors, translated by Liaison Office, Technical Information Center, MCLTD, Wright-Patterson Air Force Base, Ohio, 1960, 4 Vols., 1215 pp.

Ovchininskii, Nikolai V., *Voprosy razvitiya chernoy metallurgii v tsentralnykh rayonakh SSSR* (Problems of the growth of heavy metallurgy in the central regions of the U.S.S.R.), Moscow, 1961, 137 pp. (in Russian).

Popov, V. E., *Chernaya metallurgii Sibiri* (The heavy metallurgy of Siberia), 1960, 117 pp. (in Russian).

Razvitie chernoy metallurgii U.S.S.R. (The growth of heavy metallurgy in Ukraine), Kiev, 1963, 269 pp. (in Russian).

Stepanov, Petr N., *Geografiya tyazheloy promyshlennosti SSSR* (The geography of heavy industry of the U.S.S.R.), Moscow, 1961.

Zimm, Alfred, *Industriegeographie der Sowjetunion,* Berlin, 1963, 226 pp. (in German).

NONFERROUS METALS

Shabad, Theodore, *The Soviet Aluminum Industry*, American Metal Market, New York, 1958, 25 pp.

Vvedensky, G. A., "The Soviet Copper Industry," *Bulletin of the Institute for the Study of the U.S.S.R.*, August 1967, pp. 22–27.

CHEMICALS

Dienes, Leslie, *Locational Factors and Locational Developments in the Soviet Chemical Industry*, The University of Chicago, Dept. of Geography, Research Paper No. 119, 1969, 262 pp.

Geografiya khimicheskoy promyshlennosti (Geography of the chemical industry), *Voprosy geografii*, Moscow, 1966, No. 72, 187 pp. (in Russian).

Meltzer, Yale L., *Soviet Chemical Industry*, Noyes Development Corporation, Park Ridge, N.J., 1967, 110 pp.

Shabad, Theodore and Lydolph, Paul E., "The Chemical Industries in the U.S.S.R.," *Tijdschrift voor Economische en Sociale Geografie*, August/September 1962, pp. 169–179.

MACHINE BUILDING

Omarovskiy, A. G., "Changes in the Geography of Machine Building in the U.S.S.R.," *Soviet Geography: Review and Translation*, March 1960, pp. 42–56.

TEXTILES

Khorev, B. S. and Rogov, N. A., "On Ways of Developing Former Handicraft Industries (As Illustrated by Gorky Oblast)," *Soviet Geography: Review and Translation*, April 1963, pp. 31–46.

Pryde, Philip R., "The Areal Deconcentration of the Soviet Cotton Textile Industry," *Geographical Review*, October 1968, pp. 575–592.

FISHING

Helin, Ronald A., "Soviet Fishing in the Barents Sea and the North Atlantic," *Geographical Review*, July 1964, pp. 386–408.

Kustov, E. D., *Geografiya rybnoy promyshlennosti* (Geography of the Fishing Industry), Izd. Pishchevaya promyshlennost, Moscow, 1968, 199 pp. (in Russian).

Pfeifer, W., "The Development of the Soviet Fishing Fleet," *Bulletin of the Institute for the Study of the U.S.S.R.*, 1967, Vol. 14, No. 5, pp. 22–30.

FORESTRY

Barr, Brenton M., "The Importance of Regions in Analysis of the Soviet Forest Resource: A Reply," *Canadian Geographer*, 1966, Vol. X, No. 4, pp. 234–237.

Bone, Robert M., "The Soviet Forest Resource," *Canadian Geographer*, 1966, pp. 94–116.

Bowles, Donald W., "Soviet Timber — Two Steps Forward, One Step Back," *Soviet Studies*, April 1965, pp. 377–405.

Gorovoy, V. A. and Privalóvskaya, G. A., *Geografiya lesnoy promyshlennosti SSSR* (Geography of the Wood Industry of the U.S.S.R.), Nauka, Moscow, 1966, 150 pp. (in Russian).

Pfeifer, W., "Soviet Timber Shipping," *Bulletin of the Institute for the Study of the U.S.S.R.*, March 1967, pp. 14–21.

Rodgers, Allan, "Changing Locational Patterns in the Soviet Pulp and Paper Industry," *Annals of the Association of American Geographers*, March 1955, pp. 85–104.

Tseplyaev, V. P., *The Forest of the U.S.S.R.*, translated by A. Gourevitch, Daniel Davey and Co., New York, 1966, 521 pp.

16

Transportation and Domestic Trade

The transportation system is the lifeline of the economy in the Soviet Union, as it is in any country. It moves the traffic that is generated by the disparity between production and consumption in each locale, and is the critical factor in keeping materials supplied to industrial and agricultural concerns. At times its adequacy or inadequacy has had a governing effect on the further expansion of production. The transportation system not only has the function of providing services to the general economy, its operations constitute a significant portion of that economy. The transport system of the U.S.S.R. regularly consumes about one fourth the fuel and steel production of the country and employs about one tenth of the manpower.

Freight traffic in the Soviet Union has risen from 126 billion ton-kilometers in 1913 to 3180 billion ton-kilometers in 1967. In 1926 total freight traffic by all modes of transport in the Soviet Union was about 8 per cent of that in the United States. It rose to 37 per cent in 1940, but during World War II fell back to 20 per cent. Since then it has risen to approximately 126 per cent that of the United States. This great amount of traffic in the Soviet Union is carried by a transportation system that is considerably different from that of the United States or countries in western Europe, and some understanding must be had of the underlying geographic factors and governmental policies controlling the system before it can be understood and appreciated.

Nature of the Soviet Transportation System

Vast distances, uneven distribution of population, physical environment, and party ideology concerning the development of the economy have imparted a somewhat special character and role to the transportation system of the Soviet Union. Special characteristics are: (1) an unusually close integration of the transportation system to overall resources of the economy and to the requirements of general developmental policy, (2) strict limitations on the volume and character of traffic in an effort to minimize transport, (3) limited investment in transport facilities, particularly in highways, which might provide a variety of transport operations, (4) especially heavy reliance on railroads for intercity movement of freight and passengers, and (5) an intensity of total railroad plant operation that is unheard of in the rest of the world.

Shortcomings of River Transport In spite of the great to-do often made about Soviet rivers in general and the Volga River in particular, the truth of the matter is that all Soviet waterways suffer from a number of disabilities, and over the years the rivers' share of total Soviet freight traffic has dwindled to less than 5 per cent at the present time. (Table 16–1) This is in spite of rather heroic efforts by the Soviet government to increase traffic on rivers and to reduce it on railroads. During the last three decades, the Soviets have put into operation a great number of huge water-construction projects, the likes of which were not even dreamed about in Tsarist times. The great Volga scheme, the Dnieper Cascade, the rejuvenated Mariinsk Canal system (Volga-Baltic waterway), the White Sea-Baltic Canal, to mention only a few of the major navigational channels, include the largest reservoirs of water in the world with lengths totaling thousands of kilometers and almost innumerable locks and wintering and repair facilities that represent large investments in money, time, and energy. In addition, in the late 1950s laws were passed that arbitrarily guaranteed that freight rates on waterways would not total more than those on rail-

Table 16–1   Freight Traffic by Means of Transport, U.S.S.R., Selected Years, and U.S.A., 1966, in Billion Ton-Kilometers and Per Cents of Total

	U.S.S.R. (Within Present Boundaries)						U.S.A.,
	1913	1928	1940	1950	1960	1967	1966
Total, billion ton-kilometers	126.0	119.5	487.6	713.3	1,885.7	3,180	2,520
Railroad							
Billion ton-kilometers	76.4	93.4	415.0	602.3	1,504.3	2,162	1,109
Per cent	60.6	78.2	85.1	84.5	79.8	68.1	44
Sea [a]							
Billion ton-kilometers	20.3	9.3	23.8	39.7	131.5	523	—
Per cent	16.1	7.8	4.9	5.6	7.0	16.5	—
River							
Billion ton-kilometers	28.9	15.9	36.1	46.2	99.6	144	371 [b]
Per cent	22.9	13.3	7.4	6.5	5.3	4.5	15
Oil pipeline							
Billion ton-kilometers	0.3	0.7	3.8	4.9	51.2	183	485
Per cent	0.3	0.5	0.8	0.7	2.7	5.8	19
Automobile							
Billion ton-kilometers	0.1	0.2	8.9	20.1	98.5 [c]	166	554
Per cent	0.1	0.2	1.8	2.8	5.2	5.2	22
Airplane							
Billion ton-kilometers	0.0	0.0	0.02	0.14	0.56	1.68	3.3

Sources: Transport i svyaz SSSR, Moscow, 1967, p. 25; *Soviet Economic Performance: 1966–67,* p. 38; and *Statistical Abstract of the United States,* 1968, p. 541.

[a] U.S.S.R. statistics apparently include foreign trade. An atlas published by the Soviets in 1967 shows interregional trade in the U.S.S.R. to be carried 82.4 per cent by railroads, 8.1 per cent by rivers, 7.1 per cent by pipelines, and only 2.4 per cent by seas.

[b] Includes river, Great Lakes, and intracoastal shipping.

[c] Includes 70 billion ton-kilometers moved by trucks owned by industrial and agricultural enterprises. These shares probably are about the same in 1967.

Nature of the Soviet Transportation System   553

ways for identical shipments. According to these laws, penalties as high as 100 per cent would be levied against rail shipments that paralleled navigable waterways during the navigation season, and discounts of as much as 30 per cent would be awarded for mixed shipments utilizing combinations of water and rail movement. All these measures have increased river freight turnover absolutely by almost five times, from 28.9 billion ton-kilometers in 1913 to 144 billion ton-kilometers in 1967. But as can be seen from Table 16–1, traffic on rivers has been increasing at a slower rate than on any other type of carrier, and its share of total traffic decreased from 22.9 per cent in 1913 to only 4.5 per cent in 1967. And in spite of greatly improved navigational conditions and penalties levied against railroad transport, the major water artery in the country, the Volga, which still accounts for about two thirds of river traffic in the entire country, is working at only about one fifth capacity, whereas paralleling railroads work at nearly full capacity. Along the most heavily traveled section of the Volga, from Kuybyshev to Volgograd, average freight densities per mile are somewhat lower than they are on the paralleling railroad along the west bluff. Along the major right-bank tributary, the Oka River, where navigational facilities are not as good, railroad traffic exceeds river traffic by fourteen times.

Some of the obvious drawbacks of river transportation are winter freezing, slow speeds, and circuitous routes. On the Volga, the average speed of commodities is 48 miles per day, as compared to a commodity speed on the paralleling railroad of about 126 miles per day. And in a circuitous section of the river such as that between Gorky and Saratov, the river distance is 806 miles against a rail distance of 341 miles. On the average Volga freight travels 50 per cent farther than it would by rail. And even at the mouth of the Volga, the river is closed by ice more than 3 months of the year. In the Moscow area it is closed 5 months and more. (Table 16–2)

The river-construction projects have not been entirely beneficial. Initial construction costs involved capital investment per additional ton-kilometer freight traffic capacity that was 2 to 2.5 times as high as it would have been for railroad construction, and the years involved in the completion of these projects tied up capital and labor that could have yielded returns far more quickly in other types of endeavor. Once the construction projects are completed, this is not the end of expenditures, either. Docking and port facilities have to be maintained, and in many cases along

Table 16–2   Average Annual Length of Shipping Season, U.S.S.R., at Major Rivers and Ports

Location	Length of Season (Days)	Percentage of Time Navigable
River		
Dnieper at Kiev	267	73.2
Lower Volga	264	72.3
Upper Volga	224	61.4
Western Dvina	236	64.7
Northern Dvina	177	48.5
Ob at Salekhard	152	41.6
Irtysh at Tobolsk	189	51.8
Yenisey at Krasnoyarsk	197	54.0
Southern (Upper) Lena	145	39.7
Northern (Lower) Lena	88	24.1
Seaport		
Odessa	328	89.9
Zhdanov	288	79.8
Taganrog	252	69.0
Astrakhan	238	65.2
Tallin	283	77.5
Leningrad	200	54.8
Murmansk	365 [a]	100.0
Archangel	175	47.9
Nizhne-Kolymsk	110	30.1
Vladivostok	255	69.9

Source: Holland Hunter, *Soviet Transportation Policy,* 1957, p. 13.

[a] Kept open by icebreaker for 50 days.

the shallow gradients of the European streams frequent dredging is required. So the Soviets are finding out, as other countries have, that a waterway is not free to operate once it is in existence.

The huge reservoirs themselves have proved to be more of a hazard to transportation than an asset. The fetch of the wind over them is so great that huge waves are generated during storms which tend to capsize self-propelled vessels and render the towing of barges impossible. It has been estimated that along the Volga, tow barges lose 15 to 20 per cent of the navigational season laying over in wave shelters. This no doubt accounts for the seemingly irrational Soviet effort to place more and more self-propelled vessels on their waterways. Soviet planners contend that self-propelled vessels are 25 per cent cheaper than barges, which is surprising in light of experience in other parts of the world. At the present time apparently more than one quarter of the river tonnage is carried by self-propelled vessels, most of which have Diesel engines. The lack of a perceptible current in the reservoirs makes the rafting of timber impossible, and the wood has to be loaded on self-propelled vessels. Ice remains on the reservoirs 12 to 14 days longer than it did on the original rivers, which further shortens the navigational season. And, finally, the locks that are necessary for boats to change water levels at each dam have proved to be quite a bottleneck, as ships back up for miles and await passage.

Although water channels along the Volga and other major waterways are now adequate, river craft and port facilities are not. Until recently most of the Soviet tows averaged about 300 horsepower each, as compared to over 500 in the United States, and only recently the Soviets have been converting their barges to the push type, which was found to be more efficient than the pull type in the United States years ago. Ports are very poorly mechanized, and transshipments are costly and time consuming. Large industries located directly on river flood plains along navigable waterways, such as the Volgograd tractor plant and the Moscow automobile plant, do not even have docks. Obviously they are making no use of the river as a means of transport for their bulky supplies and products. Thus industrialization along such major waterways as the Volga has not been accompanied by a corresponding construction of river facilities and growth of river traffic.

Since the major rivers of the country flow off to the edges of the land mass and fail to join together the major concentrations of natural resources and economic activity, use of waterways would usually entail transshipments to and from rail at points where the rivers ceased to flow in the right directions. Since transshipping facilities are so poor and bureaucratic red tap between ministries of railroad transport and river transport are so involved, most shippers despair of mixing modes of transport. Along the upper Kama River, for instance, where a great volume of bulky freight—lumber—moves across the region from east to west by rail and continues southward to the Ukraine, Kama River ports manage to capture only about 7 per cent of the timber crossing the area for transshipment down the Volga. Soviet economists ruefully joke that many shippers suffer from "hydrophobia."

The use of expensive canals has been rather disappointing. (Table 16–3) The White Sea-Baltic and Volga-Don Canals have been some of the most expensive to construct and the least remunerative in their operations. Perhaps the Moscow Canal is the only one that has paid for itself, and its function as an additional supplier of domestic water to Moscow is probably more important than its navigational function. The Volga-Baltic Waterway, the old Mariinsk system, may eventually pay for itself since it connects the important industrial areas of Moscow and Leningrad with each other and with resource regions of bulky materials such as apatite, iron ore, coal, and timber.

The huge river systems of Siberia unfortunately flow northward rather than in an east-west direction, and hence do not provide direct connections with European Russia. Connection of these streams, by way of the Northern Sea Route, from their mouths westward to Archangel and Murmansk is severely limited by the short shipping season and the high cost of navigating the northern seas. The Amur River in the Soviet Far East has proved to be of slight value in developing the territory around it.

In earlier days the Dnieper and the rivers of northwestern European Russia were the main traffic arteries of the territories through which they ran, but with the coming of the railroads the role of the rivers has steadily declined, and even the building of several canals during the interwar period has failed to reestablish their former positions. All in all, the evidence indicates conclusively that the rivers of the U.S.S.R. do not mesh with the main traffic flows.

Shortcomings of Maritime Shipping
Maritime shipping in the Soviet Union suffers from many of the same ills that river transportation does. The borders of the U.S.S.R. total approximately 37,000 miles, 70 per cent of which are bounded by water. Yet only a small fraction of the surrounding water is suited to the carriage of freight between points of the U.S.S.R. Except for canal connections on Soviet territory, which are closed by ice during the winter, commodity movements between north and south European U.S.S.R. by sea require trips around the whole circumference of western Europe, and sea passage from southern ports along the Black Sea to the Soviet Far East entails a voyage almost half way around the world by way of the Suez canal, skirting India and China. Thus the movement of commodities by sea between major producing

and consuming areas of the Soviet Union entails extremely circuitous routes which involve unwarranted periods of time for shipments. The more direct route between European Russia and the Far East, the Northern Sea Route, is closed by ice at least 9 months of the year, and during the short navigational season it can only be navigated by the use of ice breakers moving ships in convoy aided by aircraft, weather stations, and other support equipment to survey ice conditions and chart the course ahead of the ships. So far, traffic along it has remained very nominal, and it appears

Table 16–3   Canals and Reservoirs Included in Navigable Waterways in 1965

	Length in Kilometers	Freight in Tons
Canals		
Karakum	535	
Volga-Baltic	362	5,288,000
White Sea-Baltic	222	3,308,000
Dnieper-Bug	202	
Moscow	125	11,172,000
Volga-Don	106	7,655,000
Reservoirs		
Kuybyshev		
Volga branch	522	
Kama branch	316	
Volgograd	526	
Bratsk	440	
Gorky	430	
Votkinsk	360	
Tsymlyansk	302	
Kama	272	
Rybinsk		
Leningrad branch	140	
Moscow branch	96	
Novosibirsk	182	
Uglich	143	
Ivankovo	134	
Pavlovsk	126	
Kakhovka, Kremenchug, and others on Dnieper River	743	
Bukhtarma	396	

Source: Transport i svyaz SSSR, Moscow, 1967, p. 174.

that it will continue to remain so. The Caspian Sea, which in the past, because of bulky oil shipments, has handled at least 50 per cent of Soviet sea movements, was landlocked until 1952 when it was joined with the Black Sea by the Volga-Don Canal, but even now this canal is closed by ice 5 months of the year.

In view of all these difficulties, sea traffic was allowed to lapse during the early part of the Soviet period. (Table 16–1) In 1940 sea traffic was barely more than it had been in 1913 and its share of total traffic had dwindled from 16.1 per cent in 1913 to 4.9 per cent in 1940. However, it appears that sometime after 1940 the decision was made to attempt to increase sea movements, and since then absolute amounts of sea traffic have been increasing rapidly and the relative share of total trade has been increasing as well. For the period 1951–1965, marine transport was the second most rapidly increasing mode of traffic after pipelines. (Table 16–4) And during the 7 years from 1960 to 1967, the share of sea traffic in total movement of freight in the Soviet Union more than doubled, from 7 per cent of the total in 1960 to 16.5 per cent in 1967. The absolute amount of sea traffic during this 7-year period increased almost four times.

Undoubtedly the reason behind this recent jump in sea traffic has been the

Table 16–4   Average Annual Growth Rates of Freight Turnover by Types of Transport, U.S.S.R. and U.S.A., 1951–1965, in Per Cents

	U.S.S.R.	U.S.A.
Total	9.4	2.3
Railroads	8.1	1.0
Marine	16.4	−0.2
River	7.4	3.1
Automobile	14.0	5.5
Pipeline	25.4	5.4

Source: Transport i svyaz SSSR, Moscow, 1967, p. 45.

stress during the past decade on the building of the Soviet merchant marine, which is tied to both commercial and strategic motives. In 1960 the Soviet merchant fleet consisted of about 650 ships totaling 4,000,000 tons dead weight which ranked thirteenth among the world's merchant marines. At the end of 1967 the fleet consisted of about 1200 ships totaling 10 million tons dead weight which ranked seventh in the world. To keep pace with the growth of the fleet and expanding foreign trade, sea ports are being improved and modernized rapidly.

Previously, much of Soviet foreign trade was carried in foreign bottoms, and no doubt the Soviets were loath to carry any domestic trade in this way. Now, with the greatly expanded merchant marine of their own, they probably are willing to devote a significant portion of space on their own ships to domestic trade, even if this is not a particularly economical practice. It might be that much of the domestic trade between, for instance, European Russia and the Soviet Far East, is integrated with foreign trade between European Russia and, for instance, Japan—the same ships stopping off at Soviet Pacific ports that continue on to Japan or some other country in the Far East. This might make for more efficient usage of ships which otherwise would make long trips partially unfilled. At any rate, it appears that the U.S.S.R. has restored sea traffic to a relative position similar to that which it held before the Revolution. But it is doubtful whether sea traffic can be expanded to handle much more of the total domestic trade of the U.S.S.R. than it is doing at the present time.

Geographical Factors Favor Railroads
The broad plains of the U.S.S.R. are unusually favorable for the construction and low-cost operation of railroads. According to 1933 data, only 4 per cent of the total main track operated had ruling gradients in excess of 1 per cent, whereas more than a quarter of the line was horizontal and more than 60 per cent had gradients below

0.5 of a per cent. Railroad operation is hampered to some extent by climate, extreme cold and snow in winter, and lack of water in the southern deserts, but the seasonality induced in railroad traffic by climatic factors is much less than that induced in the traffic of other carriers. Such considerations have induced the Soviets to stress the railroads at the expense of all other types of transport. What investments the Soviet government reluctantly put into the transport system during the 1920s and 1930s went almost exclusively into the railroads, which had already carried as much as 60 per cent of the total domestic traffic before the Revolution. By 1940 the railroads' share in total trade had risen to 85.1 per cent and it remained there throughout World War II and for about a decade thereafter. Not until approximately the mid 1950s did the Soviets make the decision to rejuvenate the merchant marine and to embark on a grandiose plan of rapid pipeline building which by the early 1960s began to cut into the railroads' share of the growing traffic. In spite of such inroads, in 1967 railroads still carried 68 per cent of total Soviet trade turnover. (Table 16–1)

Lack of Highways and Automotive Transport The reluctance of the Soviet administration to divert capital from the industrialization effort to the transportation system, coupled with the lack of public demand for good automobile roads, has resulted in an almost complete neglect of the building of highways in the country. Compared to other modes of freight movement, motor transport is highly inefficient except on short hauls and requires inputs of fuel, labor, repair parts, and rates of vehicle replacement that are unacceptable to Soviet planners. Hence intercity truck traffic does not really exist; trucks are used almost exclusively for short-haul distribution of materials from rail sidings in urban areas or for transport of farm produce from collective and state farms to rail heads in rural areas. The average length of truck haul in 1966 was only 13.3 kilo-

meters. Concrete, black-top, and gravel highways in 1966 totaled only 405,600 kilometers. By comparison, the United States had almost 6,000,000 kilometers of surfaced roads.

The areas having the densest road nets, the Center, Ukraine, Baltic, Transcaucasia, and Volga-Urals, have only about 100 kilometers of surfaced roads per 1000 square kilometers of territory. Over most of the country, the density is less than 10 kilometers of road per 1000 square kilometers. Huge areas have no roads at all. (Fig. 16–1) Those roads designated as major highways are usually only two-lane blacktop. At the end of 1967, the U.S.S.R. had about 4 million trucks in civilian use, whereas the United States had over 15.5 million. Many of these United States trucks were large semitrailers which hauled goods long distances between major cities, whereas most of the Soviet trucks were the small military type performing only collecting and disseminating functions for the railroads. Although the Soviet Union experienced a significant relative growth in automotive freight transport from 1940 to 1960, since 1960 this has leveled off, and in fact a slight relative decrease was experienced between 1966 and 1967. (Table 16–1) Although the U.S.S.R. recognizes that the lack of good roads is a real handicap to its economy, particularly in the critical agricultural sector, a tightness of investment resources has forced the Soviets to progress painfully slowly in the grading and surfacing of roads. During the period 1961–1966, about 22,500 kilometers of hard-surfaced roads were added per year. This rate has tapered off since then to about 13,000 kilometers of new construction in 1968.

Pipelines

Until the mid 1950s, the relatively small volume and geographical dispersion of oil movements did not warrant the construction of many pipelines for the transport of

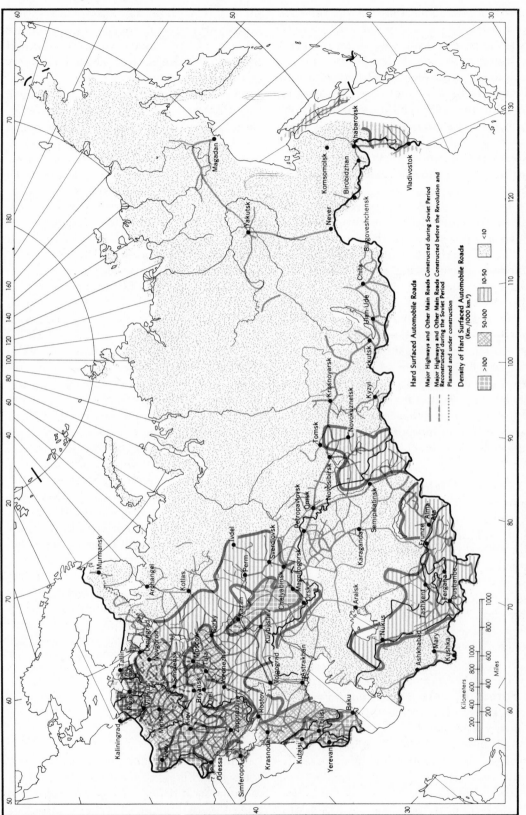

Figure 16–1   Highways and highway densities. From Atlas razvitiya khozyaystva i kultury SSSR, pp. 86–87.

petroleum and petroleum products, and the use of natural gas was virtually undeveloped. The only relatively concentrated oil movement was that from Baku across the Caspian and up the Volga to the Central Industrial Region, which moved by lake and river steamers. There was also considerable waterborne oil traffic on the Black Sea as tankers picked up oil and refined products at the Batumi end of the pipeline that traversed the Kura-Rioni Synclinal Valley, and also at Tuapse at the end of a short pipeline that traversed the low western end of the Caucasus from Maykop, and carried them to the markets in Ukraine. But the rest of the distribution of oil products to markets was done almost entirely by railroads.

With the policy trend started in 1955 to develop rapidly the usage of oil and natural gas, the Soviets realized that such an expansion of such bulky products would probably completely break down the already overworked railway system, and therefore they concomitantly decided upon a rapid construction of trunk pipelines. This is still going on, and pipes are continually being constructed in larger and larger diameters. By the end of 1967, oil pipelines in the U.S.S.R. totaled 32,200 kilometers, almost double the length in service at the end of 1960, and gas pipelines totaled 52,800 kilometers, 31,800 more than in 1960. Oil pipelines alone now account for about 6 per cent of total freight traffic in the Soviet Union, whereas in 1950 they accounted for less than 1 per cent. Priority during the last few years has been given to the construction of gas pipelines as part of a drive to substitute cheap natural gas for coal.

Despite this remarkable expansion of pipeline usage, the Soviet Union's network of oil and gas pipelines is still dwarfed by the U.S.A., which at the end of 1966 had 321,900 kilometers of oil pipelines and 420,000 kilometers of gas pipelines in service. The Soviets still have a long way to go in pipeline construction if they are going to exploit fully the huge newly discovered resources of oil and gas in such areas as western Siberia and the Central Asian deserts. Petroleum products still are moved almost as much by rail as they are by pipe and constitute the second most bulky freight traffic on the railroads. (Tables 16–5 and 16–9) As long as this situation exists, the rate of expansion of the petroleum and natural gas industries will be determined by the availability of transport facilities.

The Railroads

Policies and Realities Determining the Development of the Rail Network Governmental policies and several economic counterpressures have controlled the development of the railroad system in the U.S.S.R. Rapid industrialization with the emphasis on heavy industry at the expense of services and conveniences has led to a stringent policy in the outlay of capital for railroad plants and equipment. This stringency has resulted in a railway system that at present carries almost twice the freight traffic and five times the passenger traffic that railroads in the United States do on little more than one third the trackage that exists in the United States. (Table 16–6) The Soviet Union has the greatest railroad freight traffic densities in the world. (Fig. 16–2)

Whether considered in relation to land area, population, or traffic volume, the Soviet rail network is minimal. It is a planned system of main routes without competitive overlap and with feeder lines developed sufficiently to provide necessary minimum service to only the major sources of tonnage. Industrial plant location has often been determined by railway location, and farms have been forced to convey their produce to rail headings, usually by primitive means.

The rail net is most adequate in Ukraine and the Baltic Republics where rail densi-

Table 16–5 Movements of Main Commodities by Modes of Transport, 1966, in Millions of Tons [a,b]

	Railroad	Sea	River	Pipeline	Automobile [c]
Coal and coke	583	9	16		87
Petroleum and petroleum products	240	Not available	27	248	22
Ferrous metals	154	5	1		79
Timber	142	7 [d]	88 [d]		
Grain	86	6	6		58
Ores	203	11	4		19
Firewood	20				
Mineral construction materials	594	14	123		17
Mineral fertilizers	98	4	1		28
Other	412	14	13	0	

Source: Transport i svyaz SSSR, Moscow, 1967, pp. 102–103, 154, 180–181, and 238–239.

[a] Rounded to nearest million.

[b] Commodity breakdown for freight hauled by trucks and airplanes is not available. These modes of transport are relatively insignificant in intercity freight transport.

[c] Very short distances (data for 1965).

[d] Includes firewood.

ties are 36.1 and 35.2 kilometers of line per 1000 square kilometers of territory respectively. In the Center the density is only 21.3, and in the Urals 12.1. For the entire country, the rail density has risen very slowly to 5.9 kilometers of line per 1000 square kilometers of territory. Freight movement in the Baltic Republics is hampered by the necessity to transship goods on about half the lines which are of narrower west European gauge, whereas lines in the rest of the Soviet Union are all wide gauge.

The benefits of economy of scale and the urgency for speed of industrialization, which led to gigantomania in industrial plant construction, also led to super-trunklining of railroads between a few major producing areas at the expense of extending new lines into underdeveloped areas.

In the late 1920s the transportation system contained a good deal of slack, but by the mid 1930s this slack had been taken

Table 16–6 Total Railroad Mileage, U.S.S.R. and U.S.A., at Ends of Selected Years, in Thousands of Kilometers

	U.S.S.R. [a]	U.S.A. [b]
1950	111.8	343.6
1960	120.6	333.7
1964	124.6	328.7
1965	126.8	324.8
1966	128.2	338.9

Sources: Transport i svyaz SSSR, Moscow, 1967, pp. 46 and 95, and *Soviet Economic Performance: 1966–67,* p. 36.

[a] Figures include only wide-gauge railroads operated by the Ministry of Transport. At the end of 1965 the U.S.S.R. also had 4.7 thousand kilometers of narrow gauge operated by the Ministry of Transport and 113.9 thousand kilometers of other railways operated by individual industries and other organizations.

[b] Includes only first-class lines, which make up about 95 per cent of all lines in the U.S.A.

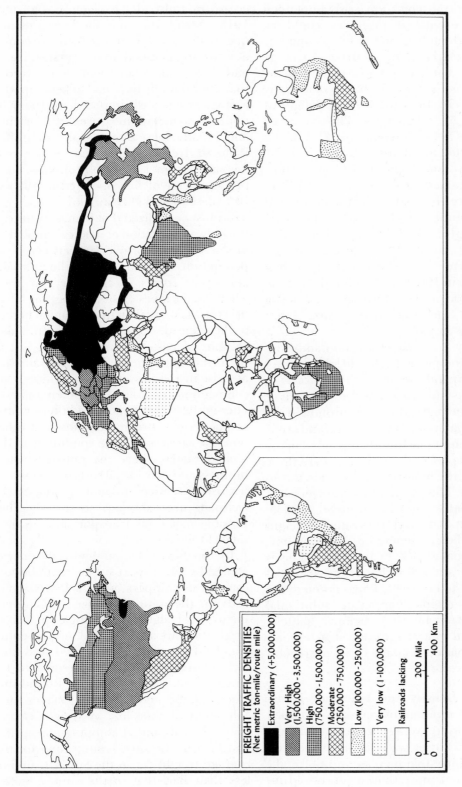

Figure 16–2   Freight traffic densities on the world's railroads. Adapted from Wallace, William H., "Railroad Traffic Densities and Patterns," Annals of the Association of American Geographers, December 1958, p. 353.

FREIGHT TRAFFIC DENSITIES
(Net metric ton-mile/route mile)

Extraordinary (+5,000,000)

Very High
(1,500,000 - 3,500,000)

High
(750,000 - 1,500,000)

Moderate
(250,000 - 750,000)

Low (100,000 - 250,000)

Very low (1 - 100,000)

Railroads lacking

0   200 Mile

0   400 Km.

up and a transportation crisis impended unless preventative measures could be taken. Although it had been planned to locate industrial plants so that the average length of haul would decrease, actually the average length of haul consistently increased. In 1928 the average length of haul was 598 kilometers. This increased steadily to 794 kilometers in 1945. When it was reported again after the war, in 1950, it appeared smaller, only 722 kilometers, but it increased again to a peak of 815 in 1957. Since then it has fluctuated up and down around the 800 mark. The years 1960, 1961, and 1962 were below 800 kilometers, but in 1963 it shot up to 811, after which it dropped a little, and then rose again in 1966 to 812. Thus during the past decade it seems to have reached a plateau at a level about one third higher than it was in 1928.

A policy to adjust production and shipments to the present railroad plant rather than to expend capital on the railroads to make them more adequate for the needs of industry and agriculture has prompted the demand that more coal, iron ore, and other bulky resources be found and mined in the European part of the country where three fourths of the industrial production is concentrated. This is an obvious reversal of the heralded eastward movement. In 1965, 67 per cent of the country's railroad freight was still being generated by economic activity situated west of the Urals. This is not significantly different from what had been reported in 1949. Thus, although the Bolshevik regime has made substantial modifications in the regional pattern bequeathed to it, the present structure is a recognizable descendant of its prerevolutionary ancestor.

Freight Density and Efficiency Measures   The rapid industrialization coupled with the rising average length of haul according to Soviet statistics has produced almost a thirty-fold increase in rail freight turnover and more than a seven-fold increase in railroad passenger traffic since 1913. During this time the length of line operated has less than doubled. Although Soviet bureaucrats tend to overstate traffic and understate equipment, it is obvious that the railroads have had to keep up with a tremendous task imposed on them by utilizing stringent measures of efficiency and greatly increasing density of traffic. Railroad freight traffic density per year increased from 1.1 million ton-kilometers per kilometer of line operated in 1913 to 10.7 in 1958 and 16.2 in 1967.

It must be realized that in most countries the railway operation embodies a good deal of slack because of overlap between competing railroads and between the railroads and other forms of transport. In areas where traffic taxes existent transport facilities, this slack is taken up and much higher traffic densities are achieved. In small sections of eastern United States, just as high traffic densities exist on the railroads as exist in the Soviet Union. There is no competition, of course, between railroad lines in the Soviet Union, and there is little competition between railroads and other types of carriers. Unlike conditions in the United States where the railroads solicit business and provide all sorts of excessively luxurious services to gain it, the Soviet railroads urge shippers to use all other possible means of transport and to limit total shipments.

In the Soviet Union high efficiency is gained by a transport system that does not cater to its shippers but which sets standards for the shippers to live by. Consignments of freight from single points of origination are accumulated until an entire trainload is ready to be shipped, and similarly entire trainloads are designated for single points of termination. Round-the-clock loading and unloading makes for a minimum of time lost by freight cars in railroad yards and at shipping enterprises and has cut the turn-around time for the average freight car in the Soviet Union to less than half that in the United States.

Whereas in the United States box cars often are used as temporary warehouses on industrial plant rail sidings until the plant gets ready to use the shipment, in the Soviet Union enterprises are penalized for delaying a freight car more than 24 hours. Such measures lead to service conditions that would be intolerable in the United States or western Europe, but they certainly make for efficient use of railroad equipment.

Greater frequency of trains in the Soviet Union counterbalances slower train speeds and lighter train weights than in the United States. During the years 1951–1955, average net freight train weights in the U.S.S.R. were 83 per cent of those in the United States, net ton-miles per freight train-hour were 67 per cent that of the United States, and freight train frequencies (train-miles per mile of road operated) were 3.3 times those of the United States. The resultant freight traffic density on all Soviet railroads was 2.8 times that on railroads in the United States. Since then freight train weights and speeds in the Soviet Union have increased and train frequencies have remained high, with the result that freight traffic density on all Soviet railroads is now five times that on United States railroads. And United States railways have the second highest freight densities in the world.

Technological Advances   With the present equipment and operating techniques it appears that the freight traffic on the railroads in the U.S.S.R. can hardly be pushed any higher, but there are two technological advances that can be and are being made that will allow for a considerably higher freight traffic on the existing lines. One innovation is the conversion from steam to electric and Diesel traction, and the other is the installation of a countrywide system of automatic block-signaling. As late as 1950, 110,800 kilometers of line out of a total of 116,900 kilometers were operated by steam locomotives which hauled almost 95 per cent

of the total rail traffic. Since that time there has been a significant shift to electric and Diesel traction. By 1966, 27,000 kilometers had been electrified out of a total of 132,500 kilometers operated by the Ministry of Transport. These were the main trunk lines, which that year carried 42 per cent of the total freight traffic. Diesel-electric accounted for another 47 per cent. This process is continuing. In 1967 steam locomotion traveled on only 28 per cent of the total trackage and pulled only 8 per cent of the total freight traffic. These changes are allowing heavier trains to be pulled at greater speeds by more powerful engines and are eliminating large amounts of coal that had been hauled simply for consumption by the locomotives. (Table 16–7)

New Railroad Construction   Some railroad construction continues all the time. About 7100 kilometers of new track were commissioned during 1961–1967. The greatest amount of construction probably takes place in the double tracking of existing lines to handle increasingly heavy flows of traffic between major concentrations of population and industry. The Soviets report about 75 per cent more track mileage than they do line mileage, which signifies the amount of double tracking that has been done in the country. In general, what new lines have been built have been built for very specific purposes in response to urgent demands that already exist or are immediately imminent. It has not been the practice of the Soviets to extend rails into remote areas of the country with the vague purpose of stimulating settlement, as has so often been the case in the past in many other countries of the world, particularly in the United States during the nineteenth century. Current railroad construction is being made in response to three types of needs: to facilitate the exploitation of large new mineral deposits in areas that have not been served by railroads previously; to complete links in existing lines that will

Table 16–7   Types of Railroad Traction and Relative Advantages, U.S.S.R., 1966

	Steam	Electric	Diesel-Electric
Rail lines (per cent of total)	33	20	47
Freight turnover (per cent of total)	11.2	42	46.8
Average freight car speeds (kilometers per hour)	25.6	40.3	32.7
Average road speeds (kilometers per hour)	39.6	50.1	44.5
Net tonnage per train (tons)	927	1465	1397
Fuel usage (conventional units per 10,000 ton-kilometers)	224	—	48

Source: Transport i svyaz SSSR, Moscow, 1967, pp. 112–114.

provide necessary alternate routes for heavy flows of traffic between major regions; and to provide adequate access into and out of newly settled areas whose population densities and aggregate production have generated adequate demands for market outlets and incoming supplies.

Probably the two most outstanding examples of the first type of railroad building in the last few years have been the railroad to the Mangyshlak Peninsula, completed in June 1964, and the Tyumen-Tobolsk-Surgut Railroad, part of which has already been completed in western Siberia. Both are being built rapidly in response to the discovery and initial exploitation of large oil deposits in those two areas. Another such line is the Arctic Railroad running about 100 miles eastward from Salekhard, near the mouth of the Ob River, to Nadym to serve a new collecting and supply center for the large west Siberian gas fields that are to be developed in this area. This project was started in the late 1940s using forced labor, but then it was abandoned.

Now it is being rehabilitated because of the new finds of gas in this region. Its construction entails, among other things, a very long bridge across the lower Ob. In the European North, a similar railroad is being laid eastward from Archangel to the Pinega River to open up new timber areas. And a 105-kilometer line opened in 1968 to provide a more direct route from the iron mines at Zheleznogorsk in the Kursk Magnetic Anomaly to Orel, from whence the ore will be shipped to the steel mill of Tula and Lipetsk. Other short lines of this type have been extended northward from the Trans-Siberian Railroad in Central Siberia to some of the new hydroelectric sites.

The most important railroad being laid at the present time is a good example of the completion of an alternate route to relieve heavy flows of traffic between major regions. This is the so-called Beyneu-Kungrad line of Kazakhstan, which will link up with the Astrakhan-Guryev Railroad that was opened in October 1967 and the rail line that starts at Kungrad near the mouth of the Amu-Darya and continues southeastward paralleling the Amu-Darya upstream to where it joins the Trans-Caspian Railroad at Chardzhou. (Fig. 16–3) The remaining section across the Ustyurt Plateau is expected to be completed in 1970. Then the line will form a new direct route between Middle Asia and European Russia.

Another such alternate route was opened in December 1962 when the important Omsk-Barnaul Railroad went into operation. This line runs southeastward from Omsk to Barnaul and then eastward to the Kuznetsk Basin, and thereby provides an alternate route to the Omsk-Novosibirsk section of the Trans-Siberian Railroad, which, linking the Kuznetsk heavy industry with the Urals heavy industry, carries the heaviest traffic of any railroad in the world.

In January 1963 the Achinsk-Abalakovo Railroad was opened to connect Achinsk, an industrial city on the Trans-Siberian Railroad, with Abalakovo, the center of a lumbering and wood-processing district on the left bank of the Yenisey just below the mouth of the Angara River. This railroad is to be one of two feeder lines which eventually are supposed to join up with a future North Siberian Railroad which, it is envisioned, will run somewhat north of the present Trans-Siberian to the Pacific. This, then, is a good example of a railroad which is being built into a newly settled area in response to the needs of that area, with an eye to the future for possible linkage with an envisioned integrated rail network.

The Pattern of Commodity Movement

Around 1900 By the turn of the century three main flows of commodities had developed. Grain moved out of central European Russia and Ukraine northwestward to markets around Moscow and St. Peters-

burg and to the ports of the Baltic for overseas shipment; it also moved southwestward to Black Sea ports for shipment to southern European markets. Coal, iron, and steel moved out of eastern Ukraine in all directions, but particularly northward toward Moscow, and inflowing freight focused on the Moscow and St. Petersburg areas. The flow of timber and wood products southward to the industrialized and heavily populated areas of central European Russia and Ukraine was significant, but it was in no way commensurate to the other three flows.

The river systems of the Volga, the Dnieper, and various smaller streams facilitated this movement of goods to a certain extent, but the railroad pattern had by this time developed to serve these routes of flow, and the railroads carried the bulk of the traffic. The Black and Baltic Seas handled much of the foreign trade, and the Caspian was becoming important for the shipment of oil from Baku northward into the Central Industrial Region.

In succeeding years, the grain traffic diminished somewhat, coal became the dominant commodity after 1907, the petroleum traffic on the Caspian and Volga system became very heavy, and some diversification in products and geographical distributions took place. Some grain now moved westward out of western Siberia into European Russia, and some cotton moved northwestward out of Middle Asia into the textile centers around Moscow.

From 1929 to 1939 With the advent of the 5-year plans, and the industrialization of the Urals and western Siberia, a large flow of traffic developed eastward into those regions. The resulting pattern of traffic was a crossbar consisting of a broad north-south flow in European Russia and a long, slender flow perpendicular to it extending eastward into Siberia. Toward the end of the 1930s rapid development of industry in eastern Siberia and the Far

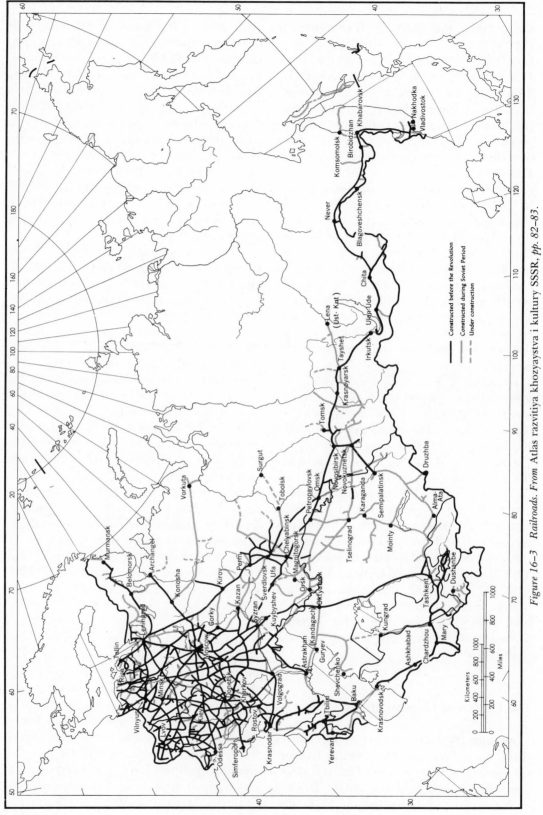

Figure 16–3 Railroads. From Atlas razvitiya khozyaystva i kultury SSSR, pp. 82–83.

East gave rise to increased freight traffic at this farthest end of the U.S.S.R. Traffic was overbalanced in the eastward direction, since the eastern regions were importing a greater volume than they were exporting. There was very little export abroad from this end of the country.

Industrial growth around Moscow and Leningrad intensified the net import balance of those regions and the northward flow of heavy freight to them. Industrial growth in the Urals and western Siberia stimulated a considerable two-way freight flow between this part of the U.S.S.R., Moscow and Leningrad, and eastern Ukraine. Other elements of the pattern were less important, although the constant flow of timber and wood products was, of course, intensified by the industrialization, and the northward flow of petroleum from the Caucasus increased appreciably.

During and Since World War II World War II brought on a trend for a significantly higher industrial growth in the eastern regions than in the south of European Russia. Also, the Volga Valley, which tended to lag behind some other regions during the 1930s, became the scene of exceptionally rapid growth during and after the war. Whereas there used to be primarily through traffic crossing the Volga Region to and from Middle Asia, Kazakhstan, and the Southern Urals, the through traffic is now combined with significant local originations and terminations of heavy freight. The crossbar of the interwar period has been modified by a diagonal connecting the Donbass with the "second iron and steel base," passing through the Volga Valley. Moreover, the concentrated shuttle of coal and iron ore between the two ends of the Ural-Kuznetsk Combine has become somewhat diffused at both ends, and a larger north-south freight flow between this region and Middle Asia has developed. Consequently, the lateral east-west flow of the crossbar is broadening and the area between the two arms is filling in.

In the Far East there is now less evidence of rapid industrial development and increased freight generation than there was in the late 1930s, but during the 1950s an increasing volume of freight traffic to and from China moved over the Trans-Siberian Railroad and south through Manchuria, or, since 1955, through the Mongolian Peoples Republic. Though this China traffic has dropped sharply since 1960, the through transit of military and other supplies to North Vietnam in recent years has largely sustained this southeasterly flow of goods.

In all freight originations on carriers other than pipelines, the Donets-Dnieper Region of Ukraine is by far the most important. This is followed by the Urals, the Center, the Volga, the Northwest, and western Siberia. (Table 16–8) Except for the Center it is obvious that each of these regions ships some bulky products. The Donets and western Siberia ship coal, the Urals ship ores and oil, the Volga ships oil, and the Northwest ships lumber. In total terminations, the Donets-Dnieper Region ranks first again, the Urals second again, the Center third again, the Northwest fourth, the Volga fifth, and western Siberia sixth. Thus those regions originating the most also receive the most, although in a slightly different order. The greatest net exporter by far is the Donets-Dnieper Region. This is followed by the Volga, west Siberia, and east Siberia. It must be remembered that these balances are computed only in terms of weight, not value. Thus eastern Siberia may be a net exporter of weight, but it is a rather significant net importer of value of products. Eastern Ukraine and the Urals concentrate on primary industries based on local raw materials and hence are net exporting regions. The Center, on the other hand, is a manufacturing area for finished products and depends on the import of great quantities of raw materials to sustain these industries. It is therefore a region where tons terminated greatly exceed tons originated. This is also true of the Baltic area.

Table 16–8   Regional Movements of Freight on Railroads, Rivers, and Seas, 1965, in Millions of Tons

Economic Reporting Regions	Freight Origina- tions	Freight Termina- tions	Intra- regional Movements	Regional Exports	Regional Imports	Net Exports (+) or Imports (−)
Northwest	220	209	157	64	52	+12
Center	228	262	154	74	108	−34
Volga-Vyatka	65	74	29	36	45	−9
Central Chernozem	62	81	34	28	47	−19
Volga	227	186	106	121	80	+41
North Caucasus	146	146	77	68	68	0
Ural	309	305	196	113	109	+4
Western Siberia	215	174	131	84	43	+41
Eastern Siberia	122	97	79	43	18	+25
Far East	78	88	71	7	17	−10
Donets-Dnieper	521	421	341	180	80	+100
Southwest	118	161	77	42	84	−42
South	59	87	30	29	57	−28
Baltic	53	88	41	12	48	−36
Transcaucasia	80	84	59	21	25	−4
Middle Asia	66	80	51	16	29	−13
Kazakhstan	134	119	73	61	45	+16
Belorussia	37	68	25	12	42	−30
Moldavia	10	18	7	3	11	−8

Source: Transport i svyaz SSSR, Moscow, 1967, pp. 74–77.

In 1965 the Donets-Dnieper Region exported a total of 74.7 million tons of coal, 69.3 million tons of which went by rail, 3.8 by river, and 1.7 by sea. It imported 6.9 million tons of coal, all by railroad. One can see what little use is made of the Volga-Don Canal for the product that one would most expect to provide much of the bulk traffic. In 1965 coal provided about 42 per cent of the materials exported from this region. Iron and manganese ores and steel make up much of the other exports, although some grain is still exported. Much of the movement of these heavy commodities is within the region itself, however, coal moving westward to the Dnieper and iron and manganese moving eastward to Donets. Thus the heaviest rail traffic in the country flows between the two nodes of this heavy industry area, which com-

plement each other in coal and iron ore resources, although no single railroad in this region has traffic equal to that which moves along the Omsk-Novosibirsk section of the Trans-Siberian Railroad. (Fig. 16–4)

In addition to eastern Ukraine and the Urals-Kuznetsk regions, very heavy rail traffic moves along the three main lines connecting the Donets Basin with the Central Industrial Region. Northbound freight predominates on all these lines since heavy raw materials and steel are moving northward to the Central Industrial Region and lighter finished goods are moving southward out of the Central Industrial Region.

Four main rail lines connect the Central Industrial Region eastward with the Urals and western Siberia. Westbound traffic predominates on all these rail lines, although farther east along the Trans-

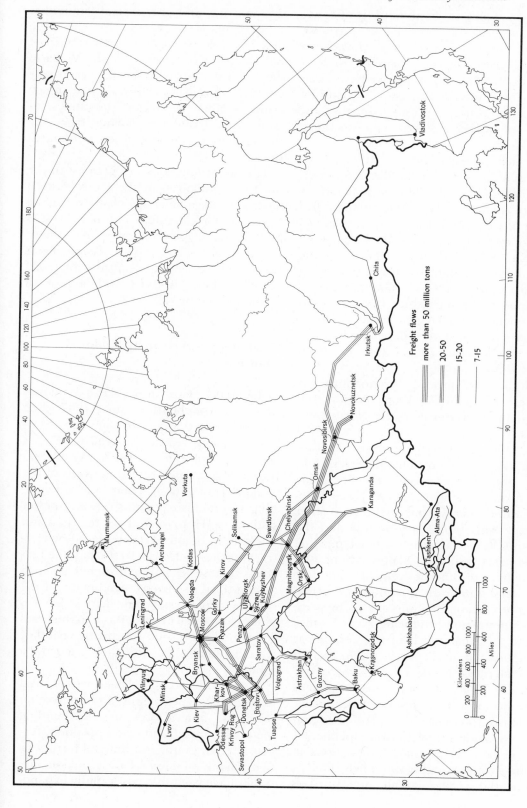

Figure 16–4 Annual freight flows on main railroads. After Nikolskiy.

Siberian Railroad eastbound traffic exceeds westbound east of the Kuznetsk Basin. The heavy westbound movements of coal, ores, and steel between western Siberia and European Russia have been augmented during the past 15 years by large movements of grain from the new lands of western Siberia and northern Kazakhstan.

Annual freight flows on the Omsk-Novosibirsk section of the Trans-Siberian Railroad exceed 70 million ton-kilometers per kilometer of route, which is about five times greater than the national average. Heavy coal movements to the Urals from the Kuznetsk Basin greatly imbalance the insignificant amounts of iron ore moving in the other direction, and these coal movements are augmented by a westward movement of lumber and grain, which together produce a very imbalanced traffic that moves about 70 per cent westward along this section.

Oil and oil product originations are highest by far in the Volga Region, followed by Transcaucasia, the North Caucasus, the Center, the Urals, and Middle Asia. Unfortunately these originations include traffic only on railroads, rivers, and seas, and therefore omit pipelines, for which data are not available. Since pipelines run primarily from the Volga to other regions and from Transcaucasia and the North Caucasus to other regions, pipeline movements probably simply strengthen the pattern of other movements. The fact that very significant quantities of petroleum product originations are taking place in nonpetroleum-producing areas testifies to the fact that much of the refining is being done in market areas rather than in raw materials areas. It is interesting to note in Table 16–8 that the Center originates more than it receives and is a net exporter. Obviously this must be explained by imports of crude petroleum via pipeline. Of the oil and oil products originations in Transcaucasia, roughly two thirds remains within the region, about one third is

shipped out, and only a small amount is shipped in. It is evident that the large flow of crude petroleum northward from Baku across the Caspian up the Volga to the Central Industrial Region has greatly diminished, and there is no longer much evidence that significant quantities of crude petroleum are moving from the Volga Region southward for refining in Baku.

Timber originations are greatest in the northwest, followed by the Urals, eastern Siberia, western Siberia, Volga-Vyatka, the Volga, and the Center. The northwest is by far the biggest exporter of lumber, mostly by rail. The Urals are second, about two thirds by rail and one third by river. Eastern Siberia is third, with almost all exports going by rail.

Commodity Structure by Modes of Transport

Railroads Coal and coke have dominated rail freight traffic since 1907 when they surpassed grain in tonnage transported. They reached a peak of 37 per cent of all rail traffic in 1947, and in 1966 they still accounted for 20 per cent of the traffic. (Table 16–9) Their role is beginning to diminish as industries and power stations switch to oil and gas for fuels and as steam locomotives are replaced by electric and Diesel-electric. In the past the railroads themselves have consumed as much as one third of the coal production of the country. Coal trains pulled by steam engines from the Kuznetsk Basin to the Urals consumed about one fourth the coal they were hauling by the time they reached the Urals.

In rail traffic, coal and coke are followed in order by petroleum and petroleum products, mineral ores, mineral building materials, timber and wood products, ferrous metals, grain, and mineral fertilizers. Short hauls of mineral construction materials have been the most rapidly expanding type of railroad freight traffic in recent years, and mineral fertilizers in significant amounts are a relatively new commodity on railroads. In 1966 mineral construction materials actually led in tons of railroad freight originated, but the short average length of haul dropped them behind coal and petroleum in ton-kilometers of traffic. Timber and oil moved farthest of all railroad freight, with average hauls of 1593 and 1257 kilometers respectively. Ferrous metals moved on the average 1159 kilometers, and grain moved 945 kilometers.

By comparison, railroad traffic in the United States is more diversified, although it is also dominated by coal and coke. Mineral construction materials and ores make up a larger percentage of the total, and petroleum products make up a very small percentage. Most of the fluid fuels in the United States are moved by pipeline.

Railroads in the Soviet Union in 1966 transported almost all the coal, coke, metals, and ores, 85 per cent of the grain, 75 per cent of the mineral construction materials, 60 per cent of the timber, and

almost 50 per cent of the petroleum produced in the country. (Table 16–5)

Main coal flows on the railroads move out of the Donets Basin in all directions to the Dnieper Bend, Moscow, the North Caucasus, and other destinations in European Russia; from the Kuznetsk Basin westward to the Urals and the Volga Region, from Karaganda westward to the Urals and southward to Middle Asia; and from Pechora southwestward to Cherepovets and Leningrad. (Fig. 16–5) Oil on the railroads moves east and west from the Volga-Urals fields to Siberia, the Center, and Ukraine and from Baku northwestward to Ukraine. (Fig. 16–6) The heaviest flows of ferrous metals move out of eastern Ukraine northward to the Central Industrial Region, out of the Urals westward to the Volga, and out of the Kuznetsk Basin westward along the Trans-Siberian Railroad. Lesser flows move primarily out of these three regions to all parts of the country. (Fig. 16–7)

With the continued development of lumbering areas in the European North,

Table 16–9   Railroad Freight Traffic Composition, U.S.S.R., 1966, and U.S.A., 1958

	U.S.S.R.				U.S.A.
Commodity	Million Tons	Average Haul in Kilometers	Billion Ton-Kilometers	Per Cent of Traffic	Per Cent of Traffic
Total	2,482	812	2,016	100	100
Coal and coke	584	676	394.5	20	29.0
Petroleum products	241	1,257	301.9	15	2.8
Mineral construction materials	594	402	238.8	12	15.7
Timber	142	1,593	226.7	11	6.1
Ferrous metals	153	1,159	178.0	9	–
Ores	200	570	114.1	6	7.9
Grain	86	945	80.9	4	8.0
Mineral fertilizers	47	1,073	50.9	3	–

Sources: Transport i svyaz SSSR, 1967, pp. 101–104, and Ernest W. Williams, Jr., Freight Transportation in the Soviet Union, p. 82.

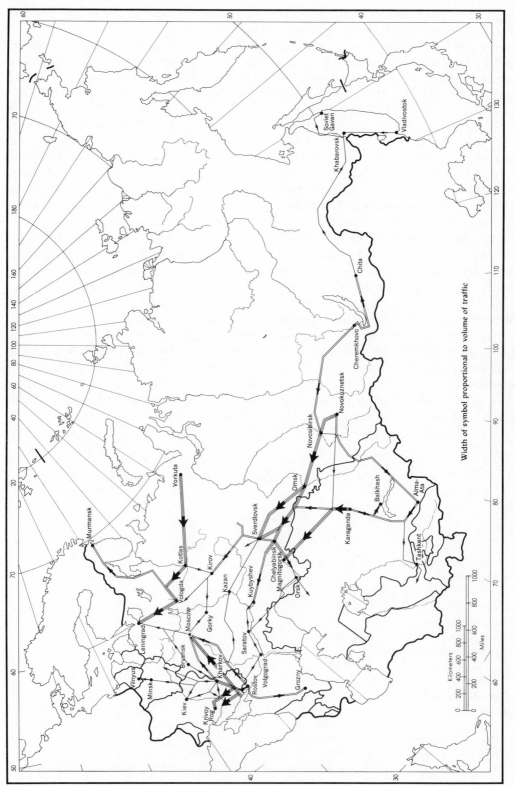

Width of symbol proportional to volume of traffic

Figure 16–5   Coal traffic on railroads. After Nikolskiy.

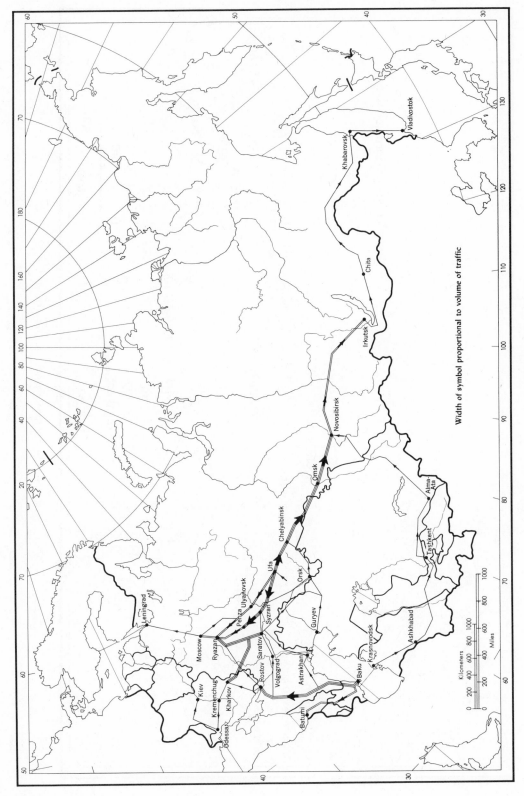

Width of symbol proportional to volume of traffic

Figure 16-6   Oil traffic on railroads. After Nikolsky.

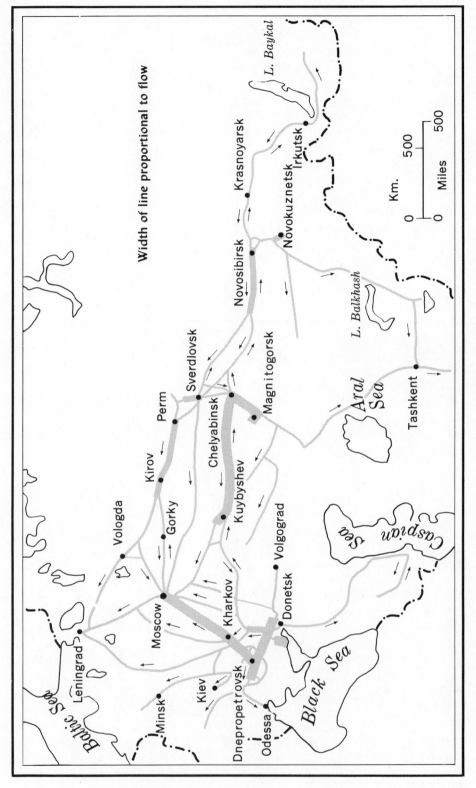

Figure 16–7   Main flows of ferrous metals. After Galitsky, et al., p. 121.

the Urals, and Siberia, the average rail haul of timber has increased from 415 kilometers in 1913 to 1593 kilometers in 1966. Sixty per cent of all sawn wood is produced in the wood-consuming areas, 20 per cent of which is in the Center; consequently 72 per cent of railroad traffic in forest products is raw timber. The heaviest flow moves southward from Archangel on the Northern Railroad. (Fig. 16–8) It is joined at Konosha by wood coming from the northeast on the Pechora Railroad and at Danilov by wood coming from the east on the Kirov-Buy line. From Danilov it flows to Moscow and fans out to the south beyond. There is also a very heavy flow along the Trans-Siberian Railroad in eastern Siberia westward from Irkutsk to the Kuznetsk Basin.

Large grain flows move out of Ukraine, the North Caucasus, and the Volga Region to the Center, the Northwest, and Belorussia. Since the opening of the virgin lands in 1953 there has been a sharp increase in grain flow from the southern Urals, western Siberia, and northern Kazakhstan to European Russia. This traffic increased from approximately 1 million tons in 1950 to more than 12 million tons in 1956. Grain loadings on the railroads of northern Kazakhstan and western Siberia increased twenty times between 1953 and 1956. Out of total loadings in 1956 grain accounted for 31.4 per cent on the Omsk Railroad, 28.8 per cent on the Orenburg Railroad, and 13.5 per cent on the South Urals Railroad. The heaviest flow moves from Novosibirsk to Chelyabinsk.

Grain flow from the northern Caucasus has largely shifted away from destinations in the Volga Region and the Center to ports for foreign export and to Transcaucasia. There has been a reduction of grain sent from the Black Sea Steppes of Ukraine to Transcaucasia and a cessation of grain shipments from the northern Caucasus to Middle Asia. In fact, there has been a reversal of this flow. Grain now moves from Kazakhstan to Transcaucasia via Krasnovodsk and Baku. (Fig. 14–29)

River River transport has long been dominated by timber and firewood, and this dominance increased until 1960 at the expense of the second most important item, oil and oil products. (Table 16–10) Since then the gap has been narrowed a bit. In 1966, 87.9 million tons of timber were shipped on river transport facilities, but only 27 million tons of oil and oil products were shipped. The average length of haul for timber is less than one third that for oil, however, so that in total freight turnover the difference is not very much. The short hauling of mineral construction materials by river barge has increased rapidly since 1940, and they now constitute the largest freight originations. Because the average haul is only about 150 kilometers, however, they make up less than 10 per cent of river traffic. Coal and grain make up minor portions.

European rivers typically have carried most of the river traffic of Russia, the Volga system alone accounting for about two thirds of total traffic. In 1955, the latest date for which data are available, the Volga and its tributaries still carried about 48 per cent of river freight traffic of the U.S.S.R. and 58 per cent of river passenger traffic. (Table 16–11) In terms of tonnage, the Northern Dvina is second only to the Volga, because of large-scale floating of timber, but since the distance is relatively short, its freight turnover is not as large as some other streams. (Fig. 16–9)

Marine The Soviets have not published shipping statistics by seas, nor have they distinguished between domestic shipping and foreign trade. Therefore it is difficult to assess the relative significance of the various ports of the country or the role of domestic shipping in total maritime transport. As has been pointed out before, the Soviets have been expanding their merchant marine very rapidly during the past few years, and total maritime shipping has

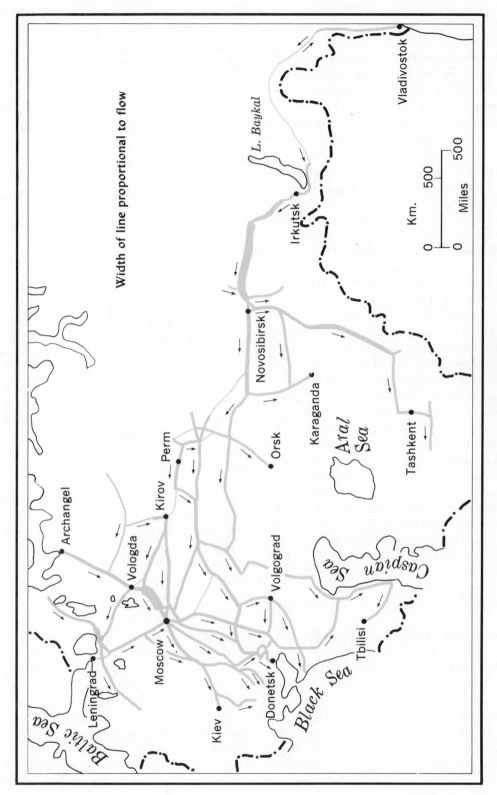

Width of line proportional to flow

Figure 16–8   Main flows of timber. After Galitskiy, et al., p. 133.

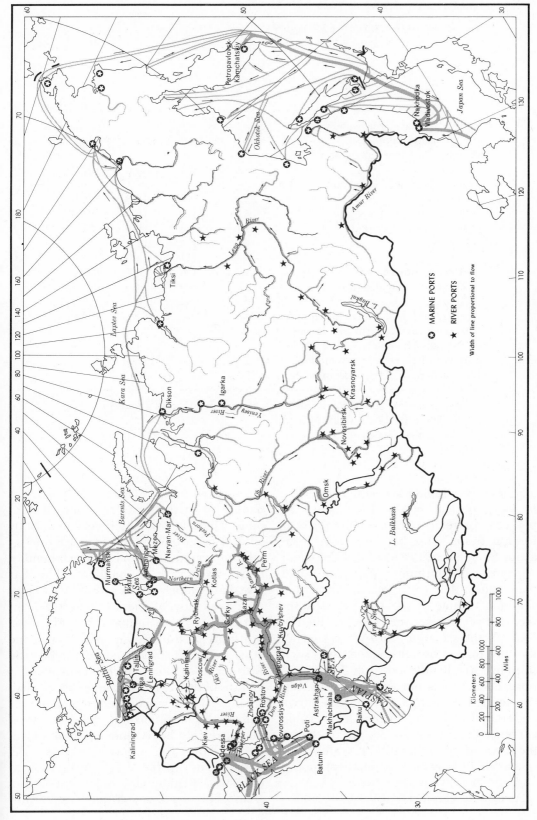

MARINE PORTS ✪

RIVER PORTS ★

Width of line proportional to flow

Figure 16–9 *Freight flows on waterways. After Galitsky, et al., pp. 73–74.*

577

Table 16–10   River Transport

	1913 (Within Present Boundaries)	1940	1960	1966
Length of navigable waterways in thousand kilometers	64.6	107.3	137.9	142.7 [b]
Freight turnover in billion ton-kilometers	28.9	36.1	99.6	137.6
Freight originations, in millions of tons	35.1	73.1	210.3	279.0
Oil and oil products	5.4	9.7	18.5	27.0
Timber and firewood	11.0	40.2	89.4	87.9
Coal	0.9	2.2	11.0	15.5
Ore	—	0.1	2.0	3.8
Mineral construction materials	1.5	7.6	70.3	127.7
Metals and metal scrap	0.6 [a]	0.5	1.0	1.3
Grain	6.1	5.2	6.8	6.0
Average length of haul in kilometers	823	494	474	493
Passenger turnover, in billion passenger kilometers	1.4	3.8	4.3	5.1
Number of passengers, in millions	11.5	73.0	118.6	145.6
Average length of trip, in kilometers	125	52	36	35

Sources: Narodnoe khozyaystvo SSSR v 1960 godu, p. 545, and *Transport i svyaz SSSR*, 1967, pp. 178–181 and 186.
[a] Without metal scrap.
[b] 1965.

increased very rapidly since the mid 1950s. It was reported that in 1960 about 30 per cent of total maritime shipping was foreign trade. This had increased from about 20 per cent in 1957, and the trend appears to be continuing. The long-range plan states that by 1980 the maritime shipping volume of the U.S.S.R. is to increase five times over 1960, primarily through the expansion of overseas trade. By this time it is anticipated that such shipping will handle not only Soviet exports and imports but will also be serving the foreign exchange of other countries and thereby will be earning convertible currency for the Soviets. It appears that at the present Soviet maritime traffic consists of about 50 per cent domestic shipping and 50 per cent foreign trade.

As can be seen in Fig. 16–10, the southern ports along the Black and Caspian Seas handle by far the greatest volume of shipping, which is dominated very heavily by oil and oil products. The third most significant region is the Baltic, which handles more diversified commodities. The Far East has a much smaller volume of shipping than any of these other areas, but shipping is more important to the total transport of this region than it is in the other areas. The scattered ports along the Northern Sea Route operate only about 3 months of the year and handle rather small volumes. The Caspian used to handle over half of the maritime shipping because of the extremely heavy and bulky oil movements from the Caucasus across the Caspian and up the Volga to the Central Industrial Region and other consuming areas. This trade is still quite significant, although it has decreased relatively through the years. At the present time it appears that the ports of the Black Sea handle at least 50 per cent of the total shipping of the country, probably three quarters or more of which is domestic shipping. Ports along the coasts of the Black and Azov Seas handle oil from the Caucasus; coal, iron ore, iron and steel from Ukraine; lumber from the Upper Volga-Kama Region; and machinery and grain from European Russia and Ukraine.

The few shipping statistics that exist for the Black and Caspian Seas are complicated by the fact that they are not reported for seas but for standard economic administrative regions which do not coincide well with sea coasts. For instance, the so-called South consists of the southwestern portion of Ukraine which borders the northwestern coast of the Black Sea and a small part of the Sea of Azov along the Crimean Peninsula. The Donets-Dnieper Region includes only the northwestern coast of the Sea of Azov. The North Caucasus includes the southeastern shore of the Sea of Azov, part of the northeastern coast of the Black Sea, and part of the northwestern coast of the Caspian. The Trans Caucasus includes the eastern end of the Black Sea and the southwestern part of the Caspian Sea. The rest of the Caspian Sea is included in the Volga, Central Asia, and Kazakhstan regions. Hence the difficulty in presenting figures for the Black Sea or the Caspian Sea as an entity in itself. What better example exists of man's fragmentation of statistics that logically would be grouped according to natural features of the earth's surface!

Statistical reporting of shipping from ports along the Baltic is somewhat simpler but no more logical than that in the south. Most of the ports are included in the so-called Western region, but the so-called Northwest region separates the largest port, Leningrad, and also the far western port of Kaliningrad, in a noncontiguous territory that is separated from the rest of the Northwest region by the Western region. Again it is obvious that political considerations have overruled the geographic ones, and Kaliningrad is included in the Northwest region because it is a part of the Russian Republic, even though its trade probably is more related to the adjacent Baltic Republics than to the area around Leningrad. Baltic statistics are further complicated by the fact that the large Northwest region extends to the Arctic Coast and thus includes the important ice-free port of Murmansk, along the far northern shores of the Kola Peninsula, and the big lumber port of Archangel on the White Sea, as well as a number of smaller ports.

If one looks at the Baltic as a whole it appears that this sea handles considerably less marine freight than does either the Black or Caspian Seas. But in contrast to these two seas, whose intraregional and

Table 16–11   Freight and Passenger Traffic by River Basins and Areas, 1955, in Per Cents of Total

	Freight Traffic	Passenger Traffic
Volga	29.6	33.6
Kama	12.1	12.5
European North	6.3	7.1
Dnieper	6.0	9.2
Irtysh	4.8	4.5
Moscow	3.9	8.5
Yenisey	3.8	4.9
European Northwest	3.5	3.4
Amur	2.1	2.7
Lena	2.1	2.4
Ob	2.0	4.0
Volga-Don Canal	2.0	3.4
Belomorsk-Onega Canal system	0.9	0.3
Pechora	0.8	0.5
Belaya	0.5	1.8
Eastern Siberia	0.5	0.8
Middle Asia	0.5	0.1
Neman	0.2	0.3
Other	19.4	0.0

Source: Transport i svyaz SSSR, 1957, p. 140.

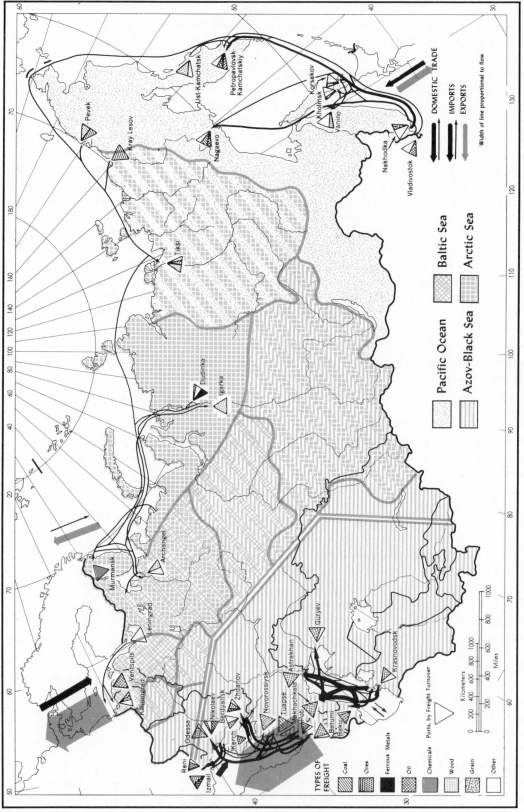

Figure 16–10 *Marine transport. After Atlas razvitiya khozyaystva i kultury SSSR, p. 81.*

interregional trade greatly exceed foreign trade, the trade of the Baltic ports is concentrated as much as 80 per cent on export-import traffic. This is definitely a transit area through which freight moves. Most of the exports leaving these ports have not originated in the local area but have come from the Central Industrial Region and other inland areas. The ports of Leningrad, Kaliningrad, and the three Baltic Republics appear to handle about 20 per cent of the overseas shipping of the Soviet Union. These ports handle coal, crude oil, oil products, iron and steel, ores, grain, lumber, sugar, and other industrial and agricultural goods. Transit goods account for about 75 per cent of the regions export-import traffic. Leningrad undoubtedly handles more shipping than any other port in this area, but it is hampered by ice in the narrow Gulf of Finland from December through May. During that time some of its traffic is diverted through the far northern port of Murmansk, which, in spite of its northerly location, is ice-free much of the time because of the northeasterly extension of the Gulf Stream. This is a very round-about way of shipping goods, and some of the more westerly ports along the Baltic, such as Riga and Kaliningrad, probably will handle more traffic in the future. Once the Soviets are more sure of themselves in the Kaliningrad area, they will probably greatly expand the port facilities there, since this logically is the best port for them along the Baltic. It is virtually ice-free and is situated most satisfactorily for trade with the west.

Archangel is the Soviet Union's greatest exporting port for lumber. As can be seen in Fig. 16–10 there are few imports coming into Archangel, so the traffic here is almost one-way. Murmansk handles great quantities of apatite ore which is shipped to other parts of the Soviet Union for the chemical industries. Only a little goes to foreign countries. By far the greatest amount of the shipping of these northern ports is domestic trade, rather than foreign trade.

Soviet Far Eastern shipping is almost entirely intraregional traffic. There is practically no connection by ship with other regions of the country except for the narrow stream of traffic flowing northward through the Bering Strait and along the Northern Sea Route during the short summer shipping season. About 13 per cent of the maritime traffic of the Far East is foreign trade. This is expected to rise significantly in the next few years as the Soviet Union increases its trade, primarily with Japan. The major ports in this area are the naval and fishing port of Vladivostok and the commercial port of Nakhodka, in a less ice-bound position just a short distance to the east of Vladivostok.

In total marine transport petroleum has long dominated the scene, particularly on the Caspian and Black Seas. Although its relative role has diminished somewhat with the development of the Volga-Urals oil fields in the North, 1966 statistics show that liquids, which must be predominantly oil products, made up 46 per cent of total marine freight. Among the solid commodities, mineral construction materials have shot well ahead of any other single commodity, and they are now followed by ores, coal, timber and firewood, metals, machinery, grain, and chemical products, primarily mineral fertilizers. (Table 16–12) These figures represent only domestic trade.

Passenger Traffic

Railroads traditionally have also carried the bulk of passenger traffic of the U.S.S.R., but this is changing now. The railroads' share of total passenger-kilometers has diminished from 90 per cent in 1950 to less than 54 per cent in 1966. Most of this relative decrease has been due to the exceedingly rapid increase of bus traffic and, to a lesser extent, air traffic. Buses have displaced railroads, particularly in suburban commuting. Bus traffic increased twelve-fold from 1950 to 1960

Table 16–12 Marine Transport of Main Commodities (Excluding Petroleum) in Petty Cabotage, in Millions of Tons

	1940	1960	1966
Total	10.3	20.2	35.6
Coal	1.6	5.7	5.3
Timber and fire-wood	1.3	2.2	2.0
Ore	1.5	5.7	6.9
Mineral construction materials	0.7	9.3	12.0
Metals	0.1	0.59	0.9
Machinery	0.2	0.5	0.8
Chemical products	0.2	0.3	0.5
Grain	1.5	1.4	0.7

Source: Transport i svyaz SSSR, Moscow, 1967, p. 155. In 1966 liquids (oil) made up 46 per cent of all marine freight.

and more than doubled again between 1960 and 1966. Its relative share of total passenger traffic increased from 5.3 per cent in 1950 to 33.4 per cent in 1966. The average trip for bus passengers was only 29 kilometers and less than 1 per cent of the passengers crossed oblast boundaries. If one discounts this type of traffic and concentrates only on intercity movements, the rails' share is still about 70 per cent and the share of air lines is significantly higher than is shown in Table 16–13. Commuters in 1966 still accounted for more than 25 per cent of the total passenger-kilometers traveled on railroads and for 89 per cent of all railroad passengers, but this is significantly lower than it used to be, and the change to buses for commuting distances is continuing at a rapid rate.

Air passenger transport has had an equally phenomenal growth. It also increased about twelve times between 1950 and 1960, since which it had quadrupled again. And, of course, all of this is intercity transport. In 1950 airlines provided a little over 1 per cent of the total passenger

transport, but by 1966 this portion had risen to over 11 per cent. In 1967 Aeroflot, the official Soviet airlines, carried more than 53 million passengers, which was three times the number it carried in 1960. This compares to 129 million passengers carried by U.S. airlines in 1967. At the end of 1967 Aeroflot operated over 500,000 kilometers of scheduled routes, of which more than 115,000 kilometers were international. (Fig. 16–11) The international routes have been the fastest growing part of the network.

Since 1955 average air trips have shown a sharp decrease in length because of the burgeoning development of local air lines in virtually every region of the Soviet Union, which have given a great impetus to air travel over medium distances. These local lines now handle more than half of the total air passengers and have cut deeply into the expected increase of passenger traffic on railroads for medium-length hauls. In most cases air rates have been set rather arbitrarily at levels comparable to first-class rates on the railroads, which puts them within the financial reach of many of the ordinary workers in the country. On most domestic routes, all airplanes are jammed to capacity with ordinary citizens and their families who are moving from one job to another or are going on scheduled vacations.

The Soviet Union has been a pioneer in the field of jet propulsion and the development of large high-speed transport planes. People in remote areas that used to be almost inaccessible because of vast distances or lack of surface transport facilities now find themselves within easy reach of the main centers of the country through only a few hours' flight by jet aircraft. Although the line-haul costs of airplanes are high, the initial outlays of capital for facilities and equipment are low, and this consideration has proved to be of most importance in the Soviet Unions' desire to overcome the time factor in catching up with the West.

Table 16–13   Passenger Traffic by Type of Carrier, U.S.S.R., Selected Years, and U.S.A., 1966, in Billions of Passenger-Kilometers and Per Cents of Total

	U.S.S.R.					U.S.A., 1966 [a]
	1913	1928	1950	1960	1966	
Total	32.7	26.9	98.3	249.5	407.3	1553
	100	100	100	100	100	100
Railroad	30.3	24.5	88.0	170.8 [b]	219.4	27.6
	92.7	91.1	89.6	68.4	53.9	2
Bus	–	–	5.2	61.0	136.1	39.3
	–	–	5.3	24.4	33.4	3
Air	–	–	1.2	12.1	45.1	111
	–	–	1.2	4.8	11.1	7
River	1.4	2.1	2.7	4.3	5.1	5.6 [c]
	4.3	7.8	2.7	1.7	1.3	1
Sea	1.0	0.3	1.2	1.3	1.6	–
	3.1	1.1	1.2	0.5	0.4	–
Private car	–	–	–	–	–	1370
	–	–	–	–	–	88

Sources: Transport i svyaz SSSR, 1967, p. 28, and *Statistical Abstract of the United States,* 1968, p. 541.

[a] Intercity only.

[b] Long-distance passenger traffic involving 237,000,000 passengers averaging 549 kilometers per trip accounted for 130,100,000,000 passenger-kilometers, and commuting involving 1,713,000,000 passengers traveling an average of 23.8 kilometers accounted for 40,700,000,000 passenger-kilometers.

[c] Includes rivers, Great Lakes, and coastal traffic.

At the other end of the scale, the initial capital outlays for automotive traffic are exceedingly high, involving the construction of hundreds of thousands of kilometers of good roads and the production of millions of automobiles. The strict competition for investment capital in the Soviet Union has thus relegated automotive traffic to a very low priority, and intercity automobile traffic is practically undeveloped. In contrast, in the United States the private automobile accounts for 88 per cent or more of all passenger traffic. The number of passenger automobiles in existence in the Soviet Union in 1966 appears to be roughly 1 million, which, for a country of 235,000,-000 people, is a very small stock of passen-

ger cars indeed. Whereas the ratio of the population to automobile registrations in the United States is about 2.7 to 1, and in West Germany, France, and the United Kingdom about 6 to 1, in the Soviet Union it is more than 200 to 1. If one realizes that this limited stock of automobiles in the Soviet Union is to a large extent in the hands of state organizations rather than private individuals, and that approximately one fifth of the existing stock is always out of service awaiting repairs, then it appears that there are more than 500 people for every car in unrestricted private use in the U.S.S.R.

During the 1960s the annual production of passenger cars has been around 200,000, of which about 40,000 have been exported

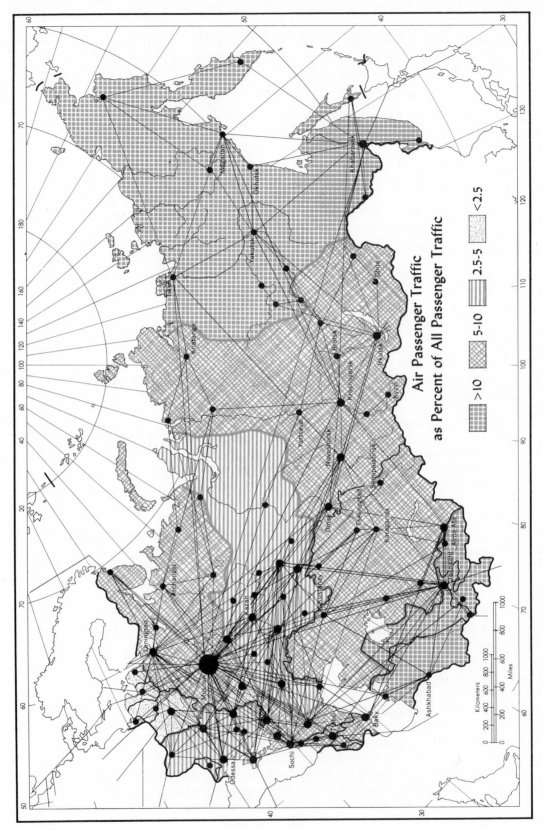

Air Passenger Traffic
as Percent of All Passenger Traffic

>10   5-10   2.5-5   <2.5

Figure 16–11   Airline routes. After Atlas razvitiya khozyaystva i kultury SSSR, p. 85.

584

to east European countries. Taking into account normal depreciation, the addition of cars to the total fleet in the Soviet Union has been taking place at a rate of only about 75,000 per year. Not only are cars in short supply, but also filling stations and garages. In 1963 it was reported that there were approximately 1500 filling stations in the entire Soviet Union. Servicing and repair facilities were even more scarce. In some cities with over 250,000 people there is only one gas station. This has led to the illegal acquisition of gas by car owners from truck drivers or through other devious channels. In some cities illegal transactions have grown to such magnitudes that a system has been imposed whereby gas can be bought only for trading stamps or special coupons which are issued for cash at government offices, and new coupons will be issued only if the mileage shown on the car is consistent with the previous record of gas purchases. The ownership of a car has often put the owner in an advantageous position for taking advantage of wide price differentials existing in produce between points separated by only short distances, such as between farms and cities. This has led certain car-owning opportunists to engage in the capitalistic practice of purchasing vegetables and fruit at cheap prices on the farms and selling them for high prices in the cities only a few miles away. Such practices, combined with illegal dealings in gas and natural jealousies of "have-nots," have almost placed a stigma on the ownership of a car and have sometimes even led to criminal action resulting in confiscation of the automobile and exile of the individual from his place of abode.

More than half of the passenger cars in the Soviet Union are assigned to people who warrant such assignments because of their positions. Party and government bureaucrats, plant managers, farm chairmen, and high-ranking academic and professional people generally have one or more cars and chauffeurs assigned to them

for their own use. Most of the time these cars and chauffeurs are sitting idle, which is a very poor usage of a very short supply of equipment and labor. Recognizing this, certain civic-minded individuals in various cities have attempted to set up some sort of cooperative system whereby such automobiles would be held in a common pool and use could be made of them by a wider group of individuals. In most cases where this has been attempted, however, the natural greed of individuals has come to the forefront and many officials have applied for exemptions from these car pools. This has resulted in a wide array of emblems plastered on windshields and bumpers signifying special vehicles. The government has experimented with the rent-a-car approach, but this has not solved any problems either. Municipal rent-a-car fleets are now available in many cities for Soviet citizens who want to take a car for a vacation trip or some other approved use. The renter of the car is liable for all sorts of injury, damage, and loss, however, and the legal authorities have withheld the availability of insurance against personal liability under the premise that this will increase the feeling of responsibility of the individual driver and minimize accidents. In addition, the renter must have a driver's license, which is usually hard to qualify for, and he always must go through a good deal of red tape to prove his eligibility for the use of a car. All these things have made most citizens very reluctant to rent cars.

The present 5-year plan calls for an expanded production of both trucks and passenger cars to an annual output of about 700,000 to 800,000 units each by 1970. Since the plan was drawn up, these figures seem to have been augmented by the agreement concluded with the Italian Fiat Corporation in May 1966 for the construction of a Fiat plant at the renamed town of Togliatti on the Volga with an annual production capacity of about 730,-000 passenger cars, and another agreement during the same month with the Renault firm of France to expand the capacity of the Moscow plant producing the small Moskvich car to 200,000 passenger cars annually. Also plans have been announced for a new plant at Izhevsk in the Udmurt A.S.S.R. with a scheduled annual capacity of 300,000 small cars by 1970. Taking all these things into account, it appears that the Soviet Union should have a production capacity of 1.5 to 2 million passenger cars by 1970. This significant planned increase in automobile production capacity might signify the beginning of an automotive age in the U.S.S.R. which has been prompted by the growing bourgeois desires of the Soviet citizens. Now that the Soviet Union has greatly expanded its petroleum production, there is no particular problem in the supply of gasoline except for adequate outlets in the form of filling stations and service garages. However, any attempt to lift the Russian "muzhik" out of the springtime muds of the dirt roads in a country as large as the Soviet Union is going to necessitate a mass construction of highways which will take many years. Intercity travel by private car will be a long time coming, and any expanded ownership of private cars will take place primarily in the cities where the cars will be used for short trips to commute to work and shopping and for occasional drives into the country. A modern double highway has been built in a ring around Moscow, and several new modernistic motels have been built at intersecting highways coming into this ring, but such facilities are more novellus than functional in the Soviet Union at the present time.

Passenger traffic on the waterways of the country, which many years ago was very significant, has remained at about the same absolute level throughout the Soviet period, and thus relatively has almost dropped out of the total picture. In view of the slowness of this type of transport, no resurgence of its importance can be expected. At the present time much of the river passenger traffic is for commuting or pleasure purposes within cities such as Moscow, where the Moscow River has been canalized and lined with frequent river stations. These are often combined with amusement facilities to provide pleasure-seeking citizens the opportunity to take a short evening cruise of a few kilometers length and combine it with an evening of eating and dancing on one of the old river boats lashed to the bank to serve as a combination river station and amusement hall. Longer cruises of several days duration have been organized on some of the newer canal and waterway systems, such as the 2-day cruise from Volgograd southward down the Volga River, across the Volga-Don Canal, and down the Don River to Rostov at the head of the Sea of Azov. Such cruise boats also serve the function of local transport facility for peasants living along the streams. The boat stops frequently, and native passengers constantly embark and debark.

Since the private automobile is a negligible factor in passenger traffic in the Soviet Union, public transportation systems within cities are crowded by swarms of urban dwellers who are either commuting to work, going shopping, or simply killing time. Since most living quarters are cramped, and frequently more than one family is living in the same apartment, leisure time is not easily spent at home, and many people simply wander the streets trying to amuse themselves when they are not on the job. The governmental policy to reduce fares continually on public transportation within cities until eventually it is all free has not brought about any reduction in the number of persons riding on public conveyances. At any time of day, it seems that the buses, street cars, trolleys, and subways are jammed to capacity. In recent years there has been a rather rapid conversion from street cars and trolleys to buses. In 1965 passenger transportation in all Soviet cities was 55 per cent by bus, 14 per cent by trolley bus, 26 per cent by street car, and 5 per cent by subway. This was a very significant change from 1939 when street cars carried 61 per cent of the traffic and buses only 13 per cent. At the present time subways exist in Moscow, Leningrad, Kiev, Tbilisi, and Baku. Detailed plans are now being worked out for a 20-kilometer, 13-station, earthquake-proof subway in Tashkent, and general plans have been approved for subways in Kharkov. The first subway lines were built in Moscow and subsequently the system there has been expanded until now the city is underlain by a criss-cross of three major systems and a circular connecting system. (Fig. 16–12)

Subways seem to have captured the imagination of Russian planners; they are one thing in the Soviet Union that has been built right. The subways of Moscow are world renowned not only for their good service but for their beauty and cleanliness. Built far underground, to cross beneath the Moscow River, they are well lighted and ventilated and are lined with large murals and chandeliers. The escalators leading down into the subways themselves are something at which to marvel; they pitch at angles of 45 degrees and go so deeply into the earth that one cannot see the bottom when he enters the top.

Intercity passenger flows resemble freight flows. (Fig. 16–13) The heaviest movement by far is between the Center and eastern Ukraine. Part of this flow continues southeastward to the Caucasus. Moderately heavy flows also move eastward from the Center along the Trans-Siberian Railroad, particularly between Omsk and Novosibirsk in western Siberia.

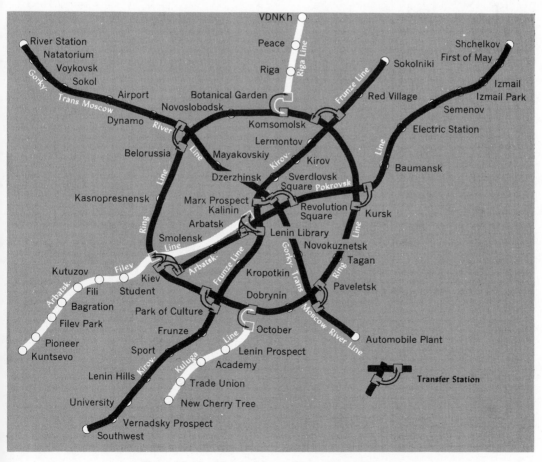

Figure 16–12   Moscow subways. From a Soviet tour map.

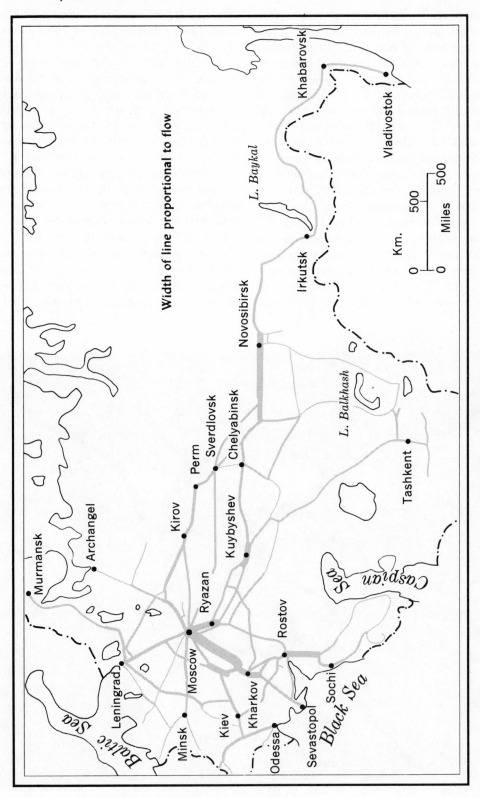

Width of line proportional to flow

Figure 16–13   Intercity passenger flows. After Galitskiy, et al., p. 173.

They also move between the larger cities of European U.S.S.R., particularly between Moscow and Leningrad.

Reading List

Automotive Industries, January 1, 1958; Entire issue devoted to Soviet transportation.

Galitskiy, M. I., Danilov, S. K., and Korneev, A. I., *Ekonomicheskaya geografiya transporta S.S.S.R.,* Moscow, 1965, 303 pp. (in Russian); translated into English by Joint Publications Research Service, JPRS 31647, August 23, 1965.

Guest, B. Ross, "The Growth of Soviet Air Cargo," *Journal of Geography,* October 1966, pp. 323–327.

———, "Soviet Gas Pipeline Development during the Seven-Year Plan," *The Professional Geographer,* July 1967, pp. 189–192.

Hunter, Holland, *Soviet Transportation Policy,* Harvard University Press, Cambridge, 1957, 416 pp.

———, "Soviet Transportation Policies — A Current View," in *Comparisons of the United States and Soviet Economies,* Joint Economic Committee, Congress of the United States, Washington, 1959, Part I, pp. 189–199.

———, "The Soviet Transport Sector," in *New Directions in the Soviet Economy,* Studies Prepared for the Subcommittee on Foreign Economic Policy of the Joint Economic Committee, Congress of the United States, Washington, 1966, Part II-B, Section 5, pp. 571–591.

———, *Soviet Transport Experience: Its Lesson for other Countries,* The Brookings Institution, Washington, 1968, 194 pp.

Kish, George, "Railroad Passenger Transport in the Soviet Union," *Geographical Review,* July 1963, pp. 363–376.

———, "Soviet Air Transport," *Geographical Review,* July 1958, pp. 309–320.

Krypton, Constantine, *The Northern Sea Route and the Economy of the Soviet North,* Praeger, New York, 1956, 219 pp.

Mazanova, M. B., "Marine Transport as a National Specialized Activity of a Major Economic Region," *Soviet Geography: Review and Translation,* May 1963, pp. 3–9.

Muckleston, Keith W. and Dohrs, Fred E., "The Relative Importance of Transport on the Volga before and after the Communist Revolution," *The Professional Geographer,* March 1965, pp. 22–25.

Nikolskiy, I. V., *Geografiya transporta S.S.S.R.,* Moscow, 1960; Excerpted in English in *Soviet Geography: Review and Translation,* June 1961, pp. 39–92.

Parakhonskiy, B. M., Kibalchich, O. A., and Kravets, F. P., *Voprosy ekonomiki i perspektivnogo planirovaniya passazhirskikh perevozok* (Economic Problems and Perspective Plans for Passenger Traffic), Moscow, 1963 (in Russian).

Petrov, Victor P., *Geography of the Soviet Union, Volume V: Transportation,* Victor Kamkin, Washington, 1967, 93 pp.

Soviet Life, June 1967, "Soviet Merchant Marine in 1967."

Spulber, Nicolas, "The Danube-Black Sea Canal and the Russian Control over the Danube," *Economic Geography,* July 1954, pp. 236–245.

Taaffe, Robert, *Rail Transportation and the Economic Development of Soviet Central Asia,* Department of Geography Research Paper No. 64, University of Chicago Press, 1960, 186 pp.

———, "Transportation and Regional Specialization: The Example of Soviet Central Asia," *Annals of the Association of American Geographers,* March 1962, pp. 80–98.

———, "Volga River Transportation: Problems and Prospects," in Richard S. Thoman and Donald J. Patton, *Focus on Geographic Activity,* McGraw-Hill, New York, 1964, pp. 185–193.

———, "Interregional Passenger Movement in the Soviet Union," *The East Lakes Geographer,* October 1967, pp. 47–79.

Transport i svyaz SSSR (Transport and Communications in the U.S.S.R.), Moscow, 1967, 332 pp. (in Russian).

Westwood, J. N., *A History of the Russian Railways,* Allen and Unwin Ltd., London, 1964, 326 pp.

———, *Soviet Railways Today,* The Citadel Press, New York, 1964, 192 pp.

Williams, Ernest W., Jr., *Freight Transportation in the Soviet Union,* Princeton, 1962, 214 pp.

———, "Some Aspects of the Structure and Growth of Soviet Transportation," in *Comparisons of the United States and Soviet Economies,* Joint Economic Committee, Congress of the United States, Washington, 1959, Part I, pp. 177–187.

Zvonkov, V. V., *Principles of Integrated Transport Development in the U.S.S.R.,* University of Chicago Press, Chicago, 1957, 63 pp.

17

Foreign Trade, Aid, and International Relations

The Background of Soviet Foreign Policy

The Russian Empire sprawled across the length of Eurasia and thereby came into contact with or close proximity to all the countries of that huge land mass. The Soviet Union has inherited that pivotal position, along with the long histories of interaction that have gone on between major powers down through time: The Tatar Hordes, the Livonian Knights, Byzantium, the Polish-Lithuanian State, the Mongol Empire, the Persian Empire, the Chinese Dynasties, the Ottoman Empire; the Swedes, the Prussians, the Austro-Hungarians; and in modern history the British, the French, and the Germans: the Russian Empire spanned them all. Over more than a millennium the Russians perfected the tactics of advance and retreat while always holding to the same long-term goals. Thus the Soviet Union is a state little more than 50 years old; it is also a state with over a thousand years of history. The Bolshevik Revolution did not effect a geographical transplantation; the Soviets inherited all the Russian legacy. Present policy has been molded by a long history of events, most of which have resulted in fear, suspicion, and reactionary aggression. It is only against this background that present foreign dealings can

be understood, that apparent incongruities, abrupt changes of tactics, and seeming stupidity in the face of world opinion understandably fall into place.

Old Russia was always faced with the duality of aims and reality. Its aims were vaguely that of expansionism, at the same time holding the lid on internal revolt. The realities that engulfed it were successive threats of first one, then another, strong adversary from the outside, particularly from the west, and abject poverty and seething rebellion internally, particularly in the peripheral areas where the Russians had gobbled up whole nations of people which they never had time to digest. No wonder the Russian Empire had often been called a "prison of nations." The Russian Empire was beset with international problems within its own boundaries, as well as without. This, together with an unbridgeable gulf between a small urban elite and a great peasant mass, led to extreme repressive measures on its own people.

To this duality of cause, the Bolsheviks have added a third dimension, Marxian ideology. And this has made the causes for Soviet actions ever more intricate, ever more obscure, than those of the Russian Tsars. But when the chips are down, the Soviets generally talk ideology and act according to self-interests and realities. Thus there has been no great shift in the basis of action from that which controlled the Tsarist governments. Preservation of the old Russian Empire intact as the Soviet Socialist State is the primary purpose, along with the maintenance of the Soviet regime in power.

The underlying fact that maintains the Soviet leadership in the position of the bad boys of the world is that the Soviets, as well as the Russians before them, have never been willing to accept a status quo. They are constantly trying to effect major changes, both in their own country and in the world setup. Therefore they feed upon instability and look upon general chaos as a time of opportunity rather than one of danger. This can only be done, of course, if one trusts his adversaries more than he trusts himself. This action alone is irrefutable evidence that the Soviets know the United States and the Western powers by and large are responsible political entities which will tend to act with reason and moderation in the face of provocation. This knowledge, of course, allows the unruly bull in the china shop to get away with many atrocious actions, up to a certain point. Such actions kept the jittery nerves of the world on edge during the late 1940s and the early 1950s as the Soviets exploited opportunities in the chaotic and rapidly changing areas of Africa and Asia, as well as in some areas of Europe and Latin America, where new states or new borders were coming into being.

One of the saving graces of the Soviets has been that, like greedy children, they have developed guilt complexes (which they also inherited from their Tsarist ancestors) which have made them want to be liked by the world. Thus, often after committing some aggressive act, they have turned around and gone to the other extreme to lavish oil on the troubled waters. Khrushchev was the personification of this national neurosis—on the one hand a ruthless, bullheaded opportunist; on the other, an almost pitiful comic character seeking to gain approval from the rest of the world. If one understands this adolescent psychology of rebellion and affection, one can better follow the reverses in action that take place while continuing down the same path. The more adult governments of the world have recognized this immature quality of the Soviet state and have sought to contain dangerous actions from without, while hoping for an evolution of improvement from within. As generations change and the educational level of the entire population is improved, it is inevitable that an evolutionary process in the political thinking of the Soviet Union will take place. However, one must not expect changes overnight. Under pressure, one can expect a reversion to earlier ways of reacting.

The world was rather lulled into overoptimism by the relative political stability that prevailed during the latter 1950s and much of the 1960s, a stability that was made even more evident by the relatively minor eruptions that were imbedded in the period. The Berlin Crisis, the Dominican Republic, the Bay of Pigs, the Middle East, even the Vietnam War, have served more than anything else to demonstrate that localized crises can exist and be dealt with without developing a major confrontation that will plunge the entire world into war. The nuclear Sword of Damocles has served as a real deterrent to conventional war that has tempered Soviet actions, which always have been fraught with a greater fear of the West than even the West's fear of the East. In the face of all this, during the past decade the Soviet leadership has acted with real restraint, and in some instances, such as the Tashkent rapprochement of the India-Pakistan conflict, with nobility. Little wonder, then, that the world began to think that the Soviet evolution had indeed taken place and that the Soviets were going to continue with great restraint, a progressively liberal outlook, and close attention to world opinion.

Western analysts and journalists in July and early August 1968 confidently wrote the boldly optimistic predictions that 1968 was not 1956 and that the Czechs, within the new milieu of world affairs, were going to pull off what the Hungarians had been unable to do. The rude shock of the invasion of Czechoslovakia in late August 1968 first flabbergasted the world that the Russians could be so stupid in the light of world opinion, and then jolted the world back to the reality that the Soviets were not particularly concerned about world opinion; they were still confident that they could act recklessly and count upon the other major powers to act responsibly for the good of the world. Therefore they could exploit the situation in eastern Europe confident that the Western world would realize that its hands were tied while the Soviets ran rampant as they pleased. Thus it appeared that the Brezhnev-Kosygin collective leadership, which had seemed so self-effacing and seriously concerned about the preservation of world order, could act with as much duplicity as its predecessor governments. The world was thrown back 15 years to the reign of Stalin and was made to realize that a long wait lay still ahead before the Russian psyche would emerge from the effects of previous traumas, and would evolve to be on a par with those of the other major powers.

Foreign Trade

Although at times Tsarist governments sought trade and other relations with outside countries, particularly the major powers of western Europe, in general Russian policy was one of isolation and as much self-sufficiency as possible. The early part of the Soviet period, if anything, intensified these tendencies. Initially the Soviets were so obsessed with the fears of allied intervention and a resurgent Ger-

many on the outside and so preoccupied with economic recoupment and maintenance of political stability inside the country, that they followed extremely isolationistic policies and strove for 100 per cent self-sufficiency. Although such aims have been far from 100 per cent attainable, the Soviet Union has consistently been characterized by foreign trade that is strictly limited in total value, in number of commodities exchanged, and in number of trading partners. With the second largest economy in the world, the Soviet Union now ranks sixth in foreign trade and comprises only 4 per cent of total world trade turnover, which gives it a lower per capita trade than all European and most western hemisphere countries. (Table 17–1)

In the past, imports have been looked upon as the last resort to provide only critically necessary prototype machinery, skilled personnel, and materials to further the industrialization of the Soviet Union and to provide consumer goods to improve incentives for increased labor productivity. And exports were made simply to pay for necessary imports. Since 1955 the Soviets more and more have been using trade as a political and propaganda instrument, and therefore their present foreign trade and international relations are inexorably tied

Table 17–1   Foreign Trade of Leading Countries, 1966

Country	Trade Turnover (Billions of U.S. Dollars)	Per Capita Trade (Dollars)
United States	55.5	282
West Germany	38.2	664
United Kingdom	30.2	552
France	22.7	459
Japan	19.3	195
Soviet Union	16.8	72

Sources: Computed from *United Nations Yearbook of International Trade Statistics,* 1966, pp. 12–19, and *United Nations Demographic Yearbook,* 1967, pp. 124–131.

together and cannot very well be considered separately. In addition, during the past few years Soviet trade has begun to reflect the form of a more mature economy which seeks to exploit comparative production advantages, importing products which can be produced more cheaply elsewhere and conserving its own capital and labor for more advanced types of production which can be sold at a premium on the world market. This procedure, which is the basis for trade among the developed countries of the world, has not progressed very far yet in the Soviet Union. However, the structural profile of Soviet trade has become nearly the mirror image of that of Imperial Russia. Before the Revolution, roughly two thirds of the

exports were raw materials, principally timber and grain, whereas at present nearly two thirds are manufactured goods. (Table 17–2) The export-import profile shown in Fig. 17–1 has been quite consistent for the past 20 years or more. The only major change took place in the early 1960s when the Soviet Union changed from a significant exporter of grain to a significant importer.

Soviet trade is also much changed from Tsarist trade in terms of trading partners. During the latter part of the nineteenth and early part of the twentieth centuries, the Russian Empire was carrying on a lively trade with the developed countries of western Europe and the United States in order to buy equipment and get technological

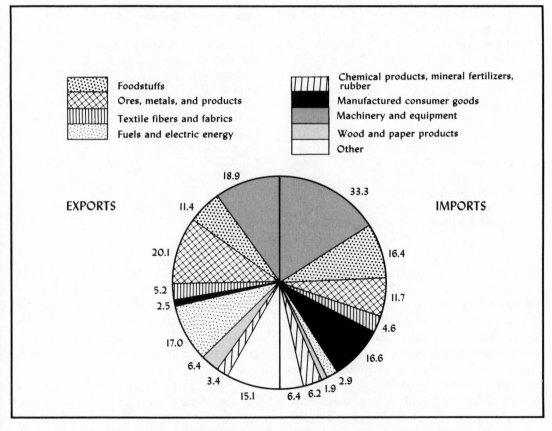

Figure 17–1   Commodity structure of U.S.S.R. exports and imports in percentages of total averaged over the period 1961–1966. Updated from Adams, Russell B., "Soviet Foreign Trade," Focus, American Geographical Society, June, 1968, p. 9.

Table 17–2   Main Exports and Imports of the U.S.S.R., 1966, in Per Cents of Total Value

Exports		Imports	
Product	Per Cent	Product	Per Cent
Total	100.0	Total	100.0
Machinery and equipment	20.8	Machinery and equipment	32.4
Coal	3.1	Oil products and liquid fuels	0.7
Coke	0.9	Rolled steel	1.3
Crude oil	7.4	Steel pipe	1.6
Oil products and liquid fuels	4.6	Copper	0.1
Iron ore	2.7	Wire and cables	1.0
Maganese ore	0.3	Chemical products	2.4
Asbestos	0.4	Natural rubber	1.9
Pig iron	2.1	Cotton fiber	1.8
Ferrous alloys	0.6	Wool	1.5
Rolled steel	6.8	Hides	1.1
Steel pipe	0.7	Raw tobacco	0.9
Copper	1.2	Small grains	6.2
Aluminum	1.3	Coffee, cocoa, and tea	1.0
Rolled light metals	0.6	Meat and meat products	0.9
Chemical products	1.2	Rice	0.6
Mineral fertilizers	1.5	Vegetables, fruit, and berries	2.5
Timber	2.2	Raw sugar	3.2
Lumber	3.5	Cotton cloth	0.5
Cotton fiber	4.2	Wool cloth	0.3
Furs and skins	0.8	Silk cloth	0.2
Small grains	2.6	Clothing	6.4
Butter	0.5	Leather shoes	2.0
Refined sugar	0.8	Furniture	2.1
Vegetable oil products	1.4	Drugs	1.4
Cotton cloth	0.4		
Household equipment	0.7		

Source: *Vneshnyaya torgovlya SSSR za 1966 god*, pp. 20 and 38.

know-how for its industrial revolution which was going on at that time. The industrialized West was the logical supplier of Russia's needs and also the largest logical market for its minerals, lumber, and grain. This trade lapsed with the advent of the Revolution and its subsequent civil war and the renouncement by the Soviets of Tsarist debts. Though there was some rejuvenation in the early 1930s, when the industrialization drive in the Soviet Union and the depression in the West made it mutually beneficial for the two to trade,

importations from the West were held strictly to a minimum and they were again interrupted by World War II. With the new political order after World War II, the Soviets switched their foreign trade primarily to the countries of eastern Europe. (Table 17–3)

Since the early 1950s Soviet trade has been expanding at a rapid rate (Table 17–4), and during the past decade there has been some tendency to shift back toward prior trading partners as the Soviets have found it more profitable for their industrialization drive to expand their trade with the industrialized western part of Europe. But they have not gone very far down this road; total trade remains small for the size of the economy, and the lion's share of it is still with east European countries, although they cannot always best serve the trade interests of the Soviet Union. Thus trade is strongly politically motivated. An additional facet to this political motivation has been added since the mid 1950s with the entrance of the Soviet Union into the "third world," trade and aid with the less developed countries.

The tactics that the Soviet Union has used with individual countries has varied by country according to ideology, geographical position, level of achievement, and historical perspective. The most intimate relations have been carried on generally with those countries immediately adjacent to the Soviet Union. Along the western border in recent times this has meant generally states much weaker militarily but more advanced culturally and economically. In the past, some of these states have been stronger and were direct contenders with the Russian Empire for supremacy on the east European Plain. Thus, although present conditions dominate present policies, the Soviets never forget the lessons of history and particularly are quite fearful of a resurgent unified Germany. Along the southern borders at the present time the countries are much smaller in military capability and less developed economically. Thus most of these countries can be categorized in the dual roles of border states and also LDC's (Less Developed Countries). However, here too in past times the Ottoman Empire and the Persian Empire vied with Russia for supremacy. In the Far East lies the ponderous giant of China which has a common border with the Soviet Union as long as that between the United States and Canada. The two facing opponents in this region have never reached an

agreement that has been very acceptable to either side. Hence potential instability exists.

Outside of this immediate contact zone lies on the one hand the industrialized West, whose power politics with the Soviet Union have largely been responsible for the continuing existence of the small border states, and on the other hand the less developed countries of Africa and part of Asia and to a certain extent Latin America, which have had disproportionate influences on world affairs in recent years. On top of all this is imposed the ideological schism between communism and the "free world," which has produced some strange bedfellows, aligning the Soviet Union in certain cases with countries immediately adjacent to it, in other cases with far-flung territories. Thus the picture is very complicated, and one cannot consider even the countries with common borders with the Soviet Union as a group, because some of these countries are economically and militarily aligned with the Soviet Union, whereas others, in reaction to policies of their big neighbor, have sought to align themselves with opposing powers wherever they might be. In the following pages an attempt will be made to unravel Soviet foreign relations, including foreign trade, by dealing with somewhat identifiable groups of countries. But it must be realized that many of these countries play dual and even triple roles in the milieu of border states, communist allies, underdeveloped countries, and so forth. And certain countries individually have figured so prominently that they will be singled out for expanded discussions.

The CEMA Countries

At the close of World War II, the Russians found their armies in occupation of all the countries of eastern Europe south to beyond the Danube and west to beyond Berlin. Thus World War II had thrown

Table 17–3 Soviet Exports and Imports, by Principal Countries, 1958 and 1966, in Millions of Rubles and Per Cents of Total

	Exports				Imports			
	1958		1966		1958		1966	
	Amount	Per Cent	Amount	Per Cent	Amount	Per Cent	Amount	Per Cent
Total	3,868	100	7,957	100	3,915	100	7,122	100
Socialist countries	2,823	73.0	5,286	66.4	2,932	74.9	4,738	66.4
CEMA countries	2,146	55.5	4,365	54.9	2,028	51.8	4,072	57.2
East Germany	720	18.6	1,266	15.9	734	18.7	1,114	15.6
Czechoslovakia	402	10.4	805	10.1	461	11.8	828	11.6
Poland	339	8.8	723	9.1	239	6.1	660	9.3
Bulgaria	181	4.7	627	7.9	183	4.7	587	8.2
Hungary	181	4.7	454	5.7	146	3.7	461	6.5
Rumania	226	5.8	348	4.4	210	5.4	365	5.1
Mongolia	58	1.5	142	1.8	43	1.1	56	0.8
Other Socialist countries	677	17.5	921	11.6	904	23.8	666	9.4
Cuba	—	—	432	5.4	14	0.4	257	3.6
Yugoslavia	46	1.2	193	2.4	46	1.2	174	2.4
China	571	14.8	158	2.0	793	20.2	129	1.8
North Korea	52	1.3	77	1.0	42	1.1	83	1.2
North Vietnam	7	0.2	61	0.8	9	0.2	23	0.3

Industrialized West	632	16.3	1,581	19.9	591	15.1	1,601	22.5
United Kingdom	131	3.4	297	3.7	66	1.7	152	2.1
Finland	105	2.7	231	2.9	124	3.2	195	2.7
Japan	18	0.5	215	2.7	16	0.4	202	2.8
West Germany	59	1.5	167	2.1	65	1.7	125	1.8
France	78	2.0	117	1.5	73	1.9	144	2.0
Italy	35	0.9	140	1.8	32	0.8	86	1.2
Austria	20	0.5	43	0.5	57	1.5	64	0.9
Netherlands	51	1.3	72	0.9	16	0.4	35	0.5
Sweden	27	0.7	64	0.8	25	0.6	40	0.6
U.S.A.	24	0.6	42	0.5	4	0.1	57	0.8
Developing countries	413	10.1	1,091	13.7	392	10.0	784	11.0
India	117	3.0	174	2.2	46	1.2	172	2.4
United Arab Republic	79	2.0	179	2.2	96	2.5	135	1.9
Malaysia	0	0	0	0	106	2.7	113	1.6
Argentina	16	0.4	6.7	0.1	14	0.4	97	1.4
Afghanistan	21	0.5	66	0.8	11	0.3	17	0.2
Pakistan	1.8	0	35	0.4	6.7	0.2	26	0.4
Brazil	0	0	25	0.3	0.8	0	28	0.4
Iran	25	0.6	28	0.4	24	0.6	18	0.3
Turkey	8.5	0.2	25	0.3	10.3	0.3	17	0.2
Syria	14	0.4	20	0.3	21	0.5	18	0.3
Iraq	0	0	32	0.4	0	0	2.9	0
Indonesia	25	0.6	4.3	0.1	10	0.3	28	0.4

Sources: Computed from *Vneshnyaya torgovlya SSSR za 1963 god,* pp. 10–15, and *za 1966 god,* pp. 10–15. Individual figures do not add to totals because not all countries are included and amounts have been rounded from different sources.
Note: Within each group, countries are listed in descending order of trade turnover with the U.S.S.R. in 1966.

Table 17–4   Soviet Trade, Selected Years, 1938–1966, in Millions of Rubles

	Turnover	Exports	Imports
1938	0.5	0.2	0.3
1946	1.3	0.6	0.7
1955	5.8	3.1	2.7
1960	10.1	5.0	5.1
1965	14.6	7.4	7.2
1966	15.1	8.0	7.1

Source: Vneshnyaya torgovlya SSSR za 1966 god, p. 8.
Note: Unless otherwise specified, all ruble values are in terms of the present ruble, which since 1961 has been valued at $1.11.

into their laps much of the territory for which they had striven for more than a thousand years against strong adversaries. It also included territories which had never been part of the Russian Empire but which also had been parts of states at one time or another that vied with Moscow for supremacy in Eastern Europe. Desiring to create a broad buffer zone against Western aggression, particularly a resurgent Germany, the Soviets were quick to set up puppet governments in the east European countries and to establish the area as a sphere of Soviet influence, excluding any sort of entry from the West.

To a certain extent, the east European countries initially found this mutually beneficial, since Germany had collapsed and with it much of their export market. The pre-war economy of countries such as Czechoslovakia and, to some extent, Poland had been geared to the rapid industrialization of Nazi Germany; they had built up their industries to serve the German industrial market. With the collapse of the Nazi war machine, these countries found themselves dangling without any visible outside markets for their industrial goods. Thus immediately after the war, some of these countries turned to the Soviet Union to find markets for their

products. Since the Soviet Union had so much war damage to repair, it was in great need of all sorts of industrial supplies. However, the relationship did not turn out to be one of simple trading between equal partners. First, many of the east European states, most of whom had been part of the Axis powers, were required by the Soviet Union to pay heavy war reparations in the form of industrial plants and equipment. And even those countries which had not been on the Nazi side, such as Poland, somehow found themselves in a similar pinch. Poland for a number of years was required to deliver coal at very cheap prices to the Soviet Union, as a sort of war booty, in spite of the fact that Poland had never fought against the Russians and had itself suffered probably the worst of any nation during the war.

Very quickly, the east European countries began to realize what was happening and immediately tried to reestablish trade with western Europe and the United States. Some of them also anticipated applying for reconstruction aid through the Marshall Plan that the United States was beginning to initiate. In order to curb any such actions, the Soviet Union in 1947 refused to participate in the Marshall Plan program and evolved its own Molotov Plan with the east European countries. This utilized bilateral trade agreements, credit on favorable terms, and scientific-technical collaboration commissions between the Soviet Union and individual east European countries. This rather loose conception was codified more precisely in 1949 with the establishment of the Council for Economic Mutual Assistance, or "Comecon" (CEMA), which was to integrate the economies of the east European countries with that of the Soviet Union (and Mongolia!) in order to effect greater efficiencies of labor and capital expenditures in individual countries and to rationalize trade among them.

In addition the Soviets set up companies owned and operated jointly by the Soviet Union and the country concerned, with production and trade strongly controlled by the Soviets. Most of these companies emanated from firms which had originally been owned by foreign capital, particularly German, and which during the war had fallen into the hands of the recipient countries, mainly through the Russian occupation. Thus there was no legal ownership, and the Soviets found it very easy to manipulate control. Naturally most of these companies were managed by Russian managers and were oriented directly toward the Soviet Union, and, in fact, enjoyed what amounted to extraterritorial rights within the countries in which they were located.

Thus until about 1954, the Soviets ruled the east European countries with a strong hand through the mechanisms of war reparations, Comecon, and Russian-owned and "mixed" companies. By 1954 it became evident even to the Soviets that economic conditions in the east European satellites were so bad that something was going to have to give or there would be mass revolt. In fact the East Berlin revolt of 1953 showed these tendencies very clearly. Therefore in 1954 the Soviet Union did somewhat of an about-face and cancelled any further war reparations and returned the Russian-owned companies to their respective countries. Also the Russians began to extend credit to the east European satellites and to provide aid in various forms for their economic reconstruction. By this time, the east European satellites were so far within the orbit of Soviet influence that such mechanisms as mixed companies were no longer needed.

As the east European countries began to recuperate, they began looking toward the West for normalization of relations and resumption of trade. Also they were chafing under the strong control of Moscow, and eventually this led to the disastrous revolts of Hungary and Poland in 1956. This brought on a tightening of controls by the Soviets and a desire by them to integrate the economies of the east European countries more fully with that of the Soviet Union through the mechanism of CEMA. Such intentions went contrary to the individual desires of the east European satellites, and the Soviet Union was voted down on this proposal in 1963. Since that time the individual east European countries have been going more and more their own ways in developing their economies and establishing trade. The Soviet Union has turned somewhat away from the CEMA organization and more toward the Warsaw Pact to try to establish tight political and military control over the countries where economic control has failed.

As far as can be discerned, the east European satellites do not necessarily want to break away from the so-called Soviet Bloc, although the Bloc is becoming cracked in all directions. What they would like is more autonomy within the Bloc, particularly in terms of the development of their own economies and the liberalization of their own ways of life. One of the reasons that they refused to integrate their economies more closely with the Soviet Union was the fact that the Soviet Union was unable to offer them sophisticated types of machinery and equipment for the industrialization that they desired, and in later years it was unable to maintain shipments of grain and other foodstuffs. Thus the countries have been forced to turn toward sources in the West where such commodities are available. This trend has only just begun, though, and the trade of east European satellites is still overwhelmingly with the Soviet Union.

This trade is very important to the Soviet Union. As can be seen in Table 17–3, in 1966, 54.9 per cent of the exports of the Soviet Union still went to the CEMA countries and 57.2 per cent of Soviet imports came from them. More important, certain east European countries, particularly East Germany and Czechoslovakia, supplied three quarters of the total Soviet imports of machinery and equipment during that year. (Table 17–5) They also supplied much manufactured consumer goods. Soviet exports to these countries have con-

Table 17–5   Principal Origins and Destinations of Some Major Soviet Imports and Exports, 1966

Imports		Exports	
Machinery and equipment		Machinery and equipment	
(million rubles)	2,308	(million rubles)	1,654
East Germany	616	Bulgaria	288
Czechoslovakia	442	Czechoslovakia	137
Poland	233	Poland	130
Hungary	220	United Arab Republic	121
Bulgaria	172	Cuba	111
Japan	95	Hungary	109
United Kingdom	91	East Germany	108
West Germany	88	Coal (million tons)	21.8
Oil products and liquid fuels		East Germany	5.9
(million tons)	1.7	Bulgaria	3.0
Rumania	1.0	Czechoslovakia	2.1
East Germany	0.3	Japan	1.6
Plastics and plastic production		France	1.5
equipment (million rubles)	45.3	Italy	1.4
Italy	10.3	Poland	1.2
East Germany	8.8	Crude oil (million tons)	50.3
Japan	8.1	Italy	8.0
Netherlands	4.5	Czechoslovakia	6.4
United Kingdom	4.4	East Germany	6.1
Paints, lacquers, and tanning fluids		Cuba	3.8
(million rubles)	52.7	Poland	3.3
Poland	10.9	West Germany	3.3
East Germany	9.4	Japan	2.8
Czechoslovakia	8.0	Bulgaria	2.6
United Kingdom	5.9	Finland	2.6
Austria	3.4	Hungary	2.5
Natural rubber (thousand tons)	311	Brazil	2.2
Malaysia	243	France	1.7
Indonesia	57	Oil products and liquid fuels	
Ceylon	12	(million tons)	23.3
Cotton fiber (thousand tons)	173	Sweden	3.7
United Arab Republic	99	Finland	3.5
Syria	24	Poland	1.7
Brazil	15	Bulgaria	1.4
Afghanistan	9	Japan	1.4
Sudan	7	Cuba	1.3
Iran	6	India	1.2
Jute (thousand tons)	34	West Germany	1.2
India	19	France	1.0
Pakistan	12	Iron ore (million tons)	26.1
Wool (thousand tons)	61	Poland	7.8
Australia	14	Czechoslovakia	7.7
Mongolia	11	East Germany	2.6
New Zealand	9	Hungary	2.6
Argentina	6	Rumania	2.4

Table 17–5   Principal Origins and Destinations of Some Major Soviet Imports and Exports, 1966 (Continued)

Imports		Exports	
Coffee (thousand tons)	28	Manganese ore (thousand tons)	1,218
Brazil	14	Poland	317
India	7	East Germany	198
Colombia	2	Czechoslovakia	149
Ethiopia	1	United Kingdom	134
Cocoa (thousand tons)	57	France	116
Ghana	54	Japan	106
Brazil	2	Chrome ore (thousand tons)	920
Tea (thousand tons)	21	United States	289
India	17	West Germany	100
Ceylon	3	France	99
Meat and meat products		Poland	67
(thousand tons)	133	Pig iron (thousand tons)	4,383
China	90	Japan	1,193
Bulgaria	17	Poland	737
Hungary	10	East Germany	671
Rice (thousand tons)	275	Rumania	342
Pakistan	90	Italy	220
United Arab Republic	73	Yugoslavia	176
North Korea	72	United States	146
Oranges (thousand tons)	142	Bulgaria	137
Morocco	46	Hungary	130
Spain	32	Rolled steel (thousand tons)	5,019
Algeria	30	East Germany	1,937
Raw sugar (thousand tons)	1,841	Rumania	829
Cuba	1,841	Bulgaria	396
Clothing (million rubles)	453	Poland	342
East Germany	79	Czechoslovakia	341
Bulgaria	74	Timber (thousand cubic meters)	12,747
Poland	45	Japan	3,522
Hungary	43	West Germany	1,825
China	42	China	1,451
Shoes (million pairs)	33.7	Hungary	1,405
Czechoslovakia	14.1	East Germany	831
Poland	4.3	Norway	700
Hungary	4.0	Lumber (thousand cubic meters)	7,991
Yugoslavia	3.1	United Kingdom	2,056
		East Germany	1,325
		Hungary	670
		West Germany	462
		Finland	432
		Italy	353
		Cuba	310
		Food grains (thousand tons)	3,557
		Czechoslovakia	1,242
		East Germany	1,148
		Netherlands	504
		Cuba	492
		North Korea	118

Source: Compiled from *Vneshnyaya torgovlya SSSR za 1966 god,* pp. 97–116.

sisted of fuels and industrial raw materials, 50 per cent; followed by machinery, 17 per cent; and foodstuffs, 10 per cent or more. The commodity structure of trade between the U.S.S.R. and the CEMA countries has remained quite consistent over the years except for the rather widely fluctuating food component, which reflects weather conditions in the U.S.S.R. East Germany and Czechoslovakia, the two most industrialized of the CEMA countries, supply by far the highest portions of Soviet imports from this region of the world, while these two countries plus Poland and Bulgaria receive many of the exports. East German exports of forge and press equipment, machinery for the food and chemical industries, railroad rolling stock, and ships regularly amount to about 40 per cent of Russia's total machinery imports. Poland also has become an important supplier of ships to the Soviet Union, which is in the process of rapidly expanding both its navy and merchant marine. East Germany, Czechoslovakia, Poland, and Hungary are the most industrialized nations of eastern Europe, and all supply significant amounts of fairly advanced industrial equipment to the Soviet Union. In return from the Soviet Union they receive mineral raw materials and, except for bad years, some grain. The less developed satellites, such as Rumania and Bulgaria, import certain mineral raw materials and heavy industrial equipment from the Soviet Union in exchange for agricultural produce, certain mineral raw materials, and a limited quantity of consumer items.

In the last few years there has been a direct link-up for the flow of fluid fuels and electrical power from the Soviet Union to many of the satellite countries. The Druzhba (friendship) oil pipeline system has been built to carry Volga-Urals oil to refineries in Poland, East Germany, Czechoslovakia, and Hungary. During 1967 it was reported that this pipeline carried 17 to 18 million metric tons of crude oil to these four east European countries, which was virtually all of the Soviet exports to these countries during that year. This is a quantity of oil about double the annual amount produced by Russia before the Revolution. In 1968 a second parallel pipeline was started at both ends which eventually is to expand this trade greatly. High-voltage electrical transmission lines also carry energy from the Soviet Union to the satellite countries. In the future, this is destined to increase with the perfection of the use of very high-voltage direct-current transmission lines which can carry electrical power over large distances all the way from the huge hydroelectric power plants of the Soviet Union to the east European satellites. Thus the east European countries have become very dependent upon the Soviet Union for energy sources.

Czechoslovakia The Soviet Union's role in eastern Europe, and the relationship of the eastern European countries to the Soviet Union, can best be exemplified by Czechoslovakia in 1968. Since the coming to power of the Communist Party in Czechoslovakia shortly after World War II, the country had been a rather surprisingly docile follower of the Soviet Union. Surprising, because previously Czechoslovakia had been one of the more democratic small countries in Europe, with very idealistic leadership. The nonresistance policy of the Czechs allowed for rapid recovery economically from the war and a continuation of their industrialization. Material life there quickly became relatively better than in the rest of eastern Europe, but political life was quite squelched. Hence the anecdote of the Czech and Polish dogs who met crossing their common boundary. The Czech dog asked the Polish dog why he was going into Czechoslovakia, whereupon the Polish dog replied that he was looking for something to eat. Then the Polish dog asked, "But why in the world are you going to Poland?" Whereupon the Czech dog said, "I had an urge to bark."

As the years passed, the Czechs found

themselves more and more dependent upon the Soviet Union for vital imports of oil, iron ore, and other raw materials to keep their industrial machine going. Also they became very dependent upon the Soviet market for disposal of the products of their machine and textile industries. Almost every vehicle in Czechoslovakia was run on gasoline from Soviet oil, and much of the bread that was baked in Czechoslovakia was made from Soviet wheat. Thus every facet of life was pervaded by the presence of the Soviet Union. The Czechs pointed out that the Soviet Union was also dependent upon them for such things as undisclosed quantities of uranium for Soviet nuclear projects, experts for advice on the development of their economy, and, to a certain extent, heavy machinery. Be this as it may, the Czechs would have been hard put to compete in the roughly competitive market of the West if they suddenly had to switch their sales from the relatively sheltered market of the Soviet Union to the open market of the free world.

Inevitably, as generations changed and world conditions relaxed, the Czechs desired greater degrees of freedom, and in the tradition of their earlier days they successfully replaced old hard-line communists with newer liberal leaders who quickly moved the country farther along the road to freedom than had been dared in any of the other east European satellites since World War II. Such rapid political and social developments not only alarmed the Soviet communists but also the communist leaders in East Germany, Poland, Hungary, and Bulgaria. All of these regimes feared that they would be toppled if the Czechs were allowed to liberalize, as they obviously intended to do. The Soviet leaders also envisioned the ultimate cracking of the entire east European Bloc which might lay the Soviet Union vulnerable to renewed attacks from the West. Thus the buffer zone that the Soviet Union had been so intent on developing after World War II would disappear. Therefore

after long negotiations which seemed to indicate to the hopeful world that the Soviets had been successfully "Czechmated" diplomatically, the Soviet Union and its four fearful allies risked condemnation by the world and swiftly sent troops crossing the Czech border from all sides in the dead of the night of August 20–21, 1968, to occupy the country militarily. The shock to the world, and Czechoslovakia, as well as to the populace of the other east European countries, rudely jolted everyone into the reality that the Soviet Union was not going to allow liberalization and fragmentation to occur in its dominated bloc of eastern Europe. Though slow evolution might eventually bring all things about, personal and national freedoms in eastern Europe do not exist yet by any means. And the mere geographical fact of the juxtaposition of these countries with the Soviet Union ties the hands of Western nations that would want to help them.

Other Socialist Countries

The Soviet Union has not been successful in molding a cohesive bloc out of communist countries that are not as near to it. China, Cuba, and Yugoslavia are the outstanding examples of communist countries that have been more successful in going their own ways. Although Yugoslavia is not very far removed geographically from the Soviet Union, it was the first to bolt the common cause of the socialist countries and take a course of its own. A strong personality as a leader coupled with adequate relations with the West have allowed Yugoslavia to walk a tightrope between the West and the Soviet Union and maintain semi-independence while developing a socialist order of its own design. For this it has been condemned by the Soviet Union, but with the ascension of Khrushchev the world witnessed the strange attempt to woo Yugoslavia back into the common fold, which resulted in Yugoslavia cooperating just as much, but no more, than she wanted to. Since then, she has been adept at deriving certain benefits from relations with the Soviet Union and other east European countries, while at the same time maintaining aloofness from involvements in that group. As far as Yugoslavia's trade is concerned, it is fairly well diversified with only that portion going to the Soviet Union that might normally be expected to. There has been a considerable increase in trade between the two countries during the last 10 years since the Soviets have effected some sort of rapprochement with Yugoslavia.

China   China, of course, has been the great dilemma to the Soviet Union. One might conclude that the Soviets somewhat anticipated this when the Chinese Communists came to power in 1948, for it was through no effort of the Russian Communists that the Chinese Revolution was successful. Nevertheless the Soviets immediately recognized the Chinese Communist regime and offered economic assistance and other sorts of relations. Much of the industrial equipment that had been stripped from the plants of Manchuria immediately after the war was returned to the Chinese, and monetary grants, long-term loans, credits, and technical assistance were offered. Within a short while, the Government of Mao Tse-tung had proclaimed its alignment with the Soviet Union and its isolation from the rest of the world. This was strengthened by Soviet military assistance to China during the latter part of the Korean War.

The Communist Chinese faithfully copied the Soviet development model during the years 1953–1957, but some rumblings of discord occurred as early as October 1954 when the Chinese demanded the return of the joint stock companies that the Soviets had set up in Manchuria and renewed territorial claims against the Soviet Union along the Russo-Chinese border. The Chinese finally abandoned the Soviet model altogether in 1958 when they launched their "great leap forward." After

that they became so overt in their verbal attacks on the Soviet Union that the Soviets withdrew most of their expert advisers during mid 1960 and sent most of the Chinese students home who had been attending universities in the Soviet Union, although a few students survived the 1960–1964 sharp attacks between the two countries and some even remained in Soviet institutions until early 1967. During the spring of 1967, Sino-Soviet relations took a definite turn for the worse and entered a new phase in which Soviet diplomats were expelled from Peking and Chinese diplomats from Moscow in an unprecedented breakdown of relations between two socialist states. With the launching of the so-called cultural revolution in China in 1966, a coarse element in Chinese society came to the forefront and made themselves very obnoxious to those Soviets who had the closest dealings with them. Soviet officials protested unorthodox modes of action by Chinese embassy members in Moscow who were not appearing for prearranged meetings and who were provoking the Soviets by using foul, slanderous language in meetings which normally should have been conducted with considerable decorum. At the same time the Soviet government withdrew embassy officials from China and cited them for exemplary performance of official duties in the face of most difficult working conditions. Previously, the Soviet press had refrained from direct candid criticism of Chinese actions, apparently in the hope that the rift still could be patched, but after 1966, when apparently the Soviets had abandoned all hope of ever bridging the gap, the Soviet press became quite outspoken about all sorts of things that were going on in China.

Soviet aid to China has been very difficult to decipher, since so many complex arrangements were involved and since the Soviets exclude military materials from trade statistics. However, some estimate can be gleaned from looking at the Soviet-

Chinese trade figures. From 1949 through 1955, the Soviets exported about $1,063,-000,000 more to the Chinese than they received in imports. Apparently this trade imbalance was covered by credits to the Chinese. From 1956 through 1965, however, the Chinese exported about $1,555,-000,000 more to the Soviets than they received. In 1966 the trade again reversed, and China imported more from the Soviet Union than they exported to the Soviet Union. Apparently the Chinese repaid their debt during the 1956–1965 period, and after that more normal trade relations, although on a much reduced scale, were entered into. The repayment period was not a time of affluence in China, and obviously the repayments worked hardships on the Chinese people who were not eager to pay back their debts to the Soviet Union and were not happy about the shift in balance of trade forced upon them in 1956 by the Soviets who were beginning to get worried about relations with China.

Aid agreements had been readily signed in 1950 and 1954 and given wide publicity, but four other agreements signed in May 1953, April 1956, August 1958, and February 1959 have hardly been mentioned by the Soviets, who apparently signed very reluctantly. Although the last Soviet loan to China was made in 1961 as an emergency loan of 45 million dollars to purchase sugar, Chinese drawdowns on Soviet aid and technical help apparently continued as late as 1965, despite the shift in the balance of trade and the deterioration of relations between the two countries. Therefore aid peaks were probably reached somewhere around 1959–1960 when relations were just reaching the breaking point, and aid materials continued to arrive in China long after Soviet technicians left in 1960. In total, Soviet aid probably amounted to at least 2 billion dollars. Some of this might have included military deliveries, which reached their peak during the Korean War and declined sharply thereafter, although some MIG fighters

and a small amount of other military equipment were delivered after that. The net effect of aid between the two countries left both sides quite disgruntled.

Trade between the Soviet Union and Communist China reached a peak of over 2 billion dollars in 1959, but dropped precipitously between 1960 and 1961 and has been declining steadily ever since. Whereas Chinese exports to the Soviet Union in 1958 made up over 20 per cent of total Soviet imports, at the present they constitute less than 2 per cent of such imports. Similarly, Soviet exports to China have dropped from around 15 per cent of total Soviet exports to less than 2 per cent. (Table 17–3) During the period 1955–1959 the Soviet Union accounted for about half of the foreign trade turnover of China, whereas at present it accounts for less than 15 per cent.

Ever since 1950 the Soviet exports to China have consisted mainly of capital goods, among which machinery and equipment, including many complete plants, petroleum products, and metals and metal products have been most important. Together, these three categories have accounted for approximately 90 per cent of Soviet sales to China. Chinese exports to the U.S.S.R. have at all times been dominated by processed and unprocessed foods, especially meat and dairy products, metals, metal ores, nonmetallic minerals, and textiles. The large amounts of food exported by China to the Soviet Union seem rather strange, because the Chinese were so in need of food themselves. However, this apparently was one of the few products that they could muster to pay for needed imports of machinery and other equipment, and so they made the sacrifice. On the other hand, the Soviet government showed its willingness to accept consumer goods in exchange for capital equipment, which was somewhat of a windfall for the Soviet consumer but something of a headache for the government since the Chinese were in the habit of changing their sales offers frequently and at very short notices.

The decline in Soviet exports to China can be attributed to three factors: (1) the unwillingness of the Soviets to sell potentially strategic goods, such as petroleum products, aircraft components, and so forth; (2) the disruption of sales of Soviet plants, machinery, and industrial equipment after the withdrawal of Soviet experts and blueprints from China in mid 1960, (3) and Chinese attempts to save on imports in order to pay off the debt as rapidly as possible. Equipment for complete plants accounted for 46 per cent of the Chinese imports in 1960, but fell to 9 per cent in 1964, and was not reported at all in 1965. Obviously it would not have made much sense for China to import such equipment after the withdrawal of Soviet technicians. Soviet exports of gasoline to China decreased from 1 million metric tons in 1960 to 30,000 in 1965. The Chinese claim that they were fully self-sufficient in oil after 1963. However, they did need highly refined petroleum products, such as jet fuel, which Russia held back precisely at the time they needed it in 1962 when the Chinese were expressing military ambitions along the Indian frontier. This was the first case of major proportions in which a communist country had supported a non-communist country against another communist country, and it somewhat repaid China for having engaged in the duplicity ever since 1955 of receiving aid from the Soviets while at the same time supplying aid to certain less developed countries in direct competition to the Soviets, who were already active in those areas.

During the last 15 years the communist giants have been vying with each other for favors in other areas instead of cooperating for their mutual benefit. The most intense struggles for influence between the Soviet Union and China have taken place in North Korea, North Vietnam, Mongolia, and Cuba. Although the Chinese hold the trumps of race and revolutionary theory in North Korea and North Vietnam, these are poor substitutes for technological expertize, scientific skill, and general material aid which the Soviets have to offer. After the escalation of the Vietnam War it became very clear to the leaders in Hanoi that anti-aircraft guns and SAM's were more important than dated advice on self-reliance in infantry warfare, and that the outcome of the war was not going to hinge on the brave and inspiring talk from Peking. Thus Hanoi turned more and more toward the Soviets for military aid, which brought on the Chinese accusation that the Soviets were sending military support to North Vietnam in order to gain the right to strike a political deal with the United States in that area.

Since 1964 the Soviets have spent hundreds of millions of dollars in military assistance to North Vietnam consisting of primarily defensive hardware such as rocket installations, anti-aircraft artillery, airplanes, tanks, coastal guns and war ships, and the training of pilots, rocket personnel, tank drivers, and artillery men. This heavy military assistance to North Vietnam required some negotiations with China regarding the question of transit rights across Chinese territory. Rail shipments of Soviet war materials through China have been subjected to harassment and delay by Chinese authorities who have said that such materials did not have proper papers for transit and that they, the Chinese, did not know whether Vietnam needed this war material anyway. Each flight across Chinese territory has had to be cleared specifically by the Chinese authorities, and often the planes have been required to stop at Peking airport and made to refuel with all passengers on board, while jeering crowds subjected the representatives of Soviet power to insults and indignities. Soviet vessels laden with munitions for Hanoi have run into all kinds of bureaucratic delays at Chinese ports. At one time in 1965 the Soviets reported that the Chinese had demanded from the U.S.S.R. payment in U.S. dollars for the transport of Soviet supplies across China to North Vietnam. The controversy over military aid to North Vietnam has become an Aesopian way of translating fundamental ideological, national, and cultural discord into issues of the moment. One of the strongest points made by the Soviets regarding the humiliation of their diplomats in Peking by teenage practitioners of Mao's Cultural Revolution in early 1967 was that the officially sponsored hooliganism had obstructed the flow of Soviet military shipments to North Vietnam.

Such communist polemics are not likely to affect Sino-Soviet relations much one way or the other, because these relations did not begin with the communist ascension to power in China in 1949, nor even the communist ascension to power in the Soviet Union in 1917. Competition for supremacy in the Far East between these two land giants began as far back as the early part of the seventeenth century when the Russian Cossacks swept across Siberia to the Pacific Coast. Border disputes have flared up between the two powers ever since. During the past century the Russians have generally had the upper hand and have forced their conditions upon the Chinese. The Russian acquisition of much of the Soviet Far East took place as late as 1860, only a short time ago if measured against the many centuries that these bordering countries have existed, and the Chinese have never accepted this settlement and have been rankling under it ever since. As relations between the Soviets and the Chinese have worsened in recent years the Chinese have become more and more outspoken about some of the disputed territories along their common boundary. (Fig. 17–2)

Conflict between the two powers has arisen not only in the areas indicated, but also in the puppet states of Mongolia and Tanu-Tuva as well as the old area of Turkestan which is peopled primarily by native groups, neither Russian nor Chinese, who have been in almost constant revolt against both of their squabbling neighbors. Tanu-Tuva was finally secretly annexed by the Soviet Union in October 1944 after it had been made nominally independent two decades earlier, and in 1921 a communist Peoples Republic of Mongolia was proclaimed by the Soviets under China's nose. After 1955 the Chinese became quite active in Mongolia, particularly through hordes of Chinese workers brought in on construction projects, but the Russians manned a massive aid program of at least 670 million dollars and accepted 95 per cent of Mongolia's export trade, which assured the orientation of Mongolia toward the U.S.S.R. At the present time, the Chinese seem to be quietly waiting for an opportunity to get a foothold in Mongolia once more.

Further west in the desert areas of Turkestan the drama of Russian-Chinese struggle for the large area sparsely populated by Turkic peoples took place from 1860 to the communist accession of power in China in 1949. Pacts were made and broken between the Soviet Union and China regarding this area, while at the same time almost constant native uprisings proclaimed various types of independence for the area and rejected both Soviet and Chinese rule. The present international boundary between the Soviet Union and China arbitrarily divides a region occupied by Kazakhs, Kirgiz, Uighurs, and other Turkic peoples of common ethnic, cultural, and religous characteristics. As late as 1944, the Soviets marched into the region and set up a Soviet-style East Turkestan Republic in the area east of their recognized boundary after a local leader in 1942 had decided that the U.S.S.R. had lost the war with Germany and liquidated thousands of local communists and Soviet agents in the area. Thus a Soviet puppet state seemed to be in the making in territory that had long been claimed by the Chinese Empire. But

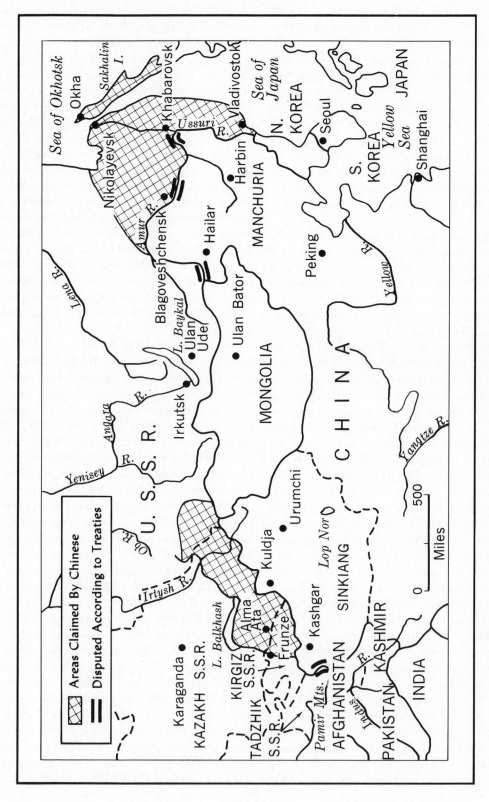

Figure 17–2 Chinese claims on Soviet Territories. Map prepared by Ludwig Cinatl to accompany an article by Hopkins, Mark, "Soviet, Chinese Nerves Grating on Long Border," Milwaukee Journal, February 11, 1967, Part 1, p. 11.

in 1949 when the Chinese Communists moved into Sinkiang Province, the Soviets agreed that this area should become the Sinkiang-Uighur Autonomous Region within the newly formed Chinese Peoples Republic. In recent years, however, the Soviets have shown sympathy for local rebels who are struggling against the Chinese and have allowed large flows of refugees into the Soviet Union. Apparently a secret school exists in the U.S.S.R. for the training of partisans, and a former major general from Sinkiang commands a 60,000-man army stationed in Alma-Ata waiting for an opportunity to "liberate" the area. Obviously such goings on rankle the Chinese and provoke them into constantly claiming large chunks of land west of the present Soviet-Chinese boundary which are similar physically and culturally to the Sinkiang area.

Probably these border disputes are minor among the major issues forming differences of opinion between the Chinese and the Soviets. Such things as the disposition of Taiwan, the development of Chinese military power, and the struggle for international communist supremacy at the present time far overshadow territorial disputes in inner Asia. But these contact zones, with their long histories of alternating Russian and Chinese control, provide tempting opportunities to express concretely friction generated by more abstract issues. Such actions as those taken by the Chinese in April 1966 to apply strict regulations to "foreign ships on bordering rivers," which obviously were aimed at Soviet shipping on the Amur, the Ussuri, and on Lake Khanka, were well calculated to antagonize the Soviet Union. In an atmosphere where two adversaries are looking for conflicting issues, the long border between the Soviet Union and China provides ample opportunities. The two giant powers have little in common other than an ideology whose subtle differences render the two ideological adversaries so inflexible as to be completely unable to negotiate. Race, history, and customs are against the two countries' acting harmoniously. China might well prove to be the greatest ultimate threat to the Soviet Union.

North Korea and North Vietnam After the capitulation of Japan in World War II, Korea, which had been under the control of the Japanese, was up for grabs, and the Soviet Union forced a settlement on the United States for its few days' participation in the Pacific War which left Korea artificially cut across the middle of the peninsula between North and South. Subsequently, North Korea very quickly became part of the Soviet sphere with a communist puppet government, and South Korea attempted to recoup its economy and form some sort of democratic republic. Exactly what the aims of the Soviets were in Korea is uncertain, other than the traditional Russian vague aim of expansion wherever possible, although port facilities might have been specific objectives, since the Korean ports are less hampered by ice than is the Soviet port of Vladivostok to the north. As it has worked out, however, North Korea has probably been more of a liability than an asset to the Soviet Union, since the Soviets have been unable to accomplish any easy aggressive expansionism, and with an unfriendly China next door the Soviets are even less apt to carry on an aggressive policy now in this area than they were in the early 1950s. The North Koreans now seem to be acting much on their own in keeping things very tense in that area, and all indications are that neither Moscow nor Peking were consulted before the North Korean seizure of the American ship *Pueblo*. Nothing worries Moscow more at the present time than the impending crisis they see inevitably building in Korea, spurred on by the rather irresponsible actions of the North Korean government. They regard Korea along with Berlin as powder capable of unleashing a catastrophic third world war. Except for military goods, there seem to be no signs of any rejuvenated trade between the Soviet Union and North Korea.

If the Soviets are wondering how they got themselves into this situation with North Korea, they are even more bewildered by their commitment to North Vietnam. Vietnam is nowhere near their own border, and so it could not conceivably serve any purposes such as Korea might, and now the Soviets find themselves in direct competition with their militant communist adversary, China, in a struggle to persuade and control the development of the government of North Vietnam, while at the same time trying to sustain the military effort of North Vietnam against the United States. Obviously, both tasks are distasteful, and undoubtedly the Soviet Union would like to disassociate itself if it could. However, the Soviets find themselves trapped in the situation much as the Americans do and continue to pour military aid into North Vietnam, which since the escalation of the war in 1964 has amounted to about 4 billion dollars. Most of this has been in the form of artillery pieces, missiles, mortars, and other heavy weapons, primarily for the defense of North Vietnam against air attacks from the United States. In addition to the Soviet help, the Rumanians have been induced to send oil and the East Germans and other communist countries to send consumer goods to North Vietnam. Red China on its own volition has been aiding at the rate of about 250 million dollars per year. Much of this is in the form of small arms for aggressive actions in South Vietnam. The Soviets have announced recently that they have completed more than 140 industrial enterprises in North Vietnam which account for 40 per cent of the country's total business turnover. What the future will bring for the Soviets in Vietnam is as unclear as what it will bring for the Americans. At the present time the biggest problem to the Soviet Union in this area is the irrationally competitive actions of the Chinese who are making it very difficult for the Soviets to ship their materials into North Vietnam and who are making it equally difficult for the Soviet Union to effect any negotiations between Hanoi and Washington because the Chinese keep screaming that the Soviet Union is in collusion with the United States and has sold out Vietnam.

Cuba The Soviets did not create Cuba. In fact, at the time of the Castro takeover, the Soviet government was purchasing fairly large amounts of raw sugar from Batista's government, which helped to finance his stay in power, and local communists in Cuba originally resisted Castro. But after it was evident that Castro was going down the communist line, the Soviet Union eagerly entered the scene in what it conceived to be the opportunity it had been waiting for to get a foothold in the western hemisphere and establish military bases close to the American land mass, much as the United States had sought to ring the Soviet Union. Accordingly, in February 1960 the Soviets extended a loan of 100 million dollars to Cuba and agreed to furnish technical advisers to construct thermo electric plants, an oil refinery, a fertilizer plant, and so forth. The Soviets also agreed to make geological and climatological surveys of the island and to build a fishing port. To help the Cubans pay for such heavy equipment and technical advice, the Soviets agreed rapidly to expand their imports of raw sugar, which by 1961 reached a value of more than 300 million dollars, six times the amount imported in 1957 before Castro came to power.

It is difficult to unravel Soviet-Cuban economic arrangements, but from 1960 through 1962 trade figures showed an enlarged Cuban surplus of exports which were probably paying for military imports. Since that time Soviet exports have considerably exceeded imports, and the Cuban trade deficit has been underwritten through balance-of-payments credits. At the same time Castro himself has acknowledged that the Soviets have been supplying military equipment free of charge. Since the Cuban missile crisis of October 1962, however, relations between Cuba and the Soviet Union have tended to become more and more strained, and military and economic aid has been extended by the Soviets more and more reluctantly. By 1964 Soviet aid to Cuba, which had been running somewhere between 400 and 600 million dollars annually, was severely cut, and Castro was bluntly told to look elsewhere when he applied for economic aid to recoup the damage caused by hurricane Flora in 1964. On this occasion Red China took the opportunity to advance 1 million dollars help to the hurricane victims of Cuba, which did not enhance Cuban-Soviet relations any. Later the Soviets began dragging their feet on the supply of oil to Cuba, which in certain years had made up as much as two thirds of Cuban imports from the Soviet Union. This further infuriated Castro and was perhaps instrumental in his decision to try and convict 37 pro-Soviet subversives in 1968 and condemn the U.S.S.R. for resuming diplomatic and trade relations with Latin America's "Oligarchy regimes" against whom Castro's guerilla warfares had been widely publicized.

It is obvious that as time has gone on, the Soviets have become embarrassed by their relationship with Castro and have tried to disassociate themselves from him. They have been unable to go along with his militant attitude toward the entire Latin American area and have rather attempted to establish diplomatic and trade relations with existent regimes in Latin America which would enhance their own standing. Their entry into Cuba in the first place obviously was not primarily in the defense or aid of Cuba against the United States, but was rather a clumsy attempt on their part to emulate the actions of the United States in countries surrounding the Soviet Union. The decision to install missiles in Cuba in 1962 was a crass attempt to force the United States to accept a settlement of the German issue on Soviet terms or to bring about the removal of U.S. missiles from Turkey. Neither Khrushchev nor Castro anticipated the strong stand that President Kennedy took in encircling the island with American warships, and the resultant backdown and removal of the missiles was a humiliating experience both for the Kremlin and for Havana. Castro's recent actions in condemning the ideology of all communist countries other than his own and the relations of the Soviet Union with those of Latin America and the United States signifies a virtual end to any agreeable relations with the Soviet Union. Although aid and trade are continuing, they are continuing on a much reduced scale, and it is probably only a matter of time before the Soviets withdraw completely.

The Industrialized "West"

Although Soviet trade is still overwhelmingly with other socialist countries, this trade is on the decrease, and much of the slack is being taken up by trade with the highly industrialized countries of the world. Much of the decline in the U.S.S.R.'s trade with socialist countries is due to the widening split between the Soviet Union and China. China was the leading trading partner for the Soviet Union as late as 1960, but since then it has dropped to about fifteenth place and is no more significant than some of the industrialized countries or even the two foremost less-developed countries, India and the United Arab Republic. Soviet exports have also decreased a little bit to the CEMA countries. The Soviets have been unable to satisfy east European needs for more sophisticated types of machinery and other equipment for industrial growth. More and more, the east European satellites are acting independently to seek their own best trade relations wherever they might be. This is also true of the Soviet Union, who must look to the West for the more advanced types of industrial equipment and know-how. Thus in 1958 socialist countries occupied about 74 per cent of the Soviet trade turnover, but in 1966 they occupied only 66.4 per cent. During this same period, exports to the CEMA countries decreased from 55.5 per cent to 54.9 per cent of total Soviet exports, whereas imports from the CEMA countries increased from 51.8 per cent to 57.2 per cent. (Table 17–3) During the 1958–1966 period, the industrialized West increased its imports from the Soviet Union from 16.3 per cent to 19.9 per cent of total Soviet exports and increased its exports to the Soviet Union from 15.1 per cent to 22.5 per cent of total Soviet imports. The Soviets imported more than twice as much from the industrialized West in 1966 as they did from the less-developed countries of the world, in spite of the fanfare that is attached to their trade with the less-developed countries.

Before the Revolution, Imperial Russia traded much more with the west European countries and the United States than the Soviets do today. Since the Tsarist trade was carried on largely between private enterprises or separate governmental agencies, largely in response to supply and demand or relative cost advantages, it can be concluded that the industrialized countries of the West are more natural trading partners for the Soviet Union than are their new-found partners in eastern Europe or the less-developed areas of the world, where trade has been promoted since World War II somewhat artificially under the auspices of the state trade monopoly in the Soviet Union and political-strategic maneuvers in both the Soviet Union and the industrial West. And this natural orientation of the country can be extended beyond the trading sphere into diplomatic spheres as well. Old Russia always competed with the western countries and has always been considered

heavily in the world balance of power in spite of the fact that its internal economy and standard of living could ill-afford such lofty national stature. This was one of the primary enigmas of the old Russian Empire; it constantly found itself thrust into the forefront along with the other major powers of the world because of its sheer size which gave it a total importance. But from a per capita standpoint, its production was way below that of the western countries, and it found itself straining to the utmost to compete on a quasi-equal basis, which worked untold personal hardships on the people of the country. Nevertheless, Russia has always identified with the more advanced countries, not with the smaller, underdeveloped countries whose living standards have been more comparable to her own. Although perhaps Russia was never one of the "in members" of the top echelon, she constantly found herself thrust into the military and diplomatic milieu of this group, and her relations with lesser countries were only incidental to those with major power blocs.

Thus it might be considered that the recent slow trend of the Soviet Union to increase its trade with the West is simply a coming back to the proper orientation that it should occupy if this trade were not hampered by various artificial restrictions imposed upon it by the Western powers and political orientations imposed upon it by the Soviet Union.

Punitive Restrictions of Soviet Trade
During the last half century the trade of the Soviet Union has almost always been subject to some form of restriction or discrimination by the nations of the West. For the first 20 years the discrimination was mainly in the form of higher interest rates because of distrust of the Soviets resulting from the annulment of all pre-Revolutionary debts. In addition to such discrimination by private individuals and firms, definite discrimination against trade with the Soviet Union has been applied by several Western governments on four

specific occasions. These governmental actions were: (1) a blockade of the Soviet Union from 1918 to 1920 during the period of civil war and intervention, (2) embargoes in 1930 and 1931 to counteract dumping of grain and lumber, (3) failure to issue export licences for military goods in 1940 when the Soviets were fighting the Finns, and (4) the various restrictions on trade with the Soviet Union and other bloc countries dating from 1948.

Much of the difficulty that the Soviet Union has with world trade organizations stems from the arbitrary limitations it has imposed on its trade by the institution of state monopoly and the policy of economic self-sufficiency. The practice of carrying on only absolutely necessary trade, usually under bilateral agreements, allows for very little flexibility in trade arrangements. When the Soviet Union finds that it must purchase certain raw materials, such as foodstuffs, from a country which is already an integral part of a well-established trade system or from an underdeveloped country, it must make some adjustments to gain the necessary imports.

In the case of importing goods from one of the primary producing countries, such as from one of the Commonwealth of Nations, the Soviet Union often finds that it cannot balance its imports because that country does not want to buy anything. Also, it finds it difficult to pay for imports in rubles since the foreign trade of the Soviet Union has been so limited that the ruble has no real world trade value. The ruble has led too sheltered a life to have acquired any value in the world monetary system; it simply has a value which the Soviets have arbitrarily fixed within their own sphere of influence. Hence when dealing with a country that is a part of the sterling or dollar bloc, the Soviet Union must seek to balance imports from that country with exports to some other country of the same monetary system. It is forced to sell whatever commodity it has available, whether the market for selling is

favorable or not. In such cases, in order to make a market for itself, the Soviet Union has frequently found it necessary to offer certain items at prices considerably below those previously established by critically balanced supply and demand. Hence the accusations of "dumping" by the established traders of the western world.

In 1931, to pay for large imports of equipment to start the industrial machine rolling, the Soviets bent every effort to increase their exports of grain and lumber to pay for greatly expanded imports. Within a few months world grain prices dropped to less than half of what they had been, and other major grain exporting countries cried, "dumping." Again, in 1957, to acquire sterling credit to balance imports from Australia, New Zealand, and other members of the sterling bloc, the Soviet Union decided to sell aluminum to Britain at 2 cents per pound under the price charged by Britain's main supplier, Canada. Again the Soviet Union was accused of dumping with the object of upsetting the world market, which was at a critical stage anyway. Actually a price reduction was necessary in order for the Soviet Union to break into a long-established trade between sister members of the Commonwealth of Nations, but the effect on the world market was the same regardless of Soviet motives. Had the Soviet Union developed a broader base for its foreign trade, it would have been unnecessary to balance imports with exports over such a short-run period, and the Soviets could have held their commodities for export until the market was more favorable. It also would not have had to break into already well-established trade relations by cutting prices below prevailing levels. Most recently, rapidly expanding sales of Soviet petroleum and petroleum products to west European countries have drastically altered long-established arrangements in this important commodity of world trade.

When the Soviet Union wants to import

raw materials or foodstuffs from an under-developed country it often finds that markets in this underdeveloped country for exports from the Soviet Union can be established only by extending long-term credit on such items as major construction projects, heavy machinery, and metallurgical items. The underdeveloped country simply does not have the market potential to buy the necessary heavy goods from the Soviet Union. Yet the Soviets wish to sell these goods to pay for imports. The only solution is for the Soviets to extend credit on large items of export which is to be paid off by the underdeveloped country in raw materials and foodstuffs over a period of years. This, of course, ties up the export trade of the underdeveloped country during the period and very often leads to other concessions, sometimes political, from the underdeveloped country to the Soviet Union. Thus the plan of long-term credit to underdeveloped countries initiated by the Soviets in 1951 has been branded by many members of the Western world as a device to control the international relations of underdeveloped countries. Again, as in the case of dumping, Soviet actions perhaps can be justified on economic grounds, but the associated results have occurred and have affected the rest of the world.

The Soviets might well solve many of their economic problems at home and keep themselves off the black list of world trading organizations while better achieving their political goals in underdeveloped countries if they would only expand and broaden their base of foreign trade. Importation of consumer items that can be more cheaply and better supplied by foreign areas than by the Soviets themselves would release their productive forces to concentrate even more intensely on the industrial build-up of their own country. At the same time a great expansion of trade would allow for much greater flexibility in dealing with individual countries and individual commodities.

The Western world is willing to trade with the Soviet Union as long as economic exchanges are reliable and political relations are stable. The Western powers reduced restrictions on the sale of goods to the Soviet Bloc in 1954 and again in 1958. And during the following decade it appeared that a general rapprochement was taking place between the Soviet Union and much of western Europe. But the Czechoslovakia incident in 1968 again muddied the waters, and it now seems unlikely that further significant progress will be made as long as Russia continues a foreign policy of expansion of Soviet control and world communism.

Current Conditions and Trends During the 1960s Soviet trade with the West has increased considerably, and imports have increased about three times as rapidly as exports, so the U.S.S.R. faces a widening hard-currency gap which is covered primarily through gold sales and to a lesser extent through the use of Western credit facilities. Largely as a result of wheat purchases following the poor harvest in 1963, the U.S.S.R.'s currency deficit in 1963–1964 was about 1 billion dollars. The Soviet Union purchased the bulk of its 10.3 million tons of wheat imports in 1963 and 1964 from hard-currency countries. Canada supplied 6.2 million tons, the United States 1.8 million, and Australia 1.7. Purchases from the United States were curtailed somewhat from original intentions because the United States insisted on a 50–50 shipping clause in the sales agreements, whereby at least 50 per cent of the wheat would be carried in U.S. ships. This, of course, added to the cost of the wheat, and the Soviets wanted to carry it all in their own ships. Therefore the Soviets consider the United States to be a supplier of wheat only as a last resort when they cannot find it elsewhere.

Soviet exports to the West continue to be dominated by raw materials, with petroleum and petroleum products the most important single category, followed by the traditional wood and wood products, metals and ores. Food exports, which have been as high as 15 per cent of all Soviet exports to western Europe, have dwindled to less than 5 per cent, mainly because of shrinking grain supplies. The Soviets are pushing for expanded machinery sales in the West, but since in general the Western countries are more advanced in technology than is the Soviet Union, there is little sale for Soviet machinery in the West. Therefore the Soviets are hard put to balance their trade with the West, and generally they have to pay for large amounts of their imports in gold.

Although the Soviet Union allocates to the industrial West less than 20 per cent of its global exports, there are a number of individual commodities for which it is substantially dependent upon Western markets. (Table 17-5) The Soviet Union regularly markets about 55 per cent of its exported forest products and refined petroleum; 43 per cent of its crude oil; 40 per cent of its exported manganese, iron ore, and fish products; over 30 per cent of its coal and aluminum; 60 per cent of its potash; 85 per cent of its chrome; and over 95 per cent of its fur skins in the West. On the import side, the Soviet Union receives from the West more than 50 per cent of all its imports of chemical equipment, 45 per cent of its merchant ships, around half of its chemical products and synthetic rubber, and almost all of its staple fibers and, recently, wheat. These are percentages of imports, not total usages within the U.S.S.R., which produces considerable quantities itself. In general, total imports of these items would constitute only very minor parts of total Soviet usages.

Much of the time since World War II, the main Soviet trading partners in western Europe have been Finland, the United Kingdom, and West Germany. It is only natural that Finland should have a lively trade with the Soviet Union since it lies in juxtaposition to it. Trade between the two

countries covers quite a large array of commodities going in both directions, with various types of machinery and equipment being of most importance in both directions. Most recently the Finns have been buying practically all of their petroleum and petroleum products from the Soviet Union.

Finland Finland, of course, has had a long history of relations with the Russian Empire and the Soviet Union, none of them very favorable for Finland. For a long time Finland was booty of a sort to be traded back and forth between Sweden and Russia in the course of peace settlements after wars, in exchange for other concessions. It was finally gained permanently from Sweden in 1809 and incorporated into the Russian Empire where it remained until the Revolution. It gained its independence in 1918, largely through the efforts of the Allied powers. Since that time it has maintained political independence from the Soviet Union, but with great difficulty. After the German invasion of east Europe in 1939, the Soviets took the opportunity to declare war on the Finns to enforce territorial demands in Karelia and other points along the common boundary with the excuse that these territories were needed for the defense of the Soviet Union against the imminent possibilities of conflict with Germany. This skirmish ended in March 1940, but after Germany invaded the Soviet Union in June 1941, the Finns then took the opportunity to declare war on the Soviet Union. Thus World War II saw two periods of fierce conflict between the two countries. Since the Soviet Union came out of this second war victorious, the Finns were forced to concede the Karelian Isthmus to the Soviet Union along with narrow strips of territory all along the boundary, including a fairly large chunk of land along the Arctic Coast in the area known as Petsamo (Pechenga). Also, immediately after the war the Soviets demanded the use of a naval and a military base along the coast of Finland southwest of Helsinki. Since then, the Soviets have relinquished these bases, although they still retain all the territory that they gained along the Finnish border. The Soviets recently have made further overtures to better relations between the two countries and have even cooperated with the Finns in the reestablishment of the Saimaa Canal which gives the Finns an important all-water route from the Eastern Lake Country to the Gulf of Finland, the southern part of which now runs through Soviet territory. The long years of one-sided relationships have left the Finns with a rather embittered attitude toward the Soviets, but they accept reality as it is and realize they must get along with their much larger neighbor.

England   England has been a major trading partner of Russia ever since the days of Ivan the Terrible, and although the ups and downs of political relations between the countries have had their effects on foreign trade, general economic complementarity has tended to override any political differences and has caused the two countries to seek considerable amounts of trade with each other. England has always needed the lumber, grain, and mineral raw materials that Russia has had to offer, and Russia has needed the industrial machinery and consumer goods that England has had to offer. Although trade relations broke down somewhat after the beginning of the Cold War in 1948, the United Kingdom has been quicker to relax controls over its export commodities than has the United States, and there has been an accelerating trend for the reestablishment of normal trade relations between the Soviet Union and the United Kingdom during the past decade. This has been augmented by several contracts for complete plants for the manufacture of chemicals, mineral fertilizers, and synthetic fibers which have been placed by the Soviets with British firms, with British lending agencies extending credits of up

to 12 or 15 years. Through such arrangements, by 1966 the United Kingdom had replaced Finland as the foremost trading partner in the industrialized West.

Germany   Before the Revolution, Imperial Russia allowed, and sometimes encouraged, foreign capital, particularly from Germany and France, as well as from Sweden, to develop large-scale industries, such as the oil industries of Baku, the iron and steel industry of Ukraine, and the railroad locomotive and rolling stock industries of European Russia, to spur the industrialization effort of the 1880s and 1890s, and again during 1905–1911. Again, after the Revolution, in the early 1930s the Germans particularly were active in aiding the new Soviet industrialization effort. The United States entered the scene at this time, too, and supplied a good deal of equipment and technical help to the young Soviet country, which was beginning to industrialize at the auspicious time when the Western countries were in the depths of an economic depression. Thus the Western countries were very eager to supply equipment and engineering personnel to the Soviets. All this was interrupted by World War II, and the strained relations since the war have allowed only much reduced activity in this sphere. However, as tensions have declined, more and more trade has sprung up between the Soviet Union and Western Germany, and during the last decade West Germany has been the third or fourth most important Soviet trader in western Europe. The Soviet Union finds a ready market for its oil products, pig iron, timber, and various agricultural produce and mineral ores, particularly manganese and chromium. In return, West Germany exports machinery for light industry and chemicals, ships and other marine equipment, iron and steel pipes, wire and cables, and various types of chemicals and pharmaceuticals. Obviously this trade with West Germany is completely economically motivated, since politically the two countries are in totally different spheres, and the Soviets still fear a united Germany more than any other single factor in the world today. The West Germans cannot afford to trust the Soviet government, either, as long as Germany remains divided and the Berlin crisis continues.

France In general, Tsarist Russia maintained a better rapport with France than it did with Germany, and French language and culture became quite fashionable among the aristocracy of the country. This Russian ardor for French frills cooled somewhat after the Napoleonic invasion of 1812, which, except for the Nazi invasion in recent times, has left the greatest impression on Russian minds of any single military effort. Nevertheless Russian military contact with the French has never been as direct as it has been with the Germans, and so in general the Russians have been more positively disposed toward the French than they have the Germans. France has never held the economic attraction for Russia that Germany has, however, and this has been true during the Soviet period too. In 1966 de Gaulle made a state visit to the Soviet Union and was accorded a lavish welcome by the Soviet leadership. De Gaulle's opposition to the American participation in Vietnam and his general disruption of NATO cast him in the light of a potential balance to West Germany on the European continent, according to Soviet views. It appeared that a close alliance was rapidly developing between France and the Soviet Union. Moscow adopted French color television technology, and French and Soviet scientists began work on a joint launching of a French satellite, which still has not taken place. Soviet-French trade increased considerably in one year. However, the strong showing of the French Communist Party in the French elections of March 1967 and the general chaos of the social revolution in France during the spring of 1968 caused de Gaulle to withdraw from such close relationships with the Soviet Union and

actually to denounce the communist threat in France. At the same time, the French Communist Party has condemned the Soviets for their actions in Czechoslovakia during August 1968, and this, along with the condemnation by the Italian Communist Party, has probably hurt the Soviet Union as much in their relations with the rest of the communist world as anything that has happened in eastern Europe. The French and Italian Communist Parties are the largest communist parties in the world outside of the communist bloc itself. In the past they have been more or less subservient to Moscow, but now they have diverged from the Soviet line, realizing that Moscow communism is for the benefit of Moscow rather than any general world communist movement. Thus the quick flash of the unholy entente that seemed to be developing between the Soviet Union and France appears to have been damped and perhaps extinguished.

Italy Political and economic relations with Italy have always been more tenuous than those with France, and that has been true up to the present time, except for the contract that was signed with Fiat in 1966 whereby the Italians are to build a large motor vehicle plant on the Volga to expand greatly automobile production in the Soviet Union. This contract initially was estimated at 320 million U.S. dollars, which was by far the largest single contract for plant construction that had been consummated with the western countries up to that time. (Table 17–6) There have also been some contracts with Italy for textile spinning plants and some chemical plants. In 1966 Italy ranked sixth among the Western powers in Soviet trade turnover, after France which was fifth. That year Italy was the biggest importer of Soviet crude oil, having considerably surpassed even Czechoslovakia and East Germany in this commodity.

United States Trade between the two principal producing countries of the

Table 17-6   Selected Soviet Contracts for Western Machinery and Equipment, 1958–May 1966

Year	Type of Plant(s)	Supplying Country	Estimated Price (Million U.S. Dollars)
1958	Polyethylene (2)	West Germany	30
1959	Tires	United Kingdom	43
1959	Acetylene, ethylene, titanium dioxide, maleic anhydride	Italy	25
1960	Cellulose	France	25
1960	Textiles	United States	25
1961	Pulp mill equipment	Japan	31
1961	Meat packing	Sweden	30
1961	Ammonia and methanol (2)	Italy	24
1962	Cargo ships and tankers	Japan	96
1962	Pulp and paper	Japan	32
1962	Phosphoric acid	West Germany	25
1963	Fish factory and refrigerator ships	Japan	135
1963	Fish factory ships	West Germany	64
1963	Ethylene and polyethylene (6)	United Kingdom	63
1963	Phosphoric acid	Belgium	22
1964	Terylene (dacron)	United Kingdom	87
1964	Caprolactam (2)	Netherlands	30
1965	Polyvinyl chloride	France	22
1965	Textile spinning	Italy	20
1965	Cardboard (11)	France	12
1966	Motor vehicles manufacturing plant and related facilities	Italy	320

Source: New Directions in the Soviet Economy, p. 946.

world, the United States and the U.S.S.R., is almost negligible, accounting for less than 0.2 per cent of total United States' trade and about 0.7 per cent of Soviet trade. This has not always been the case. During the period 1937–1940, the United States was the leading source of imports into the Soviet Union. In 1938 the United States accounted for 18.5 per cent of total Soviet trade and supplied 55 per cent of all Soviet imports of machinery. In 1940 the United States accounted for 31 per cent of all Soviet imports. The lend-lease program during World War II no doubt sent the figure considerably higher. (Table 17–7) The cold war since World War II has artificially restricted trade between the two countries; the United States has placed trade embargoes on all sorts of strategic and semistrategic materials. This in turn induced the Soviet Union to discontinue exports of manganese ore to the United States and curtail the exports of several other mineral raw materials. United States' exports to the Soviet Union dwindled from 149 million dollars in 1947 to 27 million in 1948 and from there continued to drop to a minimum of 19,000 dollars in 1953. At the same time U.S. imports from the Soviet Union dropped from a maximum of 86,825,000 dollars in 1948 to a minimum of 10,791,000 dollars in 1953. Since 1953 there has been a general trend upward in both exports and imports, although there have been rather extreme annual fluctuations in both of these. Soviet grain purchases temporarily boosted U.S. exports to the Soviet Union to 146 million dollars in 1964, but this figure has settled back down since then. In 1965 U.S.S.R. sales to the United States more than doubled as a result of a large U.S. platinum metals import.

As might be expected in a trade which has developed around restrictions on the most important items, the commodity makeup of the trade between the United States and the Soviet Union consists of small quantities of a considerable variety of relatively unessential items, and the list changes considerably from one year to another. In general, the most important exports from the United States to the Soviet Union have been such things as sheet steel, textile machinery, chemical products, and so forth, while the most important exports from the Soviet Union to the United States have been such things as certain rare metals, furs, and so forth. In 1966 furs and skins made up almost one eighth of all Soviet exports to the United States, and these were followed by pig iron, chrome ore, textile raw materials, precious stones, wool, and so forth. (Table 17–8) Leather raw materials made up almost half the Soviet imports from the United States in 1966, followed by chemical products, animal fats, machinery and equipment, and cellulose.

There does not seem to be much prospect for greatly expanded Soviet exports to the United States in the near future. Except for certain raw materials, the U.S. market has little need for the types of commodities the U.S.S.R. generally has to export to the West. The Soviet government is now making an effort to export more and more finished products and less and less raw materials, and this sort of trend will not enhance the U.S. trade, since the United States can produce almost any finished good it needs or find it on the world market at a price cheaper than the Soviets can supply it. The outlook is somewhat more favorable for Soviet imports from the United States, if the United States continues to lift embargoes on semi-strategic exports. The United States spends

Table 17–7 Wartime Trade of the United States, United Kingdom, and Canada with the U.S.S.R., in Thousands of Dollars

	U.S.S.R. Imports			U.S.S.R. Exports		
Year	United States	United Kingdom	Canada	United States	United Kingdom	Canada
1941	107,524	118,025	5,331	30,095	4,450	78
1942	1,425,442	300,281	36,814	24,656	13,015	0.1
1943	2,994,828	237,543	57,916	29,850	7,156	2.5
1944	3,473,252	226,349	103,438	49,649	8,708	16
1945	1,838,282	118,976	58,906	53,793	15,354	1,747

Source: George B. Huszar and Associates, *Soviet Power and Policy,* 1955, p. 352.

Table 17–8   Principal Items of Trade Between the U.S.S.R. and the U.S.A., 1966, in Millions of Rubles

Soviet Exports		Soviet Imports	
Total	42.0	Total	57.0
Furs and skins	5.3	Leather raw materials	25.4
Pig iron	4.3	Chemical products	8.6
Chrome ore	3.8	Animal fats	7.9
Textile raw materials	3.7	Machinery and equipment	6.7
Precious stones	3.2	Cellulose	4.4
Wool	2.7		
Goat hair	2.5		

Source: Vneshnyaya torgovlya SSSR za 1966 god, pp. 330–332.

about 3.5 per cent of its gross national product on research and development, the highest proportion by a considerable margin of any country in the West. This is just what the Soviets are looking for. They are eager to import prototype machinery and equipment to conserve their own investment in research and development. Also the Soviets have long been intrigued by the high labor productivity in the United States and the general way that the United States goes about doing things. The fact that the U.S. economic operations in manufacturing, mining, power generation, transport, and farming are organized on large scales, in contrast to the economies of western Europe, also appeals to the Soviets, who by necessity must organize on a similar scale. The wide variety of production materials offered for sale by a large number of competing enterprises also makes the United States attractive to the Soviet Union, since they can find almost anything they want in this diversified market. And finally, the United States has a rather wide range of surplus agricultural commodities for sale. If the Soviet Union continues to import large quantities of foodstuffs, there is a potential for this sort of trade. If commercial considerations are allowed once more to govern the flow of trade, the United States could quickly become one of the major suppliers to the Soviet Union.

Since World War II the United States and the Soviet Union have been thrust into the unfortunate position of being the two big opposing powers in the world. Both countries and their allies went through very critical times during the late 1940s and early 1950s as adjustments were being made toward a more stable coexistence. It now appears that the crisis has passed, and although many lingering ailments exist, nuclear war does not seem nearly so imment now as it did 15 years ago. Such temporary crises that have developed during the past decade—the Vietnam War, the Soviet invasion of Czechoslovakia, the continuing crisis in Berlin, and so forth—individually have been severe blows to East-West relations, but in the aggregate they have proved that the United States and the Soviet Union could keep communications open in the face of these threats. And this in itself is very encouraging. The restraint that the Soviet Union has shown regarding the war in Vietnam and its ability to back down in the face of impossible consequences during the Cuban missile crisis have been matched by the United States' restraint with respect to such things as Czechoslovakia and the Berlin wall. And though the brief Arab-Israeli war of 1967 again aligned the two great powers against each other, both were able to keep from getting directly involved.

In the face of all these world tensions, the U.S.A. and the U.S.S.R. were finally able to consummate a 10-year negotiation on a consular agreement and to put into effect direct air flights between New York City and Moscow on July 15, 1968.

Japan The other important trading partner and significant power that has risen rapidly since World War II among the industrialized countries of the "West" lies in the east—Japan. The recovery of its economy since the war has been no less surprising than that of West Germany. It has rapidly become one of the world's leading producers of such heavy industries as iron and steel, in spite of its great lack of raw materials. As tensions have eased between the Soviet Union and Japan, the Soviets have looked more and more toward Japan as a means of rationalizing their economy in the Soviet Far East. It appears now that the Soviets have abandoned their plan of integrating the economy of this far-flung part of the country with the major populated area in European Russia. Rather, they are trying to make the area somewhat self-sufficient through foreign trade. Large contracts have been given to the Japanese for the purchases of ships, and in turn large amounts of Soviet oil have been delivered to Japan. In 1964 Japan actually became the U.S.S.R.'s leading trading partner among the industrially developed countries, replacing the United Kingdom, as the Soviets held back on machinery imports that year in order to pay for large imports of wheat from Canada, the United States, and Australia. Though Britain regained its first position by 1966, the future may find that Japan will far outstrip some of the west European countries in trade with the Soviet Union. In 1966 Japan still retained first place among "Western" exporters to the Soviet Union. (Table 17–3) As the Soviets develop their apparently large oil supplies in western Siberia, they are looking more and more toward Japan as a market, and the Japanese have offered to construct an oil pipeline from Irkutsk to the Pacific in order to facilitate this trade. The Japanese have also offered to help in the development of certain minerals in eastern Siberia and the Soviet Far East, such as aluminum. Soviet timber exports from the Maritime Province and Sakhalin Island to Japan have been quite large for some time now, and there is considerable room for expansion.

Southern Neighbors

It is only natural that through the years the Tsarist and Soviet regimes have carried on considerable trade with the countries immediately to the south. In most cases this trade has not been very vital to the Soviet Union's economy, and considerable political overtones have been involved in the trade negotiations. In the distant past such empires as the Ottoman Turks and the Persians were as strong or stronger than Russia and vied for supremacy in the area. But this type of power struggle no longer exists, since the Soviet Union at the present time is so much larger and more powerful than any single country along its border. Nevertheless old scars heal slowly, and there is a good deal of animosity and suspicion on both sides of the border.

Turkey Turkey has been one of the most anti-Russian nations in the world. Although it accepted Soviet economic aid as early as 1932, it has generally reacted to all Soviet overtures with more than a moderate degree of skepticism. In the 1920s when both the young Soviet and young Turkish governments were struggling for world recognition, a number of agreements were signed concerning friendship and neutrality. As early as 1923, however, the new Turkish regime began investigating overtures from Western powers, and by the end of the 1920s Turkey was definitely leaning away from Moscow. As the Soviets became more insistent about discussing the control of the

Straits in the late 1930s, the Turkish government took stronger measures to guarantee its sovereignty in that area by signing a Friendship Pact with Iran, Iraq, and Afghanistan, and finally on the eve of World War II in 1939 Turkey concluded a military alliance with Britain and France. In 1941 Turkey also signed a nonaggression pact with Germany, which enabled her to maintain neutrality throughout the war. Thanks to this neutrality Turkey probably escaped the fate of the satellite countries and was not occupied by Soviet troops after the war. If she had joined either side she probably would have found herself under Soviet occupation, either because of her defeat or as part of her "liberation." In March 1945 the Soviets renounced the Soviet-Turkish Treaty of 1925 and made claims on several eastern territories of Turkey. A little later the Soviets demanded a revision of the control of the Straits set up by the Montreux Convention of 1936, proposing in its place that the Straits be defended jointly by the U.S.S.R. and Turkey. This culminated the deterioration of the postwar relations between the two countries, and as the Soviets applied further pressure Turkey became more closely bound to the Western powers, receiving economic and military aid under the Truman Doctrine in 1947–1948 and joining the North Atlantic Treaty Organization in 1952. In 1955 she was one of the original signatories to the Baghdad Pact, which later developed into the Central Treaty Organization. All this further isolated her from the Soviet Union.

After the death of Stalin in 1953, the Soviet government began making overtures to normalize Soviet-Turkish relations, and renounced any territorial claims that the Armenian and Georgian Republics of the Soviet Union had had on the eastern areas of Turkey. Turkey took a very skeptical attitude toward these early overtures, and was particularly doubtful after the Soviet intervention in the Hungarian revolt in 1956 and the Syrian crisis which was artificially created by the Soviets toward the end of 1957. Turkey seemed to be quite satisfied with the 2 billion dollars of economic and food aid from the United States and 2.3 billion dollars in military aid. Toward the end of the 1950s, however, Turkey became bitter toward the United States and some of the other NATO nations when they did not support Turkey in Cyprus, and the Turks began listening to overtures from the Soviets even though the Soviet Union showed an even less sympathetic attitude toward Turkey in the Cyprus area than was true in the NATO countries. Governmental changes in Turkey in 1961 and 1965 brought on a new constitution which guaranteed complete freedom of expression and coalition governments which were more conservative in nature and more disposed to seek a balance of relations with all powers. The Cuban crisis further endeared the Soviets to the Turks, because it ultimately brought about the removal of American rocket bases from Turkey. In 1963 an official Turkish delegation visited the Soviet Union for the first time in 30 years. This was followed in 1965 by a visit of President Podgorny of the Soviet Union to Turkey and in 1966 of Premier Kosygin. In 1964 the Soviets agreed upon a 168 million dollar loan to Turkey which was to cover river construction projects, a steel mill, an oil refinery, a tractor factory, and so forth. In 1965 Turkey further expressed its independence of Western alliances by refusing to consider participation in an American-backed multilateral nuclear fleet.

However, it is evident that Turkey does not want to foster friendship with the Soviet Union at the expense of losing its Western allies. The broad middle spectrum of political thought in Turkey now favors accepting the hand of friendship offered to them by their large northern neighbor while at the same time maintaining membership in NATO and CENTO and maintaining economic and political independence from either side. Significantly, in 1966 Kosygin in his trip to Turkey was astute enough to accept this posture of the Turks and conceded the point that friendship with the Soviet Union did not mean breaking friendships with the West.

The consequence of this recent rapprochement between the two traditional rivals has been a significant increase in trade. Soviet-Turkish trade in 1964 amounted to 19 million dollars; in 1966 it was 50 million dollars. It is still not obvious how the Turkish government is going to react to Kosygin's wish that the development of political and economic ties should go hand in hand, supplementing one another. It will not be easy for a member of NATO, whose economy is based on the principal of a free market and who is particularly alert against communist infiltration, to accept such a line from the Soviet Union. The Turks are quite aware that NATO undoubtedly was responsible for removing the danger of Soviet aggression in the early years after the war. Should the Moscow-Peking axis be reestablished, Turkey realizes that she will have nothing to turn to except NATO for defense against communist engulfment.

The Arab States and Israel   Since World War I and the demise of the Ottoman Empire, the Soviet Union and Britain, and to some extent France, have vied for control in the Near and Middle East. The Soviets have continued the Russian interest in extending their influence throughout the eastern Mediterranean, the Suez Canal, the Persian Gulf, and the Indian Ocean. The Western powers on the other hand have been just as eager to establish and maintain the buffer zone between the southern boundary of the Soviet Union and the Persian Gulf. Thus both sides have striven to exert their influence in the area and to curry favor with the numerous new states that evolved from the old Ottoman and Persian empires. After World War I Britain and France, through the

League of Nations, secured a mandate to oversee the operation of the politically disintegrating area. The Soviets were quick to renounce this mandate and to recognize newly emancipated Arab states. In 1926 they recognized the Kingdom of Hejas which came into being under Ibn-Saud, and in 1928 they recognized the complete independence of the new state of Yemen and consummated a treaty of friendship and trade that committed the U.S.S.R. to supply Yemen with the major portion of its imports. Subsequent trade treaties have extended this relationship to the present time. After the beginning of World War II the Arab countries began to evolve from their semicolonial status, and the U.S.S.R. took the opportunity to establish diplomatic relations with Egypt, Syria, Lebanon, and Iraq. This process continued after the war as the new states of Libya, the Sudan, Morocco, and Tunisia gained their independence. Finally, in 1960 the Soviet government gave de facto recognition to the provisional government of Algeria before the country had gained independence.

Before these diplomatic relations had been established, the Soviet leaders had tried to subvert the Arab countries through the establishment of local communist parties. However, these communist organizations met with stiff opposition right from the start from both the colonial and native authorities in the region as well as from strong Moslem religious circles, and they never exerted any noticeable influence on the masses of people. Realizing this, the Soviet leaders changed their tactics and began urging the cooperation of local communist parties with extreme nationalists and religious fanatics under the banner of liberation from colonialism. This new approach proved highly successful after World War II. Soviet representatives in the United Nations Security Council came out in full support of the demands of Syria and Lebanon for the withdrawal of French and British forces and gave equal backing to Egypt and called for an end to the condominium over the Sudan. Later the Soviets supported Libya, Morocco, Tunisia, and Algeria. Meanwhile the local communist parties in the Arab countries fanned the flames of nationalism and religious fanaticism in order to create a general anti-Western climate that would prevent Arab cooperation with the North Atlantic countries and with Turkey. Thus the Soviets largely abandoned the idea of converting the area to communism and turned to the task of isolating it from the Western powers and creating a rapport with the individual Arab states that would allow the establishment of Soviet bases in various areas ringing the eastern Mediterranean and the northern fringe of the Indian Ocean.

At one point in 1946 foreign minister Molotov demanded that the U.S.S.R. be given bases in the former Italian possessions of Libya, the Dodecanese Islands, and Eritrea on the Red Sea Coast. None of this was agreed to by the other powers. The Soviets' efforts at expansionism prompted countermeasures by the United States, Britain, and France, who in 1950 jointly guaranteed the security and territorial integrity of the Arab countries and Israel and followed up this declaration by plans to establish a Middle East Allied Command to defend the area. This eventually fell through largely because Egypt, having experienced such long British occupation, was leery of further agreements that would allow foreign troops on Egyptian soil. Nevertheless the Arab countries realized the need to take defensive actions against a stream of communist propaganda and a constant threat of communist subversion. Iraq was particularly vulnerable because of its unresolved Kurdish problem that the U.S.S.R. kept agitating by arming Kurdish emigres. In response to this threat, in 1955 Iraq induced Turkey to sign a bilateral agreement for mutual defense. This was soon joined by Great

Britain, Pakistan, and Iran. Thus the defensive alliance known as the Baghdad Pact was born, which later became known as CENTO. Shortly before this, in late 1954, Iraq had broken off diplomatic relations with the Soviet Union. Later, however, a pro-Egyptian coup put Iraq back in the Soviet orbit.

The Egyptian takeover by Nasser in 1954 opened new doors for the Soviet Union. They immediately recognized his new regime and attempted to exert as much influence as possible by approving his nationalization of the Suez Canal and offering economic and military aid. They also sought to upset the balance of power among other Arab countries. by selling massive arms supplies to Arab countries not in the Baghdad Pact. This led to further conflict between the Arabs and Israel as well as to revolutions within the Arab countries.

The Suez operation turned out to be quite beneficial for the Soviets. After Britain, France, and Israel invaded Egypt to open up the Suez Canal, the Soviet government protested strongly and promised to send volunteers to crush the aggressors and restore peace. Bluff or not, the Arabs believe to this day that it was the Soviet threat, and not U.S. intervention, that stopped the British, French, and Israelis. As a result of the affair, Egypt, Syria, and Saudi Arabia broke off diplomatic relations with Britain and France; and Iraq, the Sudan, and Jordan broke off relations with France. Jordan forbade Britain to use her military bases on Jordanian territory for operations against Egypt.

The Soviets then moved in 1957 to turn Syria into a powder keg by supplying the pro-Soviet government with heavy military equipment. Also subversive actions were planned in Jordan and Lebanon, and it was only through the invited intervention of the U.S. Marines in Lebanon and the British paratroopers in Jordan that these countries escaped a communist takeover. In the following years cooperation between the Soviet Union and the "progressive" Arab countries, the United Arab Republic (Egypt), Syria, Algeria, Iraq, and Yemen, became ever closer through numerous economic, trade, and cultural arrangements.

The Soviet role in the short Arab-Israeli War of June 1967 is not very clear, although it seems likely that the Soviets might have had a hand in provoking the conflict in order to establish their fleet in the eastern Mediterranean, military advisers in the Arab countries, control of Arabian oil and the Suez Canal, and to start a second localized conflict to divert American attention from Vietnam where the Soviets were very lax in extending aid. Nasser also had strong motives for provoking the conflict in order to strengthen Arab unity in the face of a common enemy and to divert attention from internal economic difficulties. The astonishing shortness and decisiveness of the war shocked the Arabs and the Soviet Union and frustrated any immediate attempt to further their goals. The Soviets, however, in spite of the fact that they did not directly aid the Arabs during the week of war, probably gained in status in the long run since they appeared to be the sole supporters and protectors of the Arab world in the intense United Nations' debates that followed. Thus in spite of the fact that the Israelis captured about a billion dollars worth of Soviet military equipment from the Arabs, much of which had never been paid for, the Soviets probably felt that they had experienced a net gain.

The Soviets are not particularly interested in whether Nasser and his cohorts realize their goals or not. They are interested in their own advancement in control over the region and the displacement of the NATO forces in the area. Unlike the Arabs, Moscow recognizes the right of Israel to exist as a state, and thus there is a split in basic precepts between the Soviets and the Arabs. Since Soviet influence in the area can be furthered by continued chaotic conditions, the Soviets skillfully manipulate the Arabs one against the other to maintain political upheaval.

In most recent years, most of the Arab states have striven to maintain some balance in associations between the Soviet Union and the Western powers. This is becoming increasingly true of even Iran, who has experienced a long history of struggle with the Soviet Union, particularly previous to the Revolution between the Russian Empire and the Persian Empire. At times northern Persia has been an almost exclusive market for Russia. Although much of the Russian influence in the area was displaced by the British after World War I, the Soviets have never desisted from trying to dominate Iranian affairs, and they have constantly reminded Iran of its juxtaposition with the Soviet Union. The following statement is only one example of many well-calculated missiles of correspondence that have been exchanged between the two countries.

Soviet-Iranian Relations (Pravda, January 17, 1959) On December 28, 1958, N. M. Pegov, U.S.S.R. Ambassador to Iran, visited Iranian Foreign Minister Hekmat, and, to supplement the Soviet government statement of October 31, 1958, handed the Minister a Soviet government memorandum on the proposed signing of an Iranian-American military agreement, which would result in a serious deterioration in Soviet-Iranian relations and increase tension in the Near and Middle East.

Excerpts from the text of the U.S.S.R. government memorandum to the government of Iran follows.

Memorandum. — . . . The Soviet government is disturbed by the fact that the Shah's government of Iran has for a certain period been taking foreign policy steps and military measures that can only be interpreted as a policy directed against the Soviet Union, which has a long common border with Iran. This is indicated by Iran's growing collaboration with aggressive forces of three countries which do not conceal their desire to use Iran and Iranian soil against the Soviet Union. In this connection the government of Iran is undertaking unfriendly actions against the Soviet Union, although the Soviet Union has not given the slightest pretext for such action, but, on the contrary, has been taking serious steps to strengthen friendly cooperation with Iran. In addition to the fact that Iran some time ago joined the Baghdad military bloc, which is directed against the U.S.S.R. (although the Iranian side has tried to assure of the reverse), the Shah's government of Iran is now taking steps to further strengthen the military and aggressive aspect of the Baghdad Pact. It is concluding new military agreements with states that are not in the least interested in maintaining peace and order in this region, states to which, as they have often shown, the genuine national interests of the countries in this area are alien. . . .

Unfortunately, the Iranian government is evidently inclined to believe that it can sacrifice good relations with the Soviet Union in the interests of strengthening military cooperation with the U.S.A., which, incidentally, makes Iran's chances for security highly doubtful. . . .

How can the government of Iran place its hope in a military pact with a state situated thousands of kilometers away, at the same time sacrificing Iran's friendly relations with neighboring states and the interests of peace and security in this area as well as the security interests of Iran itself?

Upon objective consideration of the situation one has to recognize that under present conditions and with modern weapons of mass destruction, plans of this type are profoundly erroneous and are based on outmoded views and conceptions. Moreover, the failures already suffered by the proponents of the notorious "brink of war" policy have clearly demonstrated the illusory nature of such plans. . . .

Who stands to gain from all this? There is no doubt that the gain will accrue only to foreign circles and the above power, which is very distant from Iran. The chief loser will be Iran, which because of such a policy would be threatened with annihilation should a military conflict break out. The Soviet government by no means intends this as a threat; these are merely the incontrovertible facts, facts which

cannot be denied without contradicting reality. . . .

The U.S.S.R. government wishes to state with complete frankness that if the Soviet Union, whose might and capabilities are difficult to compare with the might and capabilities of Iran, feels uneasiness about the possible deterioration of Soviet-Iranian relations, then it would seem that Iran should feel much uneasier. This means that good and friendly relations between the two countries are just as necessary and useful for Iran as for the Soviet Union. Nevertheless, judging by everything, the Iranian side does not duly value the importance to Iran of good relations with the Soviet Union or the Soviet Union's friendly attitude toward Iran. . . .

The Soviet Union opposes the proposed military agreement between Iran and the U.S.A. not because it is afraid of an attack by Iran on the U.S.S.R. The Soviet Union certainly has no such fears. The U.S.S.R. believes, however, that this agreement would virtually transform Iran into a springboard for military actions against the U.S.S.R. and other peace-loving states by third powers. Moreover, it goes without saying that no arguments to the effect that American troops will be allowed on Iranian soil only in the event of "extraordinary circumstances" within or outside of Iran can change the Soviet Union's position on the impermissibility of having foreign troops in Iran. Speaking bluntly and reckoning with the actual state of affairs, one must recognize that in the event of a military conflict the territory in a state that has been made available to third countries can be used without the consent of this state for the simple reason that the circumstances will be beyond the control of its government. The fact that some persons may dispute this does not alter the situation. What is involved here is not the presence or absence of good intentions on the part of the government of this state but the very logic of the matter, which may turn out to be stronger than any other logic, even if it is backed up by the best intentions today. . . .

The official representatives of the Iranian government assure the Soviet representatives that the proposed military agreement between Iran and the U.S.A. is not directed against the Soviet Union, although they are not disclosing the actual content of the agreement. However, it is known, in particular, that the plans connected with this agreement call for stationing American naval forces in the Persian Gulf area, near the shores of Iran. It is perfectly understandable that the Soviet Union cannot but regard such an agreement between Iran and the U.S.A. as an act directed against the interests of peace in the Near and Middle East and against the security of the U.S.S.R., which is inviolably linked with the interests of assuring peace in this area. . . .

It is possible to cite "considerations of prestige" which allegedly make it difficult for Iran not to sign an agreement with the U.S.A. that has already been publicly announced. The Soviet government feels that steps which would help to maintain and strengthen a country's sovereignty, strengthen peace and forestall the possibility of military conflicts would correspond to the interests of the prestige of any state. . . .

Naturally, the Soviet government considers that if the agreement between Iran and the U.S.A. were not a military agreement and did not involve, as has been pointed out above, a threat to the security of the Soviet Union but provided for various measures of economic cooperation, then the question of a dangerous turn in Soviet-Iranian relations would not arise. It is self-evident that the Soviet Union has no intention of interfering in any way in Iran's domestic affairs and is solely interested in seeing its neighbor-state of Iran an independent and prosperous state. . . .

In 1957 the Iranians began to show their independence of the United States and other Western powers and their ability to act on their own to carry on necessary trade. Accordingly, they bought military equipment from the Soviet Union as well as from the United States, and concluded a long-term loan arrangement with the Soviet Union whereby they could pay for the military equipment in manufactured goods and natural gas which was to be piped from Iran to the Baku area in Soviet Transcaucasia to supplement dwindling supplies in that area. This pipeline was scheduled to be completed in 1969. The Iranian government has stated that the United Arab Republic, not the Soviet Union, is the greatest enemy of Iran, and much of their move toward the Soviet Union has been in response to accusations by Nasser that Iran is nothing but a pawn of the West. Part of the turn toward the Soviet Union was also prompted by more stringent economic relations with the United States, which was planning to phase out the economic aid program and was reluctant to supply more arms to Iran, particularly on a free basis. Thus Iran has occupied much the same position that Turkey has in trying to maintain its economic and political independence while deriving what benefits it can from both the West and the Soviet Union. At the same time it realizes that the Soviet Union is a constant threat to its sovereignty and therefore it carries on a very cautious international policy.

Afghanistan   Afghanistan's location between Russian Middle Asia and British India, has made it a prime political target, and it has been the scene of numerous Russian-British clashes and intrigues, particularly during the nineteenth century. The British, by military force and political influence, maintained control of Afghanistan up until World War I, but when Afghanistan regained its political independence in 1919 the way was cleared for the Bolsheviks to spread their influence. Concessions were made by the Russians to the Afghans, and they have continued in various forms to the present time. Since the trade with Afghanistan is quite insignificant to the economy of the Soviet Union, its use to further political issues is apparent. Soviet trade delegations to Afghanistan have been instructed to organize communist cells, to issue slogans, and to spread dissatisfaction among soldiers and workers. So far Afghanistan has done a good job of walking a tightrope between the great powers on either side to derive what she wants from Soviet trade while largely maintaining independence from Soviet influence.

Recently, the Soviets have made Afghanistan a principal target in the extension of economic and technical aid. A number of construction projects, including grain elevators and roads, have been completed in Afghanistan by these means. Soviet technicians have advised on many phases of economic development and much of the Afghan army has been trained by the Soviets.

Soviet Policy in the Less-Developed Areas

Russia and the Soviet Union has always carried on a minimal amount of trade with a number of less-developed countries primarily to acquire various types of raw materials and foodstuffs that were not available in the Soviet orbit or to exercise political influence over some of their less-developed southern neighbors. Except for such politically motivated trade, before 1954 the Soviet Union showed little interest in developing an enlarged and stable trade with the so-called third world. However, in 1955, after years of denouncing Western foreign aid as an ill-disguised instrument of imperialism, the U.S.S.R. injected itself into this realm of economic and political instability with an aid program and dynamic political offensive that has gained astonishingly rapid momentum. It is now clear that the Soviets consider the emerging nations in Africa, Asia, and Latin America as a major force that is going to be a prime determinant in the future history of the world, and they have therefore firmly committed themselves, through the means of trade and aid, to convince the world of their power, to gain acceptance as the champion of peace and as the model for economic development, and to reduce the influence of the West in general and the United States in particular among the uncommitted countries of the world.

Economic Aid   Subsequently, the Soviet Bloc has on occasion been so presumptuous as to intimate that before its program of economic assistance there really had been no contributions. The facts are, however, that before the Soviet entry into the field, the United States alone had obligated or otherwise committed 11.6 billion dollars through bilateral economic agreements with less-developed countries, and United Nations members had donated 38 million dollars to the United Nations Technical Assistance Program. Between 1953 and 1959, the United States obligated another 20.3 billion dollars, compared to 3.8 billion obligated by the whole Sino-Soviet Bloc. During that time some of the less-developed countries themselves contributed more to the United Nations' efforts than the Soviet Bloc did. In 1958 India supplied 146 technicians and the United Arab Republic supplied 56, whereas the entire Soviet Bloc contributed 23. All told, between 1948 and the end of 1965, the United States spent over 100 billion dollars in foreign aid throughout the world including Marshall Plan aid to western Europe, whereas the Soviets committed themselves to only about 14 billion dollars, including about 10 billion to the east European satellites, and actually only about three quarters of that has been spent. If one discounts aid to respective orbits of influence, then it appears that during the 1946–1965 period the United States extended a total of over 20 billion dollars worth of aid to the less-developed, uncommitted countries of the world, whereas the Soviet Union committed somewhat over 4 billion dollars. (Table 17–9)

Yet the Russians seem to have achieved disproportionate success, at least as far as publicity is concerned. Everyone has heard about the Aswan Dam and Bhilai steel mill projects, but who knows about such equally spectacular American accomplishments as the Sharavathi Dam in India or the Eregli steel mill in Turkey? The Soviets have made their efforts con-

Table 17–9 *Economic Aid Commitments to Noncommunist Less-Developed Countries by the Soviet Union, China, and the United States, 1946–1966, in Millions of Dollars*

	Soviet Union		China, Loans and Grants	United States		
	Loans	Grants		Total	Food for Peace	Grants
Afghanistan	377	150	28	295	84	154
Algeria	228		55–60	162	158	4
Argentina	100			711	18	10
Brazil	100			2,518	603	112
Burma	10–15		84–88	111	46	26
Cambodia	12	6	55–60	256	3	253
Ceylon	30		31–41	91	68	16
Congo (Brazzaville)	9		25	4		2
Ethiopia	100	2		150	15	68
Ghana	82		42	166	7	9
Guinea	61–85		32	69	27	35
India	806 [a]			5,882	2,753	385
Indonesia	367–75		100–108	1,345	289	222
Iran	39			837	113	379
Iraq	183			53	25	19
Kenya	3		18–28	36	14	17
Laos	4		[b]	419	4	415
Mali	61		20	14	1	10
Morocco	[b]			484	192	19
Nepal	3	11	43–71	86	44	37
Pakistan	80–100		90	2,937	1,097	638
Senegal	7			17	6	7
Somalia	52		23	47	7	32
Sudan	22			89	18	55
Syria	237		16–20	83	63	2
Tanzania	42		43	44	18	9
Tunisia	29			449	213	110
Turkey	168–78			2,120	419	938
U.A.R.	821		85	1,081	851	68
Uganda	16		15	17	1	11
Yemen	92		44–49	39	10	29
Zambia			0.5	24		3
Total	4,141–4,208	169	859–938	20,636	7,167	4,094

Source: Marshall I. Goldman, *Soviet Foreign Aid,* p. 206. Figures for the U.S.A. are to mid 1965.

[a] Plus a reported 800 million dollars to be given during the fourth 5-year plan.

[b] Quantity unknown.

spicuous by concentrating on major construction projects in a few chosen countries rather than spreading grants thinly over broad areas primarily to improve social and cultural development and to raise standards of living, as the United States has. (Table 17–10) In addition, the Soviet Bloc has often experienced psychological advantages over the West from the very beginning in less-developed areas because its immediate interests coincide more closely with the current objectives of the less-developed countries that are striving to pull themselves up by their own bootstraps. Since the Soviets are still in the process of development themselves, developing countries often find it easier to identify with the Soviet Union than with more highly developed countries. Probably most important for the U.S.S.R. is the desire of all of the less-developed countries and their leaders for status and prestige. Because the development of national consciousness by its nature reduces the role of outside forces, its growth is automatically associated with the lessening of influence of the West, the outside group that in the past has been most consequential. The U.S.S.R. by supporting nationalism in less-developed countries has aided the process of alienation from the West and has thereby served its own interest.

The ultimate motivation for Soviet activity in these areas is the "national liberation" of colonial peoples and their ultimate amalgamation with world communism. In order to gain a foothold in the emerging countries, however, the Soviets generally have been forced to recognize and accept existing nationalist governments with the hope that they can bring them around to communism by fostering communist parties within the countries themselves. In order to woo young inspired leaders, however, often wildly nationalistic personalities, the Soviets have frequently found it necessary to restrain local communist activities in order not to offend the leaders that they are trying to

influence. In some instances this course has been pursued to such an extent that the interests of indigenous communist groups have been largely ignored, even while nationalist governments are sharply attacking them and even arresting and liquidating them.

In most cases the Soviets have been content to offer economic assistance to newly independent states without forcing political showdowns with incumbent governments that might be indifferent or even antagonistic to communism. Generally the bloc has been eager to discuss assistance and trade with new states as soon as they have become independent, so that maximum influence can be accomplished with least pressure during early periods of transition when situations are very fluid. As in other areas of the world, the Soviets generally are trying to change the course of events in the less-developed countries, and they find instability and chaos to their advantage. Therefore they have often injected themselves into extremely touchy situations where other countries have tried in vain to neutralize opposing forces and bring about stability. The boldest gambit so far has been in the Congo where the U.S.S.R. made a brazen attempt to exploit an especially disturbed situation. Trucks and repair materials, planes and food, and medical and technical personnel were poured hurriedly into the Congo (Leopoldville) as the U.S.S.R. dramatically came to the aid of the faltering Lumumba government, which was ready to turn anywhere for assitance. Although these efforts collapsed and the bloc personnel were ousted, the U.S.S.R. continued to seek a means of supporting a rump group in the Congo, and used the Congo crisis to expand its influence to other countries in Africa, such as Ghana, Guinea, and Mali.

Whereas much of the aid extended by the West has been in the form of outright grants, the Soviet Bloc has primarily used the extension of credit, probably to give the impression that it is interested in

Table 17-10 Delivery of Equipment and Material for Complete Plants by Soviet Union, in Thousands of Dollars

	Afghanistan	Algeria	Burma	Cambodia	Ceylon	Ethiopia	Ghana	Guinea	India	Indonesia	Iran
1955	1,007								78		
1956	1,724								5,794		
1957	3,344								43,330		
1958	9,728				482				98,136		226
1959	14,696				3				34,179		
1960	17,409							102	18,141	5,017	
1961	18,570						78	9,100	39,569	9,022	
1962	19,288		947		927		2,625	7,395	64,671	7,403	
1963	23,894	591	2,065		2,867		4,585	7,344	81,285	9,694	
1964	27,842	1,985	458	577	6,834	2,182	4,507	3,912	132,537	18,508	
1965	29,922	5,905		222	4,269	6,095	8,096	1,859	84,239	13,169	
Total	167,424	8,481	3,470	799	15,382	8,277	19,891	29,712	601,959	62,813	226

	Iraq	Mali	Pakistan	Somalia	Sudan	Syria	Tunisia	Turkey	U.A.R.	Yemen	Total
1955											1,085
1956									27		7,545
1957									485	44	47,203
1958						1,927		222	1,230	500	112,225
1959	239					1,018		1,215	15,657	2,001	69,234
1960	4,264		8			2,005		3,696	15,835	2,111	68,588
1961	15,925	577	242			8,598		1,388	35,169	463	138,701
1962	29,721	2,667	3,898	48	81	2,168		224	41,488	120	182,724
1963	25,902	3,361	4,308	2,736	2,556	1,716	666	129	48,073	50	220,704
1964	17,960	4,111	2,986	5,076	3,752	1,036	4	7	60,978	265	297,124
1965	5,375	2,526	3,332	5,659	1,000	4,367	2,188	6	86,018	1,535	267,187
Total	99,386	13,242	14,774	13,519	7,389	22,835	2,858	6,887	304,960	7,089	1,412,320

Source: Marshall I. Goldman, *Soviet Foreign Aid*, pp. 204–205.

631

business-like transactions and wishes to avoid the suspicion of political strings that may be aroused when gifts or interest-free loans are granted. Generally the Soviet Bloc has signed bilateral trade agreements with each trading country that begin with statements of willingness to trade and then proceed to the extension of credits to the underdeveloped country for the payment of construction projects or technical aid over long periods of time in products from the underdeveloped country. Ordinarily loans have been scheduled to run for 12 years at an interest rate of 2.5 per cent, which is considerably lower than rates on loans from the World Bank or other sources in the West, which again serves Soviet propaganda that the capitalistic countries are being usurious. The use of credit assures a prolonged association between the bloc and recipient country, a period during which the freedom of action by the latter may be limited because of the demands imposed by the payment conditions on its export capacity. Millions of rubles worth of credit extended for major construction projects may tie up exports of the recipient country for years while it is paying off the loan in produce. At the same time repayment eventually will greatly reduce the real cost suffered by the bloc in the agreement.

Such repayments began around 1960 and have increased at an accelerating rate since then. In 1965 it was estimated that repayments amounted to 40 per cent as much as the total drawdowns on Soviet credits that year. It is expected that in the future repayments will continue to accelerate at a faster rate than Soviet aid expenditures. Thus if things go as scheduled, the Soviets ultimately could realize a profit. Many countries have been hard put to meet their obligations, however, and it is becoming apparent that repayments will have to be stretched out over much longer periods than the original 12-year agreements. In the long run the problem of repayment is likely to be compounded by

two factors: (1) the unwillingness of the Soviet Union to accept payment in the form of run-of-the-mill manufactured goods which will be the products turned out by the industrial plants that their aid is constructing, and (2) the fact that these same goods, which are being produced by newly established industries, are not likely to find outlets in the competitive markets of the West. In some countries, particularly Indonesia, it is already evident that political and economic chaos has negated the entire effort and that Soviet aid will never generate new industries which will enable Indonesia to repay her debts. Thus many Soviet loans undoubtedly will ultimately be written off as losses.

In most cases the Soviets seem to have extended individual loans in very logical and realistic ways. Generally the country seeking aid will come forward with a list of projects included in its development plan from which the Soviet Union will select those projects to which it is willing to provide assistance. In a few instances, Soviet advisers have assisted in the drawing up of development plans, but generally they have not made the initial recommendations regarding projects to be included in the country's developmental program. The projects that they have selected to support seem to correspond well in each case with the stage of development of the country receiving aid. For instance, in India, where the human and physical resources are sufficiently developed to begin widening the industrial base, Soviet aid has been concentrated on the expansion of heavy industry and electrical power. At the opposite end of the development scale, aid to Afghanistan has emphasized the construction of transportation facilities to reach areas that have been inaccessible to modern vehicles, the development of mineral resources, and the construction of multipurpose projects. Manufacturing plants that have been supported by the Soviet Union in Afghanistan are small and require simple skills for operation. In addition, a significant amount of the aid has been allocated for constructing and equipping centers for training skilled and semi-skilled technicians. Soviet aid to African countries also has been characterized by a wide number and variety of small-scale projects.

One of the largest segments of Soviet aid, and probably the one that has proved to be most beneficial to the Soviets themselves, is the technical assistance program. This has consisted of the use of Soviet technicians in the less-developed countries, the training of technicians from less-developed countries in the Soviet Union, the provision of scholarships to the emerging elite for academic study in the Soviet Union, the establishment of technical institutes and vocational training centers in some of the less-developed countries, and the transference of simple technical skills to large numbers of workers through on-the-job training programs. Between 1955 and the end of 1965, at least 50,000 Soviet economic technicians were deployed to less-developed countries, and more than 20,000 students and technical trainees undertook training at facilities in the Soviet Union. Soviet economic technicians abroad increased from about 800 in 1956 to 9500 in 1965. Although originally Soviet technicians were sent to less-developed countries specifically to aid in the construction and inauguration of industrial and other types of plants, the inability of recipient countries to provide sufficient managerial, planning, educational, and medical personnel has induced a considerable increase in recent years in the number of Soviet technicians in less-developed countries who are not connected with specific economic aid projects. They are engaged in broad advisory capacities in various phases of development. Approximately 45 per cent of all Soviet technicians have been employed in Asian countries, and more than 30 per cent in the Middle East. In recent years the number of Soviet technicians in Africa has risen sharply. By the

end of 1965 about 7000 technical trainees from less-developed countries had been trained in the Soviet Union, most of them for employment at home on Soviet-built industrial projects. About 85 per cent of all trainees came from countries in Asia and the Middle East.

Technical training institutes for group-training purposes in the home areas have been built as part of most major aid programs. For example, four centers have been constructed in Ghana to train 5000 to 6000 trainees annually in the repair of agricultural machinery and mining equipment. In addition to group training, the usual practice has been to assign a local worker to each Soviet technician so that an adequately trained local technician is prepared to take over the job as the Soviet technician is phased out. In most instances these arrangements have worked very well, and plant operations have been turned over to local work forces without interruption of production.

The major snags that have been encountered have been due to the reluctance of the Soviets to assume overall management for the construction or operation of a major facility. This led to much frustration on both sides during the early stages of the building of the Aswan Dam in Egypt when the Egyptian managerial staff proved incompetent to provide labor and materials at the right times to assure continued progress in the work. Soviet engineering technicians became very frustrated by the resultant disorganization, and the Egyptian government and the rest of the world erroneously held the Soviets responsible for long delays that occurred during various phases of the construction. In some instances the Soviets have had to step in and take over the total management in order for their technical personnel to be utilized effectively and for heavy equipment to be properly installed.

An important program for establishing and maintaining contact with the emerging elite in many developing countries is the provision for scholarships for academic study in the Soviet Union. Of the 13,500 students who participated from 1955 to the end of 1965, about half came from African countries, largely since 1961. Costs of training are borne by the U.S.S.R. in the form of scholarships which usually cover transportation to and from the student's homeland, tuition, medical care, clothing, housing, and a personal allowance, which generally averages about 90 rubles per month, which is about equal to the average industrial wage in the Soviet Union. Thus the students are pretty well provided for by Soviet standards, but since many of these students have come from the privileged classes in their homelands, they have not always been pleased with the Soviet standard set for them, and a good deal of mutual dissatisfaction has been expressed by both foreign students and Soviet citizens. The Soviets thought they were making a generous overture toward African students when they established the Peoples Friendship University (Patrice Lumumba) in Moscow as an academic center of higher learning solely for foreign students. This boomeranged, however, and students complained of segregation, racial discrimination, and political indoctrination. They also contended that the standards at this university were not equal to those at Moscow University. The peak year of enrollments was 1962 when 3400 students initiated their academic programs. New enrollees have declined each year since then to about 1300 in 1965, which apparently reflects the mutual dissatisfaction previously stated.

The Soviets have attempted to channel all their economic assistance into the public sectors of the less-developed countries, thus exerting a strong influence on the character and direction of economic development. They hope that the strengthening of the public sector will provide the strongest basis for the genuine independence of less-developed countries from the economic dominance of Western and domestic capitalists. The Soviets encourage the emerging governments to nationalize foreign and domestic private investments, and in some cases have induced them to set up institutional forms, such as collectivization of agriculture, nationalization of banks, establishment of state monopoly on foreign trade, and so forth, which are similar or identical to institutions in the Soviet Union. Such measures largely achieved the desired results in Egypt where the nationalization of foreign and domestic private investments and agrarian reform did much to sever the close ties between foreign capitalists and small native groups of wealthy landowners, industrialists, and financiers who had controlled much of the Egyptian economy. Although these measures did not result in any conversions to communism, they did go a long way toward socializing the country. In India, a sizable portion of communist bloc aid has been allocated for the public development of such traditional preserves of private investment as the petroleum and pharmaceutical industries. During India's second 5-year plan (1956–1961), Soviet Bloc aid accounted for about 20 per cent of public investment in the industrial sector, and during the third 5-year plan, for about 25 per cent.

Military Assistance   Perhaps the most dynamic aspect of Soviet aid in the less-developed countries has been its military assistance program. This effort has had immediate impact on regional balances of power and has achieved a great deal of influence among recipients. It has tended to yield more immediate political effects than economic aid has, and ultimately has led to a greater degree of dependence upon the Soviet Union by recipient countries. In the guise of advocating national aspirations, the U.S.S.R. has exploited regional or local conflicts with the vague political objectives of diminishing Western influence in these areas. Arab-Israeli tensions, Yemen's conflict with the United

Kingdom over Aden, Afghanistan's border dispute with Pakistan, and Indonesia's territorial conflict with the Netherlands and Malaysia are all examples of prime opportunities exploited by the Soviet Union. Coming as it does during periods in which the recipient is caught up in political turmoil, assistance of this kind has served to establish a rapport which economic aid alone has not been able to do, and this provides the basis for expanding other political and economic ties.

In many cases Soviet credits for economic development follow close on the heels of arms agreements. As the recipient country becomes further entangled in the web of Soviet accommodation, it becomes very dependent on the U.S.S.R. for spare parts, ammunition, and so forth. Once the process has started, there is no end to it. Weapons are always becoming obsolete. The Soviet Union discontinues manufacture of such items, and recipient countries continually clamor for more advanced arms. Since armaments are being poured into neighboring adversaries by the Soviets and other sources, these countries have little choice but to keep on buying at accelerated rates. Political survival may well depend on Soviet willingness to continue the program. Eventually these military programs usually put severe stresses on the economies of the recipient countries, and it becomes necessary to shift trade more and more toward the communist countries in order to pay off military debts.

Initially the Soviets were reluctant to be identified openly with arms agreements, so they employed other east European countries as intermediaries. Thus Czechoslovakia concluded the first arms agreement with Egypt in 1955 and with Syria and Yemen in 1956, and Czechoslovakia and Poland signed the initial agreement with Indonesia in 1958. Eventually the Soviets became more open about their military assistance, and as of the end of 1965 they had provided at least 4 billion dollars worth of military assistance to sixteen less-developed countries. Undoubtedly Soviet military aid has accelerated considerably since 1965 as they have been called upon to supply more and more of the heavy defensive armaments for North Vietnam.

Military assistance has posed greater problems in terms of skilled manpower than economic assistance has, since military equipment has been delivered at a very rapid rate, and weapons are constantly changing and becoming more and more sophisticated. Thus it has been necessary to dispatch large numbers of Soviet military technicians to less-developed countries, and this has proved to be a very important element of the whole military program. The largest part of this technical assistance has consisted in the training of military personnel from the less-developed countries at military installations in the U.S.S.R. It has been estimated that by the end of 1965 as many as 18,000 trainees might have received such training. In addition, it has been estimated that a minimum of 15,000 Soviet military technicians have been employed in the countries receiving Soviet arms. Again, these two figures no doubt have been greatly expanded since 1965 by the intensification of the Vietnam War.

Distribution of Soviet Economic and Military Aid Since Soviet aid has been motivated primarily by political and strategic considerations, it is only natural that the Soviets have concentrated their efforts fairly close to home. Thus, excluding the east European satellites, which are not considered to be less-developed countries anyway, Soviet aid and trade efforts have been overwhelmingly concentrated in Asia in general and in the Near and Middle East in particular. Thus many of the countries along the southern margins of the Soviet Union play the dual role of next-door neighbor and less-developed country. And two of these, Turkey and Iran, present the additional overtones of having been parts of strong empires which in the past have carried on long and vicious struggles with the Russian Empire. Thus the present role of the Soviets in these areas is not prompted solely by the fact that here is a less-developed area which is open to Soviet efforts to alienate the West. In other areas of the world, such as Cuba, the less-developed country is also a communist country and more or less part of the Soviet Bloc. Hence again the analyst is faced with dual purposes. Thus it is not always possible to ferret out for individual cases relations that would have developed purely from Soviet attitudes toward less-developed countries. Nevertheless we will look at some of the major recipients of Soviet aid and attempt to analyze some of the more important aspects regarding individual countries.

Of the 4 or 5 billion dollars worth of economic credits and grants that have been committed to noncommunist less-developed countries since 1954, the Soviet Union has extended more than 40 per cent to Asian countries and another 40 per cent to Middle Eastern countries. The largest recipients have been the United Arab Republic, India, Afghanistan, Indonesia, and Syria, which together received about two thirds of all Soviet aid. The United Arab Republic and India alone have received about 40 per cent. (Table 17–9) Major military assistance has gone to essentially the same group of recipients, although there has been some juggling in their relative positions. The United Arab Republic and Indonesia each received more than 1 billion dollars worth of military equipment out of the 4 billion dollars that had been supplied up to the end of 1965. Other important recipients have been India, Iraq, and Syria. Within the communist realm, of course, huge outlays of military assistance have been given during the last few years to North Vietnam and Cuba, as well as a continuation of military aid to North Korea.

The Middle East Probably the most dramatic example of immediate political impact of large-scale arms purchases from the U.S.S.R. is presented by the Middle East. Such agreements provided the primary entry for the U.S.S.R. into that area and preceded economic aid agreements with Egypt, Iraq, Syria, and Yemen. The first arms agreement, concluded between Czechoslovakia and Egypt in September 1955, opened the door to other Soviet activities, decreased the strategic value of the newly created Baghdad Pact, and set off a chain of events which included Western refusal to construct the Aswan Dam and Egyptian nationalization of the Suez Canal. Egyptian willingness to conclude agreements with the Soviet Bloc obviously stemmed from a feeling of inferiority with respect to Israel and Iraq; at that time, the latter, as a member of the newly formed Baghdad Pact, loomed as a potential adversary. The large purchases of communist armaments caused a rapid reorientation of Egyptian exports. From 1954 to 1958 the Soviet Bloc countries purchased more than 60 per cent of Egyptian exports of cotton. Part of this no doubt would have taken place anyway, since the Egyptians were already looking for new markets for their cotton in a world of expanding cotton production and more intensive competition, but nevertheless the assumption of such large military debts demanded that Egypt pay for this equipment primarily in her major export.

The largest single economic agreement between the Soviet Union and Egypt was signed on August 27, 1960 for the contruction of the Aswan Dam. The total cost was to be 1,165,000,000 dollars, of which the Soviets were to pay 325 million or 27.8 per cent. This was to build a dam whose hydroelectric plant was to have a capacity of 2,700,000 kilowatts and whose reservoir was to have an irrigation potential for 2 million acres of land. When completed in 1970 the dam would increase Egypt's arable land by one third. Hence the project was of primary importance to the Egyptians, and the fact that the West had refused to build it provided the Soviets with the golden opportunity of stepping in and making a big splash early in the period of their aid commitments. Except for initial difficulties encountered in the organization of the project during the first 2 or 3 years, the work has gone pretty much on schedule and the Russians have made a good impression in showing their capabilities of tackling and completing a major project.

By the end of 1965 the Soviets had committed over 800 million dollars to the United Arab Republic for aid projects. The amount of aid actually disbursed by that time was around 300 million dollars. During the United Arab Republic's first 5-year plan, 1960–1965, drawings on Soviet economic credits were equal to about 10 per cent of gross investment and accounted for about one quarter of the aggregate United Arab Republic investment in industry, electric power, and the Aswan High Dam. The U.A.R. officials claim that during this period national income generated by the industrial sector increased about 45 per cent. (By way of comparison, during the years 1946–1966, the United States committed 1,081,000,000 dollars worth of aid to the U.A.R., 851 million of which went for "food for peace." Thus the United States poured considerably more money into the U.A.R. than did the Soviet Union during the same period, but its resources were spread so thinly throughout the economy to better living conditions for the masses of people that it was not particularly noticed.)

Although the Egyptians have in general been satisfied with Soviet aid, this has not induced them to become communistic or even particularly pro-Soviet. In fact, Nasser on occasion has verbally attacked the Soviet Union and has banned the Egyptian Communist Party. He has carried

on an effort at pan-Arabism which is entirely counter to any Soviet aspirations in the area. Thus Soviet aid in the United Arab Republic has succeeded economically in involving a significant proportion of Egypt's trade with the Soviet Union, but it has not accomplished anything particularly favorable to the Soviets on the political scene. And at the same time, Nasser has often put the Soviets in embarrassing positions by making rather rash unilateral moves and then expecting them to back him up. The prime example of this, of course, was the short Arab-Israeli War of June 1967.

Algeria and Iraq have been the next two largest recipients of Soviet aid in the Middle East, and here too the Soviets have often met with political hostility. Iraq has periodically persecuted the local communists and has maintained its membership in the Baghdad Pact, or CENTO. After the 1967 Arab-Israeli War, the premier of Algeria flew to Moscow to ask the Soviets why they had not offered direct military aid. The Soviets in turn asked him what he thought about the prospects of an atomic war.

Turkey and Iran are rather latecomers on the Soviet aid scene, but in recent years have made use of some Soviet aid in order to lessen their dependence upon the United States and other Western powers. They are currently following courses of diplomacy that would allow them some latitude for independent action while maintaining favorable relations with both the East and the West.

India India has been a close second to the United Arab Republic in the receipt of Soviet aid. During the 1946–1966 period India received 806 million dollars of Soviet economic aid. She also received an unspecified amount of military aid. Incidentally, India is the major recipient of United States' aid and during the same period of years received 5,882,000,000 dollars in economic aid commitments from the United States. Again, the Soviet Union seems to have reaped a disproportionate share of favorable publicity in this area with its construction of the Bhilai steel mill. Here was a finite project which could be displayed to the world, whereas American aid was scattered widely in a rather vain attempt to better the living conditions of the teeming hundreds of millions of people in India, a country where a few billion dollars hardly makes a dent in the poverty.

The Bhilai steel mill started out as a three-way effort by the West Germans, the English, and the Soviets to provide India with a steel industry. It became a vigorous competitive race in which the Soviet Union put its rivals to shame. There were three mills of 1 million tons capacity each built, one by the British, one by the Germans, and one by the Soviets. The Soviets built the simplest one and ran into far less complications than did the other two countries. They also loaned money at only 2.5 per cent interest, whereas the German and British loans ranged from 4.5 to 6.3 per cent. Also the Soviets showed a willingness to accept payment in rupees, whereas West Germany and Britain insisted on convertible currency. The Soviets then proceeded to build the Ranchi heavy-machine-building plant, which gained a good deal of publicity in India, and then agreed to build a fourth steel plant at Bolaro, after years of Indian negotiations with the Americans had come to naught. The Soviets cleverly used the Bolaro plant to justify the Ranchi plant, which was turning out so many pieces of heavy equipment that there was no market for them in the Indian area. Thus two birds were killed with one stone.

The second most impressive action by the Soviets in India has been in the field of oil. They succeeded in breaking a monopoly among American oil companies, and sold Russian crude petroleum to India to be utilized in its own refineries that it

wished to build. Then Soviet geologists went on to find oil in three different places in India, which by 1966 were supplying one third of India's needs. All this, after American oil companies had supposedly prospected thoroughly and pronounced India barren of oil. This prompted the Soviets to reiterate what they had said concerning several previous cases in other countries—American oil companies have, in fact, found oil but have kept the discovery secret so they could sell their own oil.

The Soviets have supplied a modest amount of military aid to India, and during the Indian-Chinese border conflicts in 1962 and 1965 the Soviets supported the Indian effort against the Chinese and stepped up their military aid. This was an unprecedented case of a communist country helping an uncommitted country against a "fraternal" communist country.

Of course, the Soviets have been antagonized by the entry of China into the aid business in the very areas where they themselves have strong aspirations. In the early stages of the entry of China into the aid business, it must have been rather galling to the Soviets to run into competition from the Chinese in areas like India where China was extending aid in competition with the Soviets and at the same time receiving aid from the Soviets.

Even stranger in this area is the case of Nepal. Nepal is in the curious position of receiving aid not only from the richer nations of the world but also from the poor, since it is being wooed both by China and India, between which it lies. It has also received aid from the United States, the Soviet Union, and the United Kingdom. In view of the fact that these three countries have all made grants and loans totaling hundreds of millions of dollars to India, and the Soviet Union has granted large sums to China, one can imagine the mixed emotions that these three countries feel as they watch India and China compete with them for favors in Nepal. One of the biggest conflicts between the Russians and Chinese in aid programs has been in Yemen where the Chinese have asked the people of Yemen to align themselves with the "Men of the East," which has prompted the Soviets to accuse the Chinese of racism.

The Soviet negotiation of the India-Pakistan border disputes in 1965 was also a first for the Soviet Union and marked an entry into a new stage whereby a communist country acted as a peacemaker between two noncommitted countries. Thus the Soviets seem bent on currying favor in India, after having coveted the area for centuries during Russian Empire days only to be stymied by the British who were in control of the area. Now the Soviets seem content to act as the magnanimous richer neighbor who is happy to extend a helping hand in time of need. Although India is considered a less-developed country, this is purely in terms of per capita economy and living standards. The total population is so great, and the civilization so mature that India swings a lot of weight in world opinion. In view of this and the great need for material aid, it is little wonder that both the Soviet Union and the United States have expended major efforts in this area.

Afghanistan The Soviets seem to have singled out Afghanistan as a model for the successful extension of economic and military aid and to prove to the world that the Soviet Union can be benevolent to a smaller less-developed neighbor. The Soviets have committed a higher per capita aid to Afghanistan than to any other country. During the period 1946–1966 the Soviet Union committed loans totaling 377 million dollars and grants totaling another 150 million, about twice the aid that was committed by the United States to Afghanistan in the same period. (Table 17–9) Since Afghanistan is at a low level of economic and social development, the Soviet aid has been spread rather widely over a number of small projects, many of which have to do with agriculture, transportation, and so forth. One of the more spectacular engineering feats accomplished by the Soviets in Afghanistan is the first-class highway built through the Hindu Kush which runs 67 miles from Kabul to the northern border. This highway was opened on September 3, 1964 and eliminated 125 miles of tortuous highway in the previous system. The biggest challenge was the completion of a tunnel 2 miles long at an elevation of 11,000 feet, which had to be engineered so that it could be used by camel and donkey caravans as well as by automobiles. During Afghanistan's first 5-year plan, 1956–1961, about one third of total gross investment was represented by Soviet expenditures, and during the second plan, 1962–1967, about half of total Afghan investment was supplied by the Soviets.

Indonesia The one place in which the Soviets have completely failed is Indonesia. As the Dutch, Americans, and British could have predicted, the Soviets have been utterly unable to cope with the chaos of the Indonesian economy and political system. They are not the only ones; a great deal of the much larger American aid has gone to naught in this area also. As of 1966, the Soviets had extended approximately 370 million dollars in loans to Indonesia, while the United States had committed 1,345,000,000 dollars in various loans, grants, and food for peace. Other countries have also sunk money into this unrewarding area, including many communist countries. China loaned around 100 million dollars, Poland 75 million, Czechoslovakia 60 million, Hungary 60 million, Rumania 50 million, and East Germany 15 million. After 10 years of aid, the Soviets have failed to complete a single industrial project, and consequently the Indonesians have been unable to generate any new income, so the Soviets obviously have no hope of collecting on the debts.

While Sukharno was in power, he was obviously much more interested in driving the Dutch out of their last foothold in New Guinea and in creating a military confrontation with Malaysia than he was in devising economic programs and balancing his budget. The Soviets also wasted an unspecified amount of military aid in this respect. Their reward for all their efforts was that Sukharno showed a more favorable disposition toward the Chinese than toward the Soviets, although he was not favorably disposed toward communists in general, and in fact he persecuted them at times in Indonesia.

Africa   The Soviets today are encountering experiences in sub-Saharan Africa similar to those of their west European predecessors. Guinea was the first new country to break away from its colonial ancestor and seek the alternate route of aid from the communist bloc. Trade and aid agreements signed between Guinea and the Soviet Union in 1959 gave the Soviets their first penetration into sub-Saharan Africa. During the next year it appeared that Guinea was an ardent admirer of the Russian model of economic development and was on the verge of becoming an African Cuba. By December 1960 there were reports that the Soviets had obtained permission to establish a submarine base on Guinea's coast. Yet, within one year, the Soviet ambassador was accused of meddling in Guinea's internal affairs and was expelled. Ironically enough, the Guineans seem to have become disenchanted with the Soviets largely because the Soviets gave them everything they wanted during the period of nationalistic fervor that existed immediately after Guinea broke away from France. Most of the things that the Soviets built, such as hotels, stadia, and the polytechnical institute, were much too large for this country of only 3 million people, and rather than realizing profits, they became a drag on the economy. Thus the Soviets were victims of

circumstances because of miscalculations, and the Guinean government began blaming them for all sorts of economic ills. The final blow to the Soviets came during the Cuban missile crisis in the fall of 1962 when Guinea denied a request by the Soviets to land Cuban-bound planes at the Conakry Airport, an airport which the Soviets had reconstructed only a few months before. The United States found itself, for once, in the advantageous position of entering the field second after the first entrant had made all the blunders.

Communist efforts in other parts of sub-Saharan Africa have not been much more rewarding than in Guinea. Expulsion of the Soviet officials from the Congo is a well-known story. In Ghana, until Nkrumah's ouster in 1966, Soviet foreign aid experience was probably more politically effective but no more successful economically. The most impressive aid project in Ghana has been the Volta Dam, which was built with American money.

The Soviets have also been dealing with Mali, Sudan, Ethiopia, and Somalia, but the Chinese have also been active in all of these areas and have probably been more successful than the Soviets have. Chinese aid exceeded Soviet aid in Congo (Brazzaville), Kenya, and Tanzania.

It is evident that despite the mistakes they have made, the Soviets consider sub-Saharan Africa a major area of interest and promise. In terms of relative amounts of resources devoted to the area, the Soviets have attached more importance to it than the Americans have. This is a new area, where the Tsarist government never trod, and the Soviets seem to be trying to carve out a sphere of influence similar to that of the European powers before World War I.

Latin America   Latin America is so far away from the Soviet Union that, except for Cuba, the Soviets seem to have accepted this area as the American sphere of influence and are not eager to create any serious confrontations, unless the effort is not too great. Cuba is the only less-developed country to join the socialist camp since the inception of the Soviet aid program, but this was not due to Soviet efforts; Cuba fell into Moscow's lap. In the past the Soviets have shown their willingness to deal with anyone, including dictators Peron of Argentina and Batista of Cuba, wherever it has been to their advantage to do so. Although Argentina, Brazil, Uruguay, and Chile have had some trade relations with the Soviet Union in recent years, there has not been much in the way of aid programs except credits extended in one direction or another to accommodate trade. Brazil has received more attention than any of the other Latin American countries except Cuba. For what appeared to be political reasons, the Soviet Union, a traditional tea-drinking country, in 1959 consummated an agreement to purchase rather large quantities of Brazilian coffee. The Soviets were to provide Brazil with wheat in exchange, but in 1964 when the Russian wheat supply was short they switched their exchange offer to petroleum. Since then they have been supplying about one third of Brazil's oil needs. Petroleum has proved to be a very handy commodity in recent years, for which the Soviet Union could always find eager acceptance in exchange of goods. As has generally been the case with Latin American countries, Brazil exported more to the Soviet Union that it imported and found itself with an excess of rubles which could not be spent on the world market. Therefore it asked the Soviet Union to finance the construction of a dam on the Parana River, but instead the Soviets agreed to provide 100 million dollars in credit for industrial equipment to be installed by Soviet technicians. Thus trade and aid were interconnected.

Soviet aid has largely prevented Cuba from sliding into an economic collapse. Since early 1960 the Soviet Union has extended about 1.1 billion dollars in economic aid to Cuba. About 70 per cent of this aid has been in the form of balance-of-payments subsidies to cover annual Cuban deficits in the bilateral trade between the two countries. In addition, credits have been extended for industrial development, and a great deal of military aid has been extended. It appears that at least 15,000 Soviet technicians have been employed in Cuba on economic aid activities engaged in agricultural, industrial, and geological surveys. In 1965 about 4500 Cuban students were enrolled in Soviet academic institutions. In spite of all the Soviet aid received, Castro has decided that the Soviet brand of communism is too conservative for him and he has largely repudiated his political and ideological ties with the Soviets. Like Nasser, he has gone off on his own to promote his own interests in what he considers to be his sphere of influence. And also like Nasser, he has involved the Soviets in a highly embarrassing world situation, the missile crisis of 1962. The biggest issue of dispute between Castro and the Kremlin is the approach to other Latin American countries. Instead of supporting guerrilla movements, as Castro would like them to do, the Soviets have been establishing diplomatic and trade relations with many of the existing regimes in Latin American countries.

Evaluation of Soviet Aid Programs   The continuing high level of economic aid extensions suggests that the results of the Soviet political-economic offensive are satisfactory to the Soviet leadership. Actually, relatively small amounts of resources have been involved, and with these the U.S.S.R. has established a strong presence throughout much of the underdeveloped world. Their entry into the aid business has provided an alternate source of economic, military, and political aid to which the leaders of many new countries could turn without being afraid of provoking Western boycotts. It has also encouraged certain countries to assume a much more aggressive posture than would have been possible without the Soviets in the background. Nasser's seizure of the Suez Canal and Sukharno's adamant policy toward Dutch New Guinea are good examples of this. The establishment of long-term credits with many less-developed countries has given the Soviet Union vested interests in current regimes, which will probably induce a measure of political stability in the recipient countries, since the Soviets are interested in being repaid eventually. Generally the Soviets are more interested in maintaining their own material gains than in bringing to power another communist party in some remote corner of the world, which, likely as not, will prove to be very self-willed anyway.

Trade with Less-Developed Countries
At the first United Nations Conference on Trade and Development in 1964, the Soviets presented delegates from less-developed countries with impressive multiples regarding Soviet trade development during the previous decade and prospects for the future, and gained considerable propaganda mileage out of promises to abolish external tariffs on certain commodities, expressions of concern with respect to general tendencies for world trade to work against primary producers, and nebulous universalities about promotion of multilateral trade agreements. However, the harsh realities are that Soviet trading practices have remained inflexibly bilateral, and the Soviets have not hesitated to take advantage of falling world prices on such things as natural rubber and cocoa beans, as well as many other primary products which make up much of the exports from the less-developed countries. Events since 1964 have pretty much convinced interested nations that Soviet trade with the developing world is of marginal global significance. The total turnover of Soviet trade with nonsocialist developing nations has amounted to about

5 per cent of the developing nations' total trade, about 70 per cent of which has been with the industrially developed Western nations, and the remaining 25 per cent of which has been among themselves.

In spite of the fact that official Soviet statements have encouraged developing countries to believe that they might find markets for their growing surpluses of manufactured products, about 60 per cent of such exports from less-developed countries has been finding markets in the Western countries, whereas the entire socialist bloc has been taking about only 4 per cent. Other countries in the socialist bloc have been more active in this trade than the Soviet Union has. This is especially true of Czechoslovakia. Although Soviet trade with the developing countries has been growing slowly, it has not been growing at any faster rate than total Soviet trade. The developing countries' share of Soviet trade turnover has hovered around 10–11 per cent during the past decade or more. The Soviet gesture to abolish high import tariffs on certain items from less-developed countries is meaningless, because there is no direct relationship in the Soviet Union between civilian demand for goods and the amount that is imported. The Soviet government arbitrarily decides on volumes of imports and retail prices. For example, after the Soviet Union abolished the high tariff on cocoa, the state retail prices for cocoa and chocolate remained unaltered at prices approximately eight times those for the same commodities in London or Paris, and this was in spite of falling prices paid for cocoa beans on the world market. Even at what in the West would seem to be prohibitive retail prices, there is still an unsatiated demand for chocolate in the Soviet Union which the government does not endeavor to fulfill. The primary determinant of how much cocoa will be imported from Ghana will continue to be the value of fabricated products which the U.S.S.R. is prepared to sell to Ghana under rigid bilateral trade deals, many of which have political overtones.

Except for certain products, the economy of the Soviet Union is not particularly complementary to those of the less-developed countries, and therefore markets for many commodities cannot be expected to be expanded significantly in the Soviet Union. As a matter of fact, the U.S.S.R. is a major net exporter of seven of the ten commodities that the delegates at the First U. N. Conference agreed upon as being suitable for price stabilization. This fact apparently has led occasionally to the rather unorthodox practice of re-exporting some of the products that have been imported by the Soviet Union from some of the less-developed countries. Although there is no real proof of this, except in the case of re-export of cocoa beans and coffee to East Germany, the less-developed countries on certain occasions have accused the Soviet Union of doing just this and of offering their original produce at prices below prevailing world levels. Egypt has taken the precaution of carefully dividing her sales of cotton almost equally between the communist bloc and various countries of western Europe, and has insisted on delaying sales to the Soviet Union until all agreements have been consummated with the Western countries at specified Egyptian prices.

Although overall communist trade with less-developed countries has occupied only about 5 per cent of the total trade of these countries, the fact that communist trade has been concentrated on a relatively few countries means that the communists have occupied significant shares of total trade of certain developing countries. For instance, the communist world has been accounting for approximately 30 per cent of the total trade of Afghanistan, the United Arab Republic, Mali, and Guinea, although the percentage appears now to be decreasing in the latter two countries. During the past decade, 50 per cent or more of Egypt's annual exports of cotton

has gone to communist countries. On the other hand, relative shares of certain commodity exports from less-developed countries, to which the Soviet Union has given a great deal of publicity, really are not that significant. In 1960 the Soviet Union rather conspicuously announced the beginning of imports of coffee from Brazil and certain other countries, in spite of the fact that the Soviet Union traditionally is a tea-drinking country. And for a long time the Soviets have been buying cocoa, primarily from Ghana, and recently they have been trying to impress the world with the expansion of these purchases. Yet the United States still imports eight times as much cocoa as the Soviet Union does and seventy times as much coffee. The per capita consumption of these two commodities in the U.S.S.R. is the lowest in Europe. Brazilian exports of coffee to communist countries has amounted to no more than 4 per cent of total Brazilian exports of coffee.

Probably the most striking feature of the pattern of commodity imports by communist countries from the less-developed countries is the relatively unchanging composition of this flow of goods. (Table 17–11) This alone would seem to indicate that the Soviet imports have been more economically than politically motivated, that the Soviet Union has really wanted these commodities. And this is no doubt true. But on the other hand, abrupt shifts in suppliers of these commodities, where alternatives exist, do strongly reflect political fortunes. For instance, the shifts of Soviet imports of rice away from China largely to the United Arab Republic and Burma, and then away from Burma to North Korea, Pakistan, Brazil, and Uruguay, without a doubt reflect Soviet desires to disassociate or associate themselves with different countries at different times. The shift in purchases of oranges away from Israel to Algeria and Morocco is another good example of politically motivated changes in suppliers while maintaining a constant or increasing level of com-

Table 17–11   Soviet Trade with Major Trading Partners Among the Less-Developed Countries, 1966, in Millions of Rubles

	Trade Turnover	Soviet Imports	Major Products Imported and (Value)
Cuba	689.2	257.3	Raw sugar (225.8), ores (24.6)
India	346.0	172.0	Burlap bags (37.8), hides (22.7), tea (21.0), cashew nuts (16.8), jute (9.4)
United Arab Republic	313.8	135.0	Cotton (115.1), rice (10.0)
Mongolia	255.2	56.1	Meat (25.2), wool (21.3)
North Korea	160.1	83.1	Pig iron, steel, and rolled steel (65.2), construction materials (11.5), rice (9.0)
Malaysia	113.0	113.0	Rubber (106.7)
Argentina	103.3	96.6	Wheat (71.9), leather (11.0), wool (10.4)
North Vietnam	84.2	22.8	Clothing (8.3), alcoholic beverages (3.5)
Afghanistan	82.9	16.9	Cotton and wool (11.8), fruit (2.1)
Pakistan	61.5	26.4	Rice (16.1), jute (3.7)
Greece	61.3	26.7	Fruit (10.6), tobacco (9.9)
Brazil	52.4	27.5	Coffee (11.1), cotton (6.7), rice (2.2)
Iran	45.4	17.5	Cotton, wool, and leather (7.2), lead and zinc ores (5.2)
Turkey	41.6	16.9	Nuts (7.3), raisins (3.1)
Syria	38.7	18.3	Cotton and wool (15.6)
Iraq	35.2	2.9	Cotton, wool, and leather (1.3)
Ceylon	34.8	15.6	Rubber (5.2), tea (4.6), cocoa butter (4.4)
Ghana	34.4	21.8	Cocoa beans (21.2)
Indonesia	32.0	27.7	Rubber (24.5)
Algeria	22.2	5.3	Oranges (3.6)
Morocco	18.2	8.5	Oranges (6.1)
Iceland	17.6	9.0	Fish (6.6)
Sudan	13.3	6.6	Cotton (5.1)
Guinea	12.9	3.2	Bananas (1.2), pineapples (1.1)
Yemen	12.0	1.4	Cotton (0.9), coffee (0.4)
Tunisia	11.2	3.4	Olive oil (2.3)
Mexico	9.9	9.3	Corn (7.3)
Mali	9.1	1.4	Arrock (0.8), cotton (0.6)
Uruguay	8.8	8.3	Wool (7.6), rice (0.7)
Burma	5.0	0.3	Rice (0.3)

Source: Compiled from *Vneshnyaya torgovlya SSSR za 1966 god,* pp. 117–334.

modity import. The Soviets have a great unsatisfied market for citrus fruits which they are increasingly trying to satisfy, largely through imports, but while doing this they have turned away from one of their earliest major suppliers because of the participation of Israel in the British-French-Israeli invasion of the Suez Canal zone.

Raw materials for metal industries and textile industries have consistently made up more than half of total imports, and food stuffs have comprised around one quarter. Two commodities, cotton and rubber, have been very high on communist import lists. In certain years they have accounted for 70 per cent of crude material imports and about 45 per cent of total imports by communist countries from less-developed areas. Rubber has decreased somewhat recently with Soviet attempts to become more self-sufficient in synthetic rubber. Since 1960 cotton alone has accounted for almost 40 per cent of crude material imports to all the communist countries from less-developed areas. The United Arab Republic provides most of this cotton, and smaller quantities have been supplied by Syria, Afghanistan, Iran, Brazil, and a few minor suppliers. If one excludes the large raw sugar imports from Cuba, the most valuable food imports from less-developed countries are the beverages tea, cocoa, and coffee. The second most important food group are fruits, berries, and nuts, including both fresh and dried fruits.

Soviet exports to developing countries have remained heavily machinery and equipment, generally accounting for 50 per cent or more, followed by petroleum and petroleum products, 11 to 12 per cent, and food products, 6 to 13 per cent. In certain countries like India and the United Arab Republic where Soviet aid has been a big part of trade, much of the machinery and equipment has been in the form of complete plants.

The countries of eastern Asia and the Middle East by far account for the largest share of Soviet trade with the less-developed world, which attests to the important stimulus that Soviet aid has given to trade. In general, the largest trading partners are also the ones who have received the most Soviet aid. During the past few years sub-Saharan Africa has accounted for about 10 per cent of the U.S.S.R. trade with less-developed countries. Ghana remains the first partner in Africa, because of large cocoa bean export. Sudan recently has climbed to second place because of its newly developed cotton exports. Excluding Cuba, the volume of Soviet trade with Latin America has been quite small and has varied erratically. Brazil has been about the only country which has sustained a significant trade with the U.S.S.R., but

in recent years Argentina has shot into first place because of its wheat exports. Over 90 per cent of the Argentine trade with the Soviets consists of Soviet imports from Argentina. Although Brazil has maintained some favorable trade balance with the Soviet Union, imports and exports are more nearly balanced than in Argentina. Although the Soviets have had some trade relations with Chile, Uruguay, and Mexico, trade there has remained insignificant.

If one includes Communist Cuba among the other less-developed countries, then its trade turnover can be seen to far exceed even India and the United Arab Republic. (Table 17–11) Practically all of this Soviet trade has sprung up as a consequence of political events, since very little existed before Castro took over. Most of the Soviet exports to Cuba consist of heavy industrial and military equipment, petroleum, skilled technical services, and so forth to further the industrial development and military aspirations of Cuba, whereas over 85 per cent of Cuban exports to the Soviet Union has been raw sugar and much of the rest has been certain mineral ores.

Soviet Intentions Toward the Sea One of the major reorientations by the Soviets in the world scene in recent years has been their sudden turn to the sea for rapid expansion and dominance. They are building up their fleet in all respects—the merchant marine, the fishing fleet, and the navy. Although at the present time the expansion of the navy is probably the most conspicuous, in the long run it might well be the merchant marine expansion that puts Russia in the driver's seat. Since 1951 the Soviet Union has moved from eighth to probably second place among the world's merchant marines, as ranked by number of ships. By 1970 they hope to exceed the American merchant marine and then to be the largest in the world. (Fig. 17–3) In order to do this they have initiated a concerted program of ship building them-

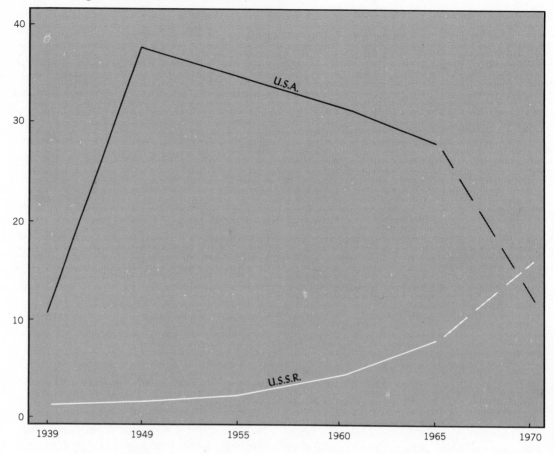

Figure 17–3   Secular changes in merchant ships, U.S.S.R. and U.S.A., in millions of tons deadweight. Adapted from Hopkins, Mark, "Russia Looks Seaward," Milwaukee Journal, *June 5, 1966, Part 5, p. 1. Originally published in* Soviet Life.

selves and have let large contracts for purchasing of ships abroad. Major suppliers in the "West" are Japan, West Germany, Italy, France, Finland, and Denmark. East Germany and Poland are building ships within the Soviet sphere. In 1966 Japan alone was constructing 319 ships for the Soviet Union. At that time the Soviets had contracts out with various countries which totaled 24 per cent of all the ships under construction in the world. *Lloyd's Register of Shipping* shows that between 1954 and 1960 the U.S. merchant marine decreased 310,000 tons per year, whereas the Soviet fleet increased 450,000 tons per year. In 1961 and 1962 the Soviet Union added about 1 million tons, whereas

the United States lost half a million. At this rate, by 1970 the Soviet Union might well have 2000 merchant ships in active duty totaling 16 million tons, while the United States might have about 900 merchant ships active totaling about 14 million tons. Although the United States has many more ships registered, most of these are reserve fleet ships built before World War II which are now inactive and by 1970 will probably be on the scrap heap.

The Soviets have long been concerned that much of their foreign trade has been carried in foreign bottoms, and they are determined to save these outlays of money to foreign vessels. This is probably the chief motivation for the rapid expansion of their merchant marine, although there have been speculations that they may well go beyond this goal and try to dominate world trade. Expansion of the Soviet merchant marine raised the share of Soviet overseas trade carried in Soviet bottoms from 37 per cent in 1962 to 52 per cent in 1965. By 1970 they may well carry all of their overseas trade in their own ships. At present the Soviet merchant marine operates primarily out of three major ports: Odessa in southwestern Ukraine, Leningrad on the Baltic, and Vladivostok in the Far East. There are a number of other ports, but these generally handle local domestic trade. (Fig. 16–10)

It appears that the Soviet Union is attempting to acquire the largest merchant fleet in the world, to operate the largest and most modern fishing fleet in the world, and to control the narrow sea bottlenecks of global shipping: the Panama Canal, the Strait of Gibralter, the Suez Canal, and the Strait of Malacca. In this regard, they are very eager to establish port facilities and stockpiles of materials in areas around the Mediterranean, the Gulf of Aden, and the Singapore region. In these areas, of course, it is not only the merchant marine, but the Soviet navy that comes into play. The Soviets took the opportunity during the 6-day Arab-Israeli War in 1967 to move forty-six ships through the Dardanelles into the eastern Mediterranean, which now almost exactly counterbalances the fifty-ship U.S. fleet in that area. One of their major objectives in negotiations with the Arab world after the war was Soviet naval rights in the ports of the area. They have been quick to establish relations with the new state of South Yemen in the hopes of taking over the abandoned British naval port at Aden to control the Red Sea entrance to the Suez bottleneck and to give them an entree into the northern Indian Ocean. There is also some speculation that they might move into the Algerian naval base at Mers-El-Kebir which the French evacuated in January 1968.

This is only 315 miles east of Gibralter. Thus, NATO would be somewhat outflanked.

The Soviets have turned the Baltic into a virtual Red Sea where their warships now outnumber NATO's ships by five to one. There is some speculation that this will happen in Singapore when the British Royal Navy pulls out in 1971. The Soviets are obviously courting Malaysia with the hope that they will be able to use the big British naval base at Singapore.

One of the most revealing power plays that has definitely established the Soviet navy as a force to be reckoned with was the flotilla of sixteen Soviet cruisers and frigates that shouldered its way between the coast of North Korea and the U.S. Navy task force that had been sent into the area to bring pressure upon North Korea to return the *Pueblo* and its crew. The Soviet naval presence effectively checkmated the U.S. naval pressure on North Korea and stalled any release of the *Pueblo* that might have been effected by these means.

In other areas, the Soviets have carried on a rather childish game of harassment, probing, and provocation, even getting so cocky as to maneuver boldly into the midst of formations of U.S. ships where the intruders would suddenly cut across the bows of American ships to test the skill of American helmsmen. There have been several instances of actual minor collisions between Soviet and American ships in such cases. Other provocations are the obvious spying by "fishing vessels" which ply most of the strategic coastlines of the world. These ships are fishing, but they are fishing for information as well as fish. They have come so close inshore along the northeastern coast of the United States that they have on a couple of occasions interrupted the Atlantic Cable. They are fishing the shallow coastal waters for shrimp and other game along the entire Atlantic and Gulf coasts of the United States and are moving up and down the west coast of North America in the Pacific.

The Soviet fishing fleet is already the world's largest and most modern. Their ships vary all the way from small trawlers to huge whaling vessels and factory ships which can stay at sea for months. As is true with the merchant marine and the navy, the fishing fleet has mostly been built during the last decade and so has all the modern equipment. In addition to the dual-purpose "fishing vessels," the Soviet Union has produced the largest and best-equipped oceanographic fleet, whose two hundred ships plumb the earth's waters for data on depths, currents, bottom topography, and other valuable information. As a result, the Soviets have produced a world *Maritime Atlas* which is unequaled anywhere.

Current Trends and Prospects for the Future Although Soviet foreign trade has been increasing at a relatively rapid rate since World War II, this rate has tapered off during the 1960s from a peak annual increase of about 14 per cent in 1962 to an increase of only 3.4 per cent in 1966. These trends reflect primarily a deceleration in the growth of trade with communist countries and a relative stagnation of trade with developing areas. Trade with the industrial West has increased considerably, mainly on the import side. In the short run this has been greatly stimulated by Soviet grain purchases necessitated by poor grain harvests in 1963 and 1965, but in the long run it will probably be sustained by the Soviets looking to the West for advanced industrial equipment and consumer items. Since other east European socialist countries are also looking more toward the West for the same types of items, intra-socialist trade is beginning to decline, and the trend will probably accelerate in the future. In fact Rumania already trades more with the West than with other east European countries.

The trend toward economic disintegration of the CEMA group is paralleled by a trend toward political disintegration. The main objectives of the Soviets in creating CEMA, to isolate West Germany and to keep the U.S.A. out of Europe, have not been particularly successful. Their preaching of Europe for the Europeans has been somewhat ambivalent anyway, since the last thing that the Soviets would like to see is a united Europe. The success of the Common Market in the West, as against the failure of CEMA in the East, is just the reverse of what their original expectations had been. Originally the Soviets sneered at the Common Market as a vain attempt to unite traditional adversaries, but they have been rather unhappily surprised to see this organization work superbly, whereas CEMA has never functioned as an integrated unit.

The general fragmentation of the communist world has probably been the single most important factor influencing power balances and world tension during the past decade or so. The abandonment of the Soviets by the Chinese and Albanians, and, to some extent, the Yugoslavs, the Rumanians, the Cubans, and others, has added to the general cracking of the east European bloc. It has also produced strong Soviet adversaries within the communist orbit that in many ways have been even harder to deal with than has the U.S.A. or other Western adversaries, since cooperation is almost impossible between communist countries in secular conflicts which are clothed in ideological absolutes that can allow neither to yield. The presence of China has caused the Soviet Union to withdraw somewhat from world revolutionary activity and to follow a somewhat subdued policy of moderation and containment, terms which had been more familiar on the other side of the fence in earlier days. The Soviets supported India against China in the border quarrels of 1959, and the Soviet mediation of the India-Pakistan War of 1965, which, among other things, limited Pakistan's rapprochement with China, were unprecedented moves by a communist state. Such actions have been furthered in Vietnam where much of Moscow's aid to Hanoi has been for the express purpose of reducing Peking's influence in that area. The fact that both the Soviet Union and the United States have been engaged in containing China has not resulted in outright Soviet-American cooperation, but it has very much tempered the Soviet approach toward the United States and furthered the course of peaceful coexistence. After the experiences of China, Yugoslavia, Rumania, and Czechoslovakia, one wonders what the Soviets would do if they were suddenly confronted with a communist Germany or a communist United States.

In the less-developed areas of the world, the Soviets no doubt will hold on to whatever gains they have made in entries into these areas and will continue to curry the favor of the "third world" which they obviously feel is going to have a large part to play in the future history of the world. In general, Soviet aid has bettered most of the recipient countries, except in places like Indonesia or Guinea where the economic and political situations were so chaotic anyway that no outside help has been able to generate any improvement. On the Soviet side, they have gained a good deal of prestige by the building of impressive construction projects in places like India and Egypt and they have established some sort of rapport with a broad group of countries. There has not been a single convert to communism, however, and the very countries into which they have poured the most money have in general given them the most worries. The Soviet Union still has limited resources for such foreign dealings, and one wonders how many "friends" like Castro or Nasser the Soviets can afford to support. Obviously the Soviets are going to have to continue to be very selective in their extensions of aid and they are going to have to continue to tread very lightly on the toes of strongly nationalistic aspirants without any hopes of converting them to communism.

The Soviet Union more and more is taking on the posture of a "have" nation rather than a "have-not" one, which has vested interests in the current world order and is unwilling to risk its own material gains for the "national liberation" of some remote African or Latin American republic. The fact that major war has virtually been eliminated as a possibility, because of the high probability of ultimate annihilation of both sides, has no doubt sobered the Soviets more than any other single factor and has driven them a little farther away from the use of old tactics of alternating hard and soft attitudes in order to harass the world into what they want. Also, the incessant proclaiming of peace by the Soviet regime as a propaganda tactic might well come home to roost as a logical consequence of years of drumming into the Soviet people, from peasants to nuclear scientists, that waging war is immoral. After all, how can one hang a bright red peace banner immediately above the lathe of an industrial worker for a quarter of a century and then suddenly provocate a holocaust? As the Soviet citizenry moves toward 100 per cent education and broader participation in the running of the country, it seems inevitable that the Soviet government will be less likely to commit capricious acts. (As I write this in August 1968 the world is witnessing the current folly of the Soviet leadership in the handling of Czechoslovakia and the imminent danger of Soviet occupation of Rumania and perhaps even Berlin. One can only hope that this crisis will pass, as many others have before it, and that the upward trend of peaceful coexistence will steadily continue.)

Reading List

Adams, Russell B., "Soviet Foreign Trade," *Focus*, American Geographical Society, New York, June 1968, pp. 8–11.

Allen, Robert Loring, "A Note on Soviet Foreign Trade Statistics," *Soviet Studies*, April 1959, pp. 360–369.

The American Review of East-West Trade; a translation journal published quarterly since

January 1965 by International Arts and Sciences Press, Inc., White Plains, N.Y.

Baykov, Alexander, *Soviet Foreign Trade*, Princeton University Press, Princeton, N.J., 1946, 100 pp.

Berliner, Joseph S., *Soviet Economic Aid*, Praeger, New York, 1958, 232 pp.

Bromke, Adam and Uren, Philip E., eds., *The Communist States and the West*, Praeger, New York, 1967, 256 pp.

Brown, J. F., *The New Eastern Europe: The Khrushchev Era and After*, Praeger, New York, 1966, 313 pp.

Bush, Keith, "The Soviet Position at the Second U. N. Conference on Trade and Development," *Bulletin of the Institute for the Study of the U.S.S.R.,* March 1968, pp. 38–41.

Campbell, John C., "The Soviet Union in the International Environment," in Allen Kassof, *Prospects for Soviet Society*, Praeger, New York, 1968, pp. 473–496.

Communist Economic Policy in the Less Developed Areas, United States Department of State Publication 7020, July 1960, 38 pp.

Comparisons of the United States and Soviet Economies, Subcommittee on Economic Statistics, Joint Economic Committee, Congress of the United States, Washington, 1959, Part II, pp. 403–466.

Dillon, Douglas, *Economic Activities of the Soviet Bloc in Less Developed Countries,* United States Department of State Bulletin No. 8:469, March 24, 1958.

Dimensions of Soviet Power, Joint Economic Committee, Congress of the United States, Washington, 1962.

Gittings, John, *Survey of the Sino-Soviet Dispute,* Oxford University Press, London, 1968, 410 pp.

Goldman, Marshall I., *Soviet Foreign Aid,* Praeger, New York, 1967, 265 pp.

Helin, Ronald A., "Finland Regains an Outlet to the Sea: The Saimaa Canal," *The Geographical Review,* April 1968, pp. 167–194.

Horelick, Arnold L. and Rush, Myron, *Strategic Power and Soviet Foreign Policy,* Praeger, New York, 1966, 223 pp.

International Boundary Studies, The Geographer, U.S. Department of State; occasional monographs pinpointing various boundary problems.

Jackson, W. A. Douglas, *Russo-Chinese Borderlands,* Van Nostrand, Princeton, 1968, 2nd ed., 156 pp.

Kaser, Michael, *Comecon: Integration Problems of the Planned Economies,* Oxford University Press, London, 1967, 2nd ed., 279 pp.

Librach, Jan, *The Rise of the Soviet Empire: A Study of Soviet Foreign Policy,* Praeger, New York, 1966, revised ed., 407 pp.

Mosely, Philip E., ed., *The Soviet Union, 1922–1962: A Foreign Affairs Reader,* Praeger, New York, 1963, 512 pp.

New Directions in the Soviet Economy, Part IV, The World Outside, Studies Prepared for the Subcommittee on Foreign Economic Policy of the Joint Economic Committee, Congress of the United States, Washington, 1966, pp. 919–974.

Prybyla, Jan S., "Recent Trends in Sino-Soviet Economic Relations," *Bulletin of the Institute for the Study of the U.S.S.R.,* May 1967, pp. 11–21.

Pryor, Frederic L., "Foreign Trade Theory in the Communist Bloc," *Soviet Studies,* July 1962, pp. 41–61.

Roucek, Joseph S., "Changing Aspects of the Comecon," *Central Europe Journal,* August–September 1967, pp. 223–237.

Rubinstein, Alvin Z., ed., *The Foreign Policy of the Soviet Union,* Random House, New York, 1960, 457 pp.

"Russia's Navy: A New Challenge at Sea," *Time,* February 23, 1968, pp. 23–28.

Saunders, M. G., *The Soviet Navy,* Praeger, New York, 1958, 340 pp.

Sawyer, Carole A., *Communist Trade with Developing Countries: 1955–1965,* Praeger, New York, 1966, 126 pp.

Smith, Glen A., *Soviet Foreign Trade: Organization and Operations,* PhD Dissertation, Stanford, 1959.

Soviet and East European Foreign Trade; a translation journal published quarterly since January 1965 by International Arts and Sciences Press, Inc., White Plains, N.Y.

Soviet Economic Performance, 1966–1967, Materials Prepared for the Subcommittee on Foreign Economic Policy of the Joint Economic Committee, Congress of the United States, Washington, May 1968, pp. 97–116, 124–128, and 248–264.

Starr, Richard F., *The Communist Regimes in Eastern Europe: An Introduction,* Hoover Institution, Stanford, 1967, Chapter 9, "The Warsaw Treaty Organization," and Chapter 10, "The CEMA."

Stokke, Baard Richard, *Soviet and Eastern Euro-*

pean Trade and Aid in Africa, Praeger, New York, 1967, 327 pp.

Stolte, Stefen C., "Three Problems Facing the Soviet Bloc," *Bulletin of the Institute for the Study of the U.S.S.R.,* July 1967, pp. 20–28.

Tekiner, Suleyman, "Sinkiang and the Sino-Soviet Conflict," *Bulletin of the Institute for the Study of the U.S.S.R.,* August 1967, pp. 9–16.

———, "Soviet Policy toward the Arab East," *Bulletin of the Institute for the Study of the U.S.S.R.,* March 1968, pp. 29–37.

———, "Soviet-Turkish Relations and Kosygin's Trip to Turkey," *Bulletin of the Institute for the Study of the U.S.S.R.,* March 1967, pp. 3–11.

The Threat of Soviet Economic Policy, United States Department of State Publication 7234, October 1961, 25 pp.

Ulam, Adam B., *Expansion and Coexistence: The History of Soviet Foreign Policy, 1917–1967,* Praeger, New York, 1968, 784 pp.

United Nations Yearbook of International Trade Statistics, yearly.

Vneshnyaya torgovlya SSSR (Foreign Trade of the U.S.S.R.), Moscow, yearly (in Russian).

Walters, Robert S., *American and Soviet Aid to Less Developed Countries: A Comparative Analysis,* Doctoral Dissertation, University of Michigan, 1967.

World Trade Information Service, Statistical Reports, *Foreign Trade of the U.S.S.R.,* 1958–1959, Part 3, No. 61-9, and *Trade of the United States with the Soviet Bloc,* No. 61-17, 1959–1960.

Zablocki, Clement J., ed., *Sino-Soviet Rivalry: Implications for U.S. Policy,* Praeger, New York, 1966, 242 pp.

Equivalent Measures

Weight

1 kilogram = 2.2 pounds
1 pood   = 36 pounds
1 centner   = 1 quintal = 100 kilo-
              grams = 220 pounds
1 metric ton = 1.1 short tons = 2200
              pounds

Length

1 kilometer = 0.625 miles
1 verst   = 1.067 kilometers
             = 0.6629 miles
1 millimeter = 0.04 inches

Area

1 hectare   = 2.471 acres
1 dessiatine   = 2.7 acres
1 square kilometer = 0.39 square miles

For the following crops one centner per hectare equals the corresponding figures in United States bushels per acre:

Wheat	1.48
Rye	1.59
Barley	1.85
Oats	2.78
Maize	1.59
Paddy rice	1.98
Potatoes	1.48

During the following periods the United States dollar equaled the corresponding numbers of rubles:

1913–1923	1.94
1924	1.99
1925–1932	1.94
1933	1.57
1934	1.16
1935	1.15
1936	5.03
1937–1949	5.30
1950–1960	4.00
1961–present	0.90

1 ruble = 100 kopeks

Appendix

Preliminary Data from the 1970 Soviet Census

Table 1   Populations of Cities with More than 100,000 People and Other Political Centers, Listed in Order of 1970 Population

City	January 15, 1959	January 15, 1970	% Increase
Moscow			
Metropolitan Area	6,044,000	7,061,000	17
City	6,009,000	6,942,000	16
Leningrad			
Metropolitan Area	3,321,000	3,950,000	19
City	2,985,000	3,513,000	18
Kiev	1,110,000	1,632,000	47
Tashkent	927,000	1,385,000	49
Baku			
Metropolitan Area	968,000	1,261,000	30
City	643,000	847,000	32
Kharkov	953,000	1,223,000	28
Gorky	941,000	1,170,000	24
Novosibirsk	885,000	1,161,000	31
Kuybyshev	806,000	1,047,000	30
Sverdlovsk	779,000	1,026,000	32
Minsk			
Metropolitan Area	509,000	916,000	80
City	509,000	907,000	78
Odessa	664,000	892,000	34
Tbilisi	703,000	889,000	27
Donetsk (Stalino)	708,000	879,000	24
Chelyabinsk	689,000	874,000	27
Kazan	667,000	869,000	30
Dnepropetrovsk	661,000	863,000	31
Perm	629,000	850,000	35
Omsk	581,000	821,000	41
Volgograd (Stalingrad)	591,000	818,000	38
Rostov-on-Don	600,000	789,000	32
Ufa	547,000	773,000	41
Yerevan	493,000	767,000	55
Saratov	579,000	758,000	31
Riga	580,000	733,000	26
Alma-Ata	456,000	730,000	60
Voronezh	447,000	660,000	48
Zaporozhye	449,000	658,000	46
Krasnoyarsk	412,000	648,000	57
Krivoy Rog	401,000	573,000	43
Lvov	411,000	553,000	35
Karaganda	383,000	522,000	36
Yaroslavl	407,000	517,000	27
Novokuznetsk (Stalinsk)	382,000	499,000	31
Krasnodar	313,000	465,000	48
Tula	351,000	462,000	32

Table 1   Populations of Cities with More than 100,000 People and Other Political Centers, Listed in Order of 1970 Population (Continued)

City	January 15, 1959	January 15, 1970	% Increase
Irkutsk	366,000	451,000	23
Vladivostok	291,000	442,000	52
Barnaul	303,000	439,000	45
Khabarovsk	323,000	437,000	35
Frunze	220,000	431,000	96
Izhevsk	285,000	422,000	48
Ivanovo	335,000	419,000	25
Zhdanov	284,000	417,000	47
Astrakhan	305,000	411,000	35
Makeyevka	371,000	393,000	6
Kemerovo	289,000	385,000	33
Voroshilovgrad (Lugansk)	275,000	382,000	39
Nizhniy Tagil	338,000	378,000	12
Dushanbe (Stalinabad)	227,000	374,000	65
Penza	255,000	374,000	46
Vilnyus	236,000	372,000	57
Magnitogorsk	311,000	364,000	17
Tallin	282,000	363,000	29
Kishinev	216,000	357,000	65
Ulyanovsk	206,000	351,000	71
Ryazan	214,000	351,000	64
Kalinin	261,000	345,000	32
Orenburg	267,000	345,000	29
Archangel	258,000	343,000	33
Grozny	250,000	341,000	37
Tomsk	249,000	339,000	36
Gorlovka	308,000	335,000	9
Kirov	252,000	332,000	32
Nikolayev	235,000	331,000	40
Bryansk	207,000	318,000	53
Murmansk	222,000	309,000	39
Kaunas	219,000	306,000	40
Kaliningrad	204,000	297,000	46
Lipetsk	157,000	290,000	85
Kursk	205,000	284,000	39
Prokopyevsk	282,000	275,000	−2
Gomel	168,000	272,000	62
Tyumen	150,000	269,000	79
Samarkand	196,000	267,000	36
Kherson	158,000	261,000	65
Taganrog	202,000	254,000	26
Ulan-Ude	174,000	254,000	46
Ashkhabad	170,000	253,000	49
Toglyatti (Stavropol)	72,000	251,000	247
Simferopol	186,000	250,000	34
Chimkent	153,000	247,000	62
Kurgan	146,000	244,000	67

Table 1   Populations of Cities with More than 100,000 People and Other Political Centers, Listed in Order of 1970 Population (Continued)

City	January 15, 1959	January 15, 1970	% Increase
Chita	172,000	242,000	41
Ordzhonikidze	164,000	236,000	44
Semipalatinsk	156,000	236,000	51
Vladimir	154,000	234,000	52
Orel	150,000	232,000	55
Vitebsk	148,000	231,000	56
Ust-Kamenogorsk	150,000	230,000	53
Tambov	172,000	229,000	33
Sevastopol	144,000	229,000	59
Dneprodzerzhinsk	194,000	227,000	17
Orsk	176,000	225,000	28
Sochi	127,000	224,000	77
Kostroma	172,000	223,000	30
Dzerzhinsk	164,000	221,000	35
Poltava	143,000	220,000	54
Rybinsk	182,000	218,000	20
Komsomolsk-on-Amur	177,000	218,000	23
Cheboksary	104,000	216,000	108
Vinnitsa	122,000	211,000	73
Kaluga	134,000	211,000	57
Smolensk	147,000	211,000	43
Shakhty	196,000	205,000	5
Angarsk	135,000	204,000	51
Mogilev	122,000	202,000	66
Stavropol	141,000	198,000	41
Saransk	91,000	190,000	109
Kirovabad	136,000	190,000	39
Cherepovets	92,000	189,000	104
Kirovograd	132,000	189,000	43
Andizhan	131,000	188,000	44
Dzhambul	113,000	188,000	66
Chernovtsy	152,000	187,000	23
Pavlodar	90,000	187,000	107
Biysk	146,000	186,000	28
Makhachkala	119,000	186,000	56
Sterlitamak	112,000	185,000	66
Petrozavodsk	135,000	185,000	37
Zlatoust	161,000	181,000	12
Tselinograd (Akmolinsk)	99,000	180,000	82
Vologda	139,000	178,000	28
Namangan	123,000	175,000	42
Syzran	148,000	174,000	17
Petropavlovsk (North Kazakhstan O.)	131,000	173,000	32
Podolsk	129,000	169,000	30
Kamensk-Uralskiy	141,000	169,000	20
Temirtau	77,000	167,000	117

Table 1   Populations of Cities with More than 100,000 People and Other Political Centers, Listed in Order of 1970 Population (Continued)

City	January 15, 1959	January 15, 1970	% Increase
Yoshkar-Ola	89,000	166,000	87
Leninakan	108,000	164,000	51
Novocherkassk	123,000	162,000	32
Kutaisi	128,000	161,000	26
Zhitomir	106,000	161,000	52
Sumy	98,000	159,000	63
Chernigov	90,000	159,000	78
Cherkassy	85,000	159,000	87
Kopeysk	162,000	156,000	−4
Bratsk	43,000	155,000	259
Petropavlovsk-Kamchatsky	86,000	154,000	80
Belgorod	72,000	151,000	109
Kramatorsk	115,000	151,000	30
Aktyubinsk	97,000	150,000	55
Kremenchug	87,000	148,000	71
Nalchik	88,000	146,000	67
Armavir	111,000	146,000	31
Berezniki	106,000	145,000	37
Rubtsovsk	111,000	145,000	30
Severodvinsk	79,000	145,000	84
Volzhskiy	67,000	142,000	113
Klaypeda	90,000	140,000	56
Lyubertsy	95,000	139,000	47
Bobruysk	98,000	138,000	41
Kadiyevka	123,000	137,000	12
Melitopol	95,000	137,000	45
Norilsk	118,000	136,000	15
Kolomna	118,000	136,000	15
Uralsk	99,000	134,000	36
Novomoskovsk	107,000	134,000	26
Kokand	105,000	133,000	27
Novorossiysk	93,000	133,000	42
Grodno	73,000	132,000	82
Miass	98,000	132,000	34
Engels	91,000	130,000	43
Novgorod	61,000	128,000	111
Blagoveshchensk	94,000	128,000	136
Leninsk-Kuznetskiy	132,000	128,000	−3
Kerch	98,000	128,000	30
Ussuriysk	104,000	128,000	23
Pskov	81,000	127,000	56
Kiselevsk	128,000	126,000	−1
Syktyvkar	69,000	125,000	82
Nikopol	83,000	125,000	50
Sumgait	51,000	124,000	142
Slavyansk	99,000	124.000	26

*Table 1   Populations of Cities with More than 100,000 People
and Other Political Centers, Listed in Order of 1970 Population (Continued)*

City	January 15, 1959	January 15, 1970	% Increase
Serpukhov	106,000	124,000	17
Kovrov	99,000	123,000	25
Kustanay	86,000	123,000	43
Kommunarsk	98,000	123,000	26
Elektrostal	97,000	123,000	27
Kzyl-Orda	66,000	123,000	87
Brest	74,000	122,000	65
Osh	65,000	120,000	85
Orekhovo-Zuyevo	108,000	120,000	11
Mytishchi	99,000	119,000	20
Pervouralsk	90,000	117,000	29
Lisichansk	104,000	117,000	13
Rovno	56,000	116,000	106
Salavat	61,000	114,000	88
Khmelnitskiy	62,000	113,000	81
Gurev	79,000	113,000	43
Bukhara	69,000	112,000	61
Fergana	72,000	111,000	55
Maykop	82,000	111,000	35
Belaya Tserkov	71,000	109,000	54
Belovo	100,000	108,000	8
Yakutsk	74,000	108,000	45
Chirchik	66,000	108,000	64
Kirovakan	49,000	107,000	116
Andzhero-Sudzhensk	116,000	106,000	−8
Yuzhno-Sakhalinsk	86,000	106,000	24
Konstantinovka	89,000	106,000	19
Kaliningrad (Moscow O.)	72,000	106,000	47
Tirispol	63,000	106,000	69
Ivano-Frankovsk	66,000	105,000	58
Nakhodka	64,000	105,000	64
Noginsk	93,000	104,000	12
Novokuybyshevsk	63,000	104,000	65
Balakovo	36,000	103,000	181
Leninabad	77,000	103,000	38
Krasnyy Luch	94,000	102,000	9
Sukhumi	65,000	102,000	57
Beltsy	66,000	102,000	54
Novoshakhtinsk	104,000	102,000	−2
Baranovichi	58,000	102,000	75
Batumi	82,000	101,000	23
Orsha	64,000	101,000	56
Elets	78,000	101,000	29
Daugavpils	65,000	101,000	54
Serov	98,000	100,000	3
Berdyansk	65,000	100,000	53
Lutsk	56,000	94,000	69

Table 1   Populations of Cities with More than 100,000 People and Other Political Centers, Listed in Order of 1970 Population (Continued)

City	January 15, 1959	January 15, 1970	% Increase
Magadan	62,000	92,000	48
Abakan	56,000	90,000	60
Ternopol	52,000	85,000	62
Kokchetav	53,000	81,000	53
Urgench	44,000	76,000	74
Nukus	39,000	74,000	89
Karshi	33,000	71,000	117
Cherkessk	42,000	67,000	61
Uzhgorod	47,000	65,000	37
Taldy-Kurgan	41,000	61,000	46
Birobidzhan	41,000	56,000	37
Kyzyl	34,000	52,000	50
Elista	23,000	50,000	115
Termez	22,000	35,000	57
Gorno-Altaysk	28,000	34,000	25
Nakhichevan	24,000	33,000	37
Gulistan	18,000	31,000	68
Tskhinvali	22,000	30,000	40
Stepanakert	20,000	30,000	54
Khorog	8,000	12,000	50

Table 2 Populations of Political Units

Region	Population January 15, 1970	% Urban	% Rural
U.S.S.R.	241,748,000	56	44
R.S.F.S.R.	130,090,000	62	38
Altay Kray	2,670,000	46	54
Gorno-Altay A.O.	168,000	24	76
Khabarovsk Kray	1,346,000	78	22
Jewish A.O.	173,000	69	31
Krasnodar Kray	4,511,000	47	53
Adyge A.O.	386,000	40	60
Krasnoyarsk Kray	2,962,000	62	38
Khakass A.O.	446,000	60	40
Taymyr N.O.	38,000	62	38
Evenki N.O.	13,000	28	72
Maritime Kray	1,722,000	73	27
Stavropol Kray	2,306,000	42	58
Karachay-Cherkess A.O.	345,000	33	67
Amur Oblast	793,000	62	38
Arkhangel Oblast	1,402,000	66	34
Nenets N.O.	39,000	55	45
Astrakhan Oblast	868,000	61	39
Belgorod Oblast	1,261,000	35	65
Bryansk Oblast	1,582,000	47	53
Chelyabinsk Oblast	3,289,000	78	22
Chita Oblast	1,145,000	57	43
Aga-Buryat N.O.	66,000	21	79
Gorky Oblast	3,683,000	65	35
Irkutsk Oblast	2,314,000	72	28
Ust-Orda Buryat N.O.	146,000	17	83
Ivanovo Oblast	1,338,000	75	25
Kalinin Oblast	1,718,000	57	43
Kaliningrad Oblast	732,000	73	27
Kaluga Oblast	995,000	52	48
Kamchatka Oblast	287,000	76	24
Koryak N.O.	31,000	34	66
Kemerovo Oblast	2,918,000	82	18
Kirov Oblast	1,726,000	55	45
Kostroma Oblast	871,000	53	47
Kurgan Oblast	1,085,000	43	57
Kursk Oblast	1,474,000	33	67
Kuybyshev Oblast	2,752,000	72	28
Leningrad City Soviet	3,950,000	100	
Leningrad Oblast	1,436,000	61	39
Lipetsk Oblast	1,224,000	44	56
Magadan Oblast	352,000	75	25
Chukchi N.O.	101,000	69	31
Moscow City Soviet	7,061,000	100	
Moscow Oblast	5,774,000	69	31
Murmansk Oblast	799,000	89	11
Novgorod Oblast	722,000	53	47
Novosibirsk Oblast	2,505,000	65	35

Table 2   *Populations of Political Units (Continued)*

Region	Population January 15, 1970	% Urban	% Rural
Omsk Oblast	1,824,000	55	45
Orel Oblast	931,000	39	61
Orenburg Oblast	2,050,000	53	47
Penza Oblast	1,536,000	44	56
Perm Oblast	3,024,000	67	33
Komi-Permyak N.O.	212,000	19	81
Pskov Oblast	876,000	43	57
Rostov Oblast	3,832,000	63	37
Ryazan Oblast	1,412,000	47	53
Sakhalin Oblast	616,000	78	22
Saratov Oblast	2,454,000	65	35
Smolensk Oblast	1,106,000	48	52
Sverdlovsk Oblast	4,319,000	81	19
Tambov Oblast	1,511,000	39	61
Tomsk Oblast	786,000	59	41
Tula Oblast	1,953,000	71	29
Tyumen Oblast	1,407,000	49	51
Khanti-Mansy N.O.	272,000	63	37
Yamal-Nenets N.O.	80,000	43	57
Ulyanovsk Oblast	1,225,000	52	48
Vladimir Oblast	1,512,000	68	32
Volgograd Oblast	2,324,000	66	34
Vologda Oblast	1,296,000	48	52
Voronezh Oblast	2,527,000	46	54
Yaroslavl Oblast	1,400,000	70	30
Bashkir A.S.S.R.	3,819,000	48	52
Buryat A.S.S.R.	812,000	45	55
Chechen-Ingush A.S.S.R.	1,065,000	42	58
Chuvash A.S.S.R.	1,224,000	36	64
Dagestan A.S.S.R.	1,429,000	35	65
Kabardino-Balkar A.S.S.R.	589,000	48	52
Kalmyk A.S.S.R.	268,000	34	66
Karelian A.S.S.R.	714,000	69	31
Komi A.S.S.R.	965,000	62	38
Mari A.S.S.R.	685,000	41	59
Mordovian A.S.S.R.	1,030,000	36	64
North-Osetian A.S.S.R.	553,000	64	36
Tatar A.S.S.R.	3,131,000	52	48
Tuva A.S.S.R.	231,000	38	62
Udmurt A.S.S.R.	1,417,000	57	43
Yakut A.S.S.R.	664,000	56	44
Ukrainian S.S.R.	47,136,000	55	45
Cherkassy Oblast	1,536,000	37	63
Chernigov Oblast	1,560,000	35	65
Chernovtsy Oblast	845,000	35	65
Crimea Oblast	1,814,000	63	37
Dnepropetrovsk Oblast	3,344,000	76	24
Donetsk Oblast	4,894,000	87	13
Ivano-Frankovsk Oblast	1,250,000	31	69

Table 2   *Populations of Political Units (Continued)*

Region	Population January 15, 1970	% Urban	% Rural
Kharkov Oblast	2,826,000	69	31
Kherson Oblast	1,031,000	54	46
Khmelnitsky Oblast	1,616,000	27	73
Kiev City	1,632,000	100	
Kiev Oblast	1,836,000	36	64
Kirovograd Oblast	1,260,000	44	56
Lvov Oblast	2,428,000	47	53
Nikolayev Oblast	1,148,000	53	47
Odessa Oblast	2,390,000	56	44
Poltava Oblast	1,706,000	40	60
Rovno Oblast	1,048,000	28	72
Sumy Oblast	1,505,000	44	56
Ternopol Oblast	1,153,000	23	77
Transcarpathia Oblast	1,057,000	30	70
Vinnitsa Oblast	2,132,000	25	75
Volyn Oblast	975,000	32	68
Voroshilovgrad Oblast (Lugansk)	2,749,000	83	17
Zaporozhye Oblast	1,775,000	66	34
Zhitomir Oblast	1,626,000	35	65
Belorussian S.S.R.	9,003,000	43	57
Brest Oblast	1,295,000	35	65
Gomel Oblast	1,534,000	40	60
Grodno Oblast	1,121,000	33	67
Minsk City Soviet	916,000	100	
Minsk Oblast	1,540,000	27	73
Mogilev Oblast	1,227,000	43	57
Vitebsk Oblast	1,370,000	45	55
Uzbek S.S.R.	11,963,000	36	64
Andizhan Oblast	1,060,000	24	76
Bukhara Oblast	934,000	31	69
Fergana Oblast	1,330,000	33	67
Kashkadarya Oblast	802,000	17	83
Khorezm Oblast	554,000	19	81
Namangan Oblast	847,000	29	71
Samarkand Oblast	1,470,000	27	73
Surkhandarya Oblast	662,000	16	84
Syrdarya Oblast	737,000	23	77
Tashkent City	1,385,000	100	
Tashkent Oblast	1,480,000	40	60
Kara-Kalpak A.S.S.R.	702,000	36	64
Kazakh S.S.R.	12,850,000	51	49
Aktyubinsk Oblast	550,000	45	55
Alma-Ata City	730,000	100	
Alma-Ata Oblast	713,000	18	82
Chimkent Oblast	1,128,000	41	59
Dzhambul Oblast	795,000	40	60
East Kazakhstan Oblast	846,000	57	43
Guryev Oblast	499,000	66	34

Table 2   Populations of Political Units (Continued)

Region	Population January 15, 1970	% Urban	% Rural
Karaganda Oblast	1,552,000	81	19
Kokchetav Oblast	590,000	30	70
Kustanay Oblast	985,000	39	61
Kzyl-Orda Oblast	492,000	55	45
North Kazakhstan Oblast	557,000	38	62
Pavlodar Oblast	697,000	49	51
Semipalatinsk Oblast	712,000	44	56
Taldy-Kurgan Oblast	610,000	39	61
Tselinograd Oblast	881,000	50	50
Uralsk Oblast	513,000	31	69
Georgian S.S.R.	4,688,000	48	52
Abkhaz A.S.S.R.	487,000	44	56
Adzhar A.S.S.R.	310,000	44	56
South-Osetian A.O.	100,000	37	63
Azerbaydzhan S.S.R.	5,111,000	50	50
Nagorno-Karabakh A.O.	149,000	38	62
Nakhichevan A.S.S.R.	202,000	24	76
Lithuanian S.S.R.	3,129,000	50	50
Moldavian S.S.R.	3,572,000	32	68
Latvian S.S.R.	2,365,000	62	38
Kirgiz S.S.R.	2,933,000	37	63
Osh Oblast	1,233,000	31	69
Tadzhik S.S.R.	2,900,000	37	63
Gorno-Badakhshan A.O.	98,000	13	87
Armenian S.S.R.	2,493,000	59	41
Turkmen S.S.R.	2,158,000	48	52
Estonian S.S.R.	1,357,000	65	35

Table 3 Populations of SSRs and Economic Regions

Region	January 15, 1959	January 15, 1970	% Increase
U.S.S.R.	208,827,000	241,748,000	16
R.S.F.S.R.	117,534,000	130,090,000	11
Northwest	10,865,000	12,160,000	12
Center	25,718,000	27,653,000	8
Volga-Vyatka	8,252,000	8,348,000	1
Central Black Earth	7,769,000	7,997,000	3
Povolzhye	15,975,000	18,377,000	15
North Caucasus	11,601,000	14,285,000	23
Ural	14,184,000	15,184,000	7
West Siberia	11,252,000	12,110,000	8
East Siberia	6,473,000	7,464,000	15
Far East	4,834,000	5,780,000	20
Kaliningrad Oblast	611,000	732,000	20
Ukraine S.S.R.	41,869,000	47,136,000	13
Donets-Dnieper	17,766,000	20,059,000	13
South West	19,078,000	20,694,000	9
South	5,075,000	6,383,000	26
Belorussia S.S.R.	8,056,000	9,033,000	12
Uzbek S.S.R.	8,261,000	11,963,000	45
Kazakh S.S.R.	9,153,000	12,850,000	40
Georgia S.S.R.	4,044,000	4,688,000	16
Azerbaydzhan S.S.R.	3,698,000	5,111,000	38
Lithuania S.S.R.	2,711,000	3,129,000	15
Moldavia S.S.R.	2,885,000	3,572,000	24
Latvia S.S.R.	2,093,000	2,365,000	13
Kirgiz S.S.R.	2,066,000	2,933,000	42
Tadzhik S.S.R.	1,981,000	2,900,000	46
Armenia S.S.R.	1,763,000	2,493,000	41
Turkmen S.S.R.	1,516,000	2,158,000	42
Estonia S.S.R.	1,197,000	1,357,000	13

The author acknowledges the help of Mrs. Ann Healy and Mr. Steven Pease in translating and arranging the above information.

Index

Abakán, 285
Abkház A.S.S.R., 184, 186, 187
Abkházian people, 357
Abovyan, 206
Achak, 232, 256
Achinsk, 300, 320, 524
Ádler, 213
Administrative subdivisions, 23, 24
Adygé A. O., 184, 186
Adzhár A.S.S.R., 184, 186, 187
Afghanets, 243
Afghanistan, 10, 13, 627, 628, 632, 639
Africa, 634, 640
Afrosiab, 6, 10; see also Samarkánd
Agá Buryát N.O., 298, 300
Agriculture, 20, 21, 22, 23, 38, 72, 98, 108,
    109, 120, 122, 128, 130, 157, 159, 165,
    175, 202, 239, 243, 278, 308, 311, 313,
    398–459
    settlements, 314
Agrogorods, 406
Aid, economic, 590, 628, 629, 630, 631, 632, 633,
    636, 637, 638, 640, 641
Air transport, 582, 584
Akademgorodok (Academic Town), 291
Ákhtuba, 72, 73
Akmólinsk, city of, 221
    Oblast, 216, 294
    see also Tselinográd
Aksáy, 8, 9
Akstafá, 189
Aksú River, 235
Aktáu, 256; see also Shevchénko
Aktyúbinsk, city of, 272, 293
    Oblast, 218, 270, 272
Alaska, 6, 8
Alaverdí, 186, 208, 521
Aláy, Range, 237
    Valley, 232, 237
Alchévsk, see Kommunársk

Aldán Plateau, 307, 308
Aleksándrovsk, 300, 328
Alekséyevka, 62
Alexander I, 10
Alexander Nevsky, 7
Alfalfa, 22, 73, 202, 239, 241, 247, 448, 455
Algeria, 624, 625
Alluvial fans, 239
Almá-Atá, city of, 216, 218, 232, 243, 260
    Oblast, 216, 218
Almalýk, 232, 521
Almáznaya, 104, 107
Almétyevsk, 82
Altáy, Kray, 270, 272
    Mountains, 13, 14, 272, 274
Aluminum, 107, 126, 133, 151, 157, 171, 206, 208,
    209, 254, 287, 316, 320, 522, 523, 524, 525
Alunite, 524
Alúshta, 118
Amú-Daryá, 232, 233, 234, 237, 239, 245, 246, 250,
    251, 253, 254
Amúr, Oblast, 22, 298, 300
    Provinces, 10, 303
    River, 8, 17, 300, 311
Anabár Shield, 307
Anádyr Mountains, 308
Andizhán, city of, 218, 262
    Oblast, 216
Angará River, 300, 307, 310, 316
Angársk, 300, 316, 325, 490
Angrén, city of, 232
    River, 243, 255
Anzhéro-Súdzhensk, 272, 293
Apatite, 39, 40, 64, 150, 154, 528; see also Phosphate
Apples, 115
Apsherón Peninsula, 189
Arab-Israeli War, 625
Arabs, 219
Aragáts, Mount, 195
Aráks River, 189, 202, 204, 205

Arál Sea, 13, 14, 218, 232, 233, 234
Ararát, Mount, 189, 195
Archangel, city of, 148, 154, 158
  Oblast, 146, 147, 148, 154
Argún River, 311
Ariqs, 259
Arkalýk, 272, 273, 287, 524
Arménian, people, 187, 350
  Plateau, 188, 189, 195, 202, 211
  S.S.R., 10, 184, 186
Artémovsk, 102, 107, 526
Arýs River, 245
Asbestos, 175, 288
Ashkhabád, 216, 218, 243, 247, 261
Aŝtrakhan, city of, 5, 72, 73, 82, 86
  Oblast, 66, 67
Aswan Dam, 636
Atasúskiy, 273
Atomic power, 63, 151, 175, 233, 501, 503
Atrék River, 247
Automobile, 50, 209, 212, 532, 557, 583, 585, 586
Autonomous oblast (A.O.), 24
Autonomous Soviet Socialist Republic (A.S.S.R.), 24
Avars, 5
Azerbaydzhánian, people, 187
  S.S.R., 10, 184, 186
Azóv Sea, 9, 44

Baghdad Pact, 624
Bakál, 172
Bakchar, 286
Bakú, city of, 10, 75, 82, 86, 185, 186, 189, 207, 208, 209
  oil fields, 487
Balakhná, 51
Balakóvo, 81
Balkars, 364
Balkhán Mountains, 230, 232
Balkháŝh, city of, 218, 232, 257, 287
  Lake, 218; see also Lake Balkháŝh
Baltic, Republics, 125, 126, 127
  Sea, 5, 7, 9, 44
Baltic–White Sea Canal, 132, 160
Barába Steppe, 279, 280
Bárents Sea, 148, 151, 153
Barley, 20, 22, 38, 60, 398, 439, 454
Barnaúl, 221, 272, 293
Barsuki, 234
Bashkír, A.S.S.R., 69, 75, 82, 164, 168
  oil fields, 487
  people, 167
Baskunchák, Lake, 83; see also Lake Baskunchák
Basmachi Revolt, 222
Batúmi, 17, 186, 189, 208, 212
Bauxite, 132, 157, 171, 522, 524; see also Aluminum
Bayrám-Ali, 232, 256
Begovát, 263; see also Bekabád
Bekabád, 218, 263, 512; see also Begovát
Bekdash, 232, 233
Bélaya River, 167

Bélgorod, chalk, 61
  city of, 64
  Oblast, 39, 56, 60, 61, 62
Belogórsk, 524
Belomórsk, 148, 151, 154
Belorétsk, 168
Belorússian S.S.R. (White Russia), 7, 10, 24, 124, 127
  oil fields, 489
Belóvo, 272, 293
Belozerka iron deposit, 106, 515
Béltsy Steppe, 120
Bereznikí, 168, 175, 182, 526, 528
Berézovo, 289
Bering, Sea, 14, 300
  Straits, 8
Bessarábia, 6, 9, 10, 11, 93, 119
Betpák-Dalá, 232, 235
Bhilai steel mill, 638
Bidzhán River, 311
Birá River, 311
Birobidzhán, 300, 311, 327
Birth rate, 336, 340, 341
Biysk, 272, 293
Black earth belt, 20, 22, 425
Black Sea, 7, 9, 10, 13, 14, 17, 22, 44, 59, 96
  Germans, 365
  Steppes, 114, 115, 116
Blagodát, 172
Blagovéshchensk, 300, 311, 327
Bodaybó, 300, 321
Boksitogórsk, 126, 132, 522
Bolshié Barsukí, 232, 234
Bolshoy Theater, 47
Bora wind, 191
Boxer Rebellion, 10
Bozshakúl, 272, 276, 521
Bratsk, city of, 300, 320, 327, 524
  Dam, 316
Brest Oblast, 124, 126
British, 10
Bryánsk, City of, 63, 126, 142
  Oblast, 124, 126
Buckwheat, 131, 454
Budzhák Steppe, 120
Bukhará, city of, 10, 218, 222, 223, 263
  Khanate, 6
  Oblast, 216
  The People's Soviet Republic of, 222
Bukhtarmá Dam, 276
Bukovína, 9, 10, 11, 93, 119
Bulgar, 67
Buréya, coal field, 315
  River, 311
Buryát A.S.S.R., 298, 300, 303, 311
Byrránga Mountains, 308
Byzantine Empire, 7

Cabbage, 20
Camels, 240, 241, 453, 456
Canals, 555

Caravan route, 241, 259
Carpathian Mountains, 12, 13, 22, 95, 103, 114
Cáspian, Basin, 230, 252
   Lowland, 81, 83
   Sea, 5, 10, 13, 14, 17, 20, 22, 44, 69, 72, 82, 234, 251, 253
Catherine II (The Great), 9, 23, 29, 139
Cattle, 60, 73, 449, 456
Caucasian people, 345
Caucasus, 9, 10, 13, 22, 40, 43, 184, 185, 186, 188, 189; *see also* North Caucasian Foreland; Transcaucasia
Caviar, 83
C E M A, 595–602
Cement, 61, 62, 64, 73, 76, 87, 209, 212
Census, 335, 657–667
C E N T O, 624; *see also* Baghdad Pact
Central Black Earth Region, 52, 56–65
Central Committee of the Communist Party, 26
Central Industrial Region, 29, 30, 34–54
Central Lenin Stadium, 48
Central Russian Uplands, 11, 12, 38, 58
Central Siberian Uplands, 13, 14, 300, 307
Chapli Island, 101
Chardara Dam, 249
Chardzhoú, 218, 263
Charentsavan, 206
Charles XII, 9
Cheboksáry, 81
Chechén-Ingúsh, A.S.S.R., 184, 186
   people, 364
Chelekén Peninsula, 218, 232, 233
Chelyábinsk, city of, 168, 172, 178, 515
   Oblast, 164, 168
Chemicals, 53, 106, 107, 133, 134, 143, 157, 175, 176, 182, 208, 212, 257, 291, 525, 527
Cheremkhóvo, city of, 300, 314, 325
   coal basin, 484
Cherepovéts, 62, 83, 148, 151, 157, 159, 160, 512
Chernígov, 487
Chernozem, 20, 22, 58
Chérskiy Mountains, 308
Chiatúra, 189, 207, 518
Chimként, city of, 218, 232, 257, 262
   Oblast, 216, 218, 522
China, 10, 14, 303, 330, 604, 605, 606, 608, 609, 638
Chinese, Eastern Railway, 302
   people, 8, 222, 223, 224
Chirchík, city of, 218, 262
   River, 243, 245, 255
Chitá, city of, 300, 311, 327
   Oblast, 298, 300
Chkálov, 180
Chrome, 172, 287, 518
Chrome-Tau, 172
Chu, River, 232, 235, 238
   Valley, 245
Chudskóe, 7; *see also* Lake Peipus
Chu–Ili Mountains, 232, 238
Chúkchi N.O., 298, 300

Chukótsk Mountains, 308
   Sea, 300
Chulák-Táu, 258
Chusováya River, 167
Chusovóy, 168, 172, 515
Chuvásh A.S.S.R., 66, 67, 69
Cities, manufacturing types, 543–547
   sizes of, 380–385, 657–662
Citrus fruits, 22, 194, 195, 197, 198, 199, 200, 247, 446, 455
Civil war, 10
Climate, of the Caucasus, 190, 191, 192, 193, 195, 196, 198, 201, 203
   of the Central Black Earth Region, 58
   of the Central Industrial Region, 38
   of Eastern Siberia and the Soviet Far East, 304
   of the European North, 150
   of the European West, 130
   of Middle Asia and Southern Kazakhstan, 217, 233, 238
   of the Povolzhye and Lower Don, 69, 70, 72
   of Ukraine and Moldavia, 96, 115, 120
   of the Urals, 176
   of the U.S.S.R., 11, 14, 17, 20, 22, 58, 69, 72, 96, 109, 120, 130, 147, 216, 425
   of Western Siberia and Northern Kazakhstan, 274
Clover, 447, 455
Coal, 38, 39, 42, 62, 75, 93, 101, 102, 104, 105, 107, 111, 151, 157, 173, 207, 257, 283, 284, 314, 477, 479, 480, 481, 482, 483, 484, 485, 486, 487, 572
Cólchis Lowland, 17, 22, 189, 195, 201
Cold pole, 305
Collective farms, 405, 410, 411, 412, 413, 422; *see also* Kolkhoz
Collectivization, 405
Communist Party, 26; *see also* Central Committee of the Communist Party
Congo, 630
Coniferous forests, 17, 20
Constantinople (Istanbul), 5, 7
Constitution of the U.S.S.R., 24, 359
Copper, 11, 151, 171, 208, 257, 287, 320, 519, 520
Corn, 17, 22, 60, 61, 73, 108, 110, 115, 122, 193, 201, 415, 417, 420, 433, 435, 436
Cossack, 8, 9, 59, 93, 113, 114, 220, 289, 301, 304
Cotton, 22, 40, 41, 100, 202, 239, 241, 243, 247, 263, 404, 425, 445, 455, 534
Council for Economic Mutual Assistance, *see* C E M A
Council of Ministers, 26
Crimea, Mountains, 13, 103, 117, 118
   Oblast, 90
   Peninsula, 5, 13, 20, 93, 95, 96, 99, 105, 107, 115, 116, 118
   Tatars, 364
   War, 8, 119
Crystalline shield, 149, 150
Cuba, 610, 611
Cuestas, 11, 69, 109, 130, 150
Cyclonic storms, 14, 17, 20
Czechoslovakia, 11, 598, 602, 603

Dagestán A.S.S.R., 184, 186, 187, 207
Dairying, 20, 38, 73, 159, 456
Danube River, 94, 103, 114
Darvazá, 232, 256
Dasháva, 102, 111, 112, 134, 494
Dashkesán, 189, 208
Dáugava River, *see* Western Dviná River
Death rate, 336
Denikin, 10
Derbént, 186, 189, 208
Desalinization, 233, 503
Desert, 13, 14, 20, 22, 72, 73
Desná, 113
Diamonds, 321
Dneprodzerzhinsk, 99, 101, 103, 104, 107
Dnepropetróvsk, 97, 101, 103, 104, 107
Dneprorudnoye, 102, 104, 106, 515
Dniéper, Dam, 99, 100, 105
   River, 5, 9, 94, 95, 96, 99, 103, 105, 110, 113, 114,
      115, 130
Dniéster River, 9, 94, 103, 113, 114, 115, 119
Don Cossack, 8, 9, 59
Donéts, Basin, 62, 90, 101, 104, 105, 106, 107, 481,
      484, 486, 506, 508
   Ridge, 11, 95, 103, 105
   River, 104
Donétsk, city of, 94, 97, 102, 103, 104, 106, 107
   Oblast, 105, 109
   see also Stálino
Donkey, 241, 256
Don River, 8, 9, 58, 63, 67, 69, 73, 78, 80, 84, 103,
      108
Dórpat, 142; *see also* Tártu
Drainage, 20
Drogóbych, city of, 102
   Oblast, 111
Drúzhba, 267
Drúzhba oil pipeline, 490, 602; *see also* Friendship
   pipeline
Dry farming, 22
Dungans, 223
Dushanbé, 216, 218, 261; *see also* Stalinabád
Dzerzhinsk, 51
Dzhalínda, 300
Dzhambúl, city of, 218, 221, 232, 262
   Oblast, 216, 218
   see also Yangi
Dzhezkazgán, 273, 287, 521
Dzungária, 224
   Alatáu, 223, 232, 238
   Gate, 13, 223, 238, 267

Eastern Sayan, 308, 310
East Germany, 602
East Kazakhstán Oblast, 270, 272
East Prussia, 125, 374
East Siberian Sea, 300
Ebe, 241
Economic regions, 26, 29

Educational system, 386, 387, 389
Egypt, 623, 624, 625
Ekibastúz, 174, 272, 273, 276, 285
Elbrús, Mount, 13, 193
Electric power, 40, 41, 44, 63, 75, 76, 81, 83, 86, 96,
      99, 101, 105, 135, 159, 174; *see also* Hydro-
      electricity; Thermal electricity
Electric transmission line, 40
Eltón, Lake, 83
Émba, oil fields, 230, 256, 488
   River, 230, 232, 233, 239, 272, 276
Éngels, 86
England, 616
Estonian S.S.R., 10, 11, 124, 125, 126, 498
Ethnic groups, 271; *see also* Nationalities
European North, 146—162
European Plain, 11
Evaporation rates, 14
Evénki N.O., 298, 300

Fallow, 421
Far East, 8, 10, 11, 14, 22, 23, 298
Farkhád Dam, 244, 249
Farming, 20, 22, 38, 60, 73, 109, 242
Fergána, Basin, 232, 237, 238, 243, 245, 248, 488
   city of, 218, 262
   Oblast, 216
Fertilizer, 106, 134, 135, 150, 160, 208, 256, 418,
      422, 528, 529; *see also* Industry, fertilizer
Fiat, 84, 87, 533, 585
Finland, 6, 9, 10, 11, 149, 615, 616
Finno-Ugrian people, 64, 69, 167, 350
Fish, 75, 82, 83, 86, 117, 119, 131, 151, 152, 323,
      324, 536, 537, 538, 645, 647, 648
Flax, 20, 22, 38, 40, 60, 72, 129, 398, 444, 455
Foehn winds, 196, 240
Foreign policy, 590—592
Foreign trade, 592—602
Forest, 22, 131, 154, 290, 321
Fort Ross, 8
France, 617
Franz Josef Land, 154
Freight traffic, 42, 76, 77, 78, 551, 552, 567, 568, 569,
      570, 571, 575, 578, 577
Friendship pipeline, 82, 113, 134; *see also* Druzhba oil
   pipeline
Frolóvo, 86
Fruit, 38
Frúnze, 216, 218, 260
Fuels, 40, 43, 53; *see also* Coal; Gas; Oil
Furs, 8, 87, 303, 374

Galicia, 93
Garden Ring, 45; *see also* Sadovaya Ulitsa
Gas, natural, 40, 43, 63, 75, 76, 82, 83, 86, 101, 102,
      111, 112, 135, 157, 160, 173, 174, 205, 207, 209,
      212, 254, 256, 283, 288, 289, 316, 477, 479, 481,
      493, 494, 495, 496, 497
Gaurdák, 232

Gay, 168, 171, 521
Gazli, 232, 256, 494
Genghis Khan, 5, 220
Georgia, 10
Georgian, Military Highway, 190
  people, 187
  S.S.R., 184, 186
Germans, 7, 67, 105, 352, 365
Germany, 10, 11, 598, 616
Ghana, 633
Gimóly, 148, 151
Gissár Mountains, 237
Glaciation, 38, 96, 114, 127, 128, 130, 147, 149
Glauber's salt, 526
Glint, the, 126, 129
Goats, 452, 456
Gold, 171, 287, 304, 320, 321, 525
Golódnaya Steppe, 245; *see also* Hungry Steppe
Gómel, city of, 126, 142
  Oblast, 124, 126
Góri, 186, 208
Gorky, city of, 35, 36, 39, 40, 44, 50, 51, 53, 67, 83,
  492, 531
  Kray, 67
  Oblast, 34, 36, 66, 67
  Park, 49
  Sea, 44
  see also Nizhny Novgorod
Górlovka, 103, 106
Górnaya Shóriya, 273, 285, 515
Górno-Altáy A.O., 270, 272
Górno-Badakhshán A.O., 216, 218
Gorodéts, 44
Goths, 5
Government, of the U.S.S.R., 26
Grain, 42
  Sorghums, 22
Grapes, 22, 200, 455
Grazing, 22, 38, 114, 193, 202, 239, 240
Great Caucasus, 9, 13, 189
Great Fergana Canal, 247, 248
Great Turkmen Canal, 251
Greeks, 9
Green belt, 46
Gródno Oblast, 124, 126
Gross national product, 460, 461
Grózny, 186, 189, 207, 208, 212, 487, 492
Gruzian people, 350; *see also* Georgian
Gúbkin, 62, 515
Gulf of Finland, 126, 130, 137, 140, 150, 160
Gulf of Pénzhina, 323
Gulf of Ríga, 126, 130, 131
GUM (state department store), 46, 47
Gúryev, city of, 218, 256, 263, 489
  Oblast, 216, 218
Gúryevsk, 272

Hanseatic League, 5, 141, 143
Hay, 20, 22, 38, 73

Hemp, 60, 455, 535
Hermitage Museum, 137, 138, 139
Hero cities, 140
Highways, 42, 46, 557, 558
Hindu Kush, 13, 236
Hogs, 38, 60, 451, 456
Horses, 456
House of Nationalities, 26
House of the Union, 26
Housing, 378
Hungary, 602
Hungry Steppe, 235, 249; *see also* Golódnaya Steppe
Huns, 5
Hydroelectricity, 41, 75, 76, 81, 83, 96, 99, 101, 105,
  107, 132, 151, 174, 204, 206, 249, 254, 255, 276,
  277, 316, 318, 448, 500, 501, 502, 503
Hydrology, 238

Igárka, 300, 322
Igrim, 289
Ilétsk, 175
Ili, District, 224
  River, 232, 235, 239
Ilmen, Lake, 6
India, 10, 637, 638
Indigirka River, 300, 308
Indonesia, 632, 639
Industrialization, 39, 73, 471, 472, 473, 474
Industrial location, 473, 476, 478
Industrial Revolution, 140
Industry, 26, 75, 127, 133, 141, 460–549
  chemical, 38, 39, 40, 41, 63, 83, 84, 85, 86, 113
  fertilizer, 39, 52, 61, 83
  iron and steel, 39, 40, 41, 52
  lumbering, 42, 75, 77, 81, 82, 83, 101; *see also*
    Lumber; Timber
  machine building, 40, 50, 52, 84, 85
  oil and gas, 42, 43, 76, 77, 82, 86
  textiles, 40, 41, 52
  see also Cement; Chemicals; Fertilizer; Gas; Iron and
    steel; Oil; Ship building; Synthetic rubber
Inguri River, 204
Ingursk, 204
International relations, 590–651
Iran, 10, 13, 625, 626, 627; *see also* Persia
Iraq, 623, 624, 625
Irkútsk, Basin, 311
  city of, 300, 325
  hydroelectric plant, 316
  Oblast, 298, 300
Iron and steel, 62, 64, 85, 93, 105, 106, 151, 159, 160,
  170, 172, 173, 176, 180, 208, 212, 263, 284, 285,
  286, 287, 315, 316, 505–519
Iron ore, 39, 52, 61, 101, 102, 104, 105, 107, 119, 171,
  172, 173, 180, 208, 284, 285, 286, 505, 506, 507,
  508, 509, 514, 515, 516, 517
Irrigation, 13, 17, 22, 72, 80, 81, 82, 96, 100, 116, 122,
  159, 193, 201, 202, 203, 204, 206, 238, 239, 243,
  277, 423, 424, 425

Irtýsh-Karaganda Canal, 276, 278
Irtýsh River, 272, 274, 276
Ishím, River, 274, 276
 Steppe, 279, 280
Ishimbáy, 173
Islam, 220
Israel, 623, 625
Issýk-Kul, 232, 237, 238
Italy, 617
Iván III (the Great), 6
Ivan IV (the Terrible), 7, 8
Ivánkovo, 43
Ivánovo, city of, 39, 40, 52, 83, 534
 Oblast, 34, 36, 44
Izba, 60, 110
Izhévsk, 168, 179
Izmail District, 115, 117

Japan, 10, 11, 302, 303, 316, 330, 609, 621
Japanese, 365
Jaxartes River, 219, 220; *see also* Syr Darya
Jewish, A. O., 298, 300, 311, 313, 327
Jews, 352, 365, 366
Jordan, 624
Jute, 455, 535

Kabardíno-Balkár A.S.S.R., 184, 186
Kachkanár, 172, 515
Kádievka, 104, 107
Kakhóvka, city of, 99
 Dam, 100, 116
Kalínin, city of, 34, 36, 39, 40, 43, 52
 Oblast, 34, 35, 36, 40, 43, 124, 126
 see also Tver
Kaliningrád, city of, 126, 131, 142
 Oblast, 6, 11, 124, 126, 127, 143, 365, 374
 see also Koenigsberg
Kálmyk, A.S.S.R., 66, 67, 68
 people, 67, 68, 220, 364
Kalúga Oblast, 34, 36, 124, 126
Kálush, 102, 113, 528
Káma River, 81, 159, 165, 167, 174, 182
Kamchátka, Oblast, 298, 300, 302, 309
 Peninsula, 14
Kamen, 272
Kámensk-Urálskiy, 168 ,171, 182, 524
Kamýshin, 87
Kandaláksha, Bay, 148
 city of, 148, 151, 524
Kánev, 99, 101
Kansk, 300
Kansk-Áchinsk, 215, 285, 315
Karabásh, 168, 171, 521
Kará-Bogáz-Gol, 218, 230, 232, 233, 252, 253, 526
Karacháy-Cherkéss A. O., 184, 186
Karacháy people, 364
Karadág, 189, 205, 207, 494
Karagandá, city of, 272, 286
 coal basin, 284, 285, 291, 481, 484

Oblast, 216, 218, 270, 272
Kára-Kalpák, A.S.S.R., 216, 218, 241, 247
 people, 228
Karakúl, 218, 240
 sheep, 241, 452
Kara-Kúm, 232, 234
 Canal, 233, 244, 250, 251
Kára Sea, 300
Karatál River, 232, 235
Karatáu, 230, 232, 235, 238, 258, 528; *see also*
 Chulák-Táu
Karélian, A.S.S.R., 146, 147, 148, 149, 357
 Isthmus, 11, 149
 people, 357
Karélo-Fínnish, Republic, 357
 S.S.R., 119, 149
Karsakpáy, 521
Karst topography, 188
Kashka-Daryá, 246, 254
Kashkadarya Oblast, 216
Káunas, 126, 132
Kazákh, folded country, 273
 people, 220, 224, 225, 226
 S.S.R. (Kazakhstán), 22, 26, 31, 217, 222, 270, 271
Kazalinsk Line, 266, 272
Kazán, 5, 7, 69, 73, 81, 83, 84, 85
Kelif, city of, 250
 Uzboy, 251
Kem, 148, 151
Kémerovo, city of, 272, 293
 Oblast, 270
Kenaf, 455
Kerch, city of, 101, 102, 104, 106, 107
 Peninsula, 105, 118, 119
Khabárovsk, city of, 8, 300, 311, 492
 Kray, 298, 300, 324
Khakáss A. O., 298, 300
Khalílovo, 515; *see also* Orsk-Khalílovo region
Khanate, of Bukhará, 6
 of Khivá, 6, 10, 221
Khantý-Mansí N.O., 270, 272
Khárkov, 97, 103, 107, 113, 114
Khartsýzsk, 104, 106, 107
Khata, 60, 110, 111
Khersón, 103, 117
Khibiny Mountains, 148, 150, 151
Khivá, city of, 218, 221, 222
 Khanate, 6
 Oasis, (Khorezm), 243, 247
Khlýnov, 86; *see also* Kírov
Khodzhént, 221; *see also* Leninabád
Khorézm, city of, 221, 225
 Oasis, 243; *see also* Khivá Oasis
 Oblast, 216, 247
 The Peoples Soviet Republic of, 222
Khozraschet, 422
Khrom-Tau, 273, 287
Kíev, 5, 9, 94, 96, 97, 101, 102, 108, 112, 113, 114
Kievan Rus, 5, 113, 142, 143

Kímry, 44
Kirgiz, A.S.S.R., 220, 222
  people, 220, 228, 229, 362
  S.S.R., 216, 218
Kírishi, 126, 133, 492
Kírov, city of, 86
  Oblast, 66, 67, 72, 146, 147, 148, 159
  Railroad, 151, 152
  see also Khlýnov; Vyátka
Kirovabád, 186, 189, 208, 209, 212, 524
Kirovakán, 186, 208
Kirovográd, city of, 103, 107, 110, 114
  Oblast, 90
Kirovsk, 148, 150, 154, 524, 528
Kiselévsk, 293
Kishinév, 103, 112, 120
Kízel, 168, 173
Kizelévsk, 272
Kizýl-Arvát, 218, 243
Kláypeda, 126, 142; *see also* Mémel
Klyázma River, 39
Kódry, 120
Koenigsberg, 125, 131, 142; *see also* Kaliningrád
Kokánd, city of, 6, 218, 221, 223, 232, 250, 262
  Khanate, 10
Kokchetáv Oblast, 270, 272
Kókhtla–Yárve, 126, 134
Kok–Sagyz, 60, 404
Kóla, Fjord, 148, 151, 153
  Peninsula, 11, 148, 149
Kolchak, 10
Kolkhoz, 405
  market, 408
  see also Collective farms
Kolómna, 39, 53
Kolymá River, 300, 308
Kómi, A.S.S.R., 146, 147, 148, 154
Kómi-Permyák, N.O., 164, 168
  people, 167, 357
Kommunársk, 104, 106; *see also* Alchévsk
Komsomólsk-on-Amur, 314, 327, 492, 512
Konakóvo, 40
Konstantinov Kámen, 165
Konstantínovka, 104, 107, 526
Kopét Dag, 13, 232, 233, 235
Kopéysk, 168, 182
Koryák Mountains, 308
  N.O., 298, 300
Kostromá, city of, 39, 40, 41, 52, 53, 534
  Oblast, 34, 35, 36, 146, 147, 148, 159
Kótlas, 148, 157
Kounrád, 257
Kovdor, 148, 151
Kóvzha River, 148, 160
Kramatórsk, 104, 107
Krásnaya–Shápochka, 171, 524
Krasnodár, city of, 185, 186, 189, 207, 211
  Kray, 184, 186, 193, 494
  see also Yekaterinodár

Krasnoturínsk, 524
Krasnourálsk, 521
Krasnovódsk, city of, 230, 233, 263
  Plateau, 230, 232
Krasnoyársk, city of, 218, 300, 320, 324, 524, 530
  hydroelectric plant, 316
  Kray, 22, 298, 300
Kray, 23, 24, 26
Kremenchúg, 99, 101, 102, 104, 106, 113
Kremlin, Gorky, 51
  Moscow, 44, 46, 47, 49, 84, 139
  Novgorod, 143
Krestovyy Pass, 212
Kirvóy Rog, 61, 62, 101, 102, 103, 104, 105, 106,
  107, 506, 512, 515, 518
Kronshtádt, 126, 141
Kubán, District, 22
  River, 89, 193
Kulundá Steppe, 277, 279, 280
Kuma River, 189, 193
Kurá, Lowland, 22, 201, 204
  River, 189, 195, 200
Kurgán, city of, 272, 293
  Oblast, 270, 272
Kuril Islands, 6, 11, 300, 302, 309
Kursk, city of, 63, 105
  Magnetic Anomaly (KMA), 52, 61, 62, 105, 518
  Oblast, 39, 56, 60, 62
Kushmurún coal field, 285
Kustanáy, city of, 272, 293
  Oblast, 270, 272, 515
Kutaisi, 186, 208, 209, 212, 533
Kúybyshev, city of, 69, 72, 75, 82, 83, 84, 489
  Dam, 69, 81
  Oblast, 66, 67, 75, 82, 83, 487
  Sea, 69, 80, 81
Kuznétsk, Ala-Táu, 273, 274
  Basin, 272, 273, 274, 284, 285, 481, 484, 486
Kyákhta, 300
Kyshtým, 168, 171, 521
Kyzýl–Kúm, 232, 234
Kzyl–Ordá, city of, 218, 245, 263
  Oblast, 216, 218

Labor force, 370, 386, 387, 389, 391, 392, 404, 411,
  414, 423, 462
Lake Balkhásh, 13, 20, 22, 232, 235, 521; *see also*
  Balkhásh, Lake
Lake Baskunchák, 526; *see also* Baskunchák, Lake
Lake Baykál, 14, 20, 310
Lake Beloe, 148, 160
Lake Chudskóe, 126, 132; *see also* Peipus
Lake Eltón, 526
Lake Ílmen, 6, 126, 143
Lake Ímandra, 148, 151
Lake Khanká, 300, 311
Lake Kúbeno, 148, 161
Lake Ládoga, 126, 132, 148, 150, 160
Lake Onéga, 126, 148, 160

Lake Peipus, 7; *see also* Chudskóe
Lake Seván, 189, 202, 203, 205
Lake Tengiz, 272
Lake Vygózero (Crescent Lake), 148, 152
Lake Zaysan, 272, 274, 276
Landform, of the Caucasus, 188–191, 193, 195
  of the Central Black Earth Region, 57–58
  of the Central Industrial Region, 37–38
  of Eastern Siberia and the Soviet Far East, 307–311
  of the European North, 149–150, 154
  of the European West, 127–130
  of Middle Asia and Southern Kazakhstan, 230–238
  of the Povolzhye and Lower Don, 69
  of the Ukraine and Moldavia, 95–96
  of the Urals, 165–167
  of the U.S.S.R., 11–14
  of Western Siberia and Northern Kazakhstan, 273–274
  see also Topography
Land use, 20, 400
Languages, 362, 363
Láptev Sea, 300
Látgale, 126, 129
Latin America, 640, 641
Latvian, people, 352
  S.S.R., 10, 11, 124, 125, 126
Lead, 171, 207, 257, 287, 520, 521
Lebanon, 623
Legislature, 26
Léna, coal field, 300
  River, 14, 17, 300, 308, 310, 311
Lénin, 10, 87
Lenin Hills, 48
  Library, 47
Leninabád, 218, 221, 262; *see also* Khodzhént
Leningrád, city of, 9, 11, 124, 126, 131, 136, 140, 148, 526
  Oblast, 124
  see also St. Petersburg; Petrográd
Leninogórsk, 272, 287, 295, 522
Léninsk–Kuznétsky, 272, 293
Lenkorán Lowland, 17, 22, 186, 189
Lépsa River, 235
Lesozavódsk, 300, 322
Less developed countries, 642, 643, 644, 645
Lesser Caucasus, 195
Libermanism, 470
Libya, 623, 624
Liépaya, 126, 131, 142
Linen, 40, 41, 53
Lipetsk, city of, 39, 62, 64, 518
  Oblast, 56, 61
Lisichánsk, 492
Lithuanian, people, 7, 352
  S.S.R., 7, 10, 11, 124, 125, 126, 142
Livestock, 20, 22, 430, 431, 433, 456
Livonian Knights, 7, 126
Locomotives, 40, 532
Loess, 22, 113, 239, 242
Lower Tunguska River, 300, 307

Lugánsk, 102, 103, 105, 106, 108; *see also* Voroshilovgrád
Lumber, 43, 75, 77, 81, 82, 83, 101, 114, 150, 157, 159, 175, 176, 290, 322, 538, 539, 540, 543; *see also* Timber; Industry
Lusavan, 206
Lvov, 94, 97, 102, 103, 111, 113, 114

Machine construction, 41, 133, 135, 531
Machine tractor stations (MTS), 409, 410, 417
Magadán, city of, 300, 328
  Oblast, 298, 300
Magnítnaya, 172
Magnitogórsk, 62, 83, 168, 172, 179, 180, 510, 512
Magnitogórsk–Kuznétsk Combine, *see* Urál–Kuznetsk Combine
Makéyevka, 103, 105, 107
Makhachkalá, 186, 189, 208, 212
Makhorka, 60, 61
Málye Barsukí, 232, 234
Manchuria, 10, 22, 303
Manganese, 101, 102, 107, 172, 207, 230, 257, 506, 518
Mangyshlák Peninsula, 230, 232, 233, 255, 256, 488, 489
Manpower, 370, 373, 376, 386, 387, 389, 390; *see also* Labor force
Mánych Depression, 189, 191
Márganets, 105
Margelán, 218, 262
Marí, A.S.S.R., 66, 67, 69, 72
  people, 69
Mariinsk Canal, 160; *see also* Volga-Baltic Waterway
Marine transport, *see* Sea traffic
Maritime, Kray, 17, 20, 22, 23, 26, 298, 300, 303
  shipping, 555, 578, 580, 581, 582
  see also Primórskiy
Mariúpol, 107; *see also* Zhdánov
Marx, 86
Marý, 218, 243
Mátochkin Shar, 154
Maykóp, 186, 189, 207, 212
Mediterranean Sea, 17
Megion, 288
Mémel, 142; *see also* Kláypeda
Merchant marine, 645, 646, 647
Merv Oasis, 221
Mezén, city of, 148, 156
  River, 148, 156, 157
Miáss, 533
Michúrinsk, 63, 64
Middle Asia, Soviet, 17, 216–269
Middle Volga Kray, 67
Migrations, 369, 370, 371, 372, 373, 374, 377, 379, 391
Military assistance, 634, 635, 636
Millet, 60, 73
Minerálnye Vódy, 186, 212, 213
Minerals, 38, 153, 157, 167, 170, 232, 273, 283, 314

Mingechaur Reservoir, 189, 202, 204
Minsk, city of, 124, 126, 136, 141
    Oblast, 124, 126
Minusinsk Basin, 310, 311
Mogilev Oblast, 124, 126
Moldavia, 6, 11, 91, 93
    A.S.S.R., 119
    people, 119, 352
    S.S.R., 119
Monchegorsk, 521
Monche Tundra, 151
Mongolia, 14, 607
    people, 219, 220, 355
    Peoples Republic, 302, 303
Monsoon, 14, 17, 20, 22, 305, 311, 312
Mordovian, A.S.S.R., 34, 56, 62, 64
    people, 361
Morocco, 623, 624
Moscow, Canal, 43, 44, 554
    city of, 6, 17, 34, 36, 38, 40, 41, 43, 44–50, 52, 53,
        492, 531
    coal basin, 38–39, 481, 484
    Grand Duchy of, 6, 9
    Oblast, 34, 36, 41
    River, 43, 44, 48, 49
Moslem, 10
Mount Aragats, 195
Mount Ararat, 189, 195
Mount Communism, 236; *see also* Mount Stalin
Mount Elbrus, 189
Mount Klyuchevskaya, 14, 309
Mount Lenin, 236
Mount Stalin, 236; *see also* Mount Communism
Mozyr, 134, 492
Msta River, 130
Mud volcanoes, 233
Mugodzhar Mountains, 166, 167, 230, 273
Mulberry trees, 201, 202, 245, 455
Murgab River, 232, 236, 249, 247, 251
Murmansk, city of, 148, 151, 152, 153
    Oblast, 146, 147, 148, 149
Muskovy, 7, 8, 84
Muslim, 221
Muyun Kum, 232, 235

Nadvoitsy, 148, 151, 524
Nagorno–Karabakh A.O., 184, 186, 187
Nakhichevan A.S.S.R., 184, 186, 187
Nakhodka, 326
Namangan, city of, 262
    Oblast, 216, 218
Narodnaya Gora (People's Mountain), 165
Narva, city of, 9, 134
    River, 132
Naryan–Mar, 148, 156
Naryn River, 232, 238
National Okrug (N.O.), 24
Nationalities, 10, 23, 24, 26, 143, 187, 188, 219, 226,
    271, 335, 344, 345, 356, 357, 359, 362, 364, 365, 366

Natural zones, 22
Navigation, 80, 81, 82, 96, 105, 113, 132, 182
Navoy, 256
Navy, 645, 647
Nazarovo, 300
Nebit–Dag, 218, 232, 233, 256, 488, 494
Neman River, 101, 126, 130, 132
Nenets National Okrug, 146, 147, 148, 156
Nephelite, 133, 151, 154, 524
Nerchinsk, Treaty of, 8
Neva River, 7, 126, 132, 137, 138, 160
Nevsky, Alexander, 7
    Prospect, 138
Nickel, 11, 151, 172, 320, 518
Nikolayev, 103, 107, 112, 117
Nikolayevsk, 300, 302
Nikopol, 101, 102, 103, 105, 107, 506, 518
Nitrogen, 528
Niva River, 148, 151
Nizhnekamsk, 83
Nizhnevartovskiy, 288
Nizhniy Tagil, 168, 172, 179, 515
Nizhny Novgorod, 39, 51; *see also* Gorky
Nogay Steppe, 189
Norilsk, 300, 320, 327, 518, 521
North Caucasian Foreland, 22, 188, 191; *see also*
    Caucasus
North Kazakhstan Oblast, 270, 272
North Korea, 22, 609, 610
North Osetian A.S.S.R., 184
North Vietnam, 609, 610
Northern Dvina River, 148, 154
Northern Sea Route, 153, 328, 555
Novaya Zemlya, 148, 154
Novgorod, city of, 6, 134, 142
    Oblast, 5, 124, 126
Novocheboksarsk, 81
Novokuznetsk, 272, 292, 515, 524; *see also* Stalinsk
Novolipetsk, 62
Novomoskovsk, 52, 104, 105; *see also* Stalinogorsk
Novorossiisk, 61, 186, 189, 208, 209, 212
Novosibirsk, city of, 272, 291, 490
    Islands, 300
    Oblast, 75, 270, 272
Novotroitsk, 168, 172, 182, 287, 515
Novovoronezhskiy, 63
Nukus, 218, 263
Nura River, 272, 276
Nurek Dam, 244, 254

Oats, 20, 22, 38, 60, 421, 438, 454
Ob, Basin, 13
    River, 13, 272, 274, 276
Oblast, 23, 24, 26, 29
Obozerskaya Bypass, 148, 152
Obshchiy Syrt, 166, 167
Odessa, 9, 97, 103, 108, 117
Oil, 42, 43, 63, 75, 76, 77, 82, 83, 86, 101, 102, 111,
    113, 134, 135, 157, 173, 174, 207, 208, 209, 230,
    233, 255, 256, 283, 288, 315, 477, 479, 481, 486–
    493, 602

pipelines, 112–113, 491
refining, 40, 52, 53, 84, 212, 291, 315, 316, 491
shale, 73, 76, 83, 126, 132, 134; *see also* Shale
transport, 573
see also Petroleum; Industry, oil and gas
Oká–Don Lowland, 58
Oká River, 35, 36, 38, 39, 50, 52, 53, 58
Okhá, 300, 315, 328, 492, 494
Okhótsk, city of, 8
Sea, 300, 537
see also Sea of Okhótsk
Olenegórsk, 148, 151
Omsk, city of, 221, 272, 291, 490, 530
Oblast, 270, 272
Onéga, city of, 148, 156
Lake, 150
River, 132, 148, 156
Orchards, 122
Ordzhonikídze, 185, 189, 207, 212, 522; *see also*
Vladikavkáz
Orékhovo–Zúevo, 53
Oról, city of, 62, 64
Oblast, 56, 58
Orenbúrg, city of, 10, 168, 180, 220
Oblast, 164, 168
see also Chkálov
Orsk, 168, 181
Orsk–Khalílovo region, 172, 518
Osh, city of, 6, 218, 262
Oblast, 216
Ostrogs, 300
Ottoman Turks, 7, 9, 59
Outer Mongolia, 302
Oxus, 219, 220; *see also* Amú Daryá
Oymyakón, 305
Oyrót, 220

Pacific Ocean, 8, 17, 20
Pakhtá–Arál (Cotton Island), 235, 245, 249
Paleo–Asiatic, 8, 355
Pamír–Aláy Mountains, 13, 22, 232, 236, 237
Pamír Knot, 236
Pamirs, 13, 14
Paper, 176, 542
Park of Economic Achievements, 49, 50
Patóm Plateau, 307, 308
Pavlodár, city of, 221, 272, 276, 293, 525
Oblast, 270, 272
Páy–Khoy, 154
Peat, 102, 132
Péchenga, 6, 11, 148, 149, 151, 521; *see also* Petsamo
Pechóra, coal basin, 157, 483, 484, 485
Railroad, 157
River, 148, 154, 156, 167
Pechóra–Výchegda diversion project, 158, 252, 253
Peipus, 7; *see also* Lake Chudskóe
Pensions, 388
Pénza, city of, 63
Oblast, 56, 57

Perekop Isthmus, 99, 115, 116
Pereyáslav, 52; *see also* Ryazán
Perguba, 148, 151
Perm (Mólotov), city of, 168, 179
Oblast, 164, 168
Permafrost, 17, 20, 307
Persia, 10, 13; *see also* Iran
Peter I (the Great), 9, 136, 138
Peterhóf, 139, 140; *see also* Petrodvoréts
Petersburg, 139; *see also* Leningrád
Petrodvoréts, 139, 140; *see also* Peterhóf
Petrográd, 9, 11, 136; *see also* Leningrád; St. Petersburg
Petroleum, 42, 43, 63, 76, 77, 82, 86, 233
Petropávlovsk (North Kazakhstán Oblast) 272,
293
Petropávlovsk–Kamchátsky, 300, 302, 328
Petróvsk, 300, 319
Petrozavódsk, 148, 151, 154
Petsamo, 6, 11, 149; *see also* Péchenga
Phosphate, 39, 40, 64, 76, 83, 101, 102, 230, 258,
528; *see also* Apatite
Pinega River, 157
Pipelines, 40, 43, 75, 82, 83, 86, 106, 111, 112, 132,
133, 134, 173, 207, 208, 256, 315, 316, 389
490, 492, 494, 496, 497, 498, 557, 559
Pishpék, 6; *see also* Frúnze
Plavinas, 126, 132
Podólian Plateau, 11, 12, 95, 103, 111, 119
Poland, 7, 9, 10, 11, 598, 602
Poles, 7, 352, 365
Polésye, 96, 101, 103, 113, 114, 126, 127, 128
Polish–Lithuanian state, 9, 93, 125 141
Political subdivisions, of the U.S.S.R., 24, 25, 26, 29
Pólotsk, 126, 133, 492
Poltáva, 9, 102, 103, 114
Poltorátsk, 261; *see also* Ashkhabád
Population, 23, 74, 95, 126, 127, 130, 187, 188, 210,
225, 231, 292, 325, 334–397
Port Arthur, 302, 303
Port Dairen, 302, 303
Ports, 117, 119, 131, 134, 141, 142, 154, 579–581,
647
Potash, 101, 102, 113, 126, 132, 133, 135, 175, 528
Potatoes, 20, 22, 38, 60, 73, 398, 440, 454
Poultry, 38, 456
Povólzhye, 67–88
Precipitation, 14, 15, 16, 17, 20, 38, 70, 72, 192, 238
Pridnepróvsk, 101
Primorskiy, *see* Maritime Kray
Prípyat, Marshes, 91
River, 101, 114, 126, 132
Private plots, 406, 407, 408, 411, 413, 414, 422
Prokópyevsk, 272, 293
Prussians, 9, 11
Prut River, 94, 103, 119
Pskov, city of, 142
Oblast, 124, 126
Púdozhgora, 148, 151
Púshkin, 140

Putorán Mountains, 307
Pyandzh River, 232, 237
Pyatigórsk, 186, 213

Railroad, 42, 43, 46, 75, 79, 86, 87, 101, 113, 153,
    190, 556, 559, 560, 561, 562, 563, 564, 565, 566
  Locomotives, 40, 108
Rayon, 23, 24
Razdán, city of, 524
  River, 202, 204, 205
Red Square, 46, 47
Refineries, 82, 84, 113, 133, 173, 174, 208, 489, 490,
    492; *see also* Oil, refining
Regár, 525
Regionalization, 26, 29–32
Reindeer, 453
Réni, 117
Reservoirs, 43, 555
Resort areas, 118, 212, 213
Réval, 141; *see also* Tallin
Rice, 22, 73, 100, 116, 193, 201, 201, 247, 441, 454
Riga, 141
Rióni River, 195, 189, 204
River, fleet, 554
  routes, 555
  traffic, 43, 75, 552–555, 575, 578, 579
Rostóv, city of, 8, 9, 66, 87, 90, 103, 108, 185, 492
  Oblast, 66, 67, 90
Róvno, 94
R.S.F.S.R., 24
Ruble, 613, 653
Rubtsóvsk, 272, 293
Rúdnyy, Altáy, 273, 287
  city of, 273, 286
Rumania, 10, 11
Rurik, 5, 142
Russian, Museum, 137
  people, 345, 358, 359, 360, 361, 376, 377
Russification, 127, 136, 143, 361, 363–366, 377
Russo-Japanese War (1905), 10, 302
Rustávi, 189, 208, 212, 512
Ruthenian people, 11
Ryazán, city of, 39, 40, 52, 492
  Oblast, 34, 36, 57
  see also Pereyáslav
Rybáchy Peninsula (Fishermen's Peninsula), 148, 149
Rýbinsk, city of, 43, 52, 53
  Reservoir, 43, 53, 148, 159, 160
  see also Shcherbakóv
Rye, 20, 22, 38, 60, 398, 437, 454

Sadovaya Ulitsa, 45, 46; *see also* Garden Ring
Sakhalin, Island, 6, 10, 14, 302, 311, 315, 488, 492
  Oblast, 11, 298, 300
Sal River, 189
Salair Ridge, 273, 274
Salavát, 173
Salekhárd, 272
Salt, 75, 76, 83, 86, 101, 105, 107, 230, 258, 526
  domes, 230

lakes, 83
Samára, city of, 67, 84
  Bend, 69, 84
  River, 84
  see also Kúybyshev
Samarkánd, city of, 6, 10, 218, 221, 232, 261
  Oblast, 216
  see also Afrosiab
Samovar, 227
Saráí, 5, 52, 58
Saránsk, 62, 64
Sarátov, city of, 67, 72, 83, 86
  hydroelectric plant, 81
  Oblast, 66, 67
Sarysú River, 232, 235
Saudi Arabia, 624
Saxaul trees, 22, 242
Sayán Mountains, 308, 310
Scandinavian Shield, 147
Scythians, 5
Sea of Azóv, 9, 67, 73, **94, 95,** 103, 107, 108, 115;
    see also Azóv Sea
Sea of Okhotsk, 310, 323; *see also* Okhotsk, Sea
Sea traffic, 555, 556, 575, 578–580
Selengá River, 310
Semipalátinsk, city of, 221, 272, 293
  Oblast, 270, 272
Sérnyy Zavód, 232
Seróv, 168, 173, 515
Settlement, Russian, 8, 304
Seván–Razdán Cascade, 204, 205, 206
Sevastópol, 90, 103, 119
Severnaya Zemlya, 300
Shákhty, 103, 107
Shale, 496, 498, 499; *see also* Oil, shale
Shatúra, 53
Shcherbakóv, 53; *see also* Rýbinsk
Shchigrý, 64
Shebelínka, 101, 102, 111, 112, 494
Sheep, 73, 202, 452, 456
Sheksná River, 43, 148, 160
Shélekhov, 320, 524
Shelter belts, 115, 116, 122, 405, 455
Shevchénko, 218, 232, 233, 256, 484
Shilka River, 311
Ship building, 53, 63, 73, 105, 117, 131, 141, 153, 533
Shipping season, 579, 581
Ships, 556, 647
Siberia, 8, 14, 17, 24, 270–331
Siberian High, 14, 17, 304
Sibir, 8
Sikhoté–Alin Mountains, 305, 308, 311
Silk industry, 202, 245, 263, 534
Simbírsk, 87; *see also* Ulyánovsk
Simferópol, 103, 108, 118
Sinkiang, 223, 224
Sinkiang–Uighur Autonomous Region, 225
Sivásh Sea, 116
Slavic princely states, 5, 7

Slavs, 5, 345
Slávyansk, 526
Smolénsk, city of, 9, 126, 142
    Oblast, 124, 126
Smolénsk–Moscow Ridge, 38, 126, 128, 142
Snow, 17
Sóbinka, 34, 36
Sóchi, 186, 212, 213
Soda, 526, 527
Sogd River, 220
Soils, 11, 20, 22, 38, 58, 71, 72, 96, 97, 110, 120, 147,
    150, 176, 193, 239, 274, 304, 425
Sokh River, 250
Sokólniki Park, 49
Sokolov–Sarbay, 286, 515
Sokolovsk, 172
Soligórsk, 126, 132, 135, 528
Solikámsk, 168, 175, 182, 526, 528
Sol–Ilétsk, 168
Solonchak, 233
Sorghum, 22
Southern Bug River, 94, 107, 115, 117
South Manchurian Railroad, 302
South Osétian A.O., 184, 186, 187
Soviet Middle Asia, 40, 216–269
Soviet Socialist Republic (S.S.R.), 23; see also Union
    Republic
Sovkhoz, see State farm
Soy beans, 22, 313, 454
Stalinabád, 261; see also Dushanbe
Stalingrád, 69, 72, 73, 78, 81, 82, 83, 85; see also
    Volgográd
Stálino, 106; see also Donétsk
Stalinogórsk, 52; see also Novomoskóvsk
Stálinsk, 292, 510; see also Novokuznétsk
Stanovoy Mountains, 308
State farm, 405, 410, 411, 412, 413, 422
Stávropol, city of, 83, 189, 186, 207, 494
    Kray, 68, 87, 184, 186, 212
    Plateau, 189, 191, 212
St. Basil's Cathedral, 46, 47
Stébnik, 113, 528
Steel, see Iron and steel
Steppe, 20, 22, 60, 72, 73
Sterlitamák, 526, 530
Stony Tunguska River, 307
Storm Tracks, 15, 16
St. Petersburg, 9, 11; see also Leningrád; Petrográd
Strezhevoy, 288
Stroganov, fur trading family, 8
Sts. Peter & Paul Fortress, 137, 139
Subarctic, 17
Subway, 46, 49, 50, 113, 141, 260, 587
Sudan, 623, 624
Suez Canal, 624, 625
Sugar beets, 22, 60, 61, 73, 109, 110, 112, 193, 245,
    398, 443, 454
Súkhona River, 148, 161
Súkhovey, 22, 96, 115, 193

Sukhúmi, 10, 212, 213
Sulfur, 76, 113, 175, 258
Sulfuric acid, 526, 527
Sumbár River, 247
Sumgaít, 186, 189, 208, 209, 524, 530
Sunflower, 22, 60, 73, 108, 110, 115, 193, 398, 442,
    454
Superphosphate, 135; see also Phosphate; Industry,
    fertilizer
Supreme Soviet, 26
Surámi Range, 188, 189, 195, 200, 209
Surgút, 272, 288, 289
Surkhán, Daryá, 216, 246, 254
Sverdlóvsk, city of, 168, 176, 531
    Oblast, 164, 168
    see also Yekaterinbúrg
Svir River, 126, 132, 148, 151, 160
Swedes, 7, 9
Swine, see Hogs
Syktyvkár, 148, 157, 158
Synthetic rubber, 63, 83, 87, 140, 528, 530
Syr–Daryá, Oblast, 216, 234
    River, 232, 238, 239, 245
Syria, 623, 624, 625
Sýzran, 73, 82, 84, 87, 498

Tadzhík, people, 227, 352
    S.S.R., 216, 218
Taganróg, 103, 105, 107
Taiga, 20, 307
Takyr, 233
Taláss River, 232, 235, 245
Taldý–Kurgán, city of, 218, 243
    Oblast, 216, 218
Tállin, 126, 141; see also Réval
Talysh, 189
Tambóv, city of, 64
    Oblast, 56, 58
    Plain, 58
Tamerlane, 219, 261
Tannenburg, Battle of, 7
Tánnu, Ola, 308
    Túva, 302, 303, 607
Tarbagatáy Mountains, 273, 274
Tártu, 126, 142; see also Dórpat
Tashaúz, city of, 218, 263
    Oblast, 247
Tashként, city of, 6, 10, 216, 218, 221, 232, 259
    Oblast, 216
Tas–Tumús, 300, 316, 494
Tatár, A.S.S.R., 8, 66, 67, 69, 72, 75, 82, 83, 84, 85
    invasion, 5
    oil fields, 487
    people, 7, 39, 52, 58, 59, 67, 84, 359, 561
    Strait, 311, 492
    yoke, 7
Taymýr N.O., 298, 300
Tayshét, 300, 319
Tbilisi, 10, 185, 186, 189, 209, 211

Tea, 22, 194, 195, 196, 197, 198, 199, 446, 455
Tedzhén, city of, 218, 247
  River, 232, 236, 239, 247, 251
Temir–Táu, 272, 286, 291, 530
Temperature, 18, 19, 20, 72, 192
Térek River, 189, 193, 204
Terméz, 218, 232
Ternópol, 94
Territorial-production complexes, 26
Tetyukhé, 320, 522
Textile industries, 41, 534–535
Thermal electricity, 41, 63, 76, 83, 96, 99, 101, 105,
    134, 205, 206, 207, 255, 498, 500, 501, 503; *see*
    also Electric power
Tikhorétsk, 189, 208, 492
Tikhvin, 126, 132
Timán Ridge, 148, 154
Timber, 42, 73, 75, 77, 81, 82, 83, 101, 113, 114, 155,
    156, 541, 542, 576; *see also* Lumber; Industry
Timur, 220; *see also* Tamerlane
Tin, 320, 520
Tkibúli, 189, 207
Tkvarchéli, 189, 207
Tobacco, 22, 200
Toból River, 167, 272, 274, 276
Tobólsk, 272, 294, 295
Togliátti, 83, 84, 87, 530, 533, 585
Tokmák, 102
Tom River, 272, 274
Tomsk, city of, 272, 294, 295
  Oblast, 270, 272
Topography, 11, 69, 95, 149, 154, 165, 230, 273, 307;
    see also Landform
Torzhók, 157
Tractor, 61, 64, 84, 85, 108, 136, 140, 141, 178, 179,
    531
Trade, 565–581, 592–625; *see also* Foreign trade
Trans Aláy Range, 237
Transcarpáthian Ukraine, 11, 93, 114
Transcaspian Railroad, 264
Transcaucasia, 17, 20, 23, 40, 185–215; *see also* Caucasus
Transcaucasian Soviet Federated Socialist Republic, 185
Transhumance, 22, 202, 241
Trans–Kazakhstán Trunk Line, 266
Transmission lines, 81, 505, 602
Transoxania, 220
Transportation, 41, 42, 75, 265, 328, 551–589
Trans-Siberian Railway, 10, 165, 272, 290, 302, 324,
    328
Transvolga Meadows, 72, 73
Treaty, of Argún, 302
  of Kyákhta, 301
  of Nérchinsk, 8, 301
  of Peking, 302
Tsaritsyn, 85; *see also* Volgográd; Stalingrád
Tsárskoye Seló, 140; *see also* Púshkin
Tselinnyy Kray, 271
Tselinográd, city of, 272, 293, 294;
  Oblast, 270, 272
  see also Akmólinsk
Tsimlyánsk, city of, 78

Dam, 78
Sea, 78, 80
Tuapsé, 186, 189, 208, 212
Túla, city of, 35, 36, 39, 40, 52, 61, 62, 518
  Oblast, 34, 35, 36, 56, 57, 58
Tundra, 17, 20, 22, 150, 307
Tungsten, 172
Tung Trees, 200
Tungúskan Plateau, 307
Tunisia, 623, 624
Turánian Lowland
Turgaý, Lowland (Tableland), 232, 234, 273, 274, 515
  River, 272, 274, 276
Turkestán, A.S.S.R., 222
  city of, 224, 607
Turkey, 10, 621, 622, 623
Turkic people, 345
Turkmén, people, 227
  S.S.R., 216, 218
Turks, *see* Ottoman Turks
Turk-Sib Railroad, 266, 272
Tuva A.S.S.R., 298, 300, 303, 310, 311
Tuymazý, 173, 490
Tver, 39, 52; *see also* Kalínin
Twelve-Foot Roads, 82
Tyan Shans, 13, 14, 22, 229, 232, 237, 238
Tyumén, city of, 272, 294, 295
  Oblast, 270, 272

Udmúrt, A.S.S.R., 69, 164, 168
  people, 167
Ufá, city of, 168, 173, 179, 490
  Plateau, 165, 166, 174
  River, 167
Úglich Reservoir, 43
Ugrá River, 7
Uighurs, 223
Ukhtá, 133, 148, 157, 158, 494
Ukraíne S.S.R., 7, 9, 10, 11, 22, 24, 31, 40, 43,
  90–119
Ulán–Udé, 300, 310, 327
Ulu–Táu, 273, 274
Ulyánovsk, city of, 87
  Oblast, 66, 67, 83
  see also Simbírsk
Union Republic, 23, 24, 26, 31; *see also* Soviet Socialist
  Republic
United Arab Republic, 637
United Nations, 24
United States, 617–620
University of Moscow, 47, 48, 49
Urál, coal fields, 481, 484
  Mountains, 10, 13, 17, 165, 508
  River, 81, 167, 180, 230, 232, 233, 239, 272, 276
Urál–Kuznetsk Combine, 172, 180, 284, 285, 510
Urálsk Oblast, 270, 272
Uranium, 101, 102, 105, 525
Urbanization, 39, 40, 336, 340, 366, 377, 378, 379
Urgénch, 218, 263
Usá River, 69
Usólye–Sibírskoye, 300, 325

Ussúri, region, 304
   River, 311
Ussúri–Khanká Lowland, 304, 311, 313
Ussurisk, 300, 326; *see also* Voroshílov
Ust–Kamenogórsk, city of, 272, 276, 288, 295, 522
   Dam, 287
Ust–Kut, 300
Ust–Ordá Buryát N.O., 298, 300
Ust–Yurt Plateau, 232, 233
Úvaly, 165, 166
Uzbék, people, 220, 225, 226
   S.S.R., 216, 218
Uzbóy System, 232, 233, 234, 244, 251
Uzen, 232, 255
Úzhgorod, 94, 114

Vakhsh River, 232, 237, 239, 243, 246, 254
Valdáy Hills, 12, 126, 130
Varangians, 5
Vasyugánye Swamp, 274
Vaygách Island, 148, 154
Vegetables, 22, 38, 73
Vegetation, 11, 38, 71, 96, 97, 109, 165, 193, 274, 304
Véntspils, 126, 131, 134, 142, 492
Verkhoyánsk, city of, 300, 305
   Mountains, 308
Vérnyy, 6, 260; *see also* Almá–Atá
Vílnyus, 126, 141, 142
Vilyúy River, 300
Vineyards, 22, 116, 120, 446
Virgin lands, 61, 73, 122, 280, 282, 374, 415, 420
Vítebsk, city of, 124, 126, 142
   Oblast, 126
Vitím Plateau, 307, 308
Vladikavkáz, 185, 212; *see also* Ordzhonikídze
Vladímir, city of, 34, 52, 53
   Oblast, 34, 36
Vladivostók, 10, 300, 302, 326
Volcanoes, 14, 118, 309
Vólga, German A.S.S.R., 86
   Germans, 68, 86, 364
   Heights, 11, 69, 72
   River, 5, 36, 38, 40, 41, 42, 43, 44, 50, 52, 67, 69,
      72, 73, 75, 76, 77, 78, 81, 82, 83, 130, 252, 533,
      554
Vólga-Baltic Waterway, 132, 151, 160, 554
Vólga-Don Canal, 44, 67, 72, 77, 80, 84, 85, 108, 554
Vólga–Urals oil fields, 40, 69, 73, 82, 83, 84, 85, 487,
   492
Volgográd, city of, 44, 69, 72, 73, 78, 81, 82, 83, 105,
   108, 524
   Dam, 5, 83, 84, 85
   Oblast, 66, 67, 82
   Reservoir, 81
   see also Stalingrád
Volgorechensk, 41
Volhynia, 93
Vólkhov, city of, 133, 151, 522
   River, 5, 126, 143

Vólogda, city of, 35, 148, 158, 160
   Oblast, 146, 147, 148, 159
Vólzhskiy, 83, 86, 87, 530
Vorkutá, 148, 151, 157, 158
Vorónezh, city of, 63
   Oblast, 56, 58, 60
Voroshílov, 326; *see also* Ussurísk
Voroshilovgrád, 106; *see also* Lugánsk
Voskresénsk, 526
Vótkinsk, 174
Vuktyl, 157
Vyátka, city of, 87
   River, 83, 87
   see also Kirov
Výborg, 149
Výchegda River, 148, 154, 157
Vygózero, Lake (Crescent Lake), *see* Lake Vygozero
Vysókaya, 172
Výtegra River, 148, 160

Warsaw, 9
   Grand Duchy of, 6
Water buffalo, 202, 453, 456
Western Dviná River, 126, 130, 132
Western Siberia, 43, 270–296
West Siberian oil fields, 134, 488
Wheat, 22, 60, 73, 75, 84, 108, 109, 110, 115, 193,
   280, 281, 398, 415, 416, 419, 420, 433, 434
White Republics, 10
White Russia, *see* Belorússian S.S.R.
White Sea, 44, 148, 151, 160
White Sea-Baltic Canal, 151, 152, 544; *see also* Baltic-
   White Sea Canal
Wild field, 58, 59
Windbreaks, *see* Shelter belts
Winter Palace, 137, 138, 139
Wooded Steppe, 20, 22, 58
Woodworking, 53, 87; *see also* Lumber; Timber
Wool, 263, 534
World War I, 10
World War II, 10, 11, 85, 86, 93, 104, 113, 114, 140,
   143, 149, 172, 338, 364

Yablonóvyy Mountains, 308, 310
Yaila, 118
Yákhroma, 53
Yakút A.S.S.R., 298, 300, 328
Yakútsk, 300, 308, 314, 328
Yálta, 103, 118, 212
Yamál–Nenéts N.O., 270, 272
Yána River, 300, 308
Yangi, 6, 221
Yaroslávl, city of, 39, 40, 51, 52, 53, 63, 492, 531
   Oblast, 34, 36, 43
Yekaterinbúrg, *see* Sverdlóvsk
Yekaterinodár, *see* Krasnodár
Yemen, 623, 625
Yenákievo, 107
Yenisey, hydroelectric plant, 316
   River, 13, 14, 300, 310, 316

Yereván, 10, 185, 186, 189, 195, 204, 208, 209, 211, 524, 530
Yermak, 7, 9, 289
Yugoslavia, 603, 604
Yurt, 229
Yúzhno–Sakhalínsk, 300, 328

Zaglík, 189, 208, 209, 524
Zailisk, 260
Zaporózhye, 9, 94, 95, 96, 99, 100, 103, 105, 107, 522
Zeravshán River, 143, 232, 239, 245, 246
Zéya, city of, 300

River, 311
Zéya-Buréya Lowland, 304, 311, 313
Zhdánov, 103, 105, 106, 107; *see also* Mariúpol
Zheleznogórsk, 515
Zhéltyye Vódy, 102, 105
Zhigulí Mountains, 69
Zhódino, 135, 136, 533
Zinc, 171, 207, 257, 287, 520, 521
Zlatoúst, 168, 172, 173, 182

The author gratefully acknowledges help in indexing by Mary and Andy Lydolph and Irene Prohaska.